Music aesthetics in late eighteenth-century Germany has always been problematic because there was no aesthetic theory to evaluate the enormous amount of high-quality instrumental music produced by composers like Haydn and Mozart. This book derives a practical aesthetic for German instrumental music during the late eighteenth century from a previously neglected source, reviews of printed instrumental works. At a time when the theory of mimesis dominated aesthetic thought, leaving sonatas and symphonies at the very bottom of the aesthetic hierarchy, a group of reviewers was quietly setting about the task of evaluating instrumental music on its own terms. Two threads run through the over 1,300 reviews dating from 1760 to 1798: a rhetorical thread in which reviewers identified the "true German style" (especially as seen in C. P. E. Bach and Haydn) and an aesthetic thread. Reviewers first focused on correct compositional technique, but rapidly expanded their horizons to include genius and originality, non-mimetic expressivity, and unity based on purely musical elements. In doing so they laid the foundation for the aesthetic theories of the nineteenth century.

German music criticism in the

late eighteenth century

German music criticism in the late eighteenth century

Aesthetic issues in instrumental music

MARY SUE MORROW

Loyola University, New Orleans

CAMBRIDGE
UNIVERSITY PRESS

PUBLISHED BY THE PRESS SYNDICATE OF THE UNIVERSITY OF CAMBRIDGE
The Pitt Building, Trumpington Street, Cambridge, CB2 1RP, United Kingdom

CAMBRIDGE UNIVERSITY PRESS
The Edinburgh Building, Cambridge, CB2 2RU, United Kingdom
40 West 20th Street, New York, NY 10011-4211, USA
10 Stamford Road, Oakleigh, Melbourne 3166, Australia

First published 1997

Printed in the United Kingdom at the University Press, Cambridge

Typeset in 10/13 pt Monophoto Sabon by Servis Filmsetting Ltd, Manchester

A catalogue record for this book is available from the British Library

Library of Congress cataloguing in publication data

Morrow, Mary Sue, 1953–
German music criticism in the late eighteenth century : aesthetic
issues in instrumental music / Mary Sue Morrow.
p.   cm.
Includes bibliographical references and index.
ISBN 0 521 58227 X (hardback)
1. Instrumental music–Germany–18th century–History and
criticism.   2. Musical criticism–Germany.   3. Music–Germany–18th
century–Philosophy and aesthetics.   4. Nationalism in music.
5. Music and rhetoric.   I. Title.
ML499.3.M67   1997
781.1'7'094309033—dc20   96-41039   CIP   MN

ISBN 0 521 58227 X hardback

SE

In Memoriam

Virginia Sue Williamson Morrow

1920–1989

Contents

Acknowledgments

If it takes a village to raise a child, it takes a scholarly community to produce a book, and I am indebted to more people than I will be able to thank in this small space. Loyola University granted me a sabbatical leave in 1991-92; a concurrent twelve-month research fellowship from the Alexander von Humboldt-Stiftung enabled me to spend that entire year in Germany. With their support, I was able to travel to the many libraries and archives that house the sources I have used in writing this book. I wish to thank the staff of those institutions for the assistance they provided. In alphabetical order by city, they are: *Berlin*: Deutsche Staatsbibliothek Unter den Linden, Bibliothek der Humboldt-Universität, Geheimes Staatsarchiv Preussischer Kulturbesitz, Ratsbibliothek der Berliner Stadtbibliothek, Staatsbibliothek Preussischer Kulturbesitz; *Copenhagen*: Det Kongelige Bibliotek; *Dresden*: Sächsische Landesbibliothek; *Erlangen*: Universitätsbibliothek Erlangen-Nürnberg; *Göttingen*: Niedersächsische Staats- und Universitätsbibliothek; *Hamburg*: Commerzbibliothek der Handelskammer, Staats- und Universitätsbibliothek Carl von Ossietzky, Staatsarchiv; *Kiel*: Bibliothek der Christian-Albrechts-Universität, Landesbibliothek; *Leipzig*: Bibliothek der Karl-Marx Universität; *Lübeck*: Bibliothek der Hansestadt; *Munich*: Bayerische Staatsbibliothek, Stadtbibliothek – Monacensia und Handschriftensammlung; *Nuremberg*: Bibliothek des Germanischen Museums, Stadtbibliothek; *Stanford, CA*: Stanford University Library; *Vienna*: Stadtbibliothek; *Würzburg*: Universitätsbibliothek.

For advice and encouragement in the early stages of my research, I wish to thank the faculty and staff at Christian-Albrechts-Universität in Kiel, particularly Heinrich Schwab, who sponsored my application for a Humboldt fellowship, Bozena Blechert, and Carmen Debryn. At various times I have benefitted from discussions with Axel Beer, Thomas Cornell, William Horne, Howard Irving, Laurenz Lütteken, Roberta Marvin, Doris Powers, Janna Saslaw, and Gretchen Wheelock. In this regard I owe a special debt to my colleague in the field of rhetoric here at Loyola, Katherine Adams. We spent many lunches discussing eighteenth-century issues and the process of writing; every time I came away with renewed energy and at least one good idea. A number of people were kind enough to read portions of the manuscript: Katherine Adams, Hans Adler, David Beveridge, A. Peter Brown, Leslie Ellen Brown, Austin Caswell, Dane Evans, and Howard Irving. For their comments, suggestions, and encouragement, I am most grateful. I would also like to thank Corie Roberts for checking sources and running innumerable errands, and Craig McCollough for preparing the musical examples. A special word of appreciation goes to my graduate assistant, Jodi Dunnick McWilliams, for her eagle-eyed help in checking the final manuscript and to Penny Souster and Alan Finch of Cambridge University Press for their editorial patience and assistance.

I would never have been able to finish this project without the unfailing love and support of both friends and my extended family. Father, brother, sister-in-law, nephews, aunts, uncles, cousins, college friends, and my colleagues here at Loyola – all have kept me sane and reminded me continually of the World Beyond the Book. Finally, my deepest gratitude is to my mother, who was my first piano teacher and the one who suggested that I pursue a career in musicology. Though she did not live to see this project, she has been with me in spirit every step of the way. I dedicate this book to her memory.

Author's note

The eighteenth century would probably have agreed with Emerson that a foolish consistency is the hobgoblin of small minds, at least with regard to the spelling of names. Sometimes it seems as if no one spelled a name the same way twice, and German composers often used French or Italian versions of their names. In the interests of intelligibility, I have standardized all names to the preferred form listed in *The New Grove Dictionary of Music and Musicians* or *Die Musik in Geschichte und Gegenwart*. (For Czech names, I have used the most common Germanized spelling.) Only in direct quotations have I retained any eccentric versions.

I have reproduced spelling and capitalization in the titles of compositions exactly as they appeared in review headings, but will warn the reader not to expect precise conformity to the piece's actual title page. Most journals did not reproduce titles exactly, frequently shortening them, nearly always omitting diacritic accents in French and Italian, and sometimes changing spellings to conform to the house style. That house style also affected the review texts themselves; for example, some publications preferred *Stük* to *Stück*, *vortreflich* to *vortrefflich*, or even *kan* to *kann*. I have retained these variations without comment, indicating only obvious typographical errors with a *sic*. Finally, a number of the journals changed their own titles several times. All the versions are listed in the bibliography, but I have used only the earliest in my text and citations. Unless otherwise indicated, all translations are my own.

INTRODUCTION

Terms of discourse

This book addresses the fundamental change in the German perception of instrumental music that occurred around 1800, when the clear aesthetic preference for vocal music, especially opera, that pervaded the world of the German Enlightenment gave way to an exalted view of the powers of purely instrumental composition. For writers and critics like E. T. A. Hoffmann, writing in the early decades of the new century, instrumental music represented the pinnacle of aesthetic expression. The change was stunning, and the musical aesthetic that emerged, reinforced by the works of composers like Beethoven, continues to shape our attitude toward music today, nearly two centuries later.

This aesthetic shift occurred simultaneously with a change in the position of instrumental music in the larger cultural context. During the eighteenth century, instrumental music played a mostly functional role in German and Austrian society. Symphonies served to open concerts and operas, quieting down audiences and providing background music during intermissions. Concertos gave virtuosos a vehicle for displaying their talents, and also frequently turned up as intermission fillers in theaters. Keyboard sonatas (both solo and accompanied), duos, trios, string quartets – all were intended for home consumption, meant to provide musical entertainment for growing numbers of dilettante musicians in the aristocracy and wealthy bourgeoisie. If a piece fulfilled the expectations for its genre and role, it could be judged as successful, then both audience and performer would move onto something new. Instrumental music was meant to be used, enjoyed, then replaced; public enthusiasm for new works, *not* slavish devotion to a composer's older ones, was the measure of commercial and artistic success.

In the early nineteenth century, instrumental music became divorced from function and context in Germanic society, and began to separate into two distinct classes. "Lighter" works remained eminently disposable, intended for popular consumption and entertainment. "Serious" instrumental music

1

became an object for contemplation and appreciation, something to be studied and analyzed, and critics began to acknowledge that some works required repeated hearings for their complexities to be fully understood.[1] To be judged successful, a work needed to meet a set of abstract aesthetic goals not bounded by temporal or practical restraints. A composer wrote for the ages, in other words, and not for the evening concert.

However useful such schemes may be in making broad distinctions between cultural eras, they can never fully capture the complex process of historical change. A fuller understanding requires the recognition of the many cross-currents and emerging trends that both complicate and enrich the larger picture. I propose here to examine one of the emerging trends that contributed to this particular change in perspective: the development of an aesthetic vocabulary for instrumental music that occurred in Germany during the last four decades of the eighteenth century. The aesthetic consciousness that resulted helped lay the foundation for later debates about the nature of music.

The evolution of this consciousness occurred not in learned treatises, but in reviews of printed instrumental music that began to appear in German periodicals in the 1760s, a largely untapped source. For a variety of reasons, most of the scholarly attention given to German criticism has focused on the early nineteenth century. On the most pragmatic level, the *Allgemeine musikalische Zeitung*, which began publication in 1798 and is widely available in reprint, provides a virtual one-stop shopping center for anyone interested in German musical thought of the period. On a more substantive level, aesthetics as a discipline had by then been firmly established, and the body of theoretical writings that dealt specifically with music aesthetics had begun to increase significantly, especially with regard to instrumental music. Moreover, early nineteenth-century writers left us reviews of high literary quality, criticism that combines the practical aspects of reviewing with rich metaphysical speculation and still has the power to excite and inspire.

The eighteenth century has proved to be more problematic, again for a variety of reasons. The field of aesthetics, itself in its infancy, could offer music little more than the theory of mimesis, which often seems – to the modern mind – an absurd and inappropriate standard. In general, serious intellectual treatment of instrumental music remained rare, for it was (as Carl Dahlhaus has effectively argued) the age of Italian opera. Nor are the sources particularly accessible. The 1,300 instrumental music reviews I collected, for example, are scattered over forty years in nearly fifty, mostly unindexed, periodicals, many relatively unknown to music scholarship. Moreover, these instrumental music reviews have not enjoyed the best of reputations and have frequently been dismissed as superficial, inadequate, and vastly inferior to the music they treat, a viewpoint that began with nineteenth-century critics.[2] Unquestionably, they do not achieve the depth or the literary quality we have come to expect since E. T. A. Hoffmann, but it seems anachronistic to dismiss the written record of an era's thought because it does not tell us what we think is important about the music.

Because I wish to use these reviews as historical documents that reveal the evolution of a German aesthetic consciousness, I have not undertaken a critique of the reviewers' abilities as reviewers. Instead, I have sought to illuminate the issues they considered important, focusing on what they *chose to notice* (or not notice) about a piece of music, and how they chose to frame their observations. Much of recent musicological research has emphasized the different conclusions that listeners can draw about the same music, depending on their particular cultural context and aesthetic assumptions. This book is about the conclusions drawn by one group of late eighteenth-century listeners about the music of its own time. These listeners were very influential, because their opinions reached to every corner of the German-speaking world. They are voices that we cannot ignore.

1

What does *instrumental music mean?*

[1773] All symphonies, all concertos, quartets, sonatas, and solos always leave us to wander around in undefined emotions of happiness and sadness; and when a piece is over, you can still ask, as did the famous Fontenelle: "Sonate, que me veux tu?"[1]

[1786] Instead, there is a clarinet solo with bassoons, which in and of itself isn't bad; but the way it appears here, you cannot help but ask: "que me veux tu?"[2]

[1792] The remaining five sonatas are worth about the same, that is, they can pass as divertimentos, etc. But if they are considered as sonatas, then the famous question would be appropriate: "Sonate, que veux tu de moi?"[3]

"*Sonate, que me veux tu?*" "Sonata, what do you want of me?" This plaintive query, attributed to Bernard le Bovier de Fontenelle in the early eighteenth century, rapidly took on a life of its own, appearing again and again as the eighteenth century grappled with the problem of defining the aesthetic significance and exact meaning of instrumental music. That it took so long for someone to respond, "Why should it have to *mean* anything?" reflects the fact that the fledgling discipline of aesthetics lay firmly in the grip of the theory of mimesis. Mimesis was a concept resurrected from classical Greek philosophy, most notably from Aristotle's *Poetics*; in its simplest formulation it held that art should imitate nature.[4] Its resurrection in the eighteenth century was tied to the attempt to raise the arts to a level worthy of philosophical contemplation, to accord them a more exalted place than they could ever have had as mere crafts. By invoking the authority of ancient Greece, philosophers could add considerable weight to their arguments for founding the new discipline of aesthetics.

Alexander Gottlieb Baumgarten is usually given credit for formally establishing the field with his treatises *Meditationes philosophicae de nonnullis ad poema pertinentibus* (*Reflections on Poetry*, 1739) and *Aesthetica* (Part 1, 1750; Part 2, 1758).[5] Using the language and concepts inherited from his teacher Christian Wolff, whose rationalist-derived thought provided the point of departure for the eighteenth-century German Enlightenment, Baumgarten addressed the philosophical problems posed by the arts and the standard of the beautiful. While he argued that the arts need not submit to the "principles of inherited logic" that lay at the root of Enlightenment philosophy, and thus allowed them to be judged by their own, more appropriate, criteria, Baumgarten did not concern himself with the more mundane task of specifying those criteria. His lack of interest in practical aesthetics, coupled with the fact that he wrote in a somewhat complex Latin, limited his sphere of influence to academic circles.[6]

Even before Baumgarten, however, an active and more public debate had begun in France, where scholars were trying to draw a distinction between the "fine arts" (which included painting, sculpture, poetry, drama, music, and sometimes dance) and the lesser, "pleasurable arts" like cooking and gardening. One way of making the separation clear was to insist that the fine arts all adhered to a common aesthetic standard, which was mimesis. For painting and sculpture, poetry and drama, and even for dance, mimesis functioned relatively well, but for music the fit was never particularly good; it simply did not imitate nature very well. As a result, music clearly remained at the bottom of the ladder with respect to its aesthetic value. At least, however, it was on the ladder. And if maintaining its position as a fine art meant adhering to the principle of mimesis, then a way would have to be found to do so. Vocal music could more or less cope with such a standard, because its text could elucidate the meaning, making the imitation more specific and understandable. Instrumental music, on the other hand, remained hopelessly vague, incapable of expressing even the simplest objects clearly enough that listeners could figure out what was being represented. Hence, advocates of mimesis not infrequently dismissed instrumental music from serious philosophical consideration by asserting that it meant nothing at all, that it could never rise above the level of empty sound. If vocal music was *standing* on the bottom rung of the ladder of aesthetic values, instrumental music was clinging by its very fingertips. "*Sonate, que me veux tu?*"

The aesthetic debate on music proved to be both contentious and convoluted, complicated not only by the difficulty authors had in defining the terms of their elusive subject, but also by the very different intellectual and musical traditions that obtained in the French-speaking, English-speaking, and

German-speaking lands in which the discussion took place. Eighteenth-century French scholars traced their intellectual roots back to the rationalism of René Descartes, whose contribution to this particular discourse proved to be his categorization of the six basic human passions: wonder, love, hate, desire, joy, and sadness. In the musical realm, French culture had a strong slant toward opera and programmatic instrumental music, as seen, for example, in the keyboard suites of François Couperin.[7] Not surprisingly, the early aesthetic debate in France took place within this framework. In his 1719 treatise on painting and poetry, for example, Jean-Baptiste Du Bos proposed that music should imitate "all the sounds that nature herself uses to express the feelings and passions."[8] Even instrumental music, which in his discussion comprised only opera overtures, had this function: "The imitative truth of a symphony lies in its resemblance to the sound that it seeks to imitate."[9] Two and a half decades later, Charles Batteux refined the theory further by specifying that "the principal object of music and of dance should be the imitation of feeling or of passions."[10] Later writers such as Jean-Jacques Rousseau (*Essai sur l'origine des langues*, 1753) and André Morellet (*De l'Expression en musique et de l'imitation dans les arts*, 1771) continued to insist on the aesthetic necessity of this type of musical mimesis. Even the treatises of Boyé and Michel-Paul-Gui de Chabanon (both from 1779), which have sometimes been interpreted as the earliest signs of the rejection of mimetic theory,[11] do not proceed from a questioning of the validity of the theory as an aesthetic standard, but from the argument that music simply cannot meet its requirements. For both men, however, music then became little more than a "pleasure of the senses and not of the intelligence," effectively denying it any serious aesthetic value.[12] Chabanon even concluded by proposing that music can express four basic characters – tender, pleasant, happy, and passionate – making the distinction between his theory and the overtly mimetic one of Batteux merely a matter of semantics and specificity.[13] Thus, mimesis found no serious challengers in eighteenth-century France.

In England and Scotland, French theories of musical mimesis found a strong echo, particularly in the first two-thirds of the century. James Harris, Charles Avison, and Daniel Webb all insisted that music could be counted among the imitative arts, albeit as an imperfect one that needed the assistance of poetry.[14] But British writers on aesthetics came from the background of the empiricist philosophers, who were concerned with the world of the senses and with practical questions of cause and effect. Moreover, they were also influenced by the marked psychological slant in eighteenth-century British intellectual discourse, especially pronounced in the area of rhetoric. In that discipline, seminal figures like Henry Home (Lord Kames), John Ogilvie,

George Campbell, and Joseph Priestly had shifted the focus away from the classical Greek perspective (which concentrated on the proper arrangement of the arguments used by an orator to persuade an audience), to an analysis of the way in which the audience comes to believe in, or feel about, the orator's subject.[15] British aesthetic treatises reflected these intellectual predilections by their interest in *how* music could *move* human passions, an issue that they invariably linked to any discussion of its ability to imitate or express them. In the last quarter of the century, James Beattie and Thomas Twining became increasingly uncomfortable with equating imitation with the expression of the passions. They both stated unequivocally that music should not be considered an imitative art; both, however, insisted that it must engage the passions, and Beattie found instrumental music to be particularly indeterminate and vague in that task.[16] Not until the writings of Archibald Alison and Adam Smith in the 1790s do any small signs appear that instrumental music might derive firm aesthetic value from an entirely different quarter.[17]

As this quick review of French and British views on mimesis should indicate, the theory braided together several distinct but nonetheless closely related ideas and attitudes that need to be separated before we turn to a consideration of the subject in German-speaking lands. Simply stated, musical mimesis was understood in several different ways. It could mean the pure imitation of nature (the depiction of bird calls, thunderstorms, battles, etc.), or sometimes, as in Du Bos, the imitation of the sounds that nature uses to express the passions. The latter then opened the door to the possibility that music could imitate or express the passions themselves. Most authors beginning with Batteux subscribed to that view, though later writers (Twining, for example) often made a semantic distinction that excluded such expressivity from the realm of pure mimesis. But "music as an imitative art" and "music as an expressive art" remained closely entwined in mimetic theory throughout the century. Equally entwined, especially in England (and, as we shall see, in Germany as well), were the strands of thought focusing on the imitation, the expression, and/or the arousal of the passions, with the distinction among them not always clearly maintained.[18] No matter which combination of ideas was being proposed, however, it had to be admitted that music seemed incapable of complying with these aesthetic requirements in ways that were specific and immediately understandable, unless, of course, the music had words to explain it. Hence the general aesthetic valuation of vocal music over instrumental.

The question of instrumental music aesthetics in late eighteenth-century German-speaking lands is especially interesting because of the enormous amount, and high quality, of absolute (as opposed to overtly programmatic) instrumental pieces produced over the entire region, from Hamburg to Vienna. More than one twentieth-century musicologist has puzzled over the seeming incongruity of German and Austrian compositional practice and aesthetic standards. Carl Dahlhaus, for example, states baldly that by 1800 there was no classical music aesthetics that corresponded to the compositions of Haydn and Mozart.[19] After quoting Dahlhaus's statement in their study of Austrian music, Rudolf Flotzinger and Gernot Gruber continue by asserting that an appropriate aesthetic for the Viennese Classic period did not truly emerge until the early nineteenth-century writings of Hegel.[20] Jakob de Ruiter notes that the problem lay in the fact that North German critics continued to be irritated by instrumental music – especially symphonies, sonatas, and concertos – that "did not express particular passions [*Leidenschaften*] or sentiments [*Empfindungen*] or was not programmatic."[21] Neal Zaslaw expresses a similar opinion in his book on Mozart's symphonies, observing that aestheticians of the eighteenth century had difficulties with the concept of "abstract" art.[22] James Webster proposes to solve the conundrum – at least partially – by speculating that many of Haydn's supposedly absolute works may have actually had extra-musical associations.[23] However one approaches the problem, one central fact remains clear: the mimetic standard *did* resound throughout the century in German philosophical and theoretical discussions of music.

During the first half of the century, aesthetic debate was dominated by music theorists who championed the concept of music as a rhetorical art, capable of expressing and arousing specific affections or passions by means of often elaborate musico-poetic compositional processes.[24] Theorists sympathetic to the latest compositional style (for example, Johann Mattheson, Johann David Heinichen, and Johann Adolf Scheibe) commonly argued for the superior aesthetic quality of a natural vocal melody backed by a simple accompaniment. As a result, complex polyphony (still much beloved in the Teutonic musical world) and all types of instrumental music were relegated to aesthetic back burners, occasional attempts to reinstate them notwithstanding.[25] With the 1751 German translation of Batteux's treatise, which precipitated a spate of other translations from both French and English sources, the issue of musical mimesis was grafted onto the German view of music as a rhetorical art, producing a particularly hardy variety of mimetic expressivity that stubbornly refused to go away. German writers rather quickly rejected the notion of music as an imitative art in the purest sense, generally heaping scorn on the programmatic bird-call-and-thunderstorm type of composition.[26] However, almost to a person, they clung to the idea that music's meaning and its intrinsic value resided in its ability to portray and arouse the

passions or – in the vocabulary of the later eighteenth century – the sentiments.[27] While debate raged around how specific that portrayal had to be, or
how many passions could be allowed in a single composition or movement,
or which passions were appropriate for musical expression, the basic premise
that music had to *mean* something in order to have aesthetic value was never
seriously questioned. As long as that premise remained, instrumental music
could never challenge the supremacy of the vocal realm or attain independent
aesthetic status.

The first two German treatises on music aesthetics published after the
German translation of Batteux sought to blend French concepts with indige-
nous ones. Christian Gottfried Krause, in his *Von der musikalischen Poesie* of
1752, discussed the advantages of musical mimesis and noted the positive
effects it could have on morals (another favorite theme in German aesthetic
thought); to this end he gave detailed directions on the procedures for arousing specific passions and imparting definite meaning to each individual
phrase.[28] In vocal pieces, both the music and the words would work "towards
the clarification of the ideas and towards the persuasion and activation of the
listeners," which constituted "the greatest superiority that vocal music has
over instrumental music."[29] Johann Adam Hiller's commentary on Batteux,
entitled "Abhandlung von der Nachahmung der Natur in der Musik" (1754),
also adopted the notion that the expression of the passions constituted
musical mimesis. Although he felt compelled to account for instrumental
pieces that did not meet this requirement by introducing the standard of the
"wonderful" (i.e. that which produces amazement), he clearly did not assign
them a very high status and went on at great length about the dangers of
"empty virtuosity."[30] (One might also note that "wonder" was one of the six
primitive passions enumerated by Descartes.) Hiller's preoccupation with
music's mimetic expressivity was long-lasting, for in 1781 he published a
translation of Chabanon's treatise, saying he found it to be well written and
substantial (*gegründet*).[31]

The concept of musical mimesis through expressivity was given both scholarly weight and broad distribution with the publication of Johann Georg
Sulzer's monumental *Allgemeine Theorie der schönen Künste*, first published
in the 1770s (the fourth edition appeared in the 1790s). In the entry entitled
"Expression in Music," Sulzer (or more likely Johann Philipp Kirnberger,
who wrote the music articles in the early volumes) stated flatly that "every
piece of music must have a definite character and evoke emotions of a specific
kind."[32] Once again, instrumental music simply could not measure up. As the
historian Johann Nikolaus Forkel pointed out in an article written during the
1780s:

All our instrumental pieces . . . are in a certain sense no more than exercises through which we can prepare ourselves for the higher purpose of music . . . Sulzer thus places them . . . at the bottom of the musical genres and says that they generally represent no more than a lively and not unpleasant noise, or a pleasant, entertaining conversation, which does not, however, engage the heart.

Though Forkel demurred that Sulzer's judgment might be somewhat severe, he nevertheless agreed with it in principle.[33]

Even during the 1780s and 1790s, German writers sought to explain the aesthetic value of music through increasingly elaborate schemes accommodating mimesis to the exigencies of composition. For example, in 1780 the literary scholar Johann Jakob Engel published a short treatise entitled *Ueber die musikalische Malerey*, which was reviewed in several journals and later reprinted in the *Magazin der Musik*.[34] After insisting that "music is actually created for sentiment [*Empfindung*], for in it everything works toward this purpose," he proposed three categories of mimesis: (1) the direct imitation of natural sounds and phenomena; (2) "transcendental" imitation, in which the music shares certain characteristics with the object portrayed, "so that the *Phantasie* can easily make the connection" (as when quick notes represent running, for example); and (3) the representation of the impression which the object makes on the soul.[35] With regard to instrumental music, Engel was quite specific: "A symphony, a sonata . . . must contain the realization of one passion, which can of course mutate into a variety of sentiments, just as they develop one after another in a soul completely immersed in passion, outwardly undisturbed in the free course of its ideas."[36] Here Engel took a position on one of the most debated points in late eighteenth-century German aesthetic discourse, i.e. how *many* passions or sentiments could legitimately be represented in a composition, and what the precise relationship among them should be. In 1786, Carl Ludwig Junker returned to the issue, distinguishing between the concrete passions and the more nebulous sentiments: "Each passion announces itself through its own music; and this sound awakens in our heart a sentiment, which itself is analogous to that which brought it forth."[37]

Caught up in the minutiae of this controversial point, scholars had no time to spend casting about for other basic premises. Even Christian Gottfried Körner's *Ueber Charakterdarstellung in der Musik*, published in 1795, could not completely break with the past, despite some undoubtedly forward-looking ideas. Some musicologists, searching for an eighteenth-century aesthetic theory that could effectively accommodate the instrumental masterworks of Haydn and Mozart, have heralded Körner's as the only eighteenth-century aesthetic theory capable of accounting for them.[38] While he does come closer than the others, his theory ultimately rested on premises that were simply no longer tenable. He went to great lengths to dismiss the theory of mimesis, rejecting both its purely imitative and expressive aspects, but then proposed a complicated system by which music should represent human character instead. His point of departure was obviously the controversy over the number of passions or sentiments allowed in a single composition, which he sought to resolve by the analogy of the multifarious feelings and emotions present in one human being. The sonata, in other words, still had to mean something.

The extent to which German-speaking musical culture assumed that musical meaning was determined by mimetic expressivity, and that instrumental music thus remained subservient to vocal, can be seen in the frequency with which those ideas turned up in other types of discourse. In his *Versuch über die wahre Art, das Clavier zu spielen* (1753), C. P. E. Bach provided a list of the affects that music could express. During the 1780s, Christian Friedrich Daniel Schubart joined the debate by proposing, as others had before him, his own list of specific characters for each key. His preference for vocal music also permeated his writings. For example, he divided his discussion of musical style into the traditional church, dramatic, pantomimic (dance) and chamber style, allotting five pages to the vocal areas of church and dramatic music, two pages to dance, and a half page to instrumental music in the chamber style.[39] As late as 1793 in a composition treatise actually emphasizing instrumental music, Heinrich Christoph Koch trotted out the standard party line, prefacing his remarks with the statement that music should express the sentiments (*Empfindungen*).[40]

Statements about music in non-music forums addressed to a general readership were, if anything, even more dogmatic. For example, the periodical *Unterhaltungen*, published in Hamburg in the late 1760s, stated bluntly in an article on musical taste: "The passions are the objects of music; it should arouse and then quiet them through regular tones. If it accomplishes this goal, you can say that it is good; otherwise, it is not."[41] An article on the wisdom of giving children music lessons published in the moral weekly *Der Greis* in 1768, praised, among other things, its positive effect on the passions.[42] In 1776, an article in *Der teutsche Merkur* somewhat grudgingly acknowledged that even "purposeless" instrumental pieces *could* enchant the listener if well performed. But the author still insisted that they would be even better if written with character and expressive purpose, because they would then affect the heart as well as the senses.[43] As late as 1792, a writer for a provincial newspaper (published in Flensburg) remarked that even a sonata by Haydn would ultimately leave the listener cold:

Music is nothing more than a succession of tones intended to express certain sentiments, or to arouse them in others, or to entertain . . .

Just as music is born through sentiment, in the same manner it affects only sentiment; the heart is the actual target of music. Words affect reason, producing in it
special ideas [*Vorstellungen*], which can, of course, then produce feelings again. But
music affects the feelings directly. As soon as it has aroused the sentiments, it has
achieved its purpose. No matter how brilliant, no matter how artfully woven together,
it is not a true artistic product if it does not arouse sentiments.

Pure instrumental music can certainly make, in and of itself, a very lively impression: a beautifully performed Haydn sonata can do a lot. But in this type of music
always lies a great deal that is vague, ambiguous, uncertain – and you have to have a
certain amount of musical training to get true pleasure from it. Such things . . . are like
an agreeable, entertaining conversation that one hears with relish, but without interest. They are more sleight-of-hand than nourishment for the heart.[44]

I do not wish to overstate my case here and imply that *no* German author
ever expressed a thought that could indicate an aesthetic direction besides
mimetic expressivity. But the persistence of the concept – and the related prejudice against instrumental music – in the discourse about music aesthetics is
nothing less than striking. Caught in the vise of mimesis, neither music theorists nor philosophers managed to articulate an aesthetic theory that could
explain the undeniable effect and increasing importance of instrumental
music as an independent, absolute genre devoid of extra-musical trappings.
To understand why they did not – and indeed could not – we must delve into
the processes of intellectual history and examine the ways in which old concepts die out and new ones emerge. One of the most influential models for
this process was developed by Thomas Kuhn in *The Structure of Scientific
Revolutions*, originally published in 1962. Kuhn, a trained physicist, proposed
a theory of intellectual change that not only provided the foundation for
current thought in the history of science, but has also been adopted, and
adapted, by other areas of history and the social sciences as well. Central to
his theory is the concept of the *paradigm*, a set of values and intellectual
assumptions that structure the mode of thought in a particular community.[45]
Kuhn demonstrates that a mature scientific field will be characterized by the
general acceptance, by all members of the scientific community, of a single
paradigm that establishes the parameters of research and experimentation.
For example, before the Copernican "revolution," astronomy was guided by
the Ptolemaic paradigm, which placed the earth at the center of the universe.[46]
Being an astronomer before Copernicus meant accepting that premise; those
who did not were excluded from the community.

Though I would not wish to argue the applicability of Kuhn's model of paradigms to all of intellectual history, it is very useful in explaining the aesthetic situation in the late eighteenth-century German-speaking lands: the writers and thinkers in that intellectual community were enmeshed in the mimetic paradigm they had adopted and were thus subject to the ramifications of paradigmatic thought in the ways that Kuhn describes. For example, once a paradigm has been accepted by a community, it will restrict the choice of problems-to-be-solved to those that have solutions within the context of the paradigm.[47] In terms of the mimetic paradigm, the "problem" of vocal music allowed for acceptable aesthetic "solutions," so it – and not instrumental music – became the focus of formal musical aesthetic thought. In addition, paradigms can blind the community to those problems that it cannot easily address: hence aesthetics could intellectually ignore the demands of instrumental music.

But when those problems become too insistent, they precipitate a crisis, leading to a revolution in which a new paradigm replaces the old.[48] For musical aesthetics, the "revolution" occurred in the years immediately surrounding 1800, and when the dust had settled, the paradigm that had completely dominated eighteenth-century Germany had been turned on its head: music had become the most exalted of all the fine arts, and instrumental music the most exalted of all music, invested not only with aesthetic, but with metaphysical significance as well.[49] Kuhn found precisely this type of radical revaluation of perception in the scientific revolutions he studied, arguing that the transition from the old to the new is not achieved "by an articulation or extension of the old paradigm," even though the new one will invariably take over much of the traditional paradigm's vocabulary.[50] Despite any semantic connections, the two paradigms will be incommensurate, because the change involves "a reconstruction of the field from *new fundamentals* [my italics], a reconstruction that changes some of the field's most elementary theoretical generalizations as well as many of its paradigm methods and applications." He compares this paradigm shift to the familiar phenomenon of "gestalt switch," in which "the marks on paper that were first seen as a bird are now seen as an antelope, or vice versa."[51] One cannot see both simultaneously.

Nearly always, such fundamental changes in perception can occur only in those not steeped in the traditions of the older paradigm, i.e. the very young or those outside the field itself.[52] And, in fact, the paradigm shift was heralded not by an established writer on musical aesthetics, but by two young figures from the literary world, Ludwig Tieck (1773–1853) and Wilhelm Heinrich Wackenroder (1773–98), in essays published in 1799. Tieck proclaimed:

Art is independent and free in instrumental music; it prescribes its own rules all by itself; it daydreams playfully and without purpose, and yet it satisfies and reaches what is highest; it completely follows its dark drives and expresses with its triflings what is deepest and most wonderful . . . Instead of portraying a single sentiment, it projects a whole world, a complete drama of human affects.[53]

Using equally rhapsodic prose, Wackenroder spoke of music's ability to express the emotions. However, his concept of "expressivity" had little use for the pedantic requirements of mimesis and turned music's "vagueness" into a virtue of metaphysical proportions. He used the vocabulary of mimesis, but with Kuhn's "gestalt switch."

> I consider music to be the most marvelous of [the fine arts], because it portrays human feelings in a superhuman way, because it shows us all the emotions of our soul above our heads in incorporeal form, clothed in golden clouds of airy harmonies, – because it speaks a language which we do not know in our ordinary life, which we have learned, we do not know where and how, and which one would consider to be solely the language of angels . . . it is also music which infuses in us true serenity of *soul* . . .
> What do they want, the faint-hearted and doubting reasoners, who require each of the hundreds and hundreds of musical pieces explained in words, and who cannot understand that not every piece has an inexpressible meaning like a painting? Are they trying to measure the richer language by the poorer and to resolve into words that which disdains words?[54]

One of the earliest comprehensive statements of the new aesthetic paradigm came from another musical outsider, the literary philosopher Johann Gottfried Herder, in what has been described as a "radical departure from much pre-romantic musical thought."[55] In his *Kalligone* (1800), Herder sought to explain the perceived emotional impact of music through a psychological and physiological response of the body, which will react involuntarily to sounds (and music) *regardless* of whether or not the music itself is a portrayal of anything. Thus he relieved music of the necessity to *mean* anything, and even of the burden of *arousing* particular passions or emotions. But he took his reasoning a step further, circumventing the charge that music would then be no more than empty sound and sensory pleasure by asserting that "Sound, the summoner of the passions, has a power that we all experience, we respond to it both physically and spiritually."[56] Rejecting the Kantian notion that our pleasure in music derives from our pleasure in its mathematical proportions, he insisted that its emotional impact must be explained by its "purely musical qualities, its functions, its procedures, fluctuations of power, its ebb and flow, its rise and fall, its strength, its weakness, its vitality, its languor."[57] In the final step, he concluded that "Music must be free to speak without encumbrance, as is the tongue. Song and speech do not adopt the same means. Music has developed into a self-sufficient art, *sui generis*, dispensing with words."[58]

Whereas Herder approached the issue from a psychological and Tieck and Wackenroder from a poetic point of view, Christian Friedrich Michaelis, a philosopher and interpreter of Kant, provided a more practical and specifically musical point of view. Writing for the *Allgemeine musikalische Zeitung* in 1806, Michaelis agreed that "musical sounds are in themselves a spiritual phenomenon," and went on to assert that precisely because of music's "representational vagueness," it comes closer to "aesthetic ideas the more it distances itself from intellectual concepts. For aesthetic ideas, products of reason and imagination, transcend all the constraints that bind the intellect to the everyday world."[59] He felt that the "magic of music" resided not in what the melodies meant or what the music expressed, but in "musical form," and that aesthetic pleasure derived from music's stimulation of our "awareness of the beautiful, the sublime, and the noble."[60] Four years later, the poet and composer E. T. A. Hoffmann opened his famous review of Beethoven's Fifth Symphony with the stirring words:

If we are talking about music as an independent art, we should mean only instrumental music, which – disdaining interference from any other art – clearly expresses the unique essence of music as nothing else does. It is the most romantic of all arts, almost – one might say – the only *pure* romantic one. Orpheus's lyre opened the door of Orkus. Music opens the door for us to an unknown realm; a world that has nothing in common with the outer world of the senses that surrounds us, one in which we can leave behind all feelings defined by concepts and give ourselves over to the ineffable. How little do they recognize the unique essence of music, those composers that sought to represent those definite sentiments, or even events, thus handling in a representative fashion, the art that is the very opposite of representation![61]

Together, these writers had effected a dramatic paradigm shift that laid the foundation for the nineteenth-century debate on music aesthetics.[62] As Kuhn points out, the adoption of a new paradigm will invariably make many of the old problems and questions simply irrelevant. Whether or not music *could* mean something ceased to be an issue, simply because it did not have to. In a historical blink of the eye, it was no longer necessary to provide an answer to Fontenelle's question, because no one was asking it anymore.

But one issue still remains. Where does a new paradigm get the "new fundamentals" Kuhn describes? Are they the sudden and exclusive invention of a few "great minds," bursting upon the horizon with unexpected and unprecedented brilliance? Or do the new fundamentals trace their origins to previously accepted thought? For all his emphasis on "gestalt shift" and "revolution," Kuhn does not propose that new ideas materialize miraculously from the void. But his explanation of antecedents revolves around the research and experimentation typical of the sciences, activities which have no direct parallel in the practice of aesthetics and philosophy. Here we must turn to models more appropriate for intellectual and cultural shifts in humanistic endeavors, an issue addressed by a wide range of twentieth-century literary scholars, historians, and rhetoricians. Despite the differences in perspective among these disciplines, most major scholars agree about one central point. They reject the notion that a culture can reverse itself instantaneously and suddenly accord general acceptance to completely new ideas that are radically different from prevailing ones. In his *The Mirror and the Lamp*, the literary theorist Meyer Howard Abrams argues, for example, that romanticism retained the eighteenth-century concept of expressivity, merely replacing the objective portrayal of nature and the passions with their subjective interpretation by the artist.[63]

On a broader, more theoretical level, the historian Fernand Braudel posits geographical and demographical "structures" and cultural "conjunctures" that provide both the basis for, and the limits of, human understanding and experience within a given period of time. He emphasizes the interplay between "long-term continuity . . . and the short-term surges and sequences, which break against it as against a rock, but which sometimes, like the waves of the sea, break it down, producing (in Braudel's words) 'ce passage d'un monde à l'autre.'"[64] In this "structural history," isolated events and the actions (or writings) of "great men" lose their significance as the driving force in history.[65] Even those figures singled out by traditional history as great "manipulators of events – Bismarck, for example – prove, on close inspection, to be almost entirely conditioned" by their own cultural context.[66] Lawrence Stone, who has described Braudel's structuralist history as deterministic and fatalistic, has nonetheless advocated the study of collective "mental structures" as a route to historical understanding.[67] However, he does not champion a return to the "paperchase of ideas back through the ages" variety of intellectual history, in which "great books" (written of course by "great men") were treated in a "historical vacuum" as the touchstones of progress.[68] Historical change must be understood as the intersection of many disparate, often previously ignored, factors, not all of which qualify as "great" literature or "profound" thought.[69] In other words, though a few influential thinkers will articulate the new fundamentals of a new paradigm, the fundamentals themselves are prepared and shaped by cultural conjunctures, social factors and the prevailing thought patterns of the community.

Musicologists have sought antecedents for the early nineteenth-century paradigm in a variety of ways. John Neubauer proposes that the history of music aesthetics has been characterized by the alternating prominence of

Pythagorean (where the beauty and significance of music resides in mathematical proportions) and rhetorical systems, and that the early nineteenth-century "recognition of instrumental music went hand in hand with a revival of Pythagoreanism."[70] Others have identified precedents in selected outcroppings of thought in the late eighteenth century, and where scholars look, there they usually find. Carl Dahlhaus, for example, ties E. T. A. Hoffmann's analytic and poetic Beethoven reviews to the poetics of Klopstock and the Göttinger Hainbund, and reads an exaltation of the pure power of instrumental music into Sulzer's article on the sublime in the symphony.[71] Gudrun Henneberg finds a connecting link in Forkel's early insistence on the concept of unity and in Koch's recognition of the individual work of art.[72] In a work more cognizant of cultural conjunctures, Bellamy Hosler proposes that the interaction of French mimetic theory, Italian instrumental music, and the value accorded instrumental music in the German pietistic tradition produced the romantic musical aesthetic.[73] These are but a few of the explanations offered by modern scholars, all offering defensible solutions to the question of historical connections. But to a certain extent they all *"gehen mit der Kirche ums Kreuz"* (carry the church around the cross), picking various strands of ideas out of the fabric of eighteenth-century thought and weaving them into new cloth. They fail to provide what another scholar from the history of science, Ludwik Fleck, has called a "thought collective." Fleck uses the concept to denote a "community of persons mutually exchanging ideas or maintaining intellectual interaction," whose readiness to perceive reality in a certain manner (which he terms thought-style) "provides the special 'carrier' for the historical development of any field of thought as well as for the given stock of knowledge and level of culture."[74] In other words, Fleck would say that the "readiness to perceive" instrumental music as an independent art free of any mimetic requirements had to have been firmly embedded in eighteenth-century German culture – even if it was not overtly promulgated – for the new romantic ideas to take root. It had to have been both substantial and widespread to have provided the basis for change. Where then, was the thought collective that prepared turn-of-the-century German-speaking culture to receive and accept the new twist of an independent, metaphysical instrumental music aesthetics, and can its existence be reconciled with the paradigm of mimesis that I have described?

I would like to propose a solution that takes into account certain elements that Kuhn did not consider in constructing his model but which Fleck suggests, i.e. the different levels and styles of discourse found in any national community.[75] Without question, the paradigm of mimesis structured the theoretical and philosophical discussions of music aesthetics in German-speaking lands in such a way that it simply could not engender the new fundamentals. However, concurrent with these intellectualized strata was another level of discourse, one that had an entirely different purpose and thus was not bound by the constraints of the mimetic paradigm: reviews of instrumental music that began to appear in German-language journals and newspapers during the last four decades of the eighteenth century. By and large directed at non-specialists, these reviews moved on the edge of the realm of aesthetics without manifesting much in the way of philosophical or theoretical pretenses. They directed their attention instead toward solving a specific problem: how to evaluate new instrumental music so that its "consumers" (both listeners and performers) would know what would be worth their time and money. The practical nature of this enterprise forced the reviewers (some of whom participated in the debate on the intellectual strata as well) to come up with some realistic standards that would allow them to do their job. Precisely because they were not trying to write about aesthetic theory, the reviewers could think about instrumental music in new and different ways.

Collectively, their discourse took a form and shape that had ramifications beyond the simple undermining of an outdated theory of art, for it helped to establish the aesthetic criteria that would form the core of the new one. And by exploring the practice of music reviewing itself, reviewers laid the foundation for the nineteenth-century style of criticism, ultimately one of the most important purveyors of this new romantic paradigm. In addition, the very existence of reviews treating instrumental pieces as objects suitable for aesthetic evaluation helped to undercut the notion of a purely functional role for instrumental music, thus preparing the public for its later, more exalted status. The review collective did not set out to do all these grand tasks, of course, and we might well ask how such a humble forum could have become so influential. To answer that question, we must first turn to an examination of how its discourse reached the wider German-speaking world.

2

Answering with a unified voice

[1768] [Marpurg's *Historisch-kritische Beiträge* and his *Kritische Briefe*] have had a good effect, in that music has begun to be viewed as a science again, one that can be judged just like other sciences can. In critical and scholarly journals it is being given its proper place alongside other scholarly things. In this area the *Allgemeine deutsche Bibliothek* deserves special praise. The *Leipziger gelehrten Zeitungen* has likewise taken up the task of announcing and evaluating newly published writings and works that pertain to music.[1]

[1769] What does the *Leipziger Zeitungen* do for musical criticism? It judges music rarely and usually superficially.[2]

[1778] Herr Forkel has undertaken the useful business of making musical works known through criticism . . . still a rather fallow field in need of cultivation, and one more worthy than many others . . . One writes for the learned and the unlearned; and the large number of the latter, whose approval must nonetheless be considered here, often requires a moderate use of reflective thought and a demonstrative writing style.[3]

[1795] At a time when our book catalogs are nearly half filled with magazine titles, it would be tragic for music lovers not to find a single musical journal that in some way continues the thread of its history. To keep this from happening, three different journals in Berlin (which is full of music lovers) recently tried out various formats – a weekly, a monthly, and finally a newspaper. But for naught! Each new attempt failed. The last didn't even last a year. Has poor music sunk to being no more than an amusement or a toy? Is it nothing but jangling? Among all the thousands of music lovers and devotees, are there really too few educated minds to support a journal that would cultivate the scholarly side of music, which is as pleasant and entertaining as it is necessary and useful?[4]

The reviews that formed the thought collective appeared in nearly fifty different publications, spanning a forty year period that began around 1760 and
ended in 1798, just before the emergence of the new romantic aesthetic paradigm.[5] Fortunately for the evolution of instrumental aesthetics, they were not
restricted to music magazines, which folded with almost clockwork regularity, as the last citation above implies and the dates in table 2.1 confirm. Other
types of critical journals managed to pick up the slack, providing both needed
continuity and the critical mass of opinion necessary for the formation of a
thought collective. Simply demonstrating a steady flow of reviews will not
suffice for my purposes here, however, precisely because the variety of
publications that ensured the existence of the collective also worked against
its cohesiveness. To function collectively, the reviews must have had a fundamental similarity transcending any differences in journalistic type and
purpose. Moreover, to serve as a preparation for the new romantic paradigm
in the manner that I have proposed, they must have been readily accessible to
a wide audience over all the German-speaking lands; and to explain the rapid
acceptance of the paradigm, the aesthetic concepts they contained must have
gained common acceptance. The fact that they appeared in such myriad
publications would seem to argue in favor of these last points, so before
addressing the issue of cohesiveness, let us first turn to an examination of
journalism in eighteenth-century Germany, particularly the types of publications and the size of their readership.

Though lagging somewhat behind England and France in the development
of a general readership press, Germany, Switzerland, and, to a lesser extent
Austria, did begin to produce an increasing number of journals and newspapers, stimulated by the Enlightenment goal of education for a wider
segment of the population. Newspapers reporting political events became a
regular feature of the cultural landscape in most cities; in the years between
1766 and 1790, over two thousand new German-language magazines and
journals were founded, more than three times the total from the previous
twenty-five years.[6] These periodicals included everything from the "moral
weeklies," intended as edifying entertainment for the general reading public,
to "general scholarly journals," to specialized publications in all fields,
including music. Many undertook book reviewing as a part of their journalistic mission. As the editors of the *Allgemeine deutsche Bibliothek* noted in
the journal's inaugural issue, "Aficionados of the latest literature are scattered
throughout Germany, some in small cities that do not even have a bookstore.
They should welcome having . . . an overview of the most recent literature."[7]
Beginning around 1760, a few journals and newspapers began to include

Table 2.1 *Periodicals with instrumental music reviews, 1760–1798*

Music magazines

Kritische Briefe, *1760–1763
Wöchentliche Nachrichten, 1767–1770
Musikalisch-kritische Bibliothek, 1778
Musikalischer Almanach, 1783–1789
Musikalisches Kunstmagazin, 1782, 1791
Magazin der Musik, 1783–1788
Musicalische Bibliotek, 1784–1785
Musikalische Real-Zeitung/Musikalische Korrespondenz, 1788–1792
Musikalisches Wochenblatt/Musikalische Monatsschrift, 1792
Berlinische musikalische Zeitung, 1793–1794
Journal der Tonkunst, 1795
Augsburger musikalischer Merkur, 1795

Scholarly review journals

Frankfurtische gelehrten Zeitungen, *1760–1771
Freymüthige Nachrichten, *1760–1763
Bibliothek der schönen Wissenschaften, *1760–1767
Neue Zeitungen von gelehrten Sachen, *1760–1784
Göttingische Anzeigen, *1760–1798*
Altonaischer gelehrter Mercurius, 1763–1788
Jenaische Zeitungen, 1765–1787
Allgemeine deutsche Bibliothek, 1765–1794
Unterhaltungen, 1766–1770
Realzeitung der Wissenschaften, Künste und der Commerzien, 1770–1788
Erlangische gelehrte Anmerkungen, 1770–1798
Prager gelehrte Nachrichten, 1771–1772
Gelehrte Zeitung [Kiel], 1771–1778; 1787–1790
Russische Bibliothek, 1772–1789
Frankfurter gelehrte Anzeigen, 1772–1790
Der teutsche Merkur/Der neue teutsche Merkur 1773–1798*
Gothaische gelehrte Zeitungen, 1774–1798*
Litterarische Nachrichten, 1775–1776
Allgemeines Verzeichniß neuer Bücher, 1776–1784
Erfurtische gelehrte Zeitungen, *1776–1798*
Berlinisches litterarisches Wochenblatt, 1777
Nürnbergische gelehrte Zeitung, 1777–1798*
Litteratur- und Theaterzeitung, 1778–1783
Raisonnirendes Bücherverzeichniß, 1782–1784
Strasburgische gelehrte Nachrichten, 1782–1785
Ephemereiden der Litteratur und des Theaters, 1785–1786

Table 2.1 (*cont.*)

Neue Leipziger gelehrte Zeitungen, 1785–1787
Allgemeine Litteratur-Zeitung, 1785–1798*
Wirzburger gelehrte Anzeigen, 1786–1798*
Oberdeutsche, allgemeine Litteraturzeitung, 1788–1798*
Tübingische gelehrte Anzeigen, 1783–1798*
Neue Leipziger gelehrte Anzeigen, 1789–1797
Neue allgemeine deutsche Bibliothek, 1793–1798*

Political newspapers
Hamburgischer Correspondent 1760–1798*
Berlinische Nachrichten, 1761–1798*
Hamburgische neue Zeitung, 1767–1798*
Berlinische privilegirte Zeitung, 1770–1798*

Note: Dates give the volumes examined for this survey, which encompasses the period from 1760 through 1798. Asterisks indicate that a periodical actually began before, or ended after, these dates.

reviews of published musical compositions, a trend perhaps sparked by the surge in music publishing that followed Johann Gottlob Immanuel Breitkopf's adoption of a cost-effective method of printing in the 1750s.[8] Whatever the reason, music's inclusion in review columns served to enhance its intellectual standing, as the *Neue Zeitungen von gelehrten Sachen* observed in 1763:

From time to time we are asked to consider music in these pages, ever since musical pieces and characters have become objects for the printing press. We are all the more willing to do so because we can thereby confirm music in that rank it has enjoyed among other fields since antiquity, [rather than] regarding it as merely a craft, something that many do, either out of ignorance or prejudice.[9]

Though the isolated music review could be found in a surprising variety of publications, only three types consistently featured them: music magazines, scholarly review journals, and political newspapers.[10] To better understand their features and purpose, we should examine each in turn.

Music journalism had emerged in the early eighteenth century as part of the attempt to demystify the arcane art of musical composition and shape the taste of the musical dilettante. The periodicals that appeared in this early period were single-author publications like Johann Mattheson's *Critica Musica* (1722–25) and *Der vollkommene Kapellmeister* (1739) or Lorenz Christoph Mizler's *Neu eröffnete musikalische Bibliothek* (1736–54).

Devoted mainly to the propagation of their authors' particular viewpoints, these early magazines contained mostly essays, and any criticism of specific works generally occurred as an illustrative tool within this context. The isolated instances of reviewing *per se* treated only vocal music, in keeping with the aesthetic preferences dictated by the mimetic paradigm.[11] Two of the early publications by the theorist Friedrich Wilhelm Marpurg, *Der critische Musicus an der Spree* and the *Historisch-kritische Beyträge* continued in a similar vein, but in the 82nd "letter" of his *Kritische Briefe über die Tonkunst*, in 1761, we finally encounter identifiable instrumental music reviews. Though Marpurg gave them formal headings that provided title and publication information in the manner of a standard book review, his ultimate polemical purpose negated any pretense of critical objectivity once the review began. With obvious glee, in tones dripping with sarcasm, he berated eleven of his twelve victims (sparing only a collection that he had edited) for their failure to live up to his theoretical standards:

Herr Wagenseil, who has received a lot of attention because of the amount of pieces he has produced, supposedly (I have been assured) plays the harpsichord quite nicely and – at the same time – is a very charming man. Glory enough for him! But his compositions? Even if they were correct with regard to the three necessary musical elements – melody, *Harmonie*, and phrasing – they would still only be mediocre, because in addition to the knowledge of the rules [of composition], there are an additional three things that must be present to produce something excellent: a creative spirit, fine judgment, and a diligent mind.[12]

Poor Wagenseil's music seems almost incidental, there only to provide a convenient punching bag for Marpurg's pugilistic critical commentary.

Over the next four decades, other single-author music magazines appeared, though not always with such idiosyncratic results. For the most part, the reviews in Johann Nikolaus Forkel's *Musicalisch-kritische Bibliothek* and *Musikalischer Almanach* steer clear of his particular soapboxes, but the single review in Heinrich Christoph Koch's *Journal der Tonkunst* seems specially designed to mourn the decline of the old art of counterpoint, a recurring theme elsewhere in the magazine. Though the dilettante editor Hans Adolph Friedrich von Eschtruth had no particular theoretical ax to grind in his *Musicalische Bibliotek*, he did adopt a recognizable style, described by the *Allgemeine deutsche Bibliothek* as "occasionally witty and often satirical as well."[13] An extreme personal viewpoint did not always garner praise, however, especially when it was perceived as interfering with the journalistic mission, as the *Allgemeine deutsche Bibliothek* pointed out in its review of Johann Friedrich Reichardt's *Musikalisches Kunstmagazin*.

It is obvious that Herr Reichardt feels strongly about various commonly held basic assumptions, and in these we can happily agree with him. But he also has various ones unique to him . . . We really wish, since Herr Reichardt is one of the few authors capable of writing musical criticism, that he would pay more attention to his readers than to himself. References to his own feelings simply do not help when he is discussing musical works, because the reader cannot possibly experience those feelings in the same way.[14]

Carl Friedrich Cramer also took exception to Reichardt's critical excesses and "transparent egotism," advising him to moderate the "passion of his ideas and feelings with the coolness of reflection."[15]

Part of Reichardt's reception problem stemmed from a change in standards. By the 1780s, when he published this first volume of his *Musikalisches Kunstmagazin*, music journalism had a different model to follow, one that aspired to greater objectivity and required the collaboration of several authors. The *Wöchentliche Nachrichten und Anmerkungen die Musik betreffend*, edited and published by the composer Johann Adam Hiller from 1766 to 1770, is usually cited as the earliest of this type. The extent of Hiller's authorship and the identity of any possible collaborators have never been firmly established, but his contemporaries believed that he did not write it alone.[16] In any case, he established a format that became standard journalistic practice for the rest of the century. He included not only formal articles of both informative and polemical natures, but also correspondence columns reporting on musical events in other cities, the occasional report on a musical performance, and formal reviews of recently published music. In the reviews, Hiller moved away from the fevered polemics that Marpurg had favored, muting his own aesthetic agenda in favor of an evaluation that focused on the work itself.[17] His reviews offered comments intended to assist potential consumers of the music, both listeners wanting guidance in developing their musical taste and purchasers needing advice on how best to spend their musical budget. For the most part he favored a positive tone, perhaps due to his stated reluctance to offend composers with unfavorable reviews, a position that did not go unchallenged. In a review of the magazine's first issue, the *Allgemeine deutsche Bibliothek* argued that such timidity was unwarranted. Though it acknowledged that most musicians were indeed a "*genus irritabile*," it encouraged Hiller's reviewers to stick to the truth and not worry about ruffling any feathers, especially since not all musicians would be capable of an adequate rebuttal anyway.[18]

These comments notwithstanding, both Hiller's collaborative format and his upbeat review philosophy were adopted by most of the later music magazines in the collective. In fact, the *Musikalisches Wochenblatt/Musikalische*

Monatsschrift often turned into a mutual admiration society when one of the contributors had occasion to review a piece by one of his colleagues. An even cozier arrangement might be suspected in the case of the *Musikalische Real-Zeitung/Musikalische Korrespondenz* and the *Berlinische musikalische Zeitung*, for both were issued by music publishers and frequently reviewed music from their own press. Their reviews, however, did not differ markedly in tone from other, less commercially tainted, journals, and they certainly did not hesitate to pan a bad piece, regardless of who published it. The *Berlinische musikalische Zeitung* dismissed some serenades by Anton Groene (published by its own publisher), calling them "tinkly little pieces for women and effeminate men."[19] Less succinctly, but no less damningly, Heinrich Philipp Bossler's *Musikalische Real-Zeitung* painfully dissected the compositional incompetence of Friedrich Schmoll, whose sonatas had been inflicted on the world by Bossler's press:

Sulzer remarks that much genius, science, as well as a receptive and abiding sensitivity, are required for writing good sonatas, characteristics that we miss in the composer of the above sonatas, and in almost every one of them. Even the briefest glance will immediately convince one that Herr S. doesn't have the slightest concept of a good musical periodicity . . . One might perhaps forgive him if his works had any interest with regard to the other side [of musical composition]: but the reviewer couldn't find a single thought that distinguished itself either through the allure of novelty *per se* or through a new presentation, like you find in the works of a Haydn or Kozeluch . . . In general Herr S. is too little acquainted with the actual structure of *Harmonie* and with the rules of sound taste for us even to be able to rate his products among the mediocre. Moreover, judging from this second attempt, it will probably be difficult for Herr S. ever to get far enough to succeed in larger compositions, because, in addition to all of this he lacks the primary requirement, namely the gift of invention. That is the reason for the frequent repetitions in these sonatas, that often borders on the disgusting.[20]

Though one suspects that Bossler might have pulled the plug if *all* his publications had received such brutal treatment, his willingness to give his reviewers some freedom bespeaks a certain commitment to journalistic integrity.[21]

The readership targeted by all of the music magazines that published reviews reached beyond the narrow audience of professional musicians. According to the *Hamburgischer Correspondent*, the theorist Marpurg had "his eye on more than one kind of reader" in publishing the *Kritische Briefe* and attempted "to serve the dilettante as well as the professional practitioner."[22] Likewise, Cramer justified the need for his *Magazin der Musik* by noting the lack of a "general music magazine" that could satisfy the musical curiosity of "professional musicians and dilettantes."[23] Despite these attempts to reach a larger reading public, none of the music magazines managed to survive more than a few years, a fact much deplored by contemporary observers. (See the review of Koch's journal cited at the beginning of the chapter.) Reichardt's *Musikalisches Kunstmagazin* folded after the first volume because its meager subscription list could not cover the paper and printing costs (though both the *Allgemeine deutsche Bibliothek* and the *Magazin der Musik* found its format to be needlessly and excessively splendid!).[24] Perhaps the very fact that editors made such a conscious effort to appeal to both the specialized and general reader doomed their efforts, for as the *Neue allgemeine deutsche Bibliothek* observed in its review of the *Musikalisches Wochenblatt*, "with such a mixed reading public, who can hope to meet the wishes of every individual?"[25] Moreover, especially in the area of reviewing, music magazines did not have the field to themselves; they had to compete with other types of publications which could lay claim to a much broader audience and hence a more stable financial base.

Chief among the music magazines' competitors were the scholarly review journals, which had begun to appear in the waning years of the seventeenth century. The Latin language of some of the earliest betrayed their origins with the educated elite, but most adopted the vernacular, a necessary step in reaching beyond the narrow confines of the university community. In doing so they spoke to the German Enlightenment's goal of achieving an educated and informed populace, and their interdisciplinary breadth reflected contemporary assumptions about what that education should entail. Some featured an occasional article, but many concentrated solely on book reviews; though a few focused on specific subject areas, most cast a wide net, critiquing volumes on philosophy, history, theology, mathematics, physics, medicine, midwifery, agronomy, astronomy, poetry, plays, novels, drama, etc., all between the same covers. Most regularly reviewed books *about* music, from travel books with general appeal (like Charles Burney's) to the most technical composition treatises. Only a smaller number felt called to critique musical works (see table 2.1), though whether they did so in response to reader requests, out of editorial conviction, or simply because someone offered to write the reviews, can rarely be determined. At least one editor complained in print about the lack of a qualified music reviewer. In the second volume of his *Russische Bibliothek*, H. L. C. Bacmeister printed a whole list of new musical compositions, adding in a footnote that he would like to review them, but that a search of all St. Petersburg had failed to turn up a single "scholarly musician" to join his reviewing staff. Despite an appeal to his readership, he obviously never found one, for remaining volumes of his journal included only a single music review – of a puzzle minuet – that he probably wrote himself.[26]

In choosing music for evaluation, scholarly review journals tended to prefer vocal music, reflecting both the era's stated preference for it and the attraction of reviewing the texts as well as the music. Still, the ratio of vocal to instrumental music reviews varied somewhat unpredictably from journal to journal. Nor could the likelihood of a journal's choosing to feature instrumental reviews be anticipated. For example, one might have expected the *Göttingische Anzeigen von gelehrten Sachen* to harbor a veritable treasure trove, given the fact that Forkel held the chair in music at the University of Göttingen, but its offerings are both minimal and insignificant. One of its three reviews of instrumental music took only a few lines to praise the "charming melodies, modulations, and original turns of phrase" in some pieces by a local student before adding that, "space and the purpose of these pages do not allow us to say more."[27] On the other hand, the *Erfurtische gelehrte Zeitungen*, published in a town not usually associated with music, contains a number of perspicacious reviews.

Some journals, like the *Allgemeine deutsche Bibliothek*, the *Allgemeine Litteratur-Zeitung*, and the *Frankfurter gelehrte Anzeigen*, aimed at a high scholarly level and achieved national significance, counting figures like Herder, Goethe, Schiller, and Kant among their contributors.[28] Their reputation enhanced the standing of their music reviews, and one observer praised the *Allgemeine deutsche Bibliothek* as the least partisan of all in that regard.[29] These prestigious journals usually represented a particular philosophical viewpoint; the *Allgemeine deutsche Bibliothek*, for example, openly propagated the views of the Enlightenment, while both the *Allgemeine Litteratur-Zeitung* and the *Frankfurter gelehrte Anzeigen* took stands against the *Allgemeine deutsche Bibliothek*'s "establishment" position. The *Allgemeine Litteratur-Zeitung* aimed for, and apparently achieved a less pretentious, more accessible style, while the openly rebellious *Frankfurter gelehrte Anzeigen* in particular took up the banner of the emerging *Sturm und Drang* literary movement, as reflected in the language of a C. P. E. Bach review:

For ladies? That's what the title says. I believe, however, that even men would bring honor upon themselves with them. If these sonatas are meant for the fair sex, that's splendid. But if I should ever see it tried; if Emanuel Bach's new sonatas really appeared on the music rack; if a daughter of Diderot actually succeeded in playing them, then I would steal away. – With my poetic heart – I would melt like wax – transported by the divine power of the *Harmonie*, by the power of these tones, which penetrate to the very core of the heart – performed by a Psyche at the clavichord – I would stand there, tears flowing and listen.[30]

Although these polemical stances definitely affected the tenor of the book discussions and the general writing style, they had little perceptible effect on the substance of the music reviews.

Other scholarly journals had a more local significance, although like the *Gothaische gelehrte Zeitungen* or the *Neue Zeitungen von gelehrten Sachen*, they could also achieve a broader distribution and distinguished reputation.[31] Not all achieved a credible intellectual status (a rival journal lambasted the *Erfurtische gelehrte Zeitungen* as a "botched-up patchwork" with ignorant reviewers – music reviews notwithstanding), but that did not stop them from issuing opinions.[32] Still others, devoid of any scholarly trappings (like the *Allgemeines Verzeichniß neuer Bücher*), functioned merely as book trade journals and offered only the briefest of evaluative comments. Whatever their reputation or orientation, scholarly review journals played a crucial role in the development and dissemination of the review collective's concepts, particularly since the appearance of instrumental reviews in their columns gave intellectual weight to the reviews' contents and helped to establish music's position in the aesthetic arena.

The same arguments apply to the reviews appearing in the political newspapers which had begun to dot the journalistic landscape. Though some, like the *Wienerisches Diarium* (later the *Wiener Zeitung*), were little more than mouthpieces of the local court, most functioned independently. Found in the larger German, Swiss, and Austrian cities, they generally appeared three or four times a week in issues of four to six pages that were filled with reports on political and court news in Europe and the Americas (not infrequently merely copied from other newspapers). Toward the middle of the eighteenth century, some expanded their coverage to include a regular column devoted to "gelehrte Sachen" (scholarly matters), which featured brief reviews of recent literature as well as the occasional short essay or poem. As with the scholarly review journals, not all included music reviews, but the ones that did formed an indispensable and valuable part of the thought collective (see table 2.1).

Though definitely directed at a very general readership, these columns attracted some of Germany's finest minds. Gotthold Ephraim Lessing, for example, edited the "gelehrte Sachen" section of the *Berlinische privilegirte Zeitung* from 1752 to 1755 and also wrote for the *Hamburgischer Correspondent* and the *Hamburgische neue Zeitung*.[33] Even more than the reviews in general scholarly journals, the "gelehrte Sachen" columns seem to have functioned as an educational service that directed readers along the path of enlightenment and knowledge by recommending literature and music for study and enjoyment. Perhaps for this reason, most of the reviews (both book and music) had a distinctly positive slant. As a group they are also generally shorter and less detailed than those in the general scholarly journals or the music magazines, but that did not mean they could safely be ignored. Friedrich Nicolai, the editor of the *Allgemeine deutsche Bibliothek*, for example, felt compelled to respond to attacks made in the columns of the *Hamburgischer Correspondent*, indicating that he took its opinions – or at least the power of its opinions – seriously.[34]

The profile of the reading public reached by these various types of publications can only be conjectured, but would in any case have been limited to the wealthier middle and upper classes, whose education and incomes would have allowed such printed luxuries. Modern estimates of the literate, reading public in Germany (as opposed to those only literate enough to sign their name) vary widely, but one expert places it as around 15 percent of the population in 1770, increasing to 25 percent by the end of the century.[35] Female literacy rates always lagged behind male ones, even though women could be found on the subscription lists of newspapers and often took over the function of reading aloud in educated households.[36] But because many of the other private and public opportunities for coming into contact with the press remained closed to women (see below), the audience of the publications discussed here would have largely consisted of men.

The size of the audience can be estimated by examining the circulation figures of various publications. At the smaller end of the scale, the *Neue Zeitungen von gelehrten Sachen* had achieved a print run of 1,000 by 1785, a very respectable figure for the time.[37] Even that substantial following could not match the *Allgemeine deutsche Bibliothek* at the peak of its popularity, when it could boast of 1,100 subscribers, print runs of 1,800 copies, and a distribution all over the German-speaking world.[38] For example, of the 1,200 copies printed in Berlin in 1783, 184 were sent to Hamburg, 111 to Frankfurt, 60 to Nuremberg, 55 to Breslau, 40 to Zurich, and 23 to Vienna.[39] In 1787, only two years after its founding, the *Allgemeine Litteratur-Zeitung* had 2,000 subscribers.[40] As might be expected, political newspapers tended to have a larger circulation than even the most widely distributed scholarly journals. The number of copies printed by the *Berlinische Nachrichten von Staats- und gelehrten Sachen* rose from 1,780 in 1776 to 4,000 by 1804; in the same period, the *Berlinische privilegirte Zeitung* increased its circulation from 2,000 to 7,100 copies.[41] But the most widely read newspaper in Germany was undoubtedly the *Hamburgischer Correspondent*, attaining a circulation that has been estimated as reaching 25,000 by the end of the century.[42] Though that figure may well be exaggerated, the impressive number of surviving copies in German libraries and archives dwarfs all other papers and does indicate its broad distribution and sizable readership.[43]

Moreover, because of readership patterns, circulation figures during the eighteenth century indicate only the absolute minimum numbers in terms of actual readers. While journals generally did not cost as much as books, they were still quite expensive relative to incomes, so various types of book-sharing were the norm. Hence, a single copy of any periodical could well have had dozens of readers. Booksellers often had a reading room stocked with various periodicals, and tavern and restaurant owners often provided journals for their customers.[44] For example, Samuel August Sohr, a book dealer in the provincial town of Görlitz in Silesia, notified his customers in 1783 that the following scholarly journals were available locally:

"Leipziger, Frankfurter, Hallische, Erfurter, Göttinger, Wittenberger, Altonaer, Nürnberger, Gothaische, Jenaische, Greifswalder, Büschingsche wöchentliche Nachrichten, Wiener Real=Zeitung, Buchhändler=Zeitung, Berliner Litteratur= Zeitung, Briefwechsel der Gelehrten," and others.[45]

In the far northern town of Flensburg, the musician and Gastwirt Hanke advertised that patrons of his coffee house would have access to several papers, including the *Hamburgischer Correspondent*, the *Altonaer Merkur*, and the *Kopenhagener* and the *Hamburger Adreß-Comtoir*.[46] Note that neither list includes any music titles, despite the fact that Hanke frequently sponsored concerts and otherwise contributed to Flensburg's musical life.

In addition to commercial ventures that encouraged multiple readership, Germany could boast of over four hundred reading societies during the last half of the eighteenth century. These societies (nearly all of which admitted only men) functioned as private libraries, allowing members to share the cost of journal subscriptions and expensive books. Towns as small as Wunstorf, near Hannover, (pop. 1,600) managed to support two reading clubs, one of which owned 133 titles.[47] Wealthier societies in larger cities had even more impressive collections. At the end of the century, in addition to an array of books, the Beygandische Lesekabinett in Leipzig provided 24 scholarly journals and 300 political newspapers for its membership.[48] Some of the clubs' periodical lists seem designed to cover a wide geographical range: at various times, the reading society in Trier subscribed to the *Wiener Zeitung* and the *Hamburgischer Correspondent*, the *Allgemeine deutsche Bibliothek* (Berlin), the *Allgemeine Litteratur-Zeitung* (Jena/Leipzig), the *Wirzburger gelehrte Anzeigen*, the *Oberdeutsche, allgemeine Litteraturzeitung* (Salzburg), and the *Göttingische Anzeigen von gelehrten Sachen*.[49] More importantly from our perspective, many of the periodicals most frequently chosen by the reading societies included those with instrumental reviews. A survey of thirty-one societies all over Germany, Austria, and Switzerland revealed that twenty-six subscribed to the *Allgemeine Litteratur-Zeitung*, probably a result of its accessibility described above. The *Allgemeine deutsche Bibliothek*, the *Oberdeutsche allgemeine Litteraturzeitung*, the *Gothaische gelehrte Zeitungen*, the *Leipziger gelehrte Zeitung*, and the *Hamburgischer Correspondent* also

Table 2.2 *Distribution of instrumental music reviews*

		Distribution by type of periodical	
Music	464	(−37 reprinted from other journals)	427
Scholarly	478	(−16 reprinted from other journals)	462
Political	422		422
TOTAL	1,364	(−53 reprinted from other journals)	1,311

		Distribution by decade	
1760s	145	(−13 reprinted from other journals)	132
1770s	331	(−2 reprinted from other journals)	329
1780s	501	(−34 reprinted from other journals)	467
1790–1798	387	(−4 reprinted from other journals)	383
TOTAL	1,364	(−53 reprinted from other journals)	1,311

Distribution in individual journals

Allgemeine deutsche Bibliothek/Neue allgemeine deutsche Bibliothek

| 1760s: 24 | 1770s: 63 | 1780s: 68 | 1790–1798: 73 |

Hamburgischer Correspondent

| 1760s: 8 | 1770s: 89 | 1780s: 127 | 1790–1798: 47 |

Hamburgische neue Zeitung

| — | 1770s: 84* | 1780s: 15* | 1790–1798: 17 |

Note: *An additional 13 from the 1770s and 2 from the 1780s were listed in the table of contents but missing in the copies I examined.

proved popular.[50] Music magazines, by way of contrast, apparently did not routinely figure in the societies' regular subscriptions any more than they did in the literature provided by booksellers and tavern keepers.

Thus, the importance of the over 800 instrumental reviews (nearly two-thirds of the total) appearing in scholarly review journals and political newspapers cannot be underestimated, because their wide distribution assured that the aesthetic criteria they contained reached a substantial percentage of the educated public. Moreover, these non-music periodicals could offer a type of continuity that the sporadically published music magazines could not. In particular the *Allgemeine deutsche Bibliothek* and its successor the *Neue allgemeine deutsche Bibliothek* provided a steady stream of reviews from 1765 until past the turn of the century, as to a lesser extent, the two Leipzig scholarly journals did from 1760 to 1787. In similar fashion, both the *Hamburgischer Correspondent* and the *Hamburgische neue Zeitung* continually fed aesthetically charged reviews to their reading public in small, easily absorbed doses, making it easy for the concept of instrumental music they articulated to insinuate itself into the German consciousness (see table 2.2).

Table 2.3 *Geographical distribution of periodicals*

	Berlin and Prussia
Music	*Kritische Briefe,* *1760–1763
	Musikalisches Kunstmagazin, 1782, 1791
	Musikalisches Wochenblatt/Musikalische Monatsschrift, 1792
	Berlinische musikalische Zeitung, 1793–1794
Scholarly	*Allgemeine deutsche Bibliothek,* 1765–1794
	Berlinisches litterarisches Wochenblatt, 1777
	Litteratur- und Theaterzeitung, 1778–1783
	Raisonnirendes Bücherverzeichniß (Königsberg), 1782–1784
	Ephemereiden der Litteratur und des Theaters, 1785–1786
Political	*Berlinische Nachrichten,* 1761–1798*
	Berlinische privilegirte Zeitung, 1770–1798*
	Hamburg
Music	*Magazin der Musik,* 1783–1789
Scholarly	*Unterhaltungen,* 1766–1770
	Altonaischer gelehrter Mercurius, 1763–1788
Political	*Hamburgischer Correspondent,* *1760–1798*
	Hamburgische neue Zeitung, 1767–1798*
	Kiel
Scholarly	*Gelehrte Zeitung,* 1771–1778; 1787–1790
	Neue allgemeine deutsche Bibliothek, 1793–1798*
	Leipzig
Music	*Wöchentliche Nachrichten,* 1767–1770
	Musikalischer Almanach, 1782–1789
Scholarly	*Bibliothek der schönen Wissenschaften,* *1760–1767
	Neue Zeitungen von gelehrten Sachen, *1760–1784
	Neue Leipziger gelehrte Zeitung, 1785–1787
	Neue Leipziger gelehrte Anzeigen, 1789–1797
	Allgemeines Verzeichniß neuer Bücher, 1776–1784
	Other central German cities
Music	*Musikalisch-kritische Bibliothek* (Gotha), 1778
	Musicalische Bibliotek (Marpurg), 1784–1785
	Journal der Tonkunst (Erfurt), 1795
Scholarly	*Frankfurtische gelehrten Zeitungen,* *1760–1771
	Göttingische Anzeigen, *1760–1798*
	Jenaische Zeitungen, 1765–1787
	Frankfurter gelehrte Anzeigen, 1772–1790
	Gothaische gelehrte Zeitungen, 1774–1798*
	Erfurtische gelehrte Zeitungen, 1776–1798*

Table 2.3 (*cont.*)

Allgemeine Litteratur-Zeitung (Jena and Leipzig), 1785–1798*
Der teutsche Merkur (Weimar), (1773–1798*)

Bavaria and other southern/southwest provinces

Music   *Musikalische Real-Zeitung/Musikalische Korrespondenz* (Speier), 1788–1792

Augsburger musikalischer Merkur, 1795

Scholarly   *Erlangische gelehrte Anmerkungen*, 1770–1798

Nürnbergische gelehrte Zeitung, 1777–1798*

Strasburgische gelehrte Nachrichten, 1782–1785

Wirzburger gelehrte Anzeigen, 1786–1798*

Tübingische gelehrte Anzeigen, 1789–1798

Austria and Austrian territories

Scholarly   *Prager gelehrte Nachrichten*, 1771–1772

Realzeitung (Vienna), 1777–1786

Litterarische Nachrichten (Vienna), 1775–1776

Oberdeutsche, allgemeine Litteraturzeitung (Salzburg), 1788–1798*

Switzerland

Scholarly   *Freymüthige Nachrichten* (Zurich), *1760–1763

Russia

Scholarly   *Russische Bibliothek* (St. Petersburg), 1772–1789

Note: Dates give the volumes examined for this survey, which encompasses the period from 1760 through 1798. Asterisks indicate that a periodical began before, or ended after, these dates.

The observant reader will have noticed, nonetheless, that however inclusive I have tried to be about Austria and Switzerland, the majority of the reviews appeared in journals published in a relatively small area of northern and central Germany, with an especially substantial cluster in Hamburg and Berlin (see table 2.3). That the Protestant northern lands were more "print friendly" than the Catholic south is one of the basic and inescapable facts of eighteenth-century German history.[51] Not until the 1780s did the southern and western parts of Germany become active in periodical publication,[52] having been stifled by a combination of the centralized, authoritative practices of the Catholic church and the strict censorship and high taxes in the Austro-Hungarian empire. Even then, as Margot Lindemann has observed with regard to rural Austria (her comments can be applied to Bavaria and other parts of Southern Germany as well), "the production of journals . . .

was negligible and without significance, just like the rest of the literary products."[53] Indeed, with the exception of the Bossler journals published in Speier
(near Mannheim in the Palatinate) and a few offerings in the *Wirzburger
gelehrte Anzeigen*, the music reviews from southern presses contain more hot
air than anything else. Neither of the two Viennese reviews says much of significance, and of the twenty-four found in the *Erlangische gelehrte
Anmerkungen*, the *Nürnbergische gelehrte Zeitung*, and the *Oberdeutsche
allgemeine Litteraturzeitung*, eight treat variations by Ludwig Cella (a minor
court official in Erlangen), consistently managing about one thought for every
fifty lines of text. However much Austria and the southern part of Germany
may have contributed to musical composition, they did not hold up their end
of the reviewing business. For my purposes here, though, the geographical
origins of the review collective are irrelevant: to have prepared the way for the
romantic paradigm, the reviews need not have been *written* in all parts of the
German-speaking world, they need to have been *read*, and the figures discussed above suggest they were.[54]

With the question of sufficiently wide distribution answered affirmatively,
we can now turn to the issue of the collective's cohesiveness and its validity as
aesthetic discourse, beginning with the type of music chosen for review.[55] In
their choices, all types of journals reflected the orientation of the typical
amateur musician, heavily favoring works for solo keyboard or small ensem-
bles with obbligato keyboard. Popular genres tended to fluctuate with
changes in musical fashion; in the solo keyboard area, for example, suites disappeared after the 1760s, having been overtaken by sonatas, which then lost
ground in the 1790s to variations. Keyboard concertos are fairly well represented, probably because they still remained a vehicle for (wealthy) amateur
performance, but symphonies and string quartets garnered relatively few
reviews (see table 2.4). Few amateurs would have had the means – or seen the
necessity – of purchasing a symphony, but the string quartet lay within the
dilettante's realm, making the scarcity of reviews somewhat puzzling. It
becomes less so when one remembers that both symphonies and string quartets were generally published only in parts, not in score, and as the
Allgemeines Verzeichniß neuer Bücher observed in its review of C. P. E. Bach's
four *Orchester Sinfonien*: "Studying a multi-voice work from individual parts
is tedious work if you are trying to judge the whole thing."[56] A reviewer for
the *Musikalische Korrespondenz* even went to the trouble of partially writing
out a score of Haydn's Op. 54 string quartets and convinced himself anew of
Haydn's "inexhaustible richness of ideas and his original humor," but not
everyone was willing to do so.[57]

Thus, two of the leading instrumental genres of the late eighteenth century

Table 2.4 *Genres reviewed*

Genre	1760s %	1770s %	1780s %	1790–1798 %
Solo keyboard sonatas	16	26	33	16
Keyboard variations	3	2	7	15
Organ pieces	3	5	3	8
Basso continuo sonatas	5	5	0.5	0.5
Sonatas for keyboard and violin or flute	4	9	11	5
Sonatas for keyboard with violin and cello	0	8	11	3
String quartets	0	2	3	5
Keyboard concertos	9	12	10	1
Symphonies	21	6	3	1
Symphonies in keyboard reduction	2	0	1	2
Opera overtures in keyboard reduction	0	1	1	9

Note: Collections of assorted keyboard pieces, combined vocal/keyboard collections, and various miscellaneous genres such as flute duos and divertimentos make up the bulk of the remaining types of pieces. Non keyboard concertos consistently made up about 1% of the reviews.

are dramatically underrepresented in review discourse. Though they are equally avoided in all types of publications, so that no disruption of cohesiveness can be discerned, some might wish then to question the collective's claim to aesthetic validity. Of course, if one subscribes to Braudel's view of history, as described in chapter 1, bit players like the flute duet deserve the stage as much as stars like the symphony, and may even reveal more generally-applicable truths about historical development. Those who resist this view must admit that just because *we* find the symphony and string quartet to be leading genres does not mean that the eighteenth century did, so there is no reason to undervalue its aesthetic commentary on other kinds of music. Moreover, as the later chapters will demonstrate, the utilization of aesthetic criteria crossed all genre lines, so that the basic standards applied to accompanied sonatas, for example, held for symphonies and string quartets as well.

If there is then no argument against validity and collective treatment based on the type of music reviewed, is there one based on authorship? Should we, for example, accord equal status and significance to the opinions of a dilettante like Eschtruth as we do to a distinguished scholar and musical journalist like Forkel? For several reasons, distinctions along those lines make little sense here. In the first place, dilettante reviewers should not automatically be treated as inferior, since many of them had substantial musical training. Eschtruth, for example, who held the post of Justizrath in the city of Marburg, had studied composition with one of C. P. E. Bach's students, was acquainted with Bach and had become an avid supporter of the Bach style.[58] His contemporary, Ernst Ludwig Gerber, thought his writing was ruled by "perceptiveness, great aesthetic and harmonic knowledge, and an absence of partisanship, combined with the choicest and most elegant expression."[59] (Not everyone agreed with this assessment; the *Allgemeine deutsche Bibliothek* dismissed his critical opinions as "just as insignificant as most of the works reviewed."[60]) Moreover, amateur status did not preclude musical perceptivity or an awareness of contemporary aesthetic thought any more than professional status guaranteed it, especially during the eighteenth century. Sometimes dilettantes even brought a certain whimsical perspective to the task. After praising Daniel Gottlob Türk as the best of those following in the tradition of C. P .E. Bach's "true art of playing the keyboard," a reviewer for the *Altonaischer gelehrter Mercurius* continued,

This reviewer is not a musician by profession, and therefore does not publish any sonatas himself, and also therefore did not want to take the trouble to find out if all the ideas in T's sonatas are actually his own; but even if they aren't, bringing together borrowed ideas appropriately and pleasantly is a fine art as well. Poets certainly do it.[61]

Despite the offhand tone, the reviewer was clearly aware of – if not entirely in agreement with – the growing concern for originality in composition, placing him squarely within the mainstream trends outlined in chapter 6. In addition, the participation of both dilettante and professional musicians in the thought collective speaks for the pervasiveness of its ideas. If reviewers at all levels advanced the same general criteria and discussed the same topics in their reviews (as the subsequent chapters will make clear), then the practical aesthetic they articulated can lay claim to being a common viewpoint accepted by the larger musical culture.[62]

In any case, insistence on ranking by authorship will be frustrated by the simple fact that nearly all eighteenth-century reviews, of both books and music, appeared anonymously. Only in those single-author music magazines discussed above can we securely identify the reviewer, for nearly all collaborative periodicals jealously guarded the identity of their review contributors, on the assumption that anonymity allowed a freer exchange of opinions. Thus Nicolai opened the first volume of the *Allgemeine deutsche Bibliothek* in 1765 by bragging that he was fortunate enough to have found scholars "of such well-known talent that their name alone would assure the fame of the work, if, that is, one wanted to make the names public."[63] Not until 1793, when he terminated his connection to the journal, did he provide a list of the illustrious people who had written reviews for him, but even then he included *only* those who were no longer living. Apparently, editors did not always know who wrote the reviews they received. The *Hamburgische Nachrichten aus dem Reiche der Gelehrsamkeit* had to issue a special request pleading with readers sending in reviews for publication to at least sign their names to their letters.[64] Exceptions to the rule of anonymity were few. While Cramer made a point of initialing the reviews he wrote in his *Magazin der Musik*, saying he thought it was not very noble to criticize someone "from behind a bush," the very tenor of his remarks indicates he was flying in the face of convention.[65] Many highly reputable scholars did not feel that way. (Herder, for example, wished to preserve the anonymity of the literary reviews he wrote, though he was not entirely successful in doing so.[66]) In fact, of the nearly fifty publications in this study, only the *Erfurtische gelehrte Zeitungen* ever provided an index of its contributors, but it did not do so until 1797, and even then felt compelled to give an extensive justification for revealing their names.

Sometimes reviewer identities can be gleaned from other sources. Reichardt, for example, acknowledged having written reviews for the *Allgemeine Litteratur-Zeitung*;[67] Eschtruth claimed to have written for several scholarly journals, including the *Erfurtische gelehrte Zeitungen*. He also disavowed certain reviews in the *Erfurtische gelehrte Zeitungen*, implying that he was not their only music critic.[68] According to a review in the *Neue allgemeine deutsche Bibliothek*, contributors to the *Musikalisches Wochenblatt/ Musikalische Monatsschrift* included not only the editors Reichardt and Friedrich Ludwig Aemilius Kunzen, but also Marpurg, the composers Friedrich Wilhelm Rust and Carl Friedrich Zelter, Carl Bernhard Wessely, the music director of the National Theater in Berlin, Johann Gottlieb Karl Spazier, the editor of the *Berlinische musikalische Zeitung*, plus assorted other dilettante contributors. The critique did not say that they all wrote reviews, however, so the exact nature of their various contributions remains unclear.[69] Finally, Gerber identified Joachim Friedrich Leister as the editor of the *Hamburgischer Correspondent* (beginning in 1770) and the author of many of its music reviews, calling him "an accomplished and tasteful keyboard player, with whom not only Kapellmeister Bach maintained a devoted friendship, but whose opinion had always carried great weight with the Hamburg public, and probably still does."[70] François-Joseph Fétis maintained that Leister held his position with the newspaper until at least 1795, but Gerber reported that Leister had complained to him that failing eyesight and other health problems had forced him to give up the editorship in 1792.[71] Music reviews in the *Hamburgischer Correspondent* drop off precipitously in

1795, so perhaps Fétis's date refers to the curtailment of reviewing activity that he had continued after his resignation as editor.

In the absence of any type of signature, however, the precise contributions of any of these men to the review collective cannot be determined. Fortunately, a few journals did allow contributors to sign their work with initials that can provide clues to the author's identity, although they did not always match the author's name. For example, reviewers for the *Allgemeine deutsche Bibliothek* wrote under pseudonymous initials that preserved the anonymity of the author while allowing readers to at least follow the opinions of a particular person. The editor jealously guarded the key to the ciphers, and only a serendipitous preservation of his list has disclosed the names to history (as well as the fact that a single reviewer generally wrote under several initials, so that it looked as if the journal had more collaborators than it actually did – apparently a common editorial trick). The list reveals that Johann Friedrich Agricola wrote the instrumental music reviews until his death in 1774; his successors included Reichardt; Daniel Gottlob Türk, a composer and author of a well-known keyboard method; Johann Abraham Peter Schulz, a prominent composer; Johann Gottlieb Portmann, Kantor at the Hofkapelle in Darmstadt and author of several pedagogical treatises on music; and Adolph von Knigge, a well known Enlightenment author (though a musical amateur).[72] Although the *Neue allgemeine deutsche Bibliothek* continued the practice of initialed reviews, no key to its authors has been discovered.

This feature of the *Allgemeine deutsche Bibliothek* should make us cautious about assigning names to the initials scattered through the pages of a few other publications, although some can be established with relative certainty. Hans Schneider has identified the author of fifteen reviews in the *Musikalische Real-Zeitung* signed "Zx." as Johann Friedrich Christmann, a pastor, composer, and close associate of the magazine's publisher.[73] The *Magazin der Musik* used a number of reviewers (leading the *Erfurtische gelehrte Zeitungen* to comment on its unevenness);[74] some, but not all, of its reviews bear initials. Those signed "C. F. C." clearly stem from the pen of the magazine's editor, Carl Friedrich Cramer, and the three signed "F—l." can be securely attributed to Forkel, because they were "reprinted" from the *Musikalischer Almanach*. In addition, Cramer admitted that his publisher Johann Christoph Westphal (a prominent Hamburg music dealer) not only had supplied him with music to review but contributed to its evaluation as well, signing his work with the letter "W."[75] The rather obvious conflict of interest did make his reviews sound like advertising copy, and "W." was criticized for being "almost too free with praise."[76] In his defense, though, not every word he wrote dripped with admiration:

Although the main melody isn't new, at least it is pleasant and flowing; but it's a pity Herr Schröter hasn't bothered to study the art of strict composition and compose according to correct harmonic rules. Page 45 in the sixth concerto is, as a result, almost unplayable, for the *Harmonie* he uses there is completely incorrect, and is made even worse by printing errors – at least we hope they are no more than that. W.[77]

Of the remaining initialed reviews in the *Magazin der Musik*, only the one by "H. A. Fr. v. E." can be securely identified (Eschtruth), although the reviews signed "G." and "Gld." might have been written by the porcelain manufacturer Peter Grönland, whom Gerber describes as a "bosom buddy of Cramer and Kunzen" and an industrious collaborator on the magazine.[78] An interesting connection with one of the Hamburg political newspapers discloses another possibility. Some of the reviews signed "L." in the *Magazin der Musik* had previously appeared in the *Hamburgischer Correspondent*, so that they might tentatively be attributed to Leister. The same double dipping also occurs with a number of Westphal reviews, as well as for several signed by "B.", "M.", and "N. N." Because the *Correspondent* version generally appeared first, one might suspect Cramer of simple plagiarism.[79] However, the *Correspondent* versions carry no initials, so that the reviewers might possibly have sent their copy to both publications, with only Cramer choosing to use initials.

No matter what the explanation, the duplicate reviews suggest that Leister shared the *Correspondent*'s reviewing responsibilities with one or more colleagues, a view supported by the sudden – and exceptional – appearance in its "gelehrte Sachen" column of a series of twenty reviews (nine vocal and eleven instrumental) signed with the letter "B." While no known evidence links them to C. P. E. Bach, assuming his authorship is not unreasonable, and might well have been the reaction of the typical eighteenth-century reader: Bach was far and away Hamburg's best known musician, and even if he did not write the reviews, many readers probably assumed he did. Bach did have a connection with the *Correspondent* at that time; he wrote and signed his full name to a review of Forkel's *Allgemeine Geschichte der Musik* that appeared there on 9 January 1788. Moreover, the flurry of reviews signed with a B., which had begun on 17 April 1787, ended on 2 July 1788, shortly before Bach's death in December; and the two reviews of his own compositions that appeared during that fourteen-month period bear no signature at all. However, if he did write them, they will not catapult him to fame as a penetrating and demanding critic. Plainly stated, they are bland and rather boring even for the *Correspondent*, which in the late 1780s rarely offered up more than the vaguest of complimentary platitudes. There are only six other signed instrumental reviews in the *Hamburgischer Correspondent*: three by "R.", one by

"R—r", one by "J.", and one by "B**" (in June of 1792). Although the ubiquitous Reichardt could have written the "R." reviews, his authorship – while not implausible – does not seem likely. Writing for a political newspaper was not beneath him, however, for he signed one vocal review in the *Berlinische privilegirte Zeitung* and initialed several others there and in the *Berlinische Nachrichten*.[80]

One final intriguing possibility suggests itself for the *Hamburgische neue Zeitung*, Hamburg's other main political newspaper. Beginning around 1773, the reviews in its "gelehrte Sachen" column begin to take on a definite personality that makes them stand out from the remainder of the review collective. Though they never left the aesthetic mainstream, they tended to emphasize Affect and organization to a greater extent, and at a much earlier date, than did reviews in other journals. Four of them (one in 1773 and three in 1777) carry the signature "F.", and although Forkel was certainly not the only eighteenth-century musical personality from that part of the alphabet, several things place his authorship at least within the realm of possibility.[81] From his post at the University in Göttingen, Forkel carried on an extensive correspondence with musicians in Hamburg, particularly with C. P. E. Bach, and thus would have had local connections. More significantly, according to the Forkel scholar Doris Powers, the writing style, content and criteria of some of the *Hamburgische neue Zeitung* reviews (both signed and unsigned) frequently correspond to the views and style of his known writings in a way that reviews from other journals do not. While we have not yet been able to establish his authorship with certainty, the possibility that he or one of his followers/imitators wrote for the newspaper remains a strong one.[82]

From this discussion of authorship, which has demonstrated the credentials of identifiable reviewers, comes another reason to consider the reviews as a collective: professional musicians often wrote for non-music journals, while amateurs contributed to music ones. Thus, we cannot automatically assign higher "status" to one review simply because it appeared in a music magazine, nor summarily dismiss the views of another because it was published in a political newspaper. Other features of the collective also prevent us from establishing any *a priori* hierarchy based on journal type. With regard to length, for example, the *Berlinische musikalische Zeitung* cultivated an epigrammatic style while the scholarly *Neue allgemeine deutsche Bibliothek* almost never failed to go into excruciating detail. Even within a single publication, reviews range from pungent one-liners to multi-page aesthetic ramblings: the *Allgemeine deutsche Bibliothek* could easily spend paragraph after paragraph taking apart a composer's style but could also offer a breezy "Not bad" (*Nicht übel*) as its entire opinion.[83] In similar fashion, the *Magazin der Musik* tended to short, often superficial critiques, but also published Cramer's extensive ruminations on C. P. E. Bach's *Claviersonaten und freye Phantasien* (18 pages) and Hardenack Otto Conrad Zinck's *Sechs Claviersonaten* (17 pages).[84] Nor can we make assumptions about the depth or specificity of reviews based on journal type, if only because of the "reprinting" (or plagiarism) discussed above. Though actually quite rare in view of ordinary journalistic practices of the period, which sanctioned wholesale pirating of other newspapers, the few instances found in the reviews reiterate the interconnection of journal types. The *Musikalische Real-Zeitung*, like the *Magazin der Musik*, published reviews that had appeared earlier in the *Hamburgischer Correspondent*, and if Eschtruth is to be believed, the *Magazin der Musik* took another review word-for-word from the *Staats- und gelehrte Zeitung* in Kassel.[85] Music magazines were more likely to support their points by printing actual examples from the piece reviewed, but non-music journals like the *Unterhaltungen* and the *Allgemeine deutsche Bibliothek* occasionally did so. Both space restrictions and expense undoubtedly prevented most publications from including examples, and the *Magazin der Musik* and *Musikalische Real-Zeitung/Musikalische Korrespondenz* resorted to the less expensive alternative of publishing all their examples together in a separate folder. Still, an acceptable degree of specificity could also be achieved by citing measure numbers, which even political newspapers occasionally did, or by printing the examples in tablature.

My arguments thus far have focused on aspects of behavior that allow *us* to consider the reviews together as a collective, i.e. demonstrable similarities cutting across all types of publications in the kinds of music reviewed, in authorship, in length, depth, and level of specificity. But there are also signs indicating that the reviewers saw *themselves* as engaged in a common task, recognizing "special rules of behavior" that fixed participation in the collective at a level that was "disciplined, uniform, and discreet," characteristic of thought collectives as described by Ludwik Fleck.[86] We have already seen that Reichardt was chastised for using standards deviating too far from the critical mainstream (see above, page 23); in the review of Forkel's *Musikalisch-kritische Bibliothek* cited at the beginning of the chapter, the *Nürnbergische gelehrte Zeitung* had observed that reviewers should not pretend their opinions had general validity if they were based only on "beauty and taste" (i.e. personal preference) or simply on a pedantic attention to tortuous rules.[87]

In fact, the review collective was constantly reviewing itself, whether in formal evaluations of the latest volumes of a periodical or with side comments in their own instrumental reviews. It should be mentioned that general eighteenth-century reviewing practices did not assume that a reviewer needed to find something wrong to be taken seriously as a critic; many reviews (both of books and music) offer no more than a description of the contents, and many editors expressed a preference for neutral evaluations. Nonetheless, the collective closely monitored the degree of severity visited upon composers in instrumental music reviews. Some reviewers expressed hostility toward unnamed colleagues who "strangle young geniuses at birth" with their exaggerated criticism.[88] In a less inflammatory fashion, the *Neue allgemeine deutsche Bibliothek* took the *Musikalisches Wochenblatt/Musikalische Monatsschrift* to task for adopting a tone that was "not always mild enough," an odd comment from a journal given to the relentless excoriation of perceived mediocrity.[89] The *Hamburgischer Correspondent* (which incidentally did not publish a single negative review during the 1790s) saw the matter in a more positive light, approving of the way the *Musikalisches Wochenblatt*'s reviewers "look each composer right in the face and examine the work as if the authors were no longer living and would never write reviews again," further observing that "candidness, pertinent truth and thoroughness" in reviewing could "teach the students and friends of music how to develop their own secure standards."[90]

Most of the reviews of reviews, however, complain about the lack of critical stringency. In the review of Hiller's *Wöchentliche Nachrichten* cited above, page 24, the *Allgemeine deutsche Bibliothek* urged the editors not to flinch in their critical judgments. According to the *Unterhaltungen*, Hiller's staff did not mend its ways and needed to be "more exact and strict" in its reviewing, especially in view of the "great mass of miserable music being visited upon us by France and Holland."[91] Of course, one should realize that the two journals were in competition for a similar readership, and the *Unterhaltungen* often found reason to disparage the *Wöchentliche Nachrichten*'s opinions.[92] One might also wish to consider a review of the *Unterhaltungen* several months later in the *Jenaische Zeitungen*, which remarked that its articles kept getting worse, adding: "Perhaps the journal will get better since it has acquired some new collaborators; but then, perhaps not, since we know for sure that Herr Licentiat Wittenberg is at the head of them."[93] The point here is not which journal had the higher standards (they actually seem rather similar), but that reviewers recognized the appropriateness of critical standards and rules of conduct. Those standards, and a clear acknowledgment of the role that the review collective played in German musical life, were clearly articulated two decades later by Türk in the *Allgemeine deutsche Bibliothek*:

We did read – right after the announcement of these pieces – the review in the very next issue of the *Hamburger unpartheyischen Correspondenten* (No. 150 of 1787). It was a very favorable review for the composer, but that much more disadvantageous for the customer, as we later discovered. We pity anyone who was enticed into purchasing Caspar Daniel Krohn's *Kleine Sonaten* by that review in the *Hamburger unpartheyischen Correspondenten*. We do not wish to be guilty of a similar sin, but prefer to say instead to all our readers – candidly and without deceit – that these little sonatas are dreadfully boring, trivial little things and are not worth further critical examination. If you think we are being partisan [*partheyisch*], we must ask you – but only for this reason – to buy these little sonatas of Caspar Daniel Krohn. At the top, or – better said – at the front, the Author has served up a wonderfully fine *Canon* of four courses. We wish all honored guests *bon appetit*. – The only thing that we must still say in praise of our host [*Wirth*, which also means a tavern keeper] is that the food on all six plates is very easy and light. You won't have to worry about getting a stomach ache from them . . . but you won't get any healthy nourishment either.[94]

The review that set Türk off does compliment Krohn's knowledge of proper compositional method and leaves the reader with the impression that the sonatas are acceptable pieces, but otherwise offers no ringing endorsement of their excellence. Türk took his profession seriously, however, and called his colleague to task for what he obviously saw as a unconscionable dereliction of duty.[95]

Though Türk's sarcasm had no measurable effect on the ensuing reviews in the *Hamburgischer Correspondent*, a flood of negative comments could shake up any editor. Just such a torrent greeted the initial volume of Cramer's *Magazin der Musik* in 1783. Forkel commented that none of its reviews said anything, "because their purpose appears to be merely the intentional recommendation of the work, never true inner judgment," and went on to observe that they either made no evaluation at all, gave unjust criticism, or bestowed unjust praise.[96] The *Hallische neue gelehrte Zeitungen*, the *Hamburgischer Correspondent*, and the *Hamburgische neue Zeitung* all concurred with Forkel; the *Erfurtische gelehrte Zeitungen* even compared them to the advertisements of "businessmen and snake-oil doctors." Only the *Gothaische gelehrte Zeitungen* found the reviews "appropriate and reasonable."[97] Peer pressure apparently worked, judging from a review of two of the *Magazin der Musik*'s subsequent issues in the *Hamburgische neue Zeitung*:

[The review] section has gotten a little more rigorous, though not nearly as much as one might like . . . Especially in music, so many things are praised that are only poor imitations, miserable inflated works; and hundreds, who do not have the least spark of original spirit, pass for Handels, Bachs, Haydns and Hasses.[98]

The strength of this outcry about Cramer's neglect of critical rigor indicates that the reviewers very much recognized the "special rules of behavior" that bound them into a collective.

This "psychological form" and common thought style makes collective behavior particularly attractive for historians wishing to discern generally accepted community thought patterns because, taken as a group, reviewers exhibit "more stable and consistent" behavior than a single individual.[99] In fact, this thought collective of reviewers, or "review collective," as they might be called, maintained a startling consistency of opinion at all levels of discourse across the span of forty years. At the core of this agreement lay the fundamental, and ultimately revolutionary, assumption that music should be judged by its own rules and standards. That required talking about the elements of music and musical style. Reviewers discussed melody, the symmetry and proportions of its construction, its gracefulness – or lack thereof, its suitability for the piece in question. They dissected *Harmonie*, a concept that included not only chord structure and progressions, but also voice leading procedures that enriched the texture.[100] They considered the role of modulation, the proper manipulation of tonality, and occasionally even touched on issues of form and musical structure. Just as interesting, however, as the topics chosen for discussion were the ones quietly ignored. For example, the mid-century controversy that pitted the proponents of melodically driven composition (e.g. Mattheson) against those who favored *Harmonie* (e.g. Rameau and Marpurg) found no place in the review collective. With few exceptions, reviewers assumed both elements to be equally essential, a common sense position, but one which deprived them of a possible aesthetic perspective for their evaluations. But a critical perspective and an aesthetic framework were sorely needed if the review collective was ever to go beyond purely functional judgments about a piece's suitability for purchase. If mimesis could not help, other avenues would have to be explored.

3

Answering with a German voice

Hamburgische neue Zeitung (1777): Johann Wilhelm Häßler, *Sechs Sonaten fürs Clavier.*

No one who has studied the works of our Carl Emanuel Philipp Bach will deny that the true art of playing the keyboard is at home here in Germany. It was left to this great genius to rescue the keyboard from the oblivion into which it had fallen. He showed that becoming a master of this instrument took more than cutting frisky capers, more than supporting snatches of opera tunes with constant, drumming basses – things that could never move a true, musical ear. Many worthy men have followed his example, and thereby gained renown and honor in the eyes of true connoisseurs of music. These sonatas bear the stamp of the good, idiomatic style; they are full of good *Harmonie* and touching melody, and thus distinguish themselves markedly from the recent swarm of superficial Italian works and other fashionable compositions.[1]

Hamburgische Correspondent (1789): Christian Friedrich Gottlieb Schwencke, *Drey Sonaten.*

He has chosen Bach, Haydn and Mozart as his models, and has so successfully entered into the manner of thinking of these famous men, that you can find their style with no trouble, for example that of Bach in the first and of Haydn in the second. But Schwencke is no slavish imitator and remains a genuine original, his models notwithstanding.[2]

The reviewers' rejection of the current aesthetic standards meant that the collective began its work essentially in a conceptual void, without established evaluative rules or criteria. Although it clearly could not function solely on the basis of individual taste, it could also not produce a suitable aesthetic theory instantaneously, for the reasons detailed in the previous chapters.

45

Instead, reviewers chose to adopt a rhetorical stance that succeeded in giving their discourse its initial focus, but that also had the effect of shaping a specifically Germanic aesthetic identity. With this step, Germanic musical culture, so long a step-child to the older traditions in Italy and France, began to assert its own identity and importance, and set in motion the process that would invest instrumental music with metaphysical significance.

The technique involved positing a superior Germanic Chosen in opposition to an inferior musical "Other," a simple but effective device well suited to the popular press, then as now not given to subtle distinctions. That reviewers used this bipolar, "us against them" method of organizing their aesthetic universe is not particularly surprising, for as we shall see later, argument by dualities characterized much German thought in the eighteenth century. In fact, feminist theorists like Hélène Cixous would simply label the perpetual division of the world into opposing camps as a typical masculine thought pattern, so we should expect to find it ordering an essentially masculine musical discourse.[3] It does take very little effort to produce a list of bipolar debates throughout music history: the melody/*Harmonie* controversy mentioned in the previous chapter, the *prima* and *seconda prattica* debate of the early Baroque, the quarrels about the merits of French and Italian opera, the conflict between the traditionalists and the New German School in the late nineteenth century, to name only a few. But the form the review collective's polemic took sets it somewhat apart from these examples, because the Other had no advocates and no voice in the discourse (a feminine role, Cixous might reply.) Only the Germanic Chosen got to speak.

The exclusionary techniques that reviewers used succeeded in creating a group identity for their German-speaking readers. For assistance in sorting out the various facets of their rhetorical *tour de force*, we can turn to the rhetorician Kenneth Burke and his chillingly perceptive analysis of the most scurrilous example of the "us against them" mentality, Adolf Hitler's *Mein Kampf*.[4] According to Burke, the first step will identify a common enemy that the members of the chosen group can all agree to despise, so that in uniting against the Other, they can paper over any internal differences and divisions (a device that proved handy for reviewers in dealing with the "South-German problem").[5] This enemy cannot be abstract, but should be physically present in the culture ("essentialized" – to use Burke's term) and distinctive enough to provide an easily visible target. After the Other has been given a definite face, the Chosen will define it in a simple and negative fashion, selecting characteristics that have a degree of plausibility, and always ignoring or rationalizing away any evidence to the contrary. For the optimum effectiveness, the Other should then be held responsible for some injury or wrong to the Chosen.[6]

Another facet of the rhetorical process involves defining the Chosen group, though here it is usually best to speak in generalities, lest a too-precise definition reveal unacceptable internal differences and divisions. To mask any possible confusion about the group identity, and to make their position virtually unassailable, the Chosen will unveil the ultimate weapon; they will drape their language with the mantle of moral superiority, thus rendering any opposition ineffective *a priori*.[7]

Reviewers embraced this strategy wholeheartedly, and it shaped their judgments and aesthetic pronouncements in a fundamental way. That fact may call forth an instinctive negative reaction in modern readers, who may well recoil at being asked to consider the writings of what could be called a propaganda machine as a source of critical and aesthetic commentary. But my point is precisely that the rhetorical and aesthetic agendas cannot and should not be separated, for their very intertwining shaped the emerging Germanic musico-aesthetic identity.

The rhetorical process unfolded in two chronological phases, with the first ending around 1775. In the initial phase, the review collective identified and defined a specific physical Other, in the second it moved the bipolar division onto more metaphysical grounds. It should surprise no one familiar with eighteenth-century German musical discourse to discover that, in the first phase, the Other had an Italian complexion. Still, the reviewers' preoccupation with the Italian style is worth exploring in some detail, because the habit of dividing the physical musical world into two camps – one superior to the other – shaped the more metaphysical distinctions made in the second phase. The "us against them" habit proved addictive.

Prejudice against Italian musicians had a long history in Germany (Heinrich Schütz had complained about their preferential treatment in Dresden during the previous century), but reached a peak during the middle of the eighteenth century.[8] *Outside* the review collective, when German writers heatedly debated the merits of the various national styles, most agreed on the inherent inferiority of south-of-the-border instrumental music. Typical is the *Wöchentliche Nachrichten*'s assessment of Italian symphonies, which it offered in a lengthy article on building up a musical library:

Galuppi, Jomelli, Sarti, etc. are famous names; they have written a lot of symphonies, because they all compose opera, and there is never an opera without a symphony. When you have considered the constant monotony and the great similarity of all these pieces; when – after a riotous Allegro you hear a short Andante that perhaps has two ideas, and then another bravely riotous Allegro or Presto that staggers around in the main key, you will probably decide that such a symphony might suffice to open an opera, as long as the audience hasn't quieted down. But they are worthless as chamber music.[9]

Leaving aside for the moment the question of the accuracy of this assessment, there can be little doubt that the collective had chosen its enemy cleverly, for the popularity and European distribution of Italian instrumental music reached a peak in the 1750s and 1760s.[10] Thus, the Other had a physical presence in the culture and was in a position to do some injury to the Germanic Us, a fact noted in several early reviews. Regretting the waste of good paper on some symphonies by Baldassare Galuppi, which no genuine connoisseur could hear "without disgust," the *Bibliothek der schönen Wissenschaften* asked indignantly why Breitkopf wasn't publishing the works of decent Germans but instead was forcing upon the world "the monster births of shallow Italians."[11] While delicately avoiding naming any responsible parties, the *Unterhaltungen* also complained that no one except C. P. E. Bach was publishing anything by Hasse, the Grauns, the Bendas, Quantz, Fasch, Neruda, or Riedt, thereby both endangering the spread of good taste and the honor of Germany.[12]

Prompted by this threat to German honor (and German pocketbooks), the review collective enthusiastically took up the crusade against the Italians. (The fact that many German composers chose to Italianize their first names adds a layer of irony to the discourse, but one fully ignored by reviewers.) In defining the Italian style, reviewers certainly identified its most salient characteristics: tuneful melodies with homophonic accompaniments, a conspicuous absence of counterpoint, a preference for limited modulations and hence broader areas of tonality. While a dispassionate observer might find none of these to be inherently bad or inferior, the collective unfailingly portrayed them all in the worst possible light. For example, when the *Wöchentliche Nachrichten* pounced on Vincenzo Manfredini (an Italian working in Russia), it lamented the "inharmonious din with broken chords in the left hand, something that has so often disgusted us in Italian keyboard sonatas," concluding that the sonatas had "lots of flash and trash, and occasionally a little bit of a tune, that might even be good, if it weren't buried by the accompaniment, and if you hadn't already heard it a hundred times."[13] Though reviewers might bestow the occasional grudging compliment (a little bit of a tune, that might even be good), they did so only to demonstrate the overwhelming inferiority of the style in general. The *Hamburgischer Correspondent*, for example, suggested that the young Johann Friedrich Reichardt could profit by learning about good melody during his sojourn in Italy, but only if he resisted the seductions of the Italianate "comic" art and remained faithful to his own "serious" style.[14]

Most often, reviewers attributed Italianate compositional choices, particularly in the areas of *Harmonie*, to a mixture of sheer incompetence, simple laziness, and shallow musical thought.[15] Marpurg, for example, excoriated the composer of some anonymously printed symphonies (he suspected Galuppi of being the culprit), complaining that the ninety-measure opening section stayed in the tonic for fifty-six measures and (with the exception of a few ii[7] chords) never ventured beyond arpeggiated tonic and dominant harmonies. According to Marpurg, even if Galuppi, with his prolific but superficial natural talents, could learn "orderly composition" (something Marpurg felt had long been out of fashion in Italy), he would probably never reach the level of a Graun or a Hasse, though he might at least improve his compositional reputation.[16] Agricola took a similarly snide approach, opening a review of Giovanni Rutini's Op. 6 sonatas by exclaiming, "The sixth opus already, and the composer still hasn't learned to write better and more idiomatic sonatas?" He then proceeded to fume about a left hand that either played "constant broken chords or went drumming along in the laudable manner of the Italians."[17]

According to some reviewers, such deficiencies in *Harmonie* stemmed from Italian disinterest in what German theorists considered to be the crucial final stage in the compositional process: the *Ausarbeitung*, or working out. During this stage, the subtleties of the accompanying voices took shape, rough edges were smoothed, excesses that had grown up in the heat of composition were snipped away, any remaining technical errors were corrected, and the composition as a whole received its final spit and polish.[18] Once again, perceived deficiencies in this area lay not with the individual talents of a particular composer, but with the Italian nation in general:

[Pietro Guglielmi's] melody is quite common, and there is almost no working out of musical ideas, something which – to be honest about it – is quite rare among the latest Italians ... Of course, the excellent keyboard pieces of our famous Kapellmeister Bach have made us so sensitive where this instrument is concerned that the *Harmonie*-less compositions of the latest Italians cannot possibly find favor.[19]

In fact, of all the Italian composers reviewed in the 1760s and early 1770s, only Luigi Boccherini ever managed to impress the collective, though reviewers who praised him usually did so at the expense of his countrymen. The *Hamburgische neue Zeitung* liked his Op. 9 Trios, saying that "You will find very few Italians so rich in serious, noble ideas and few who work out their pieces this well."[20] Boccherini became, in other words, the exception that proved the rule. If one might wish to object that the reviewers were just doing their job, that Guglielmi *is* dull and that Alberti bass *is* tiresome, one must also remember that the same criticisms could have been made without disparaging an entire nation in the process. Moreover, the way in which the collective used its anti-Italian rhetoric makes clear a larger, more nationalistic, agenda.

The patronizing tone that pervades the reviewers' comments often entailed allusions to "better" German composers. References to the hallowed names of Bach, Hasse, and Graun punctuate the judgments of Galuppi and Guglielmi discussed above, and the *Wöchentliche Nachrichten* concluded its hatchet job on Manfredini with the rhetorical question, "Are the keyboard works of Bach, Benda, Wagenseil, Kunz, Binder, and other German composers not known in Russia?"[21] The implication that German works maintained a much higher standard of excellence metamorphosed into overt declaration of Teutonic superiority two years later in the same magazine. Irked by some of Gaudenzio Comi's symphonies, a reviewer complained about the monotonous accompaniment and modulation of Italian symphonies, concluding with great self-satisfaction that:

It must be attributed to the genius of the Germans to have brought the symphonic style to a grade of perfection that an Italian composer would scarcely reach: besides invention, both reflection and diligence are required, an advantage that even the Italians themselves have never claimed to have over the Germans.[22]

Anti-Italian rhetoric did not simply serve as a means of defanging a threatening Other, it also served as a convenient foil to highlight the superior talents of the Germans, talents that revolved around the strict and intricate application of *Harmonie*. As the *Hamburgischer Correspondent* observed in reviewing Johann Wilhelm Hertel, if his symphonies were to be compared to any of the Italians (whom the reviewer had just dubbed as smearers instead of painters) it would be [Nicolò] Jomelli, though Hertel distinguished himself by forceful *Harmonie*.[23] Though no voice in the collective consistently called for intricate fugal writing, most reviewers clearly valued a more contrapuntal style, particularly in the genres of duets and trios, which could all too easily become infected with the Italianate preference for parallel thirds and sixths.[24] According to the *Hamburgischer Correspondent*, Johann Friedrich Wilhelm Wenkel had proved to be a composer who had "diligently studied the true principles of music" and therefore preferred "a solid, orderly compositional manner to the careless, error-ridden compositions of some recent [composers], particularly Italians." Because of that, he could write good contrapuntal duets, "with inversions, imitation, and worked out – even if only according to the rules of galant counterpoint" instead of the melodies in thirds and sixths that could "so easily become too sweet, and therefore disgusting to the ear of connoisseurs."[25] Of course, if someone *did* produce a fugue, that occasioned a burst of national pride. In hailing Johann Friedrich Gottlieb Beckmann's sonatas, the *Neue Zeitungen von gelehrten Sachen* proclaimed, "The best keyboard sonatas come from German composers. Händel, Bach, Benda have never been surpassed by any foreigner, by any Manfredini, Rutini, Düphlü." Beckmann's accomplishments, which allowed him to take his rightful place alongside his German colleagues, included idiomatic writing, good invention, good melody, and strict, ingenious *Harmonie*. The reviewer specifically mentioned a three-voice fugue and a perpetual canon, which managed – in spite of the restrictions of the genre – to have "a not unpleasant melody."[26]

This last review points up one of the collective's rhetorical *coup d'états*: the appropriation of good melody into the Germanic pantheon of virtues. While reviewers might acknowledge an Italianate ability to write good tunes, they avoided making that trait into an actual Italian *virtue* by sniffing that such "opera aria melodies" simply did not belong in instrumental music (as the allusion in the Häßler review cited at the beginning of this chapter indicates). Agricola criticized Adam Veichtner for following the latest Italian fashion by writing "melodies that rarely hang together, are often trashy, sometimes sprawling, sometimes clinging to a single note, but almost never expressive of anything," urging him to choose a better model to imitate, like Graun.[27] Particularly in slow movements, which "recent comic composers seemed to have banished from their works," good German composers like Ernst Wilhelm Wolf could appeal to the "true connoisseur of good melody."[28] These comments underscore the subversive effectiveness of this type of exclusionary rhetoric, however transparent and deceptive the device may appear to an outsider. As Burke observed, once the enemy has been essentialized, "all 'proof' henceforth is automatic."[29] Once the battle lines have been drawn, all virtues accrue to the Chosen.

This process of rhetorical accommodation also came into play when the collective's nationalistic agenda came into conflict with its critical duty: when reviewers had to contend with a bad piece of music produced by an indubitably German composer. The solution? Blame the pernicious influence of the Italians:

That [Fischer] could dedicate such symphonies to a German hero! Symphonies that are full of the Impotent, the Unmelodic, the Vulgar, the Farcical and the Chopped-up, plus the feverish attacks of alternating *Piano* and *Forte* that you find in the latest Italian fashion composers. That really surprises us. We would like to read an essay in which he justifies his procedures in accordance with the rules of good, sound musical taste. We would be willing to bet that his principal reason would be: because the Italians do it this way . . . We would like to try, with other Germans – two Grauns, a Hasse, a Bach, a Quantz, etc. – leading the way, to insure the propagation of the Noble, the Worthy, the Tender, the Touching, beautiful melody, strict *Harmonie*, and noble expression in music . . . Then listeners with a delicate, reasonable, refined sentiment will be able to judge which nation first produced a musical Raphael or Coreggio or Titian.[30]

Although here Agricola took the abstract high road of claiming general musical virtues for the Germans, at other times he used the Italian foil in more specific musical complaints. For example, he acknowledged that some sonatas for two violins and cello by Johann Schwanberger were not actual trios (i.e. not contrapuntal), but he nonetheless rated them higher than those of "many recent Italians." Schwanberger had just returned from a trip to Italy, and Agricola rejoiced to still recognize him as "one of those Germans, who, no matter what musical clothing they put on, still cannot deny the profundity of their knowledge."[31] In similar fashion the *Wöchentliche Nachrichten* admitted that the same sonatas were "not as contrapuntal and fugue-like as the excellent trios of Kapellmeister Graun" but did not find them "as simple and empty as most Italian trios."[32] Thus, even the weakest compositions of a German could rest assured of a place above the inferior Italian Other.

One wonders how Italians might have responded to the aspersions continually cast upon their music, but, as has already been remarked, they had no voice in the review collective. In the first fifteen years of the collective's existence, even neutrality about the Italian style was rare, and only two reviews expressed anything vaguely complimentary, both while noting the presence of Italianate characteristics in German composers. One characterized the style of Johann Gottfried Eckard as "Italian and easy," noting that his sonatas fell "pleasantly and smoothly on the ear. Musical critics won't declare war on them, at least not a very long one."[33] Another alluded to the collective's preference for contrapuntal composition:

A few artistic judges, who love only the colorful and ingenious, may not be pleased with [A. E. Forstmayer's violin sonatas] because the instruments don't chase each other around, and because the composer uses an Italian turn now and then, which for them is a great crime. We are not as intolerant and believe for certain that we have the approval of many connoisseurs and dilettantes on our side.[34]

Though both reviewers seem to be distancing themselves from the critical mainstream, neither appears to have had very long tenures, judging from the style of the surrounding reviews in both papers. Their open-mindedness was clearly unusual; they, like Boccherini, were the exception that proved the rule.

Several of the reviews cited above also indicate the first steps toward the ultimate rhetorical weapon: the relegation of the Other to an inferior plane of existence, almost moral in its implications. Here, and only here, did the collective ever touch upon the belief that art should ultimately be directed toward the "moral sentiments, through which human beings receive their ethical value," an important aspect of eighteenth-century German aesthetic theory.[35] I do not wish to argue this connection too strongly, for references to "sound taste" imperiled by frivolity hardly count as deep moral or ethical analysis, but the reviewers' discourse does assume that some types of music are better for you. The *Berlinische Nachrichten*, for example, recommended C. P. E. Bach's keyboard concertos to those wishing to "maintain the respectable correctness of their taste, and guard against falling into the swamps of musical triviality."[36]

In the 1760s and early 1770s, this assumption took the form of labeling the Italianate style as "comic" and opposing it with the Germanic adjective of "serious." Though relatively mild as an epithet (especially when translated into English – the German meaning incorporates a tinge of "strange" or "odd"), it carried connotations of superficiality when juxtaposed with the "Serious." The admonishment that Reichardt should avoid betraying his "serious" heritage when confronted with the "comic" style (above, page 48) and the comment that "comic" composers had banished touching slow movements from their works (above, page 51) indicate the disdain in which the style was held. Reviewers also frequently coined phrases like "comic clatter" to emphasize the essential emptiness of the Other's style.[37] Thus the *Hamburgische neue Zeitung* could praise Carl Friedrich Abel by saying that although he wrote in the new style, his Op. 10 symphonies betrayed no trace of the "comic din and clatter that so often is shrilly proclaimed as music – which could at most be music for splitting your sides, but which never moved a single nerve in a human heart."[38] Once again, the essential emptiness of the Other stands in stark contrast to the depth of the Germanic Abel. However, a quick glance at the first symphony of that set, particularly the outer movements, reveals mostly arpeggiated and scalar themes, often with measured tremolo accompaniment, all characteristic of the Italianate style; and the absolute regularity of the phrases might wear on the nerves more than move them.[39] Musical profundity, in other words, was often in the eye of the beholder.

Still this review demonstrates the collective's distinction between the approval of the "up-to-date" and the disparagement of the "merely fashionable." Like "comic," "fashionable" carried connotations of superficiality; and like "comic," reviewers invoked it in connection with Italians and Italianate composition (see the review of Fischer cited above). It also served as a handy explanation for perceived deficiencies in German composers. The *Unterhaltungen*, for example, complained about excessive chromatic appoggiaturas in Georg Simon Löhlein's Op. 2 sonatas, dismissing them as mere "fashionable prettiness" that had no good effect.[40] Unlike the "comic," though, "fashionable" also brought a whiff of the feminine into the discourse, because of fashion's perennial association with women.

Nonetheless, in the early years of the collective, overt associations of the Other with the feminine remained relatively rare. Women were assumed to have less talent and capability as players, as well as a lower level of taste in general, hence the comment in the *Hamburgischer Correspondent* that the short, easy dances in some of Löhlein's partitas would appeal to "beginners and women."[41] In a mostly positive review of sonatas by the Viennese composer I.B. Schmid, the *Wöchentliche Nachrichten* declared that certain dilettantes would find them pleasant and lively. It described the shorter movements as "playful [*tändelnd*] and agreeable," declaring that, "if Herr Schmid intended to please the musical woman, he appears to have succeeded."[42] If *tändelnd* is translated as "trifling" (another possibility), its connection with the superficial style of the Other becomes clearer. Only once, however, in these first fifteen years, did the collective specifically associate the serious, Germanic style with the masculine. In an often-cited review of symphonies by Giovanni Gabriel Meder, the *Wöchentliche Nachrichten* compared minuets in symphonies to beauty spots on a man, complaining that they gave the piece "a dandified appearance" and destroyed the "masculine impression" made by three successive "serious" movements.[43] Aside from these three reviews, the early collective showed little interest in feminizing the Other, though probably less because of any progressive tendencies than because of the preoccupation with the Italians.

At this point, we might well pause to consider where the South Germans and Austrians fit into the "us against them" system, for nearly all of the collective journals (especially in the 1760s and early 1770s) originated in northern and north-central Germany (see the discussion in the previous chapter). Were these Teutonic southerners grouped with the Italian Other or allowed into the German inner circle? Much modern scholarship has assumed the former, citing sources like a 1771 pamphlet entitled *Critischer Entwurf einer auserlesenen Bibliothek*:

The things of Heiden, Toeschi, Cannabisch, Filz, Pugnani, Campioni are getting the upper hand now. You only have to be half a connoisseur to notice the emptiness, the strange mixture of comic and serious, playful and touching, that rules everywhere. Compositional errors, particularly with regard to periodicity, and for the most part a complete lack of knowledge of counterpoint (which is essential if you want to compose a good trio) are frequently found in all of them. The only people who praise them are the ones for whom a line of brilliant melody is everything. The now-fashionable Trios were often really solos or duets, that can be played anywhere. The same goes for the quartets of these gentlemen.[44]

This writer lumps together the Austrian (Haydn) and the Mannheimers (Cannabich, Filtz and Toeschi) with the Italians, charging them all with the same compositional failings that we have seen the review collective attributing to the Italians. Similar biases surfaced in an article on musical taste printed in the *Unterhaltungen* in 1766; its comments on Haydn so enraged the normally quiescent Viennese press, that the *Wiener Diarium* printed an indignant response defending the empire's honor.[45]

The review collective, however, showed only a few signs of this internecine strife. In the early years, Agricola tended to tar South Germans, Austrians, and Italians all with the same brush. For example, he sneered at Italianate composers, saying that their "Cassations" (a title frequently used by Austrians) should really be called "Grassations" (which he said meant boisterousness, brigandage, and nocturnal adventures), and opined that many of the compositions hailing from the "Po, the Danube, and the Rhine" would be better as dances for Harlequin, or even Hanswurst (a beloved comic figure in the Viennese folk tradition).[46] Later, during the 1780s, Cramer published several reviews in his *Magazin der Musik* that described regional differences within the German-speaking realm. In reviewing a concerto by Carl Joseph Birnbach, he observed:

Appears to come from the area along the Rhine or from southern Germany, and unfortunately that says it all. You can recognize all the jingle-jangle from down there instantly by the monotonous figures, the everyday modulations, the trite Alberti basses, the constant running up and down the scale, and similarly arty things, all of which appear in so few different ways in so many different formats; but they all are sold to us as music (driving out the genuine works by better masters), and all appear on very white Imperial or Royal paper, which is too stiff for a certain other use, which would be the true destiny of such works.[47]

During the 1790s, the *Berlinische musikalische Zeitung* complained about the lasciviousness of contemporary "Klimpersachen" (trash music), which it found especially prevalent in South Germany and Austria.[48] Also in the 1790s, the *Allgemeine Litteratur-Zeitung* thought it unfortunate that the "older, difficult classical keyboard pieces from the Bach school" were being "pushed impatiently out of the way by the newer, galant, easier keyboard pieces from the Imperial (i.e. Austrian) school."[49] While these occasional outbursts did paint a south German face on the Other, their relative scarcity (only eight in forty years), and their concentration in only a few journals, works against our considering them a major trend. The review collective was not disposed to carry on such a campaign, perhaps because determining the geographical origins of a composer with a German surname could prove tricky, as Cramer learned after his review of Birnbach: in a review of the same pieces in the *Allgemeine deutsche Bibliothek*, Türk pointed out that while Cramer might have summed up the music from along the Rhine fairly well, Birnbach actually came from Breslau, which was in Silesia.[50]

Even if we were to accept these occasional digs as evidence of an underlying assumption of the inferior status of South Germans and Austrians, the fact remains that their music – unlike music of the Italians – received relatively equitable treatment from the review collective. Marpurg, for example, certainly treated Georg Christoph Wagenseil's music with contempt and contumely (while blaming his transgressions on Italianate influence), but the indisputably North German Johann Adam Hiller fared no better at his hands.[51] In later years, Viennese composers like Johann Baptist Vanhal and Leopold Kozeluch received acceptable, and sometimes even enthusiastic reviews from their North German judges,[52] and one of their Austrian colleagues even attained the status of a musical icon.

But the invocation of musical icons – composers whose compositional reputation placed them beyond the necessity of critical evaluation – moves us into the second phase of the review collective's rhetorical definition of the Germanic music-aesthetic identity. The first phase came to a startlingly abrupt end in 1775, when the relative merits of Italianate music, and indeed any discussion of national styles, quite suddenly became a non-issue. Whereas during the 1760s and early 1770s, about 10 percent of reviews contained comments lambasting the dreadful Italians, that percentage dropped to less than 1 percent after 1775.[53] During the half decade from 1785 to 1789, none of the *circa* 270 instrumental reviews mentioned the Italian style at all. Part of this abrupt change can be attributed to Agricola's death in 1774, which deprived the collective of its most vociferous anti-Italian reviewer. Part probably stemmed from the decrease in the number of Italian instrumental music pieces competing with German compositions in local presses. But perhaps, having successfully established a Germanic identity and being well on the way to establishing firm aesthetic criteria (see the following chapters), reviewers no longer needed the Italians as an "evil empire" against which they could define themselves in favorable terms.

It may also have become increasingly difficult to rail against the "Italian" style as such, the more frequently it flowed from the pens of German composers. *Before* the mid 1770s, Germans who strayed from the fold received a treatment no less scathing than those who had seduced them (see the review of Fischer cited above). But after around 1775, though reviewers continued to attack the same kinds of compositional failings, they did so without reference to Italian influence. The *Hamburgischer Correspondent*, for example, criticized the monotony of the constant Alberti bass in some sonatas by Franz Ignaz Beck, but it did so without blaming Italian influence.[54] Likewise, in the *Magazin der Musik*, N. N. avoided any national stereotypes when he praised the sonatas of Johann Gottfried Vierling, set in true idiomatic style – not "little scraps from opera arias, gussied up with drumming, Alberti basses, but movements worked out with profundity and dignity."[55] Occasionally, a pro-Italian comment surfaced as it had earlier, but without the references to main-stream biases found in the Eckard and Forstmayer reviews cited above. For example, the *Gothaische gelehrte Zeitungen* declared that Johann Paul Schulthesius's violin sonatas were excellent and "full of ravishing melodies," adding that an appropriate performance would reveal that they were "fruits ripened under Italian skies."[56] When Muzio Clementi burst onto the musical scene in the 1790s (to generally favorable treatment), reviewers made no special mention of his nationality. The *Musikalische Monatsschrift* even praised the sonatas of a German composer (August Eberhard Müller) by exclaiming that their "invention and execution could even do honor to a Clementi."[57]

The abandonment of the anti-Italian campaign did not, however, signify any move away from the "us against them" mentality, but simply a shift in the collective's rhetorical tactics. First of all, dropping the physically-present Other from their scheme forced reviewers to pay more attention to defining the Chosen. They did so in a way that Burke does not discuss, but that emerging nations have often used in shaping an identity: the creation and invocation of national heroes – the musical icons mentioned above. Several of the reviews cited from the early years mention names of German composers as examples of good composition: Graun, Hasse, C. P. E. Bach, Benda, Wagenseil (!), Kunz, Binder, Händel, Quantz. This habit continued unabated into the collective's later years (though the composers changed), but gradually two names emerged from the pack, singled out for special iconic status.

The first to emerge was C. P. E. Bach, whose age (approaching 50 when instrumental reviews first began to appear), impeccable North German pedigree (the collective had not forgotten his father), theoretical work and extensive list of compositions (he had already proved himself), made him an eminently suitable candidate for iconization. Even during the late 1760s, the tone in reviews of his music begins to lift him above the norm:

We have just wandered through a barren field filled with thorns, [the preceding review was the one of Manfredini cited above] and now we come to a pleasant region in which the beauty of nature fills our eyes ... The movements of these sonatas are all serious: no minuets or polonaises and are as rich in invention, melody, and strict, ingenious *Harmonie* as the other works of this famous composer.[58]

Wrenched out of context, the praise hardly seems extraordinary; in comparison with other positive reviews of the time, the language has been ratcheted up a notch. The metaphorical references to fields of thorns and the beauty of nature are unusual, for most reviews from the 1760s do not wax poetic. And the phrase "rich in invention" – an intensification of the stock praise "inventive" – was applied at that time *only* to C. P. E.[59] Not infrequently, reviewers crossed the line into the area of unbounded adulation:

That Herr Bach is one of the greatest and most famous musicians of our century is an eternal truth. That his lively, fertile and ingratiating Bach spirit emerges here palpably and alluringly, as in all his works, is also an undeniable truth. That along with his strengths in music he also possesses a beautiful heart and noble character, we know from our own experience.[60]

The writer clearly knew Bach – as did several other reviewers – and his warm admiration flows like honey onto the page, obscuring any possibility besides perfection. Having enthroned their icon, reviewers proved reluctant to notice anything that did not fit into the established Germanic picture, such as the arpeggios and broken chord accompaniments that dominate the keyboard *Sinfonia* from Bach's *Clavierstücke verschiedener Art* (example 3.1). Instead of screaming about stylistic betrayal, as often happened when a German composer picked up a touch of the Italian (see above, page 51), Agricola instead praised Bach's passion and richly inventive spirit, saying that the pieces needed no further recommendation.[61] Fault-finding occurred only when Bach strayed too noticeably into the area of a reviewer's compositional pet peeve, and then it was always couched in excessively apologetic tones. When in 1767 Agricola criticized the lack of counterpoint in the *Sonatine a Cembalo concertato*, he hastened to add that the keyboard part by itself would make the most beautiful sonata imaginable, excusing Bach's lapse by saying that the keyboard player in him had simply kept the upper hand.[62]

As Bach came to symbolize the true German style, reviewers could use him as a reference point in assessing other composers (although one critic did observe that expecting everyone to write like Bach was like expecting all poets to write like Klopstock or Goethe or Wieland).[63] Nonetheless, when the collective recognized men like Wolf, Häßler, or Türk, as worthy members of the Bach school, it conveyed the idea of their fundamental worth. Häßler, for example, received praise as a Bach follower whose sonatas had "good *Harmonie* and touching melody and distinguish themselves from the current swarm of dry, Italian fashion pieces."[64] The *Hamburgischer Correspondent* could tell that Türk had studied Bach because of his "good melody and correct *Harmonie*, and because he did not just take a little snippet from an

Example 3.1 C. P. E. Bach, *Sinfonia* from *Clavierstücke verschiedener Art*, Wq. 112/13, mm. 1–13

opera tune and harmonize it with an error-ridden Alberti bass."[65] Others were not so lucky. After panning some divertissements by Christian Benjamin Uber, the *Musicalische Bibliotek* observed that Uber "would always entertain those people who had not been spoiled by the "spirited works of C. P. E. Bach and other great composers."[66] The *Allgemeine deutsche Bibliothek* observed that Franz Duschek's sonata was rather nice for a fashionable piece, and that – to his credit – it seemed like he was trying to be the Czech Bach. Then came the fatal question: "But just how far is C. P. E. Bach from Duschek? Just as far as it is from Hamburg to Prague."[67]

Bach remained the icon-of-choice through the end of the century, though his star did begin to fade somewhat after his death in 1788. By that time, however, he had long been joined – and for genres like the symphony and string quartet even surpassed by – Joseph Haydn. As early as 1772, the *Hamburgischer Correspondent* had reviewed the Op. 8 string quartets of J. C. Bach by observing that while pleasant, they were not as "completely worked out as the ones by Haydn and Boccherini."[68] However, even though Haydn serves as a model here, and even though the "completely worked out" reflects the Germanic ideal, he was still keeping company with an Italian, not an association that would lead to iconic status in the reviewing community. But a few years later, the same newspaper reviewed the sonatas of a local dilet-tante composer by saying:

We found a lot of good things in these sonatas, but also a lot of shopworn phrases and modulations. Admittedly it is very difficult, given the amount of music now being pub-lished, to be new and original like Bach and Hayden.[69]

That was high-class company. As Reichardt remarked in a review of Haydn symphonies and quartets in 1782: "Even if we only had a Haydn and a C. P. E. Bach, we Germans could maintain that we have our own style, and that our instrumental music is the most interesting of all."[70]

This acceptance by the German review community should not surprise us, for Haydn's music has many of the same characteristics the reviewers pro-fessed to admire in Bach: originality, complex and unexpected modulations, skill in *Harmonie*. But reviewers never discussed Haydn in terms of Bach's style, like they did with the Häßlers and the Türks: they perceived him not as a follower, but as a new icon, *sui generis*. And while Haydn never had the same close personal connections to the review community that Bach did, a few of his reviews reach the same ecstatic heights:

(*Magazin der Musik*, 1783) This symphony is worthy of its master and certainly does not need our praise. In performance, the opening measures and the magnificent arrangements that follows, already reveal the mind of the great composer, who appears to have an inexhaustible supply of new ideas. May Haydn crown this grand symphonic epoch with more magnificent works like this, and thus silence all bad symphony composers, or at least force them to do a better job on their desultory movements, which no one except themselves can enjoy.[71]

The same key words and phrases generally applied only to Bach now appear attached to Haydn as well: inexhaustible wealth of ideas and original genius. And, if a reviewer did not find a work original or interesting enough, then the conclusion was that Haydn didn't actually write it, a distinct possibility given the number of spurious works circulating under his name.[72] As with Bach, negative comments came only on hot-button issues, and then with much qualification. In 1792, for example, the ever pedantic *Allgemeine deutsche Bibliothek* ventured a timid criticism of a sudden modulation from C major to A flat major in one of the Op. 54 string quartets; transgressions against tonal unity happened to be one of the reviewer's main pet peeves (see chapter 7), and he objected to the example Haydn thereby set for young and impressionable composers. But he did not venture this criticism until he had said:

When we tell our readers that these three quartets are fully worthy of a Haydn, we don't need to say anything more. For who doesn't know Haydn as one of the greatest living composers. These quartets will make you marvel at the original humor, musical wit, and the inexhaustible richness of the composer's ideas. We don't trust ourselves to decide which of the three is the best.[73]

To the characteristics he shared with Bach, the reviewer adds others for which Haydn was – and is – famous: wit and humor. Received opinion holds that the North Germans failed to understand or appreciate this aspect of Haydn's music, and some notably cranky comments are to be found *outside* the review collective. *Within*, however, instead of criticizing him for trivializing what should be serious music, reviewers not only accepted, but extolled his wit and humor as further evidence of his genius. When one of Haydn's followers (like Ignaz Pleyel) wrote in his style, that was usually what the reviewer missed: "The student of Haydn is recognizable in these sonatas right at the first glance – even though one does miss his delicacy and inexhaustible humor."[74]

Though Mozart showed signs of incipient iconic status by 1790 (see chapter 7), his early death and the fundamental changes in the collective's own makeup after about 1794 insured that his elevation would proceed quite differently and would serve quite a different aesthetic purpose. But during these crucial years of the formation of a national musical identity, Bach and Haydn helped to define the Germanic musical style.

Though the emphasis on a positive Germanic group identity, as defined by the icons, replaced the obsession with the negative Italian Other in the last

twenty-five years of collective discourse, threads of the earlier bipolar ordering of the musical universe continued, and even strengthened. "Fashionable,"
for example, remained a popular epithet, applied to those musical characteristics formerly labeled Italianate. When Forkel reviewed some sonatas by
Salomon Greßler in the *Musikalischer Almanach* – somewhat less than favorably – he nonetheless granted them some dignity by noting that Greßler had
avoided the worst of the fashion traps:

These sonatas are written in the true keyboard style, in which keyboard sonatas must
be written. You will not find any fashionable hocus pocus with as many octaves as both
hands can reach or with any murky or Alberti basses. Instead, [you will] find an
orderly, reasonable and solid course, far removed from that sort of jumping around."[75]

More frequently now, however, the implicit connection between fashion and
the feminine was made explicit. In reviewing a number of *pot-pourris* and
variations "intended for the admirers of the easy, fashionable, keyboard
style," the *Berlinische musikalische Zeitung* thought they would only provide
amusement for "the grand heap of ordinary dilettantes and ladies," for the
connoisseur would certainly not want them.[76] Comments like this differ
subtly from the earlier associations of light and easy compositions with
female taste (see above, page 54), for they contain an implicit devaluation of
the works as worthless junk. That they may be, but the reviewer did not
bother to discuss their specific aesthetic deficiencies; he simply dismissed
them by associating them with another easily-identifiable Other, women.

Cramer also held forth about the abilities of women as performers in a 1783
review of six of Wolf's keyboard sonatinas. According to Cramer, women
simply did not have "the nerves and the strength necessary for the firm and
characteristic representation of distinguished keyboard ideas, for their fingers
always slide over the keys too quickly, as if they were burning, and their deliv-
ery lacks the necessary light and shadow." Of course, since Wolf had dedicated the sonatinas to the wife of the Kapellmeister in Ludwigslust, Cramer
had to make her into the Boccherini-like exception that proved the rule,
calling her capable of the "most masculine, certain security" and "a genuine
student of the only real style of playing – the Bach style."[77] In the consumer-
oriented world of the review collective, of course, players' abilities determined their taste in music and thus are relevant to this discussion, particularly
when composers wrote with those tastes in mind. The *Erfurtische gelehrte
Zeitungen* observed that Charles Friedrich Vater had tried to please everyone,
giving the connoisseur a fugue in one of his sonatas, though "presumably
with the ladies in mind" had composed it in a "rather galant, free style."[78]

The perceived inability of women to master the intricacies of counterpoint, and hence to appreciate an essential component of the German style, is further revealed in reviews of the music of women composers. As might be expected, unless the woman had a local connection, reviewers greeted her works with patronizing approval at best. More importantly, the particular issues the reviewers addressed tend to equate the female with the character-istics of the musical Other. For example, the *Musikalische Korrespondenz* thought that Josepha Barbara von Auernhammer's variations on Mozart's "Ein Vogelfänger bin ich ja" could stand alongside many masculine works in the genre, though it hastened to add that one should not expect the "profound harmonic intricacies or movements based on the study of counterpoint that we find in the works of Mozart, Clementi and Vogler."[79] Several years later, the *Hamburgischer Correspondent* greeted the Op. 1 sonatas of Catérine Maier née Schiatti as follows:

An epoch-making composition in music, for until now, no woman has cultivated this art with such basic profundity as the composer of these sonatas. The excellent working out, united with naturalness, art, and an entirely new taste, give these sonatas a rightful place alongside the cleverest [male] composers' and proves at the same time, how much art can win when Euterpe embraces one of her own so securely.[80]

Like Boccherini, Maier is presented as the exception that proves the rule, a representative of the Other who succeeded in playing by the rules, using the Germanic technique of *Ausarbeitung* so critical to creating a profound work of art (though judging by her name, she only married into German-ness). For the most part though, the female part of the collective's readership got little respect, and when a reviewer wished to summarily dismiss a compositional effort, he could do so effortlessly, by merely proclaiming it to be something like "tiny tinklings for women and effeminate men."[81] However much such comments leap out at modern sensibilities, in the context of the times they would have counted simply as a part of the cultural wallpaper, so self-evident as to be unworthy of particular notice. And although they had doubled in fre-quency by the 1790s, even then they appeared in only 3 percent of reviews. Present though they may have been in the culture, women simply did not pose enough of a threat to the musical order of things to serve as a useful physical manifestation of the Other.

Gender distinctions did apply, for with increasing frequency, beginning in the 1780s, reviewers associated the Germanic ideal with masculinity. When Reichardt reviewed some symphonies and quartets of Haydn in 1782, he noted approvingly that the composer's "youthful playfulness and often boisterous hilarity" had turned into a "more masculine humor," reaching the conclusion linking Haydn with C. P. E. Bach, cited above.[82] The

Hamburgischer Correspondent had applauded Friedrich Wilhelm Heinrich Benda for "avoiding the temptations of fashion," and writing instead in "a masculine style."[83] Masculinity not only stood in opposition to the whims of fashion, it also strode forth with *power*, a term that first appeared in the 1780s and gained increasing currency in the 1790s. The *Musikalische Real-Zeitung*, a South German publication particularly fond of the powerful, complained that Leopold Kozeluch too often gave in to the dictates of fashion instead of creating his own ideals and presenting them "with masculine power." His efforts thus resulted only in "copies from common life dolled up like a girl who decks herself out with flowers and ribbons," and the reviewer made plain the extent of Kozeluch's shortcomings by comparing him unfavorably with C. P. E. Bach.[84] The *Musikalische Korrespondenz* later lauded the "German power and art" of Georg Joseph Vogler's Marlborough variations, which it felt would make other composers of variations quite jealous.[85]

Perhaps one of the most divisive and insidious techniques of the collective's later decades replaced the serious/comic pair with words that bore more directly on a composition's intrinsic value. One of the manifestations of that trend can be seen in several of the reviews already cited, i.e. the attachment of the words "true" (*wahr*) or "genuine" (*ächt*) to the approved Germanic Chosen: "The sonata is written in the genuine, serious style and rises far above many of our modern sonatas."[86] Reviewers used both *ächt* and *wahr* to refer to the *Harmonie*-rich style of the C. P. E. Bach school (and often playing off his treatise title, *Die wahre Art das Klavier zu spielen*). In actuality, though, neither are musical characteristics, nor even aesthetic ones, except by association. They are instead rhetorical code words, loaded with unstated assumptions: "We, the composers and appreciators of genuine music, have received the word; we know the truth." By implication, the compositions of the Other must then be judged as fake, not music at all. And in fact, concomitant with the surge in popularity of "true" and "genuine" was the emerging awareness of a work's "value," particularly its "inner value" or "inner merit." By the 1790s, a reader of the collective's reviews was six times as likely to encounter such evaluative code words as a reader in the 1760s had been. Once again, the icons helped to define the criteria. As early as 1779, the *Hamburgischer Correspondent* acknowledged that the "inner value" of Haydn's Op. 20 quartets (which have fugal finales) went without saying, and could be counted among his best compositions.[87] Scarcely a decade later, the *Allgemeine deutsche Bibliothek* could hold the definitely non-iconic Christian Benjamin Uber to the same standard: his pieces did not lack for ideas, but the reviewer faulted their "meager inner merit."[88]

None of the many reviewers that used the phrase ever defined what "inner value" meant, nor how one could attain it, and therein lay the insidiousness of the rhetoric. The musical world was still divided into the Chosen and the Other, but the differences had become deeper, more philosophical, and more insuperable. One might well learn to write the counterpoint and interesting *Harmonie* that provided entrée to the Chosen of the 1760s, as Boccherini did, but how would you learn to be true and genuine? What could you study to achieve inner value? With the adoption of these criteria, the review collective laid the foundation for the more nationalistic aspects of German nineteenth-century musical culture. Less threateningly, and perhaps more significantly, the concept of inner value points toward a fundamental shift in the perception of instrumental music, away from the functional and toward the metaphysical. That status, however, could not be accomplished by a simple rhetorical fiat. It required the development of secure aesthetic standards and criteria, a topic to which we now turn.

4

Answering with aesthetic criteria

Altonaischer gelehrter Mercurius (1779), review of the anonymous pamphlet *Wahrheiten die Musik betreffend, gerade herausgesagt von einem deutschen Biedermann.*

We would like to take the liberty – which the author himself takes – to
say bluntly that he knows little or nothing about the art of which he
speaks; that nearly everything he says is nothing but hogwash; and that
other people should be writing truths about an art whose aesthetic is
unfortunately still so little known.[1]

Allgemeine deutsche Bibliothek (1786): Louis Abeille, *Deux
Sonates.*

You won't find any new ideas here, and even the well-digested ones are
always found in the most beautiful – disorder – so that we can scarcely
expect to have a theory of musical aesthetics from Herr A.[2]

As the review collective busied itself with defining and encouraging true
German instrumental music, lively debates were occurring in literature, philosophy, and the other arts, debates that would provide aesthetic criteria to
fill the void left by the rejection of mimesis. Reviewers soon joined in, but they
did not simply tag along behind the leading edge of the discourse, gleaning
whatever ideas they found useful: they participated fully, contributing their
opinions and perspectives, and sometimes even anticipating issues that later
achieved general aesthetic significance. This intersection with non-musical
thought collectives – facilitated by the reviews' presence in general readership
journals – reflected the interdisciplinary nature of German thought in the last
quarter of the century.[3] Not only did it make the music reviews more intelligible to the general public, it also strengthened music's claims for serious
scholarly and aesthetic consideration.

The aesthetic issues raised do not, however, leap from the pages of individual reviews, for reviewers rarely spelled out their principles clearly. They did not have the time or the space to muse about the nature of "The Beautiful" or to develop elaborate theories of musical character. Though an occasional soul would wax eloquent on a particularly tender or compelling issue, most left their aesthetic assumptions lying gently between the lines. Whether stated or not, those assumptions did exist, for as M. H. Abrams has argued, any sustained discourse logical and original enough to be considered criticism will reveal attitudes that point to a theoretical aesthetic perspective.[4] Thus the reviewers' fundamental aesthetic concepts must be teased out of the texts by identifying key words and by recognizing related concepts as they were expressed by a variety of authors. For example, the following reviews touch on a number of issues, both directly and in a more oblique fashion. (In the interests of brevity, I have omitted passages that simply give biographical information on the composer or that deal with peripheral issues like printer's errors; otherwise, the reviews are complete.)

1   I. B. Schmid, *VI Sonates*: We could go on at length about the good things in these sonatas, but would like to state our opinion briefly: the larger movements are rather symphonic, and except for the occasional eruption of harmonic errors, should be lively and pleasant for certain dilettantes . . . We would expect even better work from him in the future, and indeed would welcome it, if he wouldn't find a small admonition too distressing, i.e. to be a little more careful about periodicity and harmonic strictness. For example, who told him to put two extraneous beats right at the beginning of the Allegretto of the first sonata, when they would have been better used later at the repetition of the melody? Who could find the following place harmonically correct? It would not be pleasant to hunt out all such mistakes and careless errors, so we have confined ourselves only to the third and fourth pages. Nonetheless, Herr Schmid's sonatas can still be pleasant for certain dilettantes, who think attention to such matters (which others consider to be the essence of composition) to be cranky pettiness . . . However, if Herr Schmid wishes to secure the approval of learned connoisseurs, we would advise him to study the rules of *Harmonie* a bit more carefully, and explore their use in composition more precisely. For not everything that we come across is worth snapping up.[5]

2   *Musikalisches Vielerley*: These two sheets contain a sonata with varied reprise by our Herr Bach. He has gone to great trouble to be easy; an author always loses when he has to restrain himself and cannot give

himself over entirely to his genius. Nevertheless, for all its easiness, this sonata still has much of the Bachian humor.[6]

3   F. S. Sander's *Sechs Clavier=Sonaten*: Herr Sander knows the nature of the instrument, has a good understanding of the rules of strict *Harmonie*, which he joins with the pleasant and tasteful melody that rules in his sonatas and must rule in all good sonatas. You won't find any familiar melodies from familiar operas accompanied by familiar, incorrect Alberti basses, the ingredients which various new composers – according to the dictates of fashion – use to increase the number of their printed pieces from Op. 1 to who knows how many. Instead you can see that Herr S. invents for himself, and puts his ideas down on paper according to the rules of art. He thus deserves the esteem and encouragement of the musical public, so that he will continue to study the rules of art, without which all the products of the greatest geniuses are imperfect, and cannot accomplish their proper effect. The sonatas are not too long.[7]

4   Joseph Haydn's *Grande Simphonie*: Each of these three symphonies uses a flute and two bassoons in addition to the usual instruments. With what artistry and subtlety these are used by the inexhaustible genius of the inimitable Haydn to assist and strengthen the expression! Words can simply not describe it; you must hear it, and who has ever heard a Haydn symphony without delight? Trying to praise works of such originality and perfection, and of such generally recognized value in a review would be laughable, and the reviewer recognizes all too well how far above his praise Haydn is.[8]

5   Louis Abeille's *Sonates*: If one wishes to proceed only from the style of Bach, which mustn't always be done, then one will find much to enjoy in these sonatas, for the *Phantasie* as well as for the fingers. They are occasionally striking, have a certain something that could be called bizarre and that disturbs the clarity, but on the whole are worked out well and industriously.[9]

6   Türk's *Sechs Sonaten*: Herr Türk has already been recognized as one of our most talented composers, and now he has added to his renown with these sonatas. They recommend themselves primarily through tunefulness and sentimentality, or through melodies that are full of feeling. Even with the strictest observance of all the rules of theory, a masterful heartfelt expression rules throughout.[10]

7   *Zwey und dreyßig Menuetten*: These minuets are entirely suited to their purpose, which is dancing. For the most part lively, joy-inducing melodies, without far-fetched modulation.[11]

Even a cursory reading reveals a wealth of potential aesthetic concepts. Review 1 focuses almost exclusively upon Schmidt's errors in *Harmonie* and phrasing, and makes brief reference to the sonata's "symphonic" nature. The reviewer thus appears to define a good piece of music as one that follows correct compositional procedures and adheres to genre expectations. In reviews 2 and 3, the characteristic of genius makes its appearance, both times in a manner suggesting that it can sometimes be fettered. While review 2 implies that unwelcome restrictions can be imposed upon it, review 3 argues that its flights of fancy need some restraint, in this case provided by a knowledge of the rules. The adulatory comments about Haydn's "inexhaustible" genius and "originality" in review 4 associate genius with the continual flow of new ideas, and the superlative "inimitable" implies an aesthetic preference for a definite personal style over the mere adherence to convention. We see the dangers of originality run amok in review 5, where the occasional "striking passages" shade into the "bizarre" and disturb the composition's "clarity," perhaps a reference to the desirability of a perceptible musical structure. Concern with music's emotional effect dominates the comments in review 6, which uses language associated with the North German *Empfindsamer* style, and also underlies the description of "joy-inducing melodies" in review 7. Thus, complex aesthetic perspectives and expectations can be found lurking under the briefest of comments.

Interpretive dangers lurk as well, however, not the least of which include problems of translation and the definition of words whose meanings have changed since the late eighteenth century, sometimes subtly, sometimes more substantially. While "Phantasie," for example, might credibly be rendered as "fantasy," that inappropriately conjures up a state of romantic hallucination for the modern reader. Its eighteenth-century English equivalent was "fancy," which had a specific meaning in Enlightenment philosophy. Most German writers (including Sulzer, Immanuel Kant, and the philosopher Johann Nicolaus Tetens) understood it as "an associative power that supplies the mind or the inner eye with numerous images," which connects it with the imagination, but denies it the power of invention.[12] Other terms had enough ambiguity just within the context of eighteenth-century German linguistics to make the interpretation of isolated instances difficult. Both "original" and the nearly untranslatable "*Laune*" (humor) could have negative associations, but reviewers seemed mostly to view them as positive (as the wording of reviews 2 and 4 indicates). Even given a relatively firm understanding of the meaning of key words, grouping them under larger conceptual headings poses further challenges. For example, although numerous sources clearly document the association of "original" with creative genius, "striking" (review 5) has a less obvious connection. However, because reviewers consistently used it as a clear compliment, in ways that connected it to originality and the unexpected, it can legitimately be included under the umbrella of creative genius.

Defining terms and reading between the lines still does not completely explicate the review collective's succinct evaluations, for we must also consider the significance of what the reviewer did *not* discuss. Does the exclusive focus on compositional correctness found in review 1 mean that the *Wöchentliche Nachrichten* considered that the only significant aesthetic standard, or were the pieces so error-ridden that it was pointless to talk about anything else? Does the emphasis on expressivity in review 6 betray a fundamental belief in the mimetic paradigm, or simply the hypersensitivity of that particular reviewer? Many of these interpretive questions, which seem unanswerable when asked about a single isolated review, become quite manageable if we draw upon the information provided by the review *collective*. If a number of reviewers in various journals obsessed about parallel fifths, we may safely conclude that they believed compositional correctness was a significant aesthetic criterion. If they mostly fail to mention mimesis, or expressivity, or clarity, or taste, then those characteristics must *not* have been fundamental to their perception of musical excellence. Even seemingly undeserved words of praise can indicate what issues are most *au courant*, for a partisan reviewer would surely not choose to promote a favorite composer by extolling out-of-date virtues.

The process I have followed in my interpretation is one of continuous and alternating induction and deduction: I started by indexing recurring words, phrases and concepts, which I then grouped together under conceptual headings. As larger concepts emerged, I began to see the connections to late eighteenth-century literary and philosophical discourse and used those writings to enhance and expand the vocabulary of my original groups. Armed with these expanded definitions, I returned to the reviews, often identifying issues and characteristics whose significance I had previously overlooked.[13] Such a method requires a certain amount of tabulation to establish the relative importance of the various categories and to ascertain any trends in thought, but it does not lend itself to precise statistical analysis. Merely counting the occurrences of the word "genius" will never adequately describe its significance, which is determined not just by the frequency of its use, but also the way in which it is presented. I have occasionally presented percentages and numerical comparisons to buttress my assertions, but they must be viewed as guideposts for a close reading of the review texts rather than as the end result.[14]

After multiple readings and rereadings of the review texts, an aesthetic picture began to coalesce in much the same way that a Seurat painting resolves itself, as the viewer steps backward, from a collection of dots into a landscape. The picture encompasses four main areas: compositional correctness, order/unity, creative genius, and expressivity. Each category can be found as a criterion for compositional excellence in all types of journals across the four decades, a sign of the collective's intellectual stability. Stability does not equal stasis, however, for each evolved considerably over the years, both in vocabulary and conceptual basis. What reviewers meant by "order" or "genius" in 1760 differed greatly from what they meant in 1798, signaling a dramatic change in the perception of music.

The evolution in the review collective's thinking had another dimension as well. If one steps back further from the picture of the four categories, the outlines of an even broader issue gradually emerge: the tension between the rational (compositional correctness and order/unity) and the irrational (creative genius and expressivity). This dichotomous thought pattern – like the one described in chapter 3 – reflected the general scholarly tendency to posit polar opposites found in German academic circles after around 1750.[15] Unlike the "us against them" construction, however, both sides of the "rational versus irrational" equation received attention. In fact, the concern for the proper balance between the two was a driving force in much late eighteenth-century German thought. During the 1780s, for example, Moses Mendelssohn and Friedrich Heinrich Jacobi carried on an extended debate about the conflict between reason and faith, with Jacobi arguing passionately that keeping one's faith might entail at least the partial abandonment of reason.[16] In his aesthetic writings, Gotthold Ephraim Lessing wrestled with the difficulty of keeping creative genius under control while still allowing its imaginative flights. Herder acknowledged that problem, but came down firmly on the side of genius, saying that "the creative joy in seeing thoughts grow and images arise is rarely coupled with thrifty exactness in ordering images and shaping thoughts."[17] Kant sought to accommodate both the rationally expressed concept of beauty and the irrational sublime into his *Critique of Judgment*. On its own practical level, the review collective also thrashed out the question of balance as well, but before proceeding to an examination of its solutions, we should first briefly clarify the nature and vocabulary of the individual aesthetic areas.

The criterion of compositional correctness can be defined not so much by specific terms as by an attitude, one that assumed a right and a wrong way of writing music. A good composition thus observed all the rules. Technical dissections of *Harmonie* and periodicity proceeded from this assumption and would thus fall into this aesthetic category, but other musical elements were also subject to the label of "correct" or "incorrect." A review by Türk in the *Allgemeine deutsche Bibliothek* listed a number of errors in Johann Christoph Friedrich Bach's *Drey leichte Sonaten*, including not only parallel fifths and cross relations, but also harsh modulations.[18] For Türk, these modulations needed "correction," he did not regard them as a matter of compositional preference, or as passages that should be evaluated in terms of their effect (or Affect). In the more in-depth journals, this Beckmesserian attitude occasionally manifested itself in references to rules laid down by various authorities on music. The collective cited Sulzer's *Allgemeine Theorie der schönen Künste* most frequently, followed by the treatises of Kirnberger, Riepel, Quantz, Marpurg, Mattheson, Scheibe, Engel (*Ueber die musikalische Malerey*), Vogler, and Türk (who cited himself).

The criterion of order/unity presents interpretive problems because the conceptual basis of its terms shifted considerably during the last half of the eighteenth century. At mid-century, Moses Mendelssohn succinctly formulated a common attitude by proclaiming that "beauty presumes unity in variety."[19] (As late as 1790 Kant still found use for the formula in his *Critique of Judgment*.) The review collective occasionally alluded to the Mendelssohnian phrase, urging, for example, a composer to limit the "fertility of his ideas, and attempt to round off each piece through unity and a closer connection among the variety of ideas."[20] However pungent as a concept, "unity in variety" did not actually prescribe how to achieve that unity, and therein resided the difficulty. Thus the review collective had to propose its own specific solutions, which it did in a number of ways, always reflecting the shifting philosophical ground and the changes in musical style. When the *Wöchentliche Nachrichten* complained about "certain composers who put together their rattling symphonies from ten different trite ideas," it was discomfited by variety without unity, which it proposed to cure by something akin to Baroque *Fortspinnung*. The prescription involved a dose of a symphony by C. P. E. Bach, through which the offenders could learn "what a main idea was, how it could be used in different keys, sometimes partially, sometimes in its entirety," as well as the "type of relationship any new subsidiary ideas should have to the main theme."[21] Thus unity could involve the proper connection of related ideas without reference to a superstructure or form. In an intersection with the paradigm of mimesis, Agricola invoked the unity of Affect, observing that "variations should retain the main Affect of the piece as much as possible."[22] Though reviewers rarely advocated mimetic solutions to problems of unity, they not infrequently called for the "unity of style," an attempt at a more holistic interpretation that relied on purely musical criteria. Some later reviewers, by making pointed reference to "the Whole" (*das Ganze*), implied a more internal and organic concept of unity that has little to do with the linear ordering of thoughts or the adherence to an abstract Affect.

One other aspect that seemed to fall into the domain of reason – taste – might be mentioned here, though it played only a peripheral role in the review collective's aesthetic deliberations. Taste had entered German aesthetic debate in the early eighteenth century with the theories of the arch rationalist Johann Christoph Gottsched, who posited two types of aesthetic judgment: the scholarly/discerning (*wissenschaftlich und einsichtsvoll*) on the one hand and taste on the other. Like many others, he was disturbed by the subjective element of taste, which could differ greatly even among educated people and thus seemed to have a slightly irrational tinge. Nonetheless, he placed taste under the control of reason, because he "couldn't put it anywhere else."[23] Others could. Herder felt that it did not belong to the realm of the rational, and the English philosopher Gerard (whose works were translated into German in the late 1770s – see below) brought the entire faculty of judgment, including taste, under the purview of the imagination rather than reason.[24] Forkel proposed a definition for musical taste that more or less straddled the fence. In an article on the F minor sonata from the third part of C. P. E. Bach's *Sonaten für Kenner und Liebhaber* [Wq. 57], he observed that enthusiasm and the passionate imagination needed to be tempered by reason and taste, which he defined as "the feeling of the true, the correct, and the beautiful that arises from a distillation of all the basic rules of music."[25] Nonetheless, his choice of the word "feeling" (*Gefühl*), which carried the connotation of an "intuitive sense," suggested that taste might still elude logical explanation.

While the review collective frequently referred to the taste of audiences and performers, it only rarely mentioned taste as an element contributing to the compositional process, i.e. as one that could count as an aesthetic criteria. Those few instances adhered to Forkel's conception of taste as an admirable quality capable of stemming compositional excess. The *Hamburgischer Correspondent* noted approvingly that the modulations in a set of Haydn piano sonatas were always done "with taste,"[26] while the *Musikalische Real-Zeitung*, in panning a particularly bad battle sonata, observed that if such "musical witticisms" were to be tolerated at all, they at least needed to be governed by "truth, clarity, order, sound judgment and taste."[27]

If taste remained a marginal issue, creative genius – which clearly weighed in on the irrational side of the spectrum – assumed center stage. Genius and the concomitant concept of the creative imagination – often thought of as the centerpiece of romantic thought – actually developed as a significant element of aesthetics during the late seventeenth and eighteenth centuries. One of the earliest advocates, the English philosopher Thomas Hobbes, called the imagination at its highest level the driving force behind artistic creation. Shaftesbury concurred, attributing the creative power of an artist or poet not to the faculty of reason or perception (the chief supports of the mimetic paradigm, incidentally) but to an independent function of the mind, to genius.[28] Gottfried Wilhelm Leibniz adopted Shaftesbury's ideas and thus transmitted them to the German Enlightenment, which wrestled with the concepts for much of the century, struggling to assimilate them into the prevailing rationalistic climate. In musical discourse, many tacitly agreed with Rousseau, who had proclaimed in typically passionate fashion: "Seek not, young artist, the meaning of *genius*. If you possess it you will sense it within you. If not, you will never know it."[29] Kirnberger, for example, finessed any questions about the source of the musical ideas that would be subject to his rules and regulations, saying that, "The invention of a single melodic unit or phrase which is an intelligible statement from the language of sentiments . . . is simply a work of genius and cannot be taught by rules."[30] Even though Kirnberger obviously still tied it to the concept of the sentiments, creative genius actually offered an alluring way out of the restrictive bounds of mimesis. Before it could be embraced wholeheartedly, however, its place in the scheme of the human mind had to be defined and discussed. Some of that discussion took place in the review collective.

In typically oblique fashion, reviewers did not offer any precise definitions, but their vocabulary incorporated many terms consistently associated with the faculty of creative genius. They used the word *Genie* as defined in Sulzer's *Allgemeine Theorie der schönen Künste*, to designate a composer's talent or gift for composition, reserving the superlative *Original=Genie*, a specific term directly traceable to Shaftesbury, for special cases – for C. P. E. Bach, Haydn, Mozart.[31] Reviewers also occasionally referred to *Phantasie*, both to denote a receptive power in the listener (as in review 5) and the creative faculty in a composer. More rarely, they discussed a composer's imagination as the source of musical ideas, as when the *Musikalische Real-Zeitung* proclaimed that two late Mozart quartets were "written with the passion of invention and the correctness for which Mozart has long been famous as one of the best composers in Germany."[32] In associating the imagination with composition, they gave music an exalted status that brought it into full equality with the other arts.

Many other terms clustered around the center of creative genius and the imagination. Gerard, whose 1774 treatise *Essay on Genius* received favorable reviews in Germany after its translation in 1776, stated that genius depended "on invention, the ability to . . . produce original works of art,"[33] an assertion also made by Voltaire. Both *originell* and *Erfindung* (invention), with its adjectives *erfinderisch* and *erfindungsreich* (rich in invention) made frequent appearances in the review collective, along with more colorful locutions like "leaving the common path in order to avoid the commonplace,"[34] or not just "sprinkling new sauce over leftovers."[35] Reviewers also frequently alluded to "newness" and "novelty," associated with the imagination by Joseph Addison in a series of essays in the *Spectator* in 1712.[36] Unfortunately, they did not always spell out what novelty entailed, and their vagueness did not escape the attention of eighteenth-century readers. According to the satirical pamphlet *Musikalische Charlatanerien*, Karl Spazier had reviewed some compositions by Augustin Gürlich and criticized them for not distinguishing themselves with "novel ideas" (*Neuheit der Gedanken*). The pamphlet's author, obviously partial to Gürlich, responded indignantly: "Does Herr C. S. know what he is saying here? Does he know what he means by new ideas?"[37]

Other concepts related to genius had to do with the variety (*Mannigfaltigkeit*) and abundance (*Reichheit*) of the new ideas. The role of variety in aesthetic pleasure had been stressed by Mendelssohn, among others, in his *Briefe über die Empfindungen* from 1755. In addition to pure sensory enjoyment, Mendelssohn located the source of pleasure in the perceptual ordering of variety and in the recognition of its purpose; the greater the variety, the greater the pleasure.[38] It would then follow that the products of genius, as the objects of aesthetic perception and pleasure, should encompass richness and variety. Because the richness and variety had to be original as well, reviewers often strengthened their praise with words like "surprising," "unexpected," or "striking" and complained about too-frequent repetitions or a paucity of ideas. As the *Allgemeine deutsche Bibliothek* sneered sarcastically, "surely genius doesn't manifest itself through poverty, barrenness, through slavish imitation, through dullness and frigidity," all characteristics it observed in the music being reviewed.[39]

Also swirling around in the cluster of concepts associated with genius, were the characteristics of wit (*Witz*) and humor (*Laune*). In general, wit denoted the ability to connect seemingly disparate ideas, possibly, but not necessarily, in a manner that could induce laughter. *Laune* had an etymological connection with the medieval "humors" and thus carried connotations of mood, both bad and good. Its primary meaning, used in a phrase like "a person with much humor," designated someone with "a cheerful disposition who had much wit in his manner, in his expression, and in his writing."[40] The association of wit and humor with genius might best be expressed by the formula: genius included them, but they did not necessarily indicate genius. Lessing, who believed that the fine arts and literature made up the realm of wit, nonetheless remarked that a person could "be without a single spark of genius, and still possess much wit and taste."[41] On the other hand, Adolf von Knigge observed in his *Über den Umgang mit Menschen*, from 1788, that "true humor and genuine wit cannot be forced or feigned; they work instead like the flights of a higher genius, rapturously, enthusiastically, awe-inspiring."[42] In musical discourse, an article by Forkel associated both wit and humor with genius. Under the essential aspects of music, he included not only the proper ordering of musical material and the expression of the sentiments, but also certain delights that cannot be defined by any rules: "They are the fruits of a lively imagination, a refined taste; in short only sublime genius can achieve them. Musical wit, humor, novelty, grandness and sublimity are among them." Later he indicated that these qualities, along with the "expression of the unexpected, the marvelous, of elegance, strength, and richness," should be topics for musical criticism.[43] A better summary of the characteristics of the creative genius cannot be found.

The review collective's other aesthetic preoccupation on the irrational side of the equation was expressivity, a category that included, but did not equal, the paradigm of mimesis. Mimesis required the portrayal or expression of specific, identifiable non-musical elements or emotions. Expressivity could encompass more vaguely defined issues of expression and emotional involvement in music. Without a doubt, it is the slipperiest of all the review collective's criteria, not only because of the conceptual haziness discussed in chapter 1, but also because of the difficulty in distinguishing between a reviewer's authentic perception of expressivity in music and the mere propensity for colorful and descriptive language. Before worrying about such subtleties, we should at least identify the possibilities for expression that reviewers considered.

Some of the terms clearly belonged under the umbrella of mimesis. *Affekten* and *Leidenschaften* (passions), for example, denoted abstract and static emotional states that could be rationally described, thus serving the demands of Cartesian rationalism. By the 1750s, the Affects and the passions had taken on more personalized, irrational connotations. A 1767 dictionary of the arts defined them as "tendencies in human disposition" and gave, as an example of being guided by the passions, a judge who was lenient on someone he wished well, and too strict on someone he bore malice.[44] In this sense they approached the related but nonetheless distinct concept of the sentiments (*Empfindungen*), which originally denoted sensory perceptions, but had gradually accumulated layers of meaning connecting them with the emotions and feelings.[45] As a concept, the sentiments had been appropriated by the cult of sensibility that developed in North German music circles in the last half of the century. According to its adherents, which included C. P. E. Bach, music should touch the heart and stir the emotions and feelings of the listener if it was to be considered aesthetically significant, and could do this only by expressing a particular sentiment. Although, as Georgia Cowart has pointed out, the vocabulary of sensibility "refers more properly to the listener than to the music,"[46] reviewers did upon occasion use it to describe the music itself. Thus pieces were found to be "touching" (*rührend*) or "full of feeling" (*gefühl-voll*), or "heartfelt expression," as in the Türk review cited above (review 6). Another term often linked to the Affects and the sentiments – *Charakter* – made an occasional appearance in the collective. Reviewers sometimes used it as the equivalent of style, as in a reference to a work's "symphonic character," a formulation that does not place it directly within the realm of expressivity.[47] On other occasions, character appeared to be synonymous with Affect.[48] More rarely, it meant a person whose characteristics were to be portrayed in the music, about the only type of directly representational tone painting the review collective was willing to take seriously. Character associated adjectives included naive, sentimental, melancholy, mournful (*schwermütig*) and similar words pertaining to human moods and personality.

While all these terms have a fairly clear connection to the concepts of expressivity in music (though not necessarily to mimesis), the relationship of others remains much more ambiguous. Did reviewers who called a piece "lively" (*lebhaft* or *munter*) imply the representation of a human personality trait, or were they just alluding to tempo and performance style? Did a work described as "tender" (*zärtlich*) express an emotion or Affect, or simply have a slow tempo and lyrical melody? What are we to make of adjectives like fiery (*feurig*), ingratiating (*einschmeichelnd*), soft (*sanft*), sweet (*süß*), sluggish (*träg*), waggish (*schalkhaft*), all of which appeared as musical descriptors? Even if the reviewers actually intended an expressive (or mimetic) connotation in their use of such terms, did they mean that the composer *intended* it to be expressive, that it *should* have been expressive of something, or simply that it *seemed* expressive to them? The *Hamburgische neue Zeitung*, for example, frequently complained about the absence of "touching, affective" slow movements and exclaimed that even in Allegros, "arpeggios seldom mean much to the heart," implying that expressivity was an essential aspect of music.[49] At other times, a plethora of adjectives seems to be no more than scribal exuberance:

The first sonata has an ingratiating Gratioso . . . and a flowing rondo that is full of feeling. The second sonata has (1) a short andante that sneaks by, a tender minuet, and a lively rondo . . . The third begins with a short, dark, mournful Andante maestoso, which soon breaks into a passionate Allegro assai that seems to die out at the end . . . [and] concludes with a lively Allegretto.[50]

Thus, more than the other aesthetic areas embraced by reviewers, the frequency with which they mentioned expressivity is open to subjective interpretation. Even given the broadest possible definition, however, references to it turn up in less than a quarter of the reviews. In pure numbers, it edges out order/unity, but lags behind both compositional correctness and creative genius.

Expressivity's significance, like that of the other criteria, resided less in its individual status than in its relationship to the others, a relationship guided by the tension between the rational and irrational elements of the aesthetic equation. Like their colleagues in other types of discourse, reviewers explored the balance between unity and variety, argued about the restrictions that rules should – or should not – impose upon a composer's genius and debated how much compositional license might be allowed in the interests of expressivity. In the 1760s, the preference lay with the rational, but the pendulum swung to the other side in the following two decades, only to return closer to equilibrium in the late 1780s and 1790s. Through the changing patterns of this dialectic, the review collective laid out the conceptual path that led to the nineteenth century.

5

The importance of being correct

Neue Zeitungen von gelehrten Sachen (1766): Christian Ernst Rosenbaum, *Sechs Sonaten*.

Given the pitiful appearance this composer makes, we didn't know whether to pity or look down on him. We would gladly do the former, if we thought there were any chance that he might improve. But it appears that all hope is in vain, because the chastisement we gave him about his song melodies did so little good that he is now daring to come forth with a half dozen sonatas that are even more miserable than his songs. How empty of ideas! What incorrect phrasing! Now a beat too many, now one too few! And the mistakes in *Harmonie*! Parallel fifths and octaves everywhere! And what about good modulation, what about the relationship of related keys to the main key? Even the ear of a Hottentot would be able to sense how unnatural most of this is. You stagger about from one key to the next, only to discover in astonishment that the piece, when the page is full, cadences again in the tonic. How masterful! . . . The only good thing that we can find to say about these sonatas is that they are short and didn't waste more than six sheets of paper.[1]

Wöchentliche Nachrichten (1769): Friedrich Schwindl, *Six Simphonies*.

[In the first symphony], the first movement was pleasant and passionate; the varied shadings and the modulations were effective. But then came a stiff, sluggish Andante, which did have some movement in the middle voices, but was so monotonous from beginning to end that it went nowhere. We did not know what to make of it until we finally realized it was a varied chorale. What? A chorale? In a symphony? Yes indeed, a chorale, followed by a right jolly minuet . . . In short, Herr Schwindl has sought out the waggish and adventurous too much to please reasonable ears with his symphonies.[2]

Mainstream German culture in the middle of the eighteenth century still bore the heavy imprint of rationalism, the legacy of the early eighteenth-century philosopher Christian Wolff. Though in their original form, Wolff's writings had circulated only within the German academic community, they gained a wider audience when none other than Gottsched published a two-volume popular summary in 1734. Gottsched had proclaimed his allegiance to rational thought with his *Versuch einer kritischen Dichtkunst* (1730), in which he attempted to impose a certain amount of qualitative control on German literature, thereby purging it of irrational, non-realistic elements. He believed that poetry and art emerged not from emotional inspiration or creative genius, but as a definable part of the rational process through the imitation of nature. Though he acknowledged that a poet (or painter or musician) "must possess a powerful imagination, much discernment, and a great wit," those qualities, granted as a gift from nature, must be shaped and tempered by reason and the rules of the art.[3] It was on those rules that he focused his attention. In the genre of tragedy, for example, he required that expression be kept in check by the exclusive use of restrained aristocratic speech patterns and imposed a number of other rigid criteria derived from classical models, including his famous dictum that dramas must observe the Aristotelian unities of time, place, and action.[4] For Gottsched, following the rules appropriate to a particular genre of literature or art counted as a primary qualification of aesthetic excellence.[5] Even though his influence began to wane in the 1750s, as a result of challenges by the subsequent generation of literary thinkers (see below, page 90), the forces of rationalism gained support from another quarter.

Beginning in the third quarter of the century, a group of Enlightenment thinkers in Berlin and Göttingen appropriated Wolff's concepts and recast them in a less pedantic, more accessible form. These so-called "popular philosophers" did not simply summarize Wolff, as Gottsched had done, but used his ideas to further their own goal of education for the general public. In articles, literary reviews and popular textbooks, they doggedly asserted the primacy of reason and sought to widen its influence on German thought and society. Though the movement did not produce much in the way of original thought, it achieved its didactic goal. It has relevance to the discussion here because it included men like Friedrich Nicolai, editor of the *Allgemeine deutsche Bibliothek*.[6] Thus, some of the earliest reviews of the collective appeared in a journal firmly associated with the rational forces of the Enlightenment. In addition, over a quarter of the instrumental reviews from the 1760s were written by two men who moved in the Enlightenment circles of

Table 5.1: *Periodicals with reviews during the 1760s*

Music

12   *Kritische Briefe*, 1760–1763
      Author: Marpurg
35   *Wöchentliche Nachrichten*, 1767–(1770)
      Author: Hiller? and others?

General scholarly

4   *Freymüthige Nachrichten*, 1760–1763
      3 taken from the *Neue Zeitungen von gelehrten Sachen*
      1 taken from the *Göttingische Anzeigen*
3   *Bibliothek der schönen Wissenschaften*, 1760–1767
9   *Frankfurtische gelehrten Zeitungen*, 1760–(1771)
      9 taken from the *Neue Zeitungen von gelehrten Sachen*
20   *Neue Zeitungen von gelehrten Sachen*, 1760–(1784)
1   *Göttingische Anzeigen*, 1760–(1798*)
1   *Jenaische Zeitungen*, 1765–(1787)
24   *Allgemeine deutsche Bibliothek*, 1765–(1794)
      Author: Agricola
21   *Unterhaltungen*, 1766–1770

Political newspapers

8   *Hamburgischer Correspondent*, 1760–(1798*)
7   *Berlinische Nachrichten*, 1761–(1798*)
TOTAL REVIEWS: 145
                      − 13 reprinted
ACTUAL TOTAL: 132

Note: Dates given indicate the years surveyed for this study. An asterisk indicates the journal continued beyond 1798.

Berlin: Marpurg and Agricola (see table 5.1). Born within two years of each other (in 1718 and 1720, respectively), they both remained loyal to the rationalist precepts that had shaped their youth and early adulthood. In 1750, for example, Marpurg published a translation of a treatise by Lecerf de la Viéville, giving his approval to its aesthetic views. Lecerf had maintained that music was to be judged both by proper adherence to rules and by an "inner aesthetic facility based on the senses and feelings," but, like Gottsched, insisted that this aesthetic facility was nonetheless subordinate to the rules of reason.[7] Marpurg consistently carried such precepts with him when he sat down to write his instrumental reviews, declaring once that "nothing can be beautiful unless it is done according to the rules. You cannot compose beautifully with parallel fifths and octaves any more than you can paint beautifully with blotches."[8] Though Agricola has a less documented rationalist pedigree, his reviews leave little doubt that he had absorbed the atmosphere in Berlin, where he had lived since 1741. His contributions to the collective ended with his death in 1774, and Marpurg's apparently stopped after his *Kritische Briefe* ceased publication in 1763 (though he lived for another thirty years), but their prominence during the collective's first decade helped to shape its strongly rationalist profile.

During the 1760s, that profile manifested itself in the review collective's penchant for pedantic, rules-oriented evaluations. Around 40 percent of the decade's 132 reviews discussed issues of compositional correctness, sometimes briefly (especially when no infractions were discovered), but more often in great and excruciating detail. It was not unusual for a reviewer to cover all other aesthetic issues in a sentence or two, then launch into a multi-page exposé of rule violations. Though such reviews may seem to offer little in the way of aesthetic insight, they did establish the crucial precedent of technically based music criticism, thus providing a secure foundation for the more extensive writings of early nineteenth-century critics.

Harmonie offered a particularly tempting target, and reviewers often leapt to the task with something akin to glee, attuned to the tiniest bleep from their error-detection machines and devoting page after page to mind-numbing lists of technical transgressions. The possibilities for compositional mishaps were legion, for parallel fifths and octaves, incorrect doublings, improperly used six-four chords, insufficiently prepared (or resolved) dissonances lay in wait to trap the unwary composer and unleash the reviewer's critical wrath. Marpurg's merciless dissection of Johann Anton Kobrich's *Wohlgeübter Organist* (The Well-practiced Organist) can serve as an example:

The title is wrong. It should read *The Unpracticed Organist Who Needs Lessons* . . . [It is] a hodge-podge of the most hackneyed, worn-out notions, which for variety are transposed *ad nauseam*, in which every now and then the pedal – in a totally arbitrary fashion, two or three times in each piece – takes part with a note that just lies there for three or four measures and then disappears in the middle of a dissonance. An endless racket with broken phrases, unprepared dissonances, unresolved dissonances, fifths and octaves, empty phrases, false basses – If anyone ever needs 24 musical Quodlibits for the barrel organ at a shadow play, Herr Kobrich's 24 Preludes will come in handy.[9]

Melody's subjection to the musical Geiger counters came through the aspect of its periodic structure, or *Rhythmus*, an issue addressed at mid century by theorists like Marpurg and Joseph Riepel, and in the 1770s by Kirnberger. Marpurg had a particular mania for symmetry and a marked preference for four-measure phrases; any three-measure interlopers had to be followed by another three-measures, then balanced by a four-measure answer.[10] Thus, when the *Unterhaltungen* expressed its dissatisfaction with a single three-measure phrase stuck in the middle of its exclusively four-measure neighbors, it was following the party line.[11] Critical displeasure also erupted when a composer displaced the beginning of a phrase to the middle of a measure or otherwise disturbed the primacy of the first beat, a technique held over from the late German Baroque. Agricola objected strenuously to "the clumsy *Rhythmus*" of some Müthel concertos, where "the phrase sometimes starts in the middle, sometimes at the beginning of the measure," further remarking that although nobody except Riepel had written on the subject, "a fine musical sentiment should teach the necessity of correct *Rhythmus*."[12]

Other rules of concern to the collective addressed the requirements for particular genres. One recurring topic – what constituted a proper duet, trio, or quartet – intersected with the anti-Italian bent of the period (and also lingered into the early 1770s). Reviewers complained constantly about chamber pieces in which the parts merely proceeded in thirds or sixths, and thus lacked the requisite amount of counterpoint. Not only did that rankle because of the association with the Italian style, it was not the "correct" way of composing chamber music genres. As the *Hamburgische neue Zeitung* observed in reviewing some sonatas by George Rush, even though they had nice melodies and a little bit of dialogue between the violin and keyboard, they were not "actual, worked-out trios" (and two even had Alberti bass figuration).[13]

The other genre question that occupied the collective during the 1760s concerned the type of movements that belonged in serious genres like the sonata or the symphony. Reviewers frequently objected to the presence of dance movements like minuets, because they introduced an inappropriate tone of frivolity (like beauty spots on a man, see p. 54). Agricola, for example, asked in exasperation if music lovers had to have minuets because they could no longer sit through three serious movements in a row.[14] Though the minuet question has loomed largest in modern scholarship, *any* subversion of genre expectations was likely to raise critical questions. In the review of Schwindl's symphonies cited at the beginning of this chapter, the *Wöchentliche Nachrichten* made clear its disapproval of the inclusion of a chorale-like movement in a symphony, a transgression compounded by its juxtaposition with a "right jolly minuet."

In this genre preoccupation, reviewers were again following the lead of Gottsched, and like him, they tended to support their opinions with appeals to the proper authority. Agricola waded into the chamber music question when he advised Johann Baptist Georg Neruda to mend his all-too-homophonic ways by reading the description of a good trio in Quantz's *Anweisung die Flöte traversière zu spielen*.[15] He also faulted Johann Friedrich Ernst Benda for indulging in an inappropriate chromatic melody in a minuet, citing Mattheson's description of the dance as expressing idle merriment, in which "chromatic whimpers" did not belong.[16] Both the *Wöchentliche Nachrichten* and the *Unterhaltungen* criticized a *Fantasie* by Löhlein because it lacked the "surprising turns of *Harmonie*" and enharmonic modulations characteristic of the genre, and the latter buttressed its comments by citing the appropriate passage in C. P. E. Bach's *Versuch über die wahre Art das Clavier zu spielen*.[17] Calling on theory treatises for support occurred more frequently during the 1760s than in later decades and proved particularly useful in specifying genre requirements.

A significant number of reviewers also devoted considerable time to linguistic *faux pas* found on title pages, particularly those in French and Italian. Misspelled words, grammatical errors, incongruous combinations of languages, and improper usage of terms all drew critical fire. In the *Allgemeine deutsche Bibliothek*, Agricola complained that he thought Ferdinand Fischer's *Six Symphonies a II Violons Haut-bois, ou flutes traversieres Cors de Chasse, Fagots, Violettes et Basses*, required a new type of instrument – the Fagot (a stick of kindling). Finally a fortuitous notation on the score cleared up the mystery: the Fagots were nothing but bassoons (*Fagotte* in German), normally, as he observed, called *des Bassons* in French.[18] While such observations have no direct bearing on issues of musical aesthetics, they did contribute to the pervasive atmosphere of error correction.

Of course, one might well have expected to find a rules-oriented approach in the rationalistic, didactic *Allgemeine deutsche Bibliothek* or in the publication of a theorist like Marpurg, but those journals differed from the others only in degree, not in substance. The *Wöchentliche Nachrichten*, often described as supporting taste over rules (as the review of Löhlein cited below might imply), frequently ran extensive reviews filled with lists of errors.[19] Though often couched in softer phrases such as "we do not like" or "we wish that the composer had," the objections and corrective suggestions that inevitably ensued nonetheless read like a list of "thou shalt nots." Sometimes the comments approach the venom of Marpurg at his most vituperative moments, as in the review of the hapless Manfredini (also see above, chapter 3). After ranting about all the errors of *Harmonie*, the reviewer moves to the topic of modulation and indignantly cites a passage that shifts surprisingly and awkwardly from F major to A minor, and makes an even less graceful transition back to the tonic (example 5.1), saying "Pfui! We cannot bear to write another word. Heaven preserve us from all Manfredini's sonatas and

Example 5.1 Vincenzo Manfredini, Trio of a Minuet from *Sei Sonate da Clavicembalo*, mm. 1–15 (Note the incorrect rhythm in the penultimate measure.)

minuets."[20] Likewise, although the reviews in the *Unterhaltungen* tended to be somewhat brief and less detailed, they paid no less attention to the observance of the rules. When confronted with some atrocious teaching pieces, its reviewer observed that the minuet variations simply teemed with errors, adding that wading through such musical trash took more patience than a human being could muster, and urging the composer *not* to devote any more time to composing.[21] Even when disinclined to join the count-the-errors game, other publications did not ignore the issue of compositional rules entirely. The *Neue Zeitungen von gelehrten Sachen* offered the stinging indictment of Rosenbaum found at the beginning of the chapter. Somewhat less flamboyantly, the *Hamburgischer Correspondent*'s review of compositions by Johann Friedrich Wilhelm Wenkel asked who would expect to find such order and correctness in galant pieces?[22]

The essential importance of following the rules was not to be questioned, even on those rare occasions when it suited a reviewer's purpose to make light of a composer's missteps. Thus while Agricola maintained, in reviewing a collection of keyboard works, that the errors in *Harmonie* "were of no greater significance than grammatical slips by a good author," he still felt compelled to point out the parallel fifths and concluded wryly that someone who sought to distinguish himself by hunting for them could certainly make a "malcontented evening" of it.[23] Once the *Wöchentliche Nachrichten* did admit to turning a blind eye to the possibility of compositional error. After heaping abundant praise on a set of Löhlein's keyboard sonatas, the reviewer continued, "If you were to ask us whether we discovered any forbidden fifths and octaves, we would have to admit that because so many good things can be said about such a man, we simply didn't bother to look."[24] Still, Löhlein did not escape entirely unscathed, for the reviewer found his treatment of the "Fantasie" at the beginning of the fourth sonata to be incorrect (see above, page 84). Only one review, in the *Berlinische Nachrichten*, took a jaundiced view of the whole process, noting that musicians made particularly merciless critics, unwilling to tolerate even the smallest error and attacking passionately when they discovered the slightest trace of an oversight.[25] Continuing in the same iconoclastic vein, the reviewer proceeded to offer the mildly laudatory remarks about the Italian style discussed above (see above, chapter 3), another deviation from the collective mainstream that reinforced the quirkiness of his opinion.

The focus on quantifiable rules derived in part from the simple fact that the collective was still in the process of establishing what constituted a music review. The anti-Italian rhetoric may have helped establish a general critical direction, but reviewers still needed some theoretical foundation for their work. As the mimetic paradigm could offer little of practical assistance for instrumental music, the only viable model came from theory treatises, which in the 1760s were dominated by page after page of compositional commandments. Marpurg's *Handbuch bey dem Generalbasse und der Composition*, published between 1755 and 1760, is a case in point. In the introduction, Marpurg proclaimed his intention of writing a compositional grammar book to present to the "reasonable [*vernünftige*] musical world." He did just that, devoting the first two sections (205 pages) to lists of rules governing the treatment of intervals and chords, part three to the specific treatment of two-voiced to nine-voiced composition, part four to examples and exercises. Readers encountered a methodical, painfully detailed approach to composition; for example, the section introducing polyphonic composition opened with the statement that the first compositional step involved (1) deciding whether the piece would be vocal or instrumental, (2) deciding whether it would be in the free or the strict style, (3) deciding on the number of voices it should contain.[26] Though any experienced teacher knows the necessity of stating the obvious, the mechanical approach Marpurg espoused certainly did not allow much room for spontaneity or creativity: locutions like "one must" and "not allowed" dot every single page. Moreover, he focused mainly on the easily quantifiable aspects of composition (like dissonance treatment) while glossing over issues like melodic structure, phrasing, or modulation – which he covered with the sentence: "Make reasonable and orderly modulations."[27] He did return to that topic in the treatise's final section on fugues, where he specified which modulations were *permitted*. With such a model, it is not surprising that the review collective of the 1760s had a penchant for compositional correctness.

Theory treatises also shaped reviewers' perception of the other rationally oriented aesthetic category: order/unity. Most of the references clearly reflect the theoretical practices of the time, still firmly grounded in the chord-by-chord thoroughbass method. In such a system, musical structure depended more on the logical progression of small musical ideas than it did on abstract unity or concrete form. Even Riepel's *Anfangsgründe zur musikalischen Setzkunst* (1752–68), which in its disdain for the prevailing mathematical and intervallic approach to composition broke significantly with the past, continued the essentially linear concept of writing music. Riepel advocated a method based upon the orderly composition of related melodic units and phrases, but his theories still pertain to the minutiae of the compositional *process* rather than to any resulting form or plan.[28] The collective adopted this process-oriented viewpoint when insisting that a successful composition should "hang together" (*zusammenhängen*), or could fail by being "chopped up" (*zerstückelt*).[29] Order was achieved by the proper relationship of one melodic segment to the next (thus intersecting with correct *Rhythmus*). Marpurg criticized Johann Georg Nicolai for not balancing the irregular and repetitive opening phrase in one of his partitas with a similar one, so that at least there would have been "order in the disorder," concluding wryly that even if the ear suffered at the repetition, the intellect would be satisfied with the sense of proportion.[30]

The disorderly phrases Agricola had criticized in the concertos of Johann Gottfried Müthel (see above, page 83) were not the only problems bedeviling the hapless composer: his inattention to proper motivic relationships provoked Agricola into a tirade on orderly composition, one of the handful of reviews that ventured into the area of formal construction. Adopting the familiar "thou shalt not" tone, he asserted that without a good reason (which he does not specify), internal ritornellos *may not* (my italics) contain ideas not found in the opening ritornello, giving the curious reason that otherwise

a listener might suppose the composer had thought of better ideas after composing the beginning, but was too lazy to go back and rewrite the opening
ritornello to include them. He likened the opening ritornello to the main
motive (*Hauptsatz*), which the composer could "take apart, use in different
ways, and decorate with the playing of the soloist." New ideas in the internal
ritornellos would only confuse and disrupt the attention of the listener (*seine
Aufmerksamkeit in Unordnung bringen* – literally "bring his attention into
disorder").[31] The trick was to incorporate enough new ideas to avoid monotony without preventing the movement from "hanging together," that is,
achieving unity in variety. In his review of Nicolai's suites cited above,
Marpurg had instructed the errant composer on the proper method of doing
so:

I call this the main motive; it may appear either at the beginning or in the first one or
two lines and must be worked out with repetition, transposition, imitation, and divi
sion. The resulting passages help to maintain the piece's unity. When the main motive,
or the ideas flowing from it, alternate with new subsidiary ideas according to an established, reasonable plan, and when the new ideas are likewise worked out in proper proportions, variety results from this connection of the main with the subsidiary
motives.[32]

By this process of carefully connecting any new material, the composer could
avoid chopped-up mish-mashes of unrelated melodies, and thus the collective's disdain.

This last review, incidentally, was the only one during the decade that used
the word "unity," a concept that implies a greater sense of overall structure
than found in contemporaneous music theory and one that had been less
essential in a compositional world governed by *Fortspinnung*. In fact, the
overall unification, of a piece or movement, either through technical means or
mimesis, received very little attention from early reviewers. The
Hamburgischer Correspondent did once allude to the unifying potential of
the Affects, finding Löhlein's partitas superior to many others because each
"was ruled by a single, skillfully realized main Affect."[33] In reviewing pieces
by Joseph Anton Steffan, Marpurg hinted at the same preference in his typically acerbic fashion:

Nowadays no schoolboy can begin to compose without decking out his exercises with
twenty or thirty perverse appoggiaturas, and no connoisseur owes him a compliment
here. You're supposed to put your hand to your breast and let out a long, empty sigh
to show how touched you are. It's enough to warm the cockles of your heart. More
often than not, from disgust. This much is certain: When chromatic appoggiaturas are
used in pieces where they do not fit the basic sentiment, and when they suddenly

disrupt the ruling Affect of happiness, you have just as much reason to protest as you would if a false friend roughly pinched your cheeks in the middle of the most pleasant caress.[34]

These two statements, along with Agricola's comment that Benda's variations should retain the main Affect as much as possible (see above, chapter 4), are the only indications that the early collective thought at all about the unifying properties of mimesis. Clearly it did not loom large in their aesthetic universe.

These allusions to the mimetic paradigm do bring us, however, to the aesthetic category I have designated as "expressivity." Though I have placed expressivity on the irrational side of the aesthetic equation, its most typical manifestation in the collective's early reviews betrays a certain association with the realm of reason. By the 1760s, thanks to the efforts of numerous philosophers and aestheticians, Descartes' six basic passions had mushroomed into long lists of human emotional states parading in rows of abstract nouns – the Magnificent, the Tragic, the Joyful, the Happy, the Sorrowful, etc. This technique effectively contained irrational feelings in tightly controlled boxes, and the fact that different commentators generally produced different sets of boxes proved only the difficulty, not the futility, of the exercise. When the reviewers took part in that exercise (which they did only rarely), they might offer comments like the *Hamburgischer Correspondent*, which thought that Hertel's symphonies "tastefully distributed the Magnificent, Passionate, Brilliant, Lively, Pleasant, and Playful," and that Löhlein showed a particular talent for "the Soft and Tender."[35] Other reviews that utilized the parade-of-nouns technique have less connection with the Affects proper than with the preference of the German language for such constructions. Agricola, for example, had railed about "the Impotent, the Unmelodic, the Vulgar, the Waggish, and the Chopped-up" in Fischer's symphonies (see chapter 3). The *Wöchentliche Nachrichten* also saw the "touching and solid" melodies of a Graun or a Hasse imperiled by "the Glittering and the Trifling" of musical fashion, sighing that only a few composers "had enough heart to pay attention to a good natural melody and touching expression instead of pretentious wit and purely vulgar notions."[36]

One might also wish to read the concept of the Affects into the adjectives reviewers commonly used in describing movement types: first movements were supposed to be passionate (*feurig*), grand (*prächtig*), or majestic; second movements needed to be both slow and pleasant (*angenehm*); and finales could exhibit a touch of the playful, though not all reviewers could stomach too much frivolity. The *Wöchentliche Nachrichten*, for example, described the first movements of some Hertel symphonies as "magnificent and passionate," the middle as "pleasing and expressive," and characterized the final movements as "a sample of the composer's playful muse." In his review of the same pieces, Agricola agreed that the first movements were "particularly passionate," and the middle ones mostly "very pleasant," but he found the finales "much too vulgar and insolent."[37] Using a similar vocabulary, the *Unterhaltungen* described the opening movements of some J. C. Bach symphonies as "passionate and Italianate good" (!), the middle ones as "melodious and pleasant," though he thought the finales approached "the vulgar style."[38] But the indignation reviewers expressed when a movement did *not* follow the expected affective pattern links these allusions not to expressivity and the outpourings of the heart, but to genre expectations. Middle movements that were *not* expressive or melodious simply violated the rules, for any *proper* sonata or symphony had to have one. As Gottsched had demonstrated, the Affects married well with rationalist thought patterns.

But mainstream aesthetic and literary discourse had begun to turn away from a reliance on the Affects to debate the role of more personalized expression in the creation of art, though without yet abandoning the restraints of reason. One of the early signs of rebellion came from the poet Friedrich Gottlieb Klopstock, particularly in his epic poem *Der Messias*, published in twenty cantos between 1748 and 1780. In it, Klopstock demonstrated his concern with the expressive force, rather than the mimetic capability, of poetic language, though without ignoring the restraint characteristic of the Enlightenment.[39] Other mid-century literary and philosophical figures addressed the relationship between expressivity and reason in aesthetics in a more specific manner. Mendelssohn had argued in his *Briefe über die Empfindungen* (see chapter 4) that the sentiments involved in the aesthetic experience actually constituted a form of knowledge, thus, like Gottsched, bringing the irrationality of the feelings within the control of reason.[40] However, Mendelssohn insisted that reason could not explain the source of aesthetic pleasure and attacked those that would derive sets of rules from antiquated sources:

Those who read classical literature only so they can dissect it, and who collect rhetorical figures like entomologists do the dried skeletons of worms, are deplorable. They seek and find the rules of eloquence; they make the laws for the fine arts; but they no longer feel the beauty that they praise. Their feeling is transformed into a logical conclusion.[41]

Rules, he insisted, prepared the artist to present his work in the most advantageous light, and that they should never disturb him "in the heat" of creation. He should guard against thinking about them too much in that moment, because they should never reign in the imagination, merely guide it from afar. Mendelssohn followed these remarks with a specific example drawn from the field of music:

Musicians might save themselves some grief if they would keep these remarks in mind. Everyone knows that, when it concerns the pleasantness of their melodies, they set greater store by the judgment of a good ear than that of a master in the art of music. The latter always want to show off their musical experience. They do not notice anything except the melody's regularity; they listen for the proper connection of the most contrary dissonances, while soft, touching beauty slips past their ears unnoticed.[42]

In arguing for some expressive breathing room, Mendelssohn sought to loosen the regulatory stranglehold on artistic creation, but the balance between expressivity and the rules needed further exploration. Lessing, one of his close friends in Berlin, took on that difficult issue. A confirmed opponent of Gottsched's classically derived rules, Lessing insisted on the expressive purpose of art and maintained that its success should be measured not by adherence to genre rules but by its impact on the observer or spectator, a view that managed to combine Du Bos's theory of affective art with the English rhetorical school's concern with convincing the audience. Even while rejecting the tyranny of rules and asserting the importance of feeling, however, he refused to arbitrarily abandon the dictates of reason and convention.[43] In his famous essay on the Greek statue of Laocoon (1766), he argued that the expression of Laocoon's pain must be veiled because the artist should not "force expression beyond the bounds of art" but "submit it to the first law of art, the law of Beauty." Furthermore, depicting an emotion at its "topmost note" would only decrease the artwork's effectiveness because "beyond it there is nothing further, and to show us the uttermost is to tie the wings of fancy and oblige her, as she cannot rise above the sensuous impression, to busy herself with weaker pictures below it, the visible fullness of expression acting as a frontier which she dare not transgress."[44]

In both Lessing's and Mendelssohn's writings, the role of the sentiments and the ability of a work of art or music to touch the heart assumed primary importance, a view also expressed in the entry on the sentiments in Sulzer's *Allgemeine Theorie der schönen Künste*. Sulzer firmly believed that the purpose of all art was primarily to "awaken the sentiments in a psychological sense," but like Lessing he cautioned that it should not go too far in that direction. The artist must never lose sight of "the general rules of wisdom," which would prevent him from "overstepping the limits of expressivity" and becoming "soft, weak and effeminate." As an example of proper restraint, he cited the tragedies of Seneca, whose characters always retained a certain grandeur even in their strongest passions, an observation that came directly from Gottsched's *Versuch einer kritischen Dichtkunst.*[45]

Reviewers of the 1760s actually showed relatively little interest in this type of expressivity in music. As a verb, *"empfinden"* most frequently appeared in its original meaning of "to sense" or "to experience" or "to notice" – as in the comment about "even the ears of a Hottentot should be able to sense" in the review of Rosenbaum cited above.[46] Writing for the *Allgemeine deutsche Bibliothek*, Agricola twice used the nominal form, not in connection with unleashed emotion, but with restrained judgment, speaking once of "reasonable work that is guided by good taste and fine sentiment," and another time observing that "a fine musical sentiment should teach how beautiful and necessary correct periodicity is" (see above, page 83).[47] Both these instances also reflect Sulzer's definition of sentiment as the facility to distinguish what pleases and displeases.[48] Though Agricola also used *Empfindung* in referring to perceptiveness on the part of listeners and performers, by his wording he again associated it with the faculty of reason. In criticizing chamber music addicted to parallel thirds and sixths, he objected that "insightful listeners capable of sentiment will truly be in danger of yawning at such music."[49] His comments that a particular piece required a "Quanz-like delicate power of sentiment (*Empfindungskraft*) and exactness not granted to all people" referred not to the music's expressive requirements but to a passage requiring the performer to mix thirty-second notes and sixteenth-note triplets at a very fast tempo.[50] For Agricola, at least, the sentiments had more of an association with the rational than with emotional expressivity, even when applied to delicacy in performance.

Only a few reviews imply the type of "sensitivity" associated with the C. P. E. Bach school. One in the *Wöchentliche Nachrichten* observed that a "particular kind of melody founded on tender feeling, which gains even more delicacy from the ornamentation Herr Müthel provides, will perhaps prove difficult to perform for many players not accustomed to express feeling while playing delicately."[51] Several others applied the word "touching," to slow movements, and the *Berlinische Nachrichten* used it to describe the melody and *Harmonie* of a Bach sonatina.[52] The *Neue Zeitungen von gelehrten Sachen* found that the works of Müller had a "certain tender expression."[53] With regard to any descriptive capability for instrumental music, only the *Unterhaltungen* offered comments along those lines, describing one of J. C. Bach's Andantes as depicting the "character of the unhappy one" and applauding the Andante of a sonata by Friedrich Gottlob Fleischer as "new and full of soft contentment."[54] Though these observations indicate critical approval, the *Unterhaltungen*'s reviewer conveyed a more sardonic attitude toward musical picture painting by deadpanning: "The passage work piled up in [Fischer's] fourth divertimento is supposed to represent the Bohemian mountains, right?"[55]

Far more significant than these remarks, in view of the eventual development of review collective thought, were the occasional comments suggesting that good composition required a certain fire or passion (*Feuer*) on the part of the composer. Mendelssohn had alluded to this characteristic when he observed that rules should never disturb the artist "in the heat" of creation (above, page 90). Although Marpurg reversed the formulation by exclaiming "even if a composer only wanted to work when he felt inflamed by his subject, he should still be able to control his passion and never forget the rules of art," at least he acknowledged the possibility of an irrational impulse in the compositional process.[56] Agricola confirmed its importance and worthiness as an aesthetic criterion by associating it with the work of C. P. E. Bach: "All the pieces are written with the richly inventive spirit and the passion that we are long accustomed to find in all the composer's works."[57] Still, detailing all these references (and possible references) to the concept of expressivity in music actually somewhat exaggerates its relative significance in the review collective's discourse. Particularly because of the brevity of the comments, which generally involved a single word or phrase, expressivity was completely dwarfed by the paragraphs filled with the dissections of correct compositional procedure. By itself, it did little to challenge the rule of reason, but it did have reinforcements from another quarter, as that last comment about Bach's "richly inventive spirit" implies.

When Marpurg insisted indignantly in one of his reviews that composition meant "putting together, not inventing," he took a position in an ongoing debate about the nature of artistic creation.[58] Gottsched's system, which demanded the strict imitation of nature or of classical models in literature and the arts, had effectively excluded any role for the imagination or individual genius. The poet (or composer) functioned merely as a conduit for ideas already present in nature, rather than as their progenitor. In the early 1740s, the Swiss literary critics Johann Jakob Bodmer and Johann Jakob Breitinger had launched an attack on Gottsched (faithfully reported, incidentally, in the "gelehrte Sachen" column of the *Hamburgischer Correspondent*).[59] While not denying that the artist should imitate nature – thus remaining within Enlightenment, mimetic bounds – they refined the concept of nature to include both the visible and the invisible world. Imitation of the visible world, along the lines of Gottsched, retained artistic viability, but to achieve true aesthetic significance, the artist had to explore the deeper realm of the invisible by exploiting the *Phantasie*, their word for the faculty of imagination.[60]

Likewise, Christian Fürchtegott Gellert, poet and writer of popular sentimental comedies, continued to believe in the aesthetic force of mimesis while
criticizing those "blinded and slavish" followers of the rules.[61] Though these
ideas eventually helped to demolish the facade of rationally directed aesthetic
theory, their authors intended them as corrective measures from within, not
as explosives hurled from without. Thus the debate focused not on the
abandonment of the rules but on what those rules should be. Even while
objecting to Gottsched's principles, both Mendelssohn and Lessing, for
example, still felt compelled to propose a set of rules dictating what art
"ought" to be.[62]

Sulzer's treatment of the term "genius" in the *Allgemeine Theorie der
schönen Künste* encapsulated the position of the creative imagination within
the German Enlightenment of the 1760s. Though published during the 1770s,
the encyclopedia – like many such monolithic efforts – reflected the aesthetic
philosophy of the mid-century Berlin Enlightenment circles, in which Sulzer
participated.[63] For Sulzer, genius had little to do with the impulsive, unrestrained individual creativity that the nineteenth century associated with the
term. Instead, genius was manifest in the ability to elevate ideas
(*Vorstellungen*) to a high degree of clarity and liveliness: "Bright daylight
reigns in the soul of a man of genius, a complete light that presents every
object [to him] as if it were a well illuminated painting close at hand. He can
comprehend it in its entirety, but still be able to notice each individual detail."
Though this "man of genius" is driven by an inner passion or fire that excites
his ability to discover the "pictures of the fantasy and the sentiments," he does
not so much invent those pictures as he simply observes them.[64] The artist's
relative passivity in the process made Sulzer's *Genie* quite compatible with a
mimetic theory of art, to which he essentially subscribed. Again showing his
essentially Enlightenment mentality, he defined invention (*Erfindung*) as
"always an undertaking of the intellect, one that discovers the exact relationship between the means and the end," although he did concede that because
of the sensual nature of the fine arts, reason must be joined by "experience, a
rich and lively *Phantasie*, and a fine instinct [*Gefühl*]." Like many of his contemporaries, he recognized that an artist who did not lack for genius and a
lively *Phantasie* might not need instruction in the art of invention, but he did
believe it could be taught, at least to a certain degree, and recommended
Mattheson's *Der Vollkommene Capellmeister* as a useful work in the field of
music.[65]

The same cautious and controlled view of creative genius reigned in the
review collective during the 1760s. Though mentioned in around 40 percent
of all reviews – about the same frequency as compositional correctness – in

terms of emphasis it did not balance out the obsession with rules anymore than expressivity did, for reviewers rarely accorded it more than a sentence. Most commonly, reviewers simply noticed the presence (or absence) of "invention" in a composition, sometimes complimenting a composer's "good invention." Two-thirds of the references to creative genius in the *Wöchentliche Nachrichten*, for example, involved no more than this. When a stronger appellation was required, the reviewer could describe a work as "richly inventive," an encomium found in the *Wöchentliche Nachrichten* and the *Allgemeine deutsche Bibliothek*, applied exclusively to C. P. E. Bach.

Unfortunately, no one specified just what made a composition inventive, although according to one review in the *Wöchentliche Nachrichten*, it did not necessarily involve startling novelty: "To be sure we did not find much in [Zingoni's *Huit Simphonies*] that was novel or unexpected, but they are pleasant and passionate. The Andantes in particular are very melodious and have good invention."[66] The reviewer gave no examples, but a later review in the same magazine included a minuet from a set of six sonatas by Paolo Fischer, which the reviewer had praised for having "much good invention everywhere."[67] (example 5.2) These are the same sonatas that the *Unterhaltungen* had panned, calling the minuets "mediocre" (see above, page 93) and not mentioning even a little bit of invention anywhere. Clearly, the *Wöchentliche Nachrichten* had a low invention threshold, for the only interesting aspect of the minuet (in 1760s terms) would seem to be the absence of an Alberti bass. Thus, though the review collective clearly endorsed at least one concept associated with the creative imagination, it did so rather cautiously, and in a manner consistent with the Enlightenment aesthetic expressed by Sulzer.

Other terms associated with the creative imagination appeared more rarely and would count as insignificant had they not later blossomed into important aesthetic criteria. The word "*Genie*," for example, never surfaced in a good half of the decade's journals, and when it did, reviewers seemed to equate it with "talent." The *Wöchentliche Nachrichten* referred (twice) to German genius, and the *Allgemeine deutsche Bibliothek* recognized Schwanberger's musical genius as "particularly good."[68] In discussing the partitas of Johann Friedrich Hobein, d. J., the *Hamburgischer Correspondent* thought they would be well received because they demonstrated "much taste and genius."[69] A closer connection to the creative urge emerged from a comment in the *Berlinische Nachrichten*, which thought that some of the comic pieces in the *Musicalisches Mancherley* demonstrated "the most fertile power of invention and the most fortunate *Genie* that a musician could possibly have."[70]

Fertile powers of invention apparently did not manifest themselves during the 1760s by means of variety, for the word rarely appeared in review columns.

Example 5.2 Paolo Fischer, Minuet from *Sei Sonate, per il Cembalo*

However, a number of comments deal with the monotonous *lack* of it, without mentioning the term itself. Reviewers complained frequently about the absence of modulation or the excessive length of sections in a single key, which made a piece "dull and boring."[71] Though most often leveled at Italians, this criticism occasionally applied to German composers as well. The *Allgemeine deutsche Bibliothek* objected to Wenkel's "ancient style of fugue that stays in one key," asking him (politely – after all, he was German) in the future to write fugues that demonstrated his ability to modulate skillfully to other keys, noting that "change is pleasant wherever it is allowed" (!) and the lack of it disagreeable.[72] Other elements associated with the Italian style received similar treatment. The *Unterhaltungen* had chastised Paolo Fischer for the yawn-inducing monotonous accompaniment in one of his sonatas, and the *Neue Zeitungen von gelehrten Sachen* took Kirnberger to task because "an Andante stretched over more than eleven lines of such a monotonous, dragging figure will always grow a little boring."[73] The collective's polemical stance on the Italian style perhaps explains this willingness to deplore harmonic and textural monotony without actually advocating variety, for endorsing the latter would have required the approval of thematic variety, more typical of Italianate than German composition during this period.

Reviewers showed similar mixed feelings about the issues of originality and novelty. Only twice did anyone use the adjective "original," neither time with the tone of a ringing endorsement. The *Unterhaltungen* mildly observed that a Löhlein sonata, despite some agreeable imitative counterpoint, "perhaps was not always original enough," and the *Wöchentliche Nachrichten* found nothing to criticize in Johann Friedrich Gottlieb Beckmann's overall style, which "though not completely original" was nonetheless "the style of the best masters and therefore beautiful."[74] Originality might well be a good thing, but it was not an aesthetic requirement. Neither was novelty, as the review of Zingoni cited above (page 95) implied. However, even those not particularly enthusiastic about creativity in composition could have their patience tested by an obviously outdated style. Marpurg, for example, complained that Joseph Ferdinand Timer's violin pieces had "much that was old, little that was new; tirades of transpositions; harmonic, melodic, and rhythmic carelessness, certain old-fashioned modulations," and expressed the hope that Timer played better than he composed.[75] The *Wöchentliche Nachrichten* made more specific observations in reviewing partitas by Georg Simon Löhlein, noting that some theorists might find the close proximity of A major and C major in the fourth partita offensive. The reviewer refused to label Löhlein's "audacity" as criminal, not only because an unnamed famous composer had done something similar, but also because "it is good to occasionally leave the main streets and thus avoid the ordinary. One always demands novelty in music, and the genius should be free to seek it in more than one way."[76]

Still, novelty, like originality and other elements of creative genius, could easily get out of hand, both from the excesses of the unchecked imagination and from the urge to strive for the new and different at all costs. The

Wöchentliche Nachrichten expressed this fear succinctly when it exclaimed, "May Herr Toeschi always remain the same. May he be less carried away by the love of the peculiar or perhaps by the fear of not being new enough."[77] A collection of dances by Johann Lorenz Albrecht caused the *Neue Zeitungen von gelehrten Sachen* to ruminate about the restraint marking a true genius: "When minuets and polonaises are created by a genius not lacking in invention, who knows how to avoid frequent and hackneyed paths without becoming artificial, nonsensical and adventurous, they can even deserve the attention of connoisseurs."[78] The same journal later praised the "passionate genius" of native son Bernhard Theodor Breitkopf, and though it offered somewhat reluctant praise for "going his own way in modulation" and at least tolerated the mixed rhythms he had introduced into one of the minuets, it stated firmly that such eccentricities should never become the norm. It concluded by observing that if he continued his study of music, he could bring honor to Germany by his invention as well as solid composition.[79] It is an interesting observation. Reviewers had certainly staked out the role of "technically competent composer" for the Germans, but now they had begun, albeit with some hesitation, to lay claim to the more irrational aspects of musical composition.

On balance, though, the forces of irrationality never seriously challenged the pedantic Beckmessers during the 1760s. Despite the acknowledgment of genius, and the limited role accorded expressivity, the review collective remained firmly in the camp of reason, keeping to sober, cool evaluation by the rules. Even the language was cool. Anything remotely pictorial or metaphorical had little to do with effusive outpourings of a musically captivated heart; one finds instead the cynical critic, as when the *Wöchentliche Nachrichten* criticized a cross-hands passage in Manfredini's wretched keyboard sonatas, saying that it would look like the performer was catching fleas.[80] In this and in the choice of aesthetic criteria, the pendulum was about to swing dramatically to the other side.

6

The reign of genius

Neue Zeitungen von gelehrten Sachen (1773): Johann Friedrich Doles's *Sechs Sonaten*

To his credit . . . [the sonatas] do not betray a slavishly imitative spirit, but one that thinks for itself, one that is inventive, lively and pleasant . . . The things that a strict harmonist might find to criticize here are minor careless mistakes that can be forgiven in a dilettante or excused by fashion. It is always wrong to make too much ado about such trifling matters that can be easily avoided with a little attention. A work of the soul isn't beautiful simply because certain artistic judges find nothing to criticize, especially when those judges only pay attention to the mechanical compliance with the rules and close their eyes to the true signs of a passionate and richly inventive genius.[1]

Gothaische gelehrte Zeitungen (1774): Wolf's *Sei Sonate*

The keyboard works of a Bach or a Benda have always been the very best a dilettante could own, but now he can confidently add the sonatas of Herr Wolf to them: the same passionate invention! The same novelty, the same audacity of ideas and turns of phrase! Soft and cantabile spots placed between ones that roll and spring; unexpected surprising modulations! And all of that combined with absolutely correct *Harmonie* in the true, idiomatic style.[2]

It would be hard to find more succinct statements of the change in perspective ushered in by the impetuous and stormy 1770s and 1780s, when the review collective began to abandon the secure precepts of rationalism and follow the siren call of genius. The statistics are telling: references to the various aspects of creative genius now outnumber those to compositional correctness by about two to one, an imbalance rendered even more dramatic by the degree of emphasis each category received. Half of the reviews that discussed compositional correctness during the 1760s had stressed its absolute necessity as an aesthetic criterion in excruciating detail. Fewer than 10 percent did so in the following two decades. Suddenly, most reviewers preferred to dispose of the entire issue with a single phrase, merely noting the presence – or absence – of "strict composition" (*reiner Satz*). Into that aesthetic void rushed the forces of creative genius, until the timid praise of "good invention" had been engulfed by oceans of imaginative superlatives. By the 1780s, two-thirds of all references to creative genius emphasized *it* as the primary aesthetic criterion. In these two areas, the review collective had reversed itself completely, and it did so with startling abruptness.

The precipitous decline in the importance of compositional correctness that began in 1770 – almost as if cued by the stroke of midnight – obviously did not occur because composers suddenly stopped committing parallel fifths. It might partly be attributed to the demise of several important journals: Marpurg's *Kritische Briefe* had not continued past 1763, and both the *Unterhaltungen* and Hiller's *Wöchentliche Nachrichten* ceased publication late in 1770. However, even before these last two disappeared, they had abandoned their rule-mongering; of the twenty-six reviews they published during 1770, only one carried even the barest allusion to the subject, praising the "strict contrapuntal writing" (*reine contrapunktische Schreibart*) of some organ preludes.[3] Their exit left only the *Allgemeine deutsche Bibliothek* to carry the Beckmesserian burden, a task even it began to shirk. Although both the frequency and length of its error lists remained relatively high (reflecting the journal's continuing didactic intentions), it pursued compositional offenders with much less ferocity, a trend apparent even before the death of Agricola in 1774. While continuing his anti-Italian campaign, Agricola tempered his line of attack on compositional mistakes, and when the much younger Reichardt assumed command in 1777, he took the newer aesthetic direction. That direction had been charted in part by the most recent additions to the review collective (see table 6.1). The new arrivals (nearly all in political newspapers and scholarly review journals) showed much less of an inclination to hunt for rule infractions, both for reasons of space and readership. Their less technical discourse dominated during the 1770s, serving to heighten the suddenness of the attitude reversal. Even with the surge of music journalism in the early 1780s, however, the review collective did not revert to its former nit-picking ways.

The burgeoning interest in creative genius was thus a collective-wide phenomenon. Most of the older journals approached the issue cautiously, unwilling to cede this manifestation of the irrational too much power; but they did approach. In 1770 the *Wöchentliche Nachrichten* used, for the first time, the

Table 6.1 *Periodicals with reviews during the 1770s and 1780s*

New periodicals with reviews

Music

2   *Musikalisch-kritische Bibliothek*, 1778
     Author: Forkel

8   *Musikalischer Almanach*, 1782–1789
     Author: Forkel

3   *Musikalisches Kunstmagazin*, 1782, (1791)
     Author: Reichardt

159   *Magazin der Musik*, 1783–1788
     33 reprinted from various sources
     Authors: C. F. C. (Cramer); H. A. Fr.v. E. (Eschtruth); W.
     (Westphal?); B. (Bach?); L. (Leister?); G. (Grönland?);
     Gld. (Grönland?); A*; A. B.; B. S.; J. L.; Lg.; M.; Mmm.; M. N.; N. N.;
     Pgl.; P. C. F. G.; R.

8   *Musicalische Bibliotek*, 1784–1785
     Author: Eschtruth

22   *Musikalische Real-Zeitung*, 1788–(1790)
     Authors: Zx. (Johann Friedrich Christmann); F.; Kr.;
     O.; P.; R.r.; R—r; W.

General scholarly

1   [1771] *Realzeitung* (Vienna), 1770–1788

7   [1771] *Erlangische gelehrte Anmerkungen*, 1770–(1798)
     3 reprinted from *Neue Zeitungen von gelehrten Sachen*

1   [1772] *Prager gelehrte Nachrichten*, 1771–1772

8   [1773] *Altonaischer gelehrter Mercurius*, 1763–1788

1   [1773] *Gelehrte Zeitung* [Kiel], 1771–1775

8   [1774] *Frankfurter gelehrte Anzeigen*, 1772–(1790)

1   [1774] *Russische Bibliothek*, 1772–1789

13   [1774] *Gothaische gelehrte Zeitungen*, 1774–(1797)

1   [1775] *Litterarische Nachrichten*, 1775–1776

23   [1776] *Allgemeines Verzeichniß neuer Bücher*, 1776–1784

4   [1776] *Der teutsche Merkur* 1773–(1798*)

23   [1777] *Erfurtische gelehrte Zeitungen*, 1776–(1798*)
     Authors: Eschtruth; H.; M.; T. H.

1   [1777] *Berlinisches litterarisches Wochenblatt*, 1777

2   [1779] *Litteratur- und Theaterzeitung*, 1778–1783
     Author(s): Christian August von Bertram?

1   [1782] *Strasburgische gelehrte Nachrichten*, 1782–1785

1   [1784] *Raisonnirendes Bücherverzeichniß*, 1782–1784

Table 6.1 (*cont.*)

---

4 [1786] *Ephemereiden der Litteratur und des Theaters*, 1785–1786
      Author(s): Christian August von Bertram?
2 [1786] *Nürnbergische gelehrte Zeitung*, 1777–(1798*)
7 [1786] *Neue Leipziger gelehrte Zeitung*, 1785–1787
11 [1787] *Wirzburger gelehrte Anzeigen*, 1786–(1798*)
      Author(s): Lehritter?

Political newspapers
99 [1770] *Hamburgische neue Zeitung*, 1767–(1798*)
      plus 13 not extant; Author(s): F. (Forkel?); E.
10 [1773] *Berlinische privilegirte Zeitung*, 1770–(1798*)
      Author(s): Reichardt?

Continuing periodicals with reviews
16 *Wöchentliche Nachrichten*, 1767–1770
9 *Neue Zeitungen von gelehrten Sachen*, 1760–1784
2 *Göttingische Anzeigen*, 1760–(1798*)
7 *Jenaische Zeitungen*, 1761–1787
131 *Allgemeine deutsche Bibliothek*, 1765–(1794)
      Authors: Agricola; Reichardt; Schulz; Türk;
        Eb.; Ek.; Qs.; Rz.; Vr.
10 *Unterhaltungen*, 1766–1770
216 *Hamburgischer Correspondent*, 1760–(1798*)
      Authors: Leister; B. (Bach?); J.; R. (M.?; N. N.?)
10 *Berlinische Nachrichten*, 1761–(1798*)
      Authors: Reichardt?; O.
TOTAL REVIEWS: 832
            −36 reprinted
ACTUAL TOTAL: 796

Note: The date in brackets indicates the year in which the first instrumental music review appeared. The inclusive dates are the years of the journal's publication through 1798. An asterisk indicates the journal continued beyond 1798.

term "original" as an unambiguous word of praise, a distinction that went to Haydn.[4] Signs of change also surfaced during the last years of Agricola's tenure at the *Allgemeine deutsche Bibliothek*. His very first review from 1770 took what was to become the typical stance, minimizing the presence of technical errors in the face of evident originality. Though a subtle shift, it marked creative genius's foot in the door:

In addition, the composer exhibits a passionate spirit, rich in invention and not inclined to mimic, even if accompanied by a few entirely insignificant weaknesses. In the minuet on page 8, the variation from correct periodicity is too great to be pleasing.[5]

Still, Agricola's choice of vocabulary revealed his basic distrust of the new tendencies, for he often used words that made originality sound quite foreign. He commented that one of Johann Gottfried Müthel's duets contained "good and very exotic ideas, which certainly have not been borrowed from anyone," and observed that although Carlo Gottlob Richter's concertos did not exhibit the "most exotic and strangest invention," they were not trivial either.[6] The *Hamburgischer Correspondent* also showed a certain reserve during the early 1770s, but it soon joined the enthusiastic newcomers in their unadulterated worship of the creative impulse.

The new arrivals to the collective seemed particularly sensitive to the activity in philosophical and literary circles that was challenging the primacy of reason and according new status to the role of creative genius. In those circles, attempts at tipping the balance toward genius and the imagination had begun to appear during the 1760s, even as Enlightenment figures like Lessing and Mendelssohn were ultimately resolving the cipher in favor of reason. The philosopher Johann Georg Hamann made one of the earliest such arguments in his *Aesthetica in nuce*, published in 1762. Hamann disagreed completely with Lessing and Mendelssohn, arguing that a work of art expressed the artist's personality and thus could not be subject to arbitrary rules. Though he never completely broke with the notion that art should imitate nature, he believed that imitation should be accomplished by the expression of feelings and sensations.[7] Thus from both angles he deprived reason (in the guise of *a priori* rules) from its leading position as the ultimate aesthetic arbiter. Hamann's ideas received forceful support from Herder, who attacked Gottschedesque normative theories of art in a series of essays written during the late 1760s.[8] Herder's advocacy of the power of creative genius runs like a thread through his works, particularly those published during the 1770s. In one essay, he hailed Shakespeare as the ultimate "original genius," not just for the power of his creative impulse, but because of the sheer variety of characters and ideas in his plays.[9] The "Correspondence on Ossian and the Songs of Ancient Peoples" praised the impulsive fire of primitive creativity at the expense of the poetry of Herder's own time, which he felt lacked "that certainty, that exactness, that full contour which comes only from the first spontaneous draft, not from any elaborate later revision."[10] Aesthetic value thus resided in the inspiration, not in the mechanics of art. Moreover, Herder took the ultimate step, which both Lessing and Mendelssohn had refused to do, of removing creative genius from the realm and control of reason entirely.[11] The *avant garde* position had been staked out.

Musical discourse *outside* the review collective did not fall immediately and completely under the spell of genius, and continued to find comfort in reason's ability to structure composition. Many, no doubt, would have agreed with the private observations of C. P. E. Bach, who described a colleague (during the late 1770s) as having "more genius than science" (*mehr Genie als Wißenschaft*), then betrayed his preference for the latter by continuing that it was a pity that almost no one learned strict composition any more. In his view, its neglect had caused the recent spate of error-ridden compositions.[12] Not that composition manuals of the 1770s had in any way abandoned traditional rules. Although Johann Philipp Kirnberger's *Die Kunst des reinen Satzes in der Musik* (published in four volumes between 1771 and 1779) devoted more space than Marpurg to the areas of melodic and rhythmic construction, its subject matter was still heavily oriented toward the rules of counterpoint and dissonance treatment. Even the chapter on the free style (a very small one!) and other less quantifiable aspects of composition betray a distinct "thou shalt not" attitude. For example, the section on modulation presents several charts detailing the keys to which the student was *allowed* to modulate, and explaining the permissible routes and aesthetic rationale for more distant tonal adventures.[13] By the time Heinrich Christoph Koch published the first volume of his composition method in 1782, the perspective had changed. Carl Friedrich Cramer noted in his review of Koch's treatise that, "for quite a while it has been felt that even the best of rules are completely insufficient for beginners in composition, so that they should also study good models."[14] As Cramer indicated, Koch avoided *a priori* rules; instead, he derived his precepts from actual compositional practice and presented them as options and recommendations rather than as rules. He talked, for example, about the unpleasant effect produced when two successive phrases cadence on the dominant, but he did not forbid their usage.[15]

Koch's procedures paralleled other more speculative aesthetic efforts to impose some control on the creative process without subjecting it to *a priori* rules *à la* Gottsched. In an essay published in the *Magazin der Musik* in 1783, Johann Nikolaus Forkel wrestled with the internal contradiction of having any rules in music "if music is the language of the sentiments and the passions, and if the sentiments of a single individual never fully agree with those of another." He recommended following the lead of other arts and sciences, letting "our feeling for the Beautiful in music be the yardstick by which we derive and establish rules and regulations, carefully and with the sagacity born of repeated experience," emphasizing that such rules must be discovered, not invented.[16] Forkel further refined his ideas in his *Allgemeine Geschichte der Musik*, maintaining that the first products of genius are freaks (*Mißgeburten*), and that only experience gives genius the rules by which it creates. Following reasonable rules (*Vorschriften*) would channel, not destroy genius, hindering "the injudicious and error-ridden outburst of genius just like a dam [hinders] the destructive flooding and mud of a wild river."[17] A French treatise translated and published by Johann Adam Hiller in 1781 (see chapter 1, page 9) also argued against *a priori* rules, granting reason only an after-the-fact role as the assimilator of genius's experience:

Rules have never been created before the examples, nor has reason ever told genius what it should do. Genius works only under the direction of feeling; it creates laws without knowing them. The intellect, which afterwards reflects on the works that genius brings forth, only then discovers the secrets of its effects. From this model, it then puts together the rules of art.[18]

Thus, while general musical discourse in the 1770s and 1780s began to move gradually toward a view of compositional rules more compatible with Herder's freer approach, it continued to question, as had Lessing, the wisdom of unbridled genius.

Only a few reviewers retained this cautious view of creative genius controlled by rational compositional restrictions. As might be expected, Forkel warned against deviating from the rules and regulations set by the masters of the art, just for the purposes of being new and different, because works that remained "true to sound reason and true nature glistened like precious stones among glass crystals."[19] He was joined in this opinion by Eschtruth, whose reviews in his *Musicalische Bibliotek* came closer than most others to the vitriolic barbs of the 1760s. In assessing some divertissements by Christian Benjamin Uber, Eschtruth did admit that simply knowing the "otherwise priceless rules of *Harmonie* and *Rhythmus*" would not suffice without the presence of *Genie*. However, never one for understatement, he continued by praising Uber for not belonging to "those noxious creatures who silently slip deadly poison into the taste-veins of their weak admirers with their rule-less, unreasonable scrawling," concluding that it would be better to be bored to tears by the lack of genius than killed by incorrect composition.[20] Eschtruth's propensity for making error lists did not, however, bring him renown as a critic. In fact, Johann Abraham Peter Schulz, writing in the *Allgemeine deutsche Bibliothek* (a journal still more inclined than most to notice parallel fifths), issued this rebuke when he reviewed Eschtruth's *Musicalische Bibliotek*:

With regard to the music reviews, we would like to remind him that the value of a work does not reside in its adherence, or non-adherence, to the grammatical rules of strict composition. Just as the ability to rhyme does not make someone a poet, Bach is not great simply because he composes correctly.[21]

Throughout the 1770s and 1780s, most reviewers concurred with Schulz, embracing the criterion of creative genius over the ability to compose according to strict compositional rules. Schulz's own review of some sonatas by J. C. Ribbe, which advised the composer to give up composition until he had thoroughly studied Kirnberger's treatise, nonetheless implied that correctness was merely a fall-back position, "because whoever cannot entertain his listeners with new, tasteful ideas, at least should compose correctly, in order to be considered tolerable."[22] Türk, Schulz's colleague at the *Allgemeine deutsche Bibliothek*, was actually much more disposed to call in the composition cops, but still could not condone mere correctness. He called a work by Richter a "concerto born thirty years too late," adding that "to be fair, one cannot deny the composer's diligence, but compositional correctness alone will not make a piece of music beautiful or entertaining."[23] While the *Hamburgischer Correspondent* acknowledged that the dilettante Hadrava's knowledge of strict composition "exceeded that of many so-called professors," it pointed out that "such knowledge alone, without *Genie*, does not make a tasteful composer," referring to the standards of originality set by Bach and Haydn (see above, chapter 3).[24] Even adherence to genre expectations began to take a back seat to the attributes associated with creative genius. When Felice Giardini brought out a set of accompanied sonatas, the *Hamburgische neue Zeitung* observed that they were "rather obbligato, in the manner of older trios," a characteristic that earlier would have occasioned an outburst of critical appreciation. But the reviewer merely continued that "the melody is often pleasant, and would have been even more pleasing with more novel ideas."[25]

Other members of the collective had even less regard for following the rules. After praising the sonatas of the Baron Dalberg, the *Erfurtische gelehrte Zeitungen* admitted that they did leave a little something to be desired in the areas of "compositional correctness, tonal and metric order, the frequent arpeggios, the cross-hands passages, and the musical orthography," but queried, "What of it? . . . Too many geniuses are quashed and suffocated at birth by excessive criticism."[26] For sheer surrender to the allure of genius, however, nothing can top the *Litteratur- und Theaterzeitung*'s critique of a set of sonatas published by none other than Johann Nikolaus Forkel. The reviewer gleefully pounced on his colleague's venture into the realm of composition, with comments literally reeking with *Schadenfreude*, an untranslatable word that means pleasure at another's problems:

The only merit these sonatas have is their musical correctness or their strict composition. One would have expected something quite different, something excellent from such a hale and hearty judge of art, from someone who wants to reform the entire musical world, instruct both connoisseur and dilettante, clean up all the garbage in music and restore it to its former dignity – or however else his quackish promises go – from someone who picks and jabs at whatever his little Lilliputian circle can't encompass . . . Twenty or thirty years ago these sonatas would have deserved a spot in a musical library; but now? . . . Even after the most painstaking search, you won't find a single idea stamped with novelty or originality. The composer has imitated the style of C. P. E. Bach without possessing his spirit. You have to feel sorry for Bach's pithy, forceful and penetrating ideas when you see them in the company of so many good-for-nothings, so many everyday, dull and boring things. Not a single new passage or new melodic figure . . . Herr Forkel must have borrowed the fifth sonata from Kapellmeister Bach and then forgotten whose it was, because it appears here as his own work. Whole periods have been borrowed. You will find the last movement's twin in C. P. E. Bach's "Sonaten zum Gebrauch der Damen." Herr F. has also studiously created from G. Benda's and Nichelmann's sonatas. No! Give me a Häßler any day; he is quite different: Bach's style every now and then, but at the same time countless traces of a passionate imagination, musical wit, and a fertile power of invention. Herr Forkel would have done more for the reputation of his *Musikalisch=kritische Bibliothek* if he had left these sonatas on his desk, or had only shown them to his adoring students.[27]

In an equally devastating review of the same pieces, the *Jenaische Zeitungen* found nothing individual about them, "except for some village schoolmaster cadences" and some "town-musician appoggiaturas," labeling everything else as either "plagiarized melodies" or "insignificant mechanics."[28] No matter how the rules were defined, no amount of correct composition would ever compensate for the lack of genius.

While the review collective of the 1770s and 1780s thus overwhelmingly favored creative genius over correctness, it could not ignore the latter entirely. The *Jenaische Zeitungen*, for example, complained about one composer who did not know that dissonances and suspensions should resolve downward.[29] Reviewers also continued to fret over periodicity and genre infractions into the 1770s, but their complaints generally lacked the indignant tone of the previous decade. An early Haydn review (of pirated, arranged baryton trios – see example 6.1) sniffed at Adagios that behaved more like dances and felt compelled to mention the irregular phrases in the "otherwise beautiful melody." Those problems did not, however, prevent the reviewer from recognizing all Haydn's new ideas and pleasant *Harmonie*.[30] Though specific theoretical dissections did occur occasionally (particularly in the *Allgemeine deutsche Bibliothek*), most comments did not go beyond an observation that the piece was (or was not) "theoretically correct," reducing the former premiere issue

Example 6.1 Joseph Haydn, keyboard reduction of the Baryton Trio, Hob. XI:9, Adagio, mm. 1–23

Example 6.1 (*cont.*)

to a modest place in a row of compositional attributes.[31] What status it retained now derived mainly from its association with the profundity and thoroughness of the "genuine style" (see chapter 3). As the *Frankfurter gelehrte Anzeigen* insured all admirers of "true good taste," they would find more "profundity, decorum, full and strict *Harmonie*, pleasant melody, and occasionally even ingenious modulations and fugal movements" in Johann Gottfried Eckard's *Sei Sonate* than in "many so-called keyboard sonatas."[32] Compositional correctness thus became another rhetorical weapon in the reviewers' campaign against the frivolous Other. And although Eckard's Op. 1 had been described as "Italianate and easy" (see page 52), presumably he was also one of those Germans (like Schwanberger, see page 52) who could ultimately "not deny the profundity of their knowledge."

The only expansion in the area of compositional correctness involved the issue of modulatory procedures, which – in the usage of the time – covered everything from non-diatonic chord progressions to secondary dominants to actual changes of tonal center.[33] 1760s reviewers had occasionally remarked on incorrect modulation, but they generally did so only when ranting about a composer's complete incompetence (as in the cases of Manfredini and Rosenbaum). Otherwise, most of the criticism had revolved around the Italianate tendency to stray no further afield than the dominant, treated as a problem of style rather than of technique. Once Kirnberger's treatise had provided a list of modulatory rules, however, reviewers could pick it apart as they did dissonance treatment, though – significantly – only a few ever connected proper procedures to the appropriate expression of Affect, as he had. In the *Allgemeine deutsche Bibliothek*, Türk did criticize the juxtaposition of an A major and a C minor triad, saying that he would allow such a progression only in pieces of "violent, stormy character." Earlier in the review, however, he had objected to an E major triad followed closely by D major simply because the swiftness of the transition did not have a good effect in the middle of the surrounding slower harmonic progressions; he had taken exception to the cross relation D#/D♮ because it sounded too harsh.[34] The *Erfurtische gelehrte Zeitungen* found an (unspecified) "false modulation" in the keyboard pieces of T. G. Beßler, and the *Hamburgischer Correspondent* called for a "greater exactness" in M. E. Grose's phrasing and modulation – giving the page numbers of the offending passages.[35] These examples notwithstanding, few of the comments on modulation, *Harmonie*, or anything else, carry the proscriptive (and prescriptive) tone of the review collective's early years. Marpurg would hardly have exclaimed, as did the *Altonaischer gelehrter Mercurius* in 1773, about "unexpected, bewitching paths of *Harmonie*."[36] When *Harmonie* could be viewed through lenses normally associated with creative genius, the perspective had definitely changed.

The importance of creative genius during the 1770s and 1780s is revealed not only by the overt declarations on its behalf, but also in the nature of the discussions themselves: they are as rich and varied as the discussions of rules and regulations had been in the 1760s. If reviewers rarely went into the same detail, that is because genius does not parse as well as six-four chords; its significance can be read most easily from the rapidly expanding treasury of words and phrases used to describe it. The terms *Genie* and "original" became relatively common words of praise associated with the power of invention and with an identifiable personal style. The *Hamburgischer Correspondent*, after briefly acknowledging the correctness of Hardenack Otto Conrad Zinck's *Harmonie*, labeled the sixth sonata of the set under review as the "most original," although it thought the others did not lack for "his own turns of phrase and original expression." It then went on to complain that "many of our young composers have so little that is their own. Instead, they put together their work from music they once heard – which admittedly can be called composing, but which lacks invention, one of the most precious talents of a musical *Genie*."[37] This assertion marked a 180-degree reversal of Marpurg's position that composition *meant* putting together (see chapter 5, page 93). When a promising young composer like Türk published his first collection of keyboard sonatas, the *Altonaischer gelehrter Mercurius* greeted him as a "man of genius," adding, "you won't find any warmed up leftovers sprinkled with a new sauce; but instead new ideas, that at least appear to be his own."[38] Once created, moreover, the reputation for originality had to be maintained, and after describing a sonata by J. F. Reinhardt (probably Reichardt) as "full of passion, lively and correctly composed," the *Hamburgische neue Zeitung* demurred that it was not nearly "as new as one might expect from a man with so much *Genie*."[39] Expectations ran particularly high for Mozart, indications that he might eventually reach iconic status. In the *Magazin der Musik*, N. N. declared that Mozart's Op. 2. violin sonatas were "the only ones of their kind." He found them "rich in new ideas, with the fingerprints of the great musical genius of the composer," and regretted it was not possible to "give a full description of these original works."[40] This context helps to explain the *Hamburgischer Correspondent*'s brief review of the Mozart Op. 1 violin sonatas: "These sonatas are more original than the others we know by Mozart, and therefore we prefer them."[41]

With genius and originality emerging as necessary compositional attributes, however, reviewers needed heightened terminology to distinguish the iconic styles of Bach and Haydn from the rest. They appropriated Shaftesbury's term *Original-Genie*, applying it to no other composer save Mozart (in a single review from the 1790s). More commonly, they added the adjective "inexhaustible" to "genius," marveling continually at Bach's and Haydn's ability to produce a seemingly endless stream of novel ideas. The *Hamburgischer Correspondent* greeted Haydn's Op. 33 quartets with nothing short of adulation, calling him "an inexhaustible genius who appears to exceed himself in each new work that he publishes" and rhapsodizing about the "magnificent melody, excellent *Harmonie*, unexpected and surprising modulations and the whole host of new, never-before-heard ideas."[42]

With originality so highly valued, reviewers could scarcely approve of "appropriating" someone else's ideas, and complaints about plagiarism abound. During the early 1770s, before the cult of genius became fully entrenched, composers caught in the act got off relatively lightly. Thus, though the *Wöchentliche Nachrichten* admitted that Veichtner's symphonies were "not very original," it concluded that "as imitations they were just as good and often better than their models."[43] In the *Allgemeine deutsche Bibliothek*, Agricola noted that Christian Gottlieb Neefe had industriously studied the latest C. P. E. Bach works, but hastened to say he was not accusing him of "servile, forbidden imitation" because "his way of imitating is good."[44] Such toleration did not last, and though reviewers always made allowances for young composers who still had not completely found their own voice (Forkel excepted!), even they could not escape censure for blatant copying. Several passages that Häßler had lifted from C. P. E. Bach pieces set Reichardt, in the *Allgemeine deutsche Bibliothek*, to musing about the proper relationship between studying other composers and developing a personal style. He advised against concentrating too much on a single composer, even a good one, for if you "made his style your own, and took on all his outward characteristics," you would still remain mediocre.[45] In any case, the perceived similarity to a greater composer might merely point up the imitator's deficiencies. The *Erlangische gelehrte Anmerkungen* immediately recognized Pleyel as a student of the "great Haydn, even though one misses [Haydn's] delicacy and inexhaustible humor."[46]

The new importance of creative genius and originality was not lost on the composers whose works were being scrutinized. Neefe, whose music generally got good marks for invention during the early 1770s (even the *Allgemeine deutsche Bibliothek* review cited above treated him gently), nonetheless felt compelled to respond. In an essay entitled "Ueber die musikalische Wiederholung," published in the *Deutsches Museum* in August of 1776, he addressed those critics who objected to repetitiveness in composition. Although he agreed that when stemming from a lack of invention, it deserved censure, he claimed that lapses often were due merely to "poor memory or simple haste" and therefore excusable. (He defended the appropriation of another composer's ideas on the same grounds!) On the other hand, when used as a means of working out the musical material, he thought repetition was completely justifiable because it helped to make the composition comprehensible and rendered expression possible.[47] A similar defensiveness emerges from a letter that Haydn wrote to Artaria in 1780, asking them to print the following disclaimer with his new set of sonatas:

Among these 6 sonatas there are two single movements in which the same subject occurs through several bars: the author has done this intentionally, to show different methods of treatment . . . I could have chosen a hundred other ideas instead of this one; but so that the whole *opus* will not be exposed to blame on account of this one intentional detail (which the critics and especially my enemies might interpret wrongly), I think that this advertisement or something like it must be appended, otherwise the sale might be hindered thereby.[48]

That Haydn felt the need to cut his critics off at the pass speaks volumes about the extent to which the criterion of creative genius had permeated critical discourse. He need not have worried too much, however, for Reichardt thought that these very pieces distinguished themselves "through original, masculine humor," and the *Hamburgischer Correspondent* recognized in them "the composer of those excellent quartets that are among the best musical pieces ever composed," particularly because of that "certain humor" that only Haydn had.[49]

The various attributes of creative genius discussed in chapter 4 made their appearance with increasing intensity over the course of the two decades. At first, reviewers simply looked for newness and novelty, and the positive cast of their remarks must be inferred from the association with other, accepted characteristics. When the *Unterhaltungen* observed in 1770 that Nicolas Dothel's *Sonates en Trio* had an acceptably contrapuntal texture and "many new features," one could reasonably assume from the connection with the hallowed former that the ambiguous latter counted as a compliment.[50] Less equivocal statements were not long in coming, however, and the same journal later praised a trio that was "full of invention," in which each voice had "something to do."[51] The *Jenaische Zeitungen* loved a quartet by Wolf because "there were new ideas everywhere," a judgment echoed by the *Hamburgische neue Zeitung* in proclaiming a set of his sonatas "rich in ideas and new."[52] The *Allgemeines Verzeichniß neuer Bücher* pronounced Christian Wilhelm Podbielsky's sonatas to be "rich in invention and full of beautiful, singing melodies."[53] *Der teutsche Merkur* offered kind words for Häßler, saying that of all of Bach's followers, he "kept right up with him," with "bold, new ideas, full of power and passion."[54]

With Bach and Haydn serving as icons, the review collective intensified its requirements for creative genius considerably: mere invention no longer sufficed; it had to have variety; it had to be bold, striking, unexpected, full of vitality; it had to seduce the listener onto previously unexplored pathways. With vivid appreciation, the *Neue Leipziger gelehrte Zeitungen* praised a set of Haydn's minuets:

Even if Haydn's name weren't on the title page, you would conclude these pieces were his as soon as you played them; for in each one, you see the creative spirit and the inexhaustible genius of a Haydn. What prevails here is not the ordinary, hum-drum minuet tone; everywhere you look you find new invention in ideas and the way they're used, charmingly surprising variation, and so something unique, which shows Haydn's genius at its very best. Lightness and art, melody and *Harmonie* are paired so successfully with each other as only a Haydn could do. When you consider that these are – and are supposed to be – such trifling things, then it is amazing how much they are able to say and express. In whole big pieces of fashionable composers, there is often not the abundance displayed here in a single minuet.[55]

Even if other composers did not call forth such extensive rhapsodies, they could garner compliments for the "boldness and novelty" of their ideas, and for distinguishing themselves from the rest of the pack.[56] The *Magazin der Musik* heralded the arrival of "another genius, whose rich treasure holds much promise," whose keyboard sonatas were guaranteed to warm the heart of music lovers everywhere, with their "invention, wealth of ideas, knowledge of *Harmonie*, humor, wit, a very delicate feeling for the true and the beautiful, power and neatness in the expression of all the sentiments and passions that can be represented by tones," which "united in these sonatas in a manner as admirable as it is rare."[57] All this from the otherwise unknown F. S. Sander.

On the flip side, dullness, trite and banal passages, empty virtuosity, and endless repetition never failed to elicit critical venom. Forkel could not find a single "real musical thought, not even something that vaguely resembled one from a distance," in all the "running, jumping, and hopping" that characterized the concertos of the same F. S. Sander. He compared Sander's fingers to a racehorse, which could run that much faster the less weight it had to carry.[58] Also resorting to sarcasm, Türk in the *Allgemeine deutsche Bibliothek* compared Uber to "a chatterbox who always has something to say – always something unimportant and usually something you already know – just when you would like some peace and quiet," faulting his symphony for its total lack of "vitality and novelty."[59] The *Neue Leipziger gelehrte Zeitungen* had even less regard for the inner merit of Christian Gottlob Saupe's sonatas (which it had found to be compositionally correct):

Mainly they lack for ideas and turns of phrase: thus a search for something new and remarkable is fruitless. There is seldom more than one idea in a piece, and it is repeated ceaselessly *ad nauseam*. As a result there is a constant cling-clang. They contain nothing emphatic and powerful, nothing considered or full of sensitivity, nothing but common-place melody without any *Harmonie*, about which the composer doesn't seem to know much either.[60]

Pinning down exactly what reviewers meant by an original piece or a novel idea is not always easy, even when they cited examples. In the *Magazin der Musik*, Cramer cited the following passage (example 6.2) from the Andante of a Wolf sonatina as "a true flight of genius," though why an extended I-IV-V-I arpeggiated cadential figuration should call forth such an effusion is not at all clear.[61] (The remainder of the review precludes interpreting the remark as ironic.) Even if the idea could count as original, one would have thought it

Example 6.2 Ernst Wilhelm Wolf, Andante from *Sechs Sonatinen für das Clavier* (*Magazin der Musik*, example 32)

vulnerable to the charge of repetitiveness, because the collective clearly disapproved of inspired thoughts developed tediously. For example, although the *Erfurtische gelehrte Zeitungen* found Uber's sonatas "rich in new and striking turns of phrase," a few themes seemed "too drawn out, and hence boring," and specifically criticized the rows of octaves on pages 6 and 8, and the "repeated monotonous runs in the Presto of the fifth sonata."[62] The *Musikalischer Almanach* voiced similar complaints about Salomon Greßler's sonatas, though it did approve of their serious style that avoided all virtuosic display. However, it deplored its paucity of ideas, particularly "the ceaseless repetition" of both the main and subsidiary themes, "sometimes with a little melodic variation, sometimes an octave higher or lower," and the "lack of varied modulation which that must entail," ending with the same metaphor that Türk had used in describing Uber (above, page 114): "This manner of expressing ourselves may be just fine. But when we repeat the same expression over and over, because we have no other thoughts, it loses its value and we become like chatterboxes – pleasant but empty."[63] In an age that valued variety over unity, excessive repetition could only be a major aesthetic sin, hence the reactions of Neefe and Haydn discussed above.

As these last two citations imply, originality could also reside in modulatory techniques and choices, for reviewers began to show acceptance of, and even preference for, increasingly distant modulations (even as modulatory procedures came under scrutiny for correctness). The *Hamburgische neue Zeitung* liked Johann Georg Witthauer's dominant to tonic modulation, not because it was correct, but because it was "new," because it accomplished something quite standard and expected in a novel, different way.[64] Other examples abound. After rhapsodizing about "Benda's charming, novel melody, which is unmistakably his" and the way he had retained his solid technique "without clinging stubbornly to old, outdated forms," the *Magazin der Musik* singled out for special mention a "striking modulation to C minor" on the very first page of an A minor sonata.[65] The *Musikalische Real-Zeitung* decided that typical characteristics of Leopold Kozeluch's keyboard works included the "bold flight of *Phantasie*, richness of *Harmonie*, precious inversions, and a torrent of beautiful modulations winding through near and distant keys" (though it did think he repeated himself far too often).[66] In contrast to the uncertain stance the *Neue Zeitungen von gelehrten Sachen* had taken *vis à vis* Breitkopf's modulations in 1769 (see above, chapter 5), six years later the *Hamburgischer Correspondent* derided the trios of Conrad Breuning (in favor of an Italian!):

The composer's modulations are the normal ones. He seldom dares the boldness that makes Boccherini's works so worthy of recommendation. Sugar bread gets revolting after a while; a good stomach requires hearty food now and then. What do we care if the weaklings can't digest it?[67]

All of these manifestations of genius found perfect expression in the music of Haydn, explaining his rise to iconic status (though one might also wish to argue that the delight in his music led to the creation of standards to explain it). The *Magazin der Musik* explained his excellence in a relatively detailed review of three piano trios:

Example 6.3 Joseph Haydn, Piano Trio, Hob. XV:2, Allegro, mm. 1–7

Among the many excellent compositions of this great man, for harpsichord and other instruments, these three sonatas rank among the best. The opening Adagio of the A major sonata [Hob. XV:9] has an indescribable charm and contrasts nicely with the ensuing Vivace. In the Allegro of the F major [Hob. XV:2], the shortening of the *Rhythmus* in the sixth measure surprises the listener, perhaps too unexpectedly for many. The theme of the concluding adagio variations is very original because of the stretching of the *Rhythmus* in the seventh measure. The most beautiful of these beautiful sonatas is however, the third one in E flat major [Hob. XV:10], where Haydn's genius takes the most lofty flight.[68]

The F major trio dates from the late 1760s, a good fifteen years earlier than the other two, and the cadence in measures 6–7 does come somewhat abruptly (example 6.3). In 1769, however, such a foreshortening would not have gotten off so lightly, and the cadential evasion that creates the irregularity in the Finale theme would not have been appreciated as original, though its smoothness would have made it less upsetting (example 6.4). Cadential evasion is carried to its utmost in the final movement of the E flat trio. After the last

Example 6.4 Joseph Haydn, Piano Trio, Hob. XV:2, Finale, mm. 1–9

statement of the rondo theme, Haydn diverts the music through a deceptive progression to a major III chord, persists in keeping the tonic in second inversion, then slides to vii°/V moving to vii°⁷/vi, which he then respells enharmonically. Finally, after thirty-six measures, he lands on a perfect authentic cadence in the tonic seven measures before the end (example 6.5). Thus Haydn's genius took its most lofty flight.

He also managed to delight through his celebrated wit and humor. Though occasionally attributed to other composers, both characteristics had a particular association with Haydn.[69] In a long and laudatory review of Zinck's *Sechs Claviersonaten* in the *Magazin der Musik*, Cramer confessed to a special fondness for the rondo of the fifth sonata, calling it "the drollest thing, full of the oddest whims, farces, and witty humor, something that Haydn himself could have been proud of composing."[70] The *Berlinische Nachrichten* thought it detected some of Haydn's style in the variations of Federigo Angiolini, saying that he could certainly write "very beautiful variations, even though he did not possess Haydn's humor."[71] The key to the inclusion of wit

Example 6.5 Joseph Haydn, Piano Trio, Hob. XV:10, Presto assai, mm. 213–68

Example 6.5 (*cont.*)

Example 6.5 (*cont.*)

Example 6.5 (*cont.*)

and humor in the category of attributes of creative genius – particularly during the 1770s and 1780s – lies in their association with a personal, idiosyncratic style and their role in creating musical surprise.

Thus, creative genius could manifest itself in many different ways, in vaguely defined novel ideas, but also through witty turns of phrase, through modulatory ingenuity, and through imaginatively varied melodic structure. If we attempt to extract a basic principle from all of the review collective's comments on the issue – whether or not we ultimately agree with their opinions – one common trait emerges: they all valued the skillful presentation of the unexpected within the confines of the familiar. This ability separated the excellent from the mediocre composer in late eighteenth-century musical style, where delight resides not so much in symmetry and predictability as in the frustration and eventual satisfaction of the listener's harmonic and melodic expectations. The review collective, by its conceptualization of creative genius, thus focused on the fundamental driving force of the music it considered, a force perfectly suited to the instrumental medium.

Reviewers also clearly associated the characteristics of genius with the chosen Germanic Us. In heralding sonatas by Wolf, the *Hamburgische neue Zeitung* proclaimed them to be "in true German taste, with almost no Alberti bass; full of variety, a fair amount of novelty, vitality, and good melody," further emphasizing the German link to genius by preferring the slow movements, which had "the most novelty in ideas and modulation."[72] As the rhetoric took the more abstract, moralistic tack described in chapter 3, genius accompanied those compositions designated as true and genuine, for without "striking *Harmonien* and unexpected, alluring melody," a composition could appeal only to those who preferred "the latest fashion" to "true good taste, touching the heart, and engaging the intellect."[73] The *Magazin der Musik*, therefore, had little good to say about the "intrinsic inner value" of Charles Frederick Horn's *Six Sonates*, with regard to both strict *Harmonie* and novelty. Moreover, because of the paucity of his ideas, Horn's distant modulations appeared bare and cold, giving the listener no pleasure, unlike the chromatic diversions of Haydn and Clementi, who "leave the broad highway and lead us aside to hidden romantic regions."[74] Like compositional correctness, genius became inextricably entwined with the rhetorical creation of a Germanic aesthetic.

With so much critical energy devoted to the aspects of genius, little remained to explore the criterion of expressivity, and the frequency with which it was mentioned declined from nearly one in three to less than one in four reviews. Moreover, much of the new vocabulary during the 1770s and 1780s seems to derive more from a change in writing style rather than aesthetic viewpoint. In describing movement types, for example, reviewers moved beyond the previous decade's "passionate first movement, pleasant slow movement, lively finale" to much more emotionally charged, pictorial prose. The *Berlinische Nachrichten* described the various slow movements of the Freiherr von Kospoth's symphonies as "ingratiating," "continually sweet," "peaceful," "soft"; a minuet finale as "entirely cheerful"; another finale not just as passionate, but as "extraordinarily passionate."[75] The reviewer for the *Wirzburger gelehrte Anzeigen* confessed that for him, the opening Andante of a Häßler sonata had "something spirited and honey-sweet" about it.[76] Particularly in the *Hamburgische neue Zeitung*, which had a higher than average number of references to expressivity, slow movements were likely to be described as "ingratiating," "full of affect" (*affektvoll*), "touching" (*rührend*), or "full of feeling" (*gefühlvoll*), but with no specificity as to what exactly was being expressed.[77] In other instances, reviewers appropriated adjectives associated with human personality and emotions, so that the *Erfurtische gelehrte Zeitungen* could compliment a minuet written "in completely singular, naive taste," as well as the concluding "laughing Allegretto."[78] On the other side of the emotional coin, reviewers could also praise "sweet melancholy melodies" and "plaintive, melancholy rondos."[79]

The most colorful language is concentrated in a few journals. The *Magazin der Musik* found darker emotions in a piece in the bound style by Zinck, calling it "a long earthworm that wriggles its way to the end," and claiming it expressed "a thought gnawing at the bile-laden soul of one who cannot get rid of his melancholy."[80] By way of contrast, the *Neue Leipziger gelehrte Zeitungen* seems almost restrained, although its reviewer clearly had a fertile imagination stimulating the lively prose:

Admittedly, these sonatas do not have Haydn's humor, or Vanhall's liveliness, or Bach's seriousness, or Kozeluch's and Clementi's passion; but they do distinguish themselves from many others through their soft, tender, engaging, and pleasant air . . . The second sonata contains (1) an Allegro, where liveliness and charm offer their hands to each other; (2) a very pretty Menuet, which has the character of an unhappy person coming to terms with a loss; (3) a Rondo allegro . . . in which a solitary and moderate joy predominates.[81]

Most passages like these offer the interpretive challenges discussed in chapter 4: were reviewers attributing specific programmatic intentions to the composer, were they describing the pictures the music conjured up in their minds, or were they simply attached to purple prose? After all, the German literary world of the 1770s and 1780s was infected with that (musically) notorious movement, the *Sturm und Drang*; its effusive writing style, laced with passionate outbursts of unrestrained emotions, bears a close resemblance to the more violet-hued passages in the review collective. We should therefore beware of imputing mimetic associations to seething storminess or wriggling earthworms when poetry commonly spoke in this ecstatic language:

> All the pealing melodies vied with each other
> Nimbly the living harmony gushed forth in deep streams
> Sometimes thundering like typhoon-driven waves
> surging onto the beach,
> When the crash of shattered ships and the wretched,
> anguished cries of men die out in the distance
> amid the dreadful tumult;
> Sometimes flowing like a brook that runs over smooth
> stones through flowers and grass and deep shade,
> Where shepherds take their repose, listening to its
> murmuring in delicious dreams.[82]

In actuality, no more than twenty of the nearly 800 reviews from the 1770s and 1780s refer definitely to the portrayal of specific sentiments or character. Most appeared in one of three journals (*Musikalisch-kritische Bibliothek*, *Magazin der Musik*, and *Musikalische Real-Zeitung*), and nearly half were written by either Forkel or Cramer. Forkel and Cramer also showed the greatest tendency to insist on the aesthetic necessity of mimesis, but inconsistencies and ambivalence about the issue pervade the reviews of both men. Forkel devoted serious attention to the issue of musical character in the two lengthy reviews in his *Musikalisch-kritische Bibliothek* (treating C. P. E. Bach's accompanied sonatas and the first set of keyboard sonatas by Türk). His conviction that music should be guided by "character" shaped the discussion, although he did not ignore other aesthetic criteria. For example, in the Bach sonatas, Forkel singled out an Andante that would please most music lovers "because its character is more comprehensible and its inner value more striking" than those of the surrounding movements. He particularly liked the modulatory passage that led to the ensuing Presto, which he described as "easing the transition from one character to another."[83] He identified the "main character" of Türk's melodies as "soft," which he felt stemmed from the composer's temperament, continuing: "Our composer is thus most successful when his expression is soft. He flows along so evenly and softly, like a softly and quietly rippling stream."[84] Forkel's association of personality traits with music composed reflected one of the continuing skirmishes between warring factions of the mimetic paradigm. One side held that a composer must actually have experienced (or be experiencing) the emotion to portray it in music, the other thought that unnecessary. His remarks here represent the only time the fighting on that particular issue spilled over into the collective's discourse. It should perhaps not be surprising that Forkel, one of the main participants in the ongoing aesthetic debate outside the collective, might adhere to aesthetic standards based on mimesis. Significantly – and herein lies the inconsistency – none of the reviews in his *Musikalischer Almanach* advocated these fervently held beliefs at all. In them, Forkel toed the collective line, following the emphasis on criteria associated with creative genius.

Cramer's viewpoint is even harder to pin down. In some reviews, he appears to apply mimetic criteria to instrumental music as a matter of course, noting that Wolf's *Sechs Sonatinen* did not spend much time "in the region of grand and passionate representations, but restricted themselves more to joyful, witty, cheerful sentiments."[85] He praised some pieces by Carl Rudolf Heinrich Ritter because they all had "their own specific character, a requirement that so many composers apparently do not know about, or do not know how to give to their works," implying that he considered the expression of character to be an essential aesthetic criterion.[86] Several years earlier, in reviewing Zinck sonatas (the ones with the earthworm – see above, page 124), he had expressed his strong support for the composer's skill in musical painting, and had judged a set of sonatas by Johann Ludwig Theodor Blum as not quite equal to Zinck's in the "invention of new ideas, passion, and picturesque expression."[87] On the other hand, when he maintained that keyboard variations by Giovanne Luigi Csaky "*could be labeled* [my italics] obstinate, witty, stubbornness," his phrasing implied that the mimetic interpretation was his own reading, not the composer's intention.[88] In addition, over half of his seventeen reviews do not mention specific mimesis – or even general expressivity – at all, with no discernible pattern governing when he used it as an aesthetic criterion.

Yet another perspective emerges from his extended review of the fourth volume of C. P. E. Bach's *Claviersonaten und freye Phantasien*. Although he discussed the pieces in terms of their expressive value and even referred to Forkel's various analytic categories for sentiments, he stopped short of actually supporting any theory of mimesis. Instead, he used his emotive and pictorial descriptions as a crutch for reviewing:

> It is always difficult to say something definite about an instrumental piece without simply breaking out in general exclamations or going into detail with barren lists of harmonic beauties, modulations, etc. Nonetheless, in order to justify my sentiments in some measure, I generally try to think of a character that could correspond to an excellent piece. Thus I perceive, for example, that this Rondo theme [example 6.6] and its realization resemble a charming girl who has set her cap for something that she wishes to achieve through humor and amiable insistence.[89]

Example 6.6 C. P. E. Bach, Rondo No. 1 in A Major from *Clavier-Sonaten und freye Fantasien*, Wq. 58/1, mm. 1–4 (*Magazin der Musik*, example 26)

Example 6.7 C. P. E. Bach, *Sonata No. 1 in G Major* from *Clavier-Sonaten und freye Fantasien*, Wq. 58/2, Gratioso, mm. 1–4 (*Magazin der Musik*, example 27)

Cramer went on to describe the Gratioso of the G major sonata as the "merry, soft joy of an innocent maiden sitting by a brook in the fragrance of a summer evening" (example 6.7). More unpleasant sentiments emerge in the ensuing Larghetto e sostenuto, where "seriousness awakens in her soul," and where tempo fluctuations and abrupt modulations into the harsh key of E major disrupt the soft flow of maidenly emotions. For Cramer, E major could never express the winsome joy of the feminine soul, but rather "the wild, brutal cry of a man, and in general designates a certain rough Affect in joy and sorrow." He found this "tone of masculinity" in the E major Rondo as well (example 6.8), disagreeing with the reviewer in the *Hamburgischer Correspondent*, who had called it a "soft, charming piece." His ensuing comments, however, did not address the theoretical challenge to mimesis posed by such conflicting interpretations, but instead attempted to justify the portrayal of harsher emotions in music. While he never actually stated that music *must* portray or evoke images or emotions, he did find the Allegretto of the second sonata the least valuable of the collection because he "could not think of any definite character that would give it unity," though he admitted that the fault may have been his, not the music's.[90] Throughout the review, however, Cramer vacillated between implying that Bach intended to portray specific emotions or characters and acknowledging that the extra-musical content served mainly as an aid to understanding devised by the listeners themselves. Moreover, he

Example 6.8 C. P. E. Bach, Rondo No. 2 in E Major from *Clavier-Sonaten und freye Fantasien*, Wq. 58/3, mm. 147–66 (*Magazin der Musik*, example 28)

discussed the two fantasies in the collection as exercise and entertainment for the intellect, disparaging those who agreed with Rousseau that music only had value when it expressed specific, identifiable sentiments or engaged in actual tone painting. All in all, Cramer's review of Bach probably says more about what he thought a *reviewer* should do in presenting and evaluating a piece of music than what he believed the music itself had to express.[91]

In general, the paucity of references to the mimetic paradigm would seem to indicate that reviewers did not consider it a practical tool for evaluation, one that could be applied consistently to all types of instrumental music. Johann Friedrich Christmann, for example, described the Adagio of the Mozart E flat violin sonata (K. 481) as "full of soft sentiments, the true expression of languishing love," presumably because of the broken, rising melodic line sweetened with chromatic appoggiaturas (example 6.9). He excused the absence of ingenious modulations in an Adagio by Johann Gottfried Gebhard by observing that Gebhard had probably used them more sparingly to avoid giving the movement, which "had the character of soft tenderness, a coloring of dark melancholy."[92] His remaining reviews (with one exception, discussed below) ignored the issue entirely. A hint of the frustrations involved in mimetic

Example 6.9 Wolfgang Amadeus Mozart, Violin Sonata, K. 481, Adagio, mm. 1–8

reviewing surfaced in the *Frankfurter gelehrte Anzeigen*'s review of C. P. E. Bach's *Six Sonate per il Clavicembalo Solo all Uso delle Donne*. The reviewer declared he was not in the mood to pedantically list what each movement expressed, because "whoever cannot feel it does not deserve to have it explained to him," and confessed that though he admired the skillfully used chromaticism in the Larghetto of the D minor sonata, he could not really figure out what the piece was supposed to express.[93]

The only time reviewers could be counted on to judge a piece of instrumental music based upon its mimetic effectiveness was when the composer had declared his intentions to write a programmatic work. As was the case outside the collective, too-graphic portrayals rarely met with critical approval. When the *Allgemeines Verzeichniß neuer Bücher* reviewed a characteristic sonata by Wolf, it observed that such pieces (this one described the separation and reconciliation of a married couple) had been more fashionable several years earlier, noting wryly that without the written description, most listeners would have difficulty figuring out just what the composer meant.[94] In evaluating G. C. Füger's *Charakteristische Clavierstücke*, Schulz concentrated on whether Füger had succeeded in expressing the specified emotions. Schulz observed that distinguishing musically between the various shades of happy emotions in the first five pieces (e.g. liveliness, happiness, merriment, etc.) would have tested the compositional mettle of a Grétry and required a "delicacy of feeling and richness in invention" that Füger apparently did not have, because he could think of nothing besides scales and arpeggiated passages for all of them. "Tenderness" called for something besides A major and an Allegretto tempo, and the noisy passage in the middle sounded more like the "jubilant shrieks of a woman than an outburst of inner tenderness." The sixteen measures of running sixteenth notes fit the "pride and boldness" of an F minor piece "like a fist in the eye." The specificity of his mimetic criticism stands out, not only because the *Allgemeine deutsche Bibliothek* avoided rhapsodic reviews, but also because pieces without programmatic labels were never subjected to anything like it anywhere in the collective. In other words, by declaring his intention to portray specific emotions, Füger opened the door to aesthetic criteria reviewers generally did not use. Even so, the *Allgemeine deutsche Bibliothek* attributed his mimetic ineptitude, not just to a lack of sensitivity, but to a deficiency in genius.[95]

The same emphasis on creativity stands out in the *Musikalische Real-Zeitung*'s review of the keyboard reduction of Haydn's *Seven Last Words*: "Haydn has already given us several character pieces, or musical paintings, if you will, but none that surpass this collection in wealth and fullness of *Harmonie*, bold modulations, energy and dignity of style." Only then does it continue that Haydn could hardly have done a better job of portraying Christ's emotions if he had "been writing directly from the soul of the dying redeemer."[96] The *Erlangische gelehrte Anmerkungen* agreed that the piece distinguished itself as one of Haydn's premiere masterworks because of the "exalted invention, the finest dissonances, the purest preparations and resolutions," and praised him for not attempting a literal portrayal:

The great Händel was – correctly – criticized for trying to express in music things that lay entirely outside her sphere, e.g. the swarming of lice, the hopping of grasshoppers in the Egyptian plagues. The same criticism could have been leveled against the excellent Haydn if he had tried to express Jesus' last words in these sonatas. The highest goal that he could set for himself was this: to intensify the sentiments dictated by the seven words and give them color and firmness through his music. Whoever picks up this composition with grander expectations will be disappointed and find himself in a dilemma if he tries (in the long Adagio of the fifth sonata) to find a relationship between his sentiment and the indicated word *Sitio*. The art of the composer can express only the languishing and the dying, and the gap between these feelings and the sensation of thirst has to be completed by the imagination.[97]

If anything, the attention paid to how well avowedly characteristic pieces accomplished their characterizing goals emphasizes the nearly complete absence of mimetic requirements elsewhere. The contrast comes into greater relief when we compare the very different aesthetic treatment of opera overtures and symphonies. The latter's closest brush with mimesis occurs in the Affect-laden adjectives used in describing movement types, as discussed in chapter 5, and in their more emotive substitutes outlined above. Overtures, on the other hand, were expected to portray graphically both the physical actions and emotions of the characters in the ensuing story. The *Magazin der Musik* thought the warlike character of the overture to Sacchini's *Partition de Renaud* did a good job of announcing the tone of the first act, and Schulz praised Salieri's specific depiction of dramatic action in the overture to his opera *Armida*.[98] In sum, only when called to do so by a composer's stated programmatic intentions did the review collective adopt the aesthetic standards of mimesis. Otherwise, though reviewers might occasionally use picturesque language as a rhetorical tool, or give themselves over to the pleasures of voluptuous prose, they showed no interest in the specific issues of the mimetic paradigm.

They did, however, generally concur on one aspect of expressivity: that music had the capacity, in some unspecified way, to touch the heart. This intersection with the cult of sensibility, at least in the collective's interpretation, granted instrumental pieces a higher aesthetic value without requiring they actually "mean" something. Even more significantly, reviewers most often attributed this ability not to any emotionally sensitive portrayal of the sentiments, but to intrinsically musical characteristics, particularly ones associated with creative genius:

Herr Schulz is one of this century's composers who has brought his broad musical talent to fruition through the most exact study of the rules and axioms of theory . . . [These pieces] are in the style of the Bachs and their worthy predecessors and followers. There are so many bold, grand, and new ideas, that they literally trip over each other, something that does not happen every day. The ear wins in every respect, but even more the heart.[99]

If the heart could win with new ideas, it could also lose in their absence, and the gift of melody played a large role in determining the outcome. The

Hamburgische neue Zeitung wanted more melodious and powerful themes in Carlo Gottlob Richter's concertos, because "arpeggios seldom have anything to say to the heart," and the *Hamburgischer Correspondent* deplored the absence of melody in Zinck's "old-fashioned" flute duets, which, despite their correctness, failed "to have the effect that all music should have: touching the heart."[100] Türk's sonatas, on the other hand, (the ones that weren't just left-overs sprinkled with a new sauce – see above, page 111) elicited praise from the *Erfurtische gelehrte Zeitung* primarily because they contained the "melodious" and "sentimental" along with "soft melody that is full of feeling" and "expression that masterfully stirs the heart."[101] After demurring that a dilettante composer like Uber should not be judged too strictly, the *Jenaische Zeitungen* somewhat defensively maintained that his accompanied sonatas were written correctly, "had melody and satisfied both heart and ear."[102] It is only a short semantic step from music that has the power to touch the heart – whether by means of variety or melody or even "bewitching paths of *Harmonie*" – to music that itself is "full of feeling" (*gefühlvoll*), "full of sentiment" (*empfindungsvoll*), or "heart-flooding" (*herzergiessend*). Significantly, though, the collective refused to make even this relatively vague expressivity into a general aesthetic requirement: while the *Magazin der Musik* praised the touching, *empfindungsvolle* melody of some Vanhal sonatas, it concluded that "such things should be regarded like candy or cookies: you mustn't enjoy too many of them too often."[103] Still, reviewers made clear their belief in instrumental music's capacity to be expressive, to touch the heart, thus tacitly undermining one of the mimetic paradigm's main objections to its aesthetic validity and laying the foundation for instrumental music's metaphysical importance in romantic aesthetics.

If the review collective's concept of expressivity did not reinforce the aesthetic claims of mimesis, it did coexist peaceably with the ruling force of creative genius. Taken together, the weight of these two aesthetic categories firmly tipped the scale completely away from the rational criteria of the 1760s. With the mania for compositional correctness muted, with taste continuing to remain on the sidelines – its minimal role as an aesthetic criterion unchanged – the reins of judgment had in effect been ceded to the powers of the irrational. Reason got little effective support from the remaining category of order/unity, which almost entirely slipped from view during the 1770s.

In theoretical writings from the 1770s, order and unity were still linked to a linear view of composition that preserved many of the musical requirements of the previous decade. For example, in the second volume of his composition treatise, published in 1776, Kirnberger stated that, "the unity of the melody requires that all periods begin on the same beat throughout the piece."[104] Connections were to be accomplished by mimetic principles and the *Fortspinnung*-like derivation of materials:

The entire spirit of a piece must be contained immediately in its initial period, and all the following periods must have some similarity with the first one so that the unity of sentiment is preserved throughout. Thus whatever rhythmic patterns occur in the first period, similar ones must be heard in the other periods.[105]

Reflecting this theoretical position, most of the references in reviews of the 1770s use the words "plan" (*Plan* or *Anlage*), "order," and "arrange," or describe ideas as "hanging together," all of which imply the proper connection of musical ideas in a linear fashion. Thus, while the *Hamburgische neue Zeitung* could jeer at the "cute little Viennese ideas" in Johann Samuel Schröter's Op. 2 sonatas, it had to conclude that he knew "how to arrange them pleasantly."[106] As was the case with "invention" during the 1760s, the exact meaning the review collective attached to words like "plan" or "ordering" is not always clear. The *Hamburgischer Correspondent*, for example, advised Beckmann to learn "to lay out the plan of his larger pieces more carefully," without indicating what caused the disorder.[107] In similarly ambiguous fashion, the *Altonaischer gelehrter Mercurius* thought the ordering of Wolf's thoughts was "natural and unforced," and Reichardt found that the "order in the plan" of Veichtner's concertos helped, along with rhythmic exactness and harmonic purity, to "give the whole the character of nobility and completeness."[108] In none of these instances does the collective's view of order and unity seem to have changed much from the 1760s.

References to order and unity became even more infrequent during the early 1780s, but toward the end of the decade, even as the effusive support for creative genius and expressivity reached its zenith, they began to make a dramatic comeback. As the forces of the irrational threatened to completely overwhelm the voice of reason, the review collective started to respond and found cause to bemoan the fact that "whatever tickles the ear or touches the heart finds more approval than that which engages the intellect."[109] Composers were urged to "curb the fecundity of their ideas" and encouraged to round off their works with "unity and a closer connection of the various ideas."[110] In the middle of the impetuous 1780s, cooler aesthetic currents began to emerge.

7

A call to order

The first duet in G major begins with something exquisite. It appears to be an imaginative introduction that touches on different leading tones in the space of eleven measures, and only then turns to the actual scale, which is abandoned two measures later. The composer's genius shows itself most clearly in this duet; only occasionally does it burst forth too much.[1]

The composer can certainly be trusted to separate the good and beautiful things in this early work from the less good, to cut out, of his own accord, the stormy confusion of his youthful *Phantasie*, which – unconcerned about strict unity – lets flow an abundance of ideas for good or ill, just as they present themselves.[2]

The third and final period of the review collective's evolution did not make as sudden and dramatic an entrance as had the second, when the rejection of compositional correctness and the embracing of creative genius happened simultaneously at the end of a decade. Reviewers continued to extol the virtues of creative genius, now firmly established as the centerpiece of aesthetic criteria. Not even the slightest of genres could escape its requirements: the *Tübingische gelehrte Anzeigen* faulted a collection of dances for their lack of novelty and the poverty of ideas, and the *Musikalische Korrespondenz* dismissed some Hungarian dances as "so devoid of charm and novelty in the ideas that the musical public would not have lost anything had the child been strangled at birth."[3] If simple dances inspired such heated language, weightier

134

genres like sonatas absolutely required the cultivation of an individual style. The *Musikalisches Wochenblatt* could issue no higher praise for Clementi's Op. 24 sonatas than this: "His style has no similarities to that of Bach, Haydn, Mozart, Kozeluch, Sterkel, or Vanhall; instead he stands there independently, and all by himself."[4] Even though a reviewer might find fault with aspects of individual pieces, composers who established their stylistic independence moved onto a higher plane.

The standards for that plane continued to be set by a small group of compositional icons, which still included C. P. E. Bach, though his name surfaced less often after his death in 1788. He began to serve more as a nostalgic symbol of the good old days, brought up whenever a reviewer wished to complain about current compositional practice. In his absence, Haydn reigned supreme, still exalted for his "original humor, musical wit and the inexhaustible wealth of his ideas."[5] His students actually had a difficult time establishing themselves with reviewers, for though the *Musikalische Real-Zeitung* immediately recognized that Anton Wranitzky's quartets "breathed the genius of his teacher," it observed that they "lacked the originality and particular humor" that distinguished Haydn's compositions.[6] After Mozart had established his reputation as a mature composer, he too began to move toward iconic status. Reviewers had always viewed his style as particularly individual, never considering him in terms of possible models like they did with most younger composers. During the 1790s, reviews of his music took on a quality that distinguished his type of excellence from that of Haydn. Whereas the older composer's striking modulations and never-before-heard ideas flowed from his inexhaustible genius and unsurpassable wit and humor, the same characteristics of genius in Mozart led to the edge of the sublime:

When you have to write about something by Mozart, you can be sure that you will find a lofty flight of ideas, knowledge of the most unusual *Harmonie*, beautiful melody (only once in a great while somewhat studied), and striking modulations. In this masterpiece of his comic muse, these things become even more unmistakable the closer it gets to the Sublime.[7]

In the "lofty flight of ideas," and the evocation of the sublime, we can see the earliest signs of the nineteenth-century attitude, which lifted Mozart to romantic heights and thus distinguished his genius from that of Haydn. He had not yet reached unassailable status, and the occasional review still found problematic areas in his compositions (as they did with Haydn), but his name was increasingly invoked as a compositional standard. Thus the *Musikalisches Wochenblatt* observed that while fans of Italian instrumental music might enjoy one of Johann Paul Aegidius Martini's overtures, it certainly did not measure up to Mozart's standards.[8] When another composer copied his style, the imitation itself might invite censure, but the transgressor would at least get credit for using a good model.[9] And just as Haydn's name had entered iconic status by his association with Bach, now Mozart's accompanied Haydn's. For example, while criticizing Vanhal's variations for not having an individual style, the *Musikalisches Wochenblatt* softened the blow by observing they were not "the worst," noting that he seemed always to have a Haydn or Mozart model in mind.[10] In the 1790s, then, the attributes of creative genius continued to define compositional excellence.

The association of the characteristics of creative genius with the sublime in the Mozart review cited above does indicate that the vocabulary describing creativity had begun to assume a slightly metaphysical tinge. During the last quarter of the eighteenth century, the sublime became a favored topic in German philosophical discourse. In the *Allgemeine Theorie der schönen Künste*, Sulzer had emphasized its capacity to make us marvel at objects that the concepts of the imagination cannot encompass.[11] By 1790, Immanuel Kant had made it a cornerstone of aesthetics in his *Critique of Judgment* (see below). The increased references to the sublime in the review collective after about 1787 indicate a cognizance of this philosophical drift. Less ambiguously metaphysical is the reviewers' new willingness to use two terms associated with the highest powers of creative genius: *Phantasie* and the imagination. *Phantasie* became a particularly popular term of praise. In the *Allgemeine deutsche Bibliothek*, Schulz expressed astonishment at the "inexhaustibility of the sublime [Bach's] ideas and the wealth of his *Phantasie*, which seems to renew itself in every new work."[12] Though one might expect its application to an icon like Bach, it also turned up in reviews of composers like Kozeluch, praised by the *Musikalische Real-Zeitung* for his "bold flights of *Phantasie*," which included both a fullness in the *Harmonie* and a torrent of beautiful modulations.[13] The term "imagination" was used less commonly and more selectively, with Bach, Haydn, and Mozart accounting for half of the ten references. As the *Musikalische Korrespondenz* rhapsodized about Mozart: "Both these quartets are written with the passionate imagination and correctness that has long given Mozart the reputation as one of the best composers in Germany."[14] Creative genius, in all its manifestations, from simple invention to the imagination and *Phantasie*, had completely captured the market, as a 1796 review from the *Neue allgemeine deutsche Bibliothek* made clear:

[Türk's] sonatas are meant for beginners. They consist of short pieces that do not violate the rules of strict composition and have quite pleasant melody, but in which you cannot expect to find robust, surprising ideas, warm *Phantasie*, bold transitions and modulations, though those are fairly easy to reconcile with the simple melody and avoidance of [technical] difficulties. Twenty years ago, when ears had not been spoiled by the wealth of musical ideas now in common currency, these sonatas would have had more success than they will today.[15]

More than two decades of emphasis on originality, novelty and individual style had definitely had an effect, so that instrumental composition without them (however they were defined) could not hope for success with the musical public.

As always, what reviewers did *not* mention often reveals as much as what they chose to discuss: this *Neue allgemeine deutsche Bibliothek* review did not allude to any aspects of expressivity in dismissing Türk's sonatas as outdated. During the 1790s, expressivity remained as much in the shadows of creative genius as it had in the previous two decades, still garnering only half as many references and much less emphasis. Nor did very much change in the concepts associated with it. Of the terms with a direct connection to mimesis, Affect and Passion disappeared nearly entirely, except on the pages of the *Hamburgische neue Zeitung*, but reviewers continued to make occasional references to the expression of the sentiments, though usually in a very non-specific fashion. ("The reviewer followed with happy inner pleasure the beautiful, full torrent of sentiment and the imagination of the composer.")[16] For the most part, "character" remained indistinguishable from "style," though sometimes descriptive modifiers like "soft" or "charming" lent the word a more emotional, pictorial shading.[17] Only once, however, did a reviewer go so mimetically far as to praise a composer of non-programmatic pieces for his "portrayal of different characters," and even then simply included that trait in a list of other virtues that included "order, wealth of ideas, strict composition, beautiful modulation, and properly balanced phrasing."[18] As had been the case for the previous three decades, the review collective restricted its overtly mimetic criticism to characteristic pieces and overtures.

With regard to the aspects of non-mimetic expressivity discussed in the previous chapter, a belief in music's ability to touch the heart remained strong. Reviewers still hesitated to link that ability unequivocally to the specific expression of the sentiments, though certain styles and genres were thought particularly evocative. For example, the *Neue allgemeine deutsche Bibliothek* described a Mozart piano trio in E major (K. 542) as "ruled by splendor and magnificence," adding that if performed well, it could "transport the listener into a rapturous passion, and induce effects that even fully orchestrated symphonies often fail to produce."[19] Though the Splendid and the Magnificent would have made most lists of the Affects, being "ruled by" splendor and magnificence does not equal "expressing" them, nor does the resultant "rapturous passion" have much to do with the delicate arousal of a particular sentiment in a sensitive listener. Instead, the allusion to passion (*Feuer*) in connection with symphonies suggests a reference to the sublime, which Sulzer had particularly associated with the symphonic genre. As we saw above, the review collective had begun to link the sublime to the attributes of creative genius rather than the Affects. This association of music's ability to touch the heart with elements like variety and originality, discussed in the previous chapter, appeared a few times in the 1790s as well. A different reviewer for the *Neue allgemeine deutsche Bibliothek* thought that Joseph Seegr's organ toccatas – which should have touched the heart – instead left it "indifferent, tired, and cold," not because of any deficiency in expressing sentiments, but because of their lack of metric variety and an obstinate insistence on "a certain melodic monotony."[20] In the *Musikalische Korrespondenz*, a reviewer had described some Pleyel pieces as distinguished by "striking *Harmonie* and grand thoughts," then followed that observation by declaring that the Cantabile movement of the sextet, when performed correctly, "could touch even the most insensitive heart."[21] If some element besides striking *Harmonie* and grand thoughts gave the Cantabile that power, the reviewer did not mention them.

None of these attitudes toward expressivity differed markedly from the perceptions of the previous two decades, and the only definite change in the review collective's attitude was its new preference for a more restrained writing style. Deprived of the purple prose offered by Cramer in the *Magazin der Musik* (which ceased publication in 1789), the art of poetic, pictorial criticism of non-programmatic pieces went into decline. The *Hamburgischer Correspondent* did refer to a Haydn symphony as a tone painting (*Tongemälde*), and the *Musikalische Real-Zeitung* praised J. Fodor L'ainé for the soft character of his Romanza, which had "a sweet melody, like one a shepherd in the golden ages might have sung to a maiden in the glow of the sunset," but such verbal excesses remained isolated phenomena.[22]

In fact, a general atmosphere of restraint permeates this final period in the collective's development. Although they had never been blind to the dangers of unrestrained genius and unbounded emotion, reviewers increasingly sought to restore balance to the aesthetic scales by paying greater attention to criteria associated with reason. The earliest signs of this trend can be observed in the late 1780s, just as the cult of genius had reached its zenith, so that no clear dividing line between the two eras can be drawn. While more gradual than the change that ushered in the second period, the alteration in vocabulary and perspective are no less striking. For example, the set of

Mozart piano trios with the potential of inducing "rapturous passion" (above, page 137) had captured the reviewer's attention because the themes were "interesting and developed with much judgment," a rather cool and analytical observation.[23] In general, the collective began to emphasize the wisdom of knowing how to unite "the treasures of a fortunate *Phantasie* with the rules of art."[24] Symptomatic of this shift in attitude was the modest comeback made by compositional correctness as an aesthetic criterion. The *Allgemeine deutsche Bibliothek* led the way, particularly when Türk joined its instrumental reviewing staff in 1786. After proclaiming variations by Friedrich Wilhelm Rust to be among the best in the genre, and noting with approval several instances of counterpoint, Türk went on to quarrel with unacceptably harsh dissonances in the seventh measure of the first variation and the second measure of the seventh, then managed to sniff out two instances of parallel octaves, a phrase in which a five-measure antecedent lacked the proper balancing consequent, and more unacceptable dissonances in the sixteenth, seventeenth, and twenty-first variations.[25] Despite the often-mentioned didactic tendencies of the *Allgemeine deutsche Bibliothek*, this type of pedantic dissection had mostly disappeared from its pages during the 1770s and early 1780s, making the reappearance all the more noticeable. The strict approach continued unabated in the journal's successor, the *Neue allgemeine deutsche Bibliothek*, which definitely took the prize for the most painstaking attention to rule infractions; only in its columns did the lopsided one-paragraph-on-creativity to several-pages-on-errors style of reviewing reappear in full-blown fashion. However, even the *Neue Leipziger gelehrte Zeitung*, one of the more ebullient publications in the collective, showed some impatience with blatant disregard for the rules, complaining about how rarely young composers understood strict composition.[26] Though none of the reviewers from the late 1780s and 1790s plumbed the depths of sarcasm the way that Marpurg and his colleagues had done, the frequency with which they detailed compositional transgressions began to climb. Composers had of course not suddenly begun writing parallel fifths in 1786 anymore than they had stopped in 1770: the review collective had simply started noticing them again.

In the interim, however, musical style had changed considerably. If dissonance control, symmetrical phrasing, and orderly chains of related musical thoughts had regulated invention in the 1760s, they no longer sufficed as control mechanisms for compositions brimming with startling, distant modulations and a profusion of melodic novelties. Something had to call the outpouring of musical enthusiasm to order, and thus the concepts of unity and form entered review collective discourse. After falling to an all-time low in the early 1780s, when it appeared in less than 5 percent of all reviews, the aesthetic category of order/unity started to regain strength during the late 1780s, until by the 1790s, nearly 20 percent of reviews found occasion to mention and – quite frequently – to emphasize it. Some of the references rely on theoretical precepts from the 1760s and 1770s. In 1792, for example, Türk faulted Friedrich August Baumbach for his phrase structure because he often started internal phrases on downbeats after the initial phrase had opened with an anacrusis, citing Kirnberger's rule against doing so. He pointed out the awkward transitions that resulted and – echoing Kirnberger again – the damage done to the unity.[27] Traces of the linear concept of composition also remained. When the *Magazin der Musik* observed dryly in 1787 that Franz Anton Hoffmeister's Op. 4 piano sonatas had little originality, it took comfort in the pleasant ordering of their ideas (*Gedankenordnung*), a judgment on his talents repeated three years later by the *Musikalische Korrespondenz*.[28] Likewise, when the *Hamburgischer Correspondent* could not find any "so-called quirks of genius" in some of Samuel David Willmann's piano quartets, it found compensation in their "order, beautiful melody and strict composition."[29] Even if these look backwards more than forwards, the stance of the reviewers – if not genius, then at least order – represents a striking reversal and revision of the typical cry from the 1770s, which had been: "Who cares about rules in the face of genius?" While not as absolute as the earlier reformulation (genius continued as a primary aesthetic requirement), an adjustment of attitude had obviously occurred.

This adjustment also resulted in the growing number of references to unity (*Einheit*), that previously overlooked half of the "unity in variety" Enlightenment formula: "In his variations, Herr Fasch never retains the main theme's *Harmonie*, but instead varies it; still, there is so much unity in the midst of so much variety."[30] Tied both to the "connection of ideas," and a "feeling for order," unity was well suited to curb creative excess.[31] Thus, though the *Allgemeine Litteratur-Zeitung* gave its stamp of approval to Schwencke's Op. 3 sonatas, it urged him to make more rigorous choices among his ideas, "with a view to unity and economy."[32] In assessing three sonatas by August Eberhard Müller, the *Musikalische Monatsschrift* had first lauded the "full rush of sentiments and the imagination of the composer" (above, page 137). The reviewer confessed to being most impressed, however, with Müller's "striving for correctness and unity, amid all the luxuriant richness, the unceasing rush of the melody, and the abundant figures."[33] As had earlier been the case with creative genius, reviewers did not always precisely identify their terms. Forkel's comment that a young composer (who knew how to begin pieces better than he knew how to end them!) needed to learn about the "development of musical ideas and the unity of style" was not followed by advice on achieving that unity.[34]

In musical discussions of the late 1780s and 1790s *outside* the review collective, aesthetic philosophers persevered in finding ways to achieve affective or mimetic unity, not an easy task given the prevailing taste for diversity in compositional style. As discussed in chapter 1, the debate often centered around the question of whether or not a piece or movement could legitimately express more than one type of sentiment (or feeling or passion or character), a problem that Christian Gottfried Körner tried to solve in 1795 with his treatise, *Ueber Charakterdarstellung in der Musik* (see chapter 1, page 10). In the reviews of the late 1780s and 1790s, however, the only evidence of any attachment to mimetic unity in non-programmatic pieces comes from a handful of reviews in the *Magazin der Musik*, the journal most taken with the notion of affect and character. A 1785 review of some concertos by Leopold Kozeluch (signed with the letter "R.") had, for example, objected to several measures of one of the adagios because they broke with the general movement character:

The first Adagio would perhaps be worth more if the last four phrases in both solo sections were omitted; they seem to weaken suddenly the impression of ardor and the outpouring of the heart that the whole thing has. These four last measures don't suit the character of the whole very well. For most of the piece it is earnest, touching, heartrending, and then, when it should be fully developed, the entire stream of the earlier torrent of emotions is hemmed in by four measures that would fit into a merry Allegretto better. This strengthens the reviewer's opinion that every piece would be better if it adopted a definite character, or at least not a contradictory one.[35]

"R." went on at some length, elaborating a theory of character unity that closely paralleled the known views of Reichardt, as found in a later review in Reichardt's *Musikalisches Kunstmagazin*. There he alluded to the difficulty of portraying specific emotions clearly and argued against the inclusion of contradictory feelings in the same piece, concluding:

Frivolity and the tendency to melancholy can certainly coexist in a single person, but probably not in a single moment, or not in such swift alternation that they could be the object of artistic portrayal. Thus, their combination may well have moral truth, but certainly not aesthetic [truth].[36]

However, this review – the only one from the 1790s to uphold unambiguously the principle of mimetic unity – treated character pieces, all of which had a stated programmatic goal. The remaining references to character unity pertain to works without stated programmatic or mimetic intention, but they do not allow as clear a connection to mimesis. For example, though the *Musikalische Korrespondenz* praised the Allegro of an E flat sonata by Zinck

Table 7.1 *Periodicals with reviews, 1790–1798*

	New periodicals with reviews
5	*Augsburger musikalischer Merkur*, 1795
1	*Journal der Tonkunst*, 1795
	Author: Koch
36	*Musikalisches Wochenblatt/Musikalische Monatsschrift*, 1792
	Authors: C.S.; n.; J.F.; lbr.; F.
28	*Berlinische musikalische Zeitung*, 1793–1794
	Authors: Spazier
1	[1795] *Neue Leipziger gelehrte Anzeigen*, (1789)–1797
	Continuing periodicals with reviews
126	*Musikalische Real-Zeitung/Musikalische Korrespondenz*, (1788)–1792
	4 reprinted from *Hamburgischer Correspondent*
	Authors: Zx. (Johann Friedrich Christmann); D. H.; Or.;
	B**; Q.
3	*Musikalisches Kunstmagazin*, (1782), 1791
	Author: Reichardt
55	*Allgemeine deutsche Bibliothek*, (1765)–1794
	Authors: Knigge; Portman; Türk; Om.; Qr.; Qs.; Rz.
18	*Allgemeine Litteratur-Zeitung*, (1785)–1798*
	Authors: Reichardt
3	*Erfurtische gelehrte Zeitungen*, (1776)–1798*
	Authors: Eschtruth; M.; H.; T. H.
3	*Nürnbergische gelehrte Zeitung*, (1777)–1798*
	Authors: G.; Rg.
3	*Erlangische gelehrte Anmerkungen*, (1770)–1798
2	*Gothaische gelehrte Zeitungen*, (1774)–1798*
18	*Neue allgemeine deutsche Bibliothek*, (1793)–1798*
11	*Oberdeutsche allgemeine Litteraturzeitung*, (1788)–1798*
	Authors: D. N.; F—k; ß; A.; Fpk.; B. R.
1	*Tübingische gelehrte Anzeigen* (1783)–1798
1	*Wirzburger gelehrte Anzeigen*, (1786)–1798*
	Authors: Lehritter?
3	*Berlinische Nachrichten*, (1760)–1798*
	Authors: O.; Reichardt?
5	*Berlinische privilegirte Zeitung*, (1770)–1798*
	Authors: Reichardt?
47	*Hamburgischer Correspondent*, (1760)–1798*
	Authors: Leister; B*; R**; R—r

Table 7.1 (cont.)

17	Hamburgische neue Zeitung, (1767)–1798*
	Authors: Forkel?; E.

TOTAL REVIEWS: 387
                −4 reprinted
ACTUAL TOTAL: 383

Note: The date in brackets indicates the year in which the first instrumental music review appeared. The inclusive dates are the years of the journal's publication through 1798. An asterisk indicates the journal continued beyond 1798.

for its "unity of character and beautiful modulation" and described another movement as having a "tender character," we cannot be sure that the reviewer was not simply using character as a synonym for style.[37]

Whatever the interpretation, the review collective's lack of interest in exploring mimetic unity left it bereft of an organizing principle to counterbalance the love of variety and the unexpected. Increasingly, in the late 1780s and 1790s, reviewers turned to purely musical elements to accomplish that task, particularly the unity of tonality. In the review of Haydn's Op. 54 cited above, Türk had criticized the shift from C major to A flat major because it disturbed the unity of tonality (example 7.1). For Türk, the problem lay in Haydn's refusal to cadence firmly in the tonic before venturing so far afield, a concern shared by other reviewers. The Musikalische Korrespondenz chided Johann Brandl for his modulatory adventures at the very beginning of a piece, objecting that his shift to the minor mode in the seventh measure transgressed against tonal unity.[38] Comments like these indicate an awareness of larger formal issues (a subject to which we shall return below), but the collective also evaluated details of foreground chordal movements in terms of tonal unity. For example, the Neue allgemeine deutsche Bibliothek disapproved of a particularly harsh chromatic progression that featured a G# in the dominant of E minor, a C# in the dominant of A minor, and a G# in the dominant of D minor, not because it was "incorrect," as a reviewer two decades earlier might have done, but because it was contrary to the unity of tonality.[39] Whether picking at a surface-level chord progression or a structural-level modulation, reviewers now chose to frame the debate in terms of their new preoccupation, unity.

A simple desire for unity – by whatever means – does not necessarily entail any cognizance of form or overall structure, but when reviewers began to connect it with the concept of "totality" or "the whole" (das Ganze), they

Example 7.1 Joseph Haydn, String Quartet, Op. 54/2, Vivace, mm. 1–25

Example 7.1 (*cont.*)

seemed to be moving in that direction. The concept of a whole that comprises distinct parts distinguishes, in a very fundamental way, the nineteenth-century theoretical approach to formal structure from the eighteenth-century one of composition-as-orderly-process, where unity depended on the ordering and proper connection of individual phrases. When Koch published the third part of his composition treatise in 1793, he helped to bridge this theoretical gap. By observing contemporary instrumental practice, he constructed a compositional theory that emphasized architectonic period structure, which imposed a larger shape on the earlier concern with *Rhythmus*. He also described a basic, two-part instrumental form defined by modulation, thereby outlining a self-referential formal principle, shaped and guided not by mimetic principles (to which Koch himself paid only ritual homage), but by purely musical ones. Nearly a decade before this section of his treatise appeared, early signs of the change in perspective had already begun to appear in the review collective, some in the *Musikalische Real-Zeitung*, a journal with which he was associated.[40] Very likely, Koch both influenced – and was influenced by – the reviewers' discourse, yet another indication of the integral role the collective played in shaping German musical thought.

Of particular interest are those reviews that discussed pieces in terms of the connection and proportional relationship of the parts, ideas simply never mentioned before the late 1780s. Forkel, for example, thought that C. L. Becker needed to learn a little more about the "inner and outer relationship of the parts of a piece" (unfortunately not specifying what those should be).[41] In similar fashion, Türk approved of a set of Häßler's sonatas, finding them ruled by "the necessary agreement of the individual parts with the whole," though he held certain colorful passages in some of the Adagios to have little purpose.[42] The review of Schwencke in the *Musikalische Monatsschrift* cited at the beginning of this chapter had chided his youthful inattention to unity, then continued by observing that in one sonata, the opening section's second half did not connect well with its first.[43] The *Allgemeine Litteratur-Zeitung* made an even more explicit connection between unity and form in a review of some teaching pieces, missing "the requisite unity" in a Minuet because the second part did not "completely suit the first."[44]

Once again, the significance lies in the change in perspective, which addressed elements that had earlier gone unnoticed and reinterpreted others in a new light. Two examples should illustrate this point. In an otherwise very favorable review of a Mozart violin sonata (K. 481), a reviewer for the *Musikalische Real-Zeitung* made specific observations about proportional relationships:

The broken-chord section on the fourth page is in part too trite, in part too extended; and the second part too long in comparison with the first. To be sure, music has no exact rules in such cases, but you can see immediately that a difference of three and a half pages is not a true relationship.[45]

The sonata in question has a first part of 92 measures followed by a second of 160, the result of a substantial modulation after the double bar. Though not unprecedented in Mozart's output and certainly found in any number of Haydn's compositions, the resulting proportional relationship suddenly proved disturbing in an aesthetic atmosphere focused on such issues. Several years later, the *Musikalisches Wochenblatt* praised an Andante by Röllig as "simple, noble, and melodious," but found the first period somewhat repetitious, and commented that "it appears that many have only one form for everything." It complained further that both halves cadenced in the tonic, expressing the wish that the first part could have cadenced in the dominant, because as it was, the two parts lay there like separate pieces, and you could simply play the first part and leave it at that.[46] In the 1760s, Agricola or Marpurg would no doubt have ranted about the same tonic cadence, but would have attributed it to the pernicious influence of non-modulating Italians. The collective of the 1780s would have expounded on the lack of variety and striking modulations. The *Musikalisches Wochenblatt* did neither, choosing instead to frame its criticism in formal terms.

Since the recognition of a self-referential formal structure forms an integral part of the concept of absolute music, we might well ask why the review collective began to notice such things when it did. Why in the late 1780s and not in the 1770s or the 1760s? The impetus may in part have been purely musical. For one thing, reviewers and performers alike were being confronted with ever longer compositions that taxed the listeners' capacity for immediate comprehension. Several reviews thus equated excessive length with compositional failure; one in the *Musikalische Real-Zeitung* felt that a keyboard concerto by J. N. Denninger was too long "by a third" and urged him to limit himself to fifteen minutes in future works, so that he could keep his audience wanting more.[47] Moreover, if these longer pieces contained the requisite amount of variety, then musical anarchy loomed threateningly on the horizon. With its unrestrained admiration for the attributes of creative genius, the review collective had, if not created, at least contributed, to the birth of a monster. Sniping about parallel fifths and unprepared dissonances, while undoubtedly satisfying, would do nothing to solve the problem of musical control. Thus the collective had to search for different guidelines.

In its concern for unity and form, reviewers proved to be on the cutting edge of German intellectual debate in the late 1780s and 1790s, where the quest for self-referential formal structures was putting the final nails in the coffin of mimesis. For example, Goethe's 1788 article entitled "Einfache Nachahmung der Natur, Manier, Stil," published in *Der teutsche Merkur*, insisted that art should not be understood merely as an imitation of nature, but as a system in and of itself. Goethe believed that at its best, art should manifest its own logical structure, which could be inspired by the observation of the order of nature, without having to copy that order exactly.[48] This conception of an autonomous art that should be judged on its own internal rules of unity and form, which were analogous to – but not identical with – the rule of order in nature, delicately bridged the gap between eighteenth- and nineteenth-century aesthetic philosophy.[49] In the same year, with his treatise entitled *Über die bildende Nachahmung des Schönen*, Karl Philip Moritz laid the basis for what Carl Dahlhaus has labeled a classical aesthetic. Moritz strictly separated the art work itself from its effect and purpose, dismissing the latter as irrelevant, thus freeing art from any social function (something reviewers had been doing implicitly for decades). Like Goethe, he insisted that it should then be judged as a formal unity within its own self-referential system.[50] Thus, aesthetic pleasure would reside partly in the perception of musical form. However, Moritz also recognized the presence of irrational creative elements as being an indispensable aspect of aesthetics, setting up the conceptual pair of freedom (the equivalent of genius) and form.[51] The rational-versus-irrational tension implicit in the earlier rules-versus-genius debate had been set into a new framework that reinterpreted the manifestation of the rational. When Immanuel Kant published his *Critique of Judgment* in 1790, he also set up a dichotomous framework that allowed aesthetic worth to reside both in the Beautiful, which involved the perception of artistic form, and in the Sublime, which involved the cognizance of limitlessness and things beyond sensory perception. Schiller contributed further to the ongoing discussion in his investigation of the relationship between form and content, in effect placing the older "unity versus variety" conflict on a more metaphysical plane.[52] No matter how the irrational element of artistic or musical production was defined, unity and form had assumed the leading position for the rational.

Since the 1760s, the review collective had taken an active role in debating both the nature and balance of rational and irrational elements involved in musical composition in ways that paralleled contemporaneous discussions in other fields. It is not my intention here to argue that the reviewers led the conceptual way, nor conversely that they merely followed in the intellectual footsteps of greater individuals. If pushed, I would take the position that their remarks contributed another level to the ongoing larger discussion, and even that would divert me from my main point: the review collective prepared the conceptual field for the early nineteenth-century paradigm of music – first by adopting musically based standards of judgment, then by incorporating the elements of creative genius as essential criteria, by acknowledging instrumental music's expressive capacity, and finally by addressing issues of unity and form. All of these were necessary conditions for the acceptance of instrumental music as an aesthetically valid art form, as defined by the early nineteenth-century German romantics.

A small but essential element is still missing, however. Throughout this discussion I have sought to emphasize the practical nature of the reviewers' task and even made the point that the very absence of aesthetic speculation enabled them to view instrumental music from a different perspective. One might, for example, wish for some evidence that they eventually began to adopt a less prosaic view of their endeavors, particularly if they are to be seen as preparing the way for the extensive and speculative reviews of E. T. A.

Hoffmann and later critics. That evidence can be found in the new references to aesthetics. Before the 1790s, the word "aesthetic" had occurred only twice in collective discourse, in two extensive reviews by Cramer in the *Magazin der Musik*.[53] Both references had, however, simply mentioned the existence of the realm of aesthetics; usage in the 1790s actually tied the review collective's criteria to that realm and acknowledged instrumental music's aesthetic capacity. The *Erlangische gelehrte Anmerkungen* mused about whether it was as true of music as it was of poetry that a composition's continuing capacity to please required a higher degree of "aesthetic completion" the shorter it was.[54] While the reviewer did not take a position on the question, or specify what that completion might entail, and while the piece in question (Ludwig Cella's *Musicalische Blätter*) hardly seems worthy of such ruminations, the salient point is that "aesthetic completion" was a consideration at all. Two of Türk's reviews from the *Allgemeine deutsche Bibliothek* provide other information about the criteria that might count as aesthetic considerations; not surprisingly, those included modulation and tonal unity. In a review of some Johann Christoph Friedrich Bach sonatas, Türk complained about the distant modulations, then proceeded to observe: "However, this has become so common that it seems as if [composers] are intentionally disregarding unity, though for what aesthetic reason this reviewer cannot imagine."[55] His complaint about Haydn's tonal adventures (see above, page 143), maintained that because of the damage to unity, "it would be worth the trouble to seriously oppose [such modulations] and, using aesthetic principles, determine the circumstances under which they might be acceptable and useful."[56] Though somewhat pedantically done, Türk's invocation of aesthetic principles nonetheless signified the entrance of the musical criteria chosen by the collective into the realm of speculative aesthetics. A review in the *Musikalische Korrespondenz* of some keyboard trios by Clementi, while lacking Türk's specificity, made more of a linguistic leap towards the nineteenth century:

With a view to inner merit, this sonata deserves a place alongside the previous works of this excellent, profound composer . . . Everywhere you look there always reigns the same epic flight, always the same truth in character, a certain delicacy in the ordering and development of ideas, a rhythmic precision, and a certain lightness in the utilization of contrapuntal rules. These leave the most enduring impressions on the soul and awaken sentiments that bear witness to the highest aesthetic power of music.[57]

The reader is free to judge whether "epic flights" and "impressions on the soul" begin to approach the metaphysical world of Wackenroder's Joseph Berlinger. For my taste, the language of this review (like that of the Mozart review cited above, page 135) does move beyond even the most enthusiastic raptures about creative genius during the 1780s. But in the attribution of "aesthetic power" to a collection of instrumental pieces (also found in three other reviews in the magazine and its predecessor, the *Musikalische Real-Zeitung*), we catch an unmistakable whiff of the nineteenth century.[58]

Here too, we have the most telling intersection of the review collective's aesthetic criteria and its rhetorical orientation. From the very beginning, the two strands had subtly reinforced each other. The focus on correctness and elaborately worked-out *Harmonie* during the 1760s, when interpreted as an indication of compositional depth and profundity, clearly delineated the German style from that of the inferior Italian Other. The emphasis on genius that followed moved the discourse to a higher, more abstract plane, one appropriate for the evaluation of "true, genuine" music. Then, in the last years of the eighteenth century, the rhetorical invocation of "inner value" and "intrinsic worth" joined with the perception of "aesthetic power" to ground the once ephemeral, functionally oriented genres of instrumental music, investing them with an enduring substance that could bear metaphysical weight. When Tieck, Wackenroder, and Hoffmann came on the scene a few years later, the German world of music was ready for them.

8

Epilogue: segue to the nineteenth century

By 1799, when Tieck and Wackenroder's essays began the chain of aesthetic events that secured the aesthetic value of abstract, non-mimetic instrumental music, the German-speaking public had already had forty years to get used to the idea. In the same way that an advertising slogan can insinuate an under-lying message into the public consciousness much more effectively than a learned essay on consumer trends, the review collective had continuously hammered home the idea of an instrumental music that could and should be judged on its own terms. That task had been accomplished by 1798, the cutoff point for this study. I did not, however, choose that date simply to provide a tidy package of concepts neatly wrapped up before the publications of Tieck and Wackenroder in 1799; other signs indicate that the collective itself had approached a significant juncture in its development.

For one thing, it had begun to shrink. Only a single new non-music period-ical joined its ranks in the 1790s (and it provided only one review), a slump that contrasted markedly with the activity of the previous twenty years (see table 7.1). In the early part of the decade, many scholarly review journals began to curtail their music reviewing; beginning in 1795, the number of instrumental reviews fell precipitously, dropping from a total of 353 during the period from 1790 to 1794 down to only 28 between 1795 and 1798 (see table 8.1). Some of the suddenness resulted from the near total absence of music magazines in those years. The equally sharp decline in numbers for scholarly review journals followed the demise of the *Allgemeine deutsche Bibliothek*, which had always provided the bulk of reviews in that category of publication. Although the *Neue allgemeine deutsche Bibliothek* made a valiant critical effort, the eleven instrumental reviews it published between 1795 and 1798 could not compensate for the silence elsewhere. Leister's retire-ment as music reviewer for the *Hamburgischer Correspondent* (see chapter 2) would partially account for the lower numbers in political newspapers, but not for the fact that the other three in that category published no instrumental

Table 8.1 *Overview of the review collective*

Music magazines	Scholarly journals	Political newspapers
	1760s	
2 titles	8 titles	2 titles
47 reviews	70 reviews	15 reviews
	1770s	
2 titles	19 titles	4 titles
18 reviews	127 reviews	184 reviews
	1780s	
5 titles	18 titles	4 titles
167 reviews	151 reviews	149 reviews
	1790–1794	
4 titles	10 titles	4 titles
189 reviews	98 reviews	68 reviews
	1795–1798	
2 titles	6 titles	1 title
6 reviews	18 reviews	4 reviews

reviews at all during the period from 1795 to 1798. While finding new reviewers had never been easy (even the *Allgemeine deutsche Bibliothek* went
without instrumental reviews during the mid 1770s before a replacement for
Agricola was secured), the collective-wide disinterest in continuing the tradition is striking.[1]

That disinterest was perhaps forced upon the collective's journals by the
social upheaval and economic hardships that followed in the wake of the
French Revolution; then, as now, music may have been the first to go when the
budget ax fell. Editors also had fewer actual pieces to review because fewer
were being published. The *Allgemeines Repertorium der Literatur*, an early
German version of *Books in Print*, lists nine pages of music titles published
in Germany between 1791 and 1795, but a scant two pages for the period from
1796 to 1800.[2] Some of the decline in instrumental reviews in non-music
periodicals may also have come in response to changes in music style and
genre. Sonatas for keyboard, both solo and ensemble, had always made up the
bulk of instrumental music chosen for review, with concertos, symphonies
and string quartets following behind. "Serious" genres all, they could legitimately lay claim to the attentions of scholarly journals and columns, espe-

Table 8.2 *Genres reviewed*[a]

Genre	1760s %	1770s %	1780s %	1790–1798 %
Genres with declining numbers of reviews				
Solo keyboard sonatas	16	26	33	16
Basso continuo sonatas	5	5	0.5	0.5
Sonatas for keyboard and violin or flute	4	9	11	5
Sonatas for keyboard with violin and cello	0	8	11	3
Keyboard concertos	9	12	10	1
Symphonies	21	6	3	1
Symphonies in keyboard reduction	2	0	1	2
Genres with rising numbers of reviews				
String quartets	0	2	3	5
Opera overtures in keyboard reduction	0	1	1	9
Keyboard variations	3	2	7	15
Dance collections	1	2	1	8
Organ pieces	3	5	3	8

Note: [a]Collections of assorted keyboard pieces, combined vocal/keyboard collections, and various miscellaneous genres, such as flute duos and divertimentos, make up the bulk of the remaining types of pieces. Non keyboard concertos consistently made up about 1% of works reviewed.

cially when reviewers discussed them in aesthetic terms familiar to their readership. Moreover, because many posed only limited technical difficulties, the average dilettante could expect to master them and hence had an interest in reading about them before making a purchase. In the early 1790s, however, reviews of variations, dance collections, and keyboard reductions of orchestral works began to increase perceptibly in both music and non-music journals (see table 8.2). Perhaps not coincidentally, the level of difficulty in the "serious" genres had also started its slow, but inexorable rise. If there seemed to be little point in reviewing a sonata that few skilled amateurs could ever hope to play, the technically more accessible music offered little food for aesthetic thought. Though reviewers did, for example, try to address the aesthetic requirements of variations, they obviously had a difficult time moving beyond mere description. Dances offered even less of an opportunity for substantial evaluations, and few reviewers went beyond comments on the relative quality of the keyboard writing when discussing symphony and overture reductions. In other words, the music their readership could perform no longer met the substantive criteria required for inclusion in a scholarly journal or column.

Whatever the reason, from 1795 to 1798, the average interested musician, whether amateur or professional, had very little information or guidance about the latest instrumental music, so that when the *Allgemeine musikalische Zeitung* began publication in October of 1798, it had practically no competition. The *AMZ* eventually changed the face of music journalism in fundamental ways, but from the perspective of instrumental music reviewing, it began firmly in the tradition of the review collective.[3] It adopted the practice – familiar from scholarly review journals – of providing both extensive reviews (labeled *Rezensionen*) and short notices (*Kurze Anzeigen*) of newly published music. In the first volume (covering October 1798 through September 1799), the *Kurze Anzeigen* clearly continued the consumer-advising function of the review collective, though rarely imparting any interesting aesthetic observations. Significantly, the *Anzeigen* included a higher percentage of variations and dance collections than did the extensive reviews, which focused mainly on the "serious" genres of sonatas, concertos, symphonies, piano trios, and string quartets. Though the longer reviews surpassed in detail anything ever produced by the collective (in part because of the *AMZ*'s willingness to include extensive musical examples), they focused on similar issues and relied on the same aesthetic criteria.

In fact, *AMZ* reviewers picked up where their immediate predecessors had left off. The renewed attentiveness to compositional correctness noted in the previous chapter grew even stronger – no doubt aided and abetted by the possibility of using copious musical examples – while interest in expressivity remained low.[4] Reviewers also continued the obsession with creative genius and originality, criticizing a sonata by Joseph Wölfl for its too-close resemblance to one by Mozart, and praising the "richness, fullness, and beauty" and the "lofty flight of *Phantasie*" in Haydn's Op. 90 string quartets.[5] However, complaints about composers trying for something new but ending up with the merely bizarre – while not unknown earlier – seem to increase in the first volume of the *AMZ*, reflecting yet another critical approach to dealing with the excesses of creative genius.[6]

Particularly in the area of modulation, *AMZ* reviewers showed a definite preference for restraint, favoring compositions that "did not stray much into distant keys."[7] Though chromatic exploration was certainly not proscribed, the demands of tonal unity required that it be limited and not shockingly abrupt. One review remarked that a modulation from E flat major to E major was "somewhat striking, but because it was well-prepared (and thus not overly fussy or excessively drawn out), it imparted a certain freshness to the movement."[8] Beethoven ran afoul of these strictures when he published his Op. 12 violin sonatas, receiving a slap on the wrist for "striving after unusual modulations."[9] If we try to set aside our twentieth-century ears and step into the critical framework of the reviewer, the comment seems not unjustified, for all three sonatas display frequent pockets of chromaticism that go well beyond Haydnesque Neapolitan or flat mediant diversions. The opening Allegro vivace of No. 2 in A major, for example, takes twenty measures to modulate to the dominant, passing through F sharp minor, G major, and F major, before suddenly and chromatically alighting in an E major that is certainly not "well-prepared." Small wonder the reviewer felt that the young composer was trying too hard to be new and different.

Such comments also reflect the continuing preoccupation with unity, which continued unabated in the first volume of the *AMZ*. In the same way that they approved of smoothly prepared distant modulations, reviewers showed a special appreciation for the composer who could skillfully incorporate the most surprising ideas into a unified whole:

[Haydn's symphony] is easier to comprehend and somewhat less learned than other of his most recent works, but is just as rich in new ideas as they are. The element of surprise in music cannot be pushed any further than it is here by the sudden invasion of the minor-mode Turkish music in the second movement. Until that moment, you have absolutely no hint that Turkish instruments are going to be used in the symphony. But here you can see not only the inventive, but the circumspect composer as well. The Andante is namely nonetheless a whole; for even with all the pleasant and easy things that the composer introduces into the first section, in order to draw attention away from the idea of his coup, it is still designed and worked out like a march.[10]

Discussions of unity and form in the last years of the review collective had, like this Haydn review, generally focused on the internal structure of a single movement; now some signs point to a growing awareness of supra-movement unity. For example, in the critique of Wölfl's sonatas cited above, the reviewer had preferred the first two sonatas of the set because the third "did not make as good a whole," with too little attention paid to unity.[11] Another reviewer praised a symphony by Boccherini by describing how each movement related to the others:

The first, which begins with a slow movement in D minor leading to an Allegro in the major, followed by a pretty, characteristic Adagio that is resolved by a lively minuet, whereupon a short slow movement takes up the first Allegro and brings it to an end. The piece has much unity, and the reviewer would hold it to be the best.[12]

All these comments demonstrate a more sophisticated awareness of the different methods for achieving unity than anything produced by the review collective; nonetheless, the early *AMZ* reviewers were clearly building on the foundation laid by their predecessors.

They also continued the collective's rejection of the mimetic paradigm. One review did invoke the concept of mimesis in discussing the difference between a sonata and the lighter divertimento,[13] but that position was more than counterbalanced by a spirited defense of absolute instrumental music in a review of some early Mozart symphonies six weeks later:

A composer can show the most genius in this [instrumental] genre; for not only must he invent entirely on his own and give himself all his material, he is also restricted to the speech of tones alone. His thoughts have precision in and of themselves, without the support of poetry.[14]

Here we see clearly stated, for the first time in an instrumental review, the aesthetic advantage that accrued to music not bound by the constraints of language. The self-referential aesthetic criteria developed over forty years by the review collective had borne fruit.

It would hardly be appropriate, in a book that is drawing to a close, to take up a completely new issue, so I do not propose to begin an examination of the aesthetic criteria applied to instrumental music in the nineteenth century. But because E. T. A. Hoffmann played such an important role in the articulation of the power of abstract instrumental music, and because his early Beethoven reviews have occasioned so much comment and discussion, it might be appropriate to point out his debt to the eighteenth century. Both Peter Schnaus and Robin Wallace have discussed Hoffmann's appreciation of originality and his preoccupation with unity in the Beethoven reviews. Though they are at pains to distinguish his criticism from the previous "polarized system with little room for fine distinctions,"[15] we might also see him as simply continuing the expansion and exploration of aesthetic criteria I have described here. Even the poetic language that he gracefully intermingled with his detailed analytical prose, so often seen as hovering uneasily between an abstract and a programmatic conception of instrumental music, has earlier precedents. Instead of imagining the "winsome joy of the female soul" or "long wriggling earthworms," as Cramer was wont to do, Hoffmann describes the "character of anxious, restless longing," and conjures up a spirit world, the "realm of the mighty and immeasurable," to explain the power of Beethoven's Fifth Symphony.[16] Like Cramer had done nearly thirty years earlier, Hoffmann the poet is giving life to his criticism to keep from "simply breaking out in general exclamations or going into detail with barren lists of harmonic beauties, modulations, etc."[17] This recognition of Hoffmann's debts to his eighteenth-century predecessors should not, however, be perceived as diminishing his achievements in any way. With his inspired prose and perceptive analyses, he transformed, almost single handedly, the enlightened craft of music reviewing into the romantic art of criticism.

But just as viewing Hoffmann solely as the inheritor of an established tradition would distort and falsify his musical and literary significance, simply making the late eighteenth-century voices of the review collective into the precursors of a more noble and elevated nineteenth-century style of criticism belies their inherent worth. In the course of their humble task, they successfully dealt with many of the major musical issues that confronted audiences and performers in the German-speaking world. They wrestled with the value of counterpoint and "correct" composition when confronted with a style based on Italianate homophonic tunefulness. They developed an appreciation for the musical surprise and artfully disrupted symmetry that distinguishes the best of late eighteenth-century composition, but also came to address the problems those elements posed for compositional unity. Perhaps the voices best suited to answer Fontenelle and tell us "what the sonata wants" are indeed the ones that never even asked the question.

Notes

Introduction: *terms of discourse*

1 *Allgemeine musikalische Zeitung* XI/17 (25 January 1809), 268, review of Beethoven's 1808 concert. See also Scott Burnham's *Beethoven Hero* (Princeton University Press, 1995), p. 122.

2 Gudrun Henneberg, *Idee und Begriff des musikalischen Kunstwerks im Spiegel des deutschsprachigen Schrifttums der ersten Hälfte des 19. Jahrhunderts* (Tutzing: Hans Schneider, 1983), p. 200.

1 *What* does *instrumental music mean?*

1 "Ueber die Gewalt der Musik," *Gelehrte Beyträge zu den Braunschweigischen Anzeigen* XIII/85 (30 October 1773), 681–86; and XIII/86 (3 November 1773), 689–94. "Alle die Sinfonien, alle die Concerte, Quartetten, Sonaten, lassen uns beständig in ungewissen Empfindungen von muntern und traurigen herumirren, und wenn ein Stück aus ist, könnte man immer wie der berühmte Fontenelle fragen: *Sonate, que me veux tu?*"

2 *Magazin der Musik* II/2 (27 December 1786), 1145–78, review of the overture to Meisner's *Lob der Musik*. "Statt dessen hört man ein Clarinettensolo mit Fagotten, daß an sich recht gut ist, hier aber so steht, daß man sich nicht enthalten kann, zu fragen, *"que me veux tu?"*

3 *Allgemeine deutsche Bibliothek* CXI/1 (1792), 119–21, review of Friedrich August Baumbach's *Six Sonates pour le Clavecin ou Piano-Forte*. Jena: Librarie Académique. "Die übrigen fünf Divertimente u.s.w. können sie hingehen; allein, als Sonaten betrachtet paßt auch auf sie die bekannte Frage: *"Sonate, que veux tu de moi?"*

4 Maria Rika Maniates discusses the various categories of nature in "Sonate, que me veux-tu?: The Enigma of French Musical Aesthetics in the 18th Century," *Current Musicology* 9 (1969), 117–40.

5 Alexander Gottlieb Baumgarten, *Reflections on Poetry*, translated with an Introduction by Karl Aschenbrenner and William B. Holther (Berkeley and Los Angeles: University of California Press, 1954).

6 Robert T. Clark, Jr., *Herder: His Life and Thought* (Berkeley and Los Angeles: University of California Press, 1969), pp. 15–16.

7 Bellamy Hosler notes this connection to French mimetic theory in her *Changing Aesthetic Views of Instrumental Music in Eighteenth-Century Germany* (Ann Arbor, MI: UMI Research Press, 1981), p. 44.

8 Jean-Baptiste Du Bos, *Réflexions critiques sur la poësie et sur la peinture* (Paris, 1719); translated in Peter le Huray and James Day, eds., *Music and Aesthetics in the Eighteenth and Early Nineteenth Centuries*, abridged edn. (Cambridge University Press, 1988), p. 18. The treatise appeared in a German translation in 1761.

9 Le Huray and Day, *Music and Aesthetics*, p. 20.

10 Charles Batteux, *Les beaux-arts réduits à un même principe* (Paris, 1746); translated in Edward A. Lippman, ed., *Musical Aesthetics: A Historical Reader*, vol. I: *From Antiquity to the Eighteenth Century* (Stuyvesant, NY: Pendragon, 1986–90), p. 261. Later writers criticized Batteux for his failure to distinguish between representation and expression. See le Huray and Day, *Music and Aesthetics*, p. 32.

11 Lippman, *Historical Reader*, vol. I, p. 257; and John Neubauer, *The Emancipation of Music from Language: Departure from Mimesis in Eighteenth-Century Aesthetics* (New Haven, CT: Yale University Press, 1986), p. 170.

12 Boyé, *L'Expression musicale, mise au rang des chiméres*, translated in Lippman, *Historical Reader*, vol.I, p. 294.

13 Michel-Paul-Gui de Chabanon, *Observations sur la musique*, translated by Johann Adam Hiller in 1781 as *Ueber die Musik und deren Wirkungen* (Leipzig: Friedrich Gotthold Jacobäer und Sohn, 1781; rpt. Leipzig: Zentralantiquariat der deutschen demokratischen Republik, 1974), pp. 53–54; 133. This last chapter, incidentally, is not translated in Lippman, *Historical Reader*.

14 James Harris, *Three Treatises Concerning Art* (1744), in Lippman, *Historical Reader*, vol. I, pp. 177–84; Charles Avison, *An Essay on Musical Expression* (1752), in Lippman, *Historical Reader*, vol. I, pp. 185–99; Daniel Webb, *Observations on the Correspondence between Poetry and Music* (1769), in Lippman, *Historical Reader*, vol. I, pp. 201–14.

15 Douglas Ehninger, "On Systems of Rhetoric," *Philosophy & Rhetoric* 1 (Summer 1968), 131–44.

16 James Beattie, *Essay on Poetry and Music as They Affect the Mind* (1776), in Lippman, *Historical Reader*, vol. I, pp. 215–42; Thomas Twining, *Two Dissertations on Poetical and Musical Imitation* (1789), in Lippman, *Historical Reader* vol. I, pp. 243–58.

17 See Archibald Alison, *Essays on the Nature and Principles of Taste* (Dublin, 1790), in le Huray and Day, *Music and Aesthetics*, pp. 149–53; Adam Smith, *Essays on Philosophical Subjects* (London, 1795), cited in Kevin Barry, *Language, Music and the Sign: A Study in Aesthetics, Poetics and Poetic Practice from Collins to Coleridge* (Cambridge University Press, 1987), pp. 107–08. Barry finds

signs of the appreciation of instrumental music as an independent art scattered throughout eighteenth-century British literature. However legitimate they may be as support of his own thesis, they are too fragmented and isolated to have any significance here.

18 During the course of the century, the more personalized and nebulous "sentiments" began to supersede the rigidly categorized "passions" or "affections" in the discussion of expressivity. While I have treated this development more fully in chapter 4, it is not germane to my arguments here. For a full discussion of this semantic development see Georgia Cowart, "Sense and Sensibility in Eighteenth-century Musical Thought," *Acta Musicologica* 45 (1984), 251–66.

19 Carl Dahlhaus, "Romantische Musikästhetik und Wiener Klassik," *Archiv für Musikwissenschaft* 29 (1972), 168. Dahlhaus, like most commentators on the subject, gets caught up in the fact that the writing on music aesthetics stemmed from North Germany, while the most progressive music came from Austria and South Germany. I have addressed this point in chapter 2.

20 Rudolf Flotzinger and Gernot Gruber, "Die Wiener Klassik und ihre Zeit," in *Musikgeschichte Österreichs*, vol. II: *Vom Barok zur Gegenwart*, edited by Rudolf Flotzinger and Gernot Gruber (Graz: Verlag Styria, 1979).

21 Jakob de Ruiter, *Der Charakterbegriff in der Musik: Studien zur deutschen Ästhetik der Instrumentalmusik 1740–1850* (Stuttgart: Franz Steiner, 1989), p. 37.

22 Neal Zaslaw, *Mozart's Symphonies: Context, Performance Practice, Reception* (Oxford: Clarendon Press, 1989), p. 148; Nicole Schwindt-Gross believes that the concept of an independent musical work, free of any functional association, did not achieve widespread acceptance until after 1800. See her article "Parodie um 1800: Zu den Quellen im deutschsprachigen Raum und ihrer Problematik im Zeitalter des künstlerischen Autonomie-Gedankens," *Die Musikforschung* 41 (1988), 16–45.

23 James Webster, *Haydn's "Farewell" Symphony and the Idea of Classical Style* (Cambridge University Press, 1991), pp. 227ff.

24 Edward Lippman, *A History of Western Musical Aesthetics* (Lincoln and London: University of Nebraska Press, 1992), p. 60.

25 Peter Benary, *Die deutsche Kompositionslehre des 18. Jahrhunderts*, Jenär Beiträge zur Musikforschung, 3 (Leipzig: Breitkopf & Härtel), pp. 37, 57, 86; and Lippman, *Western Musical Aesthetics*, p. 75.

26 Hosler maintains that the distinction between imitation and expression was never clear in the literature she surveyed, and that the actual debate revolved around whether or not music had any meaning or was simply empty sound or empty pleasure. See her *Changing Aesthetic Views*, p. xvi.

27 With his usual irreverence, Peter Kivy notes that "The doctrine of the affections hangs on to most philosophical accounts of music [in the eighteenth century] like an extraneous barnacle; and this is as true of Kant at the end of the century as it is of Hutcheson at the beginning." *Osmin's Rage: Philosophical Reflections on Opera, Drama and Text* (Princeton University Press, 1988), p. 125, quoted in *The*

Fine Art of Repetition: Essays in the Philosophy of Music (Cambridge University Press, 1993), p. 250.

28 Lippman, *Western Musical Aesthetics*, p. 120. The composer Ernst Wilhelm Wolf, in an essay entitled "Was ist wahre Musik?" written for *Der teutsche Merkur* in March 1783, also proclaimed that the only true music was that which aroused those sentiments and passions that led to virtuous behavior (p. 234).

29 Christian Gottfried Krause, *Von der musikalischen Poesie* (1752), translated in Lippman, *Historical Reader* vol. I, pp. 171–72.

30 Lippman, *Western Musical Aesthetics*, p. 119.

31 *Ueber die Musik und deren Wirkungen*, p. 5.

32 "Ausdruck in der Musik," translated in le Huray and Day, *Music and Aesthetics*, p. 101.

33 Johann Nikolaus Forkel, "Genauere Bestimmung einiger musicalischen Begriffe: Zur Ankündigung des academischen Winterconcerts von Michaelis 1780 bis Ostern 1781," *Magazin der Musik* I/2 (8 November 1783), 1039–72. "Alle unsere Instrumentalstücke . . . sind gewissermaaßen nur Vorübungen, wodurch man sich zur Erreichung der höhern Zwecke geschickt zu machen sucht . . . Sulzer setzt sie daher unter den mancherley Gattungen von Music, in Absicht auf ihre Anwendung in die letzte Classe, und sagt: daß sie insgemein nichts weiter, als ein lebhaftes nicht unangenehmes Geräusch, oder ein artiges und unterhaltendes, aber das Herz nicht beschäftigendes Geschwätz vorstellen. Obgleich dieses Urtheil, welches den erwähnten Stücken allen Inhalt und Charakter von Bedeutung abspricht, sehr streng ist; so muß man es doch in verschiedenem Betracht gelten lassen."

34 *Magazin der Musik* I/2 (1783), 1139–78; See the reviews in the *Allgemeine deutsche Bibliothek* LI/1 (1782), 227–29; and the *Berlinische privilegirte Zeitung* 80 (4 July 1780), 444–45.

35 *Magazin der Musik* I/2 (1783), 1144–46. John Neubauer notes that the latter amounts to a personalization of the Baroque theory of affects. See his *Emancipation of Music from Language*, p. 74.

36 *Magazin der Musik* I/2 (1783), 1166. "Eine Symphonie, eine Sonate . . . muß die Ausführung Einer Leidenschaft, die aber freylich in mannigfaltige Empfindungen ausbeugt, muß eine solche Reihe von Empfindungen enthalten, wie sie sich von selbst in einer ganz in Leidenschaft versenkten, von aussen ungestörten, in dem freyen Lauf ihrer Ideen ununterbrochnen Seele nach einander entwickeln."

37 Carl Ludwig Junker, *Über den Werth der Tonkunst*, p. 12, quoted in Cowart, "Sense and Sensibility," p. 264.

38 See Wolfgang Seifert, *Christian Gottfried Körner: Ein Musikästhetiker der deutschen Klassik* (Regensburg: Bosse, 1960); and Robert Riggs, "'On the Representation of Character in Music': Christian Gottfried Körner's Aesthetics of Instrumental Music," unpublished paper read at the 1990 meeting of the American Musicological Society.

39 Christian Friedrich Daniel Schubart, *Ideen zu einer Ästhetik der Tonkunst*, edited by Jürgen Mainka (Leipzig: Verlag Philipp Reclam jun., 1977), pp. 261–68.

40 Heinrich Christoph Koch, *Versuch einer Anleitung zur Komposition*, vol. III (Leipzig: Adam Friedrich Böhme, 1782, 1787, 1793; facsimile edn., Hildesheim: Georg Olms, 1969). His *Musikalisches Lexicon* of 1802 betrays an equally conservative bent. However, Koch's actual discussion of compositional technique reveals a much more progressive orientation.

41 "Abhandlung vom musikalischen Geschmack, in einem Schreiben an einen Freund," *Unterhaltungen* I/1 (January 1766), 41–59. "Die Musik hat die Leidenschaften zu ihrem Gegenstande; diese soll sie durch regelmäßige Töne erregen und wieder besänftigen. Erreicht sie ihren Endzweck, so kann man sagen, daß sie gut sey: und so im Gegentheile, daß sie schlecht sey."

42 *Der Greis* (Leipzig) 9 (1768), 87. "Sie ist eine Ergötzung des Gemüths, sie hat einen Einfluß auf die Leidenschaften und ihre Verbesserung, und sie ist ein edler und anständiger Zeitvertreib für diejenigen, die ein geschäftloses Leben und viel Muße haben."

43 *Der teutsche Merkur* (December 1776), 212–28: "Beynahe alle Concerts, Solos, Simphonien u.d.gl. sind ohne Endzweck bearbeitet, und bezaubern doch, wenn sie gut vorgetragen werden – Wahr, sehr wahr . . . Allein folge denn hieraus, daß alle diese Stücke nicht noch besser gefallen würden, wenn man sie nach obiger Richtschnur behandelte; und würde das Vergnügen, das sie vielleicht jezt nur auf unsre Sinnen verbreiten, nicht im andern Fall weit mehr aufs Herz würken?"

44 "Ueber Musik, ihre Wirkung und Anwendung," *Flensburgsches Wochenblat für Jedermann* V/11 (12 September 1792), 85–88, and V/12 (19 September 1792), 89–95. "Musik ist nichts anders, als eine Folge von Tönen, die die Absicht haben, gewisse Empfindungen zu äussern, oder bey andern zu erwekken, oder zu unterhalten . . . So wie Musik durch Empfindung geboren wird, so wirket sie gleichfals nur auf die Empfindung; das Herz ist der eigentliche Flek, der durch Musik getroffen werden soll. Worte wirken auf den Verstand, und bringen in demselben besondre Vorstellungen hervor, die nachher freylich wieder auch Gefühl bewirken können. Aber Musik wirkt geradezu aufs Gefühl. So bald sie Empfindungen erregt, so hat sie ihren Zwek erreicht. Ein Werk der Tonkunst sey noch so brillant, noch so künstlich zusammen gewebt, es ist ein unächtes Produkt der Kunst, wenn nicht Empfindungen dadurch erregt werden . . . Die bloße Instrumental=Musik kan schon, für sich allein, sehr lebhaft wirken: Eine schön ausgeführte Haydnische Sonate, was vermag die nicht? Aber es liegt doch in dieser Art von Musik immer viel Vages, Zweydeutiges, Unbestimmtes – und es gehört immer ein gewisser Grad musikalischer Bildung dazu, um einen ächten Genuß herauszubringen. Solche Sachen sind, wie ein gewisser Künstler sich ausdrükt, einen artigen unterhaltenden Geschwäz gleich, das man wol mit Wohlbehagen, aber ohne Interesse anhört. Sie sind mehr Gaukeley, als Nahrung des Herzens."

45 Thomas Kuhn, *The Structure of Scientific Revolutions*, 2nd edn. (University of

Chicago Press, 1970). Kuhn's use of the term is not always consistent, as he acknowledges in a postscript to the second edition, pp. 181–91.

46 Kuhn, *Scientific Revolutions*, pp. 68–69.

47 Kuhn, *Scientific Revolutions*, p. 37.

48 Kuhn, *Scientific Revolutions*, p. 82.

49 Kuhn notes that the crisis signaling the demise of the old paradigm is often characterized by "proliferation of versions" of the theory at its center (*Scientific Revolutions*, p. 71). We have already seen the variety of aesthetic theories attempting to accommodate mimesis that appeared toward the end of the eighteenth century.

50 Kuhn, *Scientific Revolutions*, pp. 84–85; 149. In aesthetics, for example, issues of expressivity did not go away, but they took place on a different plane, one where instrumental music could be taken seriously. Carl Dahlhaus observes that complaints about music's vagueness can also be found in the nineteenth century, in the writings of Friedrich Theodor Vischer and Gervinus. See his *Esthetics of Music*, translated by William Austin (Cambridge University Press, 1982), p. 30.

51 Kuhn, *Scientific Revolutions*, p. 85.

52 Kuhn, *Scientific Revolutions*, p. 90.

53 Cited in Neubauer, *Emancipation of Music from Language*, p. 199. "Symphonien" appeared in *Phantasien über die Kunst für Freunde der Kunst*, a collection of essays by Wilhelm Heinrich Wackenroder. Tieck published the volume after Wackenroder's death and included some of his own work written under Wackenroder's influence. See Edwin H. Zeydel, *Ludwig Tieck, the German Romanticist* (Princeton University Press, 1935; rpt. Hildesheim: Georg Olms, 1971).

54 Wilhelm Heinrich Wackenroder, *Phantasien über die Kunst für Freunde der Kunst* (1799), translated in Lippman, *Historical Reader*, vol. II, *The Nineteenth Century*, pp. 13, 24.

55 Le Huray and Day, *Music and Aesthetics*, p. 187. Herder had been deeply involved in various aspects of German aesthetic debate since the 1760s (see chapters 5 and 6), but without involvement in the discourse on mimesis.

56 Johann Gottfried Herder, *Kalligone* (Weimar, 1800), translated in le Huray and Day, *Music and Aesthetics*, p. 190. Herder's purpose here was to respond to and take issue with Kant's *Critique of Judgment*.

57 Le Huray and Day, *Music and Aesthetics*, pp. 190–91.

58 Le Huray and Day, *Music and Aesthetics*, p. 192.

59 *Allgemeine musikalische Zeitung* IX/43, IX/44, translated in le Huray and Day, *Music and Aesthetics*, p. 200.

60 *Allgemeine musikalische Zeitung* IX/43, translated in le Huray and Day, *Music and Aesthetics*, p. 201.

61 E. T. A. Hoffmann, review of Beethoven's Fifth Symphony, *Allgemeine musikalische Zeitung* XII/40 (4 July 1810), 630–42; XII/41 (11 July 1810), 652–59. "Wenn von der Musik als einer selbstständigen Kunst die Rede ist, sollte immer nur die

Instrumentalmusik gemeint sein, welche jede Hülfe, jede Beimischung einer andern Kunst verschmähend, das eigentümliche, nur in ihr zu erkennende Wesen der Kunst rein ausspricht. Sie ist die romantischste aller Künste, – fast möchte man sagen, allein *rein* romantisch. – Orpheus' Lyra öffnete die Tore des Orkus. Die Musik schließt dem Menschen ein unbekanntes Reich auf; eine Welt, die nichts gemein hat mit der äußern Sinnenwelt, die ihn umgibt, und in der er alle durch Begriffe bestimmbaren Gefühle zurückläßt, um sich dem Unaussprechlichen hinzugeben. Wie wenig erkannten *die Instrumentalkomponisten* dies eigentümliche Wesen der Musik, welche versuchten, jene bestimmbaren Empfindungen, oder gar Begebenheiten darzustellen, und so die der Plastik geradezu entgegengesetzte Kunst plastisch zu behandeln!"

62 Kuhn notes the common phenomenon that new scientific discoveries often occur simultaneously in different laboratories (*Scientific Revolutions*, p. 65).

63 Meyer Howard Abrams, *The Mirror and the Lamp: Romantic Theory and the Critical Tradition* (New York: Oxford University Press, 1953). Gudrun Henneberg makes a similar argument in her *Idee und Begriff des musikalischen Kunstwerks im Spiegel des deutschsprachigen Schrifttums der ersten Hälfte des 19. Jahrhunderts* (Tutzing: Hans Schneider, 1983). While she emphasizes the new importance accorded independent, abstract, instrumental music, she also asserts that nineteenth-century aesthetics regarded the "subjectivity of human feeling as being the content and subject of the work of art, setting the concept of feeling at the center of musical understanding" (p. 114).

64 Geoffrey Barraclough, *Main Trends in History*, expanded and updated by Michael Burns (New York and London: Holmes & Meier, 1991), p. 38.

65 Fernand Braudel, *On History*, translated by Sarah Matthews (University of Chicago Press, 1980), p. 31.

66 Barraclough, *Main Trends in History*, p. 39.

67 Lawrence Stone, *The Past and the Present* (Boston, London, and Henley: Routledge & Kegan Paul, 1981), pp. 19–20.

68 Stone, *The Past and the Present*, pp. 79, 86.

69 George G. Iggers sees a new recognition of the role of cultural factors, including language and rhetoric, in influencing political and economic change rather than in being influenced by them. See his essay "Rationality and History" in *Developments in Modern Historiography*, edited by Henry Kozick with an Introduction by Sidney Monas (New York: St. Martin's Press, 1993), pp. 19–39.

70 Neubauer, *Emancipation of Music from Language*, p. 193. His approach recalls the ideas of the literary theorist Viktor Shklovskii, who proposed that a culture will for a time be dominated by a group of ideas that eventually lose favor, but never disappear entirely and can eventually re-emerge and regain their former prominence. See Robert C. Holub, *Reception Theory: A Critical Introduction* (London and New York: Methuen, 1984), p. 22.

71 This connection appears in several publications, including *Beethoven*, 2nd edn. (Laaber: Laaber Verlag, 1988), pp. 102–04; *Esthetics of Music*, p. 27; and "E. T.

A. Hoffmanns Beethoven-Kritik und die Aesthetik des Erhabenen," *Archiv für Musikwissenschaft* 38 (1981), 79–92. Sulzer is also invoked in connection with the sublime by James Webster in *Haydn's "Farewell" Symphony*, p. 163.

72 Henneberg, *Idee und Begriff*, pp. 19–22.

73 Hosler, *Changing Aesthetic Views*, p. 35. Mark Evan Bonds argues convincingly that the eighteenth century's use of "idea" for a musical theme "reflects the growing belief in an inherent, self-referential meaning within musical works that have no text." See his *Wordless Rhetoric: Musical Form and the Metaphor of the Oration* (Cambridge, MA and London: Harvard University Press, 1991), pp. 164–9.

74 Ludwik Fleck, *Genesis and Development of a Scientific Fact*, translated and edited by Thaddeus J. Trenn and Robert K. Merton (University of Chicago Press, 1979), p. 39. Fleck's monograph originally appeared in 1935 as *Entstehung und Entwicklung einer wissenschaftlichen Tatsache. Einführung in die Lehre vom Denkstil und Denkkollektiv*. Kuhn acknowledges that some of the "almost unknown" monograph's ideas "anticipate" his own (*Scientific Revolutions*, pp. vi–vii), without indicating any specific indebtedness. Though the similarities in concepts are striking (a fact both men would attribute to the collective nature of scientific thought), Fleck advocates a gradual shift of "thought-style" as opposed to Kuhn's paradigm revolution. Conflating the two approaches helps address certain criticisms of Kuhn discussed below.

75 I am grateful to Dr. Thomas Cornell, Assistant Professor in the History of Science at the Rochester Institute of Technology, for this insight into recent critiques of Kuhn's work. For Fleck's ideas see *Genesis and Development*, pp. 98–125, and his "The Problem of Epistemology [1936]," translated from the Polish in *Cognition and Fact: Materials on Ludwik Fleck*, edited by Robert S. Cohen and Thomas Schnelle (Dordrecht, Holland: D. Reidel, 1986), pp. 79–112.

2 Answering with a unified voice

1 "Kritischer Entwurf einer musikalischen Bibliothek," in *Wöchentliche Nachrichten* III:1 (4 July 1768), 7. "Diese periodischen Schriften haben in der That das gute gestiftet, daß man die Musik wieder als eine Wissenschaft, wovon sich eben so wie von allen andern Wissenschaften urtheilen läßt, anzusehen anfängt. Man giebt ihr in den kritischen Journalen und gelehrten Zeitungen mit Vergnügen den Platz, der ihr neben andern wissenschaftlichen Dingen gehört. Besonders verdient von dieser Seite die allgemeine deutsche Bibliothek ein vorzügliches Lob. Die Leipziger gelehrten Zeitungen machen sichs ebenfalls zur Pflicht die neuen heraus gekommenen Schriften und Werke, welche die Musik angehen, anzuzeigen, und zu beurtheilen."

2 *Unterhaltungen* VII/3 (March 1769), 266–71, review of Hiller's *Wöchentliche Nachrichten*, vol. III. "Was sollen die Leipziger Zeitungen S. 7. zur musikalischen Kritik helfen? Sie urtheilen selten und gewöhnlich seicht über Musikalien."

3 *Nürnbergische gelehrte Zeitung* 23 (20 March 1778), 186–89, review of Forkel's *Musikalisch-kritische Bibliothek.* "Der H. [Forkel] unternimmt ein nützliches Geschäft, musikalische Schriften mit Kritik bekannt zu machen . . . Ein noch ziemlich brachliegendes Feld, das zumal in unsern Zeiten einer fleißigern Kultur bedarf und vor vielen andern würdig ist! . . . Man schreibt für Gelehrte und Ungelehrte, und die größere Zahl der letztern, deren Beyfall hier allerdings in Betrachtung zu ziehen ist, räth oft den mässigern Gebrauch des Tiefsinns und der demonstrativischen Schreibart."

4 *Erfurtische gelehrte Zeitungen* 34 (18 July 1795), 269–74, review of Heinrich Christoph Koch's *Journal der Tonkunst* (Erfurt: Keyser, 1795). "Zu einer Zeit, wo unsere Meßkatalogen beinahe um die Hälfte mit Zeitschriften angefüllt sind, war es doch etwas Trauriges für den Musikfreund, auch nicht ein musikalisches Journal zu sehen, welches einigermaßen den Faden der Kunst= und Künstlergeschichte unterhalten hätte. Um es nicht so weit kommen zu lassen, hatte man noch vor einiger Zeit, selbst in dem großen, an Liebhabern reichen Berlin, zwey Jahre hindurch, in einer Wochenschrift, Montasschrift und endlich in musikl. Zeitungen, alle Formen versucht. Aber umsonst, jeder neue Versuch scheiterte! Sogar erreichten die Zeitungsblätter nicht einmal das Ende des Jahres! – Also wäre die arme Musik so ganz zum Amüsement und Spielwerke herabgesunken? Wäre nichts mehr als Klimperey? Also fänden sich untern den Tausenden ihrer Liebhaber und Verehrer, nicht so viel gebildete Köpfe, als zur Unterhaltung eines Journals gehören, welche im Stande wären, die Musik auch von ihrer wissenschaftlichen, eben so angenehmen und unterhaltenden als nöthigen und nützlichen Seite, zu treiben?"

5 See the Epilogue for a discussion of the role the *Allgemeine musikalische Zeitung*, which began publication in October of 1798, played in signaling the beginning of a new era in music reviewing.

6 Joachim Kirchner, *Das deutsche Zeitschriftenwesen: Seine Geschichte und seine Probleme*, vol. I, *Von den Anfängen bis zum Zeitalter der Romantik*, 2nd rev. edn. (Wiesbaden: Otto Harrassowitz, 1958), p. 115.

7 *Allgemeine deutsche Bibliothek* I/1 (1765), ii. "Diese sind in Deutschland in vielen Städten, zum Theil in kleinen Städten, wo nicht einmal ein Buchladen befindlich ist, zerstreuet, und Ihnen ist also sehr damit gedienet, zuverläßige Nachrichten von den neuen Büchern und von ihrem wahren Werthe zu erhalten."

8 D. W. Krummel and Stanley Sadie, eds., *Music Printing and Publishing*, The Norton/Grove Handbooks in Music (New York and London: W. W. Norton, 1990), pp. 28–31.

9 *Neue Zeitungen von gelehrten Sachen* 97 (5 December 1763), 773–75. "Wir werden von Zeit zu Zeit aufgefordert, in unsern Blättern der Musik zu gedenken, seitdem die Noten und Charaktere derselben ein Gegenstand der Druckerpressen geworden sind. Wir thun es um so viel lieber, da wir dadurch eine Wissenschaft, die von vielen, entweder aus Unwissenheit, oder aus Vorurtheilen, für ein bloßes Handwerk angesehen wird, in demjenigen Range bestätigen, den sie von Alters

her unter anderen Wissenschaften behauptet hat." This review was reprinted in the *Frankfurtische gelehrten Zeitungen* in the issue of 30 December 1763, pp. 523–24. See below for a discussion of reprinted – or plagiarized – reviews.

10 In identifying and locating periodicals, I relied on two indispensable bibliographic tools: Gert Hagelweide's *Deutsche Zeitungsbestände in Bibliotheken und Archiven* (Düsseldorf: Droste Verlag, 1974) and Joachim Kirchner's *Die Zeitschriften des deutschen Sprachgebietes von den Anfängen bis 1830*, the first in his four-volume *Bibliographie der Zeitschriften des deutschen Sprachgebietes bis 1900* (Stuttgart: Anton Hiersemann, 1969). Kirchner's categories have been revised and refined by more recent scholarship. (Despite the publication date, most of his work was done before World War II.) In using the rubric "scholarly review journal," I am following the lead of the Zeitschriftenindex, an undertaking of the Akademie der Wissenschaften at the University in Göttingen. This project, headed by Klaus Schmidt, will index the reviews in 173 of these journals, focusing on the years 1688 to 1784, and has a planned completion date of 2020.

11 Dagmar Schenk-Güllich, "Anfänge der Musikkritik in frühen Periodika. Ein Beitrag zur Frage nach den formalen und inhaltlichen Kriterien von Musikkritiken der Tages- und Fachpresse im Zeitraum von 1600 bis 1770" (Ph.D. diss., Friedrich-Alexander-Universität, Erlangen-Nürnberg, 1972), pp. 85–98. I wish to thank Professor Dr. Friedhelm Krummacher at Christian Albrechts-Universität in Kiel, Germany, for bringing this source to my attention.

12 *Kritische Briefe* II/82 (17 October 1761), 141–42, review of Georg Christoph Wagenseil's *Tre Divertimenti per Cimbalo*. Nicolai, 1761; and his *VI. Divertimenti da Cimbalo*, Op. 1–3. Vienna: Agostino Bernardi, 1753. "Herr Wagenseil, der mit der Menge seiner Sachen nicht wenig Aufsehen macht, soll, wie mich jemand versichert, gar artig auf dem Flügel spielen, und zugleich, in Ansehung seines persönlichen Umganges, ein sehr liebenswürdiger Mann seyn. Ruhms genug für ihn! Aber seine Composition? Sie würden, wenn sie auch in Ansehung der drey zu einem Tonstücke erforderlichen Stücke, der Harmonie, Melodie und Rhythmik, regelmäßig wären, dennoch nur mittelmäßig gut seyn, indem sich zur Känntniß der Regeln annoch drey Stück unumgänglich gesellen müssen, wenn etwas vortrefliches herauskommen soll, ein schöpferischer Geist, eine feine Beurtheilung, und ein arbeitsamer Kopf."

13 *Allgemeine deutsche Bibliothek* LXXI/1 (1787), 118. He also adopted a "simplified" approach to spelling that omitted all unnecessary, unsounded letters, using "di" and "si" instead of "die" and "sie," "Jarzal" instead of "Jahrzahl," for example.

14 *Allgemeine deutsche Bibliothek* LIII/1 (1783), 141–42. "Man sieht, Hr. R. hat verschiedene Grundsätze stark empfunden, die sonst schon bekannt und gesagt sind, und in denselben pflichtet man ihm gern bey. Aber er hat auch verschiedene, die ihm eigen sind . . . Wir wünschten wirklich, da H. R. untern die wenigen Schriftsteller gehört, welche musikalische kritische Werke schreiben können, daß er mehr auf seine Leser, als auf sich selbst sehen wollte. Es hilft nicht, wenn er sich

gleich auf seine Empfindung beruft, wenn er gleich die Veranlaßung mancher von seinen hier gelieferten musikalischen Stücken erzählt. Die Erzählung kann unmöglich den Leser in eben die Empfindung setzen, welche der Autor gehabt hat."

15 *Magazin der Musik* I/1 (1783), 29–56; review of the *Musikalisches Kunstmagazin*.

16 See the preface to the *Magazin der Musik* (I/1 [1783], x), where Cramer observes that while Forkel wrote the *Musikalische Bibliothek* by himself, he has chosen to follow Hiller's example instead.

17 Ferdinand Krome, *Die Anfänge des musikalischen Journalismus in Deutschland* (Leipzig: Pöschel & Trepte, 1896), pp. 59–60.

18 *Allgemeine deutsche Bibliothek* VII/2 (1768), 115–16. "Bey . . . der Anzeige musikalischer Werke, äussern die Hrn. Verf. einige Verlegenheit über die Art der Abfassung ihrer Recensionen; weil sie sich dabey leicht, entweder einen und den andern Verf. (denn die meisten Musiker sind ein *genus irritabile* . . .) oder die Wahrheit zum Feinde machen könnten. Aber, wir rathen ihnen, nur auf die Beybehaltung der Gewogenheit der Wahrheit zu sehen, ohne sich um jener ihre Gunst zu bekümmern. Zudem haben sie ja noch den Trost, daß nicht alle Musiker, das was sie gern gesagt haben wollten, selbst zu Papiere bringen können . . . Folglich haben sich die Herren Verf. doch vor allzuvielen Zänkereyen nicht gar zu sehr zu fürchten Ursach."

19 *Berlinische musikalische Zeitung* 46 (30 November 1793), 183, review of Anton Groene's *Zwölf Serenaten für das Klavier oder F.P. mit einer theils obligaten, theils begleitenden Violin oder Flöte auch Bratsche oder Violoncell.* Berlin: Neue Musikhandlung. "Kleine Klimpereien für Weiber und weibische Männer." For a discussion of the occasional misogynist outbursts by reviewers, see chapter 3.

20 *Musikalische Real-Zeitung* II/15 (15 April 1789), 113–14, review of Friedrich Schmoll's *Trois Sonates pour le Clavecin ou Piano-Forte avec l'Accompagnement d'un Violon & Violoncelle*, Op. 2. Speier: Bossler. "Es gehört, sagt Sulzer, unstreitig viel Genie, Wissenschaft und eine besonders leicht fängliche und harrende Empfindbarkeit dazu, gute Sonaten zu machen, Eigenschaften, die wir an dem Herrn Verf. des angezeigten Sonatenwerks bei nahe in jeder vermißten. Schon aus dem flüchtigen Ueberblik kann man sich sogleich überzeugen, daß Herr S. noch nicht einmal einen Begriff von einer guten musikalischen Periodologie hat . . . Man könnte zwar Herrn S. dieses noch zu gut halten, wenn auf der andern Seite seine Arbeit einiges Interesse hätte: aber Rec. fand nicht einen Gedanken darinn, der sich durch Reiz der Neuheit an sich selbst, oder durch eine neue Darstellung, wie in den Werken eines Haydn, Kozeluchs u.a. auszeichnet . . . Ueberhaupt ist Herr S. mit der eigentlichen Beschaffenheit der Harmonie und mit den Regeln des gesunden Geschmaks viel zu wenig bekannt, als daß wir seine Produktionen auch nur unter die mittelmäsigen [*sic*] rechnen könnten und nach dieser zwoten Probe zu urtheilen, dürfte es der Herr V. auch schwerlich jemals so weit bringen, daß er mit grösseren Kompositionen sein Glük machen wird, weil es ihm überdies noch an der ersten dazu erforderlichen Eigenschaft, nemlich an der Gabe der Erfindung

fehlt. Daher auch die so häufige Wiederholungen in diesen Sonaten, die oft bis an Ekel grenzen. Zx."

21 For the relationship of music publishers and review journals in the early nineteenth century, see the forthcoming work by Axel Beer.

22 *Hamburgischer Correspondent* 21 (5 February 1760). "Diese musikalische Wochenschrift verdienet um desto eher, daß wir ihrer gedenken . . . weil die Verfasser auf mehr als eine Art von Lesern ihr Augenmerk gerichtet, und sowol dem Liebhaber, als dem Ausüber von Profeßion zu dienen gesucht haben."

23 *Magazin der Musik* I/1 (1783), iii–iv.

24 *Allgemeine deutsche Bibliothek* LIII/1 (1783), 141–42; *Magazin der Musik*, preface to the first issue, I/1 (1783), iii–iv. Reichardt published another issue of the journal nine years later, in 1791.

25 *Neue allgemeine deutsche Bibliothek* XII/2 (1794), 520. "Wer kann jedoch, bey einem so gemischten Lesepublikum, die Wünsche eines jeden Individuums völlig befriedigen!"

26 *Russische Bibliothek, zur Kenntniß des gegenwärtigen Zustandes der Literatur in Rußland* II, 215. The puzzle minuet is reviewed in vol. III, p. 411.

27 *Göttingische gelehrten Anzeigen* 163 (15 October 1785), 1633–34, review of Wilhelm Christoph Bernhard's *Ein Präludium und drey Sonaten*. Leipzig: Breitkopf, 1785. "Die Sonaten sind zwar mehr in moderner Form geschrieben, aber sehr reich an reizenden Melodien, Modulationen und originelle Wendungen. Mehr verstattet der Raum und die Absicht dieser Blätter nicht, von diesem Werke zu sagen."

28 Kirchner, *Das deutsche Zeitschriftenwesen*, pp. 121–23.

29 *Wahrheiten die Musik betreffend, gerade herausgesagt von einem teutschen Biedermann* (Frankfurt am Main: Bey den Eichenbergschen Erben, 1779), p. 27.

30 *Frankfurter gelehrte Anzeigen* III/61–62 (2 August 1774), 514–15, review of C. P. E. Bach's *Sex [sic] Sonate per il Clavicembalo Solo all Uso delle Donne* [Wq. 54]. Riga: Hartknoch, 1773. "Für Damen? – So stehts auf dem Titel. Ich glaube aber daß auch Mannspersonen Ehre damit einlegen können. Wenn diese Sonaten aber doch für den schönen Theil der Schöpfung bestimmt seyn sollen; so laß ich mirs gefallen. Aber wenn ich einmal in die Versuchung kommen sollte; wenn Emanuel Bachens neue Sonaten auf den Pult gelegt werden; wenn sich eine Tochter Diderots fertig macht sie zu spielen; dann stehl ich mich weg. – Mit meinem poetischen Herzen – würd' ich wie Wachs zerschmelzen – Hingerissen von der göttlichen Macht der Harmonie, von der Markdurchdringenden Kraft dieser Töne – von einer Psyche an dem Klavier ausgeübt – horcht' ich – und stünd schnell thränend."

31 Marlies Prüsener, "Lesegesellschaften im 18. Jahrhundert. Ein Beitrag zur Lesergeschichte," in *Archiv für Geschichte des Buchwesens*, vol. XIII, edited by Bertold Hack, Bernhard Wendt, and Marietta Kliess (Frankfurt am Main: Buchhändler-Vereinigung, 1978), p. 429.

32 *Hamburgische Nachrichten aus dem Reiche der Gelehrsamkeit* II/48 and 49 (11

February 1774), 337–38. "Die Erfurtische gelehrte Zeitung ist ein Geflicke von Lappen . . . So viel sieht man offenbar, daß diese Recensenten keine einzige Wissenschaft recht gelernt haben." The same journal referred to Friedrich Nicolai, the editor of the *Allgemeine deutsche Bibliothek,* as a "Halbgelehrter" (half-scholar), an insult that Nicolai brushed off in a preface to the *Allgemeine deutsche Bibliothek*'s vol. XII/1 (1770), vi.

33 *Deutsche Zeitungen des 17. bis 20. Jahrhunderts,* edited by Heinz-Dietrich Fischer (Pullach: Verlag Dokumentation, 1972), p. 33; Margot Lindemann, *Deutsche Presse bis 1815: Geschichte der deutschen Presse* (Berlin: Colloquium Verlag, 1969), vol. I, pp. 163, 178.

34 *Allgemeine deutsche Bibliothek* XII/1 (1770), vi.

35 Bernhard Fabian, "English Books and Their German Readers," in *The Widening Circle: Essays on the Circulation of Literature in Eighteenth-Century Europe,* edited by Paul J. Korschin (University of Pennsylvania Press, 1976), p. 166.

36 Rolf Engelsing, "Die periodische Presse und ihr Publikum. Zeitungslektüre in Breman von den Anfängen bis zur Franzosenzeit," in *Archiv für Geschichte des Buchwesens,* vol. IV, edited by Bertold Hack and Bernhard Wendt (Frankfurt am Main: Buchhändler-Vereinigung, 1963), p. 1502.

37 Kirchner, *Das deutsche Zeitschriftenwesen,* p. 29. It published a total of 29 instrumental and 42 vocal reviews.

38 Kirchner, *Das deutsche Zeitschriftenwesen,* p. 77. It published 228 instrumental and 265 vocal reviews.

39 Fabian, "English Books and Their German Readers," p. 149.

40 Kirchner, *Das deutsche Zeitschriftenwesen,* p. 123. It published 18 instrumental and 31 vocal reviews between 1785 and 1800.

41 Hans-Friedrich Meyer, "*Berlinische Nachrichten von Staats- und gelehrten Sachen,* Berlin (1740–1874)," in *Deutsche Zeitungen des 17. bis 20. Jahrhunderts,* p. 108.

42 Engelsing, "Die periodische Presse," pp. 1488–89. By way of comparison, the *London Times* during that period had a circulation of 8,000. See Franz R. Bertheau, *Kleine Chronologie zur Geschichte des Zeitungswesens in Hamburg von 1616–1913* (Hamburg: Lütcke & Wulff, 1914), p. 42.

43 See the locations given in Hagelweide. In the two Berlin papers, vocal reviews outnumbered instrumental ones by about two to one, but the Hamburg papers had more of a balance, with instrumental running slightly ahead in the *Hamburgischer Correspondent.* The figures are as follows: *Berlinische Nachrichten*: vocal-37, instrumental-23; *Berlinische privilegirte Zeitung*: vocal-27, instrumental-15; *Hamburgische neue Zeitung*: vocal-131, instrumental-116; *Hamburgischer Correspondent*: vocal-243, instrumental-271.

44 Engelsing, "Die periodische Presse," p. 1490.

45 *Lausitzisches Magazin, oder Sammlung verschiedener Abhandlungen und Nachrichten zum Behuf der Natur- Kunst- Welt- und Vaterlands-Geschichte, der Sitten, und der schönen Wissenschaften* XVI/1 (15 January 1783), 15–16.

46 *Flensburgisches Wochenblat*, 21 February 1799, cited in Hans Peter Detlefsen, *Musikgeschichte der Stadt Flensburg bis zum Jahre 1850* (Kassel and Basle: Bärenreiter, 1961). I am grateful to Prof. Dr. Heinrich Schwab for calling my attention to this source.

47 Fabian, "English Books and Their German Readers," pp. 161–62.

48 Engelsing, "Die periodische Presse," p. 1500.

49 Barney M. Milstein, *Eight Eighteenth Century Reading Societies* (Berne and Frankfurt am Main: Herbert Lang, 1972), pp. 61, 170–71.

50 Prüsener, "Lesegesellschaften," pp. 427–31.

51 Of the 173 review journals surveyed by the Zeitschriftensindex, 65 percent were published in central or northern Germany.

52 Kirchner, *Das deutsche Zeitschriftenwesen*, p. 117.

53 Lindemann, *Deutsche Presse*, p. 120.

54 I address the question of possible prejudice against South German and Austrian styles in chapter 3.

55 Performance reviews of instrumental music are rare before 1800 and generally treat only the capabilities of the performer, not the music itself. Although the handful found in the *Musikalisches Wochenblatt/Musikalische Monatsschrift* reinforce the aesthetic criteria found in reviews of printed music, I have chosen to exclude them from consideration here in the interests of a more cohesive collective.

56 *Allgemeines Verzeichniß neuer Bücher* V/8 (1780), 615, review of C. P. E. Bach's *Orchester Sinfonien mit zwölf obligaten Stimmen, 2 Hörnern, 2 Flöten, 2 Hoboen, 2 Violinen, Bratsche, Violoncell, Fagott, Flügel und Violon* [Wq. 183]. Leipzig: Schwickert. "Es ist eine mühselige Arbeit vielstimmige Stücke aus einzelnen Partien zu studiren, um das Ganze daraus zu beurtheilen."

57 *Musikalische Korrespondenz* 10 (8 September 1790), 75, review of Joseph Haydn's *III Quatuors pour deux Violons, Taille & Violoncelle, Op. 32. Libro 1.* [Hob. III:57–59, known as Op. 54] Berlin and Amsterdam: Hummel. "Allein Rec. hat sie durchgegangen, die Stimmen gegen einander verglichen, ja sogar eintge [*sic*] Stellen in Partitur gesezt und sich aufs neue mit Vergnügen von den großen hervorstechenden Talenten eines Haydn und dem unerschöpflichen Reichthum seiner Gedanken und seiner originellen Laune überzeugt."

58 Bach refers to Eschtruth's departure from Hamburg in a letter to Immanuel Breitkopf dated 21 September 1787. See Ernst Suchalla, ed., *Briefe von Carl Philipp Emanuel Bach an Johann Gottlob Immanuel Breitkopf und Johann Nikolaus Forkel* (Tutzing: Hans Schneider, 1985), p. 221.

59 Ernst Ludwig Gerber, *Historisch-biographisches Lexikon der Tonkünstler* (1790–92) and *Neues Historisch-biographisches Lexikon der Tonkünstler* (1812–1814); rpt. edn. by Othmar Wessely (Graz: Akademische Druck und Verlagsanstalt, 1966–1977), s.v. "Eschtruth, Hans Adolf Freyherr von (1756–1792)."

60 *Allgemeine deutsche Bibliothek* LXXI/1 (1787), 115–18. "Wir übergehen die

übrigen Recensionen, von denen manche eben so unbedeutend sind, als die meisten der recensirten Werke."

61 *Altonaischer gelehrter Mercurius* VI/19 (7 May 1778), 150, review of Daniel Gottlob Türk's *Sechs Sonaten für das Klavier*. Part 2. Leipzig: Breitkopf, 1777. "Ueberhaupt verdienet Herr T. den vornehmsten Rang unter denenjenigen, welche sich nach des grossen Bachs wahrer Art das Klavier zu spielen, gebildet haben; ein Verdienst, das eben nicht so allgemein ist, als man es bey itziger Musikliebhaberey erwarten sollte. Recensent ist kein Musiker von Profession, und giebt daher auch selbst keine Sonaten heraus, hat sich auch deswegen nicht die Mühe geben wollen, aufzusuchen, ob auch alle Gedanken in Herrn T. Sonaten seine eigene wären; gesezt nun, sie wären es nicht, ists denn doch eine feine Kunst, fremde Gedanken passend und gefällig anzubringen. Thun es doch auch die Dichter!"

62 According to Fleck, a thought collective will comprise an inner "esoteric" and an outer "exoteric" circle, a pattern that would fit the professional/amateur authorship described here. See his *Genesis and Development*, p. 105.

63 *Allgemeine deutsche Bibliothek* I/1 (1765), ii.

64 *Hamburgische Nachrichten aus dem Reiche der Gelehrsamkeit*, preface to the 1761 volume, pp. 8–9.

65 *Magazin der Musik* I/1, 56.

66 Clark, *Herder*, 171–78.

67 *Lyceum der schönen Künste*, edited by Johann Friedrich Reichardt (Berlin: Johann Friedrich Unger, 1797), I/2, 190–91.

68 *Musicalische Bibliotek* (1784), 38.

69 *Neue allgemeine deutsche Bibliothek* XII/2 (1794), 517–21. Other contributors included Konrad Gottlob Anton, professor of Oriental languages in Wittenberg; Friedrich Gottlieb Busse, professor in Dessau; Ernst Flovius Friedrich Chladni, philosophy and law professor in Wittenberg; Johann August Eberhard, philosophy professor in Halle; Johann Joachim Eschenburg, Hofrath and professor of fine arts in Braunschweig; Johann Ludwig Ewald, "General-Superintendent" in Detmold; Grönland, co-director of the royal porcelain factory in Copenhagen; Karl Gottlob Horstig, pastor in Bückeburg, and Christian Ludwig Stengel, law official in Berlin; Franz Wilhelm Jung; and Castillon.

70 Gerber, *Neues Lexikon*, s.v. "Leister, Joachim Friedrich." I am grateful to both Leta E. Miller and Stephen L. Clark for first drawing my attention to Leister's identity. Bach mentions him in his capacity as *Correspondent* reviewer in a letter to Johann Nikolaus Forkel dated 15 October 1777 (Suchalla, *Briefe von Carl Philipp Emanuel Bach*, p. 250).

71 François-Joseph Fétis, *Biographie universelle des musiciens* (Paris, 1875), s.v. "Leister, Joachim Friedrich."

72 Thomas Baumann, "The Music Reviews in the *Allgemeine deutsche Bibliothek*," *Acta Musicologica* 49 (1977), 69–85.

73 Hans Schneider, *Der Musikverleger Heinrich Philipp Bossler 1744–1812* (Tutzing: Hans Schneider, 1985), p. 159.

74 *Erfurtische gelehrte Zeitungen* 43 (12 September 1783), 340–41.

75 *Magazin der Musik* I/1 (1783), 68.

76 *Hallische neue gelehrte Zeitungen* XVIII/24 (20 March 1783), 186.

77 *Hamburgischer Correspondent* Beytrag 7 (1781); *Magazin der Musik* 1/1 (15 January 1783), 79–80. Johann Samuel Schröter, *Six Concerts pour le Clavecin ou le Forte Piano avec Accompagnement de deux Violons et Basse, Op. 6.* Paris. "Obgleich der darin herrschende Gesang nicht neu ist, so ist er doch sehr gefällig und fliessend; nur Schade, daß Herr Schröter sich nicht mehr Mühe giebt, die Kunst des reinen Satzes zu studiren, und nach richtigen harmonischen Regeln zu componiren. Seite 45 im 6ten Concert ist daher fast nicht spielbar, da die daselbst angebrachte Harmonie ganz unrichtig, und, wie wir hoffen wollen, durch Druckfehler noch mehr verstellt worden ist. W."

78 Gerber, *Neues Lexikon*, s.v. "Grönland."

79 The exception is one from issue 55 of the *Hamburgischer Correspondent* (5 April 1783), dated 4 April in the *Magazin der Musik.*

80 *Berlinische privilegirte Zeitung* 82 (10 July 1790), F. L. A. Kunzen, "Chöre und Gesänge zu Klopstocks Herrman und die Fürsten" (with full signature); *Berlinische Nachrichten* 152 (20 December 1794), Carl Spazier, "Einfache Lieder"; *Berlinische privilegirte Zeitung* 28 (6 March 1790), J. A. P. Schulz, *Aline, Königin von Golkonda.*

81 One of C. P. E. Bach's *Sei Concerti per il Cembalo concertato*, issue 4 (6 January 1773) and four from issue 189, 26 November 1777 (one work by F. G. Rust and three by J. F. Reichardt). Three are signed "E." (12 May 1789 and two from May 1793).

82 Private communication from Doris Powers, July 18, 1994.

83 *Allgemeine deutsche Bibliothek* XXII/2 (1774), 531, review of Johann Friedrich Wilhelm Wenkel's *Sonata I, a Violino solo, col Basso.* Uelzen: Wenkel; Hamburg: Bock.

84 *Magazin der Musik* I/2 (7 December 1783), 1238–55; 1259–75.

85 *Musicalische Bibliotek* II (1785), 187–226, review of the first volume of the *Magazin der Musik.*

86 Fleck, *Genesis and Development*, pp. 44, 103.

87 *Nürnbergische gelehrte Zeitung* 23 (20 March 1778), 186–89, review of Forkel's *Musikalisch-kritische Bibliothek.* "Am wenigsten gelten in diesem Fache einzelne Urtheile als gemein, wenn sie blos Schönheit und Geschmack betreffen, oder wenn diese Delikatessen nach torturmäsigen Regeln wollen geformt werden."

88 *Erfurtische gelehrte Zeitungen* 32 (12 July 1780), 255, review of Johann Friedrich Hugo, Freiherr von Dalberg's *Trois Sonates pour le Clavecin ou Forte Piano, avec accompagnement d'un Violon obligé, Op. 1.* Mannheim: Göz. "Und überhaupt däucht [sic] uns daß durch die allzuweit getriebene Kritik manches aufkeimende Genie oft nur in der Geburt erstickt und niedergeschlagen wird."

89 *Neue allgemeine deutsche Bibliothek*, XII/2 (1794), 519–20.

90 *Hamburgischer Correspondent* Beylage 7 (13 January 1792), review of the

Musikalisches Wochenblatt. "Der kritische Theil ist es auch gerade, der durch seine überaus große Freymüthigkeit und treffende Wahrheit und Gründlichkeit dieses Werk ganz vorzüglich auszeichnet. Die Recensenten sehen jeden Componisten grade ins Gesicht, und prüfen die Werke, als wären die Verfasser nicht mehr am Leben, und schrieben selbst nie wieder Recensionen. Und so ists recht. So nur wird der Kunstfreund und der studierende Künstler selbst ächt belehrt, und erhält so nach und nach seiner eignen sichern Maaßstab."

91 *Unterhaltungen* V/1 (January 1768), 69–71. "Wir können überhaupt das Lob der vorigen Herrn Verf. der Unterhaltungen bey diesen Nachrichten wiederhohlen, nur mit der kleinen Einschränkung, daß die V. der Nachrichten in den Kritiken genauer und strenger seyn mögten, welches vornehmlich bey der großen Menge elender Musikalien, womit man sonderlich aus Frankreich und Holland heimgesucht wird, sehr nöthig und nützlich seyn mögte." It had a similar comment several months later in V/5 (May 1768), 450–52.

92 Schenk-Güllich, "Anfänge der Musikkritik," p. 104.

93 *Jenaische Zeitungen* 35 (29 April 1768), 301, review of *Unterhaltungen*, vol. 4/6. "Die Aufsätze fangen an, immer schlechter zu werden . . . Vielleicht wird diese Monatsschrift künftig besser, da verschiedene neue Mitarbeiter hinzugekommen sind; vielleicht auch nicht, da, wie wir gewis wissen, Hr Licentiat Wittenberg ietzt an der Spitze stehet."

94 *Allgemeine deutsche Bibliothek* Anhang zum 53. bis 86. Bande (IV), 1907–08, review of Caspar Daniel Krohn's *Sechs kleine Sonaten fürs Clavier oder Forte=Piano u.s.w.* Hamburg: Krohn, 1787. "Zwar lasen wir nach geschehener Anzeige des Verfassers, daß diese Sonaten den Druck der Presse ausgestanden hätten, gleich in dem unmittelbar darauf folgenden Blatte des Hamburger unpartheyischen Correspondenten (No. 150 im Jahr 1787) eine für den Verfasser sehr günstige, wie wir aber hernach einsahen, desto nachtheiligere Recension für den Käufer. Denn wir bedauern in der That den, welcher durch gedachte Recension in dem Hamburger unpartheyischen Correspondenten angelockt worden ist, sich des Herrn Caspar Daniel Krohn kleine Sonaten zu kaufen. Wir mögen uns einer ähnliche Sünde nicht schuldig machen, sondern sagen lieber allen unsern Lesern ganz offenherzig und sonder Gefährde, daß diese kleine Sonaten äußerst fade und triviale Dingerchen und keiner weitern Beurtheilung werth sind. Wer uns für partheyisch halten sollte, den müssen wir freylich, aber bloß in dieser Rücksicht bitten, sich des Herrn Caspar Daniel Krohn wohlgedachte kleine Sonaten zu kaufen. Oben ein oder vielmehr voran hat der Herr Autor einen wunderschönen *Canon* von vier Gerichten aufgetischt. Wir wünschen den sämmtlich hochgeehrtesten Gästen guten Appetit. – Dieß Einzige müssen wir noch zum Lobe unsers Herrn Wirthes anmerken, daß die Speisen aller sechs Schüsseln sehr einfach und leicht sind, man hat daher keine Magenbeschwerden, oder wie diese Plagen in der Kunstsprache heißen mögen, davon zu befürchten; aber man wird auch keine gesunde Nahrung haben. Of. [Türk]"

95 *Hamburgischer Correspondent* 151 (not 150) (21 September 1787), review of
   Caspar Daniel Krohn's *Sechs kleine Sonaten fürs Clavier oder Fortepiano.*
   Hamburg: Author, 1787. "Diese sechs kleine Sonaten sind leicht, richtig im Satze,
   und machen den musikalischen Einsichten ihres Componisten Ehre. Jede derselben besteht aus einem Adagio und aus einem geschwinderen Satze, zu welchem
   letzteren bald ein Rondo, bald eine Menuett gewählt ist. Die Kenntnisse der
   Harmonie, welche der Componist in selbigen zeiget, geben ihm ein Recht zu
   größeren musikalischen Ausarbeitungen, womit er, wie wir hören, auch bereits
   beschäfftigt ist. Statt der Vorrede hat der Verfasser einen Canon à 4 geliefert."
96 *Musikalischer Almanach*, pp. 10–11. "Alle darinn enthaltene Recensionen sagen
   nichts, weil sie wirklich nie wahre innere Schätzung, sondern bloß absichtliche
   Empfehlung der Werke zum Zweck zu haben scheinen . . . Die meisten bisher im
   Magazin enthaltenen Recensionen lassen sich in drey Classen theilen. In die erste
   gehören die, welche gar keine Schätzung, sondern bloße Empfehlung; in die
   zweyte die, welche offenbar ungerechten Tadel, und in die dritte die, welche offenbar ungerechtes Lob enthalten."
97 *Hallische neue gelehrte Zeitungen* XVIII/24 (20 March 1783), 186;
   Hamburgischer Correspondent 46 (21 March 1783); *Hamburgische neue Zeitung*
   53 (2 April 1783); *Erfurtische gelehrte Zeitungen* 43 (12 September 1783), 340–41;
   Gothaische gelehrte Zeitungen 27 (2 April 1783), 221–22. "Die Beurtheilungen
   von 52 neuen musikalisch=practischen Werken, sind zwar alle kurz, aber sehr
   angemessen und billig."
98 *Hamburgische neue Zeitung* 197 (10 December 1783). "Rezensionen. Dieser
   Abschnitt nahet sich durch Strenge schon etwas mehr der Volkommenheit [*sic*],
   doch lange nicht so sehr, als es zu wünschen wäre . . . Besonders aber wird in der
   Musik so viel gelobt, was doch nur leidige Nachahmung, elende Ausschreiberei
   ist, und hunderte, die nicht einen Funken Originalgeist haben, gelten für Händel,
   Bache, Hayden und Hessen."
99 Fleck, *Genesis and Development*, p. 44.
100 The English equivalent of "harmony," at least in its modern usage, does not have
   the same degree of textural considerations, so I have chosen to leave the term
   untranslated.

3 Answering with a German voice

1 *Hamburgische neue Zeitung* 21 (5 February 1777), review of Johann Wilhelm
   Häßler's *Sechs Sonaten fürs Clavier der Hochwohlgebohrnen Frau
   Landeshauptmannin von Schönberg.* Leipzig: Schwickert, 1776. "Daß die wahre
   Art, das Clavier zu spielen, bey uns Deutschen zu Hause sey, wird niemand
   läugnen, der nur mit einiger Aufmerksamkeit die Werk unsers Carl Emanuel
   Philipp Bachs studiret hat. Diesem großen Genie war es vorbehalten, das Clavier
   aus der Vergessenheit hervorzuziehen, worin es lag. Er zeigte, daß auf diesem
   Instrumente Meister zu werden, etwas mehr gehörte als Bocksprünge zu machen,

beliebte Arienfloskeln mit immerwährenden Pauken und Trommelbässen aufzustutzen, wodurch kein wahres musikalisches Ohr jemals gerührt werden könnte. Viele brave Männer sind seinem Beyspiele gefolgt, und haben dadurch bey wahren Kennern der Musik Ruhm und Ehre erlangt. Auch gegenwärtige Sonaten haben das Gepräge der guten claviermäßigen Art, sie sind voller guten Harmonie und rührender Melodie, und unterscheiden sich also von dem Schwarm jetziger seichten italienischen und andern Modekompositionen auf diesem Instrumente gar sehr."

2 *Hamburgische Correspondent* 68 (29 April 1789), review of Christian Friedrich Gottlieb Schwenke's *Drey Sonaten für das Clavier, dem hochansehnlichen Collegio der Herren Scholarchen in Hamburg ergebenst zugeeignet.* Halle: Hendel, 1789. "Er hat Bach, Haydn und Mozart zu Mustern gewählt, und sich so glücklich in die Denkungsart dieser berühmten Männer hineingesetzt, daß man die Manier ihrer Bearbeitungen, zum Exempel die von Bach in der ersten, und die von Haydn in der zweyten Sonate ohne Mühe finden kann, obgleich Herr Schwenke nichts weniger als sclavischer Nachahmer ist, sondern, seiner Muster ungeachtet, ein wirkliches Original bleibt."

3 Hélène Cixous, "Sorties," in *The Newly Born Woman* (Minneapolis: University of Minnesota Press, 1986), p. 64.

4 Kenneth Burke, "The Rhetoric of Hitler's 'Battle,'" in *The Philosophy of Literary Form* (Baton Rouge, LA: Louisiana State University Press, 1941), pp. 191–220. I do *not* mean to suggest that this particular rhetoric is the exclusive property of the German nation, for there are far too many examples of its usage in my own country's political and cultural debates. Nor do I mean to imply any foreshadowing of National Socialism in the review collective's discourse. A number of modern rhetoricians have expounded on this particular oratorical strategy; I have chosen Burke's analysis because his has been particularly influential.

5 Burke, "Rhetoric," pp. 193–94.

6 Burke, "Rhetoric," p. 201.

7 Burke, "Rhetoric," pp. 201–05.

8 Many scholars have discussed the role that theorists and critics like Mattheson, Marpurg, Scheibe, etc. played in promoting a German identity at the expense of the French and the Italians. For a recent approach, see Ernst Lichtenhahn, "Der musikalische Stilwandel im Selbstverständnis der Zeit um 1750," in *Carl Philipp Emanuel Bach und die europäische Musikkultur des mittleren 18. Jahrhunderts*, edited by Hans Joachim Marx (Göttingen: Vandenhoeck & Ruprecht, 1990), pp. 65–77.

9 "Zehnte Fortsetzung des Entwurfs einer musikalischen Bibliothek" in the *Wöchentliche Nachrichten* III:14 (3 October 1768), 107–08; "Galuppi, Jomelli, Sarti, u.s.w. sind berühmte Nahmen; man hat eine Menge Sinfonien von ihnen; denn sie alle haben Opern componirt, und nie ist eine Oper ohne Sinfonie. Wenn man aber das beständige Einerley, und die große Aehnlichkeit unter allen diesen Stücken betrachtet, wenn man nach einem schwärmenden Allegro ein kurzes und

etwan aus zween Gedanken bestehendes Andante, und sodann wieder ein wacker schwärmendes, und immer im Haupttone herum taumelndes Allegro oder Presto gehört hat, so findet man wohl, daß eine solche Sinfonie zur Eröffnung einer Oper, so lange das Auditorium noch nicht ruhig geworden, gut genug ist; aber zur Kammermusik taugt sie so wenig, als wenig sie eine Beziehung auf das Stück hat, vor welchem sie aufgeführt wird." See also "Von dem wienerischen Geschmack in der Musik" in the Gelehrte Nachrichten of the *Wienerisches Diarium* 26 (18 October 1766); "Ueber den National-Charakter der Italiäner" in the *Gothaisches Magazin der Künste und Wissenschaften* I/1 (1776), 1–21; "Abhandlung vom musikalischen Geschmack"; and *Wahrheiten die Musik betreffend*, pp. 15–20.

10 Daniel E. Freeman, "Johann Christian Bach and the Early Classical Italian Masters," in *Eighteenth-Century Keyboard Music*, edited by Robert L. Marshall (New York: Schirmer Books, 1994), p. 245.

11 *Bibliothek der schönen Wissenschaften* IV/2 (1762), 822, review of a keyboard reduction of Baldassare Galuppi's *Vier Symphonien*. "Wir bedauern das schöne Papier, das zu diesen elenden Werken, die kein ächter Kenner ohne Ekel anhören kann, ist verschwendet worden. . . . Warum liefert uns doch Herr Breitkopf nicht lauter solche Werke rechtschaffner geschickter Deutschen, und will der Welt lieber die Mißgeburten seichter Italiäner aufdringen."

12 *Unterhaltungen* X/2 (August 1770), 158–60, review of *Musikalisches Vielerley*. Hamburg: Bock. "Wirklich unsre großen Genies sorgen sehr schlecht für ihre und Deutschlands Ehre, und für die Ausbreitung des guten Geschmacks, die sie in ihren Händen haben. Hr. Bach ist der einzige der fleißig drucken läßt; aber wo druckt man was von Hasse, den beyden Grauns, den Bendas, Quanz, Fasch, Neruda, Riedt, u.a. Wenig oder gar nichts. Was mag Schuld daran seyn? Die Notenverleger oder die Komponisten? Wir dächten beyde!" The Bendas and Neruda were Czech musicians writing in the German style; their adoption as defenders of German honor indicated the flexibility of the collective's "us" against "them" rhetoric.

13 *Wöchentliche Nachrichten* I:17 (21 October 1766), 127–31, review of Vincenzo Manfredini's *Sei Sonate da Clavecembalo*. St. Petersburg, 1765. "Unharmonisches Gepolter mit gebrochenen Accorden in der linken Hand, wodurch uns so oft schon die Claviersonaten der Italiäner zum Eckel geworden sind, findet sich hier beynahe in allen Sätzen. Gepitzeltes und Getändeltes die Menge, und bisweilen so etwas von Melodie, das vielleicht gut wäre, wenn es nicht öfters durch den begleitenden Baß verdorben würde, und man es nicht schon hundertmal gehört hatte."

14 *Hamburgischer Correspondent* 102 (26 June 1773), review of Johann Friedrich Reichardt's *Vermischte Musikalien*. Riga: Hartknoch, 1773. "Die Composition des Verfassers ist von der ernsthaftern Art, und wir ermuntern ihn, dabey zu bleiben, so sehr er auch an den Höfen, die er besuchen will, und in Italien, wohin er auch zu reisen gedenket, zur komischen Art möchte gereizet werden. Wenn er den Italienern den guten Gesang ablernet, ohne den alle Musik nichts werth ist,

und welchen wir noch in einigen seiner Ausarbeitungen vermissen . . . so wird seine Reise für ihn und die Musik vortheilhaft seyn."

15 Kirnberger's composition treatise from the 1770s, *Die Kunst des reinen Satzes*, attributed the Italian preference for I-IV-V progressions to their incompetence in *Harmonie*. See his *The Art of Strict Musical Composition*, translated by David Beach and Jurgen Thym (New Haven and London: Yale University Press, 1982), pp. 286–87.

16 *Kritische Briefe* II/86 (14 November 1761), 170–73, review of *II. Sinfonie a quatro, cioè Violino I. Violino II. Viola, Violoncello o Cembalo, composte da un famoso Maestro*. Nuremberg: Haffner. "Der Herr Galuppi besitzet die vortreflichsten Gaben der Natur, zwar nicht, neue Ideen zu erschaffen, sondern die schon vorhandenen zusammen zu setzen, und durch einige Favoritförmelchen des Geschmackes der Zeit aufzustutzen. Er schreibet viel und flüchtig. Wäre derselbe zur regelmäßigen Composition angeführet worden, eine Sache, die seit langer Zeit in Italien nicht mehr Mode ist, so würde er sich zwar vielleicht niemahls zu dem Range eines Grauns, oder Hasse, geschwungen, aber doch den Ruhm eines untadelhaften Componisten erworben haben. Damit man nicht ohne alle Känntniß der Beschaffenheit der beyden Sonaten davon komme, so will ich aus der ersten Clausel des Allegro der ersten Synfonie aus dem B dur einige Sachen bemerken. Diese erste Clausel besteht, wo ich richtig gezählt habe, aus neunzig Tacten im Zweyzweytheiltact. Bis zum sechs und fünfzigsten Tact bleibt der Componist in dem Hauptone B dur, und von dem sieben und fünfzigsten an lenket er sich in die Nebentonart F dur, in welche die erste Clausel schliesset. Wenn auch bewiesen werden könnte, daß derselbe sich nicht über die Zeit in dem Hauptone aufgehalten hätte, und daß es mit dem Verhältnisse dieses Aufhalts in Ansehung des Nebentons F seine Richtigkeit hätte, welches aber nicht bewiesen werden kann: so wird doch weder der Verstand noch das Gehör damit zufrieden seyn, daß sich in diesen sechs und fünfzig Tacten so wenig Mannigfaltigkeit in der Harmonie findet. Alle in diesem Raum gebrauchte harmonische Sätze lassen sich auf den leyermäßig herrschenden Dreyklang des Haupttons b d f, und den Dreyklang der Dominante f a c zurück führen. An einem Paar Oertern werden selbige mit dem Septimensatz c es g b oder dem davon abstammen Secunden= oder Sextquintensatz unterbrochen; und das ist die ganze Verschiedenheit der Harmonie in dem Raum von sechs und fünfzig Tacten."

17 *Allgemeine deutsche Bibliothek* X/1 (1769), 244, review of Giovanni Rutini's *Sei Sonate per Cimbalo*, Op. 6. Nuremberg: Haffner. "Schon das sechste Werk; und der Verf. hat doch noch keine bessern und claviermäßigern Sonaten zu machen gelernt? Das ist viel! der Baß in diesen geht mehrentheils, nach löblichen Gebrauch der Italiener, entweder mit fast unaufhörlichen Brechungen oder trommelnd einher. Und der Gesang oben drüber [*sic*] ist nicht sonderlich. X. [Agricola]"

18 Heinrich Christoph Koch, *Musikalisches Lexikon* (Frankfurt am Main, 1802), s.v. "Ausarbeitung." "Hier wird die Wirkung erwogen, welche durch die Neben und

Füllstimmen erhalten werden kann, die bey der Ausarbeitung ihr Daseyn erhalten. Hier wird abgerundet, was noch zu eckicht ist, und die Auswüchse werden weggeschnitten, die in dem Feuer der Arbeit bey der Ausführung entsprossen sind. Der grammatische Theil des Ganzen wird berichtiget; kurz das Tonstück wird bis auf seine kleinsten Theile ausgefeilt."

19 *Hamburgischer Correspondent* 127 (9 August 1771), review of Pietro Guglielmi's *Six Divertiments for the Harpsichord and Violin*. London: Author. "Die Melodie derselben . . . ist ganz gemein, und musikalische Ausarbeitung, die freylich bey vielen neuern Italienern höchst selten ist, findet man fast gar nicht darinn . . . Ueberhaupt haben uns die vortrefflichen Clavierstücke unsers berühmten Herrn Kapellmeisters Bach bey diesem Instrumente schon so delicat gemacht, daß uns die harmonielosen Compositionen der neuern Italiener für selbiges unmöglich gefallen können."

20 *Hamburgische neue Zeitung* 61 (18 April 1775), review of Luigi Boccherini's *Six Trios for 2 Violins and a Violoncello obligato with a thorough bass*, Op. 9. London. "Sehr wenige Italiäner wird man finden, die so reich an ernsthaften, edlen Gedanke wären, und ihre Stücke so gut bearbeiten."

21 *Wöchentliche Nachrichten* I:17 (21 October 1766), 127–31, review of Manfredini's *Sei Sonate* cited above. "Sollten denn in Rußland die Clavierarbeiten eines Bachs, Benda, Wagenseil, Kunz, Binder, und anderer deutschen Meister nicht bekannt seyn?" Daniel E. Freeman notes, incidentally, that "there is nothing especially incompetent about Manfredini's sonatas." "Johann Christian Bach and the Early Classical Italian Masters," p. 253.

22 *Wöchentliche Nachrichten*, III:19 (7 November 1768), 150, review of Gaudenzio Comi's *VI Sinfonie per due Violini, Alto e Basso, con Corni et Oboe ad libitum*. Paris: Venier. "Dem Genie der Deutschen muß es nachgerühmt werden, daß sie den Sinfonienstyl zu einem Grade der Vollkommenheit gebracht haben, den ein italiänischer Componist schwerlich erreicht: es gehört außer der Erfindung, noch Ueberlegung und Arbeitsamkeit dazu; ein Vorzug, den selbst die Italiäner den deutschen Componisten nie streitig gemacht haben."

23 *Hamburgischer Correspondent* 107 (8 July 1766), review of Johann Wilhelm Hertel's *Sei Sinfonie a due Violini, Violetta, e Basso, due Oboi, due Flaute, e due Corni di Caccia*. Hamburg: Bock. "Das Palet des Schmierers [ist] von dem Palet des Mahlers so sehr unterschieden, als die Sinfonie eines *Sassone* von der Sinfonie eines *S*ti* . . . Sollten wir aber noch die Schreibart, dieser Sinfonien mit der Schreibart irgend eines Welschen vergleichen, so müssen wir sie den Sinfonien des Jomelli an die Seite setzen, von denen sich aber die Gegenwärtigen annoch durch die dem Herrn Hertel eigene Stärke in der Harmonie um ein Merkliches unterscheiden."

24 The question of what constituted a good trio occupied German writers *outside* the collective during this period as well. For a discussion of this debate see Hubert Unverricht, *Geschichte des Streichtrios*, Mainzer Studien zur Musikwissenschaft, 2, edited by Hellmut Federhofer (Tutzing: Hans Schneider, 1969), pp. 79–86.

Unverricht asserts that critical opinion in Berlin and Hamburg insisted vehemently that the contrapuntal style should be maintained, while in Leipzig Hiller agreed, but less strongly.

25 *Hamburgischer Correspondent* 114 (17 July 1772), review of Johann Friedrich Wilhelm Wenkel's *Duetts für zwo Flöten Traversen.* Hamburg: Bock. "Der Componist dieser Duetts hat sich bereits in seinen herausgegebenen Clavierstücken als ein Tonkünstler gezeigt, der die wahren Grundsätze der Musik mit Fleiß studiret hat, und daher eine gründliche und regelmäßige Setzungsart, den flüchtigen und fehlerhaften Compositionen einiger neuern, besonders Italiener, vorziehet . . . Wir haben eben noch keinen Ueberfluß an guten Duetts, welche nach einem guten zweenstimmigen Satze, mit Umwendungen, Nachahmungen, und nach den Regeln auch nur des galanten Contrapunkts ausgearbeitet sind, ob es uns gleich an solchen nicht fehlet, welche nach stets auf einander folgenden zugleich steigenden und fallenden Sexten und Terzen eine angenehme Melodie, die aber dem Ohr des Kenners leicht zu süß, und folglich eckelhaft werden kann, hervorzubringen suchen."

26 *Neue Zeitungen von gelehrten Sachen* 1 (3 January 1771), 3–4, review of Johann Friedrich Gottlieb Beckmann's *Drey Sonaten für das Clavier.* Hamburg: Bock. "Die besten Claviersonaten rühren von deutschen Componisten her. Händel, Bach, Benda, sind noch von keinem Ausländer, von keinem Manfredini, Rutini, Düphlü, übertroffen worden. Hr. Beckmann hilft den Ruhm der Deutschen bestätigen: seine Sonaten verdienen neben den Sonaten der ersteren zu stehen, und denen der letzteren vorgezogen zu werden. Sie haben das Eigenthümlich des Instruments, gute Erfindung, guten Gesang, reine und künstliche Harmonie . . . So gar der *Canone infinito* auf der lezten Seite behält durchaus, bey allem Zwange, der dieser Gattung eigen ist, einen nicht unangenehmen Gesang. Der zweyte Theil, der auch schon heraus ist, verdienet mit dem ersten gleiches Lob. Es befindet sich in demselben, außer einem *Canone infinito*, auch eine wohlgearbeitete dreystimmige Fuge." Both French and English styles were held to be similar to the Italian/popular one, but got only a fraction of the attention from reviewers. Most of the comments about the English come from the Hamburg papers, which reviewed more London prints, presumably because they had better access to them.

27 *Allgemeine deutsche Bibliothek* XV/1 (1771), 241–42, review of Adam Veichtner's *IV. Sinfonie a II Violini, II Flauti traversi, II Oboi, II Corni da Caccia, Violetta, e Basso.* Mietau: Steidel, 1770. "Warum aber sind sie, was zumal die ersten Sätze anbetrift, doch auch ganz nach der neuesten wälschen Mode? Nach der Mode, welcher zu Folge man in Sinfonien der Oberstimme eine selten recht zusammenhängende, oft abgepitzelte, manchmal schwärmende, manchmal steif auf einem Tone klebende, fast niemals etwas ausdrückende Melodie giebt . . . Warum ahnte der Hr. V. nicht wenigstens . . . den Geschmack der prächtigen, höchst feurigen und was rechts sagenden Sinfonien unsers würdigen Concertmeisters Hrn. Grauns nach? Bm. [Agricola]"

28 *Hamburgischer Correspondent* 107 (6 July 1774), review of Ernst Wilhelm Wolf's *Sei Sonate per il Clavicembalo solo.* Leipzig: Breitkopf, 1774. "Durchgängig herrscht ein guter Gesang darinn, so wie er in einer Clavier=Sonate, die keine Opern=Arie ist, seyn muß. Jede hat einen langsamen Satz, der den wahren Kennern des guten Gesanges am angenehmsten seyn wird, obgleich die neuern komischen Componisten ihn aus ihren Arbeiten verbannt zu haben scheinen."

29 Burke, "Rhetoric," 194–95.

30 *Allgemeine deutsche Bibliothek* II/1 (1766), 270–72, review of Ferdinand Fischer's *Six Symphonies a II Violons Haut-bois, ou flutes traversieres Cors de Chasse, Fagots, Violettes et Basses.* Leipzig: Breitkopf, 1765. "Daß er aber einem deutschen Helden, Sinfonien zueignet, welche alle das Lahme, das Unmelodische, das Niedrige, Das Poßierliche, das Zerstückelte, alle die (wie Telemann einsmal gesagt) fieberhaften Anfälle des beständigen geschwinden Abwechselns des Piano und Forte u.s.w. der neuesten Italienischen Modecomponisten an sich haben; – darüber wundern wir uns wirklich. Wir möchten eine Abhandlung dieses Verfassers lesen, worinn er sein Verfahren nach den Regeln des gesunden und guten musikalischen Geschmacks rechtfertigte. Wir wetten, der Hauptgrund würde dieser seyn: weil es die neuesten Italiäner so machen ... Inzwischen wollen wir andern Deutschen, zween Graune, einen Hasse, einen Bach, einen Quanz u. an der Spitze habend, uns bemühen, das Erhabene, das Würdige, das Zärtliche, das Rührende, den schönen Gesang, die reine Harmonie, den edlen Ausdruck u.s.w. in der Musik nach unserm Vermögen fortzupflanzen ... Zuhörer von feiner, vernünftiger, geläuterter Empfindung mögen alsdenn urtheilen, welche Nation zuerst einen musikalischen Raphael, oder Coreggio oder Titian u. hervorgebracht haben wird. P. [Agricola]"

31 *Allgemeine deutsche Bibliothek* VIII/1 (1768), 272–73, review of Johann Schwanberger's *Sonate a due Violini e Violoncello.* Brunsvic: Casa degli Orsanelli. "Auch itzo, da er nun Italien gesehen hat, erkennen wir immer noch an ihm einen von den Deutschen, die sich zwar in alle musikalischen Trachten, wie man sie nur verlangt, einkleiden, aber doch nicht alles Gründliche in ihrem Wissen verleugnen können. X. [Agricola]"

32 *Wöchentliche Nachrichten* I:50 (8 June 1767), 390–91, review of Schwanberger's *Sonate a due Violini e Violoncello.* Braunschweig: Waisenhaus. "Sie sind nicht so gebunden und fugenartig, wie die vortrefflichen Trios des seel. Kapellmeister Grauns; sie sind aber auch nicht so einfach und leer wie die meisten italiänischen Trios."

33 *Berlinische Nachrichten* 78 (30 June 1764), 326–27, review of Johann Gottfried Eckard's *Six Sonates pour le Clavecin*, Op. 1. Paris. "Die Setzart des Herrn Verfassers der oben erwähnten Sonaten scheinet Italiänisch, und leicht, zu seyn; doch fällt sie angenehm, und schleichend, in das Gehör. Die musicalische Critick wird ihnen keinen Krieg, wenigstens keinen von langer Dauer, ankündigen."

34 *Hamburgische neue Zeitung* 140 (1 September 1772), review of A. E. Forstmayer's *Six Sonates pour le Clavicin [sic] avec l'accompagnement d'un Violon ou Flute,*

Op. 1. Frankfurt am Main: Haueisen. "Einigen Kunstrichtern, welche nur das Bunte und Künstliche lieben, dürften sie nun eben wohl nicht gefallen, weil die Instrumenten sich nicht mit einander herumjagen, und weil der Verf. hin und wieder einige italiänische Wendungen hat, welches bey ihnen ein grosses Verbrechen ist. Wir sind nicht so intolerant, und glauben gewiß, den Beyfall vieler Kenner und Liebhaber der Musick auf unsrer Seite zu haben."

35 See Sulzer's *Allgemeine Theorie der schönen Künste*, s.v. "Empfindung."

36 *Berlinische Nachrichten* 29 (9 March 1773), 144, review of C. P. E. Bach's *Sei Concerti per il Cembalo concertato, accompagnato da due Violini, Violetta e Basso; con due Corni e due Flauti per rinforzo*. Hamburg: Bach, 1772. [Wq. 43] "Kurz, es ist nichts an diesen Concerten vergessen, was Kennern so wohl als Liebhabern zu einem edlen Vergnügen, und einer angenehmen Unterhaltung gereichen, und dabey ihren Geschmack bey anständiger Richtigkeit erhalten, vor Fallen in die Sümpfe der musikalischen Trivialität bewahren, im Gegentheile vielmehr ihn noch verfeinern kann."

37 *Wöchentliche Nachrichten* I:27 (30 December 1766), 210–11, review of Carl Joseph Toeschi's *Six Simphonies*.

38 *Hamburgische neue Zeitung* 64 (21 April 1773), review of Carl Friedrich Abel's *Six Symphonies a 2 Violons, Taille & Basse Hautbois & Cors de Chasse*, Op. 10. London. "So neu Abel schreibt, so finden wir doch nichts von dem komischen Gepolter oder Gepitzel, das so oft für Musik ausgeschrien wird, und höchstens Musick fürs Zwerchfall seyn mag, wovon aber noch nie eine Nerve eines Menschenherzens ist bewegt worden."

39 Carl Friedrich Abel, *Six Selected Symphonies*, edited by Sanford Helm, Recent Researches in the Music of the Classical Era, 3 (Madison, WI: A-R Editions, 1977), pp. 38–55.

40 *Unterhaltungen* VII/5 (May 1769), 459–62, review of Georg Simon Löhlein's *Sei Sonate con variate repetizioni per il Clavicembalo*, Op. 2. Leipzig: Breitkopf. "Die chromatischen Vorschläge S. 19 im *Allegro assai* scheinen uns bloß eine Modeschönheit; gute Wirkung thun sie hier gar nicht."

41 *Hamburgischer Correspondent* 161 (10 October 1766), review of Löhlein's *Sei Partite per il Clavicembalo*. Leipzig. "Den Anfängern und dem Frauenzimmer werden die kleinen leicht zu behaltenden Tanzstücke angenehm seyn, die jeder Parthie angehängt sind."

42 *Wöchentliche Nachrichten* II:41 (11 April 1768), 317–19, review of I. B. Schmid's *VI Sonates de Clavecin avec accompagnement ad libitum de deux Violons et Basse continue*. "Sie sind, was die grössern Sätze anbelanget, ziemlich Sinfonienmässig, und der hin und wieder aufstoßenden harmonischen Unrichtigkeiten ungeachtet, für gewisse Liebhaber sehr angenehm und munter; die kleinern Sätze sind tändelnd und artig; und wenn Herr Schmid die Absicht hatte dem musicalischen Frauenzimmer zu gefallen, so scheint er seine Absicht nicht verfehlt zu haben."

43 *Wöchentliche Nachrichten* I:31 (27 January 1767), 243–44, review of Giovanni

Gabriel Meder's *Sei Sinfonie a due Violini, Viola e Basso, due Corni, due Oboe o Flauti traversi*, Op. 1. "Menuetten bey Sinfonien kommen uns immer vor, wie Schminkpflästerchen auf dem Angesichte einer Mannsperson; sie geben dem Stück ein Stutzerhaftes Ansehen, und verhindern den männlichen Eindruck, den die ununterbrochene Folge drey aufeinander sich beziehender ernsthaften Sätze allemal macht, und worinnen eine der vernehmsten Schönheiten des Vortrags bestehet." To "gender" the Minuet as feminine, as Matthew Head does, oversimplifies the issue, at least in terms of the reviews in this study. See his "'Like Beauty Spots on the Face of a Man': Gender in 18th-Century North-German Discourse on Genre," *Journal of Musicology* 13 (Spring 1995), 143–67.

44 Johann Christoph Stockhausen, *Critischer Entwurf einer auserlesenen Bibliothek*, 4th edn. (Berlin, 1771), 464–65, quoted in Unverricht, *Geschichte des Streichtrios*, p. 94. "Jetzt nehmen die Sachen von Heiden, Toeschi, Cannabisch, Filz, Pugnani, Campioni, sehr überhand. Man darf aber nur halber Kenner seyn, und das Leere, die seltsame Mischung vom comischen und ernsthaften, tändelnden und rührenden, zu merken, welche allenthalben herrscht. Die Fehler gegen den Satz, besonders gegen den Rhythmus, und meistentheils eine große Unwissenheit des Contrapunkts, ohne die noch keiner ein gutes Trio gemacht hat, sind in allen diesen sehr häufig. Nur der lobt sie, dem eine Zeile glänzende Melodie alles ist. Die neumodischen Trio's sind oft ehrliche Solo's oder Duetten gewesen, die man zu allem machen kann. Eben das gilt auch von den Quatuor's dieser Herren."

45 "Abhandlung vom musikalischen Geschmack," and "Von dem wienerischen Geschmack in der Musik." Both are quoted in Unverricht, *Geschichte des Streichtrios*, p. 87; the latter is mentioned with some sarcasm in one of Agricola's reviews in the *Allgemeine deutsche Bibliothek* (VIII/1 [1768], 272–73), and is cited in H. C. Robbins Landon, *Haydn: Chronicle & Works*, 5 vols. (Bloomington: Indiana University Press, 1976–80), vol. II, pp. 130–31.

46 *Allgemeine deutsche Bibliothek* VIII/1 (1768), 272–73, review of Schwanberger's *Sonate a due Violini e Violoncello*, cited above. "Wir könnten dieses hier durch eine Vergleichung seiner Arbeiten mit den Arbeiten mancher neuen Italiener, und ihrer blinden Nachsprecher oder Nachcomponirer, beweisen. Aber wir würden gewiß manche Crassationscomponisten (Grassations= soll es vielleicht heissen, und das bedeutet nach Gesners Lexikon: Ungestümmigkeit, Räuberey, nächtliches Umlaufen, lauter würdige Gegenstände der musikalischen Nachahmung!)"; and *Allgemeine deutsche Bibliothek* X/1 (1769), 245–46, review of Friedrich Hartmann Graf's *Sei Quartetti, a Flauto traverso, Violino, Viola e Basso*. "[Sie sind] aber doch besser als manche andere Quatuors und Quinquet, deren der Po, der Rhein, und die Donau itzo zuweilen zu uns schicken. Viele dieser leztern, würden bessere Tänze für den Harlequin, ja, wohl manchmal gar für den Hanswurst abgeben. Y. [Agricola]" See also his review of Hertel's *Sei Sinfonie* in IV/2 (1767), 289–90.

47 *Magazin der Musik* I/2 (7 December 1783), 1314–15, review of Carl Joseph

Birnbach's *Concert pour le Clavessin. Avec l'Accompagnement de deux Violons, deux Hautbois, deux Cors de Chasse, Taille & Basse.* "Scheint aus den Gegenden des Rheins, oder dem südlichern Deutschland zu kommen; und das ist leider genug gesagt. Alle das dortherige Geklimper kennt man den Augenblick an den einförmigen Figuren, den alltäglichen Modulationen, abgedroschnen Harfenbässen, beständigem Auf= und Herunterrennen der diatonischen Scala, und solchen Kunststücklein, die auf so wenig verschiedne Art in allerley verschiednen Formate, und gemeiniglich auf sehr weissem Imperial= oder Royalpapier, das noch dazu zu einem gewissen andern Gebrauche, der die wahre Bestimmung solcher Arbeiten wäre, zu steif ist, uns für Musik verkauft wird; und die ächten Arbeiten besserer Meister aus den dasigen Gegend verdrängt."

48 *Berlinische musikalische Zeitung* 7 (23 March 1793), 26, review of the second book of Johann Georg Witthauer's *Sechs Claviersonaten für Liebhaber und angehende Clavierspieler.* Berlin: Neue Musikhandlung.

49 *Allgemeine Litteratur-Zeitung* III/250 (20 September 1792), 632, review of the first book of Johann Georg Witthauer's *Sechs Claviersonaten für Liebhaber und angehende Clavierspieler.* Berlin: Mauer, 1792. "Die älteren schweren klassischen Claviersachen aus der Bachischen Schule werden – leider zu früh! – nach und nach bey Seite gelegt; und die neuen galanten, leichteren Claviersachen aus der Reichsschule drängen sich mit Ungestürm an ihre Stelle."

50 *Allgemeine deutsche Bibliothek* LXVIII/2 (1786), 456–58. "Kann viel Wahres enthalten: aber Hr. Birnbach lebt ja in Breßlau an der Oder! Gk. [Türk]"

51 *Kritische Briefe* II/82 (17 October 1761), 141–42, review of Georg Christoph Wagenseil's *Tre Divertimenti per Cimbalo.* Nicolai, 1761; *VI. Divertimenti da Cimbalo,* Op. 1–3. Vienna: Agostino Bernardi, 1753. *Kritische Briefe* II/83 (25 October 1761), 145–47, review of Johann Adam Hiller's *Loisir musical, contenant deux Sonates, un air Italien & quelques pieces de Galanterie, pour le clavecin.* Leipzig: Breitkopf, 1762.

52 See, for example, a review of Kozeluch's *Trois Sonates pour le Clavecin ou forte Piano,* Op. 8, in the *Magazin der Musik* I/2 (18 September 1783), 921–22. The reviewer compares him favorably to Haydn.

53 If 10 percent seems too small a percentage to have the rhetorical effect for which I am arguing, it should be remembered that compositions by Italians accounted for only about 7 percent of the reviews during that period. In addition, anti-Italian comments had to compete with other aesthetic and musical issues in limited space, and constituted a major concern in context.

54 *Hamburgischer Correspondent* Beytrag (September 1777), review of Franz Ignaz Beck's *Sonates pour le Clavecin ou le Piano forte.* "Diese Sonaten würden uns noch besser gefallen, wenn nicht in allen ohne Ausnahme ein beständiger Harfenbaß angebracht wäre, der sie zu einförmig macht. Indessen ist dieser Baß richtiger gesetzt, wie in vielen andern ähnlichen Sonaten."

55 *Magazin der Musik* I/1 (4 April 1783), 482–83, review of Johann Gottfried Vierling's *Sechs Sonaten für das Clavier.* Leipzig: Breitkopf, 1781. "Diese Sonaten

sind nach der wahren Spielmanier dieses Instruments gesetzt. Da giebt es keine Floskeln aus Oper=Arien, mit Trommel= und Harfen=Bässe geziert; sondern eigne, mit Gründlichkeit und Anstand ausgearbeitete Sätze, welche aber auch einen geübten Spieler erfodern. N. N."

56 *Gothaische gelehrte Zeitungen* 5 (17 January 1781), 39, review of Johann Paul Schulthesius's *Drey Sonaten für das Klavier, oder Piano forte, mit Begleitung einer obligaten Violine*, Op. 1. ". . . die Arbeit selbst aber vortreflich, natürlich und leicht, und voll hinreissenden Gesangs. Wird Klavier und besonders die Violine in dem eigentlichen Geschmack des Gesangs vorgetragen, so muß es empfunden werden können, daß es Früchte sind, die unter italienischem Himmel gediehen und gereift sind."

57 *Musikalische Monatsschrift* VI (December 1792), 162, review of August Eberhard Müller's *Trois Sonates pour le Clavecin ou Forte Piano*. Offenbach: André. "Es sind ganze Sätze in diesen Sonaten, die an Erfindung und Ausführung selbst einem Clementi Ehre machen könnten."

58 *Wöchentliche Nachrichten* I:17 (21 October 1766), 132, review of C. P. E. Bach's *Sechs leichte Claviersonaten*. Leipzig: Breitkopf. "Wir haben ein Feld durchwandelt, das sehr unfruchtbar, voller Dornen und Hecken war, und kommen nun in eine angenehme Gegend, in welcher uns die schöne Natur, mit allen Reizen der Kunst geschmückt, in die Augen fällt . . . Die Sätze sind alle ernsthaft; keine Menuetten und Polonoisen . . . Jeder dieser Sonaten bestehet demnach aus drey Sätzen; die eben so reich an Erfindung, an Melodie, an reiner und künstlicher Harmonie sind, als die übrigen Arbeiten dieses berühmten Verfassers."

59 Also see the *Allgemeine deutsche Bibliothek* II/2 (1766), 268, review of C. P. E. Bach's *Clavierstücke verschiedener Art*.

60 *Berlinische Nachrichten* 8 (18 January 1766), 31, review of C. P. E. Bach's *Sechs leichte Clavier=Sonaten*. Leipzig, 1766. [Wq. 53] "Daß Herr Bach einer von den größten und berühmtesten Tonkünstlern unseres Jahrhunderts ist, bleibt eine ewige Wahrheit. Daß sich der lebhafte, fruchtreiche und einschleichende Bachische Geist in diesen sechs leichten Sonaten, wie in allen seinen Werken, fühlbar und lockend zeigt, bleibt auch eine unwidersprechliche Wahrheit. Daß ihn seine höchstvorzügliche Wissenschaft in der Tonkunst niemahls stolz macht, bleibt ebenfalls eine unläugbare Wahrheit. Daß er bey seiner Stärke in der Musik ein schönes Herz, und einen edlen Charakter, besitzt, wissen wir aus eigener Erfahrung."

61 *Allgemeine deutsche Bibliothek* II/2 (1766), 268, review of C. P. E. Bach's *Clavierstücke verschiedener Art* [Wq. 112]. Part 1. Berlin: Winter, 1765. "Alle Stücke sind mit dem erfindungsreichen Geiste und dem Feuer geschrieben, welches man in allen Werken des Herrn Verfassers schon längst gewohnt ist. Sie brauchen also keiner weitern Anpreisung. P. [Agricola]"

62 *Allgemeine deutsche Bibliothek* V/2 (1767), 268–70, review of C. P. E. Bach's *Sonatina I.II.III. a Cembalo concertato, II. Flauti, II. Violini, Violetta e Basso*. Berlin: Winter. [Wq. 106–108] "In diesen Sonaten hat nicht der das wohlklingende

Reich übersehen sollende Componist, sondern der blosse Clavierist bey Hrn. Bach gar zu sehr die Oberhand behalten. Betrachten wir die für das Clavier durch und durch besonders ausgezogene Stimme: so sind es die schönsten Claviersonaten die man wünschen kann. Aber zu Sonaten von der Art, welche auf dem Titel angezeiget wird, gehörte eine ganz andere Form. P. [Agricola]"

63 *Gothaische gelehrte Zeitungen* 89 (6 November 1784), 730, review of Christian Kalkbrenner's *Trois Sonates pour le Clavecin ou le Pianoforte avec l'accompagnement d'un Violon & d'un Basse*, Op. 2. [Kassel]: Orphelin. ". . . In diesen Sonaten herrscht der Modegeschmack eines Giordani, Schröter, u.a. für den sich immer die Schönen und die meisten Liebhaber erklären werden, weil die Schule des Hamburger Bachs blos für stärkere Nerven ist, und zu fodern, daß jedermann in dieser Manier solle setzen können, wäre eben das, als angehende Dichtern zu sagen. Seyd Klopstocke, Göthe, Wielande!"

64 *Hamburgische neue Zeitung* 21 (5 February 1777), review of Johann Wilhelm Häßler's *Sechs Sonaten fürs Clavier*. Leipzig: Schwickert, 1776. "Auch gegenwärtigen Sonaten haben das Gepräge der guten claviermäßigen Art, sie sind voller guten Harmonie und rührender Melodie, und unterscheiden sich also von dem Schwarm jetziger seichten italienischen und andern Modekompositionen auf diesem Instrumente gar sehr."

65 *Hamburgischer Correspondent* 26 (14 February 1778), review of Daniel Gottlob Türk's *Sechs Sonaten für das Clavier*. Zweyte Sammlung. Leipzig and Halle: Breitkopf, 1777. "Man sieht aus selbigen, daß der Verfasser unsern Bach studirt hat. Guter Gesang und richtige Harmonie, zuweilen auch neue Einfälle geben diesen Sonaten vor hundert andern von unsern modernen Componisten einen großen Vorzug, die ein Stück aus der Melodie einer Opern=Arie nehmen, denn einen fehlerhaften Harfen=Baß dazu setzen, und nun ihre Sonate fertig haben."

66 *Musicalische Bibliotek* II (1785), 245–48, review of Christian Benjamin Uber, d. J.'s *Six Divertissements pour le Clavecin avec l'Accompagnement d'une Flute, d'un Violon, les deux Cors de chasse et de la Basse*. "Indessen Wird Herr Uber immer solche Leute unterhalten, di nicht durch C. P. E. Bach's und andrer groser Mäner geistvolle Werke bereits verwönt sind."

67 *Allgemeine deutsche Bibliothek* II/2 (1777), 481, review of Franz Duschek's *Sonate per il Clavi Cembalo*. Gerle, 1774. "Als modisches Stück betrachtet, recht artig. Zuweisen, in einzelnen Stücken, scheint es, als ob der Verfasser ein Bach für Prag seyn wolle. Aber wie weit ist C. P. E. Bach von Duschek entfernt! So weit, wie Hamburg von Prag. Mr. [Reichardt]"

68 *Hamburgischer Correspondent* 183 (14 November 1772), review of J. C. Bach's *Six Quatuor a une Flute, Violon, Alto & Basso*, Op. 8. Amsterdam: Hummel. "Nicht völlig so ausgearbeitet, als die von Hayden und Bocherini, aber für die Liebhaber wegen der reizenden Melodie und der dem Herrn Bach in London eigenthümlichen Simplicität und Eleganz derselben äußerst schätzbar."

69 *Hamburgischer Correspondent* Beytrag 8 (1779), review of Hadrava's *Six Sonates pour le Clavecin ou le Piano forte*. Berlin: Hummel. "Wir haben viel Gutes in

diesen Sonaten angetroffen, aber auch viele Sätze, Wendungen und Ausweichungen, die schon sehr gebraucht worden. Freylich ist es sehr schwer, bey der Menge der jetzt herauskommenden Musikstücke neu und original zu seyn, wie Bach und Hayden."

70 *Musikalisches Kunstmagazin* I:4 (1782), 205, review of Joseph Haydn's *Six Simphonies à 2 Violons 2 Obois 2 Flutes 2 Corps de Chasse, Viole & Basse*, Op. 18 [Hob. I:75, 63, 70, 71, 62, 74]. Amsterdam and Berlin: Hummel; and *Six Quatuors ou divertissements a Deux Violons, Taille & Basse composés*, Op. 19 [Hob. III:41, 37, 38, 39, 40, 42]. Amsterdam and Berlin: Hummel. "Wenn wir auch nur einen Haydn und einen C. Ph. E. Bach hätten, so könnten wir Deutsche schon kühn behaupten, daß wir eine eigne Manier haben und unsre Instrumentalmusik die interessanteste von allen ist."

71 *Magazin der Musik*, review of Joseph Haydn's *La Chasse, grande Sinfonie a 10 parties obl.* [Hob. I:73] Vienna: Toricella. "Diese Symphonie ist ihres Meisters eben so würdig als die neuesten Op. 18 lib. 1.2.3. und bedarf unsers Ruhms keinesweges. Bey der Anhörung derselben verrieth gleich der Anfang und die herliche Bearbeitung der Folge in allen den Kopf des grossen Verfassers, der in neuen Ideen unerschöpflich zu seyn scheinet . . . Möchte doch Heydn, diese grosse Symphonienepoche mit mehrern solcher herrlichen Arbeiten krönen, und alle schlechte Symphonienschreiber dadurch zum Stillschweigen oder zur bessern Bearbeitung ihrer flüchtigen Aufsätze bringen, durch die niemand als sie selbst Vergnügen haben."

72 See, for example, the review of symphonies [Hob. I:17, Es1, 29, 28, 9, 3] in the *Wöchentliche Nachrichten* IV:5 (29 January 1770), 37–38 (Es1 is spurious), or the review of three accompanied sonatas in the *Hamburgischer Correspondent Beytrag* 6 (1785) [possibly Hob. XV:3–5].

73 *Allgemeine deutsche Bibliothek* CXI/1 (1792), 121–22, review of Joseph Haydn's *Trois Quatuors pour deux Violons, Alto et Basse*, Op. 59 [Hob. III:57–59, known as Op. 54]. "Wenn wir unsern Lesern sagen, daß diese drey Quartette eines Haydn vollkommen würdig sind, so brauchen wir wohl zu ihrer Empfehlung weiter nichts mehr hinzuzufügen. Denn wer kennt nicht Haydn als einen der größten jetzt lebenden Tonsetzer! Auch in den vor uns liegenden Quartetten muß man die originelle Laune, den musikalischen Witz und den unerschöpflichen Reichthum des Gedanken des Verf. bewundern. Wir getrauen uns zwar nicht, zu entscheiden, welches von diesen drey Quartetten vor den übrigen beyden den Vorzug verdient. Of. [Türk]"

74 *Erlangische gelehrte Anmerkungen* 16 (15 April 1788), 228, review of Ignaz Pleyel's *Deux grandes Sonates pour le Clavecin ou Piano Forte avec accompagnement d'un Violon ad libitum*, Op. 7. "Gleich auf den ersten Anblick ist der Schüler des grossen Haydn in diesen Sonaten unverkennbar, wenn man schon seine Delikatesse und unerschöpfliche Laune vermißt."

75 *Musikalischer Almanach* III (1784), 17–19, review of Salomon Greßler's *Sechs Sonaten fürs Clavier*. Leipzig: Schwickert, 1781. "Diese Sonaten sind in der

wahren Schreibart geschrieben, worinn Claviersonaten geschrieben seyn müssen. Man findet darinnen weder das neumodische Hokuspokus von so vielfachen Oktaven als beyde Hände greifen können, noch Trommel- oder Harfenbässe, sondern einen ordentlichen, vernünftigen und gesetzten Gang, von welchem jene Creutz- und Quersprünge weit entfernt sind."

76 *Berlinische musikalische Zeitung* 39 (26 October 1793), 156, review of pieces by [Jan Ladislav] Dussek, J. G. Ferrari, Gabriel Grenier, Hermann, and Daniel Steibelt. "Für den Liebhaber eines leichteren, neumodischen Klavierspiels . . . Alle diese Sachen, mannigfaltigen Inhalts, besonders die letztere von Steibelt werden dem grossen Haufen gewöhnlicher Dilettanten und Damen Unterhaltung gewähren; wenn auch der Kenner sie nicht für sich zurücklegen würde."

77 *Magazin der Musik* I/2 (7 December 1783), 1255–59, review of Wolf's *Sechs Sonatinen für das Clavier*. Dessau: Buchhandlung der Gelehrten, 1783. "Auch hat er sie einer Virtuosinn gewidmet, die in diesem Stücke seine eigensinnigsten Foderungen zu erfüllen im Stande ist. Selten kann man dieses von dem weiblichen Geschlechte rühmen. Ihre Finger, so viel Uebung und Fertigkeit sie auch haben mögen, besitzen gewöhnlicherweise die Nerven und die Kraft nicht, die zu der prallen, characteristischen Darstellung ausgezeichneter Claviergedanken noth-wendig ist, sie schlüpfen fast immer zu schnell über die Tasten weg, als glühten sie; und ihre Sprache ermangelt des nöthigen Lichts und Schattens. Allein die Frau Capellmeisterinn Westenholzen . . . macht hiervon eine Ausnahme; verbindet mit alle dem feinen Gefühl des Ausdrucks, das der weiblichen Execution eigen ist, die männlichste, festeste Sicherheit; und weis, eine ächte Schülerinn des einzig wahren, des Bachischen Vortrags, ihrem Spiele eben so viel Kraft als Schimmer und Reiz mitzutheilen . . . C. F. C."

78 *Erfurtische gelehrte Zeitungen* 39 (17 August 1785), 311, review of Charles Friedrich Vater's *Trois Sonates pour le Clavecin avec l'Accompagnement d'un Violon*, Op. 1. Breslau: Korn, 1784. "Um es bey niemanden zu verderben . . . hat er auch in der zweyten Sonate für Kenner eine Fuge, mit Respect zu sagen, gegeben. Doch ist auch diese vermuthlich der Damen wegen in ziemlich galanten und freyen Style gearbeitet."

79 *Musikalische Korrespondenz* 25 (20 June 1792), 195–96, review of Josepha Barbara von Auernhammer's *VI Variazioni dell' Aria "der Vogelfänger bin ich ja," nell Opera die Zauberflöte, del Sigr. Mozart per Clavicembalo o Piano-Forte*. "Die Verfasserin . . . tritt nun wieder mit einem neuen Produkt unter uns auf, das manchen männlichen Werke von dieser Art an die Seite gestellt zu werden ver-dienet, und sowohl ihren Einsichten, als ihrem Geschmack Ehre macht. Tiefgedachte harmonische Verwiklungen, oder Säze, die sich auf das Studium des Kontrapunkts gründen, wie wir solche in den Werken eines Mozarts, Clementi und Voglers antreffen, finden sich hier zwar nicht."

80 *Hamburgischer Correspondent* 110 (11 July 1795), review of Catérine née Schiatti's *Trois Sonates pour le Clavecin ou le Piano-Forte &c*, Op. 1. St. Petersburg: J. D. Gerstenberg & Comp. "Eine Erscheinung, welche in der

musikalischen Componisten Epoche macht; denn bis jetzt hatte noch kein Frauenzimmer diese Kunst mit solcher Gründlichkeit, wie der Verfasserin dieser Sonaten, bearbeitet. Die vortrefliche Ausarbeitung, mit Natur, Kunst und einem ganz neuen Geschmack verbunden, setzt diese Sonaten den Werken der geschicktesten Tonkünstler mit Recht an die Seite und beweiset zugleich, wie viel die Kunst gewinnt, wenn Euterpe selbst so treflich sich ihrer annimmt. R**"

81 *Berlinische musikalische Zeitung* 46 (30 November 1793), 183, review of Groene's *Zwölf Serenaten*, cited in chapter 2.

82 *Musikalisches Kunstmagazin* I:4 (1782), 205, review of Joseph Haydn's *Six Simphonies*, Op. 18 and *Six Quatuors*, Op. 19, cited above. "Gleich seine ersten Arbeiten, die vor einigen zwanzig Jahren unter uns bekannt wurden, zeigten von seiner eigenen gutmüthigen Launen: es war da aber meistens mehr jugendlicher Muthwille und oft ausgelaßne Lustigkeit, mit oberflächlicher harmonischer Bearbeitung; nach und nach wurde die Laune männlicher, und die Arbeit gedachter."

83 *Hamburgischer Correspondent* Beytrag 7 (1781), review of Friedrich Wilhelm Heinrich Benda's *Trois Sonates pour le Clavecin avec l'Accompagnement d'une Flute ou Violon*, Op. 3. Berlin and Amsterdam: Hummel. (Also found in the *Magazin der Musik* I/1: 81. 15 January 1783.) "Drey gute Sonaten, deren Verfasser sich von der Modesucht nicht hinreißen lassen, sondern in einem männlichen Styl gearbeitet hat."

84 *Musikalische Real-Zeitung* II/38 (23 September 1789), 296–97, review of Leopold Kozeluch's *III Sonates pour le Clavecin ou Piano-Forte*, Op. 20 and *III. Sonates pour le Clavecin ou Piano-Forte avec l'Accompagnement d'un Violon & Violoncelle*, Op. 21. Paris. "Nur scheint es uns, daß der Herr Verf. zu sehr dem Modegeschmak unsers Zeitalters opfere: anstatt in seiner eigenen großen Seele sich Ideale zu schaffen und sie mit männlicher Kraft darzustellen, sind es, wenn man so sagen darf, blosse Kopien aus dem gemeinen Leben niedlich aufgeputzt, wie ein Mädchen, das durch Blumen und Bänder zu gefallen sucht. Daher wird man auch zwischen den Werken des Herrn K. und Bachs nie eine Vergleichung anstellen können und dieser wird auch bei der wenigeren Volltönigkeit, die in den seinigen herrscht, in den Augen des Kenners immer einen vorzüglicheren Werth haben."

85 *Musikalische Korrespondenz* 30 (27 July 1791), 233–35, review of the Abbé Georg Joseph Vogler's *Variations sur l'air de Marlborough pour le Piano-Forte avec un Accompagnement de 2 Violons, Alte, Basse, Flûtes, 2 Fagottes & de Cors ad libitum*. Speier: Bossler, 1791. "Mit scheelen Augen werden manche unserer modischen Variationenschreiber an diesem Meisterstük deutscher Kraft und Kunst hinaufbliken." Other references to "powerful" and "power" can be found in the *Neue Leipziger gelehrte Zeitungen* II/4 123 (19 October 1786), 1966, review of Christian Gottlob Saupe's *Drey Sonaten und sechs Sonatinen für die Liebhaber der Musik*. Glachau: Saupe, 1786; and in the *Allgemeine deutsche Bibliothek* XCIV/1 (1790), 135–37, review of *Olla Potrida für Clavierspieler*. Berlin: Rellstab.

The latter takes an uncharacteristic (for this time) stab at Italian overture composers.

86 *Allgemeine deutsche Bibliothek* CIX/1 (1792), 137–38, review of Johann Georg Witthauer's *Sonata pel Clavicembalo o Piano Forte.* Berlin: Rellstab. "Sie ist im ächten, ernsthaften Style geschrieben, und erhebt sich gar sehr über viele unsrer modernen Sonaten . . . Of. [Türk]"

87 *Hamburgischer Correspondent* Beytrag 11 (1779), review of Joseph Haydn's *Six Quatuors Concertants à deux Violons, Viola & Violoncello,* Op. 16 [Hob. III:31–36, known as Op. 20]. Berlin and Amsterdam: Hummel. "Von dem innern Werthe der Quatuor selbst brauchen wir nichts zu sagen. Sie sind ihres Verfassers würdig, und gehören zu den besten, die bisher von ihm erschienen sind."

88 *Allgemeine deutsche Bibliothek* LXXV/2 (1787), 459, review of Uber's *Trois Sonates pour le Clavecin avec l'accompagnement d'un Violon et Violoncelle obligés, et de deux Cors de chasse ad libitum, de même d'une Flute pour la prémière Sonate,* Op. 1. "Es fehlt ihm zwar nicht an einiger Kunstkenntniß, aber sie erstreckt sich nicht weiter, als auf die Oberfläche der Kunst; auch nicht an Gedanken, aber sie sind mager an innerm Gehalte. Swr. [Schulz]"

4 Answering with aesthetic criteria

1 *Altonaischer gelehrter Mercurius* VII/24 (17 June 1779), 190. "Wir wollen uns der Freyheit, die der Verf. sich nimmt, bedienen, und gerade heraussagen, dass er von der Kunst, wovon er spricht, wenig oder gar nichts versteht, dass fast alles, was er sagt, lauter Froschgequäcke und Nachplauderey ist, und dass ganz andere Leute dazu gehören, um in einer Kunst, deren Aesthetik leider noch so wenig bekannt ist, Wahrheiten zu schreiben."

2 *Allgemeine deutsche Bibliothek* LXVIII/2 (1786), 461, review of Louis Abeille's *Deux Sonates pour le Claveçin, avec l'accompagnement d'un Violon etc.* Nuremberg: Schmidt. "Neue Gedanken sucht man hier vergebens; und selbst die schon oft verarbeiteten kommen immer in der schönsten – Unordnung vor, so daß wir vom Herrn A. wohl schwerlich eine Theorie der musikalischen Aesthetik zu erwarten haben. Xw. [Türk]"

3 James Engell, *The Creative Imagination: Enlightenment to Romanticism* (Cambridge, MA and London: Harvard University Press, 1981), p. 33.

4 Meyer Howard Abrams, *Doing Things with Texts: Essays in Criticism and Critical Theory,* edited with a Foreword by Michael Fisher (New York: Norton, 1989), pp. 57–58.

5 *Wöchentliche Nachrichten* II:41 (11 April 1768), 317–19, review of Schmidt's *VI Sonate,* cited in chapter 3. "Wir könnten uns hier über die Güte dieser Sonaten weitläuftig ausbreiten; aber wir wollen unsre Meynung kurz sagen: Sie sind, was die grössern Sätze anbelanget, ziemlich Sinfonienmässig, und der hin und wieder aufstoßenden harmonischen Unrichtigkeiten ungeachtet, für gewisse Liebhaber sehr angenehm und munter; die kleinern Sätze sind tändelnd und artig . . . Wir

würden künftig noch bessere Arbeiten von ihm erwarten und mit Vergnügen sehen, wenn er sich eine kleine Ermahnung nicht wollte verdrüßen lassen, auf rhythmische Symmetrie nemlich, und harmonische Reinigkeit sorgfältiger bedacht zu seyn: denn wer heißt ihn z.e. im Allegretto der ersten Sonate, gleich im Anfange zween überflüßige Tacte, den fünften und sechsten einschieben, die unten bey der Wiederholung der Melodie, der Tonwendung wegen, noch eher nöthig gewesen wären? Wer kann folgende Stellen: für harmonisch richtig erkennen? Es wäre keine angenehme Arbeit, alle dergleichen Fehler und Unachtsamkeiten im ganzen Werke aufzusuchen; wir sind daher mit unserer Untersuchung nur auf der dritten und vierten Seite stehen geblieben. Bey dem allen aber sagen wir doch, daß die Sonaten des Herrn Schmide gewissen Liebhabern angenehm seyn können, die das für Kleinigkeiten und Grillenfängerey halten, was andern das wesentliche in der Composition zu seyn scheint . . . Sollte Hr. Schmid auf den Beyfall gelehrter Kenner künftig Anspruch machen wollen, so rathen wir ihm die Regeln der Harmonie noch etwas sorgfältiger zu studiren, und ihre Anwendung in der Composition genauer zu erforschen; denn nicht alles, was uns in die Finger läuft, ist das, was wir erhaschen sollten."

6 *Hamburgische neue Zeitung* 12 (20 January 1770), review of *Musikalisches Vielerley.* Hamburg: Bock. "Diese zwey Bogen . . . enthalten . . . eine Sonate mit veränderten Reprisen von unserm Hrn. Bach. Er hat sich bemüht, leicht zu seyn; ein Autor verliert allemal, wenn er sich einen gewissen Zwang anthun muß, und sich nicht ganz seinem Genie überlassen kann, indessen hat diese Sonate bey ihrer Leichtigkeit noch immer vieles von der Bachischen Laune."

7 *Hamburgischer Correspondent* 37 (5 March 1785), review of F. S. Sander's *Sechs Clavier=Sonaten.* Part 1. Breslau: Sander, 1785. "Herr Sander kennt die Natur des Instruments, hat gute Einsichten in die Regeln einer reinen Harmonie, und verbindet die letztere mit einem angenehmen und geschmackvollen Gesange, der in seinen Sonaten herrscht und in allen guten Sonaten herrschen muß. Man findet hier keine bekannte Melodie aus einer bekannten Opernarie mit einem bekannten unreinen Harfenbasse begleitet, dergleichen Ingredienzien sich verschiedene neue Componisten nach der Mode zur Verfertigung ihrer Sonaten mit solcher Leichtigkeit bedienen, daß sie ihre in Kupfer gestochenen Opern von Nro. 1 bis wer weiß wie weit, in kurzer Zeit vermehren; sondern man sieht, daß Herr S. selbst erfinden, und seine Ideen alsdenn nach den Regeln der Kunst zu Papier bringen kann. Er verdient also Schätzung und Aufmunterung vom musikalischen Publicum, damit er die Regeln der Kunst immer mehr studire, ohne welche alle Producte des größten Genies mangelhaft sind, und ihren gehörigen Effect nicht zuwege bringen. Die Sonaten sind nicht zu lang."

8 *Allgemeine deutsche Bibliothek* LXXII/1 (1787), 164–65, review of Haydn's *Grande Simphonie à plusieurs instrumens,* Op. 38–40 [Hob. I:80, 79, 81]. Vienna: Artaria. "Bey jeder dieser drey Simfonien befinden sich außer den gewöhnlichen Instrumenten noch einer Flöte und zwey Fagotte. Mit welcher Kunst und Feinheit diese von dem unerschöpflichen Genius des unnachahmlichen Haydn zur

Mitwirkung und Verstärkung des Ausdrucks angewandt und benutzt worden sind, läßt sich durch Worte nicht beschreiben: man muß es hören; und wer hat wohl je eine Haydnsche Simfonie nicht mit Entzucken gehört? Werke von solcher Originalität und Vollkommenheit, und von so allgemein anerkanntem Werthe, in einer Recension anpreisen zu wollen, wäre lächerlich, und der Rec. fühlt zu sehr, wie weit Hr. H. über sein Lob erhalten ist. Atr. [Schulz]"

9 *Berlinische musikalische Zeitung* 7 (23 March 1793), 26, review of Abeille's *Sonates pour le Clav. ou Forte Piano.* Heilborn: Amon. "Wenn man nicht einzig von der Bachischen Manier ausgehen will, was man nicht grade überall muss, so wird man in diesen Sonaten mancherley Unterhaltung, für die Phantasie sowohl als für die Finger, finden. Sie sind hin und wieder frappant, haben etwas einiges, dass man bisarr nennen könnte und die Klarheit aufhebt, sind im ganzen aber brav und fleissig gearbeitet."

10 *Erfurtische gelehrte Zeitungen* 25 (27 March 1777), 219–20, review of Türk's *Sechs Sonaten für das Clavier.* Leipzig and Halle: Breitkopf, 1776. "Hr. Türk ist sonst schon als einer unsrer geschicktesten Tonsetzer bekannt gewesen, und nun hat er sich durch diese Sonaten noch grössern Ruhm erworben. Sie empfehlen sich vorzüglich durch das Sangbare und Sentimentalische, oder durch eine gefühlvolle Melodie. Durchgehends herrschet, bey strenger Beobachtung aller Regeln der Theorie, ein meisterhafter ans Herz dringender Ausdruck."

11 *Allgemeines Verzeichniß neuer Bücher* VI/11 (1781), 858, review of *Zwey und dreyßig Menuetten, von Böhmischen Tonkünstlern.* Rothenburg an der Fulda: Hermstadt, 1781. "Diese Menuetten sind ganz dem Zwecke gemäß, zu welchem sie da sind, das ist zum Tanz. Mehrentheils muntere freudeerweckende Melodien, ohne gesuchte Modulation."

12 Engell, *The Creative Imagination,* pp. 119, 176, 181.

13 This type of research process is described by Stephen M. North in *The Making of Knowledge in Composition: Portrait of an Emerging Field* (Portsmouth, NH: Boynton/Cook, 1987), p. 307.

14 The problems of substantiating the results of statistical analyses of raw data, one of the primary tools of quantitative history, are discussed in Stone, *The Past and the Present,* p. 33. The usefulness of quantitative history's results are outlined in Barraclough, *Main Trends,* pp. 57–60.

15 Engell, *The Creative Imagination,* p. 93.

16 Frederick C. Beiser, *The Fate of Reason: German Philosophy from Kant to Fichte* (Cambridge, MA and London: Harvard University Press, 1987), p. 94.

17 *Über Thomas Abbts Schriften, der Torso zu einem Denkmal* (1768), cited in Clark, *Herder,* p. 77.

18 *Allgemeine deutsche Bibliothek* CVIII/1 (1792), 143–44, review of Johann Christoph Friedrich Bach's *Drey leichte Sonaten fürs Klavier oder Piano Forte.* Rinteln: Bösendahl, 1789.

19 Moses Mendelssohn, *Briefe über die Empfindungen* (1755), in *Schriften zur Philosophie, Aesthetik und Apologetik,* edited by Moritz Brasch, vol. II: *Schriften*

zur Psychologie, Aesthetik sowie zur Apologetik des Judentums (Hildesheim: Georg Olms, 1968), p. 28. "Schönheit setzt Einheit im Mannigfaltigen voraus."

20 *Allgemeine deutsche Bibliothek* LIX/1 (1784), 134–35, review of M. C. Grosse's *Sechs Sonaten für das Klavier oder Fortepiano*. Dessau: Gelehrte Buchhandlung, 1784. "Wenn Hr. G. in seinen künftigen Ausarbeitungen der Fruchtbarkeit seiner Einfälle mehr Schranken setzen und suchen wird, jedem Stück durch Einheit und nähere Verbindung der mannichfaltigen Gedanken mehr Ründung zu geben, so hat sich das klavierliebende Publikum viel Gutes von seiner Feder zu versprechen. Smz. [Schulz]"

21 *Wöchentliche Nachrichten* IV (29 October 1770), 344, review of the *Musikalisches Vielerley*. Hamburg: Bach. "Gewisse Componisten, die aus zehnerley abgedroschenen Gedanken ihre rasselnden Sinfonien zusammen setzen, können hier lernen, was ein Hauptgedanke sey, wie sie in den Wendungen durch verschiedene Tonarten, bald ganz, bald zum Theil, Gebrauch davon machen, und was für ein Verhältniß die neu hinzu kommenden Nebengedanken zu diesem Hauptthema haben sollen."

22 *Allgemeine deutsche Bibliothek* VIII/2 (1768), 284–86, review of Friedrich Ernst Benda's *Minuetto per il Cembalo, con Variazioni*. Leipzig: Breitkopf, 1768. "Die Variationen müssen doch, wenn es recht seyn soll, den Hauptaffekt des Stüks daß sie variiren, so viel möglich, beybehalten. X. [Agricola]"

23 Schenk-Güllich, "Anfänge der Musikkritik," pp. 130–31.

24 Clark, *Herder*, p. 216; Engell, *The Creative Imagination*, p. 80.

25 *Musikalischer Almanach* III (1784), 22–38. "Wenn dort die Vernunft und hier der Geschmack (unter Geschmack verstehe ich im musikalischen Verstande nichts anders, als das aus den gesammten musikalischen Grundsätzen entstehende abgezogene Gefühl des Wahren, Richtigen, und Schönen) nicht gehörig zu überdenken und anzuordnen wüßte, was die feurige Einbildungskraft und Begeisterung für einen Weg nehmen soll." This article, which takes the form of a letter to an unidentified nobleman, develops Forkel's aesthetic theories in depth.

26 *Hamburgischer Correspondent* 40 (10 March 1781), review of Haydn's *Six Sonates pour le Clavecin ou le Piano forte*, Op. 17 [Hob. XVI:37, 39, 38, 35, 36, 20]. Berlin and Amsterdam: Hummel.

27 *Musikalische Real-Zeitung* III/16 (21 April 1790), 121–23, review of Freystädtler's *Die Belagerung Belgrads, eine historisch=Türkische Fantasie oder Sonata für das Klavier, mit Begleitung einer Violine*. Vienna, 1789. "Aber dann müßte bei solchen musikalischen Wizelein auf der einen Seite schleppende Weitschweifigkeit und Aufhaschen falscher Objekte vermieden werden; auf der andern Seite hingegen Wahrheit, Deutlichkeit, Ordnung, gesunde Beurtheilungskraft und Geschmak darin herrschen."

28 Engell, *The Creative Imagination*, pp. 15–23.

29 *Dictionnaire de musique*, quoted in le Huray and Day, *Music and Aesthetics*, pp. 85–86.

30 Kirnberger, *The Art of Strict Musical Composition*, p. 416.

31 Victor Lange, *The Classical Age of German Literature 1740–1815* (New York: Holmes & Meier, 1982), p. 59. In the review collective, it was applied to C. P. E. Bach five times in three different publications and once each to Haydn and Mozart.

32 *Musikalische-Realzeitung* 48 (30 November 1791), 377–78, review of Mozart's *Quatuor à 2 Violons, Alto e Violoncello*. Vienna; and *Quartetto per il Clavicembalo o Forte Piano con l'Accompagn. d'un Violino, Viola & Violoncello*, Op. 13 [K. 493]. Vienna: Artaria. "Auch diese beede Quartetten sind mit dem Feuer der Einbildungskraft und Korrektheit geschrieben, wodurch sich Hr. M. schon längst den Ruhm eines der besten Tonsezer in Deutschland erworben hat."

33 Engell, *The Creative Imagination*, p. 80.

34 *Wöchentliche Nachrichten* I:4 (22 July 1766), 28–31, review of Georg Simon Löhlein's *Sei Partite per il Clavicembalo*. "Es ist gut sich bisweilen von der gemeinen Straße zu entfernen, um dem Alltäglichen zu entgehen."

35 *Altonaischer gelehrter Mercurius* V/8 (20 February 1777), 61–62, review of Daniel Gottlob Türk's *Sechs Sonaten für das Clavier*. Leipzig: Breitkopf, 1776. "aufgewärmte Materie mit neuer Brühe übergossen."

36 Engell, *The Creative Imagination*, p. 38.

37 *Musikalische Charlatanerien*, pp. 20–21: "Weiß Herr C. S. wohl, was er hier spricht? Weiß er wohl genau was er sich unter neue Gedanken denkt?" The review in question, of a performance of the "Cantata auf den Geburtstags des Königs," appeared in the *Musikalisches Wochenblatt* I (January 1792), 67.

38 Mendelssohn, *Schriften*, p. 79. Mendelssohn believed music was the only art that could do all three.

39 *Allgemeine deutsche Bibliothek* XXXV/2 (1778), 521–22, review of Uber's *Ein Divertiment für den Flügel, mit 2 Violinen, 2 Flöten, 2 Waldhörnern, Bratsche und Baß*. Breslau: Korn, 1777. "Genie äußert sich doch wohl nicht durch Armuth und Dürftigkeit, durch sclavische Nachahmung, durch Trägheit und Kälte? und dennoch sind dieses die charakteristischen Züge dieses Divertiments und anderer Arbeiten des Hrn. U. F [Reichardt]"

40 Christian Wilhelm Kindleben, *Studenten Lexicon* (Halle: Johann Christian Hendel, 1781). "Laune, wird in verschiedener Bedeutung gebraucht. Der Mensch hat viel Laune, heist: er hat in seinem Umgange, in seinem Ausdruck, in seinen Schriften viel Witz, viel aufgeräumtes Wesen."

41 Wolfgang Schmidt-Hidding, Karl Otto Schütz, and Wido Hempel, *Humor und Witz* (Europäische Schlüsselwörter, 1.) (Munich: Mach Hueber Verlag, 1963), pp. 169–70.

42 Schmidt-Hidding, *Humor und Witz*, pp. 192–93: "Wahrer Humor und ächter Witz lassen sich nicht erzwingen, nicht erkünsteln, aber sie würken, wie das Umschweben eines höheren Genius, wonnevoll, erwärmend, Erfurcht erregend."

43 "Von der Theorie der Musik in so fern sie Liebhabern und Kennern nothwendig und nützlich ist," *Magazin der Musik* I/2 (1 September 1783), 896–903. "Sie sind die Früchte einer lebhaften Einbildungskraft, eines geläuterten Geschmacke;

kurz, nur das erhabene Genie kan [*sic*] sie erreichen. Musicalischer Witz, Laune, Neuheit, Grösse und Erhabenheit gehören hierher . . . Auch der damit verbundene Ausdruck des musicalischen Witzes, der Laune, des Neuen, Unerwarteten, Wunderbaren, der Anmuth, Stärke, des Reichthums, der Grösse und Erhabenheit u.s.m. sind wichtige Gegenstände der musicalischen Kritik."

44 Johann Theodor Jablonskies, *Allgemeines Lexicon der Künste und Wissenschaften*, new edition by Johann Joachim Schwaben (Königsberg and Leipzig: Zeisens Witwe und Hartungs Erben, 1767), s.v. "Affekten."

45 Cowart, "Sense and Sensibility," pp. 251–66.

46 Cowart, "Sense and Sensibility," p. 266.

47 *Ephemereiden der Litteratur und des Theaters* IV/54 (11 November 1786), 302, review of Uber's *Trois Sonates pour le Clavecin avec l'accompagnement d'un Violon et Violoncelle obligés et de deux Cors de Chasse ad libitum*. Breslau: Uber. "Die erste dieser Sonaten mit D dur hat einen Sinfonie-Charakter . . . die dritte aus E dur hat einen tändelnden Charakter."

48 Jakob de Ruiter maintains that both Türk and Sulzer used it in this fashion. See his *Charakterbegriff*, p. 31.

49 *Hamburgische neue Zeitung* 40 (10 March 1773), review of Carlo Gottlob Richter's *Concerto I & II. per il Cembalo concertato accompagnata da 2 Viol. Violetta e Basso*. Riga: Hartknoch, 1772. "Sehr selten sagen Herpeggio's [*sic*] dem Herzen etwas."

50 *Neue Leipziger gelehrte Zeitungen* III/2 39 (31 March 1787), 618–19, review of *Trois Sonates pour le clavecin par Mdslle Edelmann, Msr Darondeau, Msr Pin*. [Dresden]: Hilscher. "Die erste Sonate besteht (1) aus einem schmeichelhaften Gratioso . . . [und] aus einem fließenden empfindungsvollen Rondo. Die zweite Sonate hat 1. ein kurzes und dabey schleichendes Andante; 2. eine zärtliche Menuett; ein munteres lebendes Rondo . . . Die dritte Sonate fängt an mit einem kurzen, finstern, schwermüthigen Andante maestoso, das bald in das feurigste Allegro assai ausbricht, und am Ende zu verlöschen scheint . . . den Beschluß macht ein sehr lebhaftes Allegretto." The review was reprinted (with cuts) in the *Magazin der Musik* II/2 (24 April 1787), 1337.

5 The importance of being correct

1 *Neue Zeitungen von gelehrten Sachen* 19 (6 March 1766), 146–47, review of Christian Ernst Rosenbaum's *Sechs Sonaten für das Clavier*. Rendsburg. "Aber bey der jämmerlichen Gestalt, in welcher dieser Componist auftritt, wißen wir nicht, ob wir Mitleiden oder Verachtung gegen ihm äußern sollen. Wir würden ihm gern das erste zu statten kommen laßen, wenn man noch einige Besserung von ihm hoffen dürfte; aber alle Hoffnung ist, wie es scheint, vergebens, da die Züchtigung, die er wegen seiner Liedermelodien erhielt, so wenig gefruchtet, daß er sich jetzt mit einem halben Dutzend Sonaten auf den Platz wagt, die in der That noch elender sind als alle seine Lieder. Wie leer von Gedanken! wie unrichtig im

Rhythmus! bald ein Tact zu viel, bald einer zu wenig! wie fehlerhaft in der
Harmonie! Quinten= und Octavenfehler die Menge! Und wie steht es um die gute
Modulation, um das Verhältniß der Nebentonarten zur Haupttonart aus? Gewiß,
das Ohr eines Hottentotten würde empfinden, daß hier meistentheils wider die
Natur gefehlt sey. Man schreitet nicht, sondern man taumelt aus einem Tone in
den andern; und zur höchsten Verwunderung siehet man das Stück, wenn die Seite
voll ist, sich wieder in den Haupton schlüßen. Wie meisterhaft! . . . Das einzige
Gute, das wir von diesen Sonaten zu rühmen haben, ist, daß sie kurz sind, und
nicht mehr als sechs Bogen Papier damit verderbt worden. "

2 *Wöchentliche Nachrichten* III:33 (13 February 1769), 160, review of Friedrich
   Schwindl's *Six Simphonies à quatre Parties obligées avec Cors, Hautbois ou Flutes
   ad libitum*. Paris and Liège: B. Andrez. "So ist es uns z.E. mit der ersten dieser
   Schwindlischen Sinfonien ergangen: der erste Satz war gefällig und feurig; die
   abwechselnden Schattierungen, die Modulation, thaten Wirkung auf uns; aber
   dann kam ein steifes, träges Andante, das zwar in den Mittelstimmen einige
   Bewegung hatte, aber vom Anfange bis zum Ende so einförmig, daß es so gut als
   keine Bewegung war. Wir wüssten nicht was wir daraus machen sollten, bis wir
   endlich sahen, daß es ein variirter Choral war. Was! ein Choral? in einer Sinfonie?
   Ja, ja, ein Choral, und hinter drein eine recht lustige Menuett . . . Kurz, Herr
   Schwindl hat überall zu sehr das Possierliche und Abendtheuerliche gesucht, als
   daß er mit diesen Sinfonien vernünftigen Ohren gefallen sollte. "

3 "Von dem Charakter eines Poeten," from *Versuch einer Kritischen Dichtkunst*, in
   Gottscheds Lebens- und Kunstreform in den zwanziger und dreissiger Jahren,
   edited by Fritz Brüggemann (Darmstadt: Wissenschaftliche Buchgesellschaft,
   1966), p. 24. "Und ein Poet muß . . . eine starke Einbildungskraft, viel
   Scharfsinnigkeit und einen großen Witz schon von Natur besitzen, wenn er den
   Namen eines Dichters mit Recht führen will. "

4 "Von Tragödien oder Trauerspielen," from *Versuch einer Kritischen Dichtkunst*,
   in *Gottscheds Lebens- und Kunstreform*, pp. 35–49.

5 Both Gottsched and Wolff had an impact on their contemporaries in music
   theory. See Joachim Birke, *Christian Wolffs Metaphysik und die Zeitgenössische
   Literatur und Musiktheorie: Gottsched, Scheibe, Mizler* (Berlin: Walter de
   Gruyter, 1966).

6 Beiser, *The Fate of Reason*, pp. 165–67.

7 Cowart, "Sense and Sensibility," pp. 253–60.

8 *Kritische Briefe* II/84 (31 October 1761), 156–58, review of Johann Georg
   Nicolai's *Six Parties sur le Clavecin*. Leipzig: Breitkopf, 1760. "Nichts kann schön
   seyn, was nicht regelmäßig ist. So wenig man mit Klecksen schön mahlen kann:
   so wenig kann man mit bösen Quinten und Octaven schön componiren. "

9 *Kritische Briefe* II/86 (14 November 1761), 173–74, review of Johann Anton
   Kobrich's *Wohlgeübter Organist, das ist, vier und zwanzig grosse Präludia für die
   Orgel*. Nuremberg: Haffner. "Der Titel ist falsch, und sollte heissen: Ungeübter
   und Unterricht brauchender Organist . . . Ein Sammelfuri von den abge-

droschensten und ausgepfiffensten Einfällen, die wechselsweise bis zum Eckel transponiret werden, und woran das Pedal zufälliger Weise von Zeit zu Zeit, etwann zwey= oder dreymahl in jedem Stücke, mit einer vier oder fünf Tacte liegenbleibenden, und mitten unter einer Dissonanz verschwindenden Note, Antheil nimmt; ein ewiges Gelärme mit gebrochnen Sätzen; unvorbereitete Dissonanzen, unaufgelösete Dissonanzen, Quinten und Octaven, leere Sätze, falsche Bäße – ; wer 24 musikalische Quodlibts für die Drehorgel eines Schattenspielers verlanget, dem werden die 24 Präludien des Herrn Kobrich zu statten kommen."

10 Friedrich Wilhelm Marpurg, *Handbuch bey dem Generalbasse und der Composition* (Berlin: Johann Jacob Schützens Wittwe, 1755–60; rpt. Hildesheim: Georg Olms, 1974), p. 222.

11 *Unterhaltungen* VII/5 (May 1769), 459–62, review of Löhlein's *Sei Sonate von variate repetizioni per il Clavicembalo*, Op. 11. Leipzig: Breitkopf. "Hier und da mögten wir einige Veränderung mit den Rhythmen machen. Z.E. S. 14. Z. 5.6. mißfällt uns der eingeflickte einzelne Dreyer in den ersten Takten, unter lauter Vierern." For similar comments, see Marpurg's *Kritische Briefe* II/86 (14 November 1761), 170–73, and the *Neue Zeitungen von gelehrten Sachen* 19 (6 March 1766), 146–47.

12 *Allgemeine deutsche Bibliothek* VIII/2 (1768), 204–08, review of Johann Gottfried Müthel's *Concerto 1 & 2, per il Cembalo concertato, accompagnato da due Violini, Violetta e Basso*. Riga and Mitau: Hartknoch, 1767. "Der holperige Rythmus an einigen Stellen beyder Concert, z.B. im ganzen ersten Satze des zweyten, wo der Einschnitt bald auf die Mitte, bald auf den Anfang des Tacts fällt . . . ist uns anstößig gewesen. So wenig auch noch über die Pflicht und die Art, einen richtigen musikalischen Rythmus zu beobachten, öffentlich gelehret worden seyn mag; denn wir können, ausser Riepeln niemanden nennen, der bis auf diese Zeit öffentlich davon geschrieben hätte: so sehr lehrt doch eine feine musikalische Empfindung, wie schön und wie nöthig ein richtiger Rythmus sey. X. [Agricola]" Kirnberger later (in 1776) issued similar prohibitions in *The Art of Strict Musical Composition*, pp. 406–08.

13 *Hamburgische neue Zeitung* 34 (27 February 1773), review of George Rush's *Six Sonates pour le Clavecin ou le Piano forte avec l'Accompagnement d'un Violon*, Op. 3. Amsterdam. "Diese Trios sind kurz und leicht, die Melodie sehr gefällig, und die Violine gar nicht müßig sondern auf eine angenehme Art dialogisch, die 2. und 5. Sonate sind vorzüglich schön. Eigentliche gearbeitete Trios sind es jedoch nicht. Bey der 4. und 6. Sonate liegt der itzt so gemeine Harfenbaß zum Grunde." It is not clear why the reviewer calls these trios, though perhaps they included a cello part not included in the title (papers frequently shortened longer titles to save space).

14 *Allgemeine deutsche Bibliothek* X/1 (1769), 245–46, review of Graf's *Sei Quartetti*, cited in chapter 3. "Können die Liebhaber der Musik nicht mehr in einem solchen Stücke drey ernsthafte Sätze aushalten?"

15 *Allgemeine deutsche Bibliothek* III/1 (1766), 259–60, review of Johann Baptist Georg Neruda's *VI. Sonate a tre, Violino I. Violino II. e Basso*. Leipzig: Breitkopf.

16 *Allgemeine deutsche Bibliothek* VIII/2 (1768), 284–86, review of Johann Friedrich Ernst Benda's *Minuetto per il Cembalo*, cited in chapter 4. "Wir sagen weiter, daß in der achten Variation die im siebenten Takte des ersten und im fünften und sechsten Takte des zweyten Abschnitts vorkommende chromatische Melodie, welche als eine artige Bizarrerie, an irgend einem anderen Orte gute Wirkung thun würde, sich in die Variation eines Menuets nicht recht schicket. Ein Menuet soll, wie Mattheson schreibt, eine mäßige Lustigkeit ausdrücken. Dazu schikt sich das chromatische Gewinsel gar nicht. X. [Agricola]"

17 *Wöchentliche Nachrichten* II:48 (30 May 1768), 375–76, review of Löhlein's *Sei sonate con variate repetizioni per il Clavicembalo*, Op. 2. Leipzig. "Wenigstens hätten wir mehr kühne und unerwartete Wendungen der Harmonie allhier gewünscht; denn die *Inganni*, die enharmonische Modulirart sind der Fantasie eigen." *Unterhaltungen* VII/5 (May 1769), 459–62.

18 *Allgemeine deutsche Bibliothek* II/1 (1766), 270–72, review of Ferdinand Fischer's *Six Symphonies*. Leipzig: Breitkopf, 1765. "Der Titel ist lang, er hätte uns beynahe auf den Argwohn gebracht, daß unter andern auch zwey neue Instrumente bey diesen Sinfonien angebracht wären, die Reisbundel hießen, wenn uns nicht zum Glücke noch die Ueberschriften zweyer gedruckter halber Blätter dieses Werkes belehret hätten, das es Fagotte wären, welche sonst auf Französisch *des Bassons* genennet werden. P. [Agricola]"

19 Schenk-Güllich, "Anfänge der Musikkritik," p. 128. Her characterization of Hiller and Marpurg as representatives of the "taste" faction makes sense because she is contrasting their views with those of the early writers Mizler and Scheibe, adherents to the "rules" philosophy.

20 *Wöchentliche Nachrichten* I:17 (21 October 1766), 127–31, review of Manfredini's *Sei Sonate*, cited in chapter 3. "Pfui! es ist uns nicht möglich, weiter zu schreiben. Der Himmel bewahre uns vor allen manfredinischen Sonaten und Minueten!" The incorrect number of beats in the penultimate measure is an example of the pieces' errors.

21 *Unterhaltungen* VI/3 (September 1768), 244–48, review of C. G. Stubel's *Kurzer Unterricht von der Musik nebst den dazu gehörigen Piecen für diejenigen, welche das Clavecin spielen*. Amsterdam: Johannes Covens. "No. 48. ist ganz Unsinn. Die Variation zur Menuet wimmelt von Fehlern; und es erfodetre wohl mehr als menschliche Geduld, diesen musikalischen Schutt durchzuwühlen. Wir wollen deswegen dem Hrn. V. wohlmeynend rathen, seine müßigen Stunden künftig nicht mehr der Musik zu weihen; denn weder der Unterricht, noch das Vergnügen wird durch seine Arbeiten unterstützt."

22 *Hamburgischer Correspondent* 102 (26 June 1765), review of Johann Friedrich Wilhelm Wenkel's *Versuche in Clavierstücken verschiedener Art*. "Wer würde zum Exempel . . . in Galanteriestücken Ordnung und Reinigkeit suchen?"

23 *Allgemeine deutsche Bibliothek* II/1 (1766), 267–70, review of *Musikalisches*

Magazin in Sonaten, Sinfonien, Trios und andern Stücken für das Clavier beste-hend. Leipzig: Breitkopf. "Die harmonischen Unrichtigkeiten, – ob sie zwar von nicht viel größerer Erheblichkeit sind, als grammatische Schnitzer bey einem guten Schriftsteller, – so wollten wir doch einige Herren Verfasser dieses Magazins geben habe, auf deren Vermeidung etwas aufmerksamer zu seyn . . . Widrigenfalls könnte sich doch mancher, der sein größtes Verdienst in Quintenjagen sucht, darüber einen misvergnügten Abend machen. P. [Agricola]"

24 *Wöchentliche Nachrichten* II:48 (30 May 1768), 375–76, review of Löhlein's *Sei sonate*, cited above. "Wenn man uns fragt, ob wir verbotene Quinten und Octaven entdeckt haben, so müssen wir gestehen, daß wir bey einem Manne, von dem sich so viel gutes sagen läßt, nicht darauf Achtung gegeben haben."

25 *Berlinische Nachrichten* 78 (30 June 1764), 326–27, review of Eckard's *Six Sonates*, cited in chapter 3. "Es ist wahr, daß die Critick nirgends schärfer ver-fährt, als bey den Herren Tonkünstlern. Sie schenken sich einander nicht den kleinsten Fehler, sondern gehen, wenn sie auch nur die geringste Spur eines Versehens entdecken, feurig darauf los."

26 Marpurg, *Handbuch*, p. 215.

27 Marpurg, *Handbuch*, p. 219. "Man mache vernünftige und ordentliche Ausweichungen."

28 Lester, *Compositional Theory*, pp. 266–67.

29 *Wöchentliche Nachrichten* I:26 (23 December 1766), 202–03, review of P. Vanmaldere's *Sei Sinfonie*. Paris and Lyon: Venier; and *Allgemeine deutsche Bibliothek* II/1 (1766), 270–72, review of Fischer's *Six Symphonien*, cited above and in chapter 3.

30 *Kritische Briefe* II/84 (31 October 1761), 156–58, review of Nicolai's *Six Parties*, cited above. "Hätte der Herr N. in der Folge der ersten Clausel einen ähnlichen Fall vorgebracht, so würde, so zu sagen, eine Ordnung in der Unordnung gewesen seyn. Man hätte in dem Zahlmaaß ein gewisses Verhältniß bemerket, und das würde alsdenn wenigstens den Verstand befriediget haben, wenn auch das Gehör zwey=oder dreymahl dabey gelitten hätte."

31 *Allgemeine deutsche Bibliothek* VIII/2 (1768), 204–08, review of Müthel's *Concerto 1 & 2*, cited above. "Neue Gedanken in den Zwischenritornellen, welche im Anfangsritornelle nicht da gewesen sind, dürfen nicht ohne wichtige Ursachen, die zu rechter Zeit eine besondere Neuigkeit einführen, angebracht werden. Sonst könnte mancher Zuhörer gar auf die Gedanken gerathen, als hätte der Setzer erst in der Folge des Schreibens bessere Einfälle bekommen, und nur nicht Lust gehabt, das schon niedergeschriebene erste Ritornell darnach zu ändern oder zu ergänzen. Das Ritornell soll eigentlich einen kurzen Begriff vom ganzen Satze geben. Es soll gleichsam der Hauptsatz seyn, welcher abzuhandeln ist. Die einzelnen Gedanken im Ritornelle kann also der Componist hernach beym Concertiren zerlegen, verschiedentlich wenden, und mit dem Spiele des Concertisten ausputzen. Neue Gedanken in den Zwischenritornellen aber, werden dem Zuhörer, dem sich schon das erste und Hauptritornell eingedrükt

haben muß, nicht recht deutlich: sie bringen vielmehr seine Aufmerksamkeit in Unordnung."

32 *Kritische Briefe* II/84 (31 October 1761), 156–58, review of Johann Georg Nicolai's *Six Parties sur le Clavecin.* "Dieses etwas, es mag nun sogleich zum Anfange, in der ersten Sectionalzeile, oder in der zweyten vorkommen, nenne ich den Hauptsatz, der durch Wiederhohlungen, Versetzungen, Nachahmungen und Zergleiderungen bearbeitet werden muß. Die daraus auf verschiedne Art entstehenden Passagen dienen dazu, die Einheit des Tonstückes mit zu erhalten. Wenn man den Hauptsatz, oder die daraus fließenden Gedanken, nach einem gemachten vernünftigen Plan, mit einem neuen Nebengedanken abwechselt, und diesen ebenfals wie den vorhergehenden, in gehörigem Verhältnisse, bearbeitet: so entspringet aus dieser Verbindung des Hauptsatzes mit dem Nebensatze, und der sowohl aus diesem als jenen entspringenden Theile, die gewissermassen so viele neue Sätze in ihrer Art sind, die Mannigfaltigkeit eines Tonstückes."

33 *Hamburgischer Correspondent* 161 (10 October 1766), review of Löhlein's *Sei Partite per il Clavicembalo.* Leipzig. "Allein, die größern Stücke scheinen uns doch den Vorzug zu haben, vornehmlich, weil sie dieses vor vielen andern voraus haben, daß ein Hauptaffect in jedem herrscht, und geschickt durchgeführt wird."

34 *Kritische Briefe* II/83 (25 October 1761), 143–45, review of Joseph Anton Stephan's *VI. Divertimenti da Cimbalo* and *VI. Sonate da Cimbalo.* Vienna: Agostino Bernardi. "Ueberhaupt bemerket man, daß kein Schulknabe heutiges Tages zu componiren anfängt, der nicht sein Exercitium mit etlichen zwanzig oder dreyßig schiefen Vorschlägen ausschmücken sollte; und der ist kein Kenner, der ihm an diesen Oertern das Compliment schuldig bleibt. Man muß sofort mit der Hand eine Bewegung nach der Brust zu machen, und durch einen langen hohlen Seufzer zu erkennen geben, wie sehr man gerührt worden sey. Es muß einem ganz warm ums Herz werden – . Ja öfters warm genug, vor Ueberdruß. So viel ist gewiß, daß wenn die Vorschläge ausserhalb der Tonart in solchen Tonstücken, wo sie der zum Grunde liegenden Empfindung nach nicht hingehören, angebracht werden, und wenn der herrschende Affect der Freude damit plötzlich unterbrochen wird, daß man alsdenn eben so viele Ursache hat, darwider zu protestiren, als wider das Betragen eines falschen Freundes, der jemanden mitten unter den angenehmsten Liebkosungen derbe in die Backen kneipet."

35 *Hamburgischer Correspondent* 107 (8 July 1766), review of Hertel's *Sei Sinfonie*, cited in chapter 3. "Das Prächtige, Feurige, Brillante, Muntre, Angenehme und Scherzhafte, ist überall mit Geschmack verbreitet." *Hamburgischer Correspondent* 161 (10 October 1766), review of Löhlein's *Sei Partite*, cited above. "Wir müßten sehr irren, oder Herr Löhlein ist im Sanften und Zärtlichen besonders glücklich."

36 *Wöchentliche Nachrichten* I:50 (8 June 1767), 390–91, review of Schwanberger's *Sonate a due Violini e Violoncello*, cited in chapter 3. "Das Schimmernde und Tandelnde ist in unserer heutigen Musik so Mode geworden, daß man die rühren-

den und gründlichen Gesänge eines Graun und Hasse bald als veraltete Schönheiten ansehen wird; unsere neuern Componisten geben der herrschenden Mode nach, die auf einige wenige, die noch Herz genug haben, mehr auf einen guten natürlichen Gesang und einen rührenden Ausdruck, als auf gedrechselten Witz und bloß niedliche Einfälle zu sehen."

37 *Wöchentliche Nachrichten* I:3 (15 July 1766), 19–23, review of Hertel's *Sei Sinfonie a due Violini, Violetta e Basso, due Oboi, due Flauti, e due Corni di Caccia*. Hamburg: Bock. "Sonst sind die ersten Sätze alle prächtig und feurig . . . Die mittlern Sätze sind gefällig und ausdrückend . . . Die letzten Sätze sind eine Probe von der scherzhaften Muse des Herrn Hofcomponisten." *Allgemeine deutsche Bibliothek* IV/2 (1767), 289–90, review of the same pieces. "Die ersten Allegro dieser Sinfonien sind besonders feurig . . . Die mehresten Andante sind auch sehr angenehm . . . Eben so halten wir auch einige der lezten Allegros für allzu niedrig und frech. P. [Agricola]"

38 *Unterhaltungen* I/3 (March 1766), 283, review of J. C. Bach's *Six Simphonies*, Op. 3. Amsterdam: Hummel. "Die ersten Sätze sind feurig, und italienisch gut: . . . Die mittlern Sätze sind singend und angenehm . . . Die letzten Sätze nähern sich dem niedern Stile."

39 Lange, *The Classical Age*, p. 49.

40 Lange, *The Classical Age*, p. 17.

41 Moses Mendelssohn, "Briefe über die Empfindungen," in *Schriften*, pp. 18–19. "Die, welche die Schriften der unsterblichen Alten nur desswegen lesen, um sie zu zergliedern und rhetorische Figuren, so wie ein Insektenkenner die getrockneten Geripppe der Würmer, zu sammeln, sind zu bedauern. Sie suchen und finden die Regeln der Wohlredenheit, sie werden Gesetzgeber in den schönen Wissenschaften; aber sie empfinden die Schönheiten nicht mehr, die sie uns anpreisen. Ihr Gefühl verwandelt sich in einen logischen Schluss."

42 Mendelssohn, *Schriften*, pp. 25–26. "Auch die Tonkünstler könnten einer schimpflichen Erniedrigung überhoben sein, wenn sie diese wichtige Anmerkung nie aus den Augen lassen wollten. Es ist bekannt, dass sie, was die Annehmlichkeit ihrer Melodien betrifft, einen grössern Werth auf das Urtheil eines blos geübten Ohres, als auf das Urtheil eines Meisters in der Tonkunst setzen. Die letztern wollen ihre Erfahrenheit in der Kunst niemals verleugnen. Sie merken auf nichts, als auf die Regelmäßigkeit einer Melodie, sie lauern auf glückliche Verbindung zwischen den allerwidersinnigsten Uebellauten, und die sanft rührenden Schönheiten schleichen unbemerkt vor ihren Ohren vorüber."

43 René Wellek, *A History of Modern Criticism: 1750–1950*, vol. I: *The Later Eighteenth Century* (New Haven, CT: Yale University Press, 1955), p. 170.

44 *Laocoon, or On the Limits of Painting and Poetry*, translated by W. A. Steel in *The Origins of Modern Critical Thought*, edited by David Simpson (Cambridge University Press, 1988), pp. 33–34.

45 Johann Georg Sulzer, *Allgemeine Theorie der schönen Künste in einzeln, nach alphabetischer Ordnung der Kunstwörter auf einander folgenden Artikeln*

abgehandelt, 4th edn. (Leipzig, 1792–99; rpt. Hildesheim: Georg Olms, 1967), s.v. "Empfindung."

46 _Wöchentliche Nachrichten_ I:27 (30 December 1766), 210–11; III:33 (13 February 1769), 160; III:35 (27 February 1769), 276; _Neue Zeitungen von gelehrten Sachen_ (9 February 1764), 95–96.

47 _Allgemeine deutsche Bibliothek_ VIII/1 (1768), 272–73, review of Schwanberger's _Sonate a due Violine e Violoncello_, cited in chapter 3. ". . . von vernünftiger und durch guten Geschmak und feine Empfindung geleiteter Arbeit."

48 _Allgemeine Theorie_, s.v. "Empfindung."

49 _Allgemeine deutsche Bibliothek_ V/2 (1767), 268–70, review of C. P. E. Bach's _Sonatina I.II.III. a Cembalo concertato_, cited in chapter 3. "Widrigenfals stehen einsehende und der Empfindung fähige Zuhörer bey einer solchen Musik wirklich in Gefahr zu gähnen."

50 _Allgemeine deutsche Bibliothek_ VIII/2 (1768), 204–08, review of Müthel's _Concerto I & II_, cited above. "Schon zwey geschwänzte Triolen und zwey und dreyßig Theile im ersten und lezten Satze eines nach gewöhnlicher Art eingerichteten Concerts, geschikt mit einander zu vermischen, daß bey den erstern keine Mattigkeit bemerkt werde, ist schwer, und wird dazu benahe immer eine, nicht allen Leuten gegeben, Quanzische feine Empfindungskraft und Genauigkeit erfodert."

51 _Wöchentliche Nachrichten_ II: 23 (7 December 1767), 178, review of Johann Gottfried Müthel's _Concerto I per il Cembalo concertato da due Violini, Violetta e Basso; Concerto II. &c._ Riga: Hartknoch, 1767. ". . . ein gewisser auf ein zärtliches Gefühl gegründeter Gesang, der durch die Art der Auszierung, die ihm Herr Müthel giebt, noch eine Feinheit mehr erhält, aber auch dadurch vielleicht für manchen Spieler, der nicht gewohnt ist bey feinem Spielen zu empfinden, ein wenig schwer in Vortrage wird."

52 _Berlinische Nachrichten_ 55 (8 May 1764), 219, review of C. P. E. Bach's _Sonatina I. a Cembalo concertato, Il Flauti Traversi, II. Violini, Violetta e Basso._ Berlin: Winter, 1764. "Beydes, sowohl die Melodie als Harmonie, sind rührend."

53 _Neue Zeitungen von gelehrten Sachen_ 51 (27 June 1765), 404–06, review of _Musicalisches Allerley von verschiedenen Tonkünstler._ "Es [fehlt] seinen [Müller's] Arbeiten nicht an guten Einfällen, an gewißen zärtlichen Ausdrücken."

54 _Unterhaltungen_ I/3 (March 1766), 283, review of J. C. Bach's _Six Simphonies_, Op. 3. Amsterdam: Hummel. "Charakter des Unzufriedenen"; VIII/2 (August 1769), 162–64, review of Friedrich Gottlob Fleischer's _Sammlung einiger Sonaten, Menuetten und Polonoisen, wie auch anderer Stücke fürs Clavier._ Braunschweig: Waisenhaus. "neu und voll sanfter Zufriedenheit."

55 _Unterhaltungen_ VI/4 (October 1768), 334–35, review of Paolo Fischer's _Sei Sonate per il Cembalo._ Leipzig: Breitkopf. "Das vierte _Divert._ soll wohl wegen seiner aufgethürmten Passagen das Böhmische Gebürge vorstellen?"

56 _Kritische Briefe_ II/83 (25 October 1761), 145–47, review of Johann Adam Huller's [_recte_ Hiller] _Loisir musical_ (Leipzig: Breitkopf, 1762): "Wenn doch ein

Tonkünstler zu keiner andern Zeit arbeiten wollte, als wenn er sich zwar von seinem Gegenstande völlig erhitzt fühlte, aber doch sein Feuer dergestalt in der Gewalt hätte, daß er die Regeln der Kunst niemahls darüber vergässe!"

57 *Allgemeine deutsche Bibliothek* II/2 (1766), 268, review of Bach's *Clavierstücke verschiedener Art*, cited in chapter 3.

58 *Kritische Briefe* II/84 (31 October 1761), 156–58, review of Nicolai's *Six Parties*, cited above. "(Componiren heißt ja zusammensetzen, und nicht erfinden.)"

59 Bertheau, *Geschichte des Zeitungswesens in Hamburg*, p. 29.

60 Helga Madland, "Imitation to Creation: The Changing Concept of Mimesis from Bodmer and Breitinger to Lenz," in *Eighteenth-Century German Authors and their Aesthetic Theories: Literature and the other Arts*, edited by Richard Critchfield and Wulf Koepke (Columbia, SC: Camden House, 1988), pp. 29–30.

61 Christian Fürchtegott Gellert, *Sämmtliche Schriften* (Leipzig: Weidmann & Fritsche, 1769), 5: 166, cited in Madland, "Imitation to Creation," p. 31.

62 Robert E. Norton, *Herder's Aesthetics and the European Enlightenment* (Ithaca and London: Cornell University Press, 1991), p. 125.

63 However, it became a standard reference work for the last quarter of the century and appeared in a fourth edition in the 1790s, so that its views continued to achieve wide circulation.

64 *Allgemeine Theorie*, s.v. "Genie." "In der Seele des Mannes von Genie herrscht ein heller Tag, ein volles Licht, das ihm jeden Gegenstand wie ein nahe vor Augen liegendes und wol erleuchtetes Gemählde vorstellt, das er leicht übersehen, und darin er jedes Einzele genau bemerken kann . . . Der Mann von Genie empfindet ein begeisterndes Feuer, das seine ganze Würksamkeit rege macht; er endeket in sich selbst Gedanken, Bilder der Phantasie und Empfindungen, die andre Menschen in Verwunderung setzen; er selbst bewundert sie nicht, weil er sie, ohne mühsames Suchen, in sich mehr wahrgenommen, als erfunden hat."

65 *Allgemeine Theorie*, s.v. "Erfindung." "Die Erfindung ist allemal ein Werk des Verstandes, der die genaue Verbindung zwischen Mittel und Endzwek endeket; weil aber die Gegenstände, wodurch die zwekmäßige Würkung geschieht, in den schönen Künsten sinnliche Vorstellungen sind, so muß zu dem Verstand Erfahrung, eine reiche und lebhafte Phantasie, und ein feines Gefühl hinzukommen: diese Dinge zusammen machen die Fähigkeit zu erfinden aus."

66 *Wöchentliche Nachrichten* II:1 (6 July 1767), 6–7, review of Giovanni Battista Zingoni's *Huits Simphonies à deux Violons, Taille et Basse etc.* Amsterdam: Hummel. "Viel Neues und Unerwartetes haben wir zwar nicht darinne gefunden; aber doch viel Angenehmes und Feuriges. Besonders haben uns die Andantesätze von guter Erfindung und sehr singbar geschienen."

67 *Wöchentliche Nachrichten* III:16 (17 October 1768), 125–26, review of Paolo Fischer's *Sei Sonate, per il Cembalo*. Leipzig: Breitkopf, 1768. "Diese Schwierigkeiten weggerechnet, bleibt in denselben überall noch viel gute Erfindung und Gesang übrig." The final measure has a notational error.

68 *Allgemeine deutsche Bibliothek* VIII/1 (1768), 272–73, review of Schwanberger's

Sonate a due Violine e Violoncello, cited above. "Das besonders gute musikalische Genie des Herrn Schwanberger."

69 *Hamburgischer Correspondent* 36 (4 March 1761), review of Johann Friedrich Hobein d. J.'s *Oden und Menuetten*. Hamburg and Altona. "Musikverständige versichern, daß seine Composition gut gerathen sey, von vielem Genie und Geschmacke zeuge, und folglich unfehlbar gefallen müsse."

70 *Berlinische Nachrichten* 51 (29 April 1762), 199, review of *Musicalisches Mancherley*. Berlin: Winter, 1762. "Sie zeugen von der fruchtbarsten Erfindungs=Kraft und dem glücklichsten Genie, das jemahls ein Musiker haben konnte."

71 See, for example, Marpurg's review of Galuppi cited in chapter 3, and the *Wöchentliche Nachrichten* I:31 (27 January 1767), 243–44, review of Meder's *Sei Sinfonie*, cited in chapter 3.

72 *Allgemeine deutsche Bibliothek* V/2 (1767), 266–67, review of Wenkel's *Versuch in Clavierstücken verschiedener Art*. Stendal: Wenkel, 1765. "Da er uns itzo eine Fuge in der rechten uralten Art, die sich nicht aus der Tonart rührt, sonst aber sehr wohl gearbeitet ist, liefert; so bitten wir ihn, inskünftige auch zu zeigen, daß er in seinen Fugen auch in andere Tonarten geschikt ausweichen kann. Die Veränderung ist ja, in allen erlaubten Dingen, und folglich auch wohl in Fugen, der menschlichen Natur angenehm, so wie der Mangel der Veränderung verdrüßlich. P. [Agricola]"

73 *Unterhaltungen* VI/4 (October 1768), 334–35, review of Paolo Fischer's *Sei Sonate*, cited above; *Neue Zeitungen von gelehrten Sachen* 97 (5 December 1763), 773–75, review of the second part of Kirnberger's *Clavierübungen mit der Bachischen Applicatur*. Berlin: Birnstiel. "Aber ein Andante, das sich über eilf Zeilen weg, in so einförmigen und so schleppenden Figuren dähnt, wird ihnen doch immer ein wenig langweilig geworden seyn."

74 *Unterhaltungen* IV/3 (September 1767), 808, review of the *Collation recreative de Pieces de Clavecin concertantes avec la Flute traversiere ou le Violon &c.* "Die zweyte Sonate ist von Herrn Löhlein, eben so gut gearbeitet, und voll artiger Nachahmungen, vielleicht aber nicht immer original genug." *Wöchentliche Nachrichten* III/Anhang 9 (28 August 1769), 68–72, review of Beckmann's *Drey Sonaten für das Clavier*. Hamburg: Bock. "Wieder seine Manier im Ganzen läßt sich nichts einwenden; sie ist nicht völlig Original, aber sie ist die Manier der besten Meister, und folglich schön."

75 *Kritische Briefe* II/84 (31 October 1761), 153, review of Joseph Ferdinand Timer's *XII. Violinsolos*. "Viel altes, wenig neues, Tiraden von Transpositionen, harmonische, melodische und rhythmische Unachtsamkeiten, gewisse altfränkische Modulationen, – vielleicht spielt der Herr Timer besser, als er componirt. Keiner hat alles beysammen."

76 *Wöchentliche Nachrichten* I:4 (22 July 1766), 28–31, review of Löhlein's *Sei Partite*, cited in chapter 4. "Im vierten Allegro aber möchten einige Harmonisten den Autor wohl einer kleinen Verwegenheit beschuldigen, und die auf einander

folgenden Tonarten für allzu entfernt und fremde halten: doch wir erinnern uns, daß diese Verwegenheit nicht ohne Beyspiel ist, und daß wir in einer Sinfonie von einem sehr berühmten Meister e dur und c dur, so wie hier a dur und c dur beysammen gefunden haben. Wir machen übrigens diese Gewagte dem Herrn Verfasser zu keinem Verbrechen. Es ist gut sich bisweilen von der gemeinen Straße zu entfernen, um dem Alltäglichen zu entgehen. Man verlangt in der Musik beständig das Neue, und dem Genie steht es frey, dasselbe nicht bloß in der einen, sondern auch in der andern Sache zu suchen."

77 *Wöchentliche Nachrichten* I:27 (30 December 1766), 210–11, review of Toeschi's *Six Simphonies*. Paris. "Möchte doch Hr. Toeschi sich immer gleich bleiben! Möchte er doch durch die Liebe zum Sonderbaren, und vielleicht durch die Furcht nicht neu genung [*sic*] zu seyn, weniger hingerissen werden!"

78 *Neue Zeitungen von gelehrten Sachen* 87 (31 October 1765), 692–93, review of Johann Lorenz Albrecht's *Musicalische Aufmunterung*. Berlin: Birnstiel. "Aber Menuetten und Polonoisen, wenn sie von einem Genie hervor gebracht werden, dem es nicht an Erfindung fehlt, das sich, um nicht Alltägliches zu sagen, von dem so häufig betretenen Wege glücklich zu entfernen weiß, ohne ins Gesuchte, ins Ungereimte, und Abentheuerliche zu fallen, Menuetten von dieser Art kann man unter die artigsten musicalischen Kleinigkeiten rechen, die allemal Aufmerksamkeit, selbst bey Kennern, verdienen."

79 *Neue Zeitungen von gelehrten Sachen* 46 (8 June 1769), 367–68, review of Bernhard Theodor Breitkopf's *Menuetten und Polonoisen für das Clavier*. Leipzig: Breitkopf. "Bey seinem überaus feurigen Genie, kann man ihn nicht tadeln . . . in der Modulation ist der Verf. sogar bisweilen eigene Wege gegangen, und man muß sich freuen, daß ihm in der Menuet und Trio S. 16 und 17. die Versetzung seltsame Vermischung verschiedener Rhythmen unter einander S. 8. ist entweder eine Nachahmung gewisser Cas- oder Gassations-Menuetten, oder eine Satyre auf dieselben: man wird diese Geburten des Eigensinns allenfalls dulden; aber Muster werden sie nie werden . . . Da es ihm an Gelegenheit nicht fehlt, die Arbeiten von alten und neuen, guten und schlechten Componisten zu studieren, so versprechen wir uns in der That einst an ihm einen Mann, der die Ehre der Deutschen, so wohl durch Erfindung, als durch Gründlichkeit in der Composition, wird behaupten helfen."

80 *Wöchentliche Nachrichten* I:17 (21 October 1766) 127–31, review of Manfredini's *Sei Sonate*, cited in chapter 3. "Sieht das nicht holpricht genung [*sic*] aus? und kann man, wenn man es spielen siehet, ein natürlicher Bild in den Gedanken haben, als ob man Flöhe haschen sähe?"

6 *The reign of genius*

1 *Neue Zeitungen von gelehrten Sachen* 47 (14 June 1773), 370–71, review of Johann Friedrich Doles's *Sechs Sonaten für das Clavier*. Riga: Hartknoch. "Dieser erste von seiner Composition bekannt gemachte Versuch, macht ihm auf

alle Weise Ehre, indem man nicht einen sclavisch nachahmenden, sondern selbst denkenden, erfindsamen, muntern, gefälligen Geist darinne entdekt . . . Was ein strenger Harmonist etwan daran tadeln möchte, sind kleine Unachtsamkeiten, die einem Dilettante um so viel eher zu verzeihen sind, oder mit der Mode leicht entschuldigt werden können. Man thut immer Unrecht, wenn man über dergleichen Kleinigkeiten, die durch Aufmerksamkeit leicht vermieden werden können, allzu viel Geschrey erhebt. Ein Werk des Geistes ist deßwegen noch nicht schön, weil gewiße Kunstrichter nichts daran zu tadeln finden, die nur auf die mechanische Beobachtung der Regel sehen, und immer vor dem Augen verschließen, worinne sich wahre Züge eines feurigen und erfindungsreichen Genies wahrnehmen laßen."

2 *Gothaische gelehrte Zeitungen* 44 (15 June 1774), 352, review of Ernst Wilhelm Wolf's *Sei Sonate per il Clavicembalo*. Wolf, 1774. "Die Clavierarbeiten eines Bach und Benda waren immer das Vorzüglichste, was ein Liebhaber besitzen konnte: nun aber nehme er getrost die Sonaten des Hrn. Wolf dazu. Eben das Feuer der Erfindung! Eben die Neuheit, eben die Kühnheit der Gedanken und Wendungen! Sanfte und cantabile Stellen zwischen rollende und springende gestellt; nicht vorhergesehene überraschende Modulationen! Und das alles mit der vollkommensten Reinigkeit der Harmonie verbunden und so recht eigentlich in der wahren Art, wie das Instrument erfodert."

3 *Wöchentliche Nachrichten* IV:41 (8 October 1770), 322, review of Johann Christoph Conrad's *Vorspiele unterschiedener Art für die Orgel*.

4 *Wöchentliche Nachrichten* IV:5 (29 January 1770), 37–38, review of Joseph Haydn's *Six Simphonies à huit Parties*, Op. 7 [Hob. I:17, Es1, 29, 28, 9, 3].

5 *Allgemeine deutsche Bibliothek* XI/1 (1770), 262–63, Bernhard Theodor Breitkopf's *Menuetten und Polonoisen für das Clavier*. Leipzig: Breitkopf, 1769. "Der V. zeigt überdies, wenn auch einige ganz unbeträchtliche Schwachheiten mit untergelaufen seyn sollten, einen feurigen, erfindungsreichen, und nicht nachäffenden Geist. In dem Menuet S. 8. sind die Abweichungen vom richtigen Rhythmus zu groß, als daß sie sollten gefallen können. X. [Agricola]"

6 *Allgemeine deutsche Bibliothek* XVII/1 (1772), 238–40, review of Johann Gottfried Müthel's *Duetto für 2 Claviere, 2 Flügel, oder 2 Fortepiano*. Riga: Hartknoch, 1771; Leipzig: Breitkopf. "Das Stück an sich selbst ist von guten und sehr fremden Gedanken, die gewiß von Niemanden erborgt sind." This review is not signed, but Agricola wrote the surrounding reviews. XIX/2 (1773), 574, review of Carlo Gottlob Richter's *Concerto I & II per il Cembalo concertato accompagnato da due Violini, Violetta e Basso*. Riga: Hartknoch, 1772. "Diese Concerte zeigen zwar nicht eben die fremdeste und sonderbareste Erfindung; doch sind sie auch nicht trivial. Ka. [Agricola]"

7 Clark, *Herder*, p. 48, and Beiser, *The Fate of Reason*, pp. 34–36. He also argued for the metaphysical significance of art, but in that he was definitely swimming against the tide.

8 "Über die neuere deutsche Literatur" (1767) and *Kritische Wälder* (1769). See the

discussion in Lange, *The Classical Age*, p. 57. Many of Herder's most radical ideas about art appeared in the unpublished fourth section of the *Kritische Wälder*, which remained unknown during his lifetime. Thus no influence can be claimed for his insistence there that art should not be governed by rules or for his ruminations on the power and aesthetic primacy of music. See Clark, *Herder*, pp. 88–94.

9 Johann Gottfried Herder, "Shakespeare" (1773), excerpts translated by Joyce P. Crick in *The Origins of Modern Critical Thought*, pp. 77–84.

10 Excerpts translated by Crick in *The Origins of Modern Critical Thought*, pp. 71–76.

11 *Ursachen des gesunknen Geschmacks bei den verschiednen Völkern, da er geblühet* (1773), as discussed in Clark, *Herder*, p. 216.

12 Suchalla, *Briefe von Carl Philipp Emanuel Bach*, p. 57. "Schade, daß Niemand beynahe mehr den reinen Satz lernet. Daher kommen die fehlerhaften Producte, die man so häufig jetzt gedruckt u. geschrieben sieht."

13 Kirnberger, *The Art of Strict Musical Composition*, pp. 139–46.

14 *Magazin der Musik* I/2 (7 December 1783), 1304–08. "Uebrigens hat man von je her gefühlt, daß alle, auch die besten Regeln für Anfänger in der Composition höchst unzulänglich sind, und deswegen immer das Studium guter Muster an die Stelle zu bringen gesucht."

15 Heinrich Christoph Koch, *Introductory Essay on Composition: The Mechanical Rules of Melody*, sections 3 and 4, translated with an Introduction by Nancy Kovaleff Baker (New Haven and London: Yale University Press, 1983), p. 114.

16 Johann Nikolaus Forkel, "Von der Theorie der Musik in so fern sie Liebhabern und Kennern nothwendig und nützlich ist," *Magazin der Musik* I/2 (1 September 1783), 855–912. "Wenn Music eine Sprache der Empfindungen und Leidenschaften ist, wenn die Empfindungen keines einzigen Menschen mit den Empfindungen eines andern vollkommen übereinstimmen; würd dann nicht folgen, daß in Ermangelung gehöriger Vorschriften, und aus Natur und Erfahrung abgeleiteten Regeln, die Kunst dem Eigensinn und der Willkühr eines jeden insbesondere überlassen seyn müßte? . . . so muß auch hier in unserer Kunst, diese aufmerksame Beobachtung der Natur unsers Herzens, und unserer Gefühle für das Schöne der Tonkunst, der Maaßstab seyn, nach welchem Vorschriften und Regeln, von vielen mit Vorsicht und Scharfsinn wiederholten Erfahrungen abzuleiten und festzusetzen sind."

17 Johann Nikolaus Forkel, *Allgemeine Geschichte der Musik*, vol. I (Leipzig: Schwickert, 1788; rpt. edn. Graz: Akademische Druck und Verlangsanstalt, 1967), sections 125–26. "verhindern die zweckwidrigen und fehlerhaften Ausbrüche seines Genies eben so, wie der Damm die verwüstende Ueberschwemmung und Verschlammung des wilden Stroms."

18 Chabanon, *Observations sur la musik*, translated as *Ueber die Musik und deren Wirkungen*, p. 3. "Nie sind die Regeln eher entstanden als die Beyspiele; die Vernunft hat sich nie dem Genie voraus gesagt, was es machen soll. Dieses arbeitet

blos unter der Leitung des Gefühls; es schafft Gesetzt, ohne sie zu kennen; der Verstand, der hinterdrein über die von ihm hervorgebrachten Werke nachdenkt, entdeckt ihm sodann erst die Geheimnisse seiner Wirkungen. Aus seinen Mustern setzt er die Regeln der Kunst zusammen."

19 *Musikalisch-kritische Bibliothek* II, 275–300, review of C. P. E. Bach's *Claviersonaten, mit einer Violine und einem Violoncell zur Begleitung.* Leipzig: Bach, 1776, 1777. [Wq. 90–91] "Zu dem Ende bemerken wir hier noch, daß es äußerst gefährlich sey, von denjenigen Gesetzen und Regeln abzuweichen, welche große Meister der Kunst durch Vernunft, Erfahrung und aufmerksames Studium der Natur gefunden, und durch ihre musterhaften Werke festgesetzt haben; daß daher die stolze Begierde, sich neue Bahnen zu eröffnen . . . eine freche Bemühung sey . . . Was gewinnt man denn mit solchen eiteln Bemühungen? Glänzt ihrer ungeachtet nicht der, welcher der gesunden Vernunft und wahren Natur treu bleibt, unter ihnen, wie ein Edelstein unter gläsernen Tropfen?"

20 *Musicalische Bibliotek* II (1785), 245–48, review of Christian Benjamin Uber d. J.'s *Six Divertissements pour le Clavecin avec l'Accompagnement d'une Flute, d'un Violon, les deux Cors de chasse et de la Basse.* Leipzig: Breitkopf, 1784. "Also ist's nicht genug, dass der Componist di sonst unschäzbaren Regeln der Harmoni und des Rythmus genau inne habe; er mus auch wares Geni besitzen . . . Er [gehört] wenigstens nicht zu den schädlichen Creaturen, di durch regelloses unvernünftiges Gesudel unvermerkt ein tödliches Gift in di Geschmaks-Ader irer schwachen Anbeter flösen, und si des Gebrauchs der Sinne berauben). Wer wird aber daran zweifeln, dass es besser sei auf eine kurze Zeit einzuschlafen, als umzukommen!"

21 *Allgemeine deutsche Bibliothek* LXXI/1 (1787), 115–18, review of the *Musicalische Bibliotek.* "Nur bey den Recensionen practischer Werke wollen wir ihn doch erinnern, nicht so sehr das Verdienst eines Werks nach der blossen Befolgung oder Nichtbefolgung der grammatischen Regeln des reinen Satzes zu würdigen. Der richtige Versificateur ist darum noch kein großer Dichter; Bach ist nicht darum allein groß, weil er im Satz richtig ist."

22 *Allgemeine deutsche Bibliothek* LXXV/2 (1787), 459, review of J.C. Ribbe's *Sechs Sonaten fürs Clavier, mit Begleitung einer Flöte.* Berlin: Hesse, 1786. "Denn wer seinen Zuhörer nicht durch neue und geschmackvolle Gedanken unterhalten kann, muß wenigstens rein schreiben, um erträglich befunden zu werden. Swr. [Schulz]"

23 *Allgemeine deutsche Bibliothek* LXXX/2 (1788), 452–53, review of (Carlo Gottlob?) Richter's *Concert pour le Clavecin avec l'accompagnement de deux Violons, deux Cors, deux Flûtes de Travers, Viole et Basse.* Riga: Hartknoch, 1785. "Ein Concert, welches an 30 Jahre zu spät in die Welt kommt. Gründlichkeit kann man dem Verf. ohne unbillig zu seyn, nicht absprechen; aber Richtigkeit im Satze macht ein Tonstück noch nicht schön und unterhaltend. Xw. [Türk]"

24 *Hamburgischer Correspondent* Beytrag 8 (4 September 1779), review of Hadrava's *Six Sonates*, cited in chapter 3. "Als Liebhaber der Musik übertrifft

Herr Hadrava manchen sogenannten Professore derselben in der Kenntniß des reinen Satzes, obgleich diese Kenntniß allein ohne Genie noch keinen geschmackvollen Componisten macht."

25 *Hamburgische neue Zeitung* 39 (9 March 1773), review of Felice Degiardino's (Giardini) *Sei Sonate di Cembalo con Violino o Flauto traverso*, Op. 3. London. "Gegenwärtige Sonaten sind ziemlich obligat nach Art der ältern Trios gesetzt; die Melodie ist oftmals angenehm, und würde durch Neuheit der Gedanken noch mehr gefallen."

26 *Erfurtische gelehrte Zeitungen* 32 (12 July 1780), 255, review of Dalberg's *Trois Sonates*, Op. 1, cited in chapter 2.

27 *Litteratur- und Theaterzeitung* II/2 23 (5 June 1779), 367–68, review of Forkel's *Sechs Klaviersonaten*. Göttingen: Forkel, 1778. "Diese Sonaten haben kein andres Verdienst, als das der musikalischen Richtigkeit, oder des reinen Satzes. Von einem so rüstigen Kunstrichter, der die ganze musikalische Welt reformiren, Kenner und Liebhaber belehren, die Tonkunst zu ihrer alten Würde zurückführen, und von allem Wuste reinigen will, und wie sonst alle seine quacksalberischen Versprechungen lauten mögen, der alles zwickt und sticht, was er mit seinem kleinen lilliputischen Zirkel nicht umfassen kann, hätte man ganz etwas andres, etwas Vortrefliches erwarten sollen ... Vor 20 oder 30 Jahren hätten diese Sonaten einen Platz in einer musikalischen Bibliothek verdient; aber jetzt? ... Vergebens wird man nach dem emsigsten Suchen einen Gedanken finden, der das Gepräge der Neuheit, der Originalität hat. Der Verf. hat die Manier C. P. E. Bachs nachgeahmt, ohne dessen Geist zu besitzen. Man muß die Bachischen körnichten, starken und eindringenden Gedanken recht bedauern, wenn man sie in Gesellschaft so vieler Taugenichts, so vieler alltäglichen, faden und matten sieht. Keine einzige neue Passage oder neue melodische Figur ... Die fünfte Sonate läßt vermuthen, daß sie Herr Forkel vorzeiten vom Herrn Kapellmeister Bach gelehnt, und weil er nachher vergessen hat, wem sie zugehört, sie jetzt als seine eigne Arbeit in seine Sammlung aufgenommen habe. Wenigstens kann man beweisen, daß ganze Perioden geborgt sind. Den Zwillingsbruder zum letzten Satz eben erwähnter Sonaten beliebe man in C. P. E. Bachs Sonaten zum Gebrauch der Damen aufzusuchen. Auch hat Herr F. fleißig aus G. Benda's und Nichelmanns Sonaten geschöpft. Nein! Gott ehre mir Häßlern! das ist ein andrer Mann. Hier und da auch Bach's Manier, aber zugleich unzählige Spuren einer feurigen Imagination, musikalischen Witzes, und fruchtreichen Erfindungskraft. Herr Forkel hätte wohl mehr Glauben an seine musikalisch=kritische Bibliothek behalten, wenn er diese Sonaten auf immer seinem Schreibpulte anvertraut oder nur seinen ihn anstaunenden Schülern mitgetheilt hätte."

28 *Jenaische Zeitungen* 45 (3 June 1779), 383–84, review of Forkel's *Sechs Klaviersonaten*. Göttingen: Forkel; and Leipzig: Breitkopf, 1778. "Denn sonst könnte man sagen, diese Sonaten hätten, auser [sic] einigen Dorfschulmeisterlichen Cadenzen S. 3. Syst. 5.u. und auser den Stadtpfeifermäsigen Vorschlägen, nach dem Trille, zur folgenden Note S. 39. Syst 4. T. 5. u. nichts

Eigenes; alles übrige sey theils abgeschriebener Gesang, theils unbedeutender Mechanismus u." Two of Forkel's colleagues showed mercy on his inaugural compositional effort, but neither were known for biting critique: *Hamburgischer Correspondent* Beytrag 2 (1779); *Göttingische Anzeigen* 42 (5 April 1779), 343–44.

29 *Jenaische Zeitungen* 38 (13 May 1782), 304, review of F. A. Eylenstein's *Sonate pour le Clavecin ou Pianoforte,* Op. 1. Speier: Bossler. "Hätte Hr. Eylenstein sicher gewußt, daß die Dissonanzen, so wie die Bindungen, nicht auf – sondern abwärts aufgelößt werden müßten . . . so hätte sie alles, was man in einer schönen Sonate suchen muß."

30 *Hamburgische neue Zeitung* 170 (23 October 1773), review of Joseph Haydn's *Six Sonates a Flute, Violon & Violoncello,* Op. 11 [Hob. XI:9 with XI:6–III; XI:7; XI:6 with a different second movement; XI:II with XI:17–III; II:9–III,II,I; XI:17–I with XI:3–III]. Amsterdam: Hummel. "Der Styl ist spielend und tändelnd, voll neuer Gedanken, schöner Melodie (ausgenommen an den unrhytmischen [*sic*] Stellen) und gefälliger Harmonie. Einige Adagios haben Variationen, die aber alle Idee vom Adagiosatze aufheben: das der dritten Sonate führt nur den Nahmen, denn es ist ein Tanz."

31 *Gelehrte Zeitung* III/9 (30 January 1773), 67, review of E. C. Fricke's *Neue Englische Tänze nebst dazu gehöriger vollstim. Musik.* Blandenburg und Quedlinburg, 1773. "Die Musik ist nicht nur theoretisch richtig; sondern auch, wenigstens größtentheils, zugleich angenehm u. leicht." *Strasburgische Gelehrte Nachrichten* 87 (29 October 1782), 1035–36, review of *Musikalische Blumenlese aufs Jahr 1782, 1783.* Speier: Bossler. "Freylich enthält diese Sammlung auch mittelmäßige und schlechte Stükke . . . die oft ein bißchen zu kühn, ich möchte lieber sagen, würklich uncorrect sind."

32 *Frankfurter gelehrte Anzeigen* III/19–20 (8 March 1774), 170–71, review of Johann Gottfried Eckard's *Sei Sonate per il Clavicembalo Solo.* Riga: Hartknoch, 1773. "Wir versichern die Verehrer des wahren guten Geschmacks, daß sie darinnen mehr finden, mehr – als in vielen sogenannten Claviersonaten – Gründlichkeit, Anstand, volle und reine Harmonie, ein angenehmer Gesang, auch zuweilen kün- stliche Modulationen= und Fugensätze, charakterisiren jede dieser Sonaten."

33 Kirnberger had excluded secondary dominants from his definition of modulation in *The Art of Strict Musical Composition,* pp. 128–29, a distinction more fully developed by Koch in volume II of his *Versuch einer Anleitung zur Composition.* For recent discussion of the subject, see Richard Kramer's article "The New Modulation of the 1770s: C.P.E. Bach in Theory, Criticism, and Practice," *JAMS* 38 (1985), 551–592; and Lester's *Compositional Theory.* In traditional eighteenth-century usage, *Modulation* could also refer simply to the progress of the music itself, without any definite association with keys or tonality. In some reviews, the wording is vague enough to allow either interpretation, but those I discuss here clearly address tonal issues.

34 *Allgemeine deutsche Bibliothek* LXXX/2 (1788), 447–50, review of Johann Georg

Witthauer's *Sammlung vermischter Klavier= und Singstücke*. Hamburg: Herold. "S. 10 im 8. Takte des zweyten Theils ist uns die Wendung aus dem harten Dreyklange E in D zu geschwind vorgekommen; wenigstens thut sie, mit den vorhergehenden und folgenden langsamen Fortschreitungen der Harmonie verglichen, keine gute Wirkung . . . S. 13, T. 7. scheint uns der Querstand (dis gegen d) doch etwas zu hart, so wenig man sich auch gegenwärtig daraus macht. Nicht für das Auge schreibt der Komponist, sondern für das Ohr: wird das letztere beleidigt, (und das ist bey der erwähnten Stelle der Fall,) so sündigt der Tonsetzer auch ohne ein besonderes Verbot . . . Der ganz unerwartete Eintritt des harten Dreyklangs A nach C moll (T. 5.) ist in diesem Andante, welches so sanft hinschleicht, gewiß jedem Zuhörer äußerst frappant und störend. Rec. würde sich eine ähnliche Modulation nur in Stücken von einem heftigen, stürmischen u. Charakter erlauben. Gk. [Türk]"

35 *Erfurtische gelehrte Zeitungen* 19 (19 April 1784), 150–51, review of T. G. Beßler's *Klavierstücke, für Anfänger und mittelmäßige Spieler*. Kassel, 1784. "Falsche Modulationen . . . machen dies Werk . . . nicht mehr genießbar." *Hamburgischer Correspondent* 140 (2 September 1786), review of M. E. Grose's *Six Sonates faciles pour le Clavecin ou Fortepiano*. Berlin: Rellstab. (This review also appeared in the *Magazin der Musik*.) "Kenner werden wohl wünschen, daß der Verfasser manchmal genauer im Rhythmus und der Modulation seyn möge."

36 *Altonaischer gelehrter Mercurius* I/15 (15 April 1773), 117–18, review of C. P. E. Bach's *Sei Concerti per il Cembalo*. "unerwartete bezaubernde Gänge der Harmonie."

37 *Hamburgischer Correspondent* 184 Beylage (18 November 1783), review of Zinck's *Sechs Clavier=Sonaten, nebst der Ode: Rain am Ufer des Meers, als ein Anhang zur sechsten Sonate*. Hamburg: Herold, 1783. "Die dritte Sonate scheint unter den sechsen am meisten original zu seyn, obgleich auch in den übrigen eigenthümliche Wendungen und originaler Ausdruck vorkkommen, welches desto schätzbarer ist, da verschiedene unserer neuen Componisten wenig Eigenthümliches haben, sondern aus demjenigen, was sie sich von gehörter Musik wieder erinnern, ihre Arbeit zusammensetzen, welches denn freylich auch Componiren heißen kann, wobey aber das Erfinden, eins der schätzbarsten Talente eines musikalischen Genies, fehlt."

38 *Altonaischer gelehrter Mercurius* V/8 (20 February 1777), 61–62, review of Türk's *Sechs Sonaten für das Clavier*, cited in chapter 4. "Bey diesen zeigt sich der Mann von Genie . . . Man findet keine aufgewärmte Materie mit neuer Brühe übergossen, sondern neue, wenigstens sichtbarlich eigene Gedanken." See also the review of Türk's second collection, cited in chapter 2, page 36, where the reviewer confesses he didn't want to bother finding out whether the ideas were new.

39 *Hamburgische neue Zeitung* 22 (8 February 1775), review of J. F. Reinhardt [Reichardt?] *Clavier=Sonaten*. Berlin, 1772. "Voll Feuer und Leben, und richtig im Satze. Nicht allemal so neu, als man von einem Manne von so vielem Genie erwartet."

40 *Magazin der Musik* I/1 (4 April 1783), 485, review of Mozart's *Six Sonates pour le Clavecin, ou Piano Forte avec l'accompagnement d'un Violon*, Op. 2 [K. 374d (376), K. 296, K. 374e (377), K. 317d (378), K. 373a (379), K. 374f (380)]. Vienna: Artaria. "Diese Sonaten sind die einzigen in ihrer Art. Reich an neuen Gedanken und Spuren des grossen musicalischen Genies des Verfassers . . . Allein es ist nicht möglich, eine vollständige Beschreibung dieses originellen Werks zu geben. N. N."

41 *Hamburgischer Correspondent* Beytrag 9 (1785), review of Mozart's *Trois Sonates pour le Clavecin ou piano forte avec l'Accompagnement d'un Violon*, Op. 1 [K. 301/293a; 304/300c; 302/293b]. Amsterdam: J. Schmitt. "Diese 3 Sonaten sind mehr original, als die übrigen, die uns von dem Herrn Mozart bekannt sind, und eben deshalb haben wir sie lieber."

42 *Hamburgischer Correspondent* 132 (17 August 1782), review of Joseph Haydn's *Six Quatuors ou Divertissements a deux Violons, Taille & Basse*, Op. 19 [originally published by Artaria as Op. 33]. Berlin and Amsterdam: Hummel. "Haydn ist ein unerschöpfliches Genie, und scheint sich fast in jedem neuen Werke, welches er herausgiebt, zu übertreffen. Diese gegenwärtigen Quatuors sind über alle Lobsprüche erhaben. Man findet in selbigen herrlichen Gesang, treffliche Harmonie, unvermuthete und überraschende Ausweichungen und eine Menge neuer noch nie gehörter Gedanken."

43 *Wöchentliche Nachrichten* IV:51 (17 December 1770), 402, review of Adam Veichtner's *Vier Sinfonien*. Mietau: Steidel. "Des Herrn Veichtners Sinfonien sind gut sehr gut, feurig, Melodienreich, mit guter Harmonie unterstützt, zwar nicht sehr Original; aber doch auch als Nachahmung eben so gut und öfters besser als ihre Urbilder."

44 *Allgemeine deutsche Bibliothek* XXII/2 (1774), 525–26, review of Christian Gottlieb Neefe's *Zwölf Klavier=Sonaten*. Leipzig: Engelhart Benjamin Schwickert, 1773. "Man sieht es, daß der V. besonders Hrn. Bachs neuere Clavierarbeiten fleißig studieret hat. Doch wollen wir ihn hiemit keiner knechtischen unerlaubten Nachahmung beschuldigen. Seine Art nachzuahmen ist gut. Z. [Agricola]"

45 *Allgemeine deutsche Bibliothek* XXXV/1 (1778), 172–74, review of Häßler's *Sechs Sonaten fürs Clavier*. Leipzig: Schwickert, 1776. "Sein Nachahmer aber, der an ihm hängt, kann sich endlich durch langen Umgang seine Manier eigen machen, all' sein äußeres Wesen annehmen, kann in vielen Stücken derselbe scheinen, und doch dabey ein mittelmäßiger Kopf bleiben. Mr. [Reichardt]"

46 *Erlangische gelehrte Anmerkungen* 16 (15 April 1788), 228, review of Ignaz Joseph Pleyel's *Deux grandes Sonates pour le Clavecin ou Piano Forte avec accompagnement d'un Violon ad libitum*, Op. 7. Frankfurt am Main: Haueisen. "Gleich auf den ersten Anblick ist der Schüler des grossen Haydn in diesen Sonaten unverkennbar, wenn man schon seine Delikatesse und unerschöpfliche Laune vermißt."

47 Elaine R. Sisman, *Haydn and the Classical Variation* (Cambridge and London: Harvard University Press, 1993), pp. 16–17.

48 Gretchen A. Wheelock, *Haydn's Ingenious Jesting with Art: Contexts of Musical Wit and Humor* (New York: Schirmer, 1992), p. 96.

49 *Musikalisches Kunstmagazin* I:2 (1782), 87, review of assorted keyboard pieces, including Haydn's *Six Sonates pour le Clavecin ou le Piano forte*, Op. 17 [Hob. XVI:37, 39, 38, 35, 36, 20]. Amsterdam and Berlin: Hummel. "Dieses sind mir die wichtigsten unter denen im vorigen Jahre herausgekommenen Klaviersachen . . . Hayden [zeichnet sich] durch originälle männliche Laune [aus]." *Hamburgischer Correspondent* 40 (10 March 1781), review of the same pieces: "Man erkennt auch in diesen Clavier=Sonaten den Verfasser der vortrefflichen Quatuors, die zu den besten musikalischen Stücken gehören, die jemals componirt worden sind. In den Haydnschen Werken herrscht überhaupt eine gewisse Laune, die diesem Componisten eigenthümlich ist."

50 *Unterhaltungen* IX/3 (March 1770), 257, review of Nicolas Dothel's *Six Sonates en Trio pour deux flutes, ou deux Violons & Violoncelle*, Op. 6. "Diese Trios sind gut dialogirt, haben einen leichten Gesang, und manche neue Züge."

51 *Unterhaltungen* X/2 (August 1770), 158–60, review of a trio by Graun in the collection *Musikalisches Vielerley*, cited in chapter 3. "Das 33st Stück liefert uns ein erfindungsvolles Trio von Hrn. Concertmeister Graun. Hier haben alle Stimmen zu thun, hier ist nichts Leeres, kein Leyermanns Menuet, noch ein poßierliches Finale u. dgl."

52 *Jenaische Zeitungen* 104 (29 December 1775), 893–94, review of Wolf's *Quartetto per il Flauto Trav, Oboe overo Violino, Fagotto overo Violoncello e Basso*. Breslau, 1776. "Auch in diesem Quartette findet man überall neue Gedanken." *Hamburgische neue Zeitung* 61 (18 April 1775), review of Wolf's *Sechs Sonaten für das Clavier oder Piano forte*. Leipzig, 1775. "Diese kleinern und leichtern Sonaten eines verdienstvollen Componisten, sind gedankenreich und neu."

53 *Allgemeines Verzeichniß neuer Bücher* V/1 (1780), 38, review of Christian Wilhelm Podbielsky's *Sechs Clavier-Sonaten*. Riga: Johann Friedrich Hartknoch, 1780. "Reich an Erfindung, und voll schönen Gesangs in den Melodien."

54 *Der teutsche Merkur* (September 1776), 265, review of Häßler's *Sechs Sonaten fürs Clavier*. Leipzig, 1776. "Bach hat bisher verschiedene Nachfolger und Nacheiferer gehabt, aber Herr Häßler scheint ihn am nächsten an der Ferse zu seyn; seine Einfälle sind neu und kühn, voll Kraft und Feuer."

55 *Neue Leipziger gelehrte Zeitungen* III/4 118 (6 October 1787), 1873–74, review of Haydn's *Sei Menuetti* [Hob. IX:9a]. Leipzig: Breitkopf. "Wenn auch der Name Haydn nicht auf dem Titel stünde, so müste [sic] man sogleich doch auf ihn schließen, wenn man diese Stücke spielt; denn in jedem erblickt man den schöpferischen Geist und das unerschöpfliche Genie eines Haydn. Es herrscht in ihnen gar nicht der gewöhnliche Schlendrian des Menuettentons, sondern überall ist neue Erfindung in Gedanken, in ihren Wendungen, überall angenehm überraschende Abwechslung, und so etwas eigenes, welches das Haydnische Genie so ganz zu seinem Vortheil auszeichnet. Leichtigkeit und Kunst, Melodie und Harmonie sind so glücklich mit einander gepaart, daß nur einem Haydn eine

solche Verbindung glücken konnte. Wenn man überdenkt, daß dies nur Kleinigkeiten sind und seyn sollen, so ist es zu verwundern, wie so viel in denselben gesagt und ausgedruckt hat werden können. In ganzen großen Stücken anderer Modekomponisten findet man oft den Reichthum nicht, der hier in einer einzigen Menuet ausgelegt ist." The *Allgemeine deutsche Bibliothek*'s review of the same pieces also recognized the "inexhaustible" Haydn, though it remarked the keyboard reduction could not do them justice. *Allgemeine deutsche Bibliothek* Anhang zum 53. bis 86. Bande (III), 1878–79, review of *Sei Minuetti del Signore Giuseppe Haydn, ridotti per Cembalo Solo*. Dresden and Leipzig: Breitkopf, 1787. Unsigned, but probably by Türk.

56 *Altonaischer gelehrter Mercurius* II/50 (11 December 1788), 419–20, review of A. J. Steinfeld's *Drei Sonatinen fürs Klavier* and *Drei Sonaten fürs Klavier*. Lübeck: Donatius, 1788. "Die Kühnheit, Neuheit seiner Ideen und die Eigenheiten seiner Arbeiten unterscheiden ihn sehr merklich von den Nachbetern, deren auch im Gebiete der Tonkunst nicht wenige neuere Componisten aufzuzählen sind."

57 *Magazin der Musik* II/2 (8 February 1787), 1209–14, review of F. S. Sander's *Sechs Clavier=Sonaten*. Part 1. Breslau and Leipzig: Friedrich Gotthold Jacobäern, 1785. "Eine höchstwillkommene Sammlung vortreflicher Sonaten . . . und es dem lautern Musikverehrer recht warm ums Herz wird! . . . wieder ein Genie erscheint, aus dessen reichem Schatz wir vieles, wenigstens bald eine zweite Sammlung ähnlicher Meisterstücke zu erhalten Hofnung haben. Erfindung, Reichthum an Gedanken, Kenntniß der Harmonie, Laune, Witz, ein sehr feines Gefühl des Wahren und Schönen, Kraft und Nettigkeit im Ausdruck aller durch Töne darzustellende möglichen Empfindungen und Leidenschaften . . . vereinigen sich in diesen Sonaten auf eine so bewundernswerthe als seltene Art."

58 *Musikalischer Almanach* III (1784), 19–20, review of F. S. Sander's *III. Concerts. pour le Clavecin, accompagnès [sic] de 2 Violons 2 Hautbois, 2 Cors, Taille et Basse, Livre I; Concert pour le Clavecin, Livre II*. Breslau, 1783. "In diesen Concerten ist des Laufens, Springens und Hüpfens beynahe kein Ende . . . hier ist von solchen Dingen, die einem wirklich musikalischen Gedanken auch nur von fernerher etwas ähnlich sähen, wenig oder gar nichts zu finden, und man muß die Finger des Hrn. Sander mit der Zunge des Hudibras vergleichen, der auf die Frage, warum diejenigen, welche von den geringsten Kleinigkeiten reden, den größten Zufluß von Worten besitzen, antwortete: daß die Zunge einem Turnierpferde gleiche, welches desto geschwinder laufe, je weniger Lastes es zu tragen habe."

59 *Allgemeine deutsche Bibliothek* LXXXI/1 (1788), 124–25, review of Uber's *Trois Sonates pour le Clavecin, avec l'accompagnement d'un Violon et Violoncelle obligés, et de deux Cors de Chasse ad libitum, de même d'un Flute pour la derniere Sonate*. Part 2. Breslau. "Herr Uber gleicht einem Schwätzer, welcher immer noch etwas Unwichtiges, oft ohnedem schon Bekanntes, zu erzählen hat, wenn man nach Ruhe sehnt, und nichts mehr hören mag . . . Auch der Symphonie . . . gebricht es an Schwung und Neuheit. Rt. [Türk]"

60 *Neue Leipziger gelehrte Zeitungen* II/4 123 (19 October 1786), 1966, review of Christian Gottlob Saupe's *Drey Sonaten und sechs Sonatinen für die Liebhaber der Musik*. Glachau: Verfasser, 1786. "Ob man sie zwar eben keines Fehlers wider den Satz beschuldigen kann, so empfehlen sie sich doch nicht eben sonderlich durch ihren innern Gehalt . . . Hauptsächlich sind sie arm an Gedanken und Wendungen: man suchet also etwas neues und auffallendes vergebens. Selten ist in einem Stücke mehr als ein Gedanke, und der unzählige Mahl bis zum Eckel wiederhohlt, [*sic*] daher ist es ein beständiger Kling Klang; sie enthalten nichts Nachdrückliches und Kraftvolles, weder etwas gedachtes noch empfindungsvolles [*sic*], alltägliche Melodie ohne Harmonie, an deren tiefen Kenntniß es dem Verf. noch zu fehlen scheint."

61 *Magazin der Musik* I/2 (7 December 1783), 1255–59, review of Wolf's *Sechs Sonatinen für das Clavier*. Dessau, 1783. "Welch ein wahrer Ausflug des Genius ist z.e. folgende Stelle, die das Andante der vierten Sonatine beschließt! (32) . . . C. F. C."

62 *Erfurtische gelehrte Zeitungen* 25 (27 March 1777), 220, review of Uber's *Sechs Sonaten für das Clavier, mit einer begleitenden Violine*. Breslau: Meyer, 1776. "Sie sind reich an neuen und frappanten Wendungen: nur scheinen uns ein Paar Themata etwas zu gedehnt, folglich langweilig ausgeführt. Die Oktaventour in der 2ten Sonate S. 6 unten und S. 8. mißfällt unsern Ohren ganz und gar; so wie die oft wiederhohlten eintönigen Läufer in dem Presto der 5ten Sonate."

63 *Musikalischer Almanach* III (1784), 17–19, review of Salomon Greßler's *Sechs Sonaten fürs Clavier*. "Mangel an Reichtum der Gedanken scheint das erste zu seyn, was diesen Sonaten anhängt. Daher erstlich die unaufhörliche Wiederholung des Hauptsatzes, bald in der Melodie etwas verändert, bald um eine Octave höher oder tiefer gesetzt; zweytens die Wiederholung so vieler Nebensätze auf eben dieselbe Weise, wie mit dem Hauptsatze, und drittens der nothwendig daraus entstehende Mangel an mannichfaltigen Modulation. Die Art uns auszudrücken, mag noch so schön seyn; wenn wir aus Mangel an Gedanken einen und ebendenselben Ausdruck mehreremahle wiederholen, so verliert sie an ihrem Werthe, und macht uns jenen Schwätzern gleich, die zwar angenehm aber zugleich leer sind."

64 *Hamburgische neue Zeitung* 84 Beylage (27 May 1786), review of Witthauer's *Samlung [sic] vermischter Klavier= und Singstücke*. "In dem ersten Allegro sind die Ausweichungen, wodurch der Komponist aus dem Thema in der Dominante zu dem Haupttone, S. 13, übergeht, vorzüglich angenehm und neu."

65 *Magazin der Musik* I/2 (7 December 1783), 1285–95, review of Georg Benda's *Sammlung vermischter Clavierstücke für geübte und ungeübte Spieler*. Parts 1–3. Gotha: Ettinger. "Bendas reizender, neuer, ihm ganz eigenthümlicher Gesang . . . und das verbunden mit der harmonischsten Richtigkeit und Correction; der ächte, in jedem Stil sich gleichbleibende und stichhaltende gute Geschmack endlich, der nicht mit Eigensinn an alten, verjährten Formen kleben bleibt . . . In dem zweyten Theile, der auch mit einem besondern Titel einzeln zu haben ist, macht wieder

eine sehr gearbeitete Sonata den Anfang, aus a moll. Die frappante Ausweichung nach c moll gleich auf der ersten Seite derselben ist nicht zu übersehen."

66 *Musikalische Real-Zeitung* II/38 (23 September 1789), 296–97, review of Kozeluch's *III Sonates pour le Clavecin ou Piano-Forte*, Op. 20 und *III. Sonates pour le Clavecin ou Piano-Forte avec l'Accompagnement d'un Violon & Violoncelle*, Op. 21. Paris. "Ein kühner Flug der Phantasie, Fülle der Harmonie, niedliche Inversionen und ein Strom schöner Modulation, der sich durch nahe und entfernte Tonarten hindurchschlängelt – dies, dünkt uns, sind die charakteristische Kennzeichen der Kozeluchischen Klavierkompositionen . . . Daher wird man auch zwischen den Werken des Herrn K. und Bachs nie eine Vergleichung anstellen können . . . Bach ist überall originel, überall neu: da im Gegentheil Herr K. gewisse Lieblingsgedanken, oder Favoritpassagen hat, die man bei nahe in jedem seiner Werke, oft nur unter sehr geringen Modifikationen antrifft."

67 *Hamburgischer Correspondent* Beytrag (November 1775), review of Conrad Breuning's *Six Trio concertans a Flute ou Violon 1mier Violon & Bass*, Op. 4. Frankfurt am Main: André. "Die Ausweichungen des Verfassers sind die gewöhnlichen. Selten wagt er eine Kühne, wodurch uns doch Boccherini seine Sachen so empfehlenswürdig macht. Lauter Zuckerbrodt wird einem bald zuwider; ein guter Magen verlangt auch zuweilen starke Speisen. Was gehen uns die Schwachen an, die sie nicht verdauen können."

68 *Magazin der Musik* II/2 (24 April 1787), 1310–11, review of Joseph Haydn's *Trois Sonates pour le Clavecin ou Piano-forte accompagnées d'un Violon & Violoncelle obligées* [sic], Op. 27 [XV:9, 2, 10]. Hummel. "Unter den vielen vortreflichen Compositionen dieses großen Mannes, für den Flügel und andre Instrumente, behaupten diese drey Sonaten eine der ersten Stufen. Das Anfangsadagio der ersten aus a dur hat einen unnennbaren Reiz und contrastirt sehr angenehm mit dem darauf folgenden Vivace. In dem Allegro der zweiten aus f dur überrascht die Verkürzung des Rhythmus im sechsten Takt den Zuhörer, manchen vielleicht zu unerwartet. Das Thema des Finaladagio mit vier Veränderungen wird durch die Ausdehnung des Rhythmus im siebenden Takt sehr original. Die schönste Sonate unter diesen schönen ist indessen noch die dritte aus Es dur, worinn Haydns Genius im Fluge den höchsten Schwung nimmt."

69 See, for example, the *Litterarische Nachrichten* Anhang I/3; I. Stück (29 July 1775), 8, review of Wolf's *Sei Sonate per il Clavicembalo solo*. Leipzig: Breitkopf, 1774. "Diese Sonaten sind von guter, feuriger, zuweilen launischer Erfindung . . . kurz sie verdienen bey allen unpartheyischen Lob und Achtung."

70 *Magazin der Musik* I/2 (7 December 1783), 1259–75, review of Zinck's *Sechs Claviersonaten*, cited in chapter 2. "Dem leztern Rondo bin ich mit warmer Verliebtheit zugethan. Es ist ein gar näckisches Ding, voll der curiosesten Whims, Possen, witziger Laune; und Haydn selbst könnte es immerhin gemacht zu haben stolz seyn."

71 *Berlinische Nachrichten* 148 (9 December 1788), 1133–34, review of Federigo Angiolini's *Variazioni pel Cembalo o Fortepiano del Duetto della Cosa rara, pace*

caro mio sposo del Signor Martin. Berlin: Rellstab. "Im Ganzen scheint Hr. A. nach Fasch und Haydn's Manier zu variiren, und er kann immer sehr schöne Variationen liefern, wenn er auch nicht ganz des erstern künstlich harmonisches Gewebe und des letztern Laune besitzt."

72 *Hamburgische neue Zeitung* 101 (25 June 1774), review of Wolf's *Sei Sonate per il Clavicembalo.* Leipzig, 1774. "Im wahren deutschen Geschmacke, wie auch fast ganz ohne Harfenbässe; und doch voll Abwechselung, ziemlich viel Neuheit, Leben, guter Melodie . . . Die langsamen Sätze gefallen uns vorzüglich, weil sich hier die meiste Neuheit in Gedanken und Modulationen findet."

73 *Allgemeine deutsche Bibliothek* XXXIII/1 (1778), 175–76, review of Boccherini's *Sei Sonate per il Clavi Cembalo e Violino Obligato.* Riga: Hartknoch, 1774. "Diese Sonaten haben nicht das Eigenthümliche und Launige, so man in den Violin= und Violoncellsachen des Verf. findet. Hie und da sieht man zwar einzelne Stellen, die ihn kenntlich, frappante Harmonieen, unerwarteten reizenden Gesang; allein das Ganze ist mehr gewöhnlich . . . Diesen empfehlen wir . . . denen an neuer Mode, Ohrenkitzel, und heftiger Erschütterung des Trommelfells mehr gelegen ist, als an wahrem gutem Geschmack, Rührung des Herzens und Beschäfftigung des Verstandes. F. [Reichardt]"

74 *Magazin der Musik* II/2 (24 April 1787), 1282–85, review of Charles Frederick Horn's *Six Sonates for the Piano-forte, or Harpsichord, with an Accompanyment for a Violin and Violoncello,* Op. 1. "Von ihrer innern Güte, in Absicht auf reine Harmonie, Neuheit und Einkleidung der Gedanken, läßt sich eben nichts Erhebliches zu ihrer Empfehlung sagen . . . Er scheint aber an Gedanken überhaupt einigen Mangel zu haben; und darinn glauben wir den Grund zu sehen, warum er sich so oft in entfernter Harmonien verliehrt, woran wir, weil sie so kahl da stehen, und fast von allem Reiz einer verschönernden Melodie entblößt sind, nicht das Vergnügen finden, das Haydn, Clementi, u. erwecken, wenn sie, von der weiten Heerstraße sich entfernend, uns in seitwärts versteckte romantische Gegenden führen."

75 *Berlinische Nachrichten* 17 (7 February 1778), 87, review of Otto Charles Erdman, Freiherr von Kospoth's *Trois Symphonies a deux Violons, Taille & Basse, deux Flutes & deux Cors de Chasse.* Berlin: Hummel, 1778. "einschmeichelnd," "durchgängig schmelzend," "ruhig," "sanft"; "ganz aufheiternd," "außerordentlich feurig."

76 *Wirzburger gelehrte Anzeigen* III/80 Beylage (4 October 1788), 887–88, review of Häßler's *Sechs leichte Sonaten fürs Clavier oder Piano Forte.* Erfurt: Häßler, 1788. "Von der vierten Sonate ist das *Andante,* womit es anfängt, etwas Geistvolles und Honigsüsses für mich."

77 *Hamburgische neue Zeitung* 33 (26 February 1773); 177 (5 November 1773); 95 (12 June 1776); 21 (5 February 1777); Beylage 189 (26 November 1777); 174 Beylage (31 October 1778); 112 (15 July 86).

78 *Erfurtische gelehrte Zeitungen* 22 (8 May 1787), 170–71, review of Mlle Edelmann, Mr Darondeau and Mr Pin's *Trois Sonates pour le Clavecin ou Piano*

Forte. Leipzig: C. G. Hilscher. "Darauf folget eine im ganz eigenem naiven Geschmacke sehr lebhafte Menuett . . . Den Schluß macht ein lachendes Allegretto."

79 *Berlinische Nachrichten* 148 (9 December 1788), 1133–34, review of Angiolini's *Variazioni*, cited above. "In der fünften, welche aus der weichen Tonleiter ist, sind viel brave harmonische Wendungen, bey der reizendsten Melodie, welche süß melancholisch ist." *Hamburgischer Correspondent* 164 (13 October 1780), review of C. P. E. Bach's *Clavier=Sonaten nebst einigen Rondos fürs Forte Piano für Kenner und Liebhaber.* Part 2. Leipzig: Bach, 1780. "Das dritte aus A moll ist mehr klagend und melancholisch und das Favorit=Rondo des Recensenten."

80 *Magazin der Musik* I/2 (7 December 1783), 1259–75, review of Zinck's *Sechs Claviersonaten,* cited above. "Ein langer, bis ans Ende sich windender Regenwurm! nur quält er die Finger durch mühseelige Reckungen. Er drückt vortreflich einen dauernden in der Seele eines Schwarzblütigen wühlenden Gedanken aus, dessen seine Melancholie sich nicht entledigen kann."

81 *Neue Leipziger gelehrte Zeitungen* III/2 49 (26 April 1787), 783–84, review of Johann Ludwig Willing's *Drey Sonaten fürs Clavier oder Piano=Forte mit Begleitung einer Violine.* Leipzig: Breitkopf, 1787. "Es herrscht zwar in ihnen weder die Haydnische Laune, noch die Vanhallische Munterkeit, und der Bachische Ernst, noch das Feuer von Kozeluch und Clementi: aber dafür zeichnen sie sich durch ihr sanftes, zärtliches, einnehmendes und gefälliges Wesen vor vielen andern sehr vortheilhaft aus . . . Die zweyte Sonate enthält (1) ein Allegro, wo Munterkeit und Annehmlichkeit sich beyde die Hände bieten; (2) eine ganz hübsche Menuet, die ganz den Character eines sich über einen Verlust zufrieden stellenden Unglücklichen an sich trägt; (3) ein Rondo allegro, das eben nur mit mäßiger Geschwindigkeit vorgetragen werden muß: in welchen eine einsame und gemäßigte Freude herrscht."

82 Johann Heinrich Voss, "Luise," third Idylle, in *Sturm und Drang Werke,* vol. I: *Göttinger Hain,* edited by Renée Strasser (Zurich: Stauffacher-Verlag, 1966), p. 254. "Alle Weisen des Klangs wetteiferten, andre mit andern; / Vielgewandt, tief-strömend ergoß sich der lebende Wohllaut: / Donnerte bald wie, gestürmt vom Orkan am Gestade die Brandung / Hoch aufbraust, wann das Krachen zerscheiterter Kiel' und der Männer / Jammerndes Angstgeschrei in den grausen Tumult fern hinsterbt, / Wallete dann wie ein Bach, der über geglättete Kiesel / Rinnt durch Blumen und Gras und Umschattungen, wo sich die Hirten / Gerne legt, aufhorchend im lieblichen Traum dem Gemurmel."

83 *Musikalisch-kritische Bibliothek* II, 275–300, review of C. P. E. Bach's *Claviersonaten,* cited above. "Die Schönheiten dieses Andante von einer solchen Beschaffenheit sind, wie sie seyn müssen, wenn sie den meisten Musikfreunden gefallen sollen, das heißt: daß ihr Charakter begreiflicher, und der innere Werth desselben auffallender ist, als die Schönheiten der beyden übrigen Stücke dieser ersten Sonate . . . Die kleine Wendung der Modulation, welche am Ende dieses schönen Andante vorkommt, um das folgende Presto, welches aus A moll geht,

gleich damit zu verbinden, ist ebenfalls von besonders guter Wirkung, so wie überhaupt solche Wendungen, welchen den Uebergang von einem Charakter zum andern erleichtern."

84 *Musikalisch-kritische Bibliothek* II: 301–05, review of Türk's *Sechs Sonaten für das Clavier*. Parts 1–2. Leipzig and Halle: Breitkopf, 1776–77. "Der Hauptcharakter dieser Melodie ist sanft, und dieser Zug scheint hier eigentlich das zu seyn, was jedes Kunstwerk von dem innern Charakter seines Verfassers zu erhalten pflegt. Es scheint vom Temperamente abzuhängen. Unser Verf. ist daher auch da am glücklichsten, wo sein Ausdruck sanft ist. Er fließt so eben und sanft dahin, wie ein sanft und etwas schwach rieselnder Bach." A later review of Türk sonatas agreed that his natural disposition tended toward the easy and pleasant. See the *Raisonnirendes Bücherverzeichniß* III/6 (March 1784), 88–89, review of Türk's *Sechs leichte Claviersonaten*. Leipzig, 1783.

85 *Magazin der Musik* I/2 (7 December 1783), 1255–59, review of Wolf's *Sechs Sonatinen*, cited above. ". . . in einem herabgestimmteren Ton, weniger sich in der Region großer und leidenschaftlicher Vorstellungen aufhaltend, mehr sich auf frohe, witzige, heitre Empfindung einschränkend."

86 *Magazin der Musik* II/2 (5 August 1786), 847–48, review of Carl Rudolf Heinrich Ritter's *Versuch einer Sammlung vermischter kleiner Stücke fürs Clavier*. Bremen, 1786. "Die Stücke des gegenwärtigen Versuchs haben alle ihren besondern bestimmten Charakter; ein Erforderniß, das so viele Componisten nicht zu kennen scheinen, oder auch ihren Arbeiten nicht zu geben wissen."

87 *Magazin der Musik* I/2 (7 December 1783), 1275–76, review of Johann Ludwig Theodor Blum's *Drey Sonaten für das Clavier*. "Auch sie gehören unter die gewiß nicht schlechten Producte des vorigen Jahres fürs Clavier, ob sie gleich an Erfindung neuer Gedanken, an Feuer und mahlerische Ausdrucke dem Kleeblatte der eben recensirten drey Werke bey weitem nicht gleichkommen."

88 *Magazin der Musik* I/1 (4 April 1783), 412, review of Conte Giovanne [*sic*] Luigi Csaky's *XII Variazioni per il Cembalo solo*. Vienna: Toricella. "Recht artig und characteristisch. Das Thema, auf das die Variationen gemacht sind, könnte allenfalls überschrieben seyn: hartnäckiger launigter Eigensinn; und dieser Character wird ziemlich gut durch die Veränderungen durchgeführt."

89 *Magazin der Musik* I/2 (7 December 1783), 1238–55, review of C. P. E. Bach's *Claviersonaten und freye Phantasien, nebst einigen Rondos für Fortepiano* [Wq. 58]. Leipzig: Bach, 1783. "Das erste dieser Rondos ist aus dem A dur, im 6/8 Tact. Es ist schwer, wenn man nicht immer in allgemeine Exclamationen ausbrechen oder auch in den Detail eines kahlen Registers der harmonischen Schönheiten, der Ausweichungen, ihrer Einlenkung u. gehen will, über Instrumentalstücke etwas bestimmtes zu sagen. Indessen mache ich es gemeiniglich, um mir doch einigermaßen von meinen Empfindungen Rechenschaft geben könne, dabey so, daß ich mir irgend einen Character denke, der einem ausgezeichneten Stücke entsprechen könnte. Und so empfinde ich z.B. bey dem Thema dieses Rondos (26) und seiner Ausführung, das es einem allerliebsten Mädchen gleicht, die ihr

Köpfchen auf was gesezt hat, das sie durch Laune und artiges Pochen durchaus erreichen will." Jakob de Ruiter recognizes the tendency of eighteenth-century reviewers to use character portraits as an aid to interpretation. See his *Charakterbegriff*, p. 72.

90 *Magazin der Musik* I/2 (7 December 1783), 1238–55, review of Bach's *Claviersonaten*, cited above. "Heitere, sanfte Freude eines unschuldigen Mädchens, sitzend an einem Bache im Dufte eines Sommerabends. So sanft, so eben fließt die dämmernd wonnigliche Empfindungen hin. Aber bald lößt sie sich in widrigere Empfindungen auf, in dem drauf folgenden *Largetto e sostenuto*. Ernst erwacht in ihrer Seele … Wozu denn auch, meinem Gefühl nach wenigstens, die Tonart E dur nicht wenig beyträgt, die eines harten, rauhen Characters ist, und selbst dann, wenn sie Freude ausdrücken kann, nie die sanfte, liebliche einer Mädchenseele, sondern den wildern, rohern Jubel des Mannes, und überhaupt einen gewissen barschen Affect in Freude und Leid zeichnet. In eben diesem Tone der Männlichkeit schreitet im E dur das folgende Rondo in 3 Achtel Tact einher. Ich gestehe es, daß hier meine Empfindung nicht mit der eines andern, von mir sehr hochgeschätzten Recensenten dieser Sammlung im hamburgischen Correspondenten harmonirt, der es ein allerliebstes, sanftes Stücke nannte … Demzufolge darf ich so aufrichtig seyn zu gestehen, daß ich in meiner Classification des Inhaltes dieser Sammlung, das Allegretto der zweyten Sonate, die nun folgt, an Werth zuletzt stelle. Vielleicht liegt die Schuld an mir; aber ich empfinde nun so. Ich wüßte mir hierbey keinen solchen bestimmten und Einheit erhaltenden Character zu denken, wie bey den übrigen Rondos und Sonaten dieser Sammlung." The *Hamburgischer Correspondent* review appeared in issue 150 (19 September 1783).

91 In this context, it is interesting to note Scott Burnham's observations about the many narratives describing Beethoven's *Eroica*: "We must not for a moment think that the symphony is about these narratives, for it is precisely the other way around: the narratives are about the symphony." See his *Beethoven Hero* (Princeton University Press, 1995), p. 25.

92 *Musikalische Real-Zeitung* I/7 (13 August 1788), 49–50, review of Mozart's *Sonate pour le Clavecin avec accompagnement d'un Violon*. Speier, Bossler. "Das Adagio ist voll sanfter Empfindungen, wahrer Ausdruk schmachtender Liebe." II/27 (8 July 1789), 208–09, review of Johann Gottfried Gebhard's *Eine Sonate für das Klavier*. 1784. "Das Adagio ist . . . nicht so reich an künstlichen Modulationen, als der vorhergehende und nachfolgende Saz: aber es scheint, Herr G. habe sie mit weiser Ueberlegung sparsamer gebraucht, um seinem Adagio, das den Charakter sanfter Zärtlichkeit hat, nicht eine Tinte von finstrer Schwermuth zu geben."

93 *Frankfurter gelehrte Anzeigen* III/61–62 (2 August 1774), 514–15, review of Bach's *Sex [sic] Sonate* [Wq. 53], cited in chapter 2. "Itzt soll ich recensiren – kritisiren u. Aber dies alles weg. Ich bin diesmal nicht aufgelegt, gewisse weise Herren mit der Nase drauf zu stossen, was dies und jenes ausdrücken will … Wer nicht fühlen

kann, der verdient auch nicht, daß mans ihm sagt . . . Die 3te Son. aus D moll scheint mir die künstlichste. In dem Larghetto S. 17, find ich besonders viel Kunst. Die in dem dritten Liniensystem auf der nemlichen Seite, angebrachte chromatische Töne, thun viel Würkung. Doch versteh' ich nicht recht, was dies milde Stück ausdrücken will."

94 *Allgemeines Verzeichniß neuer Bücher* IV/8 (August 1779), 599, review of Wolf's *Sechs kleine Sonaten*. Leipzig: Breitkopf, 1779. "Die vierte derselben ist characteristisch – der erste Satz überschrieben, das entzweyte Eheparr gemeiner Leute. Der zweyte, die Versöhnung. Diese Art Composition war vor einigen Jahren noch mehr Mode als gegenwärtig. Es wird bekanntermaßen der Ausdruck der Music, durch eine derselben untergelegte, wörtliche Beschreibung erklärt, ohne welche denn freylich mancher den Componisten nicht ganz nach seinem Sinne verstehen möchte."

95 *Allgemeine deutsche Bibliothek* LXVII/2 (1786), 448–49, review of G. C. Füger's *Charakteristische Clavierstücke*. Tübingen: Füger. "Die ersten fünf Stücke bestehen aus lauter laufenden und springenden Sätzen in geschwinder Bewegung, die aber von so weniger Bestimmtheit des Ausdrucks sind, daß die Ueberschriften, ohne dem Charakter der Stücke im geringsten zu schaden, nach Willkühr verwechselt werden könnten. Die Schattirungen unter Ausgelassenheit, Lebhaftigkeit, Fröligkeit, Heiterkeit, Freude und Frolocken bestimmt durch Töne auszudrücken, würde selbst einem Gretry, der in Charakterzeichnungen so viel Stärke besitzt, schwerlich gelingen; dazu gehört eine Feinheit des Gefühls und Reichthum der Erfindung, wovon dem Hrn. F. nach diesen Stücken zu urtheilen, gar nichts zu Theil geworden ist. Das sechste Stück, Zärtlichkeit, ist in A dur und Allegretto: eine zu diesem Ausdruck nicht zum besten gewählten Tonart und Bewegung . . . dann mit einmal wird es in der Mitte des Stücks so lermend, daß man sich eher ein frolockendes Weibergeschrey, als einen Ausbruch von inniger Zärtlichkeit darunter vorstellen kann . . . Das folgende Stück, Stolz und Kühnheit, in Fis moll und Viervierteltakt fängt Allegro assai mit 16 Takt langen laufendes Sechzehnteln an, die sich zu dem gesetzten Gang des Stolzes und der Kühnheit, wie die Faust aufs Auge, passen. Atr. [Schulz]"

96 *Musikalische Real-Zeitung* I/1 (5 March 1788), 1–2, review of Joseph Haydn's *VII Sonate con un Introduzione ed al fine un Teremoto, ridotte per il Clavicembalo o Forte Piano*, Op. 49 [Hob. XX:1C]. "Herr H. hat uns schon mehrere Charakterstüke, oder wenn man lieber will, musikalische Malereien geliefert, aber noch keines, das diese Sammlung an Reichthum und Fülle der Harmonie, an kühnen Modulationen, an Energie und Würde der Schreibart übertroffen hätte. Wenn der Hr. Verf. unmittelbar aus der Seele des sterbenden Mittlers herausgeschrieben hätte: so würde er kaum im Stand gewesen sein, die Empfindungen desselben wahrer und feierlicher darzustellen."

97 *Erlangische gelehrte Anmerkungen* 17 (22 April 1788), 135–36, review of Joseph Haydn's *Composizioni del Sgr. Giuseppe Haydn sopra le sette ultime Parole del nostro Rdentore [sic] in Croce Consistenti in Sette Sonate con un Introduzione ed*

un Teremoto, Op. 49. Vienna. Artaria. "So gerecht die Vorwürfe sind, die in einigen Komposizionen den großen Händel getroffen haben, daß er Vorfälle in der Musik ausdrücken wollte, die ganz ausser ihrem Gebiete liegen, z.B. das Gewimmel der Haarinsekten, das Hüpfen der Heuschrecken, in den Plagen der Egypter, so gegründet würde der Tadel seyn, den der treffliche Haydn erfahren müßte, wenn er sich vorgenommen hätte, die letzten Worte Jesu in diesen Sonaten auszudrücken. Das höchste Ziel, das er sich vorstecken konnte, war dieß; die Empfindungen, die durch sieben Sätze schon fixirt waren, zu verstärken und durch seine Musik ihnen Kolorit und Haltbarkeit zu geben. Wer mit großern Erwartungen diese Komposizion in die Hände nimmt, wird sich getäuscht und in einer Verlegenheit finden, wenn er in dem langen Adagio der fünften Sonate ein Verhältniß seiner Empfindung zu dem beygeschriebenen Worte, *Sitio* suchen soll, indem die Kunst des Tonsetzers nur das Schmachtende und Ersterbende ausdrücken kann, und die Lücke zwischen diesem Gefühl und der Empfindung des Durstes erst durch die Einbildungskraft ergänzt werden muß. – Da das Ganze sich durch hohe Erfindung, durch die feinsten Dissonanzen, die reinsten Bindungen und Auflösungen so auffallend als eines der ersten Meisterstücke Haydns ankündiget: so ist es schwer die hervorragende Schönheit einzelner Sonaten zu bestimmen."

98 *Magazin der Musik* I/2 (1783), 939–40, review of Antonio Sacchini's *Partition de Renaud*. Paris: Sacchini. "Die Ouverture ist in einem kriegerischen Character und kündigt den Ton des ersten Acts gut an." *Allgemeine deutsche Bibliothek* LVI/2 (1783), 458–67, review of Antonio Salieri's *Armida*. Hamburg: Westphal; Kiel: Cramer. "Sie bezeichnet sehr glücklich malerisch, was unmittelbar vor dem Augenblick, wo die Handlung der Oper beginnt, vorhergeht. Smz. [Schulz]"

99 *Berlinische Nachrichten* 100 (29 August 1778), 485, review of Johann Abraham Peter Schulz's *Six diverses pieces pour le Clavecin ou le Piano Forte*, Op. 1. Berlin: Hummel, 1778. "Herr Schulz ist einer von denenjenigen Tonkünstlern unsers Jahrhunderts, Der [*sic*] Sein [*sic*] weit umspannendes musikalisches Talent, durch die genausten Regeln und Grundsätze der Theorie verschönert, und zur Reiffe [*sic*] gebracht hat ... Sie sind ganz in dem Geiste der Bache [*sic*] und ihrer würdigen Vor= und Nachgänger geschrieben. Kühne große neue Gedanken finden sich so häufig; daß immer einer den andern überrascht, ein Fall – der nicht alle Tage vorkommt – allenthalben gewinnt das Gehör noch weit mehr aber das Herz."

100 *Hamburgische neue Zeitung* 40 (10 March 1773), review of Carlo Gottlob Richter's *Concerto I & II*, cited in chapter 4. "Die Themata der ersten Allegro's in der Principalstimme hätten wir lieber melodischer und kraftvoller gehabt; sehr selten sagen Herpeggio's [*sic*] dem Herzen etwas." *Hamburgischer Correspondent* 55 (5 April 1783), review of Zinck's *Six Sonates pour deux Flutes traversieres*, Op. 1. Berlin and Amsterdam: Hummel. "Die mehrsten der ältern, die im Satze richtig sind, versäumen den guten Gesang, sind steif und gezwungen, und verfehlen daher die Wirkung, die alle Musikstücke haben sollten, Rührung des Herzens."

101 *Erfurtische gelehrte Zeitungen* 25 (27 March 1777), 219–20, review of Türk's *Sechs Sonaten*, cited in chapter 4. "Sie empfehlen sich vorzüglich durch das Sangbare und Sentimentalische, oder durch sanfte, gefühlvolle Melodie. Durchgehends herrschet, bey strenger Beobachtung aller Regeln der Theorie, ein meisterhafter ans Herz dringender Ausdruck."

102 *Jenaische Zeitungen* 49 (19 July 1786), 391–92, review of Uber's *Trois Sonates pour le Clavecin, avec l'accompagnement d'un Violon et Violoncelle obligés, et de deux Cors de Chasse ad libitum, de meme d'une Fleute [sic] pour la premiere Sonate*. Breslau, 1786. "Der Satz der Sonaten ist, so viel Recens. davon urtheilen kann, richtig. Alle haben Melodie, und befriedigen Herz und Ohr."

103 *Magazin der Musik* I/2 (18 September 1783), 924–25, review of Vanhal's *Tre Sonate per il Fortepiano o Clavicembalo*, Op. 30. Vienna: Artaria. "Freilich muß man solche Sache nur als Bonbons oder Biscuit ansehen, davon man nicht zu viel und zu oft genießen muß."

104 Kirnberger, *The Art of Strict Musical Composition*, p. 406. Mark Evan Bonds provides an excellent discussion of late eighteenth-century concepts of form in the second chapter of his *Wordless Rhetoric*.

105 Kirnberger, *The Art of Strict Musical Composition*, p. 417.

106 *Hamburgische neue Zeitung* 105 (2 July 1773), review of J. S. Schröeter [sic]'s *Six Sonates pour le Clavecin ou le Piano forte avec l'accompagnement d'un Violon & Violoncello*, Op. 2. Amsterdam: Hummel, 1773. "Wer in den Werken der neuen sonderlich Wiener Componisten erfahren ist, wird manchen niedlichen Gedanken hier wiederfinden – Rapto vivere assulti – Herr S. weiß jene Gedanken indeß recht artig zu ordnen."

107 *Hamburgischer Correspondent* 80 (19 May 1770), review of Beckmann's *Drey Sonaten für das Clavier*. Parts 1–2. Hamburg: Bock. "Wir wünschen dem Verfasser einen genauen Beurtheiler, der . . . ihn besonders den Plan seiner größern Stücke sorgfältiger anlegen lehre."

108 *Altonaischer gelehrter Mercurius* II/34 (25 August 1774), 268, review of Wolf's *Sei Sonate per il Clavicembalo Solo*. Leipzig, 1774. "Seine Gedanken sind neu und schön und die Anordnung derselben ist natürlich und ungezwungen." *Allgemeine deutsche Bibliothek* XXXV/2 (1778), 522–23, review of Veichtner's *Concerto I. per il Violino Concertato accompagnato da due Violini, Violetta, Basso continuo, e Basso di Ripieno*. Riga: Hartknoch, 1775. "Bey sehr vielem Feuer und großer Annehmlichkeit herrscht eine Ordnung im Plan, und eine rythmische Genauigkeit und harmonische Reinigkeit, die dem Ganzen den Charakter des Edlen und Vollendeten geben. Mr. [Reichardt]"

109 *Neue Leipziger gelehrte Zeitungen* III/2 39 (31 March 1787), 618–19, review of *Trois Sonates pour le clavecin par Mdslle. Edelmann, Msr. Darondeau, Msr. Pin*. Hilscher. "Wer weiß nicht, daß dies der allgemein herrschende und alles übrige verschlingende Ton in der jetzigen lieben musikalischen Welt ist, da alles das mehr Beyfall findet, was die Ohren kützelt, das Herz rührt, als das, was den Verstand unterhält."

110 *Allgemeine deutsche Bibliothek* LIX/1 (1784), 134–35, review of M. C. Grosse's *Sechs Sonaten*, cited in chapter 4. "Wenn Hr. G. in seinen künftigen Ausarbeitungen der Fruchtbarkeit seiner Einfälle mehr Schranken setzen und suchen wird, jedem Stück durch Einheit und nähere Verbindung der mannichfaltigen Gedanken mehr Ründung zu geben, so hat sich das klavierliebende Publikum viel Gutes von seiner Feder zu versprechen."

7 A call to order

1 *Hamburgischer Correspondent* 11 (19 January 1790), review of Jean Bliesenet's *Trois Duos pour deux Violons*, Op. 67. Berlin: Rellstab. "Das erste aus G dur hat etwas vorzügliches in seinem Anfang; es scheint eine phantastische Einleitung zu seyn, die in dem Raum von 11 Tacten verschiedene Leittöne berührt, und dann erst in die eigentliche Tonleiter wieder übergeht, nach zwey Tacten aber wieder verlassen wird. Das Genie des Verfassers zeigt sich in diesem Duett am deutlichsten, nur zuweilen bricht es zu sehr aus."

2 *Musikalische Monatsschrift* V (November 1792), 135–36, review of Schwencke's *Drei Sonaten für das Klavier* and *Trois Sonates pour le Clavecin ou Fortepiano avec l'Accomp. d'un Violon*, Op. 3. "[Man] kann jetzt sicher dem Hrn. Verf. anheim stellen und es ihm selbst überlassen, an dem damaligen Versuche das Gute und Schöne, das sich darin findet, von dem Minderguten; das Daherstürmende und Verworrene der jugendlichen Phantasie, die unbekümmtert um strenge Einheit, Gedanken wohl oder übel ausströmt, wie sie sich darbieten, nunmehr selbst heraus zu scheiden."

3 *Tübingische gelehrte Anzeigen* 89 (4 November 1793), 711–12, review of Johann Christian Gottlob Eidenbenz's *Vier und zwanzig leichte Klavier Belustigungen aus 6 Minuetten, 6 Angloisen, 6 Schleifern und 6. Liedern bestehend*. Stuttgart, 1793. "Man . . . vermißt dagegen Neuheit, Ungezwungenheit, Reichthum und Würde der Gedanken." *Musikalische Korrespondenz* 48 (30 November 1791), 378–79, review of J. Bengraf's *XII Ungarische Tänze für das Klavier*. Mannheim: Göz. "Die Muse des Hrn. Bengrafs ist so arm an Reiz und Neuheit an Gedanken . . . daß in der That das musikalische Publikum nicht das mindeste würde verloren haben, wenn das Kindlein in der Geburt wäre erstikt worden."

4 *Musikalisches Wochenblatt* VI, 43–44, review of Clementi's *Tre Sonate per Clavicembalo o Pianoforte*, Op. 24. "Sein Stil hat nichts ähnliches, weder mit einem Bach, noch Hayden [*sic*] weder mit einem Mozart noch Kotzeluch [*sic*], weder mit einem Sterkel noch Vanhall, sondern er steht ganz selbständig für sich allein da."

5 *Allgemeine deutsche Bibliothek* CXI/1 (1792), 121–22, review of Haydn's Op. 54 quartets, cited in chapter 3. "Auch in den vor uns liegenden Quartetten muß man die originelle Laune, den musikalischen Witz und den unerschöpflichen Reichthum des Gedanken des Verf. bewundern."

6 *Musikalische Real-Zeitung* 19 (11 May 1791), 146–47, review of Anton

Wranitzky's *III Quatuors pour deux Violons, Alto & Violoncelle*, Op. 1. "Sie athmen ganz, selbst bis auf die mechanische Einrichtung, den Genius seines Lehrers. Freilich fehlt dem Werke noch die Originalität und die besondere Laune, die Haydns Kompositionen vorzüglich karakterisiren."

7 *Hamburgischer Correspondent* Beytrag 2 (1792), review of the keyboard reduction of Mozart's *Sinfonia e Arie scielte del Opera le nozze di Figaro, oder: Sinfonie und Favoritgesänge aus Figaros Hochzeit.* Berlin. "Wenn man etwas von Mozart anzuzeigen hat, so ist man gewiß, daß dies Dinge sind, worinn hoher Ideenflug, Kenntniß der seltensten Harmonie, schöne Melodie (nur hin und wieder etwas gesucht) und frappante Modulation anzutreffen sind. Auch in diesem Meisterwerk seiner Komischen Muse läßt sich dieses um so weniger verkennen, je mehr sie sich sonst eigentlich dem Erhabenen nähert."

8 *Musikalisches Wochenblatt* XIII, 100–01, review of the *Bibliothek der Grazien*, which included the *Ouverture aus dem Liebhaber von fünfzehn Jahren von Martini.* "Freilich keine Mozartsche; indess werden die, welche sich bei italiänischer Instrumentalmusik aufhalten und das Geleier auf Einem [*sic*] Tone ertragen können, auch hieran Gefallen finden." See also the *Musikalische Korrespondenz* 35 (31 August 1791), 273–75, review of various works by Franz Anton Hoffmeister.

9 *Musikalische Korrespondenz* 47 (23 November 1791), 370, review of Giud. Lipawsky's (Joseph Lipavsky?) *XII Variationi per il Forte-Piano,* Op. 1. "Das einzige, was wir an diesen Klavierveränderungen rügen könnten, wäre die sichtbare Nachahmung Mozartscher Variationen. Nach guten Mustern zu arbeiten, verdient freilich eher Lob, als Tadel."

10 *Musikalisches Wochenblatt* XIX, 149, review of 2 variations sets by Vanhal, 2 of Mozart, and 1 of Sterkel. "Die von Wanhal haben im Grunde wenig Eignes, obgleich sie übrigens nicht die schlechtesten sind. Wie denn W. bei all seinen Arbeiten fast immer ein Musterstück von Hayd'n oder Mozart vor Augen hat."

11 Sulzer, *Allgemeine Theorie* II, 99.

12 *Allgemeine deutsche Bibliothek* LXXII/1 (1787), 165, review of C. P. E. Bach's *Clavier=Sonaten und freye Fantasien nebst einigen Rondos fürs Fortepiano für Kenner und Liebhaber.* Part 4. "Erstaunlich ist die Unerschöpflichkeit der Gedanken, und der Reichthum der Phantasie des erhabenen Verfassers dieser Sammlung, der in jedem neuen Werke sich zu verjüngen scheint. Atr. [Schulz]"

13 *Musikalische Real-Zeitung* II/38 (23 September 1789), 296–97, review of Kozeluch's *III Sonates pour le Clavecin ou Piano-Forte,* Op. 20 and his *III. Sonates pour le Clavecin ou Piano-Forte avec l'Accompagnement d'un Violon & Violoncelle,* Op. 21. Paris. "ein kühner Flug der Phantasie, Fülle der Harmonie, niedliche Inversionen und ein Strom schöner Modulation, der sich durch nahe und entfernte Tonarten hindurchschlängelt."

14 *Musikalische Korrespondenz* 48 (30 November 1791), 377–78, review of Mozart's *Quatuor à 2 Violons, Alto e Violoncello.* Vienna; and *Quartetto per il Clavicembalo o Forte Piano con l'Accompagn. d'un Violino, Viola & Violoncello,* Op. 13. Vienna: Artaria. "Auch diese beede [*sic*] Quartetten sind mit dem Feuer

der Einbildungskraft und Korrektheit geschrieben, wodurch sich Hr. M. schon längst den Ruhm eines der besten Tonsezer in Deutschland erworben hat."

15 *Neue allgemeine deutsche Bibliothek* XVI/2 (1796), 470, review of Türk's *Sechs kleine Klaviersonaten u.s.w.* Part 3. Leipzig and Halle, 1793. "Diese Sonaten sind für Anfänger bestimmt, und bestehen aus kleinen Stücken, in welchen nicht gegen die Regeln des reinen Satzes gesündigt, die Melodie auch ganz gefällig ist, wo man aber keine starke, überraschende Gedanken, warme Phantasie, kühne Uebergänge und Ausweichungen erwarten muß, welches sonst doch recht gut mit der Einfalt des Gesanges und mit Vermeidung großer Schwierigkeiten zu vereinbaren ist. Vor zwanzig Jahren, als die Ohren noch nicht durch den Reichthum der in allgemeinen Umlauf gekommenen musikalischen Ideen verwöhnt waren, würden diese Sonaten mehr Glück gemacht haben, als in unsern Tagen. Pk."

16 *Musikalische Monatsschrift* VI (December 1792), 162, review of August Eberhard Müller's *Trois Sonates pour le Clavecin ou Forte Piano.* Offenbach: André. "Mit recht frohem innigem Genuss ist Rec. dem schönen vollen Strohme der Empfindung und der Imagination des Componisten dieser Sonaten gefolgt."

17 *Musikalische Korrespondenz* 48 (30 November 1791), 378, review of Emanuel Alois Foerster's *Duetto per il Forte Piano e Flauto o Violino,* Nro. 1. Op. 5. Vienna: Hofmeister [*sic*]. See also the *Allgemeine Litteratur-Zeitung* IV/355 (30 December 1793), 620–22, review of *Carl Ludewig Traugott Gläsers kurze Klavierstücke zum Gebrauch beym Unterrichte in Minuerts (?) und Polonoisen aus Allen Tönen.* Severin, 1791.

18 *Neue allgemeine deutsche Bibliothek* XIII/2 (1794), 318–21, review of Witthauer's *Sechs Claviersonaten für Liebhaber und angehende Clavierspieler.* Berlin: Witthauer, Mauer, Neue Musikhandlung. "Auch die vor uns liegende zwölf Sonaten zeichnen sich durch Ordnung, Reichthum an Gedanken, Darstellung verschiedener Charaktere, so wie durch reinen Satz, schöne Modulation, gutes rhythmisches Verhältniß u. sehr zu ihrem Vortheil aus, und verdienen daher allgemeiner bekannt zu werden, als sie es bis jetzt zu seyn scheinen."

19 *Neue allgemeine deutsche Bibliothek* XII/2 (1794), 526, review of Mozart's *Trois Sonates pour le Clavecin ou Forte Piano avec Accompagnement d'un Violon et Violoncelle,* Op. 15 [K. 502, 548, 542]. Mannheim: Götz. "In der dritten Sonate herrscht Pomp und Pracht, und wenn die Violinbegleitung dazu gut exequirt sind, so versetzt sie den Zuhörer, wie Rec. aus gepruftet Erfahrung versichern kann, in ein hinreißendes Feuer, und bringt überhaupt Wirkungen hervor, welche man von den wohlbesetzten Symphonien oft vergebens erwartet. *"

20 *Neue allgemeine deutsche Bibliothek* XVIII/2 (1795), 509–13, review of Joseph Seegr's *Acht Toccaten und Fugen für die Orgel.* Leipzig: Breitkopf. "Das Leer in den Toccaten (welche eigentlich Vorspiele sind, welche das Herz rühren, und auf etwas Wichtiges vorbereiten sollen) besteht in der Vernachläßigung des Metrums, dessen Veränderung und Abwechselung; in der Beharrlichkeit bey einem gewissen melodischen Einerley, wobey das Herz in einer gleichgültigen Spannung bleibt, wenig fühlt oder wohl gar müde und kalt wird. Ja."

21 *Musikalische Korrespondenz* 48 (30 November 1791), 377, review of Pleyel's *III Trios concertantes pour Violon, Viole & Violoncelle* and *Sestetto à due Violini, due Viole, Violoncello & Basso*. Vienna: Hoffmeister. "Beede [*sic*] zeichnen sich durch eine frappante Harmonie und große Gedanken aus. Das Kantabile im Sextett, wenn es mit Pünktlichkeit vorgetragen wird, kann auch das unempfindlichste Herz rühren."

22 *Hamburgischer Correspondent* Beytrag 1 (1791), review of Haydn's *Sinfonia pel Clavi-Cembalo*. Berlin: Rellstab. *Musikalische Real-Zeitung* III/22 (2 June 1790), 172–73, review of J. Fodor L'ainé's (probably Josephus Andreas Fodor) *Concerto à Violino principale, Violino primo, secondo, Alto & Basso, 2 Hautbois & 2 Cors de Chasse, ad Libitum*, Op. 15. Berlin: Hummel. "einen schmelzenden Gesang, wie ihn die Hirten der goldnen Zeit im Abendschimmer der Sonne den Mädchen mochten gesungen haben."

23 *Neue allgemeine deutsche Bibliothek* XII/2 (1794), 526, review of Mozart's *Trois Sonates*, cited above. "Die gewählten Themata sind interessant, und werden, in jeder dieser Sonaten, mit Verstand durchgeführt."

24 *Berlinische musikalische Zeitung* 12 (27 April 1793), 48, review of *Hässlers vier Sammlungen leichter Sonaten für das Clavier oder Pianoforte*. Berlin: Neue Musikhandlung. "In allen Klaviersachen von diesem Künstler, besonders den ältern, sind unverkennbare Spuren von grossem Talent . . . [der] die Schütze einer glücklichen Phantasie in gute Vereinigung mit den Kunstregeln zu bringen weis [*sic*]."

25 *Allgemeine deutsche Bibliothek* LXV/1 (1786), 145–47, review of Friedrich Wilhelm Rust's *Vier und zwanzig Veränderungen für das Clavier, über das Lied: Blühe liebes Veilchen*. Dessau: Rust and Buchhandlung der Gelehrten, 1782. "Wir müssen ihm daher Gerechtigkeit wiederfahren lassen, und zählen die gegenwärtige Arbeit unter die besten Produkte in dieser Gattung. So ist z.B. die dritte Veränderung recht artig erfunden. In der fünften und sechzehnten, wo die Mittelstimme die Melodie führt, zeigt der Verf. seine Geschicklichkeit im Kontrapunkte. Die eilfte, eine Nachahmunng [*sic*] der Hörner und Klarinetten ist ebenfalls sehr unterhaltend. Mehr hiervon weiter unten! Die siebzehnte in der gebundenen Schreibart macht den Kenntnissen des Verfassers Ehre. In der 18ten und 21sten ist eine Art von Nachahmung mit gutem Erfolg angebracht. Gk. [Türk]"

26 *Neue Leipziger gelehrte Zeitung* III/2 40 (3 April 1787), 636–38, review of Siegfried Schmiedt's *Clavier= und Singstücke*. Leipzig: Breitkopf: 1786. "Man sieht, daß Herr S. den reinen Satz sehr gut versteht, welches jetzt zur Schande des guten und richtigen Geschmacks in der Musik bey unsern neu angehenden Componisten nur selten der Fall ist."

27 *Allgemeine deutsche Bibliothek* CXI/1 (1792), 119–21, review of Friedrich August Baumbach's *Six Sonates pour le Clavecin ou Piano-Forte*. Jena: Librarie Académique. "T. 31 wird der Tonschluß, zwar nicht zu plötzlich, aber doch nicht beruhigend genug, eingeleitet. Die hernach noch folgenden Takte verdienen –

weggestrichen zu werden. Auch fängt der Verf. diese Sonate in *Arsi* an, und mehrere Einschnitte z.B. Takt 21, 25, treten in *Thesi* ein. Kirnberger schreibe hiervon im zweyten Theile der Kunst des reinen Satzes S. 149: 'Wenn der erste Einschnitt mit dem Niedersschlage anfängt, so können doch die folgenden im Aufschlage anfangen: fängt aber das Stück im Aufschlage an, so müssen ordentlicher Weise auch die folgenden im Aufschlage anfangen u.s.w.' Und in der That ist auch die Leere da, wo man den Anfang des folgenden Rhythmus u.s.w. erwartet, allerdings unangenehm; die Einheit leidet darunter; man hat eine Art von Langerweile u.s.w. Wk. [Türk]"

28 *Magazin der Musik* II/2 (8 February 1787), 1313–14, review of Franz Anton Hoffmeister's *Deux grandes Sonates pour le Clavecin ou Piano forte, l'une avec Violon obligé, l'autre solo*, Op. 4. Frankfurt am Main: Haueisen. "Originalität herrscht in diesen Sonaten, so wie in den vorigen Compositionen des Hrn. Verfassers eben nicht; aber Gründlichkeit und eine gefällige Gedankenordnung verschaffen ihnen den Beifall der Liebhaber, und dem Componisten Gelegenheit, seine Talente noch oft zu zeigen." *Musikalische Korrespondenz* 7 (18 August 1790), 49, review of his *VI. Duos à deux Flûtes traversieres*, Op. 9. Berlin and Amsterdam: Hummel. "Ordnung, Uebereinstimmung, auch einzelne gute, wiewohl nicht neue Gedanken finden sich übrigens in diesen Duetten."

29 *Hamburgischer Correspondent* Beytrag 9 (1790), review of Samuel David Willmann's *Trois Quartetti pour le Fortepiano avec Violon, Flute & Violoncelle, obligés*. Berlin: Rellstab. "Sogenannte Genienicken findet man in diesen Quartetten eben nicht, aber dafür Ordnung, schöne Melodie, reinen Satz, hübsche Abwechselungen der Solostellen der verschiedenen Instrumente unter einander."

30 *Hamburgischer Correspondent* Beytrag 7 (1787), review of Carl Fasch's *Andantino con VII Variazioni pel Clavicembalo o Fortepiano*, Op. 17. Berlin: Rellstab. "Herr F. bleibt bey seinen Variazionen nie von der Harmonie des Hauptstücks, sondern weicht ab, und doch ist so viel Einheit bey aller der Mannigfaltigkeit darinn."

31 *Erfurtische gelehrte Zeitung* 36 (30 July 1785), 286–87, review of Markus Christfried Gröse's *Sechs Sonaten für das Klavier oder Fortepiano*. Dessau: Gelehrtenbuchhandlung, 1784. "In vielen Sätzen Mangel an Einheit und Zusammenhang der Gedanken . . ." *Musikalisches Kunstmagazin* II:6 (1791), 63, review of Witthauer's *Sechs Sonaten fürs Clavier*. Hamburg, 1783. "H. Witthauer zeigt in allen seinen Arbeiten ein schönes Ordnungsgefühl, daß ihn nie die wahre Einheit verfehlen läßt."

32 *Allgemeine Litteratur-Zeitung* Part II/175 (27 May 1794), 527, review of Schwencke's *Trois sonates pour le Clavecin ou Fortepiano*, Op. 3. Berlin: Neue berlinische Musikhandlung. "Sollten wir noch einen Wunsch im Allgemeinen hinzufügen; so wäre es der, dass Hr. S. künftighin, in Absicht auf Einheit und Oekonomie, eine strengere Auswahl der Gedanken treffen möchte."

33 *Musikalische Monatsschrift* VI (December 1792), 162, review of Müller's *Trois*

Sonates, cited above. "Was Rec. am meisten daran erfreut hat, ist das Bestreben, bei grossem Reichthum, der oft Ueppigkeit erzeugt, und bei unaufgehaltnem [*sic*] Fortströhmen des Gesanges und der reichhaltigen Figuren, nach Correktheit und Einheit."

34 *Musikalischer Almanach* IV (1789), 37, review of C. B. Teuthorn's *Drey Claviersonaten mit Begleitung einer Violine.* Rendsburg and Copenhagen: Teuthorn, 1788. "Der Verf. scheint noch ein junger Mann zu seyn, der seine Sachen besser anfängt, als endigt. Mit der Zeit lernt er es vielleicht, sie eben so gut zu endigen als anzufangen, wenn er sich erst Kenntnisse von der Entwickelung musikalischer Gedanken, und von Einheit des Styls erworben haben wird."

35 *Magazin der Musik* II/1 (7 March 1785), 538–43, review of Leopold Kozeluch's *Deux grands Concerts pour le Clavecin ou Piano Forte.* "Das erste würde vielleicht noch einen höhern Werth haben, wenn die letzten 4 Takte in beyden Solosätzen nicht da wären, die den Eindruck, den die Innigkeit und das Herzergiessende des Ganzen hatte, auf einmal etwas zu schwächen scheinen. Diese 4 letzten Takte passen wohl nicht genug zum Character des Ganzen. Dieser ist den größern Theil des Ganzen hindurch ernsthaft, rührend, herzergiessend und nun, da er völlig ausgebildet werden soll, wird durch 4 Takte, die besser in einem lustigen Allegretto angebracht wären, der ganze Fluß des vorigen Empfindungstroms gehemmt; wodurch R. in seiner Meinung mehr als jemals bestärkt wird, daß jedes Stück gewinnen würde, wenn es einen bestimmten, oder zum wenigsten keinen widersprechenden Character annähme . . . R."

36 *Musikalisches Kunstmagazin* II:5 (1791), 38–39, review of *Clavier-Magazin für Kenner und Liebhaber.* Berlin: Rellstab, 1787. "Leichtsinn und Hang zur Schwermuth kan wohl in Einer Person zusammen seyn, aber wohl nie bey dieser Person in Einem Moment, oder so schnell mit einander abwechselnd, daß es der Gegenstand einer momentanen Kunstbearbeitung seyn könte. Die Zusammensetzung kan also wohl moralische Wahrheit haben, aestetische hat sie gewiß nicht."

37 *Musikalische Korrespondenz* 22 (30 May 1792), 169–70, review of Zinck's *Kompositionen für den Gesang und das Klavier.* Copenhagen: Sönnichsen. "Die Sonate aus Es dur hat zum Anfang ein Allegro scherzando, worinn viele Einheit des Karakters und eine schöne Modulation herrschet . . . Den Beschluß macht ein Allegretto, das aber als Rondo behandelt ist. Das Thema hat ein sehr zärtlichen Karakter."

38 *Musikalische Korrespondenz* 8 (22 February 1792), 59, review of Johann Brandl's *Grande Simphonie à grande Orchestre.* Speier: Bossler. "Nur daß uns der Uebergang in die weiche Tonart, die schon im siebenten Takte vorkommt, zu früh angebracht und wider die Voglerschen Tonseinheit zu seyn scheint."

39 *Neue allgemeine deutsche Bibliothek* XVIII/2 (1795), 509–13, review of Joseph Seegr's *Acht Toccaten und Fugen für die Orgel*, cited above. "So findet man z.B. (Toccate V. aus C dur Takt 15.) in der einzelnen Melodie zur Dominante h von e

moll ein gis – zur Dominante e von a moll ein cis – und zur Dominante a von d moll ein gis . . . welches, weil es wider die Einheit der Tonart ist, hart klingt."

40 Nancy Kovaleff Baker gives this bit of information without specifying her sources in her translation of Koch's *Introductory Essay on Composition*, p. xiii.

41 *Musikalischer Almanach* IV (1789), 36, review of C. L. Becker's *Stücke allerley Art für Kenner und Liebhaber des Claviers und Gesanges*. Part 1. Nordheim: Becker, 1788. "An Talent zur Composition fehlt es ihm nicht, und wenn er es nach guten Mustern, an welchen es uns in diesem Fache eben nicht fehlt, auszubilden sucht, Harmonie und inneres und äußeres Verhältniß der Theile eines Stückes sorgfältig studirt, so wird er seinen Arbeiten wenigstens denjenigen Grad von Vollkommenheit geben können, der sie für eine gewisse Classe von Liebhabern vorzüglich brauchbar macht."

42 *Allgemeine deutsche Bibliothek* Anhang zu dem 53. bis 86. Bande, III: 1879–80, review of Häßler's *Sechs leichte Sonaten fürs Clavier oder Piano=Forte, wovon zwey mit Begleitung einer Flöte oder Violine, und Eine für vier Hände auf Einem Claviere*. Part 2. Erfurt: Häßler, 1787. "Wenn wir zuweilen in seinen Adagio's gewisse bunte, und, wie dem Rec. dünkt, nicht immer zweckmäßige Passagen fanden: so ist doch dieß bey der gegenwärtigen Sammlung nicht der Fall. Vielmehr herrscht auch in dieser Hinsicht eine nöthige Uebereinstimmung der einzelnen Theile mit dem Ganzen. Gk. [Türk]"

43 *Musikalische Monatsschrift* V (November 1792), 135–36, review of Schwenke's *Drei Sonaten* and *Trios Sonates*, cited above. "Rec. will so viel sagen, dass die zweite Hälfte des ersten Theils mit der ersten gar nicht recht in Verbindung steht."

44 *Allgemeine Litteratur-Zeitung* Part IV/355 (30 December 1793), 620–22, review of *Carl Ludewig Traugott Gläsers kurze Klavierstücke zum Gebrauch beym Unterrichte in Minuerts (?) und Polonoisen aus Allen Tönen*. Weissenfels and Leipzig: Severin, 1791. "Auch vermissen wir in der Menuett S. 14 die erfoderliche Einheit; denn der zweyte Theil, worinn eine bekannte Transposition vorkommt, passt nicht völlig zu dem ersten."

45 *Musikalische Real-Zeitung* I/7 (13 August 1788), 49–50, review of Mozart's *Sonate pour le Clavecin avec accompagnement d'un Violon*. Speier: Bossler. "Die Stelle der getheilten gebrochenen Accorden auf der vierten Seite theils zu abgenuzt, theils zu gedehnt, und der zweyte Theil in Vergleichung mit dem ersten viel zu lang. Man hat zwar in dem Sistem der Tonwissenschaft keine bestimmte Vorschrift in solchen Fällen; doch sieht man, daß ein Unterschied von 3 1/2 Seite kein wahres Verhältniß ist."

46 *Musikalisches Wochenblatt* XIX, 148–49, review of J. L. [*sic*] Röllig's (Karl Leopold Röllig) *Kleine Tonstücke für die Harmonika oder das Pianoforte*. "Denn erstens sind sie sehr einfach, edel und meistens melodieus [*sic*]; obgleich Schade ist, dass darin besonders der erste Period fast überall zuviel Gleichartiges hat. Es scheint, als wenn mancher für Alles nur Eine [*sic*] Form hätte . . . Auch wünscht Rec., das der erste Theil des ersten sonst recht hübschen Andante aus b Dur [*sic*] nicht einen ganzen Tonschluss haben, sondern in die Dominante hinüber geleitet

seyn möchte. Jetzt liegen die beiden Theile als einzelne Stücken da, die nicht zusammen geflügt sind; denn man kann den ersten Satz gespielt haben, und ruhig davon gehen."

47 *Musikalische Real-Zeitung* II/7 (18 February 1789), 49–52, review of J. N. Denninger's *Concerto pour le Clavecin ou Piano forte*. Munich and Dusseldorf: Götz, Marchand & Editeur de Musique.

48 Lange, *The Classical Age*, p. 116.

49 Beiser notes that the striving for unity characterized the early romantic movement in Weimar, where Goethe lived. See *The Fate of Reason*, p. 230.

50 Carl Dahlhaus, "Karl Philipp Moritz und das Problem einer klassischen Musikaesthetik," *International Review of the Aesthetics and Sociology of Music* 9 (1978), 282.

51 Dahlhaus, "Moritz," pp. 291–92.

52 Wellek, *The Later Eighteenth Century*, p. 234.

53 *Magazin der Musik* I/2 (7 December 1783), 1238–55, review of C. P. E. Bach's *Claviersonaten und freye Phantasien*; and I/2 (7 December 1783), 1285–95, review of Georg Benda's *Sammlung vermischter Clavierstücke*, both cited above, chapter 6.

54 *Erlangische gelehrte Anmerkungen* 14 (18 February 1794), 105–06, review of Ludwig Cella's *Musicalische Blätter für Freunde der Music zum Andenken in Stammbüchern seinen Gönnern und Freunden*. Erlangen: J. J. Palm. "Sollten Kenner auch der Meinung seyn, daß in der Musik gerade so wie in der Dichtkunst, ein Stük, das lange gefallen soll, einen desto höhern Grad aesthetischer Vollendung erforde, je kleiner es ist, so werden sie doch gewiß der Bescheidenheit Gerechtigkeit wiederfahren lassen, womit der Hr. Verf. diese erste Frucht seiner musikalischen Muse dem Publikum übergeben hat."

55 *Allgemeine deutsche Bibliothek* CVIII/1 (1792), 143–44, review of Johann Christoph Friedrich Bach's *Drey leichte Sonaten fürs Klavier oder Piano Forte*. Rinteln: Bösendahl, 1789. "In Ansehung der Modulation bemerken wir vorzüglich noch über die zweyte und dritte Sonate, daß Hr. B. sich ziemlich weit vom Haupttone entfernt, und in Nebentönen beynahe zu lange verweilet hat. Jedoch dies letztere wird jetzt so sehr zur Gewohnheit, daß man in dieser Rücksicht – Rec. weiß nicht, als welchen Gründen der Aesthetik? – wohl absichtlich keine Einheit beobachten will. Of. [Türk]"

56 *Allgemeine deutsche Bibliothek* CXI/1 (1792), 121–22, review of Haydn's Op. 54 Quartets, cited above. "Da aber die Einheit hierbey sehr leidet, so wäre es wohl der Muhe werth, sich ernstlich dagegen aufzulehnen, und aus Gründen der Aesthetik zu bestimmen, unter welchen Umständen ähnliche Ausweichungen allenfalls erlaubt und zweckmäßig seyn können."

57 *Musikalische Korrespondenz* 25 (20 June 1792), 193–94, review of Clementi's *Three Sonates for the Piano-Forte or Harpsichord with Accompaniments for Violin & Violoncello*, Op. 28. "Dieses Sonatenwerk . . . verdient in Absicht seines innern Gehalts den bisherigen Werken dieses gründlichen und feinen Tonsezers

an die Seite gesezt zu werden . . . Ueberall herrscht immer einer und ebenderselbe epische Schwung, und immer gleiche Wahrheit im Karakter, eine gewisse Delikatesse in der Anordnung und Ausführung der Gedanken, eine rhytmische [*sic*] Präzision, und eine gewisse Leichtigkeit in der Anwendung kontrapunktischer Regeln, die dauerhafteste Eindrüke in der Seele zurüklassen, und Empfindungen erweken, die von der höchsten ästhetischen Kraft der Tonkunst zeugen."

58 *Musikalische Real-Zeitung* II/29 (22 July 1789), 224–25, review of Joh. Ge. Bernh. Beutler's *Kleine musikalische Unterhaltungen für das Klavier oder Pianoforte, nebst einigen Gesängen.* Part 1. Mühlhausen: Beutler, 1788; *Musikalische Korrespondenz* 22 (1 December 1790), 169, review of Kozeluch's *III Sonates pour le Clavecin ou Forte piano,* Op. 30. Vienna: Kozeluch; *Musikalische Korrespondenz* 26 (27 June 1792), 201–03, review of Franz Anton Hoffmeister's *Six Duos concertants pour le Fortepiano & Violon.* Vienna: Hoffmeister.

8 Epilogue: segue to the nineteenth century

1 Interest in general scholarly journals also declined during the 1790s, so that their music reviews would have reached a smaller audience anyway. Milstein documents the shift toward specialized publications and entertainment magazines (*Unterhaltungsblätter*) in the subscriptions of German reading societies. See his *Eight Eighteenth Century Reading Societies*, pp. 41, 118.

2 Ersch, Johann Samuel, ed., *Allgemeines Repertorium der Literatur für die Jahre 1785 bis 1800*, 8 vols. (Jena and Weimar: Industrie-Comptoir, 1793–1807).

3 For a detailed discussion of German music journalism in the early nineteenth century, see Axel Beer's forthcoming study *Das musikalische Werk zwischen Komponist, Verlag und Publikum.*

4 For one extremely picky review of some Haydn symphonies, see the *AMZ* I/50 (11 September 1799), 837–49.

5 *AMZ* I/15 (9 January 1799), 236–38, review of Joseph Wölfl's *Trois Sonates pour le Pianoforte composées et dédiées à Mr. L. van Beethoven*, Op. 6; *AMZ* I/22 (27 February 1799), 343–44, review of Haydn's *Trois Quatuors pour deux Violons, Alto et Basse*, Op. 90 [I:99, I:104, I:102, arranged as quartets]. "Es herrscht darin durchaus ein Reichthum, eine Fülle und Schönheit der Gedanken, und ein so hoher Flug der Phantasie, dass es schwer seyn dürfte, zu bestimmen, welches von diesen Quartetten das vorzüglichste sey."

6 Peter Schnaus identifies the "wild, bizarre and odd" as negative irrational aspects of the creative process in the *AMZ*'s pre-Hoffmann reviews. See his *E. T. A. Hoffman als Beethoven-Rezensent*, p. 26.

7 *AMZ* I/3 (17 October 1798), 44–45, review of Sterkel's *Grand Sonate pour le Pianoforte*, Op. 36. "Der erste Satz fängt sehr brillant an, und wird unter mancherley geschickten Wendungen und zweckmässiger Modulation, ohne viel

in entfernte Tonarten auszuweichen, bis zum zweyten Theile fortgeführt." A review of a flute trio by F. H. Salingre makes it clear that "modulation" could still mean what we would designate as a borrowed chord or secondary dominant. See *AMZ* I/37 (12 June 1799), 585–86.

8 *AMZ* I/48 (28 August 1799), 810, review of Friedrich Benda's *Sonate à quatre mains pour le Clavecin ou Pianoforte*, Op. 6. "Die Ausweichung . . . aus Es dur in E dur ist zwar etwas frappant, aber doch durch allmählige Vorbereitung weder unnatürlich gesucht, noch in die Länge gedehnt . . . und giebt dem Satze etwas Frisches."

9 *AMZ* I/36 (5 June 1799), 570–71, review of Beethoven's *Tre sonate per il Clav. o Fortepiano con un Violino*, Op. 12. "Es ist unleugbar, Herr van Beethoven geht einen eigenen Gang; aber was ist das für ein bisarrer mühseligher Gang! . . . ein Suchen nach seltener Modulation, ein Ekelthun gewöhnliche Verbindung."

10 *AMZ* I/27 (3 April 1799), 422, review of Joseph Haydn's *Grand Simphonie à plusieurs Instruments*, Op. 91 [Hob. I:100]. Augsburg: Gombart. "Sie ist etwas weniger gelehrt, und leichter zu fassen, als einige andere der neuesten Werke der-selben, aber an neuen Ideen eben so reich, als sie. Die Ueberraschung kann viel-leicht in der Musik nicht weiter getrieben werden, als sie es hier ist, durch das urplötzliche Einfallen der vollen Janitscharenmusik im Minore des zweyten Satzes – da bis dahin man keine Ahndung davon hat, dass diese türkischen Instrumente bey der Sinfonie angebracht sind. Aber auch hier zeigt sich nicht nur der erfinderische, sondern auch der besonnene Künstler. Das Andante ist nehm-lich dennoch ein Ganzes; denn by allem Gefälligen und Leichten, das der Komponist, um von der Idee seines Coups täuschen abzuleiten, in den ersten Theil desselben brachte, ist es doch marschmässig angelegt und bearbeitet."

11 *AMZ* I/15 (9 January 1799), 236–38. "Die dritte Sonate . . . hat aber Rec. darum weniger, als die ersten, gefallen; weil sie kein so gutes Ganze ausmacht und in ihr zu wenig Rücksicht auf Einheit genommen."

12 *AMZ* I/36 (5 June 1799), 571–72, review of Boccherini's *Symphonie périodique*, Nos. 1 and 2. "Die erste, die mit einem langsamen Satz aus D moll anhebt, der in ein brillantes Allegro in der harten Tonart leitet, worauf ein hübsches charakter-istisches Andantino folgt, das von einem lebhaften Menuet abgelöst wird, worauf ein kurzer langsamer Satz das erste Allegro wieder aufnimmt und zu Ende bringt, hat viel Einheit, und Rec. würde diese für die vorzüglichere halten."

13 *AMZ* I/24 (13 March 1799), 376–78, review of August Eberhard Müller's *Grand Sonate pour le Pianoforte, avec Accomp. d'un Violon et Violoncelle*, Op. 17. Leipzig: Breitkopf & Härtel.

14 *AMZ* I/31 (1 May 1799), 494–96, review of Mozart's *Quatre Simphonies pour l'Orchestre*, Op. 64. Hamburg: Günther & Böhme. "Ein Tonkünstler kann in dieser [Instrumental] Gattung am mehresten Genie zeigen; denn nicht nur muss er hier ganz allein erfinden und sich selber allen Stoff geben, sondern er ist auch einzig und allein auf die Sprache der Töne eingeschränkt. Seine Gedanken haben ihre Bestimmtheit in sich selber, ohne von der Poesie unterstützt zu seyn."

15 Wallace, *Beethoven's Critics*, pp. 14–16, citing Schnaus, *E. T. A. Hoffman als Beethoven-Rezensent*, pp. 26–29.

16 *AMZ* XII/40 (4 July 1810), 630–42 and XII/41 (11 July 1810), 652–59, review of Beethoven's Fifth Symphony, cited in chapter 1.

17 *Magazin der Musik* I/2 (1783), 1238–55, review of C. P. E. Bach's *Claviersonaten und freye Phantasien*, cited in chapter 6.

Bibliography

Periodicals with reviews

Allgemeine deutsche Bibliothek. Berlin and Stettin: Friedrich Nicolai, 1765–96.
Allgemeine Litteratur-Zeitung. Jena and Leipzig: Zeitungs-Expedition, 1785–98.
Allgemeine musikalische Zeitung. Leipzig: Breitkopf & Härtel, 1798–1848.
Allgemeines Verzeichniß neuer Bücher mit kurzen Anmerkungen. Nebst einem gelehrten Anzeiger. Leipzig: Siegfried Lebrecht Crusius, 1776–84.
Altonaischer gelehrter Mercurius. Altona: Burmester, 1763–72; *Neuer gelehrter Mercurius.* Altona: Burmester, 1773–86; *Neuester Altonaischer gelehrter Mercurius.* Altona: Burmester, 1787–88.
Augsburger musikalischer Merkur auf das Jahr 1795. Augsburg: G. W. F. Späth, 1795.
Berlinische musikalische Zeitung historischen und kritischen Inhalts. Edited by Carl Spazier. Berlin: Neue Musikhandlung, 1793–94.
Berlinische Nachrichten von Staats- und gelehrten Sachen. Berlin, 1761–98.
Berlinische privilegirte Zeitung, 1770–78; *Königlich-privilegirte Berlinische Staats- und gelehrte Zeitung*, 1779–86; *Königlich-privilegirte Berlinische Zeitung von Staats- und gelehrten Sachen*, 1787–98.
Berlinisches litterarisches Wochenblatt. Berlin and Leipzig: Friedrich Wilhelm Birnstiel, 1777.
Bibliothek der schönen Wissenschaften und der freien Künste. Leipzig: Johann Gottfried Dyck, 1757–67; facsimile edn. Hildesheim: Georg Olms, 1979.
Ephemereiden der Litteratur und des Theaters. Berlin: Friedrich Mauer, 1785–86; facsimile edn. Munich: Kraus, 1981.
Erfurtische gelehrte Zeitungen. Erfurt: J. J. F. Straube, 1776–79; *Erfurtische gelehrte Zeitung.* Reval and Leipzig: Albrecht und Compagnie; Erfurt: Johann Ernst Schlegel, 1780; *Erfurtische gelehrte Zeitung.* Herausgegeben unter der Aufsicht der Kuhrmainzischen Akademie nützlicher Wissenschaften. Erfurt: Georg Adam Keyser, 1781–96; *Nachrichten von gelehrten Sachen.* Herausgegeben von der Akademie nützl. Wissenschaften zu Erfurt. Erfurt: Expedition der Nachrichten von gelehrten Sachen und in dem Kayserlichen Reichs-Oberpostamte, 1797–98.
Erlangische gelehrte Anmerkungen und Nachrichten. Erlangen: Johann Carl Tetzschner, 1770–82; *Erlangischen gelehrten Anmerkungen.* Erlangen: Georg

Wolfgang Zeltner, 1783–87; Wolfgang Walthers, 1788–89; *Erlangische gelehrte Zeitung*. Erlangen: J. J. Palms, 1790–92; *Erlanger gelehrte Zeitungen*. Erlangen: Adolph Ernst Junge, 1793–98.

Frankfurter gelehrte Anzeigen. Edited by Johann Heinrich Merck. Frankfurt am Main: Eichenberg, 1772–90.

Frankfurtische gelehrten Zeitungen. Frankfurt am Main: Heinrich Ludwig Brönner, 1760–71.

Freymüthige Nachrichten von Neuen Büchern, und andern zur Gelehrtheit gehörigen Sachen. Zurich: Heidegger und Compagnie, 1760–63.

Gelehrte Zeitung herausgegeben zu Kiel. Kiel: Victorin Bossiegel und Sohn, 1771–72; Michael Friedrich Bartsch, 1773–75; *Kielische gelehrte Zeitungen*. Kiel: Michael Friedrich Bartsch, 1787–90.

Gothaische gelehrte Zeitungen. Gotha: Carl Wilhelm Ettinger, 1774–97.

Göttingische Anzeigen von gelehrten Sachen unter der Aufsicht der Königl. Gesellschaft der Wissenschaften. Göttingen: Johann Christian Dietrich, 1760–98.

Hallische neue gelehrte Zeitungen. Vols. 15–25. Halle: Johann Jacob Curt, 1770–80.

Hamburgische Nachrichten aus dem Reiche der Gelehrsamkeit. Edited by M. Christian Ziegra. Hamburg: Christian Simon Schröder, 1760–71. *Freywillige Beyträge zu den Hamburgischen Nachrichten aus dem Reiche der Gelehrsamkeit*. Edited by M. Christian Ziegra. Hamburg: Schröder, 1772–79.

Jenaische Zeitungen von gelehrten Sachen. Jena: zu finden in den Cröckerischen, Gollnerischen und andern hiesigen Buchläden. 1765–81. *Jenaische gelehrte Zeitungen*. Jena: zu finden in der Straußischen Buchdruckerey, 1782–86. *Jenaische gelehrte Anzeigen*. Jena, 1787.

Journal der Tonkunst. Edited by Heinrich Christoph Koch. 2 vols. Erfurt: Georg Adam Keyser and Braunschweig: Musikalisches Magazin auf der Höhe, 1795.

Kaiserlich Königliche allergnädigst privilegirte Realzeitung der Wissenschaften, Künste und der Commerzien. Vienna: Joseph Kurzböck, 1770–86.

Kaiserlich-privilegirte Hamburgische neue Zeitung. Hamburg, 1767–98.

Kritische Briefe über die Tonkunst, mit kleinen Clavierstücken und Singoden begleitet von einer musikalischen Gesellschaft in Berlin. Edited by Friedrich Wilhelm Marpurg. 2 vols. Berlin: Friedrich Wilhelm Birnstiel, 1759–63; facsimile edn. Hildesheim: Georg Olms, 1974.

Litterarische Nachrichten von den Werken der besten Schriftsteller unserer Zeit. Vienna: Johann Thomas Edler von Trattner, 1775–76.

Litteratur- und Theaterzeitung. Edited by Christian August von Bertram. Berlin: Arnold Wever, 1778–83.

Magazin der Musik. Edited by Carl Friedrich Cramer. Hamburg: Musikalische Niederlage, 1783–87; facsimile edn. in 4 vols. Hildesheim: Georg Olms, 1971; Copenhagen: Johann Friedrich Schultz, 1788.

Musicalische Bibliotek. Edited by Hans Adolf Friedrich von Eschstruth. Marburg and Giesen: Krieger der Jungere, 1784–85; facsimile edn. Hildesheim: Georg Olms, 1977.

Musikalische Real-Zeitung. Speier: Expedition der Zeitung, 1788–90; facsimile edn. Hildesheim: Georg Olms, 1971; *Musikalische Korrespondenz der teutschen Filarmonischen Gesellschaft.* Speier: Expedition der Zeitung, 1790–92.

Musikalischer Almanach für Deutschland. Edited by Johann Nikolaus Forkel. Leipzig: Schwickert, 1782–89.

Musikalisches Kunstmagazin. Edited by Johann Friedrich Reichardt. 2 vols. Berlin: Reichardt, 1782, 1791; facsimile edn. Hildesheim: Georg Olms, 1969.

Musikalisches Wochenblatt/Musikalische Monatsschrift. (*Studien für Tonkünstler und Musikfreunde: Eine historisch- kritische Zeitschrift mit neun und dreissig Musikstücken von verschiedenen Meistern fürs Jahr 1792.*) Edited by Friedrich Ludwig Aemilius Kunzen and Johann Friedrich Reichardt. Berlin: Neue Musikhandlung, 1793.

Musikalisch-kritische Bibliothek. Edited by Johann Nikolaus Forkel. 2 vols. Gotha: Carl Wilhelm Ettinger, 1778; facsimile edn. Hildesheim: Georg Olms, 1964.

Neue allgemeine deutsche Bibliothek. Kiel: Carl Ernst Bohn, 1793–98.

Neue Leipziger gelehrte Anzeigen. Leipzig, 1789–97.

Neue Leipziger gelehrte Zeitungen. Leipzig: Breitkopf, 1785–87.

Neue Zeitungen von gelehrten Sachen. Leipzig: Zeitungs-Expedition, 1760–84.

Nürnbergische gelehrte Zeitung. Nuremberg: M. J. Bauer, 1777–89; *Neue Nürnbergische gelehrte Zeitung.* Nuremberg: Grattenauerische Buchhandlung, 1791–98.

Oberdeutsche, allgemeine Litteraturzeitung. Salzburg: Hauptversendungsamte der Zeitung; Mainz: P. A. Winkopp; Vienna: Georg Philipp Wucherer, 1788–89; Oberdeutsche Staatszeitungs-Comptoir, 1790–98.

Prager gelehrte Nachrichten. Wolfgang Gerle, 1771–72.

Raisonnirendes Bücherverzeichniß. Königsberg: G. L. Hartung, 1782–84.

Russische Bibliothek, zur Kenntniß des gegenwärtigen Zustandes der Literatur in Rußland. Edited by H. L. C. Bacmeister. St. Petersburg, Riga, and Leipzig: Johann Friedrich Hartknoch, 1772–89.

Staats- und gelehrte Zeitung des Hamburgischen unpartheyischen Correspondenten. Hamburg, 1760–98.

Strasburgische gelehrte Nachrichten. Strasburg: Stein, 1782–85.

Der teutsche Merkur/Der neue teutsche Merkur. Edited by Christoph Martin Wieland. Weimar, 1773–98.

Tübingische gelehrte Anzeigen. Tübingen: Wilhelm Heinrich Schramm, 1789–98.

Unterhaltungen. Hamburg: Michael Christian Bock, 1766–70.

Wirzburger gelehrte Anzeigen. Würzburg: Riennersche Buchhandlung, 1786–96; *Würzburger wöchentliche Anzeigen von gelehrten und anderen gemeinnützigen Gegenständen.* Edited by A. M. Köl. Würzburg: Kölische Buchhandlung, 1797–98.

Wöchentliche Nachrichten und Anmerkungen die Musik betreffend. Edited by Johann Adam Hiller. Leipzig: Zeitungs-Expedition, 1767–69; *Musikalische Nachrichten und Anmerkungen.* Leipzig: Zeitungs-Expedition, 1770; facsimile edn. Hildesheim: Georg Olms, 1970.

Primary sources

"Abhandlung vom musikalischen Geschmack, in einem Schreiben an einen Freund."
    Unterhaltungen I/1 (January 1766), 41–59.

Baumgarten, Alexander Gottlieb. *Reflections on Poetry*. Translated with an
    Introduction by Karl Aschenbrenner and William B. Holther. Berkeley and Los
    Angeles: University of California Press, 1954.

Ersch, Johann Samuel, ed. *Allgemeines Repertorium der Literatur für die Jahre 1785
    bis 1800*. 8 vols. Jena and Weimar: Industrie-Comptoir, 1793–1807.

F. W. V. *Musikalische Charlatanerien*. Berlin and Leipzig, 1792.

Forkel, Johann Nikolaus. *Allgemeine Geschichte der Musik*. Vol. I. Leipzig:
    Schwickert, 1788; rpt. edited with an index by Othmar Wessely. Graz:
    Akademische Druck und Verlangsanstalt, 1967.

"Genauere Bestimmung einiger musicalischen Begriffe: Zur Ankündigung des acad-
    emischen Winterconcerts von Michaelis 1780 bis Ostern 1781." *Magazin der
    Musik* I/2 (8 November 1783), 1039–72.

"Von der Theorie der Musik in so fern sie Liebhabern und Kennern nothwendig und
    nützlich ist." *Magazin der Musik* I/2 (1 September 1783), 896–903.

Gerber, Ernst Ludwig. *Historisch-biographisches Lexikon der Tonkünstler* (1790–92)
    and *Neues Historisch-biographisches Lexikon der Tonkünstler* (1812–1814).
    Rpt. edn. by Othmar Wessely. Graz: Akademische Druck und Verlagsanstalt,
    1966–1977.

Der Greis. Leipzig: Friedrich Gotthold Jacobaern, 1763–69.

Jablonskies, Johann Theodor. *Allgemeines Lexicon der Künste und Wissenschaften*.
    New edn. by Johann Joachim Schwaben. Königsberg and Leipzig: Zeisens Witwe
    und Hartungs Erben, 1767.

Kindleben, Christian Wilhelm. *Studenten Lexicon*. Halle: Johann Christian Hendel,
    1781.

Kirnberger, Johann Philipp. *The Art of Strict Musical Composition*. Translated by
    David Beach and Jurgen Thym. New Haven and London: Yale University Press,
    1982.

Koch, Heinrich Christoph. *Introductory Essay on Composition: The Mechanical
    Rules of Melody, Sections 3 and 4*. Translated with an Introduction by Nancy
    Kovaleff Baker. New Haven and London: Yale University Press, 1983.

    Musikalisches Lexikon. Frankfurt am Main: Hermann, 1802.

    Versuch einer Anleitung zur Composition. 3 vols. Leipzig: Adam Friedrich Böhme,
    1782, 1787, 1793; facsimile edn. Hildesheim: Georg Olms, 1969.

"Kritischer Entwurf einer musikalischen Bibliothek." *Wöchentliche Nachrichten* III:1
    (4 July 1768), 1–7; III:11 (12 September 1768), 81–85; III:12 (26 September 1768),
    97–99; III:14 (3 October 1768), 103–08.

Lyceum der schönen Künste. Edited by Johann Friedrich Reichardt. Berlin: Johann
    Friedrich Unger, 1797.

Marpurg, Friedrich Wilhelm. *Handbuch bey dem Generalbasse und der Composition*.

4 vols. Berlin: Johann Jacob Schützens Witwe, 1755–60; facsimile edn. Hildesheim: Georg Olms, 1974.

Mendelssohn, Moses. *Schriften zur Philosophie, Aesthetik und Apologetik.* Edited by Moritz Brasch. Vol. II: *Schriften zur Psychologie, Aesthetik sowie zur Apologetik des Judentums.* Hildesheim: Georg Olms, 1968.

Musikalischer Almanach auf das Jahr 1782. [Edited by Carl Ludwig Junker.] Alethinopel [Berlin].

Musikalisches Taschenbuch auf das Jahr 1784. Freyburg.

Reichardt, Johann Friedrich. *Briefe eines aufmerksamen Reisenden die Musik betreffend.* 2 vols. Frankfurt and Leipzig, 1774–76.

Schreiben über die Berlinische Musik. Hamburg: Carl Ernst Bohn, 1775.

Schubart, Christian Friedrich Daniel. *Ideen zu einer Aesthetik der Tonkunst.* Edited by Jürgen Mainka. Leipzig: Reclam, 1977.

Sulzer, Johann Georg. *Allgemeine Theorie der schönen Künste in einzeln, nach alphabetischer Ordnung der Kunstwörter auf einander folgenden Artikeln abgehandelt.* 4th edn. Leipzig, 1792–99; facsimile edn. Hildesheim: Georg Olms, 1967.

"Ueber den National-Charakter der Italiäner." *Gothaisches Magazin der Künste und Wissenschaften* I/1 (1776), 1–21.

Ueber die Musik und deren Wirkungen. Translated by Johann Adam Hiller. Leipzig: Friedrich Gotthold Jacobäer und Sohn, 1781; facsimile edn. Leipzig: Zentralantiquariat der deutschen demokratischen Republik, 1974.

"Ueber Musik, ihre Wirkung und Anwendung." *Flensburgsches Wochenblat für Jedermann* V/11 (12 September 1792), 85–88, and V/12 (19 September 1792), 89–95.

"Von dem wienerischen Geschmack in der Musik." *Wienerisches Diarium* 26 (18 October 1766).

Wahrheiten die Musik betreffend, gerade herausgesagt von einem teutschen Biedermann. Frankfurt am Main: Bey den Eichenbergschen Erben, 1779.

Wolf, Ernst Wilhelm. "Was ist wahre Musik?" *Der teutsche Merkur* (March 1783), 231–39.

Secondary sources

Abel, Carl Friedrich. *Six Selected Symphonies.* Edited by Sanford Helm. Recent Researches in the Music of the Classical Era, 3. Madison, WI: A-R Editions, 1977.

Abrams, Meyer Howard. *Doing Things with Texts: Essays in Criticism and Critical Theory.* Edited with a Foreward by Michael Fisher. New York: Norton, 1989.

The Mirror and the Lamp: Romantic Theory and the Critical Tradition. New York: Oxford University Press, 1953.

Baker, Nancy Kovaleff and Thomas Cristensen. *Aesthetics and the Art of Musical Composition in the German Enlightenment.* Cambridge Studies in Music Theory and Analysis. Edited by Ian Bent. Cambridge University Press, 1995.

Barraclough, Geoffrey. *Main Trends in History*. Expanded and updated by Michael Burns. New York and London: Holmes & Meier, 1991.

Barry, Kevin. *Language, Music and the Sign: A Study in Aesthetics, Poetics and Poetic Practice from Collins to Coleridge*. Cambridge University Press, 1987.

Baumann, Thomas. "The Music Reviews in the Allgemeine deutsche Bibliothek." *Acta Musicologica* 49 (1977), 69–85.

Beiser, Frederick C. *The Fate of Reason: German Philosophy from Kant to Fichte*. Cambridge, MA and London: Harvard University Press, 1987.

Benary, Peter. *Die deutsche Kompositionslehre des 18. Jahrhunderts*. Jenär Beiträge zur Musikforschung, 3. Leipzig: Breitkopf & Härtel.

Besseler, Heinrich. "Mozart und die deutsche Klassik." In *Bericht über den internationalen musikwissenschaftlichen Kongress Wien. Mozartjahr 1956*, edited by Erich Schenk. Bonn: Hermann Böhlaus Nachfolger, 1958.

Birke, Joachim. *Christian Wolffs Metaphysik und die Zeitgenössische Literatur und Musiktheorie: Gottsched, Scheibe, Mizler*. Berlin: Walter de Gruyter, 1966.

Bonds, Mark Evan. "Haydn, Laurence Sterne, and the Origins of Musical Irony." *Journal of the American Musicological Society* 44 (Spring 1991), 57–91.

Wordless Rhetoric: Musical Form and the Metaphor of the Oration. Studies in the History of Music, 4. Edited by Lewis Lockwood and Christoph Wolff. Cambridge, MA and London: Harvard University Press, 1991.

Braudel, Fernand. *On History*. Translated by Sarah Matthews. Chicago: University of Chicago Press, 1980.

Burke, Kenneth. *The Philosophy of Literary Form*. [Baton Rouge]: Louisiana State University Press, 1941.

Burnham, Scott. *Beethoven Hero*. Princeton University Press, 1995.

Cixous, Hélène. "Sorties." In *The Newly Born Woman*. Minneapolis: University of Minnesota Press, 1986.

Clark, Robert T. Jr. *Herder: His Life and Thought*. Berkeley and Los Angeles: University of California Press, 1969.

Cognition and Fact: Materials on Ludwik Fleck. Edited by Robert S. Cohen and Thomas Schnelle. Dordrecht, Holland: D. Reidel, 1986.

Cohen, Peter. *Theorie und Praxis der Clavierästhetik Carl Philipp Emanuel Bachs*. Hamburg: Karl Dieter Wagner, 1974.

Cowart, Georgia. "Critical Language and Musical Thought in the Seventeenth and Eighteenth Centuries." *College Music Symposium* 27 (1987), 14–29.

"Sense and Sensibility in Eighteenth-Century Musical Thought." *Acta Musicologica* 45 (1984), 251–66.

Dahlhaus, Carl. *Beethoven*. 2nd edn. Laaber: Laaber Verlag, 1988.

Esthetics of Music. Translated by William Austin. Cambridge University Press, 1982.

"E. T .A. Hoffmanns Beethoven-Kritik und die Aesthetik des Erhabenen." *Archiv für Musikwissenschaft* 38 (1981), 79–92.

"Karl Philipp Moritz und das Problem einer klassischen Musikaesthetik."

International Review of the Aesthetics and Sociology of Music 9 (1978), 279–94.

Klassische und romantische Musikästhetik. Laaber: Laaber Verlag, 1988.

"Romantische Musikästhetik und Wiener Klassik. *Archiv für Musikwissenschaft 29* (1972), 167–81.

"Zu Kants Musikästhetik." *Archiv für Musikwissenschaft* 10 (1953), 338–47.

Dammann, Rolf. *Der Musikbegriff im deutschen Barock*. Cologne: Arno Volk Verlag, 1967.

De Ruiter, Jakob. *Der Charakterbegriff in der Musik: Studien zur deutschen Aesthetik der Instrumentalmusik 1740–1850*. Stuttgart: Franz Steiner, 1989.

Developments in Modern Historiography. Edited by Henry Kozick with an Introduction by Sidney Monas. New York: St. Martin's Press, 1993.

Dolinski, Kurt. "Die Anfänge der musikalischen Fachpresse in Deutschland: Geschichtliche Grundlagen." Ph.D. diss., Friedrich-Wilhelms-Universität zu Berlin. Berlin: Hermann Schmidt, 1940.

Ehninger, Douglas. "On Systems of Rhetoric." *Philosophy & Rhetoric* 1 (Summer 1968), 131–44.

Engell, James. *The Creative Imagination: Enlightenment to Romanticism*. Cambridge, MA and London: Harvard University Press, 1981.

Engelsing, Rolf. "Die periodische Presse und ihr Publikum. Zeitungslektüre in Breman von den Anfängen bis zur Franzosenzeit." In *Archiv für Geschichte des Buchwesens*, vol. IV, edited by Bertold Hack and Bernhard Wendt. Frankfurt am Main: Buchhändler-Vereinigung, 1963.

Fabian, Bernhard. "English Books and Their German Readers." In *The Widening Circle: Essays on the Circulation of Literature in Eighteenth-Century Europe*, edited by Paul J. Korschin. University of Pennsylvania Press, 1976.

Faller, Max. *Johann Friedrich Reichardt und die Anfänge der musikalischen Journalistik*. Kassel: Bärenreiter, 1929.

Fellerer, Karl G. "Zur Mozart-Kritik im 18./ 19. Jahrhundert." *Mozart Jahrbuch 1959*. Salzburg: Salzburger Druckerei und Verlag, 1960.

Fischer, Heinz-Dietrich, ed. *Deutsche Zeitungen des 17. bis 20. Jahrhunderts*. Publizistik-historische Beiträge, 2. Pullach: Verlag Dokumentation, 1972.

Fleck, Ludwik. *Genesis and Development of a Scientific Fact*. Translated by Fred Bradley and Thaddeus J. Trenn. Edited by Thaddeus J. Trenn and Robert K. Merton, with a Foreword by Thomas S. Kuhn. Chicago and London: University of Chicago Press, 1979.

Flotzinger, Rudolf and Gernot Gruber. "Die Wiener Klassiker und ihre Zeit." In *Musikgeschichte Österreichs*. Vol. II: *Vom Barok zur Gegenwart*, edited by Rudolf Flotzinger und Gernot Gruber. Graz: Verlag Styria, 1979.

Freeman, Daniel E. "Johann Christian Bach and the Early Classical Italian Masters." In *Eighteenth-Century Keyboard Music*, edited by Robert L. Marshall. New York: Schirmer Books, 1994.

Gottscheds Lebens- und Kunstreform in den zwanziger und dreissiger Jahren. Edited by Fritz Brüggemann. Deutsche Literatur in Entwicklungsreihen: Reihe Aufklärung, 3. Darmstadt: Wissenschaftliche Buchgesellschaft, 1966.

Gülke, Peter. "Imitation und génie – die Konstellation zweier Zentralbegriffe bei Rousseau und deren Wirkung auf Deutschland." In *Aufklärungen: Studien zur deutsch-französischen Musikgeschichte im 18. Jahrhundert: Einflüsse und Wirkungen, II*, edited by Wolfgang Birtel and Christoph-Hellmut Mahling. Heidelberg: Carl Winter, 1986, pp. 30–44.

Hagelweide, Gert. *Deutsche Zeitungsbestände in Bibliotheken und Archiven.* Bibliographien zur Geschichte des Parlamentarismus und der politischen Parteien, 6. Düsseldorf: Droste Verlag, 1974.

Head, Matthew. "'Like Beauty Spots on the Face of a Man': Gender in 18th-Century North-German Discourse on Genre." *Journal of Musicology* 13 (Spring 1995), 143–67.

Henneberg, Gudrun. *Idee und Begriff des musikalischen Kunstwerks im Spiegel des deutschsprachigen Schrifttums der ersten Hälfte des 19. Jahrhunderts.* Mainzer Studien zur Musikwissenschaft, 17. Tutzing: Hans Schneider, 1983.

Himmelfarb, Gertrude. *The New History and the Old: Critical Essays and Reappraisals.* Cambridge, MA and London: Harvard University Press, 1987.

Hollmann, Wolfgang. *Alte deutsche Zeitungen.* Leipzig: Bibliographisches Institut, 1937.

Holub, Robert C. *Reception Theory: A Critical Introduction.* London and New York: Methuen, 1984.

Hosler, Bellamy. *Changing Aesthetic Views of Instrumental Music in Eighteenth-Century Germany.* Ann Arbor, MI: UMI Research Press, 1981.

Katz, Ruth and Carl Dahlhaus. *Contemplating Music: Source Readings in the Aesthetics of Music.* 4 vols. Aesthetics in Music, 5. Stuyvesant, NY: Pendragon Press, 1986–93.

Kirchner, Joachim. *Bibliographie der Zeitschriften des deutschen Sprachgebietes bis 1900.* 4 vols. Vol. I: *Die Zeitschriften des deutschen Sprachgebietes von den Anfängen bis 1830.* Index by Edith Chorherr. Stuttgart: Anton Hiersemann, 1969.

Das deutsche Zeitschriftenwesen: Seine Geschichte und seine Probleme. Vol. I: *Von den Anfängen bis zum Zeitalter der Romantik.* 2nd rev. edn. Wiesbaden: Otto Harrassowitz, 1958.

Kivy, Peter. *The Fine Art of Repetition: Essays in the Philosophy of Music.* Cambridge University Press, 1993.

Kramer, Richard. "The New Modulation of the 1770s: C. P. E. Bach in Theory, Criticism, and Practice." *Journal of the American Musicological Society* 38 (1985), 551–92.

Krome, Ferdinand. "Die Anfänge des musikalischen Journalismus in Deutschland." Ph.D. diss., University of Leipzig. Leipzig: Pöschel & Trepte, 1896.

Krummel, Donald W. and Stanley Sadie, eds. *Music Printing and Publishing.* The Norton/Grove Handbooks in Music. New York and London: W. W. Norton, 1990.

Kuhn, Thomas S. *The Structure of Scientific Revolutions*. 2nd edn. International Encyclopedia of Unified Science, II/2. University of Chicago Press, 1970.

Landon, H. C. Robbins. *Haydn: Chronicle & Works*. 5 vols. Bloomington: Indiana University Press, 1976–80.

Lange, Victor. *The Classical Age of German Literature, 1740–1815*. New York: Holmes & Meier, 1982.

Le Huray, Peter. "The Role of Music in Eighteenth- and Early Nineteenth-Century Aesthetics. *Proceedings of the Royal Music Association*, 105 (1978–79), 90–99.

Le Huray, Peter and James Day, eds. *Music and Aesthetics in the Eighteenth and Early Nineteenth Centuries*. Abridged edn. Cambridge University Press, 1988.

Lester, Joel. *Compositional Theory in the Eighteenth Century*. Cambridge, MA and London: Harvard University Press, 1992.

Lichtenhahn, Ernst. "Der musikalische Stilwandel im Selbstverständnis der Zeit um 1750." In *Carl Philipp Emanuel Bach und die europäische Musikkultur des mittleren 18. Jahrhunderts*, edited by Hans Joachim Marx. Göttingen: Vandenhoeck & Ruprecht, 1990.

Lindemann, Margot. *Geschichte der deutschen Presse*. Part 1: *Deutsche Presse bis 1815*. Abhandlungen und Materielen zur Publizistik, 5. Berlin: Colloquium Verlag, 1969.

Lippman, Edward A. *A History of Western Musical Aesthetics*. Lincoln and London: University of Nebraska Press, 1992.

Lippman, Edward A., ed. *Musical Aesthetics: A Historical Reader*. 3 vols. Aesthetics in Music, 4. Stuyvesant, NY: Pendragon Press, 1986–90.

Madland, Helga. "Imitation to Creation: The Changing Concept of Mimesis from Bodmer and Breitinger to Lenz." In *Eighteenth-Century German Authors and their Aesthetic Theories: Literature and the other Arts*, edited by Richard Critchfield and Wulf Koepke. Studies in German Literature, Linguistics, and Culture, 34. Columbia, SC: Camden House, 1988.

Maniates, Maria Rika. "'Sonate, que me veux tu?'. The Enigma of French Musical Aesthetics in the 18th Century." *Current Musicology* 9 (1969), 117–40.

Milstein, Barney M. *Eight Eighteenth-Century Reading Societies*. Berne and Frankfurt am Main: Herbert Lang, 1972.

Neubauer, John. *The Emancipation of Music from Language: Departure from Mimesis in Eighteenth-Century Aesthetics*. New Haven, CT: Yale University Press, 1986.

North, Stephen M. *The Making of Knowledge in Composition: Portrait of an Emerging Field*. Portsmouth, NH: Boynton/Cook, 1987.

Norton, Robert E. *Herder's Aesthetics and the European Enlightenment*. Ithaca and London: Cornell University Press, 1991.

The Origins of Modern Critical Thought: German Aesthetic and Literary Criticism from Lessing to Hegel. Edited by David Simpson. Cambridge University Press, 1988.

Pederson, Sanna Florence. "Enlightened and Romantic German Music Criticism, 1800–1850." Ph. D. diss., University of Pennsylvania, 1995.

Prüsener, Marlies. "Lesegesellschaften im 18. Jahrhundert. Ein Beitrag zur Lesergeschichte." In *Archiv für Geschichte des Buchwesens*, vol. XIII, edited by Bertold Hack, Bernhard Wendt, and Marietta Kliess. Frankfurt am Main: Buchhändler-Vereinigung, 1978.

Riggs, Robert. "'On the Representation of Character in Music': Christian Gottfried Körner's Aesthetics of Instrumental Music." Unpublished paper read at the 1990 meeting of the American Musicological Society.

Salmen, Walter. *Johann Friedrich Reichardt: Komponist, Schriftsteller, Kapellmeister und Verwaltungsbeamter der Goethezeit.* Freiburg im Breisgau and Zurich: Atlantis Verlag, 1963.

Schenk-Güllich, Dagmar. "Anfänge der Musikkritik in frühen Periodika. Ein Beitrag zur Frage nach den formalen und inhaltlichen Kriterien von Musikkritiken der Tages- und Fachpresse im Zeitraum von 1600 bis 1770." Ph.D. diss., Friedrich-Alexander-Universität, Erlangen-Nürnberg, 1972.

Schmidt, Lothar. *Organische Form in der Musik: Stationen eines Begriffs 1795–1810.* Kassel: Bärenreiter, 1990.

Schmidt-Hidding, Wolfgang, Karl Otto Schütz, and Wido Hempel. *Humor und Witz.* Europäische Schlüsselwörter, 1. Munich: Mach Hueber Verlag, 1963.

Schnaus, Peter. *E. T. A. Hoffmann als Beethoven-Rezensent der Allgemeine Musikalische Zeitung.* Freiburger Schriften zur Musikwissenschaft, 8. Munich and Salzburg: Emil Katzbichler, 1977.

Schneider, Hans. *Der Musikverleger Heinrich Philipp Bossler 1744–1812.* Tutzing: Hans Schneider, 1985.

Schwindt-Gross, Nicole. "Parodie um 1800: Zu den Quellen im deutschsprachigen Raum und ihrer Problematik im Zeitalter des künstlerischen Autonomie-Gedankens." *Die Musikforschung* 41 (1988), 16–45.

Seifert, Wolfgang. *Christian Gottfried Körner: Ein Musikästhetiker der deutschen Klassik.* Regensburg: Bosse, 1960.

Sheehan, James J. *German History 1770–1866.* Oxford: Clarendon Press, 1989.

Sieber, Paul. *Johann Friedrich Reichardt als Musikästhetiker: Seine Anschauungen über Wesen und Wirkung der Musik.* Strasburg, 1930; rpt. Baden-Baden: Verlag Valentin Koerner, 1971.

Sisman, Elaine R. *Haydn and the Classical Variation.* Cambridge, MA and London: Harvard University Press, 1993.

Stone, Lawrence. *The Past and the Present.* Boston, London, and Henley: Routledge & Kegan Paul, 1981.

Suchalla, Ernst, ed. *Briefe von Carl Philipp Emanuel Bach an Johann Gottlob Immanuel Breitkopf und Johann Nikolaus Forkel.* Tutzing: Hans Schneider, 1985.

Unverricht, Hubert. *Geschichte des Streichtrios.* Mainzer Studien zur Musikwissenschaft, 2. Edited by Hellmut Federhofer. Tutzing: Hans Schneider, 1969.

Wallace, Robin. *Beethoven's Critics: Aesthetic Dilemmas and Resolutions During the Composer's Lifetime.* Cambridge University Press, 1986.

Webster, James. *Haydn's "Farewell" Symphony and the Idea of Classical Style.* Cambridge Studies in Music Theory and Analysis, 1. Edited by Ian Bent. Cambridge University Press, 1991.

Wellek, René. *A History of Modern Criticism: 1750–1950.* 4 vols. Vol. I: *The Later Eighteenth Century.* Vol. II: *The Romantic Age.* New Haven, CT: Yale University Press, 1955.

Wheelock, Gretchen A. *Haydn's Ingenious Jesting with Art: Contexts of Musical Wit and Humor.* New York: Schirmer, 1992.

The Widening Circle: Essays on the Circulation of Literature in Eighteenth-Century Europe. Edited by Paul J. Korschin. University of Pennsylvania Press, 1976.

Zaslaw, Neal. *Mozart's Symphonies: Context, Performance Practice, Reception.* Oxford: Clarendon Press, 1989.

Zeydel, Edwin H. *Ludwig Tieck, the German Romanticist.* Princeton University Press, 1935; rpt. Hildesheim, Georg Olms, 1971.

Index

THE PELICAN SHAKESPEARE
GENERAL EDITORS

STEPHEN ORGEL
A. R. BRAUNMULLER

The Third Part of Henry the Sixth

The murder of King Henry by Richard of Gloucester (V.6), frontispiece to the play in Nicholas Rowe's Shakespeare, 1709, the first illustrated edition. The play was performed throughout the Restoration in an adaptation by John Crowne called *The Miseries of Civil War*. The costumes are a mixture of medieval and modern, the setting gothic, the decor eighteenth-century, all reflecting stage practice.

Contents

Publisher's Note

IT IS ALMOST half a century since the first volumes of the Pelican Shakespeare appeared under the general editorship of Alfred Harbage. The fact that a new edition, rather than simply a revision, has been undertaken reflects the profound changes textual and critical studies of Shakespeare have undergone in the past twenty years. For the new Pelican series, the texts of the plays and poems have been thoroughly revised in accordance with recent scholarship, and in some cases have been entirely reedited. New introductions and notes have been provided in all the volumes. But the new Shakespeare is also designed as a successor to the original series; the previous editions have been taken into account, and the advice of the previous editors has been solicited where it was feasible to do so.

Certain textual features of the new Pelican Shakespeare should be particularly noted. All lines are numbered that contain a word, phrase, or allusion explained in the glossarial notes. In addition, for convenience, every tenth line is also numbered, in italics when no annotation is indicated. The intrusive and often inaccurate place headings inserted by early editors are omitted (as is becoming standard practice), but for the convenience of those who miss them, an indication of locale now appears as the first item in the annotation of each scene.

In the interest of both elegance and utility, each speech prefix is set in a separate line when the speaker's lines are in verse, except when those words form the second half of a verse line. Thus the verse form of the speech is kept visually intact. What is printed as verse and what is printed as prose has, in general, the authority of the original texts. Departures from the original texts in this regard have only the authority of editorial tradition and the judgment of the Pelican editors; and, in a few instances, are admittedly arbitrary.

The Theatrical World

Economic realities determined the theatrical world in which Shakespeare's plays were written, performed, and received. For centuries in England, the primary theatrical tradition was nonprofessional. Craft guilds (or "mysteries") provided religious drama – mystery plays – as part of the celebration of religious and civic festivals, and schools and universities staged classical and neoclassical drama in both Latin and English as part of their curricula. In these forms, drama was established and socially acceptable. Professional theater, in contrast, existed on the margins of society. The acting companies were itinerant; playhouses could be any available space – the great halls of the aristocracy, town squares, civic halls, inn yards, fair booths, or open fields – and income was sporadic, dependent on the passing of the hat or on the bounty of local patrons. The actors, moreover, were considered little better than vagabonds, constantly in danger of arrest or expulsion.

In the late 1560s and 1570s, however, English professional theater began to gain respectability. Wealthy aristocrats fond of drama – the Lord Admiral, for example, or the Lord Chamberlain – took acting companies under their protection so that the players technically became members of their households and were no longer subject to arrest as homeless or masterless men. Permanent theaters were first built at this time as well, allowing the companies to control and charge for entry to their performances.

Shakespeare's livelihood, and the stunning artistic explosion in which he participated, depended on pragmatic and architectural effort. Professional theater requires ways to restrict access to its offerings; if it does not, and admission fees cannot be charged, the actors do not get paid, the costumes go to a pawnbroker, and there is no such thing as a professional, ongoing theatrical tradition. The answer to that economic need arrived in the late 1560s and 1570s with the creation of the so-called public or amphitheater playhouse. Recent discoveries indicate that the precursor of the Globe playhouse in London (where Shakespeare's mature plays were presented) and the Rose theater (which presented Christopher Marlowe's plays and some of Shakespeare's earliest ones) was the Red Lion theater of 1567. Archaeological studies of the foundations of the Rose and Globe theaters have revealed that the open-air theater of the 1590s and later was probably a polygonal building with fourteen to twenty or twenty-four sides, multistoried, from 75 to 100 feet in diameter, with a raised, partly covered "thrust" stage that projected into a group of standing patrons, or "groundlings," and a covered gallery, seating up to 2,500 or more (very crowded) spectators.

These theaters might have been about half full on any given day, though the audiences were larger on holidays or when a play was advertised, as old and new were, through printed playbills posted around London. The metropolitan area's late-Tudor, early-Stuart population (circa 1590–1620) has been estimated at about 150,000 to 250,000. It has been supposed that in the mid-1590s there were about 15,000 spectators per week at the public theaters; thus, as many as 10 percent of the local population went to the theater regularly. Consequently, the theaters' repertories – the plays available for this experienced and frequent audience – had to change often: in the month between September 15 and October 15, 1595, for instance, the Lord Admiral's Men performed twenty-eight times in eighteen different plays.

Since natural light illuminated the amphitheaters' stages, performances began between noon and two o'clock and ran without a break for two or three hours. They often concluded with a jig, a fencing display, or some other nondramatic exhibition. Weather conditions deter-

mined the season for the amphitheaters: plays were performed every day (including Sundays, sometimes, to cler-
ical dismay) except during Lent – the forty days before
Easter – or periods of plague, or sometimes during the
summer months when law courts were not in session and
the most affluent members of the audience were not in
London.

To a modern theatergoer, an amphitheater stage like
that of the Rose or Globe would appear an unfamiliar mixture of plainness and elaborate decoration. Much of the
structure was carved or painted, sometimes to imitate
marble; elsewhere, as under the canopy projecting over the
stage, to represent the stars and the zodiac. Appropriate
painted canvas pictures (of Jerusalem, for example, if the
play was set in that city) were apparently hung on the wall
behind the acting area, and tragedies were accompanied by
black hangings, presumably something like crepe festoons
or bunting. Although these theaters did not employ what
we would call scenery, early modern spectators saw numerous large props, such as the "bar" at which a prisoner stood
during a trial, the "mossy bank" where lovers reclined,
an arbor for amorous conversation, a chariot, gallows,
tables, trees, beds, thrones, writing desks, and so forth.
Audiences might learn a scene's location from a sign (reading "Athens," for example) carried across the stage (as in
Bertolt Brecht's twentieth-century productions). Equally
captivating (and equally irritating to the theater's enemies)
were the rich costumes and personal props the actors used:
the most valuable items in the surviving theatrical invento-
ries are the swords, gowns, robes, crowns, and other items
worn or carried by the performers.

Magic appealed to Shakespeare's audiences as much as
it does to us today, and the theater exploited many deceptive and spectacular devices. A winch in the loft above the
stage, called "the heavens," could lower and raise actors
playing gods, goddesses, and other supernatural figures to
and from the main acting area, just as one or more trap-
doors permitted entrances and exits to and from the area,

called "hell," beneath the stage. Actors wore elementary makeup such as wigs, false beards, and face paint, and they employed pig's bladders filled with animal blood to make wounds seem more real. They had rudimentary but effective ways of pretending to behead or hang a person. Supernumeraries (stagehands or actors not needed in a particular scene) could make thunder sounds (by shaking a metal sheet or rolling an iron ball down a chute) and show lightning (by blowing inflammable resin through tubes into a flame). Elaborate fireworks enhanced the effects of dragons flying through the air or imitated such celestial phenomena as comets, shooting stars, and multiple suns. Horses' hoofbeats, bells (located perhaps in the tower above the stage), trumpets and drums, clocks, cannon shots and gunshots, and the like were common sound effects. And the music of viols, cornets, oboes, and recorders was a regular feature of theatrical performances.

For two relatively brief spans, from the late 1570s to 1590 and from 1599 to 1614, the amphitheaters competed with the so-called private, or indoor, theaters, which originated as, or later represented themselves as, educational institutions training boys as singers for church services and court performances. These indoor theaters had two features that were distinct from the amphitheaters': their personnel and their playing spaces. The amphitheaters' adult companies included both adult men, who played the male roles, and boys, who played the female roles; the private, or indoor, theater companies, on the other hand, were entirely composed of boys aged about 8 to 16, who were, or could pretend to be, candidates for singers in a church or a royal boys' choir. (Until 1660, professional theatrical companies included no women.) The playing space would appear much more familiar to modern audiences than the long-vanished amphitheaters; the later indoor theaters were, in fact, the ancestors of the typical modern theater. They were enclosed spaces, usually rectangular, with the stage filling one end of the rectangle and the audience arrayed in seats or benches across (and sometimes lining) the building's longer axis. These spaces staged plays less frequently than the public theaters (perhaps only once a week) and held far fewer spectators than the amphitheaters: about 200 to 600, as opposed to 2,500 or more. Fewer patrons mean a smaller gross income, unless each pays more. Not surprisingly, then, private theaters charged higher prices than the amphitheaters, probably sixpence, as opposed to a penny for the cheapest entry.

Protected from the weather, the indoor theaters presented plays later in the day than the amphitheaters, and used artificial illumination – candles in sconces or candelabra. But candles melt, and need replacing, snuffing, and trimming, and these practical requirements may have been part of the reason the indoor theaters introduced breaks in the performance, the intermission so dear to the heart of theatergoers and to the pocketbooks of theater concessionaires ever since. Whether motivated by the need to tend to the candles or by the entrepreneurs' wishing to sell oranges and liquor, or both, the indoor theaters eventually established the modern convention of the non-continuous performance. In the early modern "private" theater, musical performances apparently filled the intermissions, which in Stuart theater jargon seem to have been called "acts."

At the end of the first decade of the seventeenth century, the distinction between public amphitheaters and private indoor companies ceased. For various cultural, political, and economic reasons, individual companies gained control of both the public, open-air theaters and the indoor ones, and companies mixing adult men and boys took over the formerly "private" theaters. Despite the death of the boys' companies and of their highly innovative theaters (for which such luminous playwrights as Ben Jonson, George Chapman, and John Marston wrote), their playing spaces and conventions had an immense impact on subsequent plays: not merely for the intervals (which stressed the artistic and architectonic importance of "acts"), but also because they introduced political and social satire as a popular dramatic ingredient, even in tragedy, and a wider range of actorly effects, encouraged by their more intimate playing spaces.

Even the briefest sketch of the Shakespearean theatrical world would be incomplete without some comment on the social and cultural dimensions of theaters and playing in the period. In an intensely hierarchical and status-conscious society, professional actors and their ventures had hardly any respectability; as we have indicated, to protect themselves against laws designed to curb vagabondage and the increase of masterless men, actors resorted to the near-fiction that they were the servants of noble masters, and wore their distinctive livery. Hence the company for which Shakespeare wrote in the 1590s called itself the Lord Chamberlain's Men and pretended that the public, money-getting performances were in fact rehearsals for private performances before that high court official. From 1598, the Privy Council had licensed theatrical companies, and after 1603, with the accession of King James I, the companies gained explicit royal protection, just as the Queen's Men had for a time under Queen Elizabeth. The Chamberlain's Men became the King's Men, and the other companies were patronized by the other members of the royal family.

These designations were legal fictions that half-concealed an important economic and social development, the evolution away from the theater's organization on the model of the guild, a self-regulating confraternity of individual artisans, into a proto-capitalist organization. Shakespeare's company became a joint-stock company, where persons who supplied capital and, in some cases, such as Shakespeare's, capital and talent, employed themselves and others in earning a return on that capital. This development meant that actors and theater companies were outside both the traditional guild structures, which required some form of civic or royal charter, and the feudal household organization of master-and-servant. This anomalous, maverick social and economic condition made theater companies practically unruly and potentially even dangerous; consequently, numerous official bodies – including the London metropolitan and ecclesiastical authorities as well as, occasionally, the royal court itself – tried, without much success, to control and even to disband them.

Public officials had good reason to want to close the theaters: they were attractive nuisances – they drew often riotous crowds, they were always noisy, and they could be politically offensive and socially insubordinate. Until the Civil War, however, anti-theatrical forces failed to shut down professional theater, for many reasons – limited surveillance and few police powers, tensions or outright hostilities among the agencies that sought to check or channel theatrical activity, and lack of clear policies for control. Another reason must have been the theaters' undeniable popularity. Curtailing any activity enjoyed by such a substantial percentage of the population was difficult, as various Roman emperors attempting to limit circuses had learned, and the Tudor-Stuart audience was not merely large, it was socially diverse and included women. The prevalence of public entertainment in this period has been underestimated. In fact, fairs, holidays, games, sporting events, the equivalent of modern parades, freak shows, and street exhibitions all abounded, but the theater was the most widely and frequently available entertainment to which people of every class had access. That fact helps account both for its quantity and for the fear and anger it aroused.

WILLIAM SHAKESPEARE OF STRATFORD-UPON-AVON, GENTLEMAN

Many people have said that we know very little about William Shakespeare's life – pinheads and postcards are often mentioned as appropriately tiny surfaces on which to record the available information. More imaginatively and perhaps more correctly, Ralph Waldo Emerson wrote, "Shakespeare is the only biographer of Shakespeare. . . . So far from Shakespeare's being the least known, he is the one person in all modern history fully known to us."

In fact, we know more about Shakespeare's life than we do about almost any other English writer's of his era. His last will and testament (dated March 25, 1616) survives, as do numerous legal contracts and court documents involving Shakespeare as principal or witness, and parish records in Stratford and London. Shakespeare appears quite often in official records of King James's royal court, and of course Shakespeare's name appears on numerous title pages and in the written and recorded words of his literary contemporaries Robert Greene, Henry Chettle, Francis Meres, John Davies of Hereford, Ben Jonson, and many others. Indeed, if we make due allowance for the bloating of modern, run-of-the-mill bureaucratic records, more information has survived over the past four hundred years about William Shakespeare of Stratford-upon-Avon, Warwickshire, than is likely to survive in the next four hundred years about any reader of these words.

What we do not have are entire categories of information – Shakespeare's private letters or diaries, drafts and revisions of poems and plays, critical prefaces or essays, commendatory verse for other writers' works, or instructions guiding his fellow actors in their performances, for instance – that we imagine would help us understand and appreciate his surviving writings. For all we know, many such data never existed as written records. Many literary and theatrical critics, not knowing what might once have existed, more or less cheerfully accept the situation; some even make a theoretical virtue of it by claiming that such data are irrelevant to understanding and interpreting the plays and poems.

So, what do we know about William Shakespeare, the man responsible for thirty-seven or perhaps more plays, more than 150 sonnets, two lengthy narrative poems, and some shorter poems?

While many families by the name of Shakespeare (or some variant spelling) can be identified in the English Midlands as far back as the twelfth century, it seems likely that the dramatist's grandfather, Richard, moved to Snitterfield, a town not far from Stratford-upon-Avon, sometime before 1529. In Snitterfield, Richard Shakespeare leased farmland from the very wealthy Robert Arden. By 1552, Richard's son John had moved to a large house on Henley Street in Stratford-upon-Avon, the house that stands today as "The Birthplace." In Stratford, John Shakespeare traded as a glover, dealt in wool, and lent money at interest; he also served in a variety of civic posts, including "High Bailiff," the municipality's equivalent of mayor. In 1557, he married Robert Arden's youngest daughter, Mary. Mary and John had four sons – William was the oldest – and four daughters, of whom only Joan outlived her most celebrated sibling. William was baptized (an event entered in the Stratford parish church records) on April 26, 1564, and it has become customary, without any good factual support, to suppose he was born on April 23, which happens to be the feast day of Saint George, patron saint of England, and is also the date on which he died, in 1616. Shakespeare married Anne Hathaway in 1582, when he was eighteen and she was twenty-six; their first child was born five months later. It has been generally assumed that the marriage was enforced and subsequently unhappy, but these are only assumptions; it has been estimated, for instance, that up to one third of Elizabethan brides were pregnant when they married. Anne and William Shakespeare had three children: Susanna, who married a prominent local physician, John Hall; and the twins Hamnet, who died young in 1596, and Judith, who married Thomas Quiney – apparently a rather shady individual. The name Hamnet was unusual but not unique: he and his twin sister were named for their godparents, Shakespeare's neighbors Hamnet and Judith Sadler. Shakespeare's father died in 1601 (the year of *Hamlet*), and Mary Arden Shakespeare died in 1608 (the year of *Coriolanus*). William Shakespeare's last surviving direct descendant was his granddaughter Elizabeth Hall, who died in 1670.

Between the birth of the twins in 1585 and a clear reference to Shakespeare as a practicing London dramatist in Robert Greene's sensationalizing, satiric pamphlet, *Greene's Groatsworth of Wit* (1592), there is no record of where William Shakespeare was or what he was doing. These seven so-called lost years have been imaginatively filled by scholars and other students of Shakespeare: some think he traveled to Italy, or fought in the Low Countries, or studied law or medicine, or worked as an apprentice actor/writer, and so on to even more fanciful possibilities. Whatever the biographical facts for those "lost" years, Greene's nasty remarks in 1592 testify to professional envy and to the fact that Shakespeare already had a successful career in London. Speaking to his fellow playwrights, Greene warns both generally and specifically:

> . . . trust them [actors] not: for there is an upstart crow, beautified with our feathers, that with his tiger's heart wrapped in a player's hide supposes he is as well able to bombast out a blank verse as the best of you; and being an absolute Johannes Factotum, is in his own conceit the only Shake-scene in a country.

The passage mimics a line from *3 Henry VI* (hence the play must have been performed before Greene wrote) and seems to say that "Shake-scene" is both actor and playwright, a jack-of-all-trades. That same year, Henry Chettle protested Greene's remarks in *Kind-Heart's Dream*, and each of the next two years saw the publication of poems – *Venus and Adonis* and *The Rape of Lucrece*, respectively – publicly ascribed to (and dedicated by) Shakespeare. Early in 1595 he was named one of the senior members of a prominent acting company, the Lord Chamberlain's Men, when they received payment for court performances during the 1594 Christmas season.

Clearly, Shakespeare had achieved both success and reputation in London. In 1596, upon Shakespeare's application, the College of Arms granted his father the now-familiar coat of arms he had taken the first steps to obtain, almost twenty years before, and in 1598, John's son – now permitted to call himself "gentleman" – took a 10 percent share in the new Globe playhouse. In 1597, he bought a substantial bourgeois house, called New Place, in Stratford – the garden remains, but Shakespeare's house, several times rebuilt, was torn down in 1759 – and over the next few years Shakespeare spent large sums buying land and making other investments in the town and its environs. Though he worked in London, his family remained in Stratford, and he seems always to have considered Stratford the home he would eventually return to. Something approaching a disinterested appreciation of Shakespeare's popular and professional status appears in Francis Meres's *Palladis Tamia* (1598), a not especially imaginative and perhaps therefore persuasive record of literary reputations. Reviewing contemporary English writers, Meres lists the titles of many of Shakespeare's plays, including one not now known, *Love's Labor's Won,* and praises his "mellifluous & hony-tongued" "sugred Sonnets," which were then circulating in manuscript (they were first collected in 1609). Meres describes Shakespeare as "one of the best" English playwrights of both comedy and tragedy. In *Remains . . . Concerning Britain* (1605), William Camden – a more authoritative source than the imitative Meres – calls Shakespeare one of the "most pregnant witts of these our times" and joins him with such writers as Chapman, Daniel, Jonson, Marston, and Spenser. During the first decades of the seventeenth century, publishers began to attribute numerous play quartos, including some non-Shakespearean ones, to Shakespeare, either by name or initials, and we may assume that they deemed Shakespeare's name and supposed authorship, true or false, commercially attractive.

For the next ten years or so, various records show

Shakespeare's dual career as playwright and man of the theater in London, and as an important local figure in Stratford. In 1608-9 his acting company – designated the "King's Men" soon after King James had succeeded Queen Elizabeth in 1603 – rented, refurbished, and opened a small interior playing space, the Blackfriars theater, in London, and Shakespeare was once again listed as a substantial sharer in the group of proprietors of the playhouse. By May 11, 1612, however, he describes himself as a Stratford resident in a London lawsuit – an indication that he had withdrawn from day-to-day professional activity and returned to the town where he had always had his main financial interests. When Shakespeare bought a substantial residential building in London, the Blackfriars Gatehouse, close to the theater of the same name, on March 10, 1613, he is recorded as William Shakespeare "of Stratford upon Avon in the county of Warwick, gentleman," and he named several London residents as the building's trustees. Still, he continued to participate in theatrical activity: when the new Earl of Rutland needed an allegorical design to bear as a shield, or *impresa,* at the celebration of King James's Accession Day, March 24, 1613, the earl's accountant recorded a payment of 44 shillings to Shakespeare for the device with its motto.

For the last few years of his life, Shakespeare evidently concentrated his activities in the town of his birth. Most of the final records concern business transactions in Stratford, ending with the notation of his death on April 23, 1616, and burial in Holy Trinity Church, Stratford-upon-Avon.

THE QUESTION OF AUTHORSHIP

The history of ascribing Shakespeare's plays (the poems do not come up so often) to someone else began, as it continues, peculiarly. The earliest published claim that someone else wrote Shakespeare's plays appeared in an 1856 article by Delia Bacon in the American journal *Putnam's Monthly* – although an Englishman, Thomas Wilmot, had shared his doubts in private (even secretive) conversations with friends near the end of the eighteenth century. Bacon's was a sad personal history that ended in madness and poverty, but the year after her article, she published, with great difficulty and the bemused assistance of Nathaniel Hawthorne (then United States Consul in Liverpool, England), her *Philosophy of the Plays of Shakspere Unfolded.* This huge, ornately written, confusing farrago is almost unreadable; sometimes its intents, to say nothing of its arguments, disappear entirely beneath near-raving, ecstatic writing. Tumbled in with much supposed "philosophy" appear the claims that Francis Bacon (from whom Delia Bacon eventually claimed descent), Walter Ralegh, and several other contemporaries of Shakespeare's had written the plays. The book had little impact except as a ridiculed curiosity.

Once proposed, however, the issue gained momentum among people whose conviction was the greater in proportion to their ignorance of sixteenth- and seventeenth-century English literature, history, and society. Another American amateur, Catherine P. Ashmead Windle, made the next influential contribution to the cause when she published *Report to the British Museum* (1882), wherein she promised to open "the Cipher of Francis Bacon," though what she mostly offers, in the words of S. Schoenbaum, is "demented allegorizing." An entire new cottage industry grew from Windle's suggestion that the texts contain hidden, cryptographically discoverable ciphers – "clues" – to their authorship; and today there are not only books devoted to the putative ciphers, but also pamphlets, journals, and newsletters.

Although Baconians have led the pack of those seeking a substitute Shakespeare, in *"Shakespeare" Identified* (1920), J. Thomas Looney became the first published

"Oxfordian" when he proposed Edward de Vere, seventeenth earl of Oxford, as the secret author of Shakespeare's plays. Also for Oxford and his "authorship" there are today dedicated societies, articles, journals, and books. Less popular candidates – Queen Elizabeth and Christopher Marlowe among them – have had adherents, but the movement seems to have divided into two main contending factions, Baconian and Oxfordian. (For further details on all the candidates for "Shakespeare," see S. Schoenbaum, *Shakespeare's Lives,* 2nd ed., 1991.)

The Baconians, the Oxfordians, and supporters of other candidates have one trait in common – they are snobs. Every pro-Bacon or pro-Oxford tract sooner or later claims that the historical William Shakespeare of Stratford-upon-Avon could not have written the plays because he could not have had the training, the university education, the experience, and indeed the imagination or background their author supposedly possessed. Only a learned genius like Bacon or an aristocrat like Oxford could have written such fine plays. (As it happens, lucky male children of the middle class had access to better education than most aristocrats in Elizabethan England – and Oxford was not particularly well educated.) Shakespeare received in the Stratford grammar school a formal education that would daunt many college graduates today; and popular rival playwrights such as the very learned Ben Jonson and George Chapman, both of whom also lacked university training, achieved great artistic success, without being taken as Bacon or Oxford.

Besides snobbery, one other quality characterizes the authorship controversy: lack of evidence. A great deal of testimony from Shakespeare's time shows that Shakespeare wrote Shakespeare's plays and that his contemporaries recognized them as distinctive and distinctly superior. (Some of that contemporary evidence is collected in E. K. Chambers, *William Shakespeare: A Study of Facts and Problems,* 2 vols., 1930.) Since that testimony comes from Shakespeare's enemies and theatrical competitors as well as from his co-workers and from the Elizabethan equivalent of literary journalists, it seems unlikely that, if any of these sources had known he was a fraud, they would have failed to record that fact.

Books About Shakespeare's Theater

Useful scholarly studies of theatrical life in Shakespeare's day include: G. E. Bentley, *The Jacobean and Caroline Stage*, 7 vols. (1941-68), and the same author's *The Professions of Dramatist and Player in Shakespeare's Time, 1590-1642* (1986); E. K. Chambers, *The Elizabethan Stage*, 4 vols. (1923); R. A. Foakes, *Illustrations of the English Stage, 1580-1642* (1985); Andrew Gurr, *The Shakespearean Stage*, 3rd ed. (1992), and the same author's *Play-going in Shakespeare's London*, 2nd ed. (1996); Edwin Nungezer, *A Dictionary of Actors* (1929); Carol Chillington Rutter, ed., *Documents of the Rose Playhouse* (1984).

Books About Shakespeare's Life

The following books provide scholarly, documented accounts of Shakespeare's life: G. E. Bentley, *Shakespeare: A Biographical Handbook* (1961); E. K. Chambers, *William Shakespeare: A Study of Facts and Problems*, 2 vols. (1930); S. Schoenbaum, *William Shakespeare: A Compact Documentary Life* (1977); and *Shakespeare's Lives*, 2nd ed. (1991), by the same author. Many scholarly editions of Shakespeare's complete works print brief compilations of essential dates and events. References to Shakespeare's works up to 1700 are collected in C. M. Ingleby et al., *The Shakespeare Allusion-Book*, rev. ed., 2 vols. (1932).

The Texts of Shakespeare

As far as we know, only one manuscript conceivably in Shakespeare's own hand may (and even this is much disputed) exist: a few pages of a play called *Sir Thomas More*, which apparently was never performed. What we do have, as later readers, performers, scholars, students, are printed texts. The earliest of these survive in two forms: quartos and folios. Quartos (from the Latin for "four") are small books, printed on sheets of paper that were then folded in fours, to make eight double-sided pages. When these were bound together, the result was a squarish, eminently portable volume that sold for the relatively small sum of sixpence (translating in modern terms to about $5.00). In folios, on the other hand, the sheets are folded only once, in half, producing large, impressive volumes taller than they are wide. This was the format for important works of philosophy, science, theology, and literature (the major precedent for a folio Shakespeare was Ben Jonson's *Works*, 1616). The decision to print the works of a popular playwright in folio is an indication of how far up on the social scale the theatrical profession had come during Shakespeare's lifetime. The Shakespeare folio was an expensive book, selling for between fifteen and eighteen shillings, depending on the binding (in modern terms, from about $150 to $180). Twenty Shakespeare plays of the thirty-seven that survive first appeared in quarto, seventeen of which appeared during Shakespeare's lifetime; the rest of the plays are found only in folio.

The First Folio was published in 1623, seven years after Shakespeare's death, and was authorized by his fellow actors, the co-owners of the King's Men. This publication was certainly a mark of the company's enormous respect for Shakespeare; but it was also a way of turning the old plays, most of which were no longer current in the play-house, into ready money (the folio includes only Shakespeare's plays, not his sonnets or other nondramatic verse). Whatever the motives behind the publication of the folio, the texts it preserves constitute the basis for almost all later editions of the playwright's works. The texts, however, differ from those of the earlier quartos, sometimes in minor respects but often significantly – most strikingly in the two texts of *King Lear,* but also in important ways in *Hamlet, Othello,* and *Troilus and Cressida.* (The variants are recorded in the textual notes to each play in the new Pelican series.) The differences in these texts represent, in a sense, the essence of theater: the texts of plays were initially not intended for publication. They were scripts, designed for the actors to perform – the principal life of the play at this period was in performance. And it follows that in Shakespeare's theater the playwright typically had no say either in how his play was performed or in the disposition of his text – he was an employee of the company. The authoritative figures in the theatrical enterprise were the shareholders in the company, who were for the most part the major actors. They decided what plays were to be done; they hired the playwright and often gave him an outline of the play they wanted him to write. Often, too, the play was a collaboration: the company would retain a group of writers, and parcel out the scenes among them. The resulting script was then the property of the company, and the actors would revise it as they saw fit during the course of putting it on stage. The resulting text belonged to the company. The playwright had no rights in it once he had been paid. (This system survives largely intact in the movie industry, and most of the playwrights of Shakespeare's time were as anonymous as most screenwriters are today.) The script could also, of course, continue to change as the tastes of audiences and the requirements of the actors changed. Many – perhaps most – plays were revised when they were reintroduced after any substantial absence from the repertory, or when they were performed by a company different from the one that originally commissioned the play.

Shakespeare was an exceptional figure in this world because he was not only a shareholder and actor in his company, but also its leading playwright – he was literally his own boss. He had, moreover, little interest in the publication of his plays, and even those that appeared during his lifetime with the authorization of the company show no signs of any editorial concern on the part of the author. Theater was, for Shakespeare, a fluid and supremely responsive medium – the very opposite of the great classic canonical text that has embodied his works since 1623.

The very fluidity of the original texts, however, has meant that Shakespeare has always had to be edited. Here is an example of how problematic the editorial project inevitably is, a passage from the most famous speech in *Romeo and Juliet,* Juliet's balcony soliloquy beginning "O Romeo, Romeo, wherefore art thou Romeo?" Since the eighteenth century, the standard modern text has read,

> What's Montague? It is nor hand, nor foot,
> Nor arm, nor face, nor any other part
> Belonging to a man. O be some other name!
> What's in a name? That which we call a rose
> By any other name would smell as sweet.
> (II.2.40-44)

Editors have three early texts of this play to work from, two quarto texts and the folio. Here is how the First Quarto (1597) reads:

> Whats *Mountague?* It is nor hand nor foote,
> Nor arme, nor face, nor any other part.
> Whats in a name? That which we call a Rose,
> By any other name would ſmell as ſweet:

Here is the Second Quarto (1599):

> Whats *Mountague*? it is nor hand nor foote,
> Nor arme nor face, ô be fome other name
> Belonging to a man.
> Whats in a name that which we call a rofe,
> By any other word would fmell as fweete,

And here is the First Folio (1623):

> What's *Mountague*? it is nor hand nor foote,
> Nor arme, nor face, O be fome other name
> Belonging to a man.
> What? in a names that which we call a Rofe,
> By any other word would fmell as fweete,

There is in fact no early text that reads as our modern text does – and this is the most famous speech in the play. Instead, we have three quite different texts, all of which are clearly some version of the same speech, but none of which seems to us a final or satisfactory version. The transcendently beautiful passage in modern editions is an editorial invention: editors have succeeded in conflating and revising the three versions into something we recognize as great poetry. Is this what Shakespeare "really" wrote? Who can say? What we can say is that Shakespeare always had performance, not a book, in mind.

Books About the Shakespeare Texts

The standard study of the printing history of the First Folio is W. W. Greg, *The Shakespeare First Folio* (1955). J. K. Walton, *The Quarto Copy for the First Folio of Shakespeare* (1971), is a useful survey of the relation of the quartos to the folio. The second edition of Charlton Hinman's *Norton Facsimile* of the First Folio (1996), with a new introduction by Peter Blayney, is indispensable. Stanley Wells, Gary Taylor, John Jowett, and William Montgomery, *William Shakespeare: A Textual Companion,* keyed to the Oxford text, gives a comprehensive survey of the editorial situation for all the plays and poems.

THE GENERAL EDITORS

Introduction

In 1592 Robert Greene, one of Shakespeare's rivals on the London stage, parodied a line from *3 Henry VI* in a pamphlet called *Greenes Groats-worth of Witte*. Greene turned York's bitter words to Margaret, "O tiger's heart wrapped in a woman's hide!" (I.4.138) into an attack on Shakespeare, whom he accused of having a "tiger's heart wrapped in a player's hide." The parody implies that *3 Henry VI* was a popular play whose memorable lines were well known to Greene's Elizabethan audience. In our own time, however, the Henry VI plays have been over-shadowed by other works, such as *Richard III* or *Henry V,* in which strong protagonists transform English history into dramas of individual psychology. In contrast to some of these more famous Shakespearean histories, the Henry VI plays represent their title character as an uncertainty at the heart of the drama rather than a central figure. Instead of showing how historical circumstances emanate from the monarch's character, these works highlight the inter-dependence of character and circumstance.

Henry VI came to the throne when he was nine months old. The king's personality was thus shaped by public events, perhaps much more than events were ever shaped by the king. This certainly seems to be the as-sumption of Shakespeare's Henry VI plays, which show Henry developing under the influence of politicians try-ing to use him instead of seeking to nurture him. Failure is reciprocal, as conspiracy and rebellion weaken King Henry, and Henry's weakness encourages disorder. In *1 Henry VI* the child-king's aristocratic guardians fight among themselves and neglect both Henry's upbringing and his empire. *2 Henry VI* expands the study of Henry's fall, to embrace all levels of English society. In *3 Henry VI,*

Shakespeare again focuses on the nobles who should be England's leaders, revealing them totally absorbed in the treachery and brutality of civil war.

2 Henry VI saw the start of open hostilities in the Wars of the Roses. After the first battle of Saint Albans, in 1455, the Lancastrians, including King Henry, fled to London. As *3 Henry VI* begins, Richard Duke of York and his followers arrive at the Parliament House in pursuit of the king. York's son Richard, later Richard III, is still carrying the head of his last battle victim, the Duke of Somerset:

> RICHARD *To Somerset's head, which he shows*
> Speak thou for me, and tell them what I did.
> RICHARD DUKE OF YORK
> Richard hath best deserved of all my sons.
> *To the head*
> But is your grace dead, my Lord of Somerset?
> (I.1.16-18)

The picture of the Yorks clowning with Somerset's head recalls the scene in *2 Henry VI* where Jack Cade and his rebels play with the severed heads of two victims, making them kiss (IV.7). Civil war, it appears, brings out barbarity at all social levels. York's son the Earl of Rutland, still a child, is shortly murdered by Clifford, and York himself is captured, humiliated, and stabbed to death by Clifford and Queen Margaret. This parade of horrors brings the play only to the end of Act I.

Like the two earlier plays in the sequence, *3 Henry VI* implicitly compares the orphaned king to several other parent-child pairs. These include York and his sons, Clifford and his dead father, Margaret and the Prince of Wales, and the characters in Act II identified only as "a soldier who has killed his father" and "a soldier who has killed his son." The two Richards, father and son, are alike in ambition and rage. When news comes of York's death, his older son, Edward, cries, "O, speak no more, for I have heard too much" (II.1.48). But Richard feeds on distress: "Say how he died, for I will hear it all" (49). Told that York was taunted by Margaret with a paper crown and a cloth dipped in young Rutland's blood, Richard refuses to mourn: "To weep is to make less the depth of grief; / Tears, then, for babes – blows and revenge for me!" (85-86). Richard reproduces and eventually surpasses York's ferocious appetite for power and revenge.

Henry VI, by contrast, offers only faint echoes of his own legendary father, Henry V. One such reminder occurs when the king arrives at the Parliament House and discovers York sitting in his chair of state:

> Think'st thou that I will leave my kingly throne,
> Wherein my grandsire and my father sat?
> No – first shall war unpeople this my realm.
>   (I.1.125-27)

Evidently this sensitive and pious king can nevertheless consider slaughtering his people to keep his seat. For a moment, he sounds as ruthless as Clifford, who dedicates himself entirely to revenge and not at all to morality:

> King Henry, be thy title right or wrong,
> Lord Clifford vows to fight in thy defense.
> May that ground gape and swallow me alive
> Where I shall kneel to him that slew my father.
>   (160-63)

A few lines later, however, York stamps his foot, his soldiers peep out from their hiding places, and Henry agrees without a whimper to make the duke his heir. This abrupt switch from a vow of total war to one of peace makes it clear that Henry's solution to York's aggression derives not from an inability to contemplate armed conflict but from a dread of carrying it out.

Audiences at the Henry VI plays can perhaps sympathize with a king unable to sustain the warlike attitudes of a father he has never seen. By entailing the crown to York and his heirs, however, Henry violates his own responsibilities as a father. To his family, the king can only say, "Pardon me, Margaret; pardon me, sweet son – / The Earl of Warwick and the duke enforced me" (229-30). Margaret and Prince Edward march out to lead the army themselves, and "bashful Henry" withdraws into his mind, where fitful anger fights a losing battle with vivid images of fear:

> Revenged may she be on that hateful duke,
> Whose haughty spirit, wingèd with desire,
> Will coast my crown, and, like an empty eagle,
> Tire on the flesh of me and of my son.
>
> (267-70)

Thereafter, Henry becomes a looker-on rather than a participant in the conflict between Lancaster and York. From the sidelines, he laments the "unnatural" savagery of civil war, which splits households apart. It seems possible to interpret the two soldiers who drag the bodies of their kinfolk on stage as projections of the king's own imagination. A lifetime of experience as a merely symbolic ruler has trained him to focus on emblematic parallels. Thus when the first soldier discovers he has killed his father in battle, and the second discovers he has killed his son, Henry grieves for the "bloody times" that have engulfed them all. Like the two soldiers, however, he regards himself as a victim and not a maker of civil war, dreading censure without admitting fault:

FIRST SOLDIER
> How will my mother for a father's death
> Take on with me, and ne'er be satisfied!

SECOND SOLDIER
> How will my wife for slaughter of my son
> Shed seas of tears, and ne'er be satisfied!

KING HENRY
>How will the country for these woeful chances
>Misthink the king, and not be satisfied!
>>(II.5.103-8)

Henry attributes events to chance, fortune, and the will of God, never to his own will. On the other side stand the self-reliant Yorks, especially Richard. Even as he struggles to maintain his brother Edward on the throne, Richard, now Duke of Gloucester, also begins a campaign for himself:

>I can add colors to the chameleon,
>Change shapes with Proteus for advantages,
>And set the murderous Machiavel to school.
>Can I do this, and cannot get a crown?
>Tut, were it farther off, I'll pluck it down.
>>(III.2.191-95)

In the end, Edward is king, but it is Richard and Henry who face off as the champions of two opposing responses to the world: complete resignation to fate and complete defiance. When Richard comes to kill Henry in the Tower, the king's only resistance is prophecy:

>Teeth hadst thou in thy head when thou wast
> born,
>To signify thou cam'st to bite the world;
>And if the rest be true which I have heard,
>Thou cam'st –

RICHARD DUKE OF GLOUCESTER
>I'll hear no more. Die, prophet, in thy speech,
> *He stabs him.*
>For this, amongst the rest, was I ordained.

KING HENRY
>Ay, and for much more slaughter after this.
>O, God forgive my sins, and pardon thee.
> *He dies.*
>>(V.6.53-60)

Richard admits the truth of Henry's perceptions, but rejects his piety. The heavens may indeed rule Richard's life, but they cannot make him like it:

> Then, since the heavens have shaped my body so,
> Let hell make crooked my mind to answer it.
> I had no father, I am like no father;
> I have no brother, I am like no brother;
> And this word "love," which graybeards call divine,
> Be resident in men like one another
> And not in me – I am myself alone.
>
> (78-84)

The audience knows that Richard does resemble his father and once loved him fiercely, yet now he denies all determining forces except self. Henry refuses to see the world as a place where he can make choices and take action, and Richard refuses to see it any other way. Henry is a good man and Richard is an evil one, but neither is fit to govern, as Shakespeare demonstrates here and in *Richard III,* the last play in the series.

3 Henry VI seems less episodic than the other two Henry VI plays because its major incidents all depict the fluctuating fortunes of the wars between Lancaster and York. Act I shows the aftermath of the first battle of Saint Albans and the death of York at the battle of Wakefield. At the start of Act II, Warwick describes the second battle of Saint Albans, and at the end of the act King Henry observes the battle of Towton (II.5). Henry is taken prisoner in Act III, until Warwick the "kingmaker" changes sides, and takes the crown from Edward (IV.3) and restores it to Henry (IV.6). Act V portrays the battle of Barnet, where Henry was recaptured, and the battle of Tewkesbury, where Margaret was defeated and her son Edward killed. Historically, these events took place over ten years, from 1461 to 1471, and the play is crowded with violent incidents as the balance between the two sides tips back and forth. Yet Shakespeare manages to

shape the narrative of these battles into a dramatic structure in which Henry's decline and Margaret's defeat are
counterpoised by Edward's rise and the ominous success
of Richard.

Although Richard and his brothers mock Clifford for
following a woman, "Captain Margaret" (II.6.75), the
queen stands in roughly the same relation to Henry as
Richard does to his brother Edward. Henry's cause depends on Margaret's military leadership, just as the Yorks'
depends on Richard's. The Yorks question Margaret's
womanhood –"O tiger's heart wrapped in a woman's
hide!" (I.4.138)– and scorn a female general, but these are
ritual insults, the equivalent of Margaret's calling Warwick "long-tongued" (II.2.102) or Richard a "foul misshapen stigmatic" (136). Like the other Henry VI plays,
this one treats women as little different from men in their
motivations and sometimes in their methods. Margaret
wants power and revenge, and like the other nobles in the
play, she pursues it on the battlefield. The motives of Lady
Grey, later Edward IV's Queen Elizabeth, are more ob-
scure. In II.2, she finds herself in the same situation as the
young Margaret did at the end of *I Henry VI*, when circumstances propelled her to the throne. Elizabeth, like
Margaret, is an ambitious female struggling to advance
herself in situations controlled by powerful males. But
whether either woman uses her sexuality to angle for marriage with a king or merely watches out for herself is hard
to say. Henry's choice of Margaret and Edward's choice of
Elizabeth lead their husbands into political trouble, and
Elizabeth's response, to seek protection, accords better
with conventional notions of how women should behave
than Margaret's increasing belligerence. Yet both women
evoke pity and fear. Margaret, like the other ruthless warriors in *3 Henry VI*, laughs at the death of her enemy's
children and suffers when her child suffers. Both Margaret and Elizabeth fix their hopes on their young sons,
both named Prince Edward. At the end of the play, Margaret's Edward is dead and Elizabeth's is still alive. But

Richard of Gloucester lives, too, and the audience has already seen him planning more dynastic butchery.

Because the plays in the Henry VI sequence, including *Richard III*, are closely related and seem to have been written at about the same time, they are known as Shakespeare's first "tetralogy," or four-play series. Although each of these plays is a full-length drama, the later ones continue several of the story lines begun earlier. Their action stretches from the funeral of Henry V in 1422 to the defeat of Richard III in 1485, but they may never have been staged as a continuous series until the twentieth century. Scholars have disagreed about the order in which Shakespeare wrote the plays, some arguing that *1 Henry VI* was drafted after *2 Henry VI* and *3 Henry VI* to provide an introduction. No matter how the Henry VI series was composed or first presented, however, the epilogue to Shakespeare's *Henry V* suggests the playwright's confidence that his audience knew all three plays and thought of them as a sequence:

> Henry the Sixth, in infant bands crowned king
>   Of France and England, did this king succeed;
> Whose state so many had the managing
>   That they lost France, and made his England
>   bleed:
> Which oft our stage hath shown.
>   (*Henry V,* Epilogue, 9-13)

Some students of the plays have also wondered whether Shakespeare wrote everything in the first tetralogy, a difficult question in the Tudor-Stuart period, when playwrights routinely collaborated and rewrote one another's work, much as screenwriters do today. Taken as a whole, however, the three Henry VI plays plus *Richard III* present a developing dramatic picture of England's political fortunes during the Wars of the Roses. (The plays of the second tetralogy, *Richard II, 1 Henry IV, 2 Henry IV,* and

Henry V, concern an earlier period, 1399-1420, and are not so closely connected as the first four.)

Although Shakespeare derives the events of *3 Henry VI* largely from the chronicle histories of Edward Hall (1548) and Raphael Holinshed (1587), many of the details are invented. Such mingling of fact and fiction is typical of Shakespeare's method in the English history plays, as he converts his narrative sources into drama. Shakespeare was one of the most important Elizabethan authors of such plays. Some scholars even consider him the first dramatist to use English history to comment on his own era. Yet his works violate most modern ideas of how history should be written. These dramas mingle source material, what we might think of as fact, with material created by the author, or fiction. It seems clear, however, that Elizabethan scholars, writers, and audiences did not look at history the way we do. The chroniclers Hall and Holinshed, for example, gathered their narratives of medieval English history not from primary documents or eyewitness accounts, but from earlier chronicles and literary stories. For the Tudors, the purpose of retelling the history of the period from Richard II to Richard III was not so much to achieve a scientific re-creation of events as to point out morals and cautionary tales. The example of a king such as Henry VI, later perceived as a failure, could help the Elizabethans avoid calamities like the Wars of the Roses. Whether the motives and actions attributed to Henry and his nobles were matters of fact or merely possible explanations seems to have mattered less than the need to avoid behaviors that might lead to similar disasters. Perhaps Henry V was in reality not the consummate warrior-politician that Shakespeare sketches at the start of the first tetralogy, and perhaps society did not really fail Henry VI in the ways shown in these plays. Nevertheless, an Elizabethan might have replied, it could have happened this way, and our era needs to understand and avoid such situations. As William Baldwin put it in

A Mirror for Magistrates (1559), "where the ambitious seek no office, there no doubt offices are duly minist'red; and where offices are duly minist'red, it cannot be chosen but the people are good, whereof must needs follow a good commonweal. For if the officers be good, the people cannot be ill. Thus the goodness or badness of any realm lieth in the goodness or badness of the rulers."

By most measures, the language of the Henry VI plays is stately and formal. The editors of the Oxford Shakespeare have devised what they call a "colloquialism-in-verse" index, charting contractions and other abbreviated linguistic forms, and find these plays to be among the least colloquial Shakespearean dramas. While much sixteenth-century language sounds ornate to the modern ear, comparison of the Henry VI plays to the body of Shakespeare's work shows that the dialogue of this series observes the conventions of formal oratory more than many of his other dramas. The characters speak in balanced, largely end-stopped lines, as when Henry stands and muses on the combatants before him:

> This battle fares like to the morning's war,
>   When dying clouds contend with growing light,
> What time the shepherd, blowing of his nails,
>   Can neither call it perfect day nor night.
> Now sways it this way like a mighty sea
>   Forced by the tide to combat with the wind,
> Now sways it that way like the selfsame sea
>   Forced to retire by fury of the wind.
>
> (II.5.1-8)

In elaborate rhetorical similes, Henry compares the civil war to the struggle of night with day and the contention of sea and wind. Pauses in thought occur at the ends of lines, which also use rhyme and repetition to enhance the impression that the king is creating an artifact in his mind, setting up an orderly construct to oppose the chaos of battle. His own image of "the shepherd, blowing of his nails" then leads Henry to envision himself as a "homely swain," happily filling up his days with pastoral duties:

> So many hours must I tend my flock,
> So many hours must I take my rest,
> So many hours must I contemplate,
> So many hours must I sport myself,
> So many days my ewes have been with young,
> So many weeks ere the poor fools will ean,
> So many years ere I shall shear the fleece.
> So minutes, hours, days, weeks, months, and years,
> Passed over to the end they were created,
> Would bring white hairs unto a quiet grave.
>   (31–40)

If being king had been like this – predictable and peaceful – Henry might have served with joy. The echoing figures of formal rhetoric, particularly *anaphora,* or repeated words at the beginnings of clauses, help create a sound picture of the soothing routine that Henry longs for.

Of course, Henry's kingship has not resembled his pastoral daydream, nor, the play implies, could a king ever be merely the shepherd of his people. Authority rests on military power, and a medieval king's power resides in the strength and loyalty of his barons. Henry's warrior father, Henry V, turned power outward to create an empire in France. In the leadership void of his son's regime, however, power turned inward and devoured civil peace. Shakespeare uses the unfortunate reign of Henry VI, whose failure was the fault of many, to explore the dangers of a weak monarchy. He also examines, in his portraits of the Yorks, the kind of mad ambition that leads to tyranny. A monarchical nation must somehow avoid both types, but the only hope offered in *3 Henry VI* seems, like Henry himself, to rely on fate. Those who know their history know the king is right when he predicts that the young

Earl of Richmond will one day provide England with a more stable monarchy:

> This pretty lad will prove our country's bliss.
> His looks are full of peaceful majesty,
> His head by nature framed to wear a crown,
> His hand to wield a scepter, and himself
> Likely in time to bless a regal throne.
> Make much of him, my lords, for this is he
> Must help you more than you are hurt by me.
> (IV.7.70-76)

At the end of *Richard III,* Richmond will finally end the Wars of the Roses by killing Richard and assuming the throne as Henry VII.

3 Henry VI takes prophecy seriously, as do most of Shakespeare's plays. But the role of fate in this political drama is anything but simple. Pious Henry expresses orthodox resignation as he watches the battle fought in his name: "To whom God will, there be the victory" (II.5.15). Yet as the play shows, Henry's passivity provokes and intensifies the civil wars. The self-reliance of the Yorks, on the other hand, does not make them immune to fate, as Richard acknowledges:

> The midwife wondered and the women cried,
> "O, Jesus bless us, he is born with teeth!"–
> And so I was, which plainly signified
> That I should snarl and bite and play the dog.
> (V.6.74-77)

Richard both admits and challenges Henry's prophecies, as he also challenges heaven, stabbing the dead king's body and cursing his soul: "Down, down to hell, and say I sent thee thither" (67). Henry's mere acceptance of divine will leads to inertia, while Richard's defiance leads to savagery.

If the play endorses any attitude toward fate, it may be

that of Somerset, who believes Henry's predictions for Richmond, but does not therefore abandon the young earl to his destiny:

> As Henry's late presaging prophecy
> Did glad my heart with hope of this young Richmond,
> So doth my heart misgive me, in these conflicts,
> What may befall him, to his harm and ours.
> Therefore, Lord Oxford, to prevent the worst,
> Forthwith we'll send him hence to Brittany,
> Till storms be past of civil enmity.
>
> (IV.7.92-98)

Henry knows that God's purposes will be fulfilled, but refuses to serve as their active instrument. Richard thinks that God's purposes will be fulfilled, but refuses to submit. Somerset and Oxford, more prudent than either Lancaster or York, manage to resolve the paradox of fate by walking a middle way. They assume that God's will must be done, but do not presume that they know what it is or how it is to be executed.

JANIS LULL
University of Alaska Fairbanks

The Third Part of Henry the Sixth
GENEALOGICAL CHART

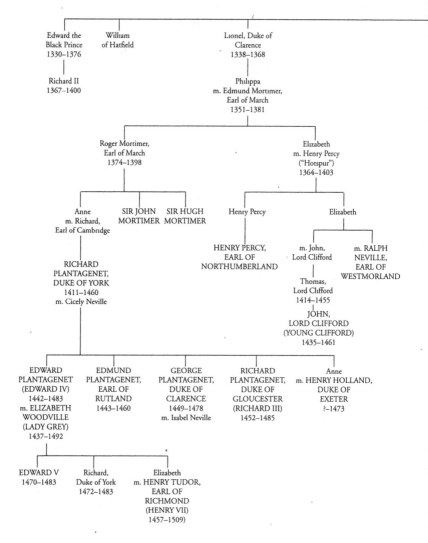

Names of characters in the play appear in capitals.
Many persons not significant to *3 Henry VI* are omitted.

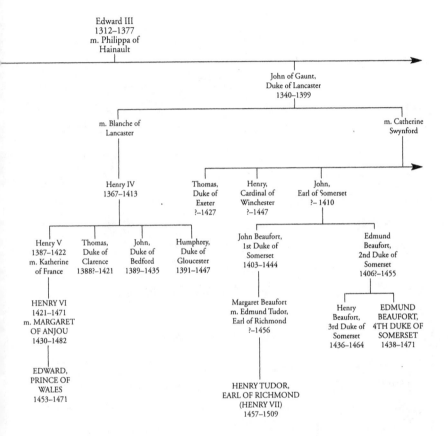

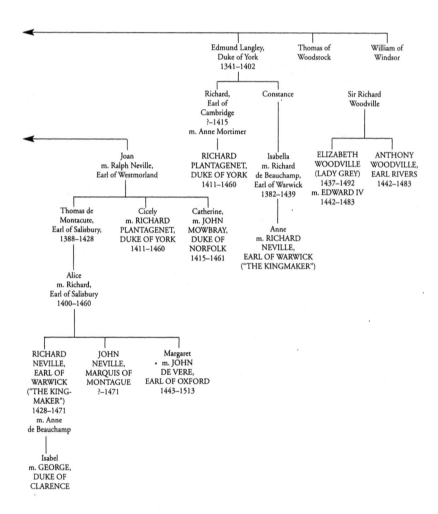

Note on the Text

TWO VERSIONS of this play survive. The first to be published, in octavo format (O, 1595), though undeniably corrupt, appears to derive from a revised, post-performance version of the play later than that included in the First Folio collection (F, 1623), which seems to have been set from a slightly damaged, pre-performance, authorial early draft.

The control text for this new Pelican edition is F, though I do take account of what I believe to be the revisions represented by O where I believe these reflect what happened onstage and where reconstruction seems practically possible.

While this edition uses the traditional folio title for this play, there are powerful arguments for preferring a form of the O title, *The True Tragedy of Richard Duke of York*. The O title is what was used when the text was (piratically) published only a few years after the play's initial performances and so was probably the title by which it was contemporarily known to the playgoing, book-buying public. Moreover, the authority of the F title is undermined because the editor of that volume seems to have regularized the titles of the history plays to conform with his organizational principle, which was that these plays be grouped together, arranged in their historical order, and clearly named after the monarchs whose reigns they cover.

This edition silently regularizes speech prefixes, expands stage directions where this appears necessary, and modernizes all spelling and punctuation. Act divisions are more or less traditional, while scene divisions are made on the basis of a stage cleared of all characters. All substantive departures from the control text apart from these exceptions are recorded below.

The adopted reading is in italics, followed by the F reading in roman.

I.1 19 *hap* hope   69 *EXETER* Westm   78 *mine* my   83 *and that's* that's   105 *Thy* My   120–24 *NORTHUMBERLAND . . . king* – Henry. Peace thou, and giue King Henry leaue to / speake. Warw. Plantagenet shal speake first: Heare him Lords, / And be you silent and attentiue too, / For he that interrupts him, shall not liue.   121 *York* Plantagenet   122 *both* both both   171 *me* (not in F)   197 *thine* an   200 *nor* neyther   255 *the utter ruin* vtter ruine   260 *with* (not in F)   262 *from* to   269 *coast* cost
I.2 40 *to Edmund Brook* vnto my   72 *uncles* Vnckle
I.4 51 *buckle* buckler   82 *thy* the   151 *passions move* passions moues
II.1 113 *And . . . thought,* (not in F)   127 *captains* Captiues   131 *an idle* a lazie   144 *his* the
II.2 92 *our brother out* out me   133 *RICHARD* War.   172 *deniest* denied'st
II.5 38 *weeks* (not in F)   119 *E'en* Men
II.6 6 *commixture* Commixtures   8 *The . . . flies,* (not in F)   42 *EDWARD DUKE OF YORK* Rich.   43 *RICHARD A* A   44 *EDWARD . . . See* See; *And* Ed. And   60 *his* is   80 *buy but* buy
III.1 17 *wast* was   24 *adversity* Aduesaries   30 *Is* I: 55 *thou that* thou   96 *in the.* the
III.2 3 *lands* Land   28 *whip me then* then whip me   30 *an* if   32 *them then*   119 *as* your   123 *honorably* honourable
III.3 11 *state* Seat   124 *eternal* externall   156 *Warwick, peace* Warwicke   228 *I'll* I
IV.1 17 *you* (not in F)   28 *my* mine   91 *thy* the   133 *near'st* neere
IV.2 2 *sort* people   12 *come* welcome   15 *towns* Towne
IV.6 4 *stands* stand   8 *Comes* Come
IV.7 11 *prisonment* imprisonment   55 *be confiscate* confiscate
IV.8 71 *MONTGOMERY* Soul.   72 *Ireland* – Ireland, &c.   73 *And* Mount. And
IV.9 12 *stir* stirre vp
V.1 75 *an* if   78 *an* in   80–83 *GEORGE . . . WARWICK* (not in F)   94 *Jephthah* Iephah   102 *brothers* Brother
V.4 35 *York* (not in F)
V.5 49 *The* (not in F)   76–77 *butcher . . . Richard?* butcher Richard?
V.6 46 *tempests* Tempest   80 *I had . . . like no father;* (not in F)   90–91 *Henry . . . the rest,* King Henry, and the Prince his Son are gone, / Clarence thy turne is next, and then the rest
V.7 5 *renowned* Renowne   21 *an* if   25 *and* an earlier state of F reads "add"; *thou* that   27 *kiss* an earlier state of F reads "'tis"   30 *QUEEN ELIZABETH* Cla.; *Thanks* Thanke   42 *rests* an earlier state of F reads "tests"

The Third Part of
Henry the Sixth

NAMES OF THE ACTORS

The House of Lancaster and its supporters:
KING HENRY THE SIXTH, *Duke of Lancaster*
QUEEN MARGARET
PRINCE EDWARD, *their only son*
Edmund Beaufort, DUKE OF SOMERSET
Henry Tudor, the young Earl of Richmond, his nephew
  (nonspeaking)
Henry Holland, DUKE OF EXETER, *brother-in-law to*
  Edward Duke of York
Henry Percy, EARL OF NORTHUMBERLAND
John, LORD CLIFFORD, *"Young Clifford" in*
  2 Henry VI
Humphrey, Lord Stafford (nonspeaking)
SOMERVILLE
A LANCASTRIAN SOLDIER *who has killed his father*
A HUNTSMAN *who guards King Edward*

The divided House of Neville:
Richard Neville, EARL OF WARWICK *("Kingmaker"),*
  nephew of Richard Duke of York; he initially
  supports York, and later Lancaster
John Neville, MARQUIS OF MONTAGUE, *Richard's*
  brother, a nephew and a supporter of York
Ralph Neville, EARL OF WESTMORLAND, *first cousin to*
  Richard and John, and a supporter of Lancaster
John de Vere, EARL OF OXFORD, *Richard and John's*
  brother-in-law, a supporter of Lancaster
William, LORD HASTINGS, *Richard and John's*
  brother-in-law, a supporter of York

The House of York and its supporters:

RICHARD PLANTAGENET, DUKE OF YORK

EDWARD PLANTAGENET, *Earl of March, his eldest son,*
later DUKE OF YORK, *and later still* KING EDWARD
THE FOURTH

ELIZABETH WOODVILLE, LADY GREY, *a widow, later*
Edward's wife, QUEEN ELIZABETH

Anthony Woodville, EARL RIVERS, *her brother*

GEORGE PLANTAGENET, *Edward's brother, later*
DUKE OF CLARENCE

RICHARD PLANTAGENET, *Edward's brother, later*
DUKE OF GLOUCESTER, *and later still King Richard*
the Third

EDMUND PLANTAGENET, EARL OF RUTLAND,
Edward's brother

Rutland's TUTOR, *a chaplain*

SIR JOHN MORTIMER, *Richard Duke of York's uncle*

Sir Hugh Mortimer, Sir John's brother, and so also
Richard Duke of York's uncle (nonspeaking)

John Mowbray, DUKE OF NORFOLK

Sir William Stanley (nonspeaking)

William Herbert, Earl of Pembroke (nonspeaking)

SIR JOHN MONTGOMERY

Sir James Harrington, a NOBLEMAN

Two GAMEKEEPERS

Three WATCHMEN

LIEUTENANT OF THE TOWER

The French:

KING LOUIS THE ELEVENTH

LADY BONNE OF SAVOY, *his sister-in-law*

Jean, Lord Bourbon, the French High Admiral,
son-in-law to King Louis (nonspeaking)

Others:

A SOLDIER *who has killed his son*
Mayor of Coventry (nonspeaking)
MAYOR OF YORK
ALDERMEN OF YORK
SOLDIERS, MESSENGERS, AND ATTENDANTS

SCENE: *England and France*
*

The Third Part of Henry the Sixth

∾ **I.1** *A chair of state. Alarum. Enter Richard Planta-genet Duke of York, his two sons Edward Earl of March and Crookback Richard, the Duke of Norfolk, the Marquis of Montague, and the Earl of Warwick, with Drummers and Soldiers. They all wear white roses in their hats.*

WARWICK
  I wonder how the king escaped our hands?
RICHARD DUKE OF YORK
  While we pursued the horsemen of the north,
  He slyly stole away and left his men;
  Whereat the great Lord of Northumberland,
  Whose warlike ears could never brook retreat,   5
  Cheered up the drooping army; and himself,
  Lord Clifford, and Lord Stafford, all abreast,
  Charged our main battle's front, and, breaking in,   8
  Were by the swords of common soldiers slain.   9
EDWARD
  Lord Stafford's father, Duke of Buckingham,   10
  Is either slain or wounded dangerous.   11
  I cleft his beaver with a downright blow.   12

I.1 The Parliament House, London **s.d.** *Alarum* a trumpet call to arms; *Crookback* hunchbacked **5** *brook* endure; *retreat* i.e., the trumpet call signaling retreat **8** *battle's* army's **9** *Were . . . slain* (in *2 Henry VI,* V.2, "Old" Clifford is killed by York) **11** *dangerous* dangerously **12** *beaver* the face piece of the helmet; *downright* downward

That this is true, father, behold his blood.
He shows a bloody sword.
MONTAGUE   *To York*
And, brother, here's the Earl of Wiltshire's blood,
He shows a bloody sword.
Whom I encountered as the battles joined.
RICHARD   *To Somerset's head, which he shows*
Speak thou for me, and tell them what I did.
RICHARD DUKE OF YORK
Richard hath best deserved of all my sons.
To the head
But is your grace dead, my Lord of Somerset?
19   Such hap have all the line of John of Ghent.
RICHARD
20   Thus do I hope to shake King Henry's head.
He holds aloft the head, then throws it down.
WARWICK
And so do I, victorious prince of York.
Before I see thee seated in that throne
Which now the house of Lancaster usurps,
I vow by heaven these eyes shall never close.
25   This is the palace of the fearful king,
And this, *(Pointing to the chair of state)* the regal seat –
    possess it, York,
For this is thine, and not King Henry's heirs'.
RICHARD DUKE OF YORK
Assist me then, sweet Warwick, and I will,
For hither we have broken in by force.
NORFOLK
30   We'll all assist you – he that flies shall die.
RICHARD DUKE OF YORK
31   Thanks, gentle Norfolk. Stay by me, my lords
32   And soldiers – stay, and lodge by me this night.

------

19 *Such . . . Ghent* i.e., may all the descendants of John of Ghent (Gaunt)
look for the same fate (Edmund, second Duke of Somerset, was a grandson
of John of Ghent, Duke of Lancaster; Henry VI was a great-grandson)   25
fearful timid, frightened   31 *gentle* noble   32 **s.d.** *They go up* (the chair of
state, which York occupies, is probably placed on a raised platform)

They go up upon the state.

WARWICK
And when the king comes, offer him no violence
Unless he seek to thrust you out perforce.   34
The Soldiers withdraw.

RICHARD DUKE OF YORK
The queen this day here holds her Parliament,
But little thinks we shall be of her council;
By words or blows here let us win our right.

RICHARD
Armed as we are, let's stay within this house.

WARWICK
"The Bloody Parliament" shall this be called,
Unless Plantagenet, Duke of York, be king,   40
And bashful Henry deposed, whose cowardice
Hath made us bywords to our enemies.   42

RICHARD DUKE OF YORK
Then leave me not, my lords. Be resolute –
I mean to take possession of my right.

WARWICK
Neither the king nor he that loves him best –
The proudest he that holds up Lancaster –   46
Dares stir a wing if Warwick shake his bells.   47
I'll plant Plantagenet, root him up who dares.
Resolve thee, Richard – claim the English crown.   49
Richard Duke of York sits in the chair. Flourish.
Enter King Henry, Lord Clifford, the Earls of
Northumberland and Westmorland, the Duke of
Exeter, and the rest. They all wear red roses in
their hats.

KING HENRY
My lords, look where the sturdy rebel sits –   50

---

34 *perforce* by force   42 *bywords* i.e., objects of scorn   46 *holds up* supports
47 *shake . . . bells* twitches (bells were fastened to the legs of hawks; their
ringing supposedly both increased the falcons' ferocity and further frightened the prey)   49 *Resolve thee* decide firmly; **s.d.** Flourish trumpet fanfare
50 *sturdy* stubborn

51 Even in the chair of state! Belike he means,
   Backed by the power of Warwick, that false peer,
   To aspire unto the crown and reign as king.
   Earl of Northumberland, he slew thy father –
   And thine, Lord Clifford – and you both have vowed
      revenge
   On him, his sons, his favorites, and his friends.

NORTHUMBERLAND
   If I be not, heavens be revenged on me.
58 The hope thereof makes Clifford mourn in steel.

WESTMORLAND
   What, shall we suffer this? Let's pluck him down.
60 My heart for anger burns – I cannot brook it.

KING HENRY
   Be patient, gentle Earl of Westmorland.

CLIFFORD
62 Patience is for poltroons, such as he. *(Indicating York)*
   He durst not sit there had your father lived.
   My gracious lord, here in the Parliament
   Let us assail the family of York.

NORTHUMBERLAND
66 Well hast thou spoken, cousin, be it so.

KING HENRY
67 Ah, know you not the city favors them,
68 And they have troops of soldiers at their beck?

EXETER
   But when the duke is slain, they'll quickly fly.

KING HENRY
70 Far be the thought of this from Henry's heart,
71 To make a shambles of the Parliament House.
   Cousin of Exeter, frowns, words, and threats
   Shall be the war that Henry means to use.
      To York
74 Thou factious Duke of York, descend my throne

---

51 *Belike* it is likely that   58 *steel* armor   62 *poltroons* cowards   66 *cousin* kinsman   67 *the city* i.e., London (as distinct from the court)   68 *beck* command   71 *shambles* slaughterhouse   74 *factious* rebellious

And kneel for grace and mercy at my feet.
I am thy sovereign.
RICHARD DUKE OF YORK   I am thine.
EXETER
For shame, come down – he made thee Duke of York.
RICHARD DUKE OF YORK
It was mine inheritance, as the earldom was.   78
EXETER
Thy father was a traitor to the crown.   79
WARWICK
Exeter, thou art a traitor to the crown   80
In following this usurping Henry.
CLIFFORD
Whom should he follow but his natural king?
WARWICK
True, Clifford, and that's Richard Duke of York.
KING HENRY   *To York*
And shall I stand and thou sit in my throne?
RICHARD DUKE OF YORK
It must and shall be so – content thyself.
WARWICK   *To King Henry*
Be Duke of Lancaster, let him be king.
WESTMORLAND
He is both king and Duke of Lancaster –
And that, the Lord of Westmorland shall maintain.
WARWICK
And Warwick shall disprove it. You forget
That we are those which chased you from the field,   90
And slew your fathers, and, with colors spread,   91
Marched through the city to the palace gates.
NORTHUMBERLAND
Yes, Warwick, I remember it to my grief,
And, by his soul, thou and thy house shall rue it.

---

78 *earldom* i.e., the earldom of March (a title inherited by York from his
mother, Anne Mortimer; it was through the Mortimers that he also claimed
the crown) 79 *Thy father . . . crown* (York's father, Richard, Earl of Cambridge, was executed during the reign of Henry V) 91 *colors* flags

WESTMORLAND *To York*
 Plantagenet, of thee, and these thy sons,
 Thy kinsmen, and thy friends, I'll have more lives
 Than drops of blood were in my father's veins.
CLIFFORD *To Warwick*
 Urge it no more, lest that, instead of words,
 I send thee, Warwick, such a messenger
100 As shall revenge his death before I stir.
WARWICK *To York*
 Poor Clifford, how I scorn his worthless threats.
RICHARD DUKE OF YORK *To King Henry*
102 Will you we show our title to the crown?
 If not, our swords shall plead it in the field.
KING HENRY
 What title hast thou, traitor, to the crown?
105 Thy father was, as thou art, Duke of York;
 Thy grandfather, Roger Mortimer, Earl of March.
 I am the son of Henry the Fifth,
 Who made the dauphin and the French to stoop
 And seized upon their towns and provinces.
WARWICK
110 Talk not of France, sith thou hast lost it all.
KING HENRY
111 The Lord Protector lost it, and not I.
 When I was crowned, I was but nine months old.
RICHARD
113 You are old enough now, and yet, methinks, you lose.
  To York
 Father, tear the crown from the usurper's head.
EDWARD *To York*
 Sweet father, do so – set it on your head.
MONTAGUE *To York*
 Good brother, as thou lov'st and honor'st arms,

---

102 *Will you we* do you wish us to 105 *Thy father . . . York* (York actually
inherited his title from his uncle; see ll. 77–79) 110 *sith* since 111 *Lord
Protector* i.e., Humphrey, Duke of Gloucester 113 *yet* even now

Let's fight it out and not stand caviling thus.   117
RICHARD
Sound drums and trumpets, and the king will fly.
RICHARD DUKE OF YORK
    Sons, peace!
NORTHUMBERLAND
Peace, thou – and give King Henry leave to speak.   120
KING HENRY
Ah, York, why seekest thou to depose me?
Are we not both Plantagenets by birth,
And from two brothers lineally descent?
Suppose by right and equity thou be king –
Think'st thou that I will leave my kingly throne,
Wherein my grandsire and my father sat?
No – first shall war unpeople this my realm;
Ay, and their colors, often borne in France,
And now in England to our heart's great sorrow,
Shall be my winding-sheet. Why faint you, lords?   130
My title's good, and better far than his.
WARWICK
Prove it, Henry, and thou shalt be king.
KING HENRY
Henry the Fourth by conquest got the crown.
RICHARD DUKE OF YORK
'Twas by rebellion against his king.   134
KING HENRY   *Aside*
I know not what to say – my title's weak.
    To York
Tell me, may not a king adopt an heir?
RICHARD DUKE OF YORK
    What then?
KING HENRY
An if he may, then am I lawful king –   138
For Richard, in the view of many lords,
Resigned the crown to Henry the Fourth,   *140*

───────

117 *caviling* quibbling frivolously 120 *leave* permission 130 *winding-sheet* shroud; *faint* lose heart 134 *king* i.e., Richard II 138 *An if* if

Whose heir my father was, and I am his.

RICHARD DUKE OF YORK

142   He rose against him, being his sovereign,
And made him to resign his crown perforce.

WARWICK

Suppose, my lords, he did it unconstrained –

145   Think you 'twere prejudicial to his crown?

EXETER

No, for he could not so resign his crown

147   But that the next heir should succeed and reign.

KING HENRY

Art thou against us, Duke of Exeter?

EXETER

149   His is the right, and therefore pardon me.

RICHARD DUKE OF YORK

150   Why whisper you, my lords, and answer not?

EXETER   *To King Henry*

My conscience tells me he is lawful king.

KING HENRY   *Aside*

All will revolt from me and turn to him.

NORTHUMBERLAND   *To York*

Plantagenet, for all the claim thou lay'st,
Think not that Henry shall be so deposed.

WARWICK

155   Deposed he shall be, in despite of all.

NORTHUMBERLAND

Thou art deceived – 'tis not thy southern power
Of Essex, Norfolk, Suffolk, nor of Kent,
Which makes thee thus presumptuous and proud,

159   Can set the duke up in despite of me.

CLIFFORD

160   King Henry, be thy title right or wrong,
Lord Clifford vows to fight in thy defense.
May that ground gape and swallow me alive

---

142 *him* i.e., Richard II; *being* who was   145 *his crown* his claim to the
crown   147 *But* without ensuring   149 *His* i.e., York's   155 *despite* spite
159 *set the duke up* i.e, as king

Where I shall kneel to him that slew my father.
KING HENRY
O, Clifford, how thy words revive my heart!
RICHARD DUKE OF YORK
Henry of Lancaster, resign thy crown.
What mutter you, or what conspire you, lords?
WARWICK
Do right unto this princely Duke of York,
Or I will fill the house with armèd men
And over the chair of state, where now he sits,
Write up his title with usurping blood.   170
He stamps with his foot, and the Soldiers show
themselves.
KING HENRY
My Lord of Warwick, hear me but one word –
Let me for this my lifetime reign as king.
RICHARD DUKE OF YORK
Confirm the crown to me and to mine heirs,
And thou shalt reign in quiet while thou liv'st.
KING HENRY
I am content. Richard Plantagenet,
Enjoy the kingdom after my decease.
CLIFFORD
What wrong is this unto the prince your son?
WARWICK
What good is this to England and himself?
WESTMORLAND
Base, fearful, and despairing Henry.
CLIFFORD
How hast thou injured both thyself and us?   *180*
WESTMORLAND
I cannot stay to hear these articles.   181
NORTHUMBERLAND
Nor I.

---

170 *usurping blood* i.e., King Henry's   **181** *articles* clauses in a legal document (i.e., further details of the agreement)

CLIFFORD
  Come, cousin, let us tell the queen these news.
WESTMORLAND   *To King Henry*
  Farewell, fainthearted and degenerate king,
185 In whose cold blood no spark of honor bides.
                              Exit with his Soldiers.
NORTHUMBERLAND   *To King Henry*
  Be thou a prey unto the house of York,
187 And die in bands for this unmanly deed.
                              Exit with his Soldiers.
CLIFFORD   *To King Henry*
  In dreadful war mayst thou be overcome,
  Or live in peace, abandoned and despised.
                              Exit with his Soldiers.
WARWICK   *To King Henry*
190 Turn this way, Henry, and regard them not.
EXETER   *To King Henry*
  They seek revenge and therefore will not yield.
KING HENRY
  Ah, Exeter.
WARWICK   Why should you sigh, my lord?
KING HENRY
  Not for myself, Lord Warwick, but my son,
  Whom I unnaturally shall disinherit.
195 But be it as it may. *(To York)* I here entail
  The crown to thee and to thine heirs for ever,
  Conditionally, that here thou take thine oath
  To cease this civil war, and whilst I live
  To honor me as thy king and sovereign,
200 And nor by treason nor hostility
  To seek to put me down and reign thyself.
RICHARD DUKE OF YORK
  This oath I willingly take and will perform.
WARWICK
  Long live King Henry. *(To York)* Plantagenet, embrace
  him.

---

185 *bides* resides   **187** *bands* bonds   **195** *entail* bequeath inalienably

Richard Duke of York descends. Henry and York
embrace.

KING HENRY   *To York*

And long live thou, and these thy forward sons.   204

RICHARD DUKE OF YORK

Now York and Lancaster are reconciled.

EXETER

Accursed be he that seeks to make them foes.   206

Sennet. Here Richard Duke of York's train comes down
from the state.

RICHARD DUKE OF YORK   *To King Henry*

Farewell, my gracious lord, I'll to my castle.   207

Exeunt York, Edward, and Richard, with Soldiers.

WARWICK

And I'll keep London with my soldiers.

Exit with Soldiers.

NORFOLK

And I to Norfolk with my followers.

Exit with Soldiers.

MONTAGUE

And I unto the sea from whence I came.   *210*

Exit with Soldiers.

KING HENRY

And I with grief and sorrow to the court.

King Henry and Exeter turn to leave.
Enter Queen Margaret and Prince Edward.

EXETER

Here comes the queen, whose looks bewray her anger.   212

I'll steal away.

KING HENRY   Exeter, so will I.

QUEEN MARGARET

Nay, go not from me – I will follow thee.

KING HENRY

Be patient, gentle queen, and I will stay.

---

204 *forward* spirited   **206** s.d. *Sennet* a trumpet call indicating a ceremonial
entrance or exit   **207** *castle* i.e, Sandal, near Wakefield, in Yorkshire   **212**
bewray expose

QUEEN MARGARET
Who can be patient in such extremes?
Ah, wretched man, would I had died a maid
And never seen thee, never borne thee son,
Seeing thou hast proved so unnatural a father.
220 Hath he deserved to lose his birthright thus?
Hadst thou but loved him half so well as I,
222 Or felt that pain which I did for him once,
Or nourished him as I did with my blood,
Thou wouldst have left thy dearest heartblood there
Rather than have made that savage·duke thine heir
And disinherited thine only son.

PRINCE EDWARD
Father, you cannot disinherit me.
If you be king, why should not I succeed?

KING HENRY
Pardon me, Margaret; pardon me, sweet son –
230 The Earl of Warwick and the duke enforced me.

QUEEN MARGARET
Enforced thee? Art thou king, and wilt be forced?
232 I shame to hear thee speak! Ah, timorous wretch,
Thou hast undone thyself, thy son, and me,
234 And giv'n unto the house of York such head
As thou shalt reign but by their sufferance.
To entail him and his heirs unto the crown –
What is it, but to make thy sepulcher
And creep into it far before thy time?
Warwick is Chancellor and the Lord of Calais;
240 Stern Falconbridge commands the narrow seas;
241 The duke is made Protector of the Realm;
And yet shalt thou be safe? Such safety finds

---

222 *that pain* i.e., the pain of giving birth   232 *shame* am ashamed   234
giv'n . . . head i.e., slackened the horse's reins so as to allow him to move his
head more freely and, hence, to run more rapidly   240 *Stern . . . seas*
(William Neville, Baron Falconbridge and Warwick's uncle, served as Warwick's deputy at Calais in 1459–60, whence he would have commanded the
Straits of Dover – the *narrow seas*)   241 *duke* i.e., Richard, Duke of York

The trembling lamb environèd with wolves.   243
Had I been there, which am a seely woman,   244
The soldiers should have tossed me on their pikes   245
Before I would have granted to that act.   246
But thou preferr'st thy life before thine honor.
And seeing thou dost, I here divorce myself
Both from thy table, Henry, and thy bed,
Until that act of Parliament be repealed   250
Whereby my son is disinherited.
The northern lords that have forsworn thy colors
Will follow mine, if once they see them spread –
And spread they shall be, to thy foul disgrace
And the utter ruin of the house of York.
Thus do I leave thee.
    To Prince Edward
                        Come, son, let's away.
Our army is ready – come, we'll after them.

KING HENRY
    Stay, gentle Margaret, and hear me speak.

QUEEN MARGARET
    Thou hast spoke too much already.
        To Prince Edward
                        Get thee gone.

KING HENRY
    Gentle son Edward, thou wilt stay with me?   260

QUEEN MARGARET
    Ay, to be murdered by his enemies.

PRINCE EDWARD   *To King Henry*
    When I return with victory from the field,
    I'll see your grace. Till then, I'll follow her.

QUEEN MARGARET
    Come, son, away – we may not linger thus.
                        Exit with Prince Edward.

---

243 *environèd* surrounded   244 *seely* helpless   245 *pikes* axlike weapons
246 *granted* conceded

KING HENRY

Poor queen, how love to me and to her son
Hath made her break out into terms of rage.
Revenged may she be on that hateful duke,
Whose haughty spirit, wingèd with desire,

269 Will coast my crown, and, like an empty eagle,
270 Tire on the flesh of me and of my son.
The loss of those three lords torments my heart.
272 I'll write unto them and entreat them fair.
Come, cousin, you shall be the messenger.

EXETER

274 And I, I hope, shall reconcile them all.

Flourish. Exeunt.

*

∾ **I.2** *Enter Richard, Edward Earl of March, and the
Marquis of Montague.*

RICHARD

1 Brother, though I be youngest give me leave.

EDWARD

No, I can better play the orator.

MONTAGUE

But I have reasons strong and forcible.
Enter Richard Duke of York.

RICHARD DUKE OF YORK

Why, how now, sons and brother – at a strife?
What is your quarrel? How began it first?

EDWARD

No quarrel, but a slight contention.

RICHARD DUKE OF YORK

About what?

RICHARD

About that which concerns your grace and us –

---

269 *coast* approach with hostility, attack, assail; *empty* hungry   **270** *Tire* feed
greedily   **272** *fair* courteously   **274 s.d.** *Flourish* a trumpet fanfare
   I.2 York's castle, Sandal (in Yorkshire)   **1** *give me leave* allow me (to
speak)

The crown of England, father, which is yours.
RICHARD DUKE OF YORK
Mine, boy? Not till King Henry be dead.   *10*
RICHARD
Your right depends not on his life or death.
EDWARD
Now you are heir – therefore enjoy it now.
By giving the house of Lancaster leave to breathe, *13*
It will outrun you, father, in the end.
RICHARD DUKE OF YORK
I took an oath that he should quietly reign.
EDWARD
But for a kingdom any oath may be broken.
I would break a thousand oaths to reign one year.
RICHARD   *To York*
No – God forbid your grace should be forsworn.
RICHARD DUKE OF YORK
I shall be if I claim by open war.
RICHARD
I'll prove the contrary, if you'll hear me speak.   *20*
RICHARD DUKE OF YORK
Thou canst not, son – it is impossible.
RICHARD
An oath is of no moment being not took   *22*
Before a true and lawful magistrate
That hath authority over him that swears.
Henry had none, but did usurp the place.
Then, seeing 'twas he that made you to depose,   *26*
Your oath, my lord, is vain and frivolous.
Therefore to arms – and, father, do but think
How sweet a thing it is to wear a crown,
Within whose circuit is Elysium   *30*
And all that poets feign of bliss and joy.   *31*
Why do we linger thus? I cannot rest
Until the white rose that I wear be dyed

---

13 *leave to breathe* i.e., a respite   **22** *moment* importance   **26** *depose* swear
30 *circuit* circumference; *Elysium* classical paradise   **31** *feign* imagine

Even in the lukewarm blood of Henry's heart.

RICHARD DUKE OF YORK

Richard, enough! I will be king or die.

To Montague

36 Brother, thou shalt to London presently
And whet on Warwick to this enterprise.
Thou, Richard, shalt to the Duke of Norfolk
39 And tell him privily of our intent.
40 You, Edward, shall to Edmund Brook, Lord Cobham,
41 With whom the Kentishmen will willingly rise.
In them I trust, for they are soldiers
Witty, courteous, liberal, full of spirit.
44 While you are thus employed, what resteth more
But that I seek occasion how to rise,
46 And yet the king not privy to my drift,
Nor any of the house of Lancaster.

Enter a Messenger.

48 But stay, what news? Why com'st thou in such post?

MESSENGER

The queen, with all the northern earls and lords,
50 Intend here to besiege you in your castle.
She is hard by with twenty thousand men,
52 And therefore fortify your hold, my lord.

RICHARD DUKE OF YORK

Ay, with my sword. What – think'st thou that we fear
them?
Edward and Richard, you shall stay with me;
My brother Montague shall post to London.
Let noble Warwick, Cobham, and the rest,
Whom we have left protectors of the king,
58 With powerful policy strengthen themselves,
And trust not simple Henry nor his oaths.

MONTAGUE

60 Brother, I go – I'll win them, fear it not.

---

36 *presently* immediately   39 *privily* secretly   41 *rise* (in rebellion)   44
what resteth more what else remains   46 *privy to* aware of; *drift* intentions
48 *post* haste   52 *hold* stronghold   58 *policy* stratagem

And thus most humbly I do take my leave.   *Exit.*
   Enter Sir John Mortimer and his brother Sir Hugh.
RICHARD DUKE OF YORK
  Sir John and Sir Hugh Mortimer, mine uncles,
  You are come to Sandal in a happy hour.   63
  The army of the queen mean to besiege us.
SIR JOHN
  She shall not need, we'll meet her in the field.
RICHARD DUKE OF YORK
  What, with five thousand men?
RICHARD
  Ay, with five hundred, father, for a need.   67
  A woman's general – what should we fear?   68
   A march sounds afar off.
EDWARD
  I hear their drums. Let's set our men in order,
  And issue forth and bid them battle straight.   70
RICHARD DUKE OF YORK   *To Sir John and Sir Hugh*
  Five men to twenty – though the odds be great,
  I doubt not, uncles, of our victory.
  Many a battle have I won in France
  Whenas the enemy hath been ten to one –   74
  Why should I not now have the like success?   *Exeunt.*
             *

∾ **I.3** *Alarums, and then enter the young Earl of*
   Rutland and his Tutor, a chaplain.

RUTLAND
  Ah, whither shall I fly to scape their hands?   1
   Enter Lord Clifford with Soldiers.
  Ah, tutor, look where bloody Clifford comes.

---

63 *happy* fortunate   67 *for a need* if necessary   68 s.d. *A march* drumbeats
70 *straight* immediately   74 *Whenas* when
   I.3 A battlefield between Sandal and Wakefield **s.d.** *young Earl* (though
historically the second eldest of York's four sons, Edmund, Earl of Rutland, is
treated in this play as if he were the youngest – only a boy, really – thereby
emphasizing the horror of his murder)   1 *scape* escape

CLIFFORD   *To the Tutor*
    Chaplain, away – thy priesthood saves thy life.
    As for the brat of this accursèd duke,
    Whose father slew my father – he shall die.

TUTOR
    And I, my lord, will bear him company.

CLIFFORD
    Soldiers, away with him.

TUTOR
    Ah, Clifford, murder not this innocent child
9   Lest thou be hated both of God and man.

                                 Exit, guarded.

     Rutland falls to the ground.

CLIFFORD
10   How now – is he dead already?
    Or is it fear that makes him close his eyes?
    I'll open them.

RUTLAND   *Reviving*
13   So looks the pent-up lion o'er the wretch
    That trembles under his devouring paws,
15   And so he walks, insulting o'er his prey,
    And so he comes to rend his limbs asunder.
    Ah, gentle Clifford, kill me with thy sword
    And not with such a cruel threat'ning look.
    Sweet Clifford, hear me speak before I die.
20   I am too mean a subject for thy wrath.
    Be thou revenged on men, and let me live.

CLIFFORD
    In vain thou speak'st, poor boy. My father's blood
    Hath stopped the passage where thy words should
      enter.

RUTLAND
    Then let my father's blood open it again.
25   He is a man, and, Clifford, cope with him.

---

9 *of* by   13 *pent-up* caged, hence fierce   15 *insulting* exulting   20 *mean* lowly   25 *cope* fight

CLIFFORD
  Had I thy brethren here, their lives and thine
  Were not revenge sufficient for me.
  No – if I digged up thy forefathers' graves,
  And hung their rotten coffins up in chains,
  It could not slake mine ire nor ease my heart.   30
  The sight of any of the house of York
  ˙Is as a fury to torment my soul.
  And till I root out their accursèd line,
  And leave not one alive, I live in hell.
  Therefore –
RUTLAND
  O, let me pray before I take my death.
    Kneeling
  To thee I pray: sweet Clifford, pity me.
CLIFFORD
  Such pity as my rapier's point affords.
RUTLAND
  I never did thee harm – why wilt thou slay me?
CLIFFORD
  Thy father hath.   40
RUTLAND   But 'twas ere I was born.
  Thou hast one son – for his sake pity me,
  Lest in revenge thereof, sith God is just,   42
  He be as miserably slain as I.
  Ah, let me live in prison all my days,
  And when I give occasion of offense,
  Then let me die, for now thou hast no cause.
CLIFFORD
  No cause? Thy father slew my father, therefore die.
    He stabs him.
RUTLAND
  Dii faciant laudis summa sit ista tuae.   48
    He dies.

---

30 *slake* lessen **42** *sith* since **48** *Dii . . . tuae* may the gods grant that this
be the height of your fame (Ovid, *Heroides,* 2:66)

CLIFFORD
    Plantagenet – I come, Plantagenet!
50   And this thy son's blood cleaving to my blade
    Shall rust upon my weapon till thy blood,
52   Congealed with this, do make me wipe off both.
              Exit with Rutland's body and Soldiers.

                        *

∾ **I.4** *Alarum. Enter Richard Duke of York.*

RICHARD DUKE OF YORK
1   The army of the queen hath got the field;
2   My uncles both are slain in rescuing me;
    And all my followers to the eager foe
4   Turn back, and fly like ships before the wind,
    Or lambs pursued by hunger-starvèd wolves.
6   My sons – God knows what hath bechancèd them.
7   But this I know – they have demeaned themselves
    Like men born to renown by life or death.·
    Three times did Richard make a lane to me,
10   And thrice cried, "Courage, father, fight it out!"
    And full as oft came Edward to my side,
12   With purple falchion painted to the hilt
    In blood of those that had encountered him.
    And when the hardiest warriors did retire,
    Richard cried, "Charge and give no foot of ground!"
16   [   ]
    And cried, "A crown or else a glorious tomb!
    A scepter or an earthly sepulcher!"

---

52 s.d. *and Soldiers* (It is possible, however, that all attendants left the stage
with the tutor at l. 9 s.d. Whether they did or not is important, for upon it
depends whether Clifford's murder of young Rutland was witnessed [and so
responded, mutely, to] by anyone other than the audience.)
    I.4 The battlefield **1** *got* won **2** *My uncles* Sir John and Sir Hugh Mor-
timer **4** *Turn back* i.e., turn their backs **6** *bechancèd* happened to **7** *de-*
meaned themselves i.e., behaved **12** *falchion* curved broadsword **16** [   ]
(a line is probably missing here, one in which Edward, like his brother
Richard, is described as having cried out encouragement to York's forces)

With this, we charged again – but out, alas –
We bodged again, as I have seen a swan   20
With bootless labor swim against the tide   21
And spend her strength with overmatching waves.   22
   A short alarum within.
Ah, hark – the fatal followers do pursue,
And I am faint and cannot fly their fury;
And were I strong, I would not shun their fury.
The sands are numbered that makes up my life.   26
Here must I stay, and here my life must end.
   Enter Queen Margaret, Lord Clifford, the Earl of
   Northumberland, and the young Prince Edward,
   with Soldiers.
Come, bloody Clifford, rough Northumberland –
I dare your quenchless fury to more rage!
I am your butt, and I abide your shot.   30
NORTHUMBERLAND
   Yield to our mercy, proud Plantagenet.
CLIFFORD
   Ay, to such mercy as his ruthless arm,
   With downright payment, showed unto my father.   33
   Now Phaëthon hath tumbled from his car,   34
   And made an evening at the noontide prick.   35
RICHARD DUKE OF YORK
   My ashes, as the phoenix, may bring forth   36
   A bird that will revenge upon you all,   37
   And in that hope I throw mine eyes to heaven,
   Scorning whate'er you can afflict me with.
   Why come you not? What – multitudes, and fear?   40

---

20 *bodged* botched, screwed up 21 *bootless* fruitless 22 *with* against; *over-matching* more powerful 26 *sands* i.e., in the hourglass 30 *butt* target for archery 33 *downright payment* i.e., vertical blow (York killed Clifford's father in *2 Henry VI*, V.3.27 s.d.) 34 *Phaëthon* the son of Apollo, who took his father's sun chariot and, unable to manage it, was dashed to pieces (a conventional symbol of presumption, appropriate here because the sun was a Yorkist device) 35 *noontide prick* mark on a sundial indicating noon 36 *phoenix* miraculous bird that died through spontaneous combustion and rose again from its own ashes 37 *bird* child

CLIFFORD
> So cowards fight when they can fly no further;
> So doves do peck the falcon's piercing talons;
> So desperate thieves, all hopeless of their lives,
> Breathe out invectives 'gainst the officers.

RICHARD DUKE OF YORK
> O, Clifford, but bethink thee once again,
46 And in thy thought o'errun my former time,
> And, if thou canst for blushing, view this face
> And bite thy tongue, that slanders him with cowardice
> Whose frown hath made thee faint and fly ere this.

CLIFFORD
50 I will not bandy with thee word for word,
51 But buckle with thee blows twice two for one.
> *He draws his sword.*

QUEEN MARGARET
> Hold, valiant Clifford: for a thousand causes
> I would prolong a while the traitor's life.
> Wrath makes him deaf – speak thou, Northumberland.

NORTHUMBERLAND
> Hold, Clifford – do not honor him so much
> To prick thy finger though to wound his heart.
57 What valor were it when a cur doth grin
> For one to thrust his hand between his teeth
59 When he might spurn him with his foot away?
60 It is war's prize to take all vantages,
61 And ten to one is no impeach of valor.
> *They fight and take York.*

CLIFFORD
62 Ay, ay, so strives the woodcock with the gin.

NORTHUMBERLAND
63 So doth the cony struggle in the net.

---

46 *o'errun* review   50 *bandy* exchange   51 *buckle* grapple, engage   57 *grin* snarl   59 *spurn* kick   60 *prize* reward; *vantages* opportunities   61 *is no impeach of* does not call into question (our)   62 *woodcock* (proverbially stupid, as was the *cony,* l. 63); *gin* engine, trap   63 *cony* rabbit

RICHARD DUKE OF YORK
     So triumph thieves upon their conquered booty,
     So true men yield, with robbers so o'ermatched.   65
NORTHUMBERLAND   *To the Queen*
     What would your grace have done unto him now?
QUEEN MARGARET
     Brave warriors, Clifford and Northumberland,
     Come make him stand upon this molehill here,   68
     That wrought at mountains with outstretchèd arms   69
     Yet parted but the shadow with his hand.   70
          To York
     What – was it you that would be England's king?
     Was't you that reveled in our Parliament,   72
     And made a preachment of your high descent?   73
     Where are your mess of sons to back you now?   74
     The wanton Edward and the lusty George?
     And where's that valiant crookback prodigy,   76
     Dickie, your boy, that with his grumbling voice
     Was wont to cheer his dad in mutinies?   78
     Or with the rest where is your darling Rutland?
     Look, York, I stained this napkin with the blood   80
     That valiant Clifford with his rapier's point
     Made issue from the bosom of thy boy.
     And if thine eyes can water for his death,
     I give thee this to dry thy cheeks withal.   ·84
     Alas, poor York, but that I hate thee deadly
     I should lament thy miserable state.
     I prithee, grieve, to make me merry, York.
     What – hath thy fiery heart so parched thine entrails
     That not a tear can fall for Rutland's death?
     Why art thou patient, man? Thou shouldst be mad,   *90*
     And I, to make thee mad, do mock thee thus.

---

65 *true* honest   68 *stand . . . here* (with allusion to the "king of the molehill,"
a term of contempt)   69 *wrought* reached   70 *but* only   72 *reveled* enjoyed
yourself   73 *preachment* sermon   74 *mess of* group of four   76 *prodigy* monster   78 *mutinies* rebellions   80 *napkin* handkerchief   84 *withal* with

Stamp, rave, and fret, that I may sing and dance.
93 Thou wouldst be fee'd, I see, to make me sport.
York cannot speak unless he wear a crown.
     To her Men
A crown for York, and, lords, bow low to him.
Hold you his hands whilst I do set it on.
     She puts a paper crown on York's head.
97 Ay, marry, sir, now looks he like a king,
Ay, this is he that took King Henry's chair,
And this is he was his adopted heir.
100 But how is it that great Plantagenet
Is crowned so soon and broke his solemn oath?
As I bethink me, you should not be king
Till our King Henry had shook hands with death.
104 And will you pale your head in Henry's glory,
And rob his temples of the diadem
Now, in his life, against your holy oath?
O, 'tis a fault too, too, unpardonable.
Off with the crown,
     She knocks it from his head.
                    and with the crown his head,
109 And whilst we breathe, take time to do him dead.
     CLIFFORD
110 That is my office for my father's sake.
     QUEEN MARGARET
111 Nay, stay – let's hear the orisons he makes.
     RICHARD DUKE OF YORK
She-wolf of France, but worse than wolves of France,
Whose tongue more poisons than the adder's tooth –
114 How ill-beseeming is it in thy sex
115 To triumph like an Amazonian trull
116 Upon their woes whom fortune captivates!

---

93 *fee'd* paid   97 *marry* by the Virgin Mary (with weakened force)   104 *pale*
encircle   109 *breathe* rest; *do him dead* kill him   111 *orisons* prayers   114
ill-beseeming inappropriate, unbecoming   115 *Amazonian* (the Amazons,
who figure in classical myth, were a legendary race of female warriors); *trull*
whore   116 *captivates* subdues

But that thy face is visorlike, unchanging,   117
Made impudent with use of evil deeds,
I would essay, proud queen, to make thee blush.   119
To tell thee whence thou cam'st, of whom derived,   *120*
Were shame enough to shame thee – wert thou not
    shameless.
Thy father bears the type of King of Naples,   122
Of both the Sicils, and Jerusalem –   123
Yet not so wealthy as an English yeoman.   124
Hath that poor monarch taught thee to insult?
It needs not, nor it boots thee not, proud queen,   126
Unless the adage must be verified   127
That beggars mounted run their horse to death.
'Tis beauty that doth oft make women proud –
But, God he knows, thy share thereof is small;   *130*
'Tis virtue that doth make them most admired –
The contrary doth make thee wondered at;
'Tis government that makes them seem divine –   133
The want thereof makes thee abominable.
Thou art as opposite to every good
As the antipodes are unto us,   136
Or as the south to the septentrion.   137
O tiger's heart wrapped in a woman's hide!
How couldst thou drain the lifeblood of the child
To bid the father wipe his eyes withal,   *140*
And yet be seen to bear a woman's face?
Women are soft, mild, pitiful, and flexible –   142
Thou stern, obdurate, flinty, rough, remorseless.
Bidd'st thou me rage? Why, now thou hast thy wish.
Wouldst have me weep? Why, now thou hast thy will.

---

117 *But that* were it not that; *visorlike* expressionless, masklike (prostitutes
sometimes wore masks) 119 *essay* try 122 *type* title 123 *both the Sicils*
i.e., Sicily and Naples 124 *yeoman* landowner (below the rank of gentleman) 126 *boots* profits 127 *adage* proverb 133 *government* self-control
136 *antipodes* (1) the other side of the world, (2) those who live there 137
septentrion seven stars of the constellation of the Great Bear (i.e., north)
142 *pitiful* compassionate

For raging wind blows up incessant showers,
147 And when the rage allays the rain begins.
148 These tears are my sweet Rutland's obsequies,
And every drop cries vengeance for his death
150 'Gainst thee, fell Clifford, and thee, false French-
woman.

NORTHUMBERLAND
151 Beshrew me, but his passions move me so
That hardly can I check my eyes from tears.

RICHARD DUKE OF YORK
That face of his the hungry cannibals
Would not have touched, would not have stained with
blood –
But you are more inhuman, more inexorable,
156 O, ten times more than tigers of Hyrcania.
157 See, ruthless queen, a hapless father's tears.
This cloth thou dipped'st in blood of my sweet boy,
And I with tears do wash the blood away.
160 Keep thou the napkin and go boast of this,
161 And if thou tell'st the heavy story right,
Upon my soul the hearers will shed tears,
Yea, even my foes will shed fast-falling tears
And say, "Alas, it was a piteous deed."
There, take the crown – and with the crown, my curse:
And in thy need such comfort come to thee
As now I reap at thy too cruel hand.
Hardhearted Clifford, take me from the world.
My soul to heaven, my blood upon your heads.

NORTHUMBERLAND
170 Had he been slaughterman to all my kin,
I should not, for my life, but weep with him,
172 To see how inly sorrow gripes his soul.

---

147 *allays* diminishes 148 *obsequies* funeral rites 150 *fell* cruel 151
Beshrew curse 156 *Hyrcania* a region of ancient Persia (the reference to the
fierceness of Hyrcanian tigers derives ultimately from the *Aeneid,* 4:366–67)
157 *hapless* luckless 161 *heavy* sorrowful 172 *inly* heartfelt; *gripes* grieves,
afflicts, distresses

QUEEN MARGARET
   What – weeping-ripe, my Lord Northumberland?   173
   Think but upon the wrong he did us all,
   And that will quickly dry thy melting tears.   175
CLIFFORD
   Here's for my oath, here's for my father's death.
      He stabs York.
QUEEN MARGARET
   And here's to right our gentle-hearted king.
      She stabs York.
RICHARD DUKE OF YORK
   Open thy gate of mercy, gracious God –
   My soul flies through these wounds to seek out thee.
      He dies.
QUEEN MARGARET
   Off with his head and set it on York gates,   180
   So York may overlook the town of York.
               Flourish. Exeunt with York's body.
                        *

∾ **II.1** *A march. Enter Edward Earl of March and*
      Richard, with a Drummer and Soldiers.

EDWARD
   I wonder how our princely father scaped,
   Or whether he be scaped away or no .
   From Clifford's and Northumberland's pursuit.
   Had he been ta'en we should have heard the news;
   Had he been slain we should have heard the news;
   Or had he scaped, methinks we should have heard
   The happy tidings of his good escape.
   How fares my brother? Why is he so sad?

---

173 *weeping-ripe* ready for weeping   175 *melting tears* tears arising from a
softened heart
   II.1 Fields in the Marches (the border between Wales and England)

RICHARD

    I cannot joy until I·be resolved

10   Where our right valiant father is become.

    I saw him in the battle range about,

12   And watched him how he singled Clifford forth.

    Methought he bore him in the thickest troop,

14   As doth a lion in a herd of neat;

    Or as a bear encompassed round with dogs,

16   Who having pinched a few and made them cry,

    The rest stand all aloof and bark at him.

    So fared our father with his enemies;

    So fled his enemies my warlike father.

20   Methinks 'tis prize enough to be his son.

       Three suns appear in the air.

    See how the morning opes her golden gates

    And takes her farewell of the glorious sun.

    How well resembles it the prime of youth,

24   Trimmed like a younker prancing to his love!

EDWARD

25   Dazzle mine eyes, or do I see three suns?

RICHARD

    Three glorious suns, each one a perfect sun;

27   Not separated with the racking clouds,

    But severed in a pale clear-shining sky.

       The three suns begin to join.

    See, see – they join, embrace, and seem to kiss,

30   As if they vowed some league inviolable.

    Now are they but one lamp, one light, one sun.

32   In this the heaven figures some event.

EDWARD

    'Tis wondrous strange, the like yet never heard of.

34   I think it cites us, brother, to the field,

---

10 *Where . . . is become* what has happened to . . .   12 *forth* out   14 *neat* cattle   16 *pinched* bitten   20 *prize* privilege   24 *Trimmed* dressed up; *younker* young man   25 *Dazzle mine eyes* do my eyes blur   27 *racking* passing   32 *figures* foretells   34 *cites* urges

That we, the sons of brave Plantagenet,
Each one already blazing by our meeds,   36
Should notwithstanding join our lights together
And overshine the earth as this the world.   38
Whate'er it bodes, henceforward will I bear
Upon my target three fair-shining suns.   40

RICHARD
   Nay, bear three daughters – by your leave I speak it – 41
   You love the breeder better than the male.   42
     Enter onè blowing a horn.
   But what art thou whose heavy looks foretell
   Some dreadful story hanging on thy tongue?

MESSENGER
   Ah, one that was a woeful looker-on
   Whenas the noble Duke of York was slain –   46
   Your princely father and my loving lord.

EDWARD
   O, speak no more, for I have heard too much.

RICHARD
   Say how he died, for I will hear it all.

MESSENGER
   Environèd he was with many foes,   50
   And stood against them as the hope of Troy   51
   Against the Greeks that would have entered Troy.
   But Hercules himself must yield to odds;
   And many strokes, though with a little ax,
   Hews down and fells the hardest-timbered oak.
   By many hands your father was subdued,
   But only slaughtered by the ireful arm
   Of unrelenting Clifford and the queen,
   Who crowned the gracious duke in high despite,   59
   Laughed in his face, and when with grief he wept,   60

---

36 *meeds* merits 38 *this* i.e., this phenomenon 40 *target* shield 41
daughters (with obvious pun on *suns*, l. 40) 42 *breeder* female; **s.d.** *blowing
a horn* (indicating that the messenger is a post rider) 46 *Whenas* when 50
Environèd surrounded 51 *hope of Troy* i.e., Hector 59 *in high despite* with
great contempt

The ruthless queen gave him to dry his cheeks
A napkin steepèd in the harmless blood
Of sweet young Rutland, by rough Clifford slain;
And after many scorns, many foul taunts,
They took his head, and on the gates of York
They set the same; and there it doth remain,
The saddest spectacle that e'er I viewed.

EDWARD

Sweet Duke of York, our prop to lean upon,
69   Now thou art gone, we have no staff, no stay.
70   O Clifford, boist'rous Clifford – thou hast slain
The flower of Europe for his chivalry,
And treacherously hast thou vanquished him –
For hand to hand he would have vanquished thee.
74   Now my soul's palace is become a prison.
75   Ah, would she break from hence that this my body
Might in the ground be closèd up in rest.
For never henceforth shall I joy again –
Never, O never, shall I see more joy.

RICHARD

I cannot weep, for all my body's moisture
80   Scarce serves to quench my furnace-burning heart;
Nor can my tongue unload my heart's great burden,
82   For selfsame wind that I should speak withal
Is kindling coals that fires all my breast,
And burns me up with flames that tears would quench.
To weep is to make less the depth of grief;
Tears, then, for babes – blows and revenge for me!
87   Richard, I bear thy name; I'll venge thy death
Or die renownèd by attempting it.

EDWARD

His name that valiant duke hath left with thee,
90   His dukedom and his chair with me is left.

RICHARD

91   Nay, if thou be that princely eagle's bird,

---

69 *stay* support   **70** *boist'rous* savage   **74** *my soul's palace* i.e, my body   **75**
she i.e., my soul   **82** *wind* breath   **87** *venge* revenge   **91** *bird* young

Show thy descent by gazing 'gainst the sun: 92
For "chair and dukedom," "throne and kingdom" say –   93
Either that is thine or else thou wert not his.
> *March. Enter the Earl of Warwick and the Marquis of*
> *Montague, with Drummers, an Ensign, and Soldiers.*

WARWICK
How now, fair lords? What fare? What news abroad?   95

RICHARD
Great Lord of Warwick, if we should recount
Our baleful news, and at each word's deliverance   97
Stab poniards in our flesh till all were told,   98
The words would add more anguish than the wounds.
O valiant lord, the Duke of York is slain.   *100*

EDWARD
O Warwick, Warwick! That Plantagenet,
Which held thee dearly as his soul's redemption,
Is by the stern Lord Clifford done to death.

WARWICK
Ten days ago I drowned these news in tears.
And now, to add more measure to your woes,
I come to tell you things sith then befall'n.   106
After the bloody fray at Wakefield fought,   108
Where your brave father breathed his latest gasp,   108
Tidings, as swiftly as the posts could run,   109
Were brought me of your loss and his depart.   110
I then in London, keeper of the king,
Mustered my soldiers, gathered flocks of friends,
And, very well appointed as I thought,   113
Marched toward Saint Albans to intercept the queen,
Bearing the king in my behalf along –
For by my scouts I was advertisèd   116

---

92 *gazing 'gainst the sun* (Eagles, according to Pliny and many later writers, could gaze at the sun without blinking. The *sun* here symbolizes the king; the *eagle* is an allusion to a Yorkist badge.)   **93** *chair* (symbol of a duke's authority, as *throne* is of a king's)   **95** *What fare?* How goes it?   **97** *baleful* deadly   **98** *poniards* daggers   **106** *sith* since   **108** *latest* last   **109** *posts* messengers   **110** *depart* death   **113** *appointed* equipped   **116** *advertisèd* informed

That she was coming with a full intent
118   To dash our late decree in Parliament
Touching King Henry's oath and your succession.
120   Short tale to make, we at Saint Albans met,
121   Our battles joined, and both sides fiercely fought;
But whether 'twas the coldness of the king,
Who looked full gently on his warlike queen,
124   That robbed my soldiers of their heated spleen,
Or whether 'twas report of her success,
Or more than common fear of Clifford's rigor –
Who thunders to his captains, "Blood and death!" –
I cannot judge; but, to conclude with truth,
Their weapons like to lightning came and went;
130   Our soldiers', like the night owl's lazy flight,
131   Or like an idle thresher with a flail,
Fell gently down, as if they struck their friends.
I cheered them up with justice of our cause,
With promise of high pay, and great rewards.
But all in vain. They had no heart to fight,
And we in them no hope to win the day.
So that we fled – the king unto the queen,
Lord George your brother, Norfolk, and myself
139   In haste, posthaste, are come to join with you.
140   For in the Marches here we heard you were,
141   Making another head to fight again.
EDWARD
Where is the Duke of Norfolk, gentle Warwick?
And when came George from Burgundy to England?
WARWICK
Some six miles off the duke is with his soldiers;
And for your brother – he was lately sent

---

118 *late* recent   121 *battles* armies   124 *heated spleen* i.e., warlike mood
131 *a flail* an instrument for threshing (a stout stick joined to a longer han-
dle by a leather thong)   139 *posthaste* as speedily as postriders   140 *Marches*
Welsh borders   141 *Making . . . head* gathering . . . force

From your kind aunt, Duchess of Burgundy,   146
With aid of soldiers to this needful war.

RICHARD
    'Twas odd belike when valiant Warwick fled.   148
    Oft have I heard his praises in pursuit,   149
    But ne'er till now his scandal of retire.   150

WARWICK
    Nor now my scandal, Richard, dost thou hear –
    For thou shalt know this strong right hand of mine
    Can pluck the diadem from faint Henry's head   153
    And wring the aweful scepter from his fist,   154
    Were he as famous and as bold in war
    As he is famed for mildness, peace, and prayer.

RICHARD
    I know it well, Lord Warwick – blame me not.
    'Tis love I bear thy glories make me speak.
    But in this troublous time what's to be done?
    Shall we go throw away our coats of steel,   160
    And wrap our bodies in black mourning gowns,
    Numb'ring our Ave Maries with our beads?   162
    Or shall we on the helmets of our foes
    Tell our devotion with revengeful arms?   164
    If for the last, say "ay," and to it, lords.

WARWICK
    Why, therefore Warwick came to seek you out,
    And therefore comes my brother Montague.
    Attend me, lords. The proud insulting queen,
    With Clifford and the haught Northumberland,   169
    And of their feather many more proud birds,   170

---

146 *aunt . . . Burgundy* (Isabel, Duchess of Burgundy, was a granddaughter
of John of Ghent and a distant cousin to Edward. Holinshed says that
George and Richard were sent for protection to the Duke of Burgundy after
York's death and remained with him until Edward was crowned.)   148
'Twas odd belike no doubt the odds were heavily against him   149 *pursuit*
i.e., of enemies   150 *scandal of retire* disgrace because of retreating   153
faint weak   154 *aweful* awe-inspiring   162 *Ave Maries* Hail Marys (prayers
to the Virgin Mary)   164 *Tell our devotion* (1) count off our prayers, as on a
rosary, (2) declare our love (ironically)   169 *haught* haughty

171   Have wrought the easy-melting king like wax.
      To Edward
    He swore consent to your succession,
173   His oath enrollèd in the Parliament.
    And now to London all the crew are gone,
    To frustrate both his oath and what beside
176   May make against the house of Lancaster.
    Their power, I think, is thirty thousand strong.
    Now, if the help of Norfolk and myself,
179   With all the friends that thou, brave Earl of March,
180   Amongst the loving Welshmen canst procure,
    Will but amount to five and twenty thousand,
182   Why, *via,* to London will we march,
    And once again bestride our foaming steeds,
    And once again cry "Charge!" upon our foes –
    But never once again turn back and fly.

RICHARD
    Ay, now methinks I hear great Warwick speak.
187   Ne'er may he live to see a sunshine day
    That cries "Retire!" if Warwick bid him stay.

EDWARD
    Lord Warwick, on thy shoulder will I lean,
190   And when thou fail'st – as God forbid the hour –
191   Must Edward fall, which peril heaven forfend!

WARWICK
    No longer Earl of March, but Duke of York;
193   The next degree is England's royal throne –
    For King of England shalt thou be proclaimed
    In every borough as we pass along,
    And he that throws not up his cap for joy,
    Shall for the fault make forfeit of his head.
    King Edward, valiant Richard, Montague –
    Stay we no longer dreaming of renown,

---

171 *wrought* persuaded; *easy-melting* softhearted, easily swayed **173** *enrollèd* officially recorded **176** *make* tell **179** *Earl of March* i.e., Edward (his title before York's death; see l. 192) **182** *via* onward **187** *he* i.e., anyone **191** *forfend* forbid **193** *degree* rank

But sound the trumpets and about our task.   *200*

RICHARD
Then, Clifford, were thy heart as hard as steel,
As thou hast shown it flinty by thy deeds,
I come to pierce it or to give thee mine.

EDWARD DUKE OF YORK
Then strike up drums – God and Saint George for us!   204
 Enter a Messenger.

WARWICK
How now? What news?

MESSENGER
The Duke of Norfolk sends you word by me
The queen is coming with a puissant host,   207
And craves your company for speedy counsel.

WARWICK
Why then it sorts. Brave warriors, let's away.   209
       March. Exeunt.

     *

∾ **II.2** *Richard Duke of York's head is thrust out, above.*
 Flourish. Enter King Henry, Queen Margaret, Lord
 Clifford, the Earl of Northumberland, and young
 Prince Edward, with a Drummer and Trumpeters.

QUEEN MARGARET
Welcome, my lord, to this brave town of York.
Yonder's the head of that arch-enemy
That sought to be encompassed with your crown.
Doth not the object cheer your heart, my lord?

KING HENRY
Ay, as the rocks cheer them that fear their wreck.   5
To see this sight, it irks my very soul.
Withhold revenge, dear God – 'tis not my fault,
Nor wittingly have I infringed my vow.   8

---

204 *Saint George* the patron saint of England   207 *puissant* powerful   **209**
sorts works out well
 II.2 Before the walls of York · 5 *wreck* ruin   8 *wittingly* knowingly

CLIFFORD

9   My gracious liege, this too much lenity
10 And harmful pity must be laid aside.
    To whom do lions cast their gentle looks?
    Not to the beast that would usurp their den.
    Whose hand is that the forest bear doth lick?
14 Not his that spoils her young before her face.
    Who scapes the lurking serpent's mortal sting?
    Not he that sets his foot upon her back.
    The smallest worm will turn, being trodden on,
    And doves will peck in safeguard of their brood.
19 Ambitious York did level at thy crown,
20 Thou smiling while he knit his angry brows.
    He, but a duke, would have his son a king,
22 And raise his issue like a loving sire;
    Thou, being a king, blest with a goodly son,
    Didst yield consent to disinherit him,
    Which argued thee a most unloving father.
26 Unreasonable creatures feed their young,
    And though man's face be fearful to their eyes,
    Yet, in protection of their tender ones,
    Who hath not seen them, even with those wings
30 Which sometime they have used with fearful flight,
    Make war with him that climbed unto their nest,
    Offering their own lives in their young's defense?
    For shame, my liege, make them your precedent!
    Were it not pity that this goodly boy
    Should lose his birthright by his father's fault,
    And long hereafter say unto his child
    "What my great-grandfather and grandsire got
38 My careless father fondly gave away"?
    Ah, what a shame were this! Look on the boy,
40 And let his manly face, which promiseth

---

9 *liege* sovereign; *lenity* gentleness   14 *spoils* destroys   19 *level* aim   22 *raise* promote; *issue* offspring   26 *Unreasonable* not endowed with reason   38 *fondly* foolishly

Successful fortune, steel thy melting heart
To hold thine own and leave thine own with him.

KING HENRY

Full well hath Clifford played the orator,
Inferring arguments of mighty force.   44
But, Clifford, tell me – didst thou never hear
That things ill got had ever bad success?   46
And happy always was it for that son   47
Whose father for his hoarding went to hell?   48
I'll leave my son my virtuous deeds behind,
And would my father had left me no more.   *50*
For all the rest is held at such a rate   51
As brings a thousandfold more care to keep
Than in possession any jot of pleasure.
Ah, cousin York, would thy best friends did know
How it doth grieve me that thy head is here.

QUEEN MARGARET

My lord, cheer up your spirits – our foes are nigh,
And this soft courage makes your followers faint.   57
You promised knighthood to our forward son.   58
Unsheathe your sword and dub him presently.   59
Edward, kneel down.   *60*
    Prince Edward kneels.

KING HENRY

Edward Plantagenet, arise a knight –
And learn this lesson: draw thy sword in right.

PRINCE EDWARD   *Rising*

My gracious father, by your kingly leave,
I'll draw it as apparent to the crown,   64
And in that quarrel use it to the death.   65

CLIFFORD

Why, that is spoken like a toward prince.   66

---

44 *Inferring* adducing   46 *success* outcome   47 *happy . . . it* were things always good   48 *for* because of   51 *rate* cost   57 *faint* fainthearted   58 *forward* high-spirited   59 *dub him* make him a knight; *presently* immediately   64 *apparent* heir   65 *quarrel* cause   66 *toward* bold

Enter a Messenger.

MESSENGER

 Royal commanders, be in readiness –
 For with a band of thirty thousand men
69 Comes Warwick backing of the Duke of York;
70 And in the towns, as they do march along,
 Proclaims him king, and many fly to him.
72 Deraign your battle, for they are at hand.

CLIFFORD *To King Henry*

 I would your highness would depart the field –
 The queen hath best success when you are absent.

QUEEN MARGARET *To King Henry*

 Ay, good my lord, and leave us to our fortune.

KING HENRY

 Why, that's my fortune too – therefore I'll stay.

NORTHUMBERLAND

 Be it with resolution then to fight.

PRINCE EDWARD *To King Henry*

 My royal father, cheer these noble lords
 And hearten those that fight in your defense.
80 Unsheathe your sword, good father; cry "Saint
  George!"

  March. Enter Edward Duke of York, the Earl of
  Warwick, Richard, George, the Duke of Norfolk,
  the Marquis of Montague, and Soldiers.

EDWARD DUKE OF YORK

 Now, perjured Henry, wilt thou kneel for grace,
 And set thy diadem upon my head –
83 Or bide the mortal fortune of the field?

QUEEN MARGARET

84 Go rate thy minions, proud insulting boy!
 Becomes it thee to be thus bold in terms
 Before thy sovereign and thy lawful king?

---

69 *backing of* in support of; *Duke of York* i.e., Edward **72** *Deraign your battle* deploy your forces **83** *bide* await; *mortal* fatal **84** *rate thy minions* chide your favorites

EDWARD DUKE OF YORK
  I am his king, and he should bow his knee.
  I was adopted heir by his consent.
GEORGE   *To Queen Margaret*
  Since when his oath is broke – for, as I hear,
  You that are king, though he do wear the crown,   *90*
  Have caused him by new act of Parliament
  To blot our brother out, and put his own son in.
CLIFFORD
  And reason too –
  Who should succeed the father but the son?
RICHARD
  Are you there, butcher? O, I cannot speak!
CLIFFORD
  Ay, crookback, here I stand to answer thee,
  Or any he the proudest of thy sort.   *97*
RICHARD
  'Twas you that killed young Rutland, was it not?
CLIFFORD
  Ay, and old York, and yet not satisfied.
RICHARD
  For God's sake, lords, give signal to the fight.   *100*
WARWICK
  What sayst thou, Henry, wilt thou yield the crown?
QUEEN MARGARET
  Why, how now, long-tongued Warwick, dare you
    speak?
  When you and I met at Saint Albans last,
  Your legs did better service than your hands.
WARWICK
  Then 'twas my turn to fly – and now 'tis thine.
CLIFFORD
  You said so much before, and yet you fled.
WARWICK
  'Twas not your valor, Clifford, drove me thence.

---

97 *sort* gang

NORTHUMBERLAND
No, nor your manhood that durst make you stay.

RICHARD

109   Northumberland, I hold thee reverently.
110   Break off the parley, for scarce I can refrain
111   The execution of my big-swoll'n heart
Upon that Clifford, that cruel child-killer.

CLIFFORD
I slew thy father – call'st thou him a child?

RICHARD

114   Ay, like a dastard and a treacherous coward,
As thou didst kill our tender brother Rutland.
But ere sun set I'll make thee curse the deed.

KING HENRY
Have done with words, my lords, and hear me speak.

QUEEN MARGARET
Defy them, then, or else hold close thy lips.

KING HENRY
I prithee give no limits to my tongue –
120   I am a king, and privileged to speak.

CLIFFORD
My liege, the wound that bred this meeting here
Cannot be cured by words – therefore be still.

RICHARD
Then, executioner, unsheathe thy sword.
124   By him that made us all, I am resolved
125   That Clifford's manhood lies upon his tongue.

EDWARD DUKE OF YORK
Say, Henry, shall I have my right or no?
A thousand men have broke their fasts today
That ne'er shall dine unless thou yield the crown.

WARWICK   *To King Henry*
129   If thou deny, their blood upon thy head;

---

109 *reverently* in respect 111 *big-swoll'n* passionate 114 *dastard* coward
124 *resolved* convinced 125 *Clifford's . . . tongue* i.e., he talks better than he
fights 129 *deny* refuse

For York in justice puts his armor on.   130
PRINCE EDWARD
If that be right which Warwick says is right,
There is no wrong, but everything is right.
RICHARD
Whoever got thee, there thy mother stands –   133
For, well I wot, thou hast thy mother's tongue.   134
QUEEN MARGARET
But thou art neither like thy sire nor dam,
But like a foul misshapen stigmatic,   136
Marked by the destinies to be avoided,
As venom toads or lizards' dreadful stings.   138
RICHARD
Iron of Naples, hid with English gilt,   139
Whose father bears the title of a king –   140
As if a channel should be called the sea –   141
Sham'st thou not, knowing whence thou art extraught,   142
To let thy tongue detect thy base-born heart?   143
EDWARD DUKE OF YORK
A wisp of straw were worth a thousand crowns   144
To make this shameless callet know herself.   145
    To Queen Margaret
Helen of Greece was fairer far than thou,   146
Although thy husband may be Menelaus;
And ne'er was Agamemnon's brother wronged
By that false woman, as this king by thee.
His father reveled in the heart of France,   150

---

133 *got* begot   134 *wot* know   136 *stigmatic* one branded (stigmatized) by
deformity   138 *venom* venomous   139 *Iron . . . gilt* i.e., you cheap Neapolitan (Naples was known for prostitution and venereal disease), whose worth-
lessness is concealed by English gold (perhaps punning on Suffolk's "guilt"
for having paid so much for her)   141 *channel* gutter   142 *Sham'st thou not*
are you not ashamed; *extraught* descended   143 *detect* reveal   144 *wisp of
straw* (traditional mark of a scold); *were* would be   145 *callet* whore   146–
48 *Helen . . . Menelaus . . . Agamemnon* (Paris of Troy abducted Helen, wife
of Menelaus, king of Sparta, who was brother to Agamemnon, king of Myce-
nae; here Helen is the typical false woman and Menelaus the typical cuckold.
There is an allusion to the belief that Prince Edward was not the son of
Henry VI.)   150 *His father* i.e., Henry V

151 And tamed the king, and made the dauphin stoop;
152 And had he matched according to his state,
     He might have kept that glory to this day.
     But when he took a beggar to his bed,
155 And graced thy poor sire with his bridal day,
     Even then that sunshine brewed a shower for him
157 That washed his father's fortunes forth of France,
     And heaped sedition on his crown at home.
159 For what hath broached this tumult but thy pride?
160 Hadst thou been meek, our title still had slept,
     And we, in pity of the gentle king,
162 Had slipped our claim until another age.
     GEORGE   *To Queen Margaret*
     But when we saw our sunshine made thy spring,
164 And that thy summer bred us no increase,
165 We set the ax to thy usurping root.
166 And though the edge hath something hit ourselves,
     Yet know thou, since we have begun to strike,
     We'll never leave till we have hewn thee down,
169 Or bathed thy growing with our heated bloods.
     EDWARD DUKE OF YORK   *To Queen Margaret*
170 And in this resolution I defy thee,
     Not willing any longer conference
172 Since thou deniest the gentle king to speak.
     Sound trumpets – let our bloody colors wave!
     And either victory, or else a grave!
     QUEEN MARGARET
     Stay, Edward.
     EDWARD DUKE OF YORK
     No, wrangling woman, we'll no longer stay –
     These words will cost ten thousand lives this day.

---

151 *dauphin* (title held by the French king's eldest son)   152 *he* i.e., Henry VI; *matched* married; *state* rank   155 *graced . . . day* i.e., did honor (grace) to your lowly father by marrying you   157 *of* from   159 *broached* started (literally, set flowing)   160 *title* claim to the throne   162 *slipped* postponed 164 *increase* harvest   165 *usurping* (because she is wife to Henry VI, regarded by the Yorkists as a usurper)   166 *something* to some extent   169 *bathed* watered   172 *deniest* forbid

Flourish. March. Exeunt York and his Men at one door,
and Queen Margaret and her Men at another door.

✳

∾ **II.3** *Alarum. Excursions. Enter the Earl of Warwick.*

WARWICK

Forespent with toil, as runners with a race,   1
I lay me down a little while to breathe;   2
For strokes received, and many blows repaid,
Have robbed my strong-knit sinews of their strength,   4
And, spite of spite, needs must I rest a while.   5

Enter Edward Duke of York, running.

EDWARD DUKE OF YORK

Smile, gentle heaven, or strike, ungentle death!   6
For this world frowns, and Edward's sun is clouded.   7

WARWICK

How now, my lord, what hap? What hope of good?

Enter George, running.

GEORGE

Our hap is loss, our hope but sad despair;   9
Our ranks are broke, and ruin follows us.   10
What counsel give you? Whither shall we fly?

EDWARD DUKE OF YORK

Bootless is flight – they follow us with wings,   12
And weak we are, and cannot shun pursuit.   13

Enter Richard, running.

RICHARD

Ah, Warwick, why hast thou withdrawn thyself?
Thy brother's blood the thirsty earth hath drunk,   15
Broached with the steely point of Clifford's lance.   16

II.3 Fields near York **s.d.** *Alarum* a trumpet call meaning "to arms"; *Excursions* attacks and counterattacks 1 *Forespent* exhausted 2 *breathe* rest 4 *strong-knit* powerful 5 *spite of spite* come what may 6 *ungentle* ignoble 7 *sun* i.e., good fortune (with allusion to the Yorkists' sun device) 9 *hap* luck 12 *Bootless* hopeless 13 *shun* avoid 15 *Thy brother's blood* (a reference to the "Bastard of Salisbury," Warwick's half brother, killed at Ferrybridge) 16 *Broached* set flowing

And in the very pangs of death he cried,
Like to a dismal clangor heard from far,
"Warwick, revenge – brother, revenge my death!"
20   So, underneath the belly of their steeds
21   That stained their fetlocks in his smoking blood,
The noble gentleman gave up the ghost.

WARWICK
Then let the earth be drunken with our blood.
I'll kill my horse, because I will not fly.
Why stand we like softhearted women here,
26   Wailing our losses, whiles the foe doth rage,
27   And look upon, as if the tragedy
Were played in jest by counterfeiting actors?
        Kneeling
Here, on my knee, I vow to God above
30   I'll never pause again, never stand still,
Till either death hath closed these eyes of mine
Or fortune given me measure of revenge.

EDWARD DUKE OF YORK   *Kneeling*
O, Warwick, I do bend my knee with thine,
And in this vow do chain my soul to thine.
And, ere my knee rise from the earth's cold face,
36   I throw my hands, mine eyes, my heart to thee,
Thou setter up and plucker down of kings,
38   Beseeching thee, if with thy will it stands
That to my foes this body must be prey,
40   Yet that thy brazen gates of heaven may ope
And give sweet passage to my sinful soul.
        They rise.
Now, lords, take leave until we meet again,
Where'er it be, in heaven or in earth.

RICHARD
44   Brother, give me thy hand; and, gentle Warwick,
Let me embrace thee in my weary arms.
I, that did never weep, now melt with woe

---

21 *smoking* steaming   26 *whiles* while   27 *upon* on   36 *thee* i.e., God   38 *stands* agrees   44 *gentle* noble

That winter should cut off our springtime so.
WARWICK
Away, away! Once more, sweet lords, farewell.
GEORGE
Yet let us all together to our troops,
And give them leave to fly that will not stay;   50
And call them pillars that will stand to us;   51
And, if we thrive, promise them such rewards
As victors wear at the Olympian games.
This may plant courage in their quailing breasts,
For yet is hope of life and victory.
Forslow no longer – make we hence amain.   *Exeunt.* 56

＊

∾ **II.4** *Alarums. Excursions. Enter Richard at one door
and Lord Clifford at the other.*

RICHARD
Now, Clifford, I have singled thee alone.   1
Suppose this arm is for the Duke of York,
And this for Rutland, both bound to revenge,
Wert thou environed with a brazen wall.   4
CLIFFORD
Now, Richard, I am with thee here alone.
This is the hand that stabbed thy father York,
And this the hand that slew thy brother Rutland,
And here's the heart that triumphs in their death
And cheers these hands that slew thy sire and brother
To execute the like upon thyself –   10
And so, have at thee!
       *They fight. The Earl of Warwick comes and rescues
       Richard. Lord Clifford flies.*
RICHARD
Nay, Warwick, single out some other chase –   12
For I myself will hunt this wolf to death.   *Exeunt.*

---

50 *leave* permission   51 *to* by   56 *Forslow* delay; *amain* quickly
   II.4 Fields near York   1 *singled* i.e., chosen one from the herd (a hunting term)
4 *environed* surrounded   12 *chase* prey

*

ᴏᴠ **II.5** *Alarum. Enter King Henry.*

KING HENRY
This battle fares like to the morning's war,
  When dying clouds contend with growing light,
3 What time the shepherd, blowing of his nails,
  Can neither call it perfect day nor night.
  Now sways it this way like a mighty sea
    Forced by the tide to combat with the wind,
  Now sways it that way like the selfsame sea
    Forced to retire by fury of the wind.
  Sometime the flood prevails, and then the wind;
10 Now one the better, then another best –
  Both tugging to be victors, breast to breast,
  Yet neither conqueror nor conquerèd.
13 So is the equal poise of this fell war.
14 Here on this molehill will I sit me down.
  To whom God will, there be the victory.
  For Margaret my queen, and Clifford, too,
  Have chid me from the battle, swearing both
  They prosper best of all when I am thence.
  Would I were dead, if God's good will were so –
20 For what is in this world but grief and woe?
  O God! Methinks it were a happy life
22 To be no better than a homely swain.
  To sit upon a hill, as I do now;
24 To carve out dials quaintly, point by point,
  Thereby to see the minutes how they run:
  How many makes the hour full complete,
27 How many hours brings about the day,
  How many days will finish up the year,

II.5 Fields near York **3** *What time* when; *of* on (for warmth) **13** *poise* balance; *fell* cruel **14** *molehill* (see the note to I.4.68) **22** *homely* simple; *swain* countryman **24** *dials quaintly* sundials artfully (perhaps alluding to shepherds' practice of cutting sundials in the turf of hillsides) **27** *brings about* completes

How many years a mortal man may live.
When this is known, then to divide the times: *30*
So many hours must I tend my flock,
So many hours must I take my rest,
So many hours must I contemplate,   *33*
So many hours must I sport myself,   *34*
So many days my ewes have been with young,
So many weeks ere the poor fools will ean,   *36*
So many years ere I shall shear the fleece.
So minutes, hours, days, weeks, months, and years,
Passed over to the end they were created,   *39*
Would bring white hairs unto a quiet grave.   *40*
Ah, what a life were this! How sweet! How lovely!
Gives not the hawthorn bush a sweeter shade
To shepherds looking on their seely sheep   *43*
Than doth a rich embroidered canopy
To kings that fear their subjects' treachery?
O yes, it doth – a thousandfold it doth.
And to conclude, the shepherd's homely curds,
His cold thin drink out of his leather bottle,
His wonted sleep under a fresh tree's shade,   *49*
All which secure and sweetly he enjoys,   *50*
Is far beyond a prince's delicates,   *51*
His viands sparkling in a golden cup,   *52*
His body couchèd in a curious bed,   *53*
When care, mistrust, and treason waits on him.   *54*
        Alarum. Enter at one door a Lancastrian Soldier with
        a dead Yorkist Soldier in his arms. Henry stands apart.
LANCASTRIAN SOLDIER
    Ill blows the wind that profits nobody.
    This man, whom hand to hand I slew in fight,
    May be possessèd with some store of crowns;   *57*

---

33 *contemplate* meditate, pray   **34** *sport* amuse   **36** *ean* give birth   **39** *end*
they end for which they   **43** *seely* innocent   **49** *wonted* accustomed   **51** *delicates* dainty foods   **52** *viands* food   **53** *curious* (1) elaborately wrought, (2)
full of cares   **54 s.d.** *Lancastrian . . . Yorkist* (we know these allegiances from
ll. 64–66, but the characters were probably visually identifiable to the audience at this point by their costumes)   **57** *crowns* money

58 And I, that haply take them from him now,
May yet ere night yield both my life and them
60 To some man else, as this dead man doth me.
He removes the dead man's helmet.
Who's this? O God! It is my father's face
62 Whom in this conflict I, unwares, have killed.
63 O, heavy times, begetting such events!
64 From London by the king was I pressed forth;
65 My father, being the Earl of Warwick's man,
66 Came on the part of York, pressed by his master;
And I, who at his hands received my life,
Have by my hands of life bereavèd him.
Pardon me, God, I knew not what I did;
70 And pardon, father, for I knew not thee.
My tears shall wipe away these bloody marks,
And no more words till they have flowed their fill.
He weeps.
KING HENRY
O piteous spectacle! O bloody times!
Whiles lions war and battle for their dens,
75 Poor harmless lambs abide their enmity.
Weep, wretched man, I'll aid thee tear for tear;
And let our hearts and eyes, like civil war,
78 Be blind with tears, and break, o'ercharged with grief.
*Enter at another door another Soldier with a dead
man in his arms.*
SECOND SOLDIER
Thou that so stoutly hath resisted me,
80 Give me thy gold, if thou hast any gold –
For I have bought it with an hundred blows.
He removes the dead man's helmet.
82 But let me see: is this our foeman's face?

---

58 *haply* by chance **62** *unwares* unknowingly **63** *heavy* miserable **64**
pressed impressed, drafted (into service against my will) **65** *man* servant
66 *part* side **75** *abide* endure **78** *o'ercharged* overfilled; **s.d.** *Soldier . . .
dead man* (In so formal a scene as this, one would expect this second pair to
reverse the allegiances of the first: here, a Yorkist soldier carrying a dead Lancastrian soldier. But here the text provides no evidence.) **82** *foeman's* enemy's

Ah, no, no, no – it is mine only son!
Ah, boy, if any life be left in thee,
Throw up thine eye! *(Weeping)* See, see, what showers
  arise,
Blown with the windy tempest of my heart,
Upon thy wounds, that kills mine eye and heart!
O, pity, God, this miserable age!
What stratagems, how fell, how butcherly,   89
Erroneous, mutinous, and unnatural,   90
This deadly quarrel daily doth beget!
O boy, thy father gave thee life too soon,
And hath bereft thee of thy life too late!   93

KING HENRY
Woe above woe! Grief more than common grief!
O that my death would stay these ruthful deeds!   95
O, pity, pity, gentle heaven, pity!
The red rose and the white are on his face,
The fatal colors of our striving houses;
The one his purple blood right well resembles,
The other his pale cheeks, methinks, presenteth.   100
Wither one rose, and let the other flourish –
If you contend, a thousand lives must wither.

LANCASTRIAN SOLDIER
How will my mother for a father's death
Take on with me, and ne'er be satisfied!   104

SECOND SOLDIER
How will my wife for slaughter of my son
Shed seas of tears, and ne'er be satisfied!

KING HENRY
How will the country for these woeful chances   107
Misthink the king, and not be satisfied!   108

LANCASTRIAN SOLDIER
Was ever son so rued a father's death?

---

89 *stratagems* bloody acts; *fell* cruel   90 *Erroneous* criminal   93 *late* recently
95 *stay* stop; *ruthful* pitiful   100 *presenteth* symbolizes   104 *Take on with*
rage against; *satisfied* comforted   107 *chances* happenings   108 *Misthink*
misunderstand, blame

SECOND SOLDIER
110   Was ever father so bemoaned his son?
KING HENRY
       Was ever king so grieved for subjects' woe?
       Much is your sorrow, mine ten times so much.
LANCASTRIAN SOLDIER   *To his father's body*
       I'll bear thee hence where I may weep my fill.
                    Exit at one door with the body of his father.
SECOND SOLDIER   *To his son's body*
114   These arms of mine shall be thy winding-sheet;
       My heart, sweet boy, shall be thy sepulcher,
       For from my heart thine image ne'er shall go.
       My sighing breast shall be thy funeral bell,
118   And so obsequious will thy father be,
       E'en for the loss of thee, having no more,
120   As Priam was for all his valiant sons.
       I'll bear thee hence, and let them fight that will –
       For I have murdered where I should not kill.
                    Exit at another door with the body of his son.
KING HENRY
123   Sad-hearted men, much overgone with care,
       Here sits a king more woeful than you are.
                Alarums. Excursions. Enter Prince Edward.
PRINCE EDWARD
       Fly, father, fly – for all your friends are fled,
126   And Warwick rages like a chafèd bull!
       Away – for death doth hold us in pursuit!
                Enter Queen Margaret.
QUEEN MARGARET
128   Mount you, my lord – towards Berwick post amain.
129   Edward and Richard, like a brace of greyhounds
130   Having the fearful flying hare in sight,

---

114 *winding-sheet* shroud   118 *obsequious* dutiful in mourning   120 *Priam*
king of Troy (whose fifty sons were killed defending the city)   123 *overgone*
overcome   126 *chafèd* angry   128 *Berwick* Berwick-on-Tweed, in
Northumberland; *post* ride; *amain* at full speed   129 *brace* pair

With fiery eyes sparkling for very wrath,
And bloody steel grasped in their ireful hands,
Are at our backs – and therefore hence amain.
        Enter Exeter.
EXETER
Away – for vengeance comes along with them!
Nay – stay not to expostulate – make speed –   135
Or else come after. I'll away before.
KING HENRY
Nay, take me with thee, good sweet Exeter.
Not that I fear to stay, but love to go
Whither the queen intends. Forward, away.   *Exeunt.*
                                    *

∾ **II.6** *A loud alarum. Enter Lord Clifford, wounded
with an arrow in his neck.*

CLIFFORD
Here burns my candle out – ay, here it dies,
Which, whiles it lasted, gave King Henry light.   2
O Lancaster, I fear thy overthrow   3
More than my body's parting with my soul!
My love and fear glued many friends to thee –   5
And, now I fall, thy tough commixture melts,   6
Impairing Henry, strength'ning misproud York.   7
The common people swarm like summer flies,
And whither fly the gnats but to the sun?   9
And who shines now but Henry's enemies?   10
O Phoebus, hadst thou never given consent   11
That Phaëthon should check thy fiery steeds,   12
Thy burning car never had scorched the earth!   13

---

135 *expostulate* argue
    II.6 Fields near York   2 *whiles* while   3 *Lancaster* i.e., the house of Lan-
caster   5 *My . . . fear* the love and respect I commanded   6 *commixture*
compound   7 *Impairing* weakening; *misproud* unjustly proud   9 *sun* (another allusion to the Yorkist sun device)   11 *Phoebus* Phoebus Apollo, the
sun   12 *Phaëthon* (see the note to I.4.34); *check* manage   13 *car* chariot

14　And, Henry, hadst thou swayed as kings should do,
　　Or as thy father and his father did,
　　Giving no ground unto the house of York,
17　They never then had sprung like summer flies;
　　I and ten thousand in this luckless realm
　　Had left no mourning widows for our death;
20　And thou this day hadst kept thy chair in peace.
21　For what doth cherish weeds, but gentle air?
　　And what makes robbers bold, but too much lenity?
23　Bootless are plaints, and cureless are my wounds;
　　No way to fly, nor strength to hold out flight;
　　The foe is merciless and will not pity,
　　For at their hands I have deserved no pity.
　　The air hath got into my deadly wounds,
28　And much effuse of blood doth make me faint.
　　Come York and Richard, Warwick and the rest –
30　I stabbed your fathers' bosoms; split my breast.
　　　　He faints.
　　　　Alarum and retreat. Enter Edward Duke of York,
　　　　his brothers George and Richard, the Earl of Warwick,
　　　　the Marquis of Montague, and Soldiers.
EDWARD DUKE OF YORK
　　Now breathe we, lords – good fortune bids us pause,
　　And smooth the frowns of war with peaceful looks.
　　Some troops pursue the bloody-minded queen,
　　That led calm Henry, though he were a king,
35　As doth a sail filled with a fretting gust
36　Command an argosy to stem the waves.
　　But think you, lords, that Clifford fled with them?
WARWICK
　　No – 'tis impossible he should escape;
　　For, though before his face I speak the words,
40　Your brother Richard marked him for the grave.

---

14 *swayed* ruled　17 *sprung* multiplied　20 *chair* i.e., of state, throne　21
cherish foster　23 *Bootless* useless; *plaints* pleas　28 *effuse* effusion　30 s.d.
retreat a trumpet call signaling recall　35 *fretting* (1) blowing in gusts, (2)
nagging　36 *argosy* large merchant ship; *stem* resist

And wheresoe'er he is, he's surely dead.
    Clifford groans.
EDWARD DUKE OF YORK
    Whose soul is that which takes her heavy leave?
RICHARD
    A deadly groan, like life and death's departing.
EDWARD DUKE OF YORK   *To Richard*
    See who it is.
        Richard goes to Clifford.
                        And now the battle's ended,
    If friend or foe, let him be gently used.
RICHARD
    Revoke that doom of mercy, for 'tis Clifford;   46
    Who not contented that he lopped the branch
    In hewing Rutland when his leaves put forth,
    But set his murd'ring knife unto the root
    From whence that tender spray did sweetly spring –   50
    I mean our princely father, Duke of York.
WARWICK
    From off the gates of York fetch down the head,
    Your father's head, which Clifford placèd there.
    Instead whereof let this *(Indicating Clifford's head)* sup-   54
        ply the room –
    Measure for measure must be answerèd.   55
EDWARD DUKE OF YORK
    Bring forth that fatal screech owl to our house,   56
    That nothing sung but death to us and ours.
        Clifford is dragged forward.
    Now death shall stop his dismal threat'ning sound
    And his ill-boding tongue no more shall speak.   59
WARWICK
    I think his understanding is bereft.   60

---

46 *doom* judgment 50 *spray* shoot 54 *supply the room* take its place 55
Measure for measure i.e., the strict rule of justice that demands "an eye for an
eye" (the allusion is to the New Testament, however: Mark 4:24); *answerèd*
given in reply 56 *fatal . . . house* doom-prophesying bird whose predictions
are directed particularly at our family 59 *ill-boding* doom-promising 60
understanding consciousness; *bereft* lost

Speak, Clifford, dost thou know who speaks to thee?
Dark cloudy death o'ershades his beams of life,
63   And he nor sees nor hears us what we say.
RICHARD
O, would he did – and so perhaps he doth.
65   'Tis but his policy to counterfeit,
Because he would avoid such bitter taunts
Which in the time of death he gave our father.
GEORGE
68   If so thou think'st, vex him with eager words.
RICHARD
Clifford, ask mercy and obtain no grace.
EDWARD DUKE OF YORK
70   Clifford, repent in bootless penitence.
WARWICK
Clifford, devise excuses for thy faults.
GEORGE
72   While we devise fell tortures for thy faults.
RICHARD
Thou didst love York, and I am son to York.
EDWARD DUKE OF YORK
Thou pitied'st Rutland – I will pity thee.
GEORGE
75   Where's Captain Margaret to fence you now?
WARWICK
76   They mock thee, Clifford – swear as thou wast wont.
RICHARD
What, not an oath? Nay, then, the world goes hard
When Clifford cannot spare his friends an oath.
I know by that he's dead – and, by my soul,
80   If this right hand would buy but two hours' life
That I, in all despite, might rail at him,
    Raising his left hand
This hand should chop it off, and with the issuing
blood

---

63 *nor . . . nor* neither . . . nor   **65** *policy* stratagem   **68** *eager* bitter   **72** *fell* cruel   **75** *fence* protect   **76** *wont* accustomed

Stifle the villain whose unstanchèd thirst   83
York and young Rutland could not satisfy.
WARWICK
Ay, but he's dead. Off with the traitor's head,
And rear it in the place your father's stands.
And now to London with triumphant march,
There to be crownèd England's royal king;
From whence shall Warwick cut the sea to France,
And ask the Lady Bonnë for thy queen.   90
So shalt thou sinew both these lands together.   91
And, having France thy friend, thou shalt not dread
The scattered foe that hopes to rise again,
For though they cannot greatly sting to hurt,
Yet look to have them buzz to offend thine ears.   95
First will I see the coronation,
And then to Brittany I'll cross the sea
To effect this marriage, so it please my lord.
EDWARD DUKE OF YORK
Even as thou wilt, sweet Warwick, let it be.
For in thy shoulder do I build my seat,   100
And never will I undertake the thing
Wherein thy counsel and consent is wanting.
Richard, I will create thee Duke of Gloucester,
And George, of Clarence; Warwick, as ourself,
Shall do and undo as him pleaseth best.
RICHARD
Let me be Duke of Clarence, George of Gloucester –
For Gloucester's dukedom is too ominous.   107
WARWICK
Tut, that's a foolish observation –   108

---

83 *Stifle* strangle; *unstanchèd* unquenchable   91 *sinew* join (as if tied with
sinew)   95 *buzz* circulate scandal   100 *in thy shoulder* with your support
107 *too ominous* (because the three immediately preceding dukes of Gloucester had died violent deaths)   108 *observation* comment

Richard, be Duke of Gloucester. Now to London
110   To see these honors in possession.
          Exeunt. Richard late Duke of York's head is removed.

                    ✱

∿ **III.1** *Enter two Gamekeepers, with crossbows in their hands.*

FIRST GAMEKEEPER
1   Under this thick-grown brake we'll shroud ourselves,
2   For through this laund anon the deer will come,
     And in this covert will we make our stand,
4   Culling the principal of all the deer.
SECOND GAMEKEEPER
     I'll stay above the hill, so both may shoot.
FIRST GAMEKEEPER
     That cannot be – the noise of thy crossbow
7   Will scare the herd, and so my shoot is lost.
8   Here stand we both, and aim we at the best.
9   And, for the time shall not seem tedious,
10   I'll tell thee what befell me on a day
11   In this self place where now we mean to stand.
FIRST GAMEKEEPER
     Here comes a man – let's stay till he be past.
          They stand apart.
          Enter King Henry, disguised, carrying a prayer book.
KING HENRY
13   From Scotland am I stolen, even of pure love,
14   To greet mine own land with my wishful sight.
     No, Harry, Harry – 'tis no land of thine.
     Thy place is filled, thy scepter wrung from thee,
     Thy balm washed off wherewith thou wast anointed.

---

110 s.d. *removed* (Clifford's head may for a while be displayed in its place, but for how long it is impossible to know)
     III.1 A forest in northern England, near the Scottish border **1** *brake* thicket **2** *laund* glade **4** *Culling* selecting; *principal* best **7** *shoot* discharge of arrows **8** *at the best* as well as we can **9** *for* so that **11** *self* same **13** *even of* precisely because of **14** *wishful* longing

No bending knee will call thee Caesar now,
No humble suitors press to speak for right,   19
No, not a man comes for redress of thee –   20
For how can I help them and not myself?
FIRST GAMEKEEPER   *To the Second Gamekeeper*
Ay, here's a deer whose skin's a keeper's fee: 22
This is the quondam king – let's seize upon him.   23
KING HENRY
Let me embrace thee, sour adversity,
For wise men say it is the wisest course.   25
SECOND GAMEKEEPER   *To the First Gamekeeper*
Why linger we? Let us lay hands upon him.
FIRST GAMEKEEPER   *To the Second Gamekeeper*
Forbear awhile – we'll hear a little more.
KING HENRY
My queen and son are gone to France for aid,
And, as I hear, the great commanding Warwick
Is thither gone to crave the French king's sister   30
To wife for Edward. If this news be true,
Poor queen and son, your labor is but lost –
For Warwick is a subtle orator,
And Louis a prince soon won with moving words.
By this account, then, Margaret may win him –
For she's a woman to be pitied much.
Her sighs will make a batt'ry in his breast,   37
Her tears will pierce into a marble heart,
The tiger will be mild whiles she doth mourn,
And Nero will be tainted with remorse   40
To hear and see her plaints, her brinish tears.   41
Ay, but she's come to beg; Warwick to give.
She on his left side, craving aid for Henry;
He on his right, asking a wife for Edward.
She weeps and says her Henry is deposed,

---

19 *speak for right* beg for justice   20 *of* from   22 *fee* i.e., perquisite of the job
of gamekeeper   23 *quondam* former   25 *it* i.e., accepting adversity   37
batt'ry breach   40 *Nero* (traditionally hardhearted and cruel); *tainted* affected   41 *plaints* pleas; *brinish* salty

He smiles and says his Edward is installed;
47   That she, poor wretch, for grief can speak no more,
48   Whiles Warwick tells his title, smooths the wrong,
49   Inferreth arguments of mighty strength,
50   And in conclusion wins the king from her
51   With promise of his sister and what else
      To strengthen and support King Edward's place.
      O, Margaret, thus 'twill be; and thou, poor soul,
      Art then forsaken, as thou went'st forlorn.
SECOND GAMEKEEPER   *Coming forward*
      Say, what art thou that talk'st of kings and queens?
KING HENRY
      More than I seem, and less than I was born to:
      A man at least, for less I should not be;
      And men may talk of kings, and why not I?
SECOND GAMEKEEPER
      Ay, but thou talk'st as if thou wert a king.
KING HENRY
60   Why, so I am, in mind – and that's enough.
SECOND GAMEKEEPER
      But if thou be a king, where is thy crown?
KING HENRY
      My crown is in my heart, not on my head;
63   Not decked with diamonds and Indian stones,
      Nor to be seen. My crown is called content –
      A crown it is that seldom kings enjoy.
SECOND GAMEKEEPER
      Well, if you be a king crowned with content,
      Your crown content and you must be contented
      To go along with us – for, as we think,
      You are the king King Edward hath deposed,
70   And we his subjects sworn in all allegiance
      Will apprehend you as his enemy.

---

47 *That* so that   48 *tells his title* explains Edward's claim to the throne;
smooths glosses over   49 *Inferreth* adduces   51 *and what else* i.e., and who
knows what other promises   63 *Indian stones* gems (probably pearls)

KING HENRY
  But did you never swear and break an oath?
SECOND GAMEKEEPER
  No – never such an oath, nor will not now.
KING HENRY
  Where did you dwell when I was King of England?
SECOND GAMEKEEPER
  Here in this country, where we now remain.
KING HENRY
  I was anointed king at nine months old,
  My father and my grandfather were kings,
  And you were sworn true subjects unto me –
  And tell me, then, have you not broke your oaths?
FIRST GAMEKEEPER
  No, for we were subjects but while you were king.   80
KING HENRY
  Why, am I dead? Do I not breathe a man?
  Ah, simple men, you know not what you swear.
  Look as I blow this feather from my face,
  And as the air blows it to me again,
  Obeying with my wind when I do blow,   85
  And yielding to another when it blows,
  Commanded always by the greater gust –
  Such is the lightness of you common men.   88
  But do not break your oaths, for of that sin
  My mild entreaty shall not make you guilty.   *90*
  Go where you will, the king shall be commanded;
  And be you kings, command, and I'll obey.
FIRST GAMEKEEPER
  We are true subjects to the king, King Edward.
KING HENRY
  So would you be again to Henry,
  If he were seated as King Edward is.
FIRST GAMEKEEPER
  We charge you, in God's name and in the king's,
  To go with us unto the officers.

---

80 *but* only   **85** *Obeying with* submitting to   **88** *lightness* fickleness

KING HENRY
    In God's name, lead; your king's name be obeyed;
    And what God will, that let your king perform;
100   And what he will I humbly yield unto.   *Exeunt.*

✳

⸰∾ **III.2** *Enter King Edward, Richard Duke of*
        Gloucester, George Duke of Clarence, and Elizabeth
        Lady Grey.

KING EDWARD
    Brother of Gloucester, at Saint Albans field
2   This lady's husband, Sir Richard Grey, was slain,
    His lands then seized on by the conqueror.
    Her suit is now to repossess those lands,
    Which we in justice cannot well deny,
    Because in quarrel of the house of York
    The worthy gentleman did lose his life.
RICHARD DUKE OF GLOUCESTER
    Your highness shall do well to grant her suit –
    It were dishonor to deny it her.
KING EDWARD
10   It were no less; but yet I'll make a pause.
RICHARD DUKE OF GLOUCESTER   *Aside to George*
    Yea, is it so?
12   I see the lady hath a thing to grant
    Before the king will grant her humble suit.
GEORGE DUKE OF CLARENCE   *Aside to Richard*
14   He knows the game; how true he keeps the wind!
RICHARD DUKE OF GLOUCESTER   *Aside to George*
    Silence.

III.2 The palace, London   2 *Sir Richard Grey* (Lady Grey's husband, actually
Sir John, was killed at the second battle of Saint Albans, where he fought the
Lancastrians. The facts are given correctly in *Richard III,* I.3.126–29.)   12 *a
thing* (1) a favor, (2) genitals   14 *knows the game* understands the nature of
his prey (Lady Grey) (Richard and George's commentary is couched in the
language of hunting and dueling; their meaning, sexual); *keeps the wind*
hunts downwind, so as not to alarm his prey

KING EDWARD *To Lady Grey*
 Widow, we will consider of your suit;
 And come some other time to know our mind.
ELIZABETH LADY GREY
 Right gracious lord, I cannot brook delay.   18
 May it please your highness to resolve me now,   19
 And what your pleasure is shall satisfy me.   20
RICHARD DUKE OF GLOUCESTER *Aside to George*
 Ay, widow? Then I'll warrant you all your lands   21
 An if what pleases him shall pleasure you.   22
 Fight closer, or, good faith, you'll catch a blow.   23
GEORGE DUKE OF CLARENCE *Aside to Richard*
 I fear her not unless she chance to fall.   24
RICHARD DUKE OF GLOUCESTER *Aside to George*
 God forbid that! For he'll take vantages.   25
KING EDWARD *To Lady Grey*
 How many children hast thou, widow? Tell me.
GEORGE DUKE OF CLARENCE *Aside to Richard*
 I think he means to beg a child of her.   27
RICHARD DUKE OF GLOUCESTER *Aside to George*
 Nay, whip me then – he'll rather give her two.   28
ELIZABETH LADY GREY *To King Edward*
 Three, my most gracious lord.
RICHARD DUKE OF GLOUCESTER *Aside*
 You shall have four, an you'll be ruled by him.   30
KING EDWARD *To Lady Grey*
 'Twere pity they should lose their father's lands.
ELIZABETH LADY GREY
 Be pitiful, dread lord, and grant it them.

---

18 *brook* endure 19 *resolve me* free me from uncertainty 20 *pleasure* (1) will, (2) (sexual) desire 21 *warrant* guarantee 22 *An if* if 23 *Fight . . . blow* fight more closely to avoid his thrusts (playing on the sense of "sexual thrust") 24 *fear* fear for; *fall* (1) stumble, (2) submit to sex 25 *vantages* opportunities 27 *beg . . . her* (1) apply to her for a wardship, a source of profit if the child were highborn; (2) ask her to bear him a child 28 *whip me* (a mild imprecation; or, perhaps, literally, for being so childish as to think so) 30 *an if*

KING EDWARD   *To Richard and George*

33   Lords, give us leave – I'll try this widow's wit.

RICHARD DUKE OF GLOUCESTER   *Aside to George*

34   Ay, good leave have you; for you will have leave,

35   Till youth take leave and leave you to the crutch.

Richard and George stand apart.

KING EDWARD   *To Lady Grey*

Now tell me, madam, do you love your children?

ELIZABETH LADY GREY

Ay, full as dearly as I love myself.

KING EDWARD

And would you not do much to do them good?

ELIZABETH LADY GREY

To do them good I would sustain some harm.

KING EDWARD

40   Then get your husband's lands, to do them good.

ELIZABETH LADY GREY

Therefore I came unto your majesty.

KING EDWARD

I'll tell you how these lands are to be got.

ELIZABETH LADY GREY

So shall you bind me to your highness' service.

KING EDWARD

44   What service wilt thou do me, if I give them?

ELIZABETH LADY GREY

What you command, that rests in me to do.

KING EDWARD

46   But you will take exceptions to my boon.

ELIZABETH LADY GREY

47   No, gracious lord, except I cannot do it.

KING EDWARD

Ay, but thou canst do what I mean to ask.

---

33 *give us leave* pardon us (i.e., please go away)   **34** *good leave* willing pardon; *have leave* take liberties   **35** *take leave* bid farewell; *leave you to* pass you on to (because you will be too old to be amorous); *crutch* (playing on the sexual sense, "crotch")   **44** *service* (1) duty, (2) sexual attention   **46** *boon* request   **47** *except* unless

ELIZABETH LADY GREY
Why, then, I will do what your grace commands.
RICHARD DUKE OF GLOUCESTER   *To George*
He plies her hard, and much rain wears the marble.   50
GEORGE DUKE OF CLARENCE
As red as fire! Nay, then her wax must melt.
ELIZABETH LADY GREY   *To King Edward*
Why stops my lord? Shall I not hear my task?
KING EDWARD
An easy task – 'tis but to love a king.
ELIZABETH LADY GREY
That's soon performed, because I am a subject.
KING EDWARD
Why, then, thy husband's lands I freely give thee.
ELIZABETH LADY GREY   *Curtsies.*
I take my leave, with many thousand thanks.
RICHARD DUKE OF GLOUCESTER   *To George*
The match is made – she seals it with a curtsy.
KING EDWARD   *To Lady Grey*
But stay thee – 'tis the fruits of love I mean.
ELIZABETH LADY GREY
The fruits of love *I* mean, my loving liege.
KING EDWARD
Ay, but I fear me in another sense.   60
What love think'st thou I sue so much to get?
ELIZABETH LADY GREY
My love till death, my humble thanks, my prayers –
That love which virtue begs and virtue grants.
KING EDWARD
No, by my troth, I did not mean such love.
ELIZABETH LADY GREY
Why, then, you mean not as I thought you did.
KING EDWARD
But now you partly may perceive my mind.

---

50 *plies* urges

ELIZABETH LADY GREY
   My mind will never grant what I perceive
68   Your highness aims at, if I aim aright.
KING EDWARD
   To tell thee plain, I aim to lie with thee.
ELIZABETH LADY GREY
70   To tell *you* plain, I had rather lie in prison.
KING EDWARD
   Why, then, thou shalt not have thy husband's lands.
ELIZABETH LADY GREY
72   Why, then, mine honesty shall be my dower;
   For by that loss I will not purchase them.
KING EDWARD
   Therein thou wrong'st thy children mightily.
ELIZABETH LADY GREY
   Herein your highness wrongs both them and me.
   But, mighty lord, this merry inclination
77   Accords not with the sadness of my suit.
   Please you dismiss me either with ay or no.
KING EDWARD
   Ay, if thou wilt say "ay" to my request;
80   No, if thou dost say "no" to my demand.
ELIZABETH LADY GREY
   Then, no, my lord – my suit is at an end.
RICHARD DUKE OF GLOUCESTER   *To George*
   The widow likes him not – she knits her brows.
GEORGE DUKE OF CLARENCE
   He is the bluntest wooer in Christendom.
KING EDWARD   *Aside*
84   Her looks doth argue her replete with modesty;
   Her words doth show her wit incomparable;
86   All her perfections challenge sovereignty.
   One way or other, she is for a king;
   And she shall be my love or else my queen.

---

68 *aim* guess; *aright* correctly   **72** *honesty* honor   **77** *sadness* seriousness   **84**
argue prove   **86** *challenge* lay claim to

To Lady Grey
Say that King Edward take thee for his queen?
ELIZABETH LADY GREY
   'Tis better said than done, my gracious lord.   *90*
   I am a subject fit to jest withal,
   But far unfit to be a sovereign.
KING EDWARD
   Sweet widow, by my state I swear to thee   *93*
   I speak no more than what my soul intends,
   And that is to enjoy thee for my love.
ELIZABETH LADY GREY
   And that is more than I will yield unto.
   I know I am too mean to be your queen,
   And yet too good to be your concubine.
KING EDWARD
   You cavil, widow – I did mean my queen.   *99*
ELIZABETH LADY GREY
   'Twill grieve your grace my sons should call you father.   *100*
KING EDWARD
   No more than when my daughters call thee mother.
   Thou art a widow and thou hast some children;
   And, by God's mother, I, being but a bachelor,
   Have other some. Why, 'tis a happy thing   *104*
   To be the father unto many sons.
   Answer no more, for thou shalt be my queen.
RICHARD DUKE OF GLOUCESTER   *To George*
   The ghostly father now hath done his shrift.   *107*
GEORGE DUKE OF CLARENCE
   When he was made a shriver, 'twas for shift.   *108*
KING EDWARD   *To Richard and George*
   Brothers, you muse what chat we two have had.   *109*

---

93 *state* kingship   **99** *cavil* quibble frivolously   **104** *other some* some others
107 *ghostly* spiritual; *father* i.e., a priest; *done his shrift* finished hearing confession   **108** *for shift* (1) as a trick to serve some purpose, (2) to gain access to her undergarments (to say that a woman was "shriven to her shift" was a common off-color joke meaning that she had been seduced)   **109** *muse* wonder

Richard and George come forward.

RICHARD DUKE OF GLOUCESTER

110 The widow likes it not, for she looks very sad.

KING EDWARD

You'd think it strange if I should marry her.

GEORGE DUKE OF CLARENCE

To who, my lord?

KING EDWARD   Why, Clarence, to myself.

RICHARD DUKE OF GLOUCESTER

113 That would be ten days' wonder at the least.

GEORGE DUKE OF CLARENCE

That's a day longer than a wonder lasts.

RICHARD DUKE OF GLOUCESTER

115 By so much is the wonder in extremes.

KING EDWARD

Well, jest on, brothers – I can tell you both
Her suit is granted for her husband's lands.
Enter a Nobleman.

NOBLEMAN

My gracious lord, Henry your foe is taken
And brought as prisoner to your palace gate.

KING EDWARD

120 See that he be conveyed unto the Tower –
To Richard and George
And go we, brothers, to the man that took him,

122 To question of his apprehension.
To Lady Grey
Widow, go you along. *(To Richard and George)* Lords,
use her honorably.   *Exeunt all but Richard.*

RICHARD DUKE OF GLOUCESTER

Ay, Edward will use women honorably.

125 Would he were wasted, marrow, bones, and all,
That from his loins no hopeful branch may spring

---

110 *sad* serious 113 *ten days' wonder* i.e., a most marvelous thing (proverbially, a novelty attracts for only nine days) 115 *in extremes* exceedingly
great 122 *question . . . apprehension* inquire about his capture 125
wasted . . . all destroyed utterly by (venereal) disease

To cross me from the golden time I look for.   127
And yet, between my soul's desire and me –
The lustful Edward's title burièd –   129
Is Clarence, Henry, and his son young Edward,   *130*
And all the unlooked-for issue of their bodies,   131
To take their rooms ere I can place myself.   132
A cold premeditation for my purpose.   133
Why, then, I do but dream on sovereignty
Like one that stands upon a promontory
And spies a far-off shore where he would tread,
Wishing his foot were equal with his eye,   .   137
And chides the sea that sunders him from thence,
Saying he'll lade it dry to have his way –   139
So do I wish the crown being so far off,   ı   140
And so I chide the means that keeps me from it,   141
And so I say I'll cut the causes off,
Flattering me with impossibilities.   143
My eye's too quick, my heart o'erweens too much,   144
Unless my hand and strength could equal them.
Well, say there is no kingdom then for Richard –
What other pleasure can the world afford?
I'll make my heaven in a lady's lap,
And deck my body in gay ornaments,
And 'witch sweet ladies with my words and looks.   150
O, miserable thought! And more unlikely   .
Than to accomplish twenty golden crowns.   152
Why, love forswore me in my mother's womb,   153
And, for I should not deal in her soft laws,   154
She did corrupt frail nature with some bribe
To shrink mine arm up like a withered·shrub,
To make an envious mountain on my back –   157
Where sits deformity to mock my body –

---

127 *cross* keep   129 *burièd* out of the way   131 *unlooked-for* unanticipated
132 *rooms* places   133 *cold premeditation* discouraging forecast   137 *equal
with* as capable as   139 *lade* ladle   140 *wish* wish for   141 *means* obstacles
143 *me* myself   144 *o'erweens* presumes   150 *'witch* bewitch   152 *accomplish* obtain   153 *forswore* abandoned   154 *for* so that   157 *envious* detested

To shape my legs of an unequal size,
160   To disproportion me in every part,
161   Like to a chaos, or an unlicked bear whelp
162   That carries no impression like the dam.
And am I then a man to be beloved?
O, monstrous fault, to harbor such a thought!
Then, since this earth affords no joy to me
166   But to command, to check, to o'erbear such
167   As are of better person than myself,
I'll make my heaven to dream upon the crown,
And whiles I live, t' account this world but hell,
170   Until my misshaped trunk that bears this head
171   Be round impalèd with a glorious crown.
And yet I know not how to get the crown,
173   For many lives stand between me and home.
And I – like one lost in a thorny wood,
That rends the thorns and is rent with the thorns,
Seeking a way and straying from the way,
Not knowing how to find the open air,
But toiling desperately to find it out –
Torment myself to catch the English crown.
180   And from that torment I will free myself,
Or hew my way out with a bloody ax.
Why, I can smile, and murder whiles I smile,
And cry "Content!" to that which grieves my heart,
And wet my cheeks with artificial tears,
And frame my face to all occasions.
186   I'll drown more sailors than the mermaid shall;
187   I'll slay more gazers than the basilisk;
188   I'll play the orator as well as Nestor,

---

161 *chaos* unformed mass; *unlicked bear whelp* (bear cubs were supposedly born as lumps of matter and licked into shape by their mothers) **162** *impression* shape; *dam* mother **166** *check* rebuke; *o'erbear* dominate **167** *person* appearance **171** *impalèd* encircled **173** *home* i.e., my goal **186** *mermaid* siren **187** *basilisk* fabulous serpent whose look killed the gazed-upon **188** *Nestor* the aged Greek warrior at the siege of Troy, noted for his wisdom

Deceive more slyly than Ulysses could,   189
And, like a Sinon, take another Troy.   190
I can add colors to the chameleon,
Change shapes with Proteus for advantages,   192
And set the murderous Machiavel to school.   193
Can I do this, and cannot get a crown?
Tut, were it farther off, I'll pluck it down.   *Exit.*

*

∾ **III.3** *Two chairs of state. Flourish. Enter King Louis*
of France, his sister the Lady Bonne, Lord Bourbon his
admiral, Prince Edward, Queen Margaret, and the
Earl of Oxford. Louis goes up upon the state, sits, and
riseth up again.

KING LOUIS
Fair Queen of England, worthy Margaret,
Sit down with us. It ill befits thy state   2
And birth that thou shouldst stand while Louis doth sit.
QUEEN MARGARET
No, mighty King of France, now Margaret
Must strike her sail and learn a while to serve   5
Where kings command. I was, I must confess,
Great Albion's queen in former golden days,   7
But now mischance hath trod my title down,
And with dishonor laid me on the ground,
Where I must take like seat unto my fortune   10
And to my humble state conform myself.

---

189 *Ulysses* the Greek warrior, the subject of the *Odyssey*, noted for his crafti-
ness 190 *a Sinon* the Greek who persuaded the Trojans to bring the
Wooden Horse into the city 192 *Proteus* the sea deity who, when captured,
changed his shape; *for advantages* as my purpose dictates 193 *Machiavel*
Machiavelli (Italian political philosopher [1469–1527], known in England as
an advocate of guile and ruthlessness in the attainment of political objectives)
    III.3 The king's palace, France **s.d.** *Two* (possibly three, one each for King
Louis, Queen Margaret, and Lady Bonne) 2 *state* status 5 *strike her sail*
lower her sail (a mark of deference paid at sea to a senior) 7 *Albion's* England's

KING LOUIS
　Why, say, fair queen, whence springs this deep despair?
QUEEN MARGARET
　From such a cause as fills mine eyes with tears
　And stops my tongue, while heart is drowned in cares.
KING LOUIS
15　Whate'er it be, be thou still like thyself,
　And sit thee by our side.

　　　Seats her by him.

　　　　　　　　　　Yield not thy neck
　To fortune's yoke, but let thy dauntless mind
　Still ride in triumph over all mischance.
　Be plain, Queen Margaret, and tell thy grief.
20　It shall be eased if France can yield relief.
QUEEN MARGARET
　Those gracious words revive my drooping thoughts,
　And give my tongue-tied sorrows leave to speak.
　Now, therefore, be it known to noble Louis
　That Henry, sole possessor of my love,
25　Is of a king become a banished man,
26　And forced to live in Scotland a forlorn,
　While proud ambitious Edward, Duke of York,
　Usurps the regal title and the seat
　Of England's true-anointed lawful king.
30　This is the cause that I, poor Margaret,
　With this my son, Prince Edward, Henry's heir,
　Am come to crave thy just and lawful aid.
　An if thou fail us all our hope is done.
　Scotland hath will to help, but cannot help;
　Our people and our peers are both misled,
　Our treasure seized, our soldiers put to flight,
　And, as thou seest, ourselves in heavy plight.
KING LOUIS
　Renownèd queen, with patience calm the storm,

---

15 *be thou . . . thyself* i.e., behave always in a way appropriate to your great-
ness　20 *France* the king of France　25 *of* instead of　26 *forlorn* outcast

While we bethink a means to break it off.   39
QUEEN MARGARET
The more we stay, the stronger grows our foe.   40
KING LOUIS
The more I stay, the more I'll succor thee.
QUEEN MARGARET
O, but impatience waiteth on true sorrow.   42
        Enter the Earl of Warwick.
And see where comes the breeder of my sorrow.
KING LOUIS
What's he approacheth boldly to our presence?
QUEEN MARGARET
Our Earl of Warwick, Edward's greatest friend.
KING LOUIS
Welcome, brave Warwick. What brings thee to France?
        He descends. She ariseth.
QUEEN MARGARET   *Aside*
Ay, now begins a second storm to rise,
For this is he that moves both wind and tide.
WARWICK   *To King Louis*
From worthy Edward, King of Albion,
My lord and sovereign, and thy vowèd friend,   50
I come in kindness and unfeignèd love,
First, to do greetings to thy royal person,
And then, to crave a league of amity,   53
And lastly, to confirm that amity
With nuptial knot, if thou vouchsafe to grant
That virtuous Lady Bonnë, thy fair sister,   56
To England's king in lawful marriage.
QUEEN MARGARET   *Aside*
If that go forward, Henry's hope is done.
WARWICK   *To Lady Bonne*
And, gracious madam, in our king's behalf
I am commanded, with your leave and favor,   60

---

39 *break it off* stop it   40 *stay* delay   42 *waiteth on* attends   53 *league* alliance; *amity* friendship   56 *sister* i.e., sister-in-law

Humbly to kiss your hand, and with my tongue
To tell the passion of my sovereign's heart,
Where fame, late ent'ring at his heedful ears,
Hath placed thy beauty's image and thy virtue.
QUEEN MARGARET
King Louis and Lady Bonnë, hear me speak
Before you answer Warwick. His demand
Springs not from Edward's well-meant honest love,
But from deceit, bred by necessity.
For how can tyrants safely govern home
70   Unless abroad they purchase great alliance?
To prove him tyrant this reason may suffice –
That Henry liveth still; but were he dead,
Yet here Prince Edward stands, King Henry's son.
Look, therefore, Louis, that by this league and marriage
Thou draw not on thy danger and dishonor,
76   For though usurpers sway the rule a while,
Yet heav'ns are just and time suppresseth wrongs.
WARWICK
78   Injurious Margaret.
PRINCE EDWARD   And why not "Queen"?
WARWICK
Because thy father Henry did usurp,
80   And thou no more art prince than she is queen.
OXFORD
81   Then Warwick disannuls great John of Ghent,
82   Which did subdue the greatest part of Spain;
And, after John of Ghent, Henry the Fourth,
Whose wisdom was a mirror to the wisest;
And, after that wise prince, Henry the Fifth,
Who by his prowess conquerèd all France.
From these our Henry lineally descends.
WARWICK
Oxford, how haps it in this smooth discourse
You told not how Henry the Sixth hath lost

---

70 *purchase* obtain 76 *sway the rule* exercise power 78 *Injurious* insulting
81 *disannuls* cancels out 82 *Which . . . Spain* (John of Ghent did campaign
in Spain, but his successes were minor)

All that which Henry the Fifth had gotten?   *90*
Methinks these peers of France should smile at that.
But for the rest, you tell a pedigree   *92*
Of threescore and two years – a silly time
To make prescription for a kingdom's worth.

OXFORD
Why, Warwick, canst thou speak against thy liege,
Whom thou obeyedest thirty and six years,
And not bewray thy treason with a blush?   *97*

WARWICK
Can Oxford, that did ever fence the right,   *98*
Now buckler falsehood with a pedigree?   *99*
For shame – leave Henry, and call Edward king.   *100*

OXFORD
Call him my king by whose injurious doom   101
My elder brother, the Lord Aubrey Vere,   102
Was done to death? And more than so, my father,   103
Even in the downfall of his mellowed years,   104
When nature brought him to the door of death?
No, Warwick, no – while life upholds this arm,
This arm upholds the house of Lancaster.

WARWICK
And I the house of York.

KING LOUIS
Queen Margaret, Prince Edward, and Oxford,
Vouchsafe, at our request, to stand aside   *110*
While I use further conference with Warwick.   111

Queen Margaret comes down from the state and, with
Prince Edward and Oxford, stands apart.

QUEEN MARGARET
Heavens grant that Warwick's words bewitch him not.

92–94 *you . . . worth* i.e., the line you describe runs for sixty-two years, a
ridiculously short time upon which to base a claim sanctioned by custom
(*prescription*) to the wealth and honor of kingship **97** *bewray* reveal **98**
fence the right defend justice **99** *buckler* shield **101** *injurious doom* insulting judgment **102** *Lord Aubrey Vere* (Holinshed reports that in 1462 the
twelfth Earl of Oxford and Lord Aubrey Vere, his eldest son, were accused of
treason and executed) **103** *more than so* yet more **104** *downfall* decline
111 *use further conference* talk further

KING LOUIS
Now, Warwick, tell me even upon thy conscience,
Is Edward your true king? For I were loath
To link with him that were not lawful chosen.
WARWICK
Thereon I pawn my credit and mine honor.
KING LOUIS
But is he gracious in the people's eye?
WARWICK
The more that Henry was unfortunate.
KING LOUIS
Then further, all dissembling set aside,
120   Tell me for truth the measure of his love
Unto our sister Bonnë.
WARWICK   Such it seems
122   As may beseem a monarch like himself.
Myself have often heard him say and swear
124   That this his love was an eternal plant,
Whereof the root was fixed in virtue's ground,
The leaves and fruit maintained with beauty's sun,
127   Exempt from envy, but not from disdain,
Unless the Lady Bonnë quit his pain.
KING LOUIS *To Lady Bonne*
Now, sister, let us hear your firm resolve.
LADY BONNE
130   Your grant, or your denial, shall be mine.
To Warwick
Yet I confess that often ere this day,
132   When I have heard your king's desert recounted,
Mine ear hath tempted judgment to desire.
KING LOUIS *To Warwick*
Then, Warwick, thus – our sister shall be Edward's.
And now, forthwith, shall articles be drawn

---

122 *beseem* befit   124 *eternal* i.e., heavenly   127–28 *Exempt . . . pain* i.e.,
Edward's love will be free from the effects of sharp criticism (*envy*) of Lady
Bonne (because of her coldness to his suit), but it will suffer from rejection
(*disdain*) unless she reward his passion for her (*quit his pain*)   130 *grant* con-
currence   132 *desert* merit

Touching the jointure that your king must make,   136
Which with her dowry shall be counterpoised.   137
   To Queen Margaret
Draw near, Queen Margaret, and be a witness
That Bonnë shall be wife to the English king.
   Queen Margaret, Prince Edward, and Oxford come
   forward.

PRINCE EDWARD
To Edward, but not to the English king.   140

QUEEN MARGARET
Deceitful Warwick – it was thy device
By this alliance to make void my suit!
Before thy coming Louis was Henry's friend.

KING LOUIS
And still is friend to him and Margaret.
But if your title to the crown be weak,
As may appear by Edward's good success,
Then 'tis but reason that I be released
From giving aid which late I promisèd.   148
Yet shall you have all kindness at my hand
That your estate requires and mine can yield.   150

WARWICK   *To Queen Margaret*
Henry now lives in Scotland at his ease,
Where having nothing, nothing can he lose.
And as for you yourself, our quondam queen,   153
You have a father able to maintain you,
And better 'twere you troubled him than France.

QUEEN MARGARET
Peace, impudent and shameless Warwick, peace!
Proud setter up and puller down of kings!
I will not hence till, with my talk and tears,
Both full of truth, I make King Louis behold
Thy sly conveyance and thy lord's false love,   160

---

136 *jointure* marriage settlement   137 *counterpoised* matched   148 *late* recently   153 *quondam* former   160 *conveyance* trickery; **s.d.** *Post* dispatch
rider

Post blowing a horn within.
For both of you are birds of selfsame feather.

KING LOUIS
Warwick, this is some post to us or thee.
Enter the Post.

POST   *To Warwick*
My Lord Ambassador, these letters are for you,
Sent from your brother Marquis Montague;
To Louis
These from our king unto your majesty;
To Queen Margaret
And, madam, these for you, from whom I know not.
They all read their letters.

OXFORD   *To Prince Edward*
I like it well that our fair queen and mistress
Smiles at her news, while Warwick frowns at his.

PRINCE EDWARD
Nay, mark how Louis stamps as he were nettled.
170   I hope all's for the best.

KING LOUIS
Warwick, what are thy news? And yours, fair queen?

QUEEN MARGARET
Mine, such as fill my heart with unhoped joys.

WARWICK
Mine, full of sorrow and heart's discontent.

KING LOUIS
What! Has your king married the Lady Grey?
175   And now to soothe your forgery and his,
Sends me a paper to persuade me patience?
Is this th' alliance that he seeks with France?
Dare he presume to scorn us in this manner?

QUEEN MARGARET
I told your majesty as much before –
180   This proveth Edward's love and Warwick's honesty.

WARWICK
King Louis, I here protest in sight of heaven

---

175 *soothe* smooth over; *forgery* deceit

And by the hope I have of heavenly bliss,
That I am clear from this misdeed of Edward's,
No more my king, for he dishonors me,
But most himself, if he could see his shame.
Did I forget that by the house of York
My father came untimely to his death?   187
Did I let pass th' abuse done to my niece?   188
Did I impale him with the regal crown?   189
Did I put Henry from his native right?   *190*
And am I guerdoned at the last with shame?   191
Shame on himself, for my desert is honor.
And to repair my honor, lost for him,
I here renounce him and return to Henry.
    To Queen Margaret
My noble queen, let former grudges pass,
And henceforth I am thy true servitor.   196
I will revenge his wrong to Lady Bonnë
And replant Henry in his former state.
QUEEN MARGARET
    Warwick, these words have turned my hate to love,
    And I forgive and quite forget old faults,   *200*
    And joy that thou becom'st King Henry's friend.
WARWICK
    So much his friend, ay, his unfeignèd friend,
    That if King Louis vouchsafe to furnish us
    With some few bands of chosen soldiers,
    I'll undertake to land them on our coast
    And force the tyrant from his seat by war.
    'Tis not his new-made bride shall succor him.
    And as for Clarence, as my letters tell me,
    He's very likely now to fall from him   209

---

187 *My . . . death* (According to the chronicles, Warwick's father, the Salisbury of *2 Henry VI*, was captured by the Lancastrians at Wakefield and beheaded. Perhaps what Warwick means is that his father would not have died in the Yorkist cause had the Yorkists never laid claim to the throne.)   188 *Did . . . niece* (Holinshed reports that Edward "would have deflowered" Warwick's "daughter or his niece")   189 *impale him* encircle his brow   191 *guerdoned* rewarded   196 *servitor* servant   209 *fall from* desert

210 For matching more for wanton lust than honor,
Or than for strength and safety of our country.
LADY BONNE *To King Louis*
Dear brother, how shall Bonnë be revenged,
But by thy help to this distressèd queen?
QUEEN MARGARET *To King Louis*
Renownèd prince, how shall poor Henry live
Unless thou rescue him from foul despair?
LADY BONNE *To King Louis*
My quarrel and this English queen's are one.
WARWICK
And mine, fair Lady Bonnë, joins with yours.
KING LOUIS
And mine with hers, and thine, and Margaret's.
Therefore at last I firmly am resolved:
220 You shall have aid.
QUEEN MARGARET
Let me give humble thanks for all at once.
KING LOUIS *To the Post*
222 Then, England's messenger, return in post
And tell false Edward, thy supposèd king,
224 That Louis of France is sending over masquers
To revel it with him and his new bride.
226 Thou seest what's passed, go fear thy king withal.
LADY BONNE *To the Post*
Tell him, in hope he'll prove a widower shortly,
228 I'll wear the willow garland for his sake.
QUEEN MARGARET *To the Post*
229 Tell him my mourning weeds are laid aside,
230 And I am ready to put armor on.
WARWICK *To the Post*
Tell him from me that he hath done me wrong,
And therefore I'll uncrown him ere't be long.

---

210 *matching* marrying **222** *post* haste **224** *masquers* participants in the courtly dramatic performances, or revels, that were staged to celebrate aristocratic marriages (here meant ironically) **226** *fear* frighten; *withal* with it **228** *willow garland* (symbol of rejected love) **229** *weeds* garments

Giving money
There's thy reward – be gone.   *Exit Post.*
KING LOUIS
But, Warwick, thou and Oxford, with five thousand
    men,
Shall cross the seas and bid false Edward battle;
And, as occasion serves, this noble queen
And prince shall follow with a fresh supply.
Yet, ere thou go, but answer me one doubt:
What pledge have we of thy firm loyalty?
WARWICK
This shall assure my constant loyalty: 240
That if our queen and this young prince agree,
I'll join mine eldest daughter and my joy   242
To him forthwith in holy wedlock bands.
QUEEN MARGARET
Yes, I agree, and thank you for your motion.   244
    To Prince Edward
Son Edward, she is fair and virtuous,
Therefore delay not. Give thy hand to Warwick,
And with thy hand thy faith irrevocable
That only Warwick's daughter shall be thine.
PRINCE EDWARD
Yes, I accept her, for she well deserves it,
And here to pledge my vow I give my hand.   250
    He and Warwick clasp hands.
KING LOUIS
Why stay we now? These soldiers shall be levied,
And thou, Lord Bourbon, our high admiral,
Shall waft them over with our royal fleet.   253
I long till Edward fall by war's mischance
For mocking marriage with a dame of France.
                    Exeunt all but Warwick.

---

242 *eldest daughter* (Actually his younger daughter, Anne, as his elder daughter, Isabella, is to marry Clarence. In the chronicles, Isabella and Clarence are
already married at this time.)   244 *motion* offer   253 *waft* transport by
water

WARWICK
    I came from Edward as ambassador,
    But I return his sworn and mortal foe.
    Matter of marriage was the charge he gave me,
    But dreadful war shall answer his demand.
260   Had he none else to make a stale but me?
    Then none but I shall turn his jest to sorrow.
    I was the chief that raised him to the crown,
    And I'll be chief to bring him down again.
    Not that I pity Henry's misery,
    But seek revenge on Edward's mockery.   *Exit.*

✻

∾ **IV.1** *Enter Richard Duke of Gloucester, George Duke of Clarence, the Duke of Somerset, and the Marquis of Montague.*

RICHARD DUKE OF GLOUCESTER
    Now tell me, brother Clarence, what think you
    Of this new marriage with the Lady Grey?
    Hath not our brother made a worthy choice?
GEORGE DUKE OF CLARENCE
    Alas, you know 'tis far from hence to France;
5   How could he stay till Warwick made return?
SOMERSET
    My lords, forbear this talk – here comes the king.
    Flourish. Enter King Edward, Elizabeth Lady Grey his
    Queen, the Earl of Pembroke, and the Lords Stafford
    and Hastings. Four stand on one side of the King,
    and four on the other.
RICHARD DUKE OF GLOUCESTER
    And his well-chosen bride.
GEORGE DUKE OF CLARENCE
8   I mind to tell him plainly what I think.

---

260 *stale* dupe
    IV.1 The palace, London   **5** *stay* wait   **8** *mind* intend

KING EDWARD
　Now, brother of Clarence, how like you our choice,
　That you stand pensive, as half malcontent?　　　　10
GEORGE DUKE OF CLARENCE
　As well as Louis of France, or the Earl of Warwick,
　Which are so weak of courage and in judgment　　12
　That they'll take no offense at our abuse.　　　　13
KING EDWARD
　Suppose they take offense without a cause –
　They are but Louis and Warwick; I am Edward,
　Your king and Warwick's, and must have my will.　16
RICHARD DUKE OF GLOUCESTER
　And you shall have your will, because our king.
　Yet hasty marriage seldom proveth well.
KING EDWARD
　Yea, brother Richard, are you offended too?
RICHARD DUKE OF GLOUCESTER
　Not I, no – God forbid that I should wish them severed　20
　Whom God hath joined together. Ay, and 'twere pity
　To sunder them that yoke so well together.　　　22
KING EDWARD
　Setting your scorns and your mislike aside,　　　23
　Tell me some reason why the Lady Grey
　Should not become my wife and England's queen.
　And you too, Somerset and Montague,
　Speak freely what you think.
GEORGE DUKE OF CLARENCE
　Then this is my opinion: that King Louis
　Becomes your enemy for mocking him
　About the marriage of the Lady Bonnë.　　　　30
RICHARD DUKE OF GLOUCESTER
　And Warwick, doing what you gave in charge,
　Is now dishonorèd by this new marriage.

---

10 *malcontent* disgusted with the world   12 *Which* who   13 *abuse* insult
16 *will* (1) way, (2) sexual desire satisfied   22 *that yoke* who are joined (in
marriage)   23 *mislike* displeasure

KING EDWARD
What if both Louis and Warwick be appeased
34   By such invention as I can devise?
MONTAGUE
Yet, to have joined with France in such alliance
Would more have strengthened this our common-
wealth
'Gainst foreign storms than any home-bred marriage.
HASTINGS
Why, knows not Montague that of itself
England is safe, if true within itself?
MONTAGUE
40   But the safer when 'tis backed with France.
HASTINGS
'Tis better using France than trusting France.
Let us be backed with God and with the seas
Which he hath giv'n for fence impregnable,
44   And with their helps only defend ourselves.
In them and in ourselves our safety lies.
GEORGE DUKE OF CLARENCE
For this one speech Lord Hastings well deserves
47   To have the heir of the Lord Hungerford.
KING EDWARD
Ay, what of that? It was my will and grant –
And for this once my will shall stand for law.
RICHARD DUKE OF GLOUCESTER
50   And yet, methinks, your grace hath not done well
To give the heir and daughter of Lord Scales
52   Unto the brother of your loving bride.
She better would have fitted me or Clarence,
54   But in your bride you bury brotherhood.
GEORGE DUKE OF CLARENCE
Or else you would not have bestowed the heir

---

34 *invention* plan   44 *only* alone   47 *heir . . . Hungerford* i.e., a wealthy heiress (George's point is that Lady Grey's upstart relatives, such as Hastings, are inappropriately being matched with wealthy partners)   52 *brother . . . bride* i.e., Lord Rivers   54 *But in* because of; *bury* forget

Of the Lord Bonville on your new wife's son,   56
And leave your brothers to go speed elsewhere.   57

KING EDWARD
Alas, poor Clarence, is it for a wife
That thou art malcontent? I will provide thee.

GEORGE DUKE OF CLARENCE
In choosing for yourself you showed your judgment,   60
Which being shallow, you shall give me leave
To play the broker in mine own behalf,   62
And to that end I shortly mind to leave you.

KING EDWARD
Leave me, or tarry. Edward will be king,
And not be tied unto his brother's will.

QUEEN ELIZABETH
My lords, before it pleased his majesty
To raise my state to title of a queen,
Do me but right, and you must all confess
That I was not ignoble of descent –
And meaner than myself have had like fortune.   70
But as this title honors me and mine,
So your dislikes, to whom I would be pleasing,   72
Doth cloud my joys with danger and with sorrow.   73

KING EDWARD
My love, forbear to fawn upon their frowns.   74
What danger or what sorrow can befall thee
So long as Edward is thy constant friend,
And their true sovereign, whom they must obey?
Nay, whom they shall obey, and love thee too –
Unless they seek for hatred at my hands,
Which if they do, yet will I keep thee safe,   80
And they shall feel the vengeance of my wrath.

RICHARD DUKE OF GLOUCESTER   *Aside*
I hear, yet say not much, but think the more.

---

56 *son* i.e., Sir Thomas Grey, Marquis of Dorset   57 *go speed* prosper (for
themselves)   62 *broker* agent   70 *meaner* persons of lower social rank; *like
fortune* (Not true: Elizabeth Woodville was the first commoner to become a
queen of England.)   72 *dislikes* disapproval   73 *danger* apprehension   74
forbear . . . frowns pay no attention to their disapproval

Enter the Post from France.

KING EDWARD
Now, messenger, what letters or what news from France?

POST
My sovereign liege, no letters and few words,
But such as I, without your special pardon,
Dare not relate.

KING EDWARD
87   Go to, we pardon thee. Therefore, in brief,
88   Tell me their words as near as thou canst guess them.
What answer makes King Louis unto our letters?

POST
90   At my depart these were his very words:
"Go tell false Edward, thy supposèd king,
That Louis of France is sending over masquers
To revel it with him and his new bride."

KING EDWARD
94   Is Louis so brave? Belike he thinks me Henry.
But what said Lady Bonnë to my marriage?

POST
These were her words, uttered with mild disdain:
"Tell him, in hope he'll prove a widower shortly,
I'll wear the willow garland for his sake."

KING EDWARD
I blame not her, she could say little less;
100   She had the wrong. But what said Henry's queen?
101   For I have heard that she was there in place.

POST
"Tell him," quoth she, "my mourning weeds are done,
And I am ready to put armor on."

KING EDWARD
Belike she minds to play the Amazon.
But what said Warwick to these injuries?

POST
He, more incensed against your majesty

---

87 *Go to* all right, don't worry 88 *guess* approximate 90 *depart* departure
94 *Belike* perhaps 101 *in place* present

Than all the rest, discharged me with these words:
"Tell him from me that he hath done me wrong,
And therefore I'll uncrown him ere't be long."

KING EDWARD

Ha! Durst the traitor breathe out so proud words?   110
Well, I will arm me, being thus forewarned.
They shall have wars and pay for their presumption.
But say, is Warwick friends with Margaret?

POST

Ay, gracious sovereign, they are so linked in friendship
That young Prince Edward marries Warwick's daughter.

GEORGE DUKE OF CLARENCE

Belike the elder; Clarence will have the younger.   116
Now, brother king, farewell, and sit you fast,
For I will hence to Warwick's other daughter,
That, though I want a kingdom, yet in marriage   119
I may not prove inferior to yourself.   120
You that love me and Warwick, follow me.
                    Exit Clarence, and Somerset follows.

RICHARD DUKE OF GLOUCESTER

Not I – *(Aside)* my thoughts aim at a further matter.
I stay not for the love of Edward, but the crown.

KING EDWARD

Clarence and Somerset both gone to Warwick?
Yet am I armed against the worst can happen,
And haste is needful in this desp'rate case.
Pembroke and Stafford, you in our behalf
Go levy men and make prepare for war.   128
They are already, or quickly will be, landed.
Myself in person will straight follow you.   130
                    Exeunt Pembroke and Stafford.
But ere I go, Hastings and Montague,
Resolve my doubt. You twain, of all the rest,
Are near'st to Warwick by blood and by alliance.
Tell me if you love Warwick more than me.

---

116 *Belike . . . younger* (see the note to III.3.242)   119 *want* lack   128 *prepare* preparation

If it be so, then both depart to him –
136   I rather wish you foes than hollow friends.
But if you mind to hold your true obedience,
Give me assurance with some friendly vow
139   That I may never have you in suspect.

MONTAGUE
140   So God help Montague as he proves true.

HASTINGS
And Hastings as he favors Edward's cause.

KING EDWARD
Now, brother Richard, will you stand by us?

RICHARD DUKE OF GLOUCESTER
Ay, in despite of all that shall withstand you.

KING EDWARD
Why, so. Then am I sure of victory.
Now, therefore, let us hence and lose no hour
146   Till we meet Warwick with his foreign power.   *Exeunt.*

* * * * *

∾ **IV.2** *Enter the Earls of Warwick and Oxford
in England, with French Soldiers.*

WARWICK
1   Trust me, my lord, all hitherto goes well.
The common sort by numbers swarm to us.
     Enter the Dukes of Clarence and Somerset.
But see where Somerset and Clarence comes.
Speak suddenly, my lords, are we all friends?

GEORGE DUKE OF CLARENCE
Fear not that, my lord.

WARWICK
Then, gentle Clarence, welcome unto Warwick –
And welcome, Somerset. I hold it cowardice
To rest mistrustful where a noble heart

---

136 *hollow* empty (i.e., untrustworthy)   **139** *suspect* suspicion   **146** *power*
army
   IV.2 Fields near Warwick   **1** *hitherto* so far

Hath pawned an open hand in sign of love,   9
Else might I think that Clarence, Edward's brother,   10
Were but a feignèd friend to our proceedings.
But come, sweet Clarence, my daughter shall be thine.
And now what rests but, in night's coverture,   13
Thy brother being carelessly encamped,
His soldiers lurking in the towns about,   15
And but attended by a simple guard,
We may surprise and take him at our pleasure?
Our scouts have found the adventure very easy;
That, as Ulysses and stout Diomed   19
With sleight and manhood stole to Rhesus' tents   20
And brought from thence the Thracian fatal steeds,
So we, well covered with the night's black mantle,
At unawares may beat down Edward's guard   23
And seize himself – I say not "slaughter him,"
For I intend but only to surprise him.   25
You that will follow me to this attempt,
Applaud the name of Henry with your leader.
        They all cry "Henry!"
Why, then, let's on our way in silent sort,   28
For Warwick and his friends, God and Saint George!
                                        Exeunt.

                    *

---

9 *pawned* pledged   13 *rests* remains; *in night's coverture* under cover of night
15 *lurking* idling   19–21 *That . . . steeds* (The oracle predicted that Troy
would not fall if the horses of Rhesus, king of Thrace, grazed on the Trojan
plain. To prevent their doing so, Ulysses and Diomedes captured them on a
night raid.)   20 *sleight* stealth; *manhood* manly actions, bravery   23 *At unawares* suddenly   25 *surprise* capture   28 *sort* manner

∽ **IV.3** *Enter three Watchmen, to guard King Edward's tent.*

FIRST WATCHMAN

1   Come on, my masters, each man take his stand.

2   The king by this is set him down to sleep.

SECOND WATCHMAN

What, will he not to bed?

FIRST WATCHMAN

Why, no – for he hath made a solemn vow

Never to lie and take his natural rest

6   Till Warwick or himself be quite suppressed.

SECOND WATCHMAN

Tomorrow then belike shall be the day,

If Warwick be so near as men report.

THIRD WATCHMAN

But say, I pray, what nobleman is that

10   That with the king here resteth in his tent?

FIRST WATCHMAN

'Tis the Lord Hastings, the king's chiefest friend.

THIRD WATCHMAN

O, is it so? But why commands the king

That his chief followers lodge in towns about him,

14   While he himself keeps in the cold field?

SECOND WATCHMAN

'Tis the more honor, because more dangerous.

THIRD WATCHMAN

16   Ay, but give me worship and quietness –

I like it better than a dangerous honor.

18   If Warwick knew in what estate he stands,

19   'Tis to be doubted he would waken him.

FIRST WATCHMAN

20   Unless our halberds did shut up his passage.

IV.3 King Edward's camp, near Warwick **1** *stand* post **2** *this* i.e., this time; *set him down* settled in a chair **6** *suppressed* defeated **14** *keeps* lodges **16** *worship* a place of dignity **18** *estate* condition; *he* King Edward **19** *doubted* feared **20** *halberds* axlike weapons on long staves; *shut up* bar

SECOND WATCHMAN
  Ay, wherefore else guard we his royal tent
  But to defend his person from night foes?
      Enter silently the Earl of Warwick, George Duke of
      Clarence, the Earl of Oxford, and the Duke of
      Somerset, with French Soldiers.
WARWICK
  This is his tent – and see where stand his guard.
  Courage, my masters – honor now or never!
  But follow me, and Edward shall be ours.
FIRST WATCHMAN   Who goes there?
SECOND WATCHMAN   Stay or thou diest.
      Warwick and the rest all cry "Warwick, Warwick!"
      and set upon the Guard, who fly, crying "Arm, arm!"
      Warwick and the rest follow them.

                    *

  ∾ IV.4 *With the Drummer playing and the Trumpeter*
      sounding, enter the Earl of Warwick, the Duke of
      Somerset, and the rest, bringing King Edward out
      in his gown, sitting in a chair. Richard Duke of
      Gloucester and Lord Hastings flee over the stage.

SOMERSET
  What are they that fly there?
WARWICK
  Richard and Hastings – let them go. Here is the duke.
KING EDWARD
  "The duke"! Why, Warwick, when we parted,
  Thou calledst me king.   4
WARWICK   Ay, but the case is altered.
  When you disgraced me in my embassade,   5
  Then I degraded you from being king,
  And come now to create you Duke of York.
  Alas, how should you govern any kingdom

IV.4 King Edward's camp   4 *the case is altered* things have changed (prover-
bial)   5 *embassade* diplomatic mission

That know not how to use ambassadors,
10 Nor how to be contented with one wife,
Nor how to use your brothers brotherly,
Nor how to study for the people's welfare,
13 Nor how to shroud yourself from enemies?
KING EDWARD *Seeing George*
Yea, brother of Clarence, art thou here too?
15 Nay, then, I see that Edward needs must down.
Yet, Warwick, in despite of all mischance,
17 Of thee thyself and all thy complices,
Edward will always bear himself as king.
19 Though fortune's malice overthrow my state,
20 My mind exceeds the compass of her wheel.
WARWICK
21 Then, for his mind, be Edward England's king.
Warwick takes off Edward's crown.
But Henry now shall wear the English crown,
And be true king indeed, thou but the shadow.
My Lord of Somerset, at my request,
See that, forthwith, Duke Edward be conveyed
26 Unto my brother, Archbishop of York.
When I have fought with Pembroke and his fellows,
I'll follow you, and tell what answer
Louis and the Lady Bonnë send to him.
30 Now for a while farewell, good Duke of York.
They begin to lead Edward out forcibly.
KING EDWARD
31 What fates impose, that men must needs abide.
32 It boots not to resist both wind and tide.
Exeunt some with Edward.
OXFORD
What now remains, my lords, for us to do

---

13 *shroud* conceal, protect 15 *needs must down* must necessarily be put
down 17 *complices* accomplices 19 *state* sovereignty 20 *compass* circumference 21 *for his* in Edward's 26 *Archbishop of York* i.e., George Neville
31 *abide* endure 32 *boots not* is no use

But march to London with our soldiers?

WARWICK
Ay, that's the first thing that we have to do –
To free King Henry from imprisonment
And see him seated in the regal throne.   *Exeunt.*

*

∾ **IV.5** *Enter Earl Rivers and his sister Queen Elizabeth.*

RIVERS
Madam, what makes you in this sudden change?   1

QUEEN ELIZABETH
Why, brother Rivers, are you yet to learn
What late misfortune is befall'n King Edward?

RIVERS
What? Loss of some pitched battle against Warwick?

QUEEN ELIZABETH
No, but the loss of his own royal person.

RIVERS
Then is my sovereign slain?

QUEEN ELIZABETH
Ay, almost slain – for he is taken prisoner,
Either betrayed by falsehood of his guard
Or by his foe surprised at unawares,
And, as I further have to understand,   *10*
Is new committed to the Bishop of York,   11
Fell Warwick's brother, and by that our foe.   12

RIVERS
These news, I must confess, are full of grief.
Yet, gracious madam, bear it as you may.
Warwick may lose, that now hath won the day.

QUEEN ELIZABETH
Till then fair hope must hinder life's decay,

IV.5 The palace, London 1 *what . . . change?* why have you suddenly
changed your mind 11 *new* recently; *Bishop* i.e., archbishop 12 *Fell* cruel;
by that i.e., because of that relationship

17   And I the rather wean me from despair
      For love of Edward's offspring in my womb.
19   This is it that makes me bridle passion
20   And bear with mildness my misfortune's cross.
      Ay, ay, for this I draw in many a tear
22   And stop the rising of bloodsucking sighs,
23   Lest with my sighs or tears I blast or drown
      King Edward's fruit, true heir to th' English crown.
RIVERS
25   But, madam, where is Warwick then become?
QUEEN ELIZABETH
      I am informèd that he comes towards London
      To set the crown once more on Henry's head.
      Guess thou the rest – King Edward's friends must down.
29   But to prevent the tyrant's violence –
30   For trust not him that hath once broken faith –
31   I'll hence forthwith unto the sanctuary,
      To save at least the heir of Edward's right.
      There shall I rest secure from force and fraud.
      Come, therefore, let us fly while we may fly.
      If Warwick take us, we are sure to die.   *Exeunt.*

                              ∗

      ∾ **IV.6** *Enter Richard Duke of Gloucester, Lord*
          Hastings, and Sir William Stanley, with Soldiers.

RICHARD DUKE OF GLOUCESTER
      Now my Lord Hastings and Sir William Stanley,
      Leave off to wonder why I drew you hither
3   Into this chiefest thicket of the park.
      Thus stands the case: you know our king, my brother,
      Is prisoner to the bishop here, at whose hands

`17 *I the rather* I am the more obliged to   19 *bridle* control   22 *bloodsucking sighs* (sighing was supposed to waste the heart's blood, which explains why *hope* can *hinder life's decay* in l. 16)   23 *blast* wither   25 *become* gone   29 *prevent* forestall   31 *sanctuary* (where I will be immune from arrest)
      IV.6 The Archbishop of York's park, or hunting ground, near Warwick
      3 *chiefest* largest; *park* hunting ground

He hath good usage and great liberty,
And, often but attended with weak guard,
Comes hunting this way to disport himself.   8
I have advertised him by secret means   9
That if about this hour he make this way   10
Under the color of his usual game,   11
He shall here find his friends with horse and men
To set him free from his captivity.
    Enter King Edward and a Huntsman with him.
HUNTSMAN
This way, my lord – for this way lies the game.
KING EDWARD
Nay, this way, man – see where the huntsmen stand.
Now, brother of Gloucester, Lord Hastings, and the
    rest,
Stand you thus close to steal the bishop's deer?   17
RICHARD DUKE OF GLOUCESTER
Brother, the time and case requireth haste.
Your horse stands ready at the park corner.
KING EDWARD
But whither shall we then?   20
HASTINGS
To Lynn, my lord,   21
And shipped from thence to Flanders.
RICHARD DUKE OF GLOUCESTER   *Aside*
Well guessed, believe me – for that was my meaning.
KING EDWARD
Stanley, I will requite thy forwardness.   24
RICHARD DUKE OF GLOUCESTER
But wherefore stay we? 'Tis no time to talk.
KING EDWARD
Huntsman, what sayst thou? Wilt thou go along?
HUNTSMAN
Better do so than tarry and be hanged.

---

8 *disport* amuse   9 *advertised* notified   11 *color* pretext; *game* hunting (i.e.,
as though he were merely hunting)   17 *close* hidden   21 *Lynn* i.e., King's
Lynn, on the Norfolk coast   24 *requite* reward; *forwardness* zeal

RICHARD DUKE OF GLOUCESTER
Come then, away – let's have no more ado.
KING EDWARD
Bishop, farewell – shield thee from Warwick's frown,
30 And pray that I may repossess the crown. *Exeunt.*

*

∾ **IV.7** *Flourish. Enter the Earl of Warwick and George
Duke of Clarence with the crown. Then enter King
Henry, the Earl of Oxford, the Duke of Somerset with
young Henry Earl of Richmond, the Marquis of
Montague, and the Lieutenant of the Tower.*

KING HENRY
Master Lieutenant, now that God and friends
Have shaken Edward from the regal seat
And turned my captive state to liberty,
My fear to hope, my sorrows unto joys,
5 At our enlargement what are thy due fees?
LIEUTENANT
6 Subjects may challenge nothing of their sovereigns –
But if an humble prayer may prevail,
I then crave pardon of your majesty.
KING HENRY
For what, lieutenant? For well using me?
10 Nay, be thou sure I'll well requite thy kindness,
For that it made my prisonment a pleasure –
Ay, such a pleasure as encagèd birds
Conceive when, after many moody thoughts,
At last by notes of household harmony
They quite forget their loss of liberty.
But, Warwick, after God, thou sett'st me free,
And chiefly therefore I thank God and thee.
He was the author, thou the instrument.

IV.7 The Tower, London **s.d.** *Lieutenant* deputy warden   **5** *enlargement* re-
lease; *fees* (due because prisoners who could afford it were charged for special
quarters and food)   **6** *challenge* demand

Therefore, that I may conquer fortune's spite
By living low, where fortune cannot hurt me,   20
And that the people of this blessèd land
May not be punished with my thwarting stars,   22
Warwick, although my head still wear the crown,
I here resign my government to thee,
For thou art fortunate in all thy deeds.

WARWICK
Your grace hath still been famed for virtuous,   26
And now may seem as wise as virtuous
By spying and avoiding fortune's malice,
For few men rightly temper with the stars.   29
Yet in this one thing let me blame your grace: 30
For choosing me when Clarence is in place.   31

GEORGE DUKE OF CLARENCE
No, Warwick, thou art worthy of the sway,   32
To whom the heav'ns in thy nativity   33
Adjudged an olive branch and laurel crown,   34
As likely to be blest in peace and war.
And therefore I yield thee my free consent.

WARWICK
And I choose Clarence only for Protector.   37

KING HENRY
Warwick and Clarence, give me both your hands.
Now join your hands, and with your hands your hearts,
That no dissension hinder government.   40
I make you both Protectors of this land,
While I myself will lead a private life
And in devotion spend my latter days,
To sin's rebuke and my creator's praise.

---

20 *low* humbly **22** *thwarting stars* (1) bad luck, (2) stars (instruments of fortune) whose influence impedes happiness and success **26** *still* always **29** *temper . . . stars* i.e., come to terms with their fate **31** *in place* here **32** *sway* rule **33** *nativity* birth (an allusion to astrological determinism) **34** *olive branch* (a symbol of peace); *laurel crown* (a symbol of victory) **37** *only* alone; *Protector* i.e., a kind of deputy king, who ruled during the minority or incapacity of the monarch (Humphrey, Duke of Gloucester, held this position in *2 Henry VI*)

WARWICK
  What answers Clarence to his sovereign's will?
GEORGE DUKE OF CLARENCE
  That he consents, if Warwick yield consent,
  For on thy fortune I repose myself.
WARWICK
  Why, then, though loath, yet must I be content.
  We'll yoke together, like a double shadow
50 To Henry's body, and supply his place –
  I mean in bearing weight of government –
  While he enjoys the honor and his ease.
  And, Clarence, now then it is more than needful
  Forthwith that Edward be pronounced a traitor,
  And all his lands and goods be confiscate.
GEORGE DUKE OF CLARENCE
  What else? And that succession be determined.
WARWICK
57 Ay, therein Clarence shall not want his part.
KING HENRY
  But with the first of all your chief affairs,
  Let me entreat – for I command no more –
60 That Margaret your queen and my son Edward
  Be sent for, to return from France with speed.
  For, till I see them here, by doubtful fear
  My joy of liberty is half eclipsed.
GEORGE DUKE OF CLARENCE
  It shall be done, my sovereign, with all speed.
KING HENRY
  My Lord of Somerset, what youth is that
  Of whom you seem to have so tender care?
SOMERSET
67 My liege, it is young Henry, Earl of Richmond.

---

50 *supply* take   57 *want* lack; *his part* (should the Lancastrian claim be dismissed and Edward proclaimed a traitor, Clarence would be next in line to the throne)   67 *Henry* (the future Henry VII; at his accession to the throne the Wars of the Roses finally ceased)

KING HENRY
  Come hither, England's hope.
    King Henry lays his hand on Richmond's head.
                            If secret powers
  Suggest but truth to my divining thoughts,   69
  This pretty lad will prove our country's bliss.   70
  His looks are full of peaceful majesty,
  His head by nature framed to wear a crown,
  His hand to wield a scepter, and himself
  Likely in time to bless a regal throne.
  Make much of him, my lords, for this is he
  Must help you more than you are hurt by me.
    Enter a Post.
WARWICK
  What news, my friend?
POST
  That Edward is escapèd from your brother
  And fled, as he hears since, to Burgundy.   79
WARWICK
  Unsavory news – but how made he escape?   80
POST
  He was conveyed by Richard Duke of Gloucester   81
  And the Lord Hastings, who attended him   82
  In secret ambush on the forest side
  And from the bishop's huntsmen rescued him –
  For hunting was his daily exercise.
WARWICK
  My brother was too careless of his charge.
    To King Henry
  But let us hence, my sovereign, to provide
  A salve for any sore that may betide.   88
    Exeunt all but Somerset, Richmond, and Oxford.
SOMERSET   *To Oxford*
  My lord, I like not of this flight of Edward's,

---

69 *divining* prophesying **79** *he* i.e., your brother, the Archbishop of York
81 *conveyed* secretly carried away **82** *attended* waited for **88** *betide* develop

90   For doubtless Burgundy will yield him help,
      And we shall have more wars before't be long.
      As Henry's late presaging prophecy
      Did glad my heart with hope of this young Richmond,
      So doth my heart misgive me, in these conflicts,
      What may befall him, to his harm and ours.
      Therefore, Lord Oxford, to prevent the worst,
      Forthwith we'll send him hence to Brittany,
      Till storms be past of civil enmity.

OXFORD
      Ay, for if Edward repossess the crown,
100   'Tis like that Richmond with the rest shall down.

SOMERSET
      It shall be so – he shall to Brittany.
      Come, therefore, let's about it speedily.   *Exeunt.*

*

∾ **IV.8** *Flourish. Enter King Edward, Richard Duke
of Gloucester, and Lord Hastings, with a troop of
Hollanders.*

KING EDWARD
      Now, brother Richard, Lord Hastings, and the rest,
      Yet thus far fortune maketh us amends,
      And says that once more I shall interchange
4   My wanèd state for Henry's regal crown.
      Well have we passed and now repassed the seas
      And brought desirèd help from Burgundy.
      What then remains, we being thus arrived
8   From Ravenspurgh haven before the gates of York,
      But that we enter, as into our dukedom?
       Hastings knocks at the gates of York.

RICHARD DUKE OF GLOUCESTER
10   The gates made fast? Brother, I like not this.

---

100 *down* fall
   IV.8 Outside the walls of York   **4** *wanèd* faded, declined   **8** *Ravenspurgh*
(on the Yorkshire coast, at the mouth of the River Humber)

For many men that stumble at the threshold   11
Are well foretold that danger lurks within.

KING EDWARD
Tush, man, abodements must not now affright us.   13
By fair or foul means we must enter in,
For hither will our friends repair to us.

HASTINGS
My liege, I'll knock once more to summon them.
He knocks.
Enter, on the walls, the Mayor and Aldermen of York.

MAYOR
My lords, we were forewarnèd of your coming,
And shut the gates for safety of ourselves –
For now we owe allegiance unto Henry.

KING EDWARD
But, Master Mayor, if Henry be your king,   20
Yet Edward at the least is Duke of York.

MAYOR
True, my good lord, I know you for no less.

KING EDWARD
Why, and I challenge nothing but my dukedom,   23
As being well content with that alone.

RICHARD DUKE OF GLOUCESTER   *Aside*
But when the fox hath once got in his nose,
He'll soon find means to make the body follow.

HASTINGS
Why, Master Mayor, why stand you in a doubt?
Open the gates – we are King Henry's friends.

MAYOR
Ay, say you so? The gates shall then be opened.
They descend.

RICHARD DUKE OF GLOUCESTER
A wise stout captain, and soon persuaded.   30

HASTINGS
The good old man would fain that all were well,   31

---

11 *stumble . . . threshold* (a sign of bad luck) 13 *abodements* omens 23
challenge claim 30 *stout* valiant 31 *would fain* desires

32 So 'twere not long of him; but being entered,
    I doubt not, I, but we shall soon persuade
    Both him and all his brothers unto reason.
        Enter below the Mayor and two Aldermen.
    KING EDWARD
    So, Master Mayor, these gates must not be shut
    But in the night or in the time of war.
    What – fear not, man, but yield me up the keys,
        King Edward takes some keys from the Mayor.
    For Edward will defend the town and thee,
39 And all those friends that deign to follow me.
        March. Enter Sir John Montgomery, with a Drummer
        and Soldiers.
    RICHARD DUKE OF GLOUCESTER
40 Brother, this is Sir John Montgomery,
    Our trusty friend, unless I be deceived.
    KING EDWARD
    Welcome, Sir John – but why come you in arms?
    MONTGOMERY
    To help King Edward in his time of storm,
    As every loyal subject ought to do.
    KING EDWARD
    Thanks, good Montgomery, but we now forget
    Our title to the crown, and only claim
    Our dukedom till God please to send the rest.
    MONTGOMERY
    Then fare you well, for I will hence again.
    I came to serve a king and not a duke.
50 Drummer, strike up, and let us march away.
        The Drummer begins to sound a march.
    KING EDWARD
    Nay, stay, Sir John, a while, and we'll debate

---

32 *So . . . him* as long as he bears no responsibility   **39** *deign* are willing   **40**
Sir John Montgomery (called Sir Thomas in the chronicles, which report that
he met Edward at Nottingham after the securing of the city of York)   **50 s.d.**
begins . . . march commences beating a march

By what safe means the crown may be recovered.

MONTGOMERY

    What talk you of debating? In few words,

    If you'll not here proclaim yourself our king

    I'll leave you to your fortune and be gone

    To keep them back that come to succor you.

    Why shall we fight, if you pretend no title?   57

RICHARD DUKE OF GLOUCESTER *To King Edward*

    Why, brother, wherefore stand you on nice points?   58

KING EDWARD

    When we grow stronger, then we'll make our claim.

    Till then 'tis wisdom to conceal our meaning.   60

HASTINGS

    Away with scrupulous wit! Now arms must rule.   61

RICHARD DUKE OF GLOUCESTER

    And fearless minds climb soonest unto crowns.

    Brother, we will proclaim you out of hand,   63

    The bruit thereof will bring you many friends.   64

KING EDWARD

    Then be it as you will, for 'tis my right,

    And Henry but usurps the diadem.

MONTGOMERY

    Ay, now my sovereign speaketh like himself,

    And now will I be Edward's champion.   68

HASTINGS

    Sound trumpet, Edward shall be here proclaimed.

    To Montgomery

    Come, fellow soldier, make thou proclamation.   70

    Flourish.

MONTGOMERY Edward the Fourth, by the grace of God

    King of England and France, and Lord of Ireland –

    And whosoe'er gainsays King Edward's right,   73

    By this I challenge him to single fight.   74

    He throws down his gauntlet.

---

57 *pretend* claim **58** *stand* dwell; *nice points* minor details **61** *wit* reasoning **63** *out of hand* immediately **64** *bruit* news **68** *champion* defender **73** *gainsays* denies **74 s.d.** *gauntlet* glove (a challenge to a duel)

ALL   Long live Edward the Fourth!

KING EDWARD

Thanks, brave Montgomery, and thanks unto you all.

77   If fortune serve me I'll requite this kindness.

Now, for this night, let's harbor here in York;

79   And when the morning sun shall raise his car

80   Above the border of this horizon,

We'll forward towards Warwick and his mates.

82   For well I wot that Henry is no soldier.

83   Ah, froward Clarence, how evil it beseems thee

To flatter Henry and forsake thy brother!

Yet, as we may, we'll meet both thee and Warwick.

Come on, brave soldiers – doubt not of the day

And, that once gotten, doubt not of large pay.   *Exeunt.*

✱

∾ **IV.9**   *Flourish. Enter King Henry, the Earl of*
Warwick, the Marquis of Montague, George
Duke of Clarence, and the Earl of Oxford.

WARWICK

1   What counsel, lords? Edward from Belgia,

2   With hasty Germans and blunt Hollanders,

Hath passed in safety through the narrow seas,

4   And with his troops doth march amain to London,

And many giddy people flock to him.

KING HENRY

Let's levy men and beat him back again.

GEORGE DUKE OF CLARENCE

A little fire is quickly trodden out,

8   Which, being suffered, rivers cannot quench.

WARWICK

In Warwickshire I have true-hearted friends,

10   Not mutinous in peace, yet bold in war.

---

77 *requite* repay   79 *car* chariot   82 *wot* know   83 *froward* perverse

IV.9 The Bishop of London's palace   1 *Belgia* the Netherlands   2 *hasty*
rash, quick-tempered; *blunt* merciless   4 *amain* speedily   8 *suffered* tolerated

Those will I muster up. And thou, son Clarence,   11
Shalt stir in Suffolk, Norfolk, and in Kent,
The knights and gentlemen to come with thee.
Thou, brother Montague, in Buckingham,
Northampton, and in Leicestershire shalt find
Men well inclined to hear what thou command'st.
And thou, brave Oxford, wondrous well beloved
In Oxfordshire, shalt muster up thy friends.
My sovereign, with the loving citizens,
Like to his island girt in with the ocean,   20
Or modest Dian circled with her nymphs,   21
Shall rest in London till we come to him.
Fair lords, take leave and stand not to reply.
Farewell, my sovereign.

KING HENRY
Farewell, my Hector, and my Troy's true hope.   25

GEORGE DUKE OF CLARENCE
In sign of truth, I kiss your highness' hand.
He kisses King Henry's hand.

KING HENRY
Well-minded Clarence, be thou fortunate.

MONTAGUE
Comfort, my lord, and so I take my leave.
He kisses King Henry's hand.

OXFORD
And thus I seal my truth and bid adieu.   29
He kisses King Henry's hand.

KING HENRY
Sweet Oxford, and my loving Montague,   30
And all at once, once more a happy farewell.   *Exit.*   31

---

11 *son* i.e., son-in-law   21 *Dian* Diana (in Roman mythology the goddess
of the moon, hunting, and chastity, with whom Queen Elizabeth was
often associated)   25 *Hector* greatest warrior of Troy; *my Troy's* (because London [New-Troy] was supposedly founded by Brutus, legendary grandson of
the Trojan hero Aeneas)   29 *seal my truth* affirm my loyalty   31 *at once* together

WARWICK

32   Farewell, sweet lords – let's meet at Coventry.

Exeunt severally.

*

∽ **IV.10** *Enter King Henry and the Duke of Exeter.*

KING HENRY
Here at the palace will I rest a while.
Cousin of Exeter, what thinks your lordship?
Methinks the power that Edward hath in field
Should not be able to encounter mine.

EXETER

5   The doubt is that he will seduce the rest.

KING HENRY

6   That's not my fear. My meed hath got me fame.
I have not stopped mine ears to their demands,

8   Nor posted off their suits with slow delays.
My pity hath been balm to heal their wounds,

10   My mildness hath allayed their swelling griefs,
My mercy dried their water-flowing tears.
I have not been desirous of their wealth,

13   Nor much oppressed them with great subsidies,

14   Nor forward of revenge, though they much erred.
Then why should they love Edward more than me?

16   No, Exeter, these graces challenge grace;
And when the lion fawns upon the lamb,
The lamb will never cease to follow him.

Shout within: "A Lancaster!" "A York!"

EXETER
Hark, hark, my lord – what shouts are these?

Enter King Edward and Richard Duke of Gloucester,
with Soldiers.

---

32 s.d. *severally* separately
    IV.10 The bishop's palace **5** *doubt* fear **6** *meed* merit, generosity; *got* won
8 *posted off* (1) treated lightly, (2) postponed **13** *subsidies* taxes **14** *forward*
of eager for **16** *challenge grace* claim favor

KING EDWARD

 Seize on the shamefaced Henry – bear him hence, 20
 And once again proclaim us King of England.
 You are the fount that makes small brooks to flow.
 Now stops thy spring – my sea shall suck them dry,
 And swell so much the higher by their ebb.
 Hence with him to the Tower – let him not speak.
    Exeunt some with King Henry and Exeter.
 And lords, towards Coventry bend we our course,
 Where peremptory Warwick now remains. 27
 The sun shines hot, and, if we use delay, 28
 Cold biting winter mars our hoped-for hay.

RICHARD DUKE OF GLOUCESTER

 Away betimes, before his forces join, 30
 And take the great-grown traitor unawares.
 Brave warriors, march amain towards Coventry.
          Exeunt.

      *

❧ **V.1** *Enter the Earl of Warwick, the Mayor of*
  Coventry, two Messengers, and others upon
  the walls.

WARWICK

 Where is the post that came from valiant Oxford?
  The First Messenger steps forward.
 How far hence is thy lord, mine honest fellow?

FIRST MESSENGER

 By this at Dunsmore, marching hitherward. 3

WARWICK

 How far off is our brother Montague?
 Where is the post that came from Montague?
  The Second Messenger steps forward.

---

20 *shamefaced* timid   27 *peremptory* overbearing   28–29 *The sun . . . hay*
we should seize this opportunity (i.e., we should make hay while the sun
shines)   30 *betimes* at once
 V.1 Before the walls of Coventry   3 *this* this time; *Dunsmore* Dunsmore
Heath, between Coventry and Daventry

SECOND MESSENGER

6   By this at Da'ntry, with a puissant troop.
Enter Somerville to them, above.

WARWICK

Say, Somerville – what says my loving son?
And, by thy guess, how nigh is Clarence now?

SOMERVILLE

9   At Southam I did leave him with his forces,

10   And do expect him here some two hours hence.
A march afar off.

WARWICK

Then Clarence is at hand – I hear his drum.

SOMERVILLE

12   It is not his, my lord. Here Southam lies.
The drum your honor hears marcheth from Warwick.

WARWICK

14   Who should that be? Belike, unlooked-for friends.

SOMERVILLE

They are at hand, and you shall quickly know.
*Flourish. Enter below King Edward and Richard
Duke of Gloucester, with Soldiers.*

KING EDWARD

16   Go, trumpet, to the walls, and sound a parley.
Sound a parley.

RICHARD DUKE OF GLOUCESTER

See how the surly Warwick mans the wall.

WARWICK

18   O, unbid spite – is sportful Edward come?
Where slept our scouts, or how are they seduced,

20   That we could hear no news of his repair?

KING EDWARD

Now, Warwick, wilt thou ope the city gates,

---

6 *Da'ntry* i.e., Daventry (about 20 miles southeast of Coventry); *puissant* strong **9** *Southam* (about 10 miles southeast of Coventry) **12–13** *It . . . Warwick* (the city of Warwick lies southwest of Coventry; the earl has slightly mistaken directions, as Somerset points out) **14** *Belike* no doubt **16** *parley* trumpet call requesting a truce for conference **18** *unbid* uninvited, unwelcome; *sportful* lascivious **20** *repair* approach

Speak gentle words, and humbly bend thy knee,
Call Edward king, and at his hands beg mercy?
And he shall pardon thee these outrages.

WARWICK
Nay, rather, wilt thou draw thy forces hence,
Confess who set thee up and plucked thee down,
Call Warwick patron, and be penitent?
And thou shalt still remain the Duke of York.

RICHARD DUKE OF GLOUCESTER
I thought at least he would have said "the king."
Or did he make the jest against his will?   30

WARWICK
Is not a dukedom, sir, a goodly gift?

RICHARD DUKE OF GLOUCESTER
Ay, by my faith, for a poor earl to give.   32
I'll do thee service for so good a gift.   33

WARWICK
'Twas I that gave the kingdom to thy brother.

KING EDWARD
Why then, 'tis mine, if but by Warwick's gift.

WARWICK
Thou art no Atlas for so great a weight;   36
And, weakling, Warwick takes his gift again;
And Henry is my king, Warwick his subject.

KING EDWARD
But Warwick's king is Edward's prisoner,
And, gallant Warwick, do but answer this: 40
What is the body when the head is off?

RICHARD DUKE OF GLOUCESTER
Alas, that Warwick had no more forecast,   42
But whiles he thought to steal the single ten,   43
The king was slyly fingered from the deck.   44
    To Warwick

---

32 *poor earl* (a duke outranks an earl) **33** *do thee service* accept you as my feudal overlord (ironically) **36** *Thou . . . for* i.e., you cannot bear (Atlas, a Titan, supported the world on his shoulders) **42** *forecast* anticipated **43** *single ten* mere ten (the ten, highest of the plain cards, is worth having, but not in comparison with the king) **44** *fingered* stolen

You left poor Henry at the bishop's palace,
And ten to one you'll meet him in the Tower.
KING EDWARD
'Tis even so – *(To Warwick)* yet you are Warwick still.
RICHARD DUKE OF GLOUCESTER
48　Come, Warwick, take the time – kneel down, kneel down.
49　Nay, when? Strike now, or else the iron cools.
WARWICK
50　I had rather chop this hand off at a blow,
And with the other fling it at thy face,
52　Than bear so low a sail to strike to thee.
KING EDWARD
Sail how thou canst, have wind and tide thy friend,
This hand, fast wound about thy coal-black hair,
Shall, whiles thy head is warm and new cut off,
Write in the dust this sentence with thy blood:
57　"Wind-changing Warwick now can change no more."
Enter the Earl of Oxford, with a Drummer and
Soldiers bearing colors.
WARWICK
O cheerful colors! See where Oxford comes.
OXFORD
Oxford, Oxford, for Lancaster!
Oxford and his Men pass over the
stage and exeunt into the city.
RICHARD DUKE OF GLOUCESTER　*To King Edward*
60　The gates are open – let us enter too.
KING EDWARD
61　So other foes may set upon our backs?
Stand we in good array, for they no doubt
63　Will issue out again and bid us battle.
If not, the city being but of small defense,

---

48 *take the time* seize the opportunity　49 *Nay, when* (an exclamation indicating impatience)　52 *bear . . . sail* be so humble as (Warwick is punning on Gloucester's use of *Strike* [=hit] in l. 49 with an allusion to sail-lowering [=strike]; see the note to III.3.5)　57 *Wind-changing* i.e., fickle, inconstant; **s.d.** *colors* flags　61 *So* so that　63 *bid* offer

We'll quickly rouse the traitors in the same.   65

WARWICK   *To Oxford, within*

O, welcome, Oxford – for we want thy help.   66
    Enter the Marquis of Montague, with a Drummer
    and Soldiers bearing colors.

MONTAGUE

Montague, Montague, for Lancaster!
                Montague and his Men pass over the stage
                        and exeunt into the city.

RICHARD DUKE OF GLOUCESTER

Thou and thy brother both shall bye this treason   68

Even with the dearest blood your bodies bear.

KING EDWARD

The harder matched, the greater victory.   70

My mind presageth happy gain and conquest.
    Enter the Duke of Somerset, with a Drummer and
    Soldiers bearing colors.

SOMERSET

Somerset, Somerset, for Lancaster!
                Somerset and his Men pass over the stage
                        and exeunt into the city.

RICHARD DUKE OF GLOUCESTER

Two of thy name, both Dukes of Somerset,   73

Have sold their lives unto the house of York –

And thou shalt be the third, an this sword hold.   75
    Enter George Duke of Clarence, with a Drummer and
    Soldiers bearing colors.

WARWICK

And lo, where George of Clarence sweeps along,

Of force enough to bid his brother battle;

With whom an upright zeal to right prevails   78

---

65 *rouse . . . in* drive . . . from (hunting terminology) 66 *want* need 68
bye atone for 73 *Two . . . name* (The Somerset being addressed is Edmund,
the fourth duke. His elder brother, Henry Beaufort, the third duke, was executed after the battle of Hexham, 1464, though his defection from Edward is
described in IV.1 and IV.2 as taking place in 1472. Their father, Edmund,
the second duke, was killed at Saint Albans, 1445; it is his head that Richard
throws down at I.1.20 s.d.) 75 *an* if 78 *to right* for justice

More than the nature of a brother's love.

GEORGE DUKE OF CLARENCE

80 Clarence, Clarence, for Lancaster!

KING EDWARD

81 *Et tu, Brutè* – wilt thou stab Caesar too?

To a Trumpeter

82 A parley, sirrah, to George of Clarence.

Sound a parley. Richard Duke of Gloucester and
George Duke of Clarence whisper together.

WARWICK

Come, Clarence, come – thou wilt if Warwick call.

GEORGE DUKE OF CLARENCE

Father of Warwick, know you what this means?

He takes his red rose out of his hat and throws it at
Warwick.

Look – here I throw my infamy at thee!

I will not ruinate my father's house,

87 Who gave his blood to lime the stones together,

88 And set up Lancaster. Why, trowest thou, Warwick,

89 That Clarence is so harsh, so blunt, unnatural,

90 To bend the fatal instruments of war

Against his brother and his lawful king?

92 Perhaps thou wilt object my holy oath.

To keep that oath were more impiety

94 Than Jephthah, when he sacrificed his daughter.

I am so sorry for my trespass made

That, to deserve well at my brothers' hands,

I here proclaim myself thy mortal foe,

With resolution, wheresoe'er I meet thee –

99 As I will meet thee, if thou stir abroad –

100 To plague thee for thy foul misleading me.

And so, proud-hearted Warwick, I defy thee,

And to my brothers turn my blushing cheeks.

---

81 *Et tu, Brutè* And you, too, Brutus? (Julius Caesar's exclamation when he realized that his friend was one of the conspirators to his murder)   **82** *sirrah* fellow (said to a social inferior)   **87** *lime* cement   **88** *trowest thou* do you believe   **89** *blunt* uncivilized   **92** *object* raise as an objection   **94** *Jephthah* (see Judges 11:30–40)   **99** *abroad* i.e., outside Coventry

To King Edward
Pardon me, Edward – I will make amends.
To Richard
And, Richard, do not frown upon my faults,
For I will henceforth be no more unconstant.   105
KING EDWARD
Now welcome more, and ten times more beloved,
Than if thou never hadst deserved our hate.
RICHARD DUKE OF GLOUCESTER   *To George*
Welcome, good Clarence – this is brotherlike.
WARWICK   *To George*
O, passing traitor – perjured and unjust!   109
KING EDWARD
What, Warwick, wilt thou leave the town and fight?   *110*
Or shall we beat the stones about thine ears?
WARWICK   *Aside*
Alas, I am not cooped here for defense.   112
To King Edward
I will away towards Barnet presently,   113
And bid thee battle, Edward, if thou dar'st.
KING EDWARD
Yes, Warwick – Edward dares, and leads the way.
Lords, to the field – Saint George and victory!
       Exeunt below King Edward and his company. March.
       The Earl of Warwick and his company descend and
       follow.

                           *

---

105 *unconstant* fickle 109 *passing* more than, unsurpassed 112 *cooped*
confined (i.e., prepared) 113 *Barnet* (about 10 miles north of London and
75 miles southeast of Coventry; by departing from the historical order of
events and having Henry captured in IV.10, Shakespeare is forced here to
treat Barnet as if it were adjacent to Coventry)

~ **V.2** *Alarum and excursions. Enter King Edward,
bringing forth the Earl of Warwick, wounded.*

KING EDWARD

    So lie thou there. Die thou, and die our fear –

2   For Warwick was a bug that feared us all.

    Now, Montague, sit fast – I seek for thee

    That Warwick's bones may keep thine company.   *Exit.*

WARWICK

    Ah, who is nigh? Come to me, friend or foe,

    And tell me who is victor, York or Warwick?

    Why ask I that? My mangled body shows,

    My blood, my want of strength, my sick heart shows,

    That I must yield my body to the earth

10   And by my fall the conquest to my foe.

11   Thus yields the cedar to the ax's edge,

12   Whose arms gave shelter to the princely eagle,

13   Under whose shade the ramping lion slept,

14   Whose top branch overpeered Jove's spreading tree

    And kept low shrubs from winter's powerful wind.

    These eyes, that now are dimmed with death's black
      veil,

    Have been as piercing as the midday sun

    To search the secret treasons of the world.

    The wrinkles in my brows, now filled with blood,

20   Were likened oft to kingly sepulchers –

    For who lived king, but I could dig his grave?

    And who durst smile when Warwick bent his brow?

    Lo now my glory smeared in dust and blood.

24   My parks, my walks, my manors that I had,

    Even now forsake me, and of all my lands

V.2 Near Barnet **2** *bug* goblin; *feared* frightened **11** *cedar* (symbol of pre-eminence) **12–13** *eagle . . . lion* (the allusion may be general – i.e., "royal creatures"; or it may be intended specifically, through the identification of the men with their emblems – i.e., *eagle:* Richard of York, as perhaps at II.1.91, and *lion:* Henry VI, three rampant lions being represented on his royal arms) **13** *ramping* rampant **14** *overpeered* overlooked; *Jove's . . . tree* i.e., the oak **24** *parks* hunting grounds

Is nothing left me but my body's length.
Why, what is pomp, rule, reign, but earth and dust?
And, live we how we can, yet die we must.
   Enter the Earl of Oxford and the Duke of Somerset.

SOMERSET
  Ah, Warwick, Warwick – wert thou as we are,
  We might recover all our loss again.   30
  The queen from France hath brought a puissant power. 31
  Even now we heard the news. Ah, couldst thou fly!

WARWICK
  Why, then I would not fly. Ah, Montague,
  If thou be there, sweet brother, take my hand,
  And with thy lips keep in my soul a while.   35
  Thou lov'st me not – for, brother, if thou didst,
  Thy tears would wash this cold congealèd blood
  That glues my lips and will not let me speak.
  Come quickly, Montague, or I am dead.

SOMERSET
  Ah, Warwick – Montague hath breathed his last,   40
  And to the latest gasp cried out for Warwick,   41
  And said, "Commend me to my valiant brother."
  And more he would have said, and more he spoke,
  Which sounded like a cannon in a vault,
  That mote not be distinguished; but at last   45
  I well might hear, delivered with a groan,
  "O, farewell, Warwick."

WARWICK
  Sweet rest his soul. Fly, lords, and save yourselves –
  For Warwick bids you all farewell, to meet in heaven.
    He dies.

OXFORD
  Away, away – to meet the queen's great power!   50
    Here they bear away Warwick's body. Exeunt.
         ✳

---

31 *puissant* strong; *power* army 35 *with thy lips . . . a while* kiss me, and
thereby briefly prolong my life (the soul was believed to escape through the
mouth at death) 41 *latest* final 45 *mote* might

∾ **V.3** *Flourish. Enter King Edward in triumph, with Richard Duke of Gloucester, George Duke of Clarence, and Soldiers.*

KING EDWARD
Thus far our fortune keeps an upward course,
And we are graced with wreaths of victory.
But in the midst of this bright-shining day
I spy a black suspicious threatening cloud
That will encounter with our glorious sun
Ere he attain his easeful western bed.
I mean, my lords, those powers that the queen
8   Hath raised in Gallia have arrived our coast,
And, as we hear, march on to fight with us.
GEORGE DUKE OF CLARENCE
10   A little gale will soon disperse that cloud,
And blow it to the source from whence it came.
Thy very beams will dry those vapors up,
13   For every cloud engenders not a storm.
RICHARD DUKE OF GLOUCESTER
14   The queen is valued thirty thousand strong,
And Somerset, with Oxford, fled to her.
16   If she have time to breathe, be well assured,
Her faction will be full as strong as ours.
KING EDWARD
18   We are advertised by our loving friends
19   That they do hold their course toward Tewkesbury.
20   We, having now the best at Barnet field,
21   Will thither straight, for willingness rids way –
And, as we march, our strength will be augmented
In every county as we go along.
Strike up the drum, cry "Courage!" and away.
                    Flourish. March. Exeunt.

V.3 Near Barnet 8 *Gallia* France 13 *engenders* begets 14 *The . . . valued*
the queen's strength is thought to be 16 *breathe* i.e., gather her strength
18 *advertised* notified 19 *Tewkesbury* a town in Gloucestershire 20 *having . . . best* having now overcome 21 *rids way* i.e., (seems to) decrease the
distance

*

∾ **V.4** *Flourish. March. Enter Queen Margaret, Prince Edward, the Duke of Somerset, the Earl of Oxford, and Soldiers.*

QUEEN MARGARET
 Great lords, wise men ne'er sit and wail their loss,
 But cheerly seek how to redress their harms.   2
 What though the mast be now blown overboard,
 The cable broke, the holding anchor lost,
 And half our sailors swallowed in the flood?
 Yet lives our pilot still. Is't meet that he   6
 Should leave the helm and, like a fearful lad,
 With tearful eyes add water to the sea,
 And give more strength to that which hath too much,
 Whiles, in his moan, the ship splits on the rock   10
 Which industry and courage might have saved?
 Ah, what a shame; ah, what a fault were this.
 Say Warwick was our anchor – what of that?
 And Montague our topmast – what of him?
 Our slaughtered friends the tackles – what of these?   15
 Why, is not Oxford here another anchor?
 And Somerset another goodly mast?
 The friends of France our shrouds and tacklings?   18
 And, though unskillful, why not Ned and I   19
 For once allowed the skillful pilot's charge?   20
 We will not from the helm to sit and weep,
 But keep our course, though the rough wind say no,
 From shelves and rocks that threaten us with wreck.   23
 As good to chide the waves as speak them fair.

V.4 Fields near Tewkesbury 2 *cheerly* cheerfully 6 *our pilot* i.e., King Henry 10 *in* at; *moan* state of grief 15 *tackles* lines and pulleys for raising sail (running rigging) 18 *shrouds* lines bracing the mast (standing rigging); *tacklings* fittings and similar equipment 19 *Ned* Prince Edward (her son) 20 *charge* responsibility (i.e., to guide the ship) 23 *shelves* sandbanks; *wreck* ruin

And what is Edward but a ruthless sea?
What Clarence but a quicksand of deceit?
27   And Richard but a raggèd fatal rock?
28   All these the enemies to our poor bark.
Say you can swim – alas, 'tis but a while;
30   Tread on the sand – why, there you quickly sink;
Bestride the rock – the tide will wash you off,
Or else you famish. That's a threefold death.
This speak I, lords, to let you understand,
34   If case some one of you would fly from us,
That there's no hoped-for mercy with the brothers York
More than with ruthless waves, with sands, and rocks.
Why, courage then – what cannot be avoided
'Twere childish weakness to lament or fear.

PRINCE EDWARD
Methinks a woman of this valiant spirit
40   Should, if a coward heard her speak these words,
41   Infuse his breast with magnanimity
42   And make him, naked, foil a man at arms.
I speak not this as doubting any here –
For did I but suspect a fearful man,
45   He should have leave to go away betimes,
Lest in our need he might infect another
And make him of like spirit to himself.
If any such be here – as God forbid –
Let him depart before we need his help.

OXFORD
50   Women and children of so high a courage,
51   And warriors faint – why, 'twere perpetual shame!
52   O brave young prince, thy famous grandfather
Doth live again in thee! Long mayst thou live
To bear his image and renew his glories!

SOMERSET
And he that will not fight for such a hope,

---

27 *raggèd* jagged   28 *bark* ship   34 *If* in   41 *magnanimity* great courage
42 *naked* unarmed; *foil* defeat; *a man at arms* an armed man   45 *betimes* immediately   51 *faint* fainthearted   52 *grandfather* i.e., Henry V

Go home to bed, and like the owl by day,
If he arise, be mocked and wondered at.
QUEEN MARGARET
Thanks, gentle Somerset; sweet Oxford, thanks.
PRINCE EDWARD
And take his thanks that yet hath nothing else.   59
    Enter a Messenger.
MESSENGER
Prepare you, lords, for Edward is at hand   60
Ready to fight – therefore be resolute.
OXFORD
I thought no less. It is his policy
To haste thus fast to find us unprovided.   63
SOMERSET
But he's deceived; we are in readiness.
QUEEN MARGARET
This cheers my heart, to see your forwardness.   65
OXFORD
Here pitch our battle – hence we will not budge.   66
    Flourish and march. Enter King Edward, Richard
    Duke of Gloucester, and George Duke of Clarence,
    with Soldiers.
KING EDWARD   *To his followers*
Brave followers, yonder stands the thorny wood
Which, by the heavens' assistance and your strength,
Must by the roots be hewn up yet ere night.
I need not add more fuel to your fire,   70
For well I wot ye blaze to burn them out.   71
Give signal to the fight, and to it, lords.
QUEEN MARGARET   *To her followers*
Lords, knights, and gentlemen – what I should say
My tears gainsay; for every word I speak   74
Ye see I drink the water of my eye.
Therefore, no more but this: Henry your sovereign
Is prisoner to the foe, his state usurped,

---

59 *that yet* who as yet   63 *unprovided* unprepared   65 *forwardness* zeal   66
pitch our battle deploy our army   71 *wot* know   74 *gainsay* forbid

His realm a slaughterhouse, his subjects slain,
His statutes canceled, and his treasure spent –
80 And yonder is the wolf that makes this spoil.
You fight in justice; then in God's name, lords,
Be valiant, and give signal to the fight.
Alarum, retreat, excursions.

Exeunt.

*

∾ **V.5** *Flourish. Enter King Edward, Richard Duke of
Gloucester, and George Duke of Clarence with Queen
Margaret, the Earl of Oxford, and the Duke of
Somerset, guarded.*

KING EDWARD
1 Now here a period of tumultuous broils.
2 Away with Oxford to Hammes Castle straight;
For Somerset, off with his guilty head.
Go bear them hence – I will not hear them speak.
OXFORD
For my part, I'll not trouble thee with words.

Exit, guarded.

SOMERSET
Nor I, but stoop with patience to my fortune.

Exit, guarded.

QUEEN MARGARET
So part we sadly in this troublous world
8 To meet with joy in sweet Jerusalem.
KING EDWARD
Is proclamation made that who finds Edward
10 Shall have a high reward and he his life?
RICHARD DUKE OF GLOUCESTER
It is, and lo where youthful Edward comes.
Enter Prince Edward, guarded.

V.5 Fields near Tewkesbury **1** *period* full stop, end **2** *Hammes Castle* an
English fortification, southwest of Calais (where Oxford was confined after
his capture in 1474, three years later than Tewkesbury) **8** *Jerusalem* i.e.,
heaven, the New Jerusalem (Revelations 21:2)

KING EDWARD

   Bring forth the gallant – let us hear him speak.

   What, can so young a thorn begin to prick?

   Edward, what satisfaction canst thou make   14

   For bearing arms, for stirring up my subjects,

   And all the trouble thou hast turned me to?

PRINCE EDWARD

   Speak like a subject, proud ambitious York.

   Suppose that I am now my father's mouth –

   Resign thy chair, and where I stand, kneel thou,

   Whilst I propose the selfsame words to thee,   20

   Which, traitor, thou wouldst have me answer to.

QUEEN MARGARET

   Ah, that thy father had been so resolved.

RICHARD DUKE OF GLOUCESTER

   That you might still have worn the petticoat   23

   And ne'er have stolen the breech from Lancaster.   24

PRINCE EDWARD

   Let Aesop fable in a winter's night –   25

   His currish riddles sorts not with this place.   26

RICHARD DUKE OF GLOUCESTER

   By heaven, brat, I'll plague ye for that word.

QUEEN MARGARET

   Ay, thou wast born to be a plague to men.

RICHARD DUKE OF GLOUCESTER

   For God's sake take away this captive scold.

PRINCE EDWARD

   Nay, take away this scolding crookback rather.   30

KING EDWARD

   Peace, willful boy, or I will charm your tongue.   31

---

14 *satisfaction* recompense   23 *still* always   24 *breech* breeches (i.e., the clothing of a man; literally, breeches are trousers that extend only just below the knee)   25–26 *Let . . . place* i.e., you lie about the relationship between my mother and father (with a gibe at Richard, for Aesop was supposedly stunted and deformed)   26 *currish* mean, cynical; *sorts not* are not appropriate   30 *crookback* hunchback   31 *charm your tongue* i.e., silence you (*charm:* cast a spell upon)

GEORGE DUKE OF CLARENCE   *To Prince Edward*
32   Untutored lad, thou art too malapert.
PRINCE EDWARD
      I know my duty – you are all undutiful.
      Lascivious Edward, and thou, perjured George,
      And thou, misshapen Dick – I tell ye all
      I am your better, traitors as ye are,
      And thou usurp'st my father's right and mine.
KING EDWARD
38   Take that, the likeness of this railer here.
      King Edward stabs Prince Edward.
RICHARD DUKE OF GLOUCESTER
39   Sprawl'st thou? Take that, to end thy agony.
      Richard stabs Prince Edward.
GEORGE DUKE OF CLARENCE
40   And there's for twitting me with perjury.
      George stabs Prince Edward, who dies.
QUEEN MARGARET
41   O, kill me too!
RICHARD DUKE OF GLOUCESTER
                    Marry, and shall.
      He offers to kill her.
KING EDWARD
      Hold, Richard, hold – for we have done too much.
RICHARD DUKE OF GLOUCESTER
      Why should she live to fill the world with words?
      Queen Margaret faints.
KING EDWARD
      What – doth she swoon? Use means for her recovery.
RICHARD DUKE OF GLOUCESTER   *Aside to George*
      Clarence, excuse me to the king my brother.
      I'll hence to London on a serious matter.
47   Ere ye come there, be sure to hear some news.

---

32 *malapert* impertinent   **38** *railer* scold (i.e., Queen Margaret)   **39** *Sprawl'st thou?* Do you struggle in your death throes?   **41** *Marry, and shall* I will indeed (*marry:* by the Virgin Mary, a mild oath)   **41 s.d.** *offers* threatens   **47** *Ere* before; *be sure to* be confident that you will

GEORGE DUKE OF CLARENCE   *Aside to Richard*
  What? What?
RICHARD DUKE OF GLOUCESTER   *Aside to George*
  The Tower, the Tower.   *Exit.*
QUEEN MARGARET
  O Ned, sweet Ned – speak to thy mother, boy.   50
  Canst thou not speak? O traitors, murderers!
  They that stabbed Caesar shed no blood at all,
  Did not offend, nor were not worthy blame,
  If this foul deed were by to equal it.   54
  He was a man – this, in respect, a child;   55
  And men ne'er spend their fury on a child.
  What's worse than murderer that I may name it?
  No, no, my heart will burst an if I speak;
  And I will speak that so my heart may burst.
  Butchers and villains! Bloody cannibals!   60
  How sweet a plant have you untimely cropped!
  You have no children, butchers; if you had,
  The thought of them would have stirred up remorse.
  But if you ever chance to have a child,
  Look in his youth to have him so cut off
  As, deathsmen, you have rid this sweet young prince!   66
KING EDWARD
  Away with her – go, bear her hence perforce.
QUEEN MARGARET
  Nay, never bear me hence – dispatch me here.   68
  Here sheathe thy sword – I'll pardon thee my death.
  What? Wilt thou not? Then, Clarence, do it thou.   70
GEORGE DUKE OF CLARENCE
  By heaven, I will not do thee so much ease.
QUEEN MARGARET
  Good Clarence, do; sweet Clarence, do thou do it.
GEORGE DUKE OF CLARENCE
  Didst thou not hear me swear I would not do it?

---

54 *by* nearby; *equal* compare with 55 *in respect* by comparison 66 *rid*
killed 68 *dispatch* kill

QUEEN MARGARET

74   Ay, but thou usest to forswear thyself.
'Twas sin before, but now 'tis charity.
What, wilt thou not? Where is that devil's butcher,
77   Hard-favored Richard? Richard, where art thou?
78   Thou art not here. Murder is thy alms deed –
79   Petitioners for blood thou ne'er putt'st back.

KING EDWARD

80   Away, I say – I charge ye, bear her hence.

QUEEN MARGARET

So come to you and yours as to this prince!

Exit, guarded.

KING EDWARD

Where's Richard gone?

GEORGE DUKE OF CLARENCE

83   To London all in post – *(Aside)* and as I guess,
To make a bloody supper in the Tower.

KING EDWARD

He's sudden if a thing comes in his head.
86   Now march we hence. Discharge the common sort
With pay and thanks, and let's away to London,
And see our gentle queen how well she fares.
89   By this I hope she hath a son for me.   *Exeunt.*

*

∾ **V.6** *Enter, on the walls, King Henry the Sixth,*
reading a book, Richard Duke of Gloucester,
and the Lieutenant of the Tower.

RICHARD DUKE OF GLOUCESTER

1   Good day, my lord. What, at your book so hard?

KING HENRY

Ay, my good lord – "my lord," I should say, rather.

---

74 *thou . . . to forswear* you have the habit of forswearing   77 *Hard-favored*
ugly   78 *alms deed* act of charity   79 *Petitioners . . . back* you never turn
away those who ask for blood   83 *post* haste   86 *common sort* ordinary soldiers   89 *this* this time
V.6 The Tower, London   1 *book* (of devotions)

'Tis sin to flatter; "good" was little better.   3
"Good Gloucester" and "good devil" were alike,
And both preposterous – therefore not "good lord."   5
RICHARD DUKE OF GLOUCESTER   *To the Lieutenant*
Sirrah, leave us to ourselves. We must confer.   6
                                              Exit Lieutenant.
KING HENRY
So flies the reckless shepherd from the wolf;   7
So first the harmless sheep doth yield his fleece,
And next his throat unto the butcher's knife.
What scene of death hath Roscius now to act?   10
RICHARD DUKE OF GLOUCESTER
Suspicion always haunts the guilty mind;
The thief doth fear each bush an officer.
KING HENRY
The bird that hath been limèd in a bush   13
With trembling wings misdoubteth every bush.   14
And I, the hapless male to one sweet bird,   15
Have now the fatal object in my eye
Where my poor young was limed, was caught and
    killed.
RICHARD DUKE OF GLOUCESTER
Why, what a peevish fool was that of Crete,   18
That taught his son the office of a fowl!
And yet, for all his wings, the fool was drowned.   20
KING HENRY
I, Daedalus; my poor boy, Icarus;
Thy father, Minos, that denied our course;
The sun that seared the wings of my sweet boy,   23

---

3 *better* i.e., better than flattery 5 *preposterous* unnatural 6 *Sirrah* fellow
(used of a social inferior) 7 *reckless* heedless 10 *Roscius* a famous Roman
actor (died 62 BC), supposed by the Elizabethans to be the greatest of all
tragedians 13 *limèd* caught with birdlime 14 *misdoubteth* suspects 15
hapless unlucky; *male* father; *bird* chick 18 *peevish* ridiculous 18–25
fool . . . life (Daedalus wished to escape from Crete, having been imprisoned
there by King Minos. He devised wings for himself and his son Icarus, fas-
tening them on with wax. The father flew to safety, but Icarus rose too near
the sun, the heat melted the wax, and he fell into the sea and was drowned.)
23–24 *sun . . . Edward* (referring to the sun insignia of York)

Thy brother Edward; and thyself, the sea,
25 Whose envious gulf did swallow up his life.
Ah, kill me with thy weapon, not with words!
27 My breast can better brook thy dagger's point
Than can my ears that tragic history.
But wherefore dost thou come? Is't for my life?

RICHARD DUKE OF GLOUCESTER
30 Think'st thou I am an executioner?

KING HENRY
A persecutor I am sure thou art;
If murdering innocents be executing,
Why, then thou art an executioner.

RICHARD DUKE OF GLOUCESTER
Thy son I killed for his presumption.

KING HENRY
Hadst thou been killed when first thou didst presúme,
Thou hadst not lived to kill a son of mine.
And thus I prophesy: that many a thousand
38 Which now mistrust no parcel of my fear,
And many an old man's sigh, and many a widow's,
40 And many an orphan's water-standing eye –
Men for their sons', wives for their husbands',
42 Orphans for their parents' timeless death –
Shall rue the hour that ever thou wast born.
The owl shriekèd at thy birth – an evil sign;
45 The night crow cried, aboding luckless time;
Dogs howled, and hideous tempests shook down trees;
47 The raven rooked her on the chimney's top;
48 And chatt'ring pies in dismal discords sung.
Thy mother felt more than a mother's pain,
50 And yet brought forth less than a mother's hope –
51 To wit, an indigested and deformèd lump,
Not like the fruit of such a goodly tree.

---

25 *envious gulf* hateful gullet   27 *brook* endure   38 *mistrust no parcel* do not
suspect any part   40 *water-standing* full of tears   42 *timeless* untimely   45
night crow bird of evil omen; *aboding* foreboding   47 *rooked her* squatted
48 *pies* magpies   51 *indigested* shapeless

Teeth hadst thou in thy head when thou wast born,
To signify thou cam'st to bite the world;
And if the rest be true which I have heard,
Thou cam'st –

RICHARD DUKE OF GLOUCESTER
I'll hear no more. Die, prophet, in thy speech.
    He stabs him.
For this, amongst the rest, was I ordained.

KING HENRY
Ay, and for much more slaughter after this.
O, God forgive my sins, and pardon thee.   60
    He dies.

RICHARD DUKE OF GLOUCESTER
What – will the aspiring blood of Lancaster
Sink in the ground? I thought it would have mounted.
See how my sword weeps for the poor king's death.
O, may such purple tears be alway shed   64
From those that wish the downfall of our house!
If any spark of life be yet remaining,
Down, down to hell, and say I sent thee thither –
    He stabs him again.
I that have neither pity, love, nor fear.
Indeed, 'tis true that Henry told me of,
For I have often heard my mother say   70
I came into the world with my legs forward.
Had I not reason, think ye, to make haste,
And seek their ruin that usurped our right?
The midwife wondered and the women cried,
"O, Jesus bless us, he is born with teeth!" –
And so I was, which plainly signified
That I should snarl and bite and play the dog.
Then, since the heavens have shaped my body so,
Let hell make crooked my mind to answer it.   79
I had no father, I am like no father;   80
I have no brother, I am like no brother;
And this word "love," which graybeards call divine,

---

64 *purple* i.e., bloody   79 *answer* accord with

Be resident in men like one another
And not in me – I am myself alone.
Clarence, beware; thou kept'st me from the light –
86 But I will sort a pitchy day for thee.
87 For I will buzz abroad such prophecies
That Edward shall be fearful of his life,
And then, to purge his fear, I'll be thy death.
90 Henry and his son are gone; thou, Clarence, art next;
And by one and one I will dispatch the rest,
Counting myself but bad till I be best.
I'll throw thy body in another room
And triumph, Henry, in thy day of doom.

Exit with the body.

*

∾ **V.7** *A chair of state. Flourish. Enter King Edward,*
Queen Elizabeth, George Duke of Clarence, Richard
Duke of Gloucester, the Lord Hastings, a Nurse
carrying the infant Prince Edward, and Attendants.

KING EDWARD
Once more we sit in England's royal throne,
Repurchased with the blood of enemies.
3 What valiant foemen, like to autumn's corn,
4 Have we mowed down in tops of all their pride!
Three dukes of Somerset, threefold renowned
6 For hardy and undoubted champions;
7 Two Cliffords, as the father and the son;
And two Northumberlands – two braver men
9 Ne'er spurred their coursers at the trumpet's sound.
10 With them, the two brave bears, Warwick and Montague,
That in their chains fettered the kingly lion

---

86 *sort* seek out (as being befitting); *pitchy* black **87** *buzz* whisper (scandal)
V.7 The palace, London **3** *corn* wheat **4** *in tops* at the peak **6** *un-*
doubted fearless **7** *as* to wit **9** *coursers* warhorses **10** *bears* (a bear chained
to a staff was the emblem of the Neville family, which included the brothers
Warwick and Montague)

And made the forest tremble when they roared.
Thus have we swept suspicion from our seat   13
And made our footstool of security.
  To Queen Elizabeth
Come hither, Bess, and let me kiss my boy.
  The Nurse brings forth the infant prince. King
  Edward kisses him.
Young Ned, for thee, thine uncles and myself
Have in our armors watched the winter's night,   17
Went all afoot in summer's scalding heat,
That thou mightst repossess the crown in peace;
And of our labors thou shalt reap the gain.   20

RICHARD DUKE OF GLOUCESTER   *Aside*
I'll blast his harvest, an your head were laid;   21
For yet I am not looked on in the world.   22
This shoulder was ordained so thick to heave;
And heave it shall some weight or break my back.
Work thou the way, and thou shalt execute.   25

KING EDWARD
Clarence and Gloucester, love my lovely queen;
And kiss your princely nephew, brothers, both.

GEORGE DUKE OF CLARENCE
The duty that I owe unto your majesty
I seal upon the lips of this sweet babe.   29
  He kisses the infant prince.

QUEEN ELIZABETH
Thanks, noble Clarence – worthy brother, thanks.   30

RICHARD DUKE OF GLOUCESTER
And that I love the tree from whence thou sprang'st,   31
Witness the loving kiss I give the fruit.
  He kisses the infant prince.
  Aside
To say the truth, so Judas kissed his master,

---

13 *suspicion* apprehension; *seat* throne   **17** *watched* stayed awake during
21 *blast* wither; *an* if; *laid* laid down (dead)   **22** *looked on* respected   **25**
thou . . . thou (he indicates first his head and then his arm or shoulder)   **29**
seal pledge   **31** *tree* i.e., the family of York

34   And cried "All hail!" whenas he meant all harm.
KING EDWARD
    Now am I seated as my soul delights,
    Having my country's peace and brothers' loves.
GEORGE DUKE OF CLARENCE
    What will your grace have done with Margaret?
    René her father, to the King of France
39   Hath pawned the Sicils and Jerusalem,
40   And hither have they sent it for her ransom.
KING EDWARD
41   Away with her, and waft her hence to France.
42   And now what rests but that we spend the time
43   With stately triumphs, mirthful comic shows,
    Such as befits the pleasure of the court?
45   Sound drums and trumpets – farewell, sour annoy!
    For here, I hope, begins our lasting joy.

                          Flourish. Exeunt.

---

34 *whenas* when   39 *the Sicils* Naples and Sicily   40 *it* i.e., the money raised
41 *waft* transport across water   42 *rests* remains (to be done)   43 *triumphs*
festivities   45 *sour annoy* bitter tribulation